TOTAL
AUTO
BODY
REPAIR

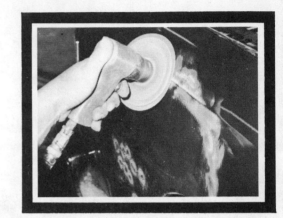

TOTAL AUTO BODY REPAIR

L. C. RHONE

HOWARD W. SAMS & CO., INC.

INDIANAPOLIS · KANSAS CITY · NEW YORK

FIRST EDITION

FIRST PRINTING—1976

International Standard Book Number: 0-672-21031-2
Library of Congress Catalog Card Number: 75-2551

To: My wife Opal, son Curtis, daughter Brenda Yates, and grandsons Eric and Mark Yates. *L.C.R.*

PREFACE

Total Auto Body Repair is the first completely new, comprehensive text on automobile body repair in over a decade. This book discusses the most up-to-date procedures and materials available to the auto body repair and refinishing industry. It may easily be used as either a text or a reference book and will be a useful tool for schools, professional body shops, and individuals doing work on their own cars.

All areas of auto body repair are thoroughly and equally discussed in this book. Included are complete discussions of major and minor metal straightening, filling, welding, brazing, heat-shrinking, and glass and trim work. A separate unit details the several different methods of panel adjustment used during auto body repairs. Complete discussions of the tools and equipment needed for auto body repair are included, as are discussions of the many types of consummable materials used during repairs.

A very detailed section of the book is concerned with the many types of automobile paint, paint products, and painting techniques in use today. Possible paint problems and their probable causes and solutions are discussed and well illustrated. Paint rub-out, restoration, and protection are discussed in a separate unit.

Body shop business management is treated thoroughly in a separate four-unit section of the book. Such procedures as estimating, insurance work, and shop personnel and management are included to provide a genuine insight into the operation of a body shop as a profitable business venture. Included in this section are procedures used for the wholesale repair work required on used cars that are reconditioned as a sideline in many body shops.

Total Auto Body Repair is arranged in 7 sections that contain a total of 28 individual units of material. If desired, the sections may be used individually or as instructional material on a given area of body shop operation or auto body repair. Taken in order and as a whole, however, the sections provide a logical learning sequence for all areas of contemporary auto body shop work and operation.

ACKNOWLEDGMENTS

The information in *Total Auto Body Repair* represents an effort to compile the most complete text available concerning all aspects of automobile body repair. The firms and individuals listed below contributed valuable time and material for this text. The author and the publisher sincerely appreciate their assistance and material furnished.

Acme Quality Paints
American Optical Corporation
Autobody and The Reconditioned Car
Bear Manufacturing Corporation, Division of Applied Power Industries, Inc.
Binks Manufacturing Company
Blackhawk Automotive Service Systems, Division of Applied Power Industries, Inc.
Channellock, Inc.
Chrysler Motors Corporation
Clark, Mr. Howe K., Jr.
The DeVilbiss Company
Ditzler Automotive Finishes Division, PPG Industries, Inc.
Refinish Division, DuPont Company
Fisher Body Division, General Motors Corporation
Ford Customer Service Division, Ford Motor Company
Grabber Manufacturing Company
Guy-Chart Sales, Inc.
Hagler Welder Sales
Harris Calorific Division of Emerson Electric Company
Hobart Brothers Company
Hobson, Mr. W. T.
Hubbard, Mr. John M.
Hutchins Manufacturing Company
Ingersoll-Rand Company
Johnson, Mr. George
Lenco, Inc., Automotive Equipment Division
Lincoln Electric Company
Hand Tools Division; Litton Industrial Products, Inc.
Lovelace, Mr. Clifton
Mac Tools, Inc.
Marson Corporation, Ingalls Associates, Inc.
The Martin-Senour Company
J. M. Merrill Motor Company
Mitchell Manuals, Inc.
Morrow, Mr. Reese
National Automobile Dealers Used Car Guide Company
Nevin, Mr. E. C.
The Norton Company
Oatey Company
Plymouth Products Corporation
PPG Industries, Inc.
Rinshed-Mason Products Division of Inmont Corporation
Road & Track Magazine
Snap-On Tools Corporation
Stanley Tools
3-M Company, Automotive Division
Tru-Way Company
The Unican Corporation
Victor Equipment Company
Wolfe Body Shop
Yates, Mr. H. David

TABLE OF CONTENTS

Section III   Body Shop Materials

Section IV   Using Heat to Work Metal

Section VII   Automotive Painting

The Body Shop as a Modern Business

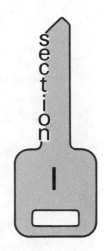

Unit 1

The Auto Body Shop Business

There are several basic types of auto body shops. Many body shops are one department of a new-car dealership's service center, as in Fig. 1-1. Other "independent" body shops (Figs. 1-2 and 1-3) come in a variety of sizes. Generally speaking, the items needed for a successful body shop are the same for a new-car dealer's service center shop as they are for an independently-owned body shop.

The three main topics of this unit are: the shop's location, the building design, and the equipment that the shop owner should provide. These three topics will be discussed in detail to provide a better understanding of the body shop as a modern business.

Fig. 1-1. Many body shops are one department of a new-car dealership.

SHOP LOCATION

There are many important reasons for considering the shop's location. The location should provide for good advertising, should be at least *near* an area where many late model cars are in use, and should provide room for automobile storage and parking. Future shop expansion should be considered, and the shop should be in a location where the rent rates and taxes are reasonable.

Locating for Advertising

Of prime importance is a building that can be easily seen. This will allow signs, lights, and other advertisements to be seen by people who are passing by. Always keep at least the approach area neat and clean, both inside and out, as in Fig. 1-4. Generally speaking, customers do not like to stop at an unclean shop.

By giving attention to the building's appearance and location, these properties become the shop's own advertisement.

Locating for Vehicle Supply

A second consideration in the body shop business is the number and type of vehicles in the area. No one can operate a profitable body shop business without vehicles on which to work. Few body men like to work on jalopies,

1

Fig. 1-2. A very large independent body shop. (Courtesy of Grabber Manufacturing Company.)

since there is usually less profit and harder work when repairing older, bent or rusty automobiles. Many owners of older-model cars will not spend the money needed to keep the cars in first-class condition.

For these reasons, a location in which people own good, late model cars is necessary to operate a profitable, modern body shop.

Locating for Storage, Parking, and Expansion

The building lot and location should be big enough to provide space for storing wrecked vehicles. It should be located in a place that will provide plenty of parking space for both workers and customers.

When looking for a building and location, keep in mind that the building and lot size should have plenty of room for easy expansion at a later date. A good parking lot with extra area for future expansion is shown in Fig. 1-5. If a business is to grow, it must have room to grow. It is better to have the room from the beginning than to try to buy or add more room later.

Location for Rent and Taxes

The shop building should be located in an area where the rent and taxes are low enough that the owner can pay these bills and still

Fig. 1-3. A smaller independent body shop.

Fig. 1-4. A nice-looking shop with an easily-identified entrance is good advertising.

Fig. 1-5. A parking lot with area for future expansion of the shop.

make a reasonable profit. The final decision on a shop's location must strike a balance between advertising, customer access, rent, and tax rates. To run a shop successfully, the rent should normally not exceed 5% of the shop's net income. (Net income is clear profit after all the expenses have been paid.)

DESIGNING A BODY SHOP

Some of the main factors to be considered in modern body shop design include the floor plan, adequate storage area, door and floor design, arrangement of equipment, and paint booth design.

Each of these points is important for efficient, well-organized work, convenience, and creating a good impression for the customer.

Floor Plan

Fig. 1-6 shows a basic floor plan for a fairly large body shop with a volume business. Here, as many as eight or more paint jobs per day could be completed. Note that in this shop, although the spray booth and drying enclosure are in one area, they are used as separate units.

This basic shop layout shows the type of floor plan for maximum shop efficiency. The vehicles are first moved into the metal-working stalls (where metal is straightened) for the basic body work. From here, they are first moved to the paint prep area where they will be prepared for painting. Here, time must be allowed for water and solvents to dry off the prepared surface. Then, after this step is completed, the vehicle is ready to enter the spray booth and be painted.

After the vehicle is painted, it is moved from the spray booth to the drying enclosure. Here, the drying oven is put into action to fast-dry the paint. This drying (heating) oven is necessary for high-speed painting. The oven shown in Fig. 1-7 is a luxury-type oven that might be used in a shop with a large-volume business.

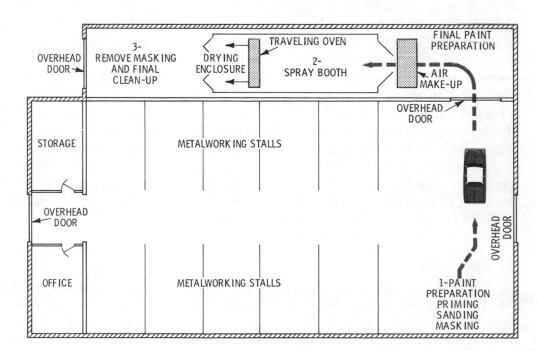
Fig. 1-6. Typical floor plan for a fairly large body shop.

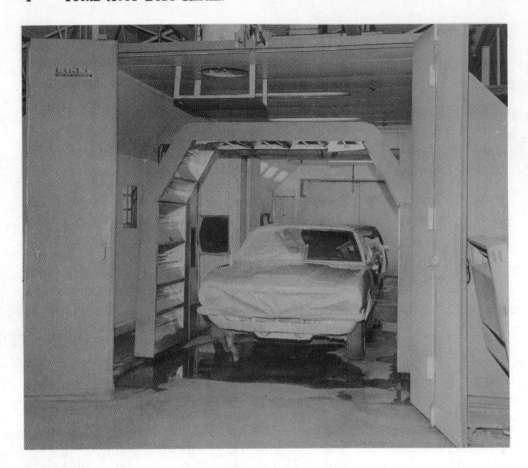

Fig. 1-7. Large paint-drying oven in a commercial body shop. (Courtesy of Binks Manufacturing Company.)

The traveling oven moves back and forth over the vehicle and shuts off after the drying time is completed. The drying time is controlled by a pre-set timer. The oven is more thoroughly explained and pictured in the painting equipment unit.

Fig. 1-8 shows a suggested layout for a smaller, independent body shop. This might be known as an average "two or three" man shop. The vehicle to be repaired is first moved into the metal-working area to basically repair the damaged metal. Then, it is moved to the sanding and taping area for paint preparation. Here, glass and chrome parts should be taped with masking tape and paper (Fig. 1-9), so that they will not be painted. The vehicle is then moved into the paint booth for painting.

Building Condition

Questions to be asked about the building's condition include: Are the building and floor area *large enough* to handle the expected volume of business? Is the ceiling *high enough* for raising automobiles so that they may be inspected and worked on underneath?

Also, are there community laws about *air pollution* (paint mist, evaporating solvents) that the building cannot be equipped to satisfy? Laws in some locations require that paint mist be filtered before the paint booth fan blows it into the street or alley.

Is the building electrically *wired* for all the tools and equipment that will be needed? Does the building have skylights or ceiling windows that allow natural sunlight into the building, or will the building need fluorescent lighting? These and other local questions must be answered when operating a modern body shop.

Storage

Wrecked vehicles require waiting time for appraisal and estimates of the repair cost. For this reason, there must be a place at the body shop for wrecked car storage until the insurance company or owner can make adjustments. Insurance appraisers are not likely to pull a

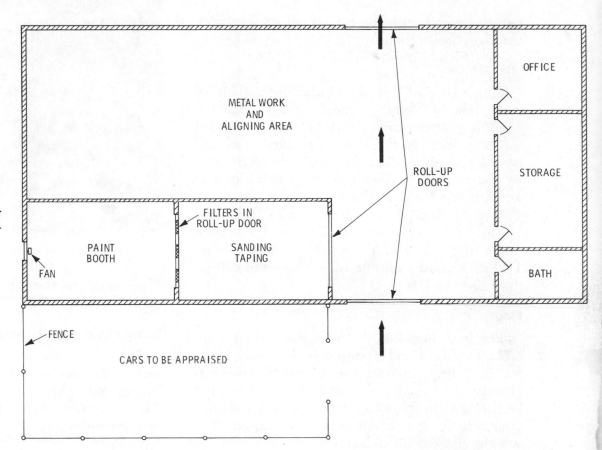

Fig. 1-8. Floor plan for a smaller shop in which two or three full-time bodymen would work.

wrecked vehicle from the shop, nor pull it to a shop that does not have enough storage room.

If the shop is located in a city's business district, storage becomes a problem because a large enough building to store several wrecked vehicles will cost a good deal of money. An extra fenced-in lot, like the one shown in Fig. 1-10, is very helpful for the storage of wrecked vehicles.

In any case, storage costs money. Some insurance companies or car owners do not pay storage costs. This fact should be kept in mind

Fig. 1-9. In the paint preparation area, glass and chrome parts are masked to avoid being painted. (Courtesy of Binks Manufacturing Company.)

Fig. 1-10. A fenced-in area will be needed around a modern body shop to store damaged cars.

and discussed with the car owner or insurance company beforehand.

Shop Doors

Figs. 1-6 and 1-8 shows the floor plans of well-planned body repair shops. Having enough proper-sized doors is very important for easy shop work. Many damaged cars will have to be towed into the shop. Therefore, it is necessary to have a wide door for entrance and another one for exit. For easy access, the doors should be about 14 feet high and 14 feet wide.

Figs. 1-1, 1-2, and 1-4 all show body shop doors of good size. The door pictured in Fig. 1-11 is a good example of a large-size roll-up door used in a typical shop.

Floor

The building should have a good, solid, concrete floor. A good example is the floor shown in Fig. 1-12. Concrete is preferred because it is strong. Most floor jacks have small rollers that work best on smooth, strong concrete floors. Concrete is also strong enough to support the weight of a car on jack stands.

Several drains must be installed in the floor when the floor is built. Fig. 1-13 shows a floor drain in front of the paint spray booth.

The purpose of any drain is cleanliness, so that the shop can be washed down with water. Also, cars need to be washed both before and

Fig. 1-12. A smooth concrete floor is the best floor for a clean shop.

after repair, so the drain is needed to keep the shop floor dry.

Shop Equipment Arrangement

There are two main ideas to keep in mind when planning or looking over the shop arrangement. The first of them is *convenience*. The equipment must be located where it is needed and where most of the workmen can get to it easily.

The second idea to keep in mind is *advertising*. A neat display of good tools and body shop equipment is one of the best ways to advertise. Power tools, panel straighteners, wheel alignment machines, etc., should all be located where they can be seen by the customer. This display of good equipment shows the customer that the shop has the tools necessary to do high-quality work. A good arrangement of equipment is also a sign of orderly working conditions. Notice the attention-getting display of equipment shown in Fig. 1-14.

Paint Booth Design

All body shops should have a paint booth if they want to do high-quality paint work. Also, some shops may need more inside ventilation to remove the paint spray dust. Both the paint booth and the shop itself will be health hazards if they are not properly ventilated.

The paint booth should be placed in one corner of the shop (Figs. 1-6 and 1-8) so that it will be as far as possible from the dust of the

Fig. 1-11. Good-sized, roll-up doors are needed in a modern body shop building.

Fig. 1-13. A floor drain should be located near the paint booth and wherever cars are washed. (Courtesy of Binks Manufacturing Company.)

FLOOR DRAIN

sanding and grinding machines. Old paint, metal, and plastic dust from grinders and sanders will often penetrate many paint booth filters. The filters are used to allow only clean air to get into the booth. If dust gets through

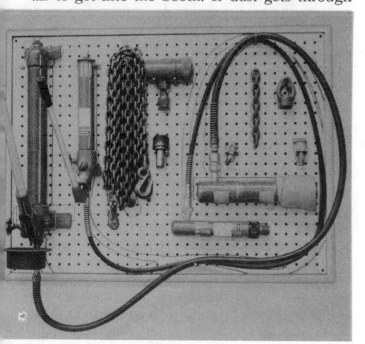

Fig. 1-14. A neat display of good equipment tells the customer a good deal about the shop's business.

the filters, the dust can cause trouble by getting into the wet paint.

All paint booths need a ventilator fan (Fig. 1-15). The fan will move the paint spray dust from the paint booth to the outside (Fig. 1-16). An air separator-regulator, Fig. 1-17, will also be needed in the paint booth, to provide the spray gun with the correct supply of clean air. A good fan, good filters, and a good separator-regulator will be needed in a paint booth for high-quality paint work.

Fast Turn-Out Spray Booth—The booth in Fig. 1-18 is one of the best designs in paint spray booths. It will allow the shop to paint several vehicles in one day. This better-design paint booth is both dust-free and self-heated. It has fluorescent lighting and plenty of air filters.

Even so, there are many less expensive paint booth designs that are built inside a body shop. These may be made with all types of building material, such as wood or concrete blocks. These may be grouped together as average turn-out spray booths.

Average Turn-Out Spray Booths—Figs. 1-19 and 1-20 show floor plans of the two different

Fig. 1-15. Typical fan on the inside of the paint booth, looking out.

types of average turn-out paint booths. They are either air-drying or oven-drying paint booths.

In an *air-drying* paint booth (Fig. 1-19), the ventilation fan pulls the fresh, filtered air over the vehicle. This air movement causes the paint solvents to evaporate until the vehicle is dry.

Fig. 1-16. The paint booth exhaust fan as seen from outside the body shop building. For safety, a screen should be placed in front of the fan blades.

In the *oven-drying* paint booth shown in Fig. 1-20, the paint is heated with an oven on roller tracks. This causes the paint solvents to dry (evaporate) faster than in the air drying booth.

EQUIPPING A BODY SHOP

There are several pieces of equipment needed by any body repair shop. These pieces may be too stationary (fixed in place), too large, or too expensive for each body man in the shop to provide for himself. The shop owner will be expected to bear the cost of this equipment, such as fire extinguishers, air compressors, frame straightening equipment, and other large or expensive items.

In this section, typical shop equipment that the shop owner needs for a well-equipped shop will be discussed. In each case, the use of each piece of equipment will be briefly discussed. Later units will discuss the equipment and use more thoroughly.

Cost—This equipment varies greatly in price. It is very difficult to closely estimate the true cost of completely equipping a new body shop. However, it is assumed that a smaller shop could be reasonably well equipped for about $25,000. Of course, this depends on the type and size of shop desired.

It *is* necessary, of course, to have the proper tools and equipment; however, it is wise to buy only what is needed to do a first-class job. Other tools may be an unwise use of the shop's money.

It is also important to know when to *sub-contract* work, also known as "farming out."

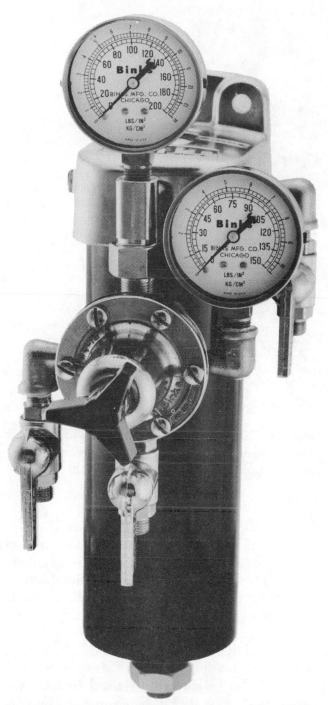

Fig. 1-17. Typical high-quality air separator-regulator. (Courtesy of Binks Manufacturing Company.)

Sending out such work as badly bent frames or wheels are typical examples of subcontracting. The equipment necessary to do these jobs is expensive; unless a shop is very large, it is usually cheaper to send out (subcontract) such jobs to a special shop for that type of work.

Fire Extinguisher

A fire extinguisher puts out a fire by a chemical process. There is always a danger of fire in an auto body repair shop. For this reason, the shop should have several fire extinguishers on hand.

Most auto body replacement panels are welded or brazed into place with a torch or arc welder. This welding creates heat and may involve a hot, open flame. Both the heat and flame are definite fire hazards. Also, many types of flammable materials (paint, cleaning solvent, cleaning rags, etc.) are frequently used in an auto body shop. These are possible fire hazards. Fig. 1-21 shows a typical shop fire extinguisher.

Air Compressor

An air compressor is a machine (usually driven by electric power) that compresses air. Then, when the air is released, its expansion may be used as a source of power for shop equipment.

A common body shop air compressor is shown in Fig. 1-22. It supplies the air needed to operate many of the tools in the shop. Paint guns, jacks, power wrenches, power chisels, and many other modern shop tools may need compressed air for power.

Polisher

A shop polisher is used to apply rubbing compound, polish, and some waxes to the paint of the automobile. A typical polisher is shown in Fig. 1-23. Most polishers in use today are electric.

Bench Grinder

The electric bench grinder has many uses in the auto body shop. It is often used several times a day, for example, to smooth rough edges on metal and to sharpen or reshape tools. Safety goggles must always be worn when using the bench grinder. A typical shop bench grinder is shown in Fig. 1-24. Sometimes, a wire brush wheel is mounted on one end of the bench grinder instead of one of the grinding wheels.

Fig. 1-18. A very large, self-contained paint booth for use in a large body shop. (Courtesy of Binks Manufacturing Company.)

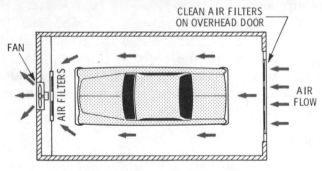

Fig. 1-19. Typical air-drying paint booth.

Vise

The shop vise is usually mounted firmly on a work bench, as can be seen in Fig. 1-25. The

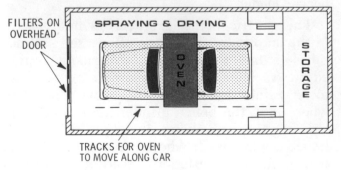

Fig. 1-20. Typical, smaller, oven-drying paint booth.

shop vise is a useful piece of equipment. It is able to clamp and hold objects together when they are being welded or for any other type of work.

Work Bench

The work bench is usually used to work on smaller parts of the car that have been removed. This might include light assemblies or other parts. By using the work bench, the parts can be held at waist level, high enough to be easily worked on.

A typical work bench, Fig. 1-25, is strong, stable, and made of steel. This is very important if the bench will be used to mount a vise, as was done in Fig. 1-25. A shelf underneath the bench can be used to store smaller shop tools such as a tap and die set, electric drills, etc.

Shop Bench

The shop bench is used as a comfortable seat while working on hard-to-reach panels that need straightening. This allows the body man to work with ease, without having to stoop

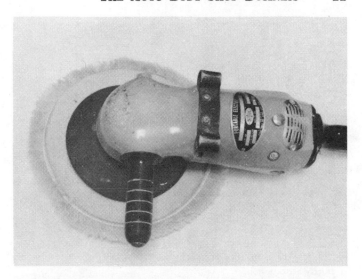

Fig. 1-23. The shop polisher is used to repair the car's topcoat paint.

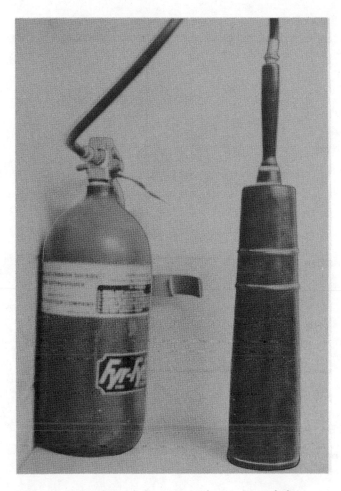

Fig. 1-21. Several good fire extinguishers are needed in every auto body shop.

Fig. 1-24. A common, useful, shop bench grinder. (Courtesy of Snap-On Tools.)

Fig. 1-22. An air compressor is used to supply compressed air to a body shop.

Fig. 1-25. The shop vise is usually bolted firmly to one corner of a sturdy workbench.

down to work in an awkward position on the floor.

The shop bench may also be used as a table for many parts that have been removed from the automobile. A shop bench is shown in Fig. 1-26.

Floor Jack

The floor jack (Fig. 1-27) is one of the most useful pieces of shop equipment. The jack must be used only to *lift* the vehicle so that jack (safety) stands can be put under the car to hold the car up. Then, wheels can be removed or the worker can get underneath the car to check or repair damage.

Wrecking Equipment (Wrecker)

Wrecking equipment, commonly called a *wrecker,* is a special truck used to safely move

Fig. 1-26. A shop bench may be used to work on the car without having to stoop over.

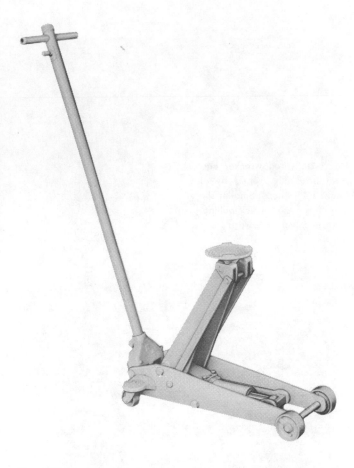

Fig. 1-27. A floor jack is used to raise the car and allow jack stands to be positioned. (Courtesy of Mac Tools.)

wrecked vehicles from one place to another. A good wrecking equipment package includes a wrecker truck with *winches* to raise the damaged vehicle from the vehicle's front or rear. A common wrecker and equipment are shown in Fig. 1-28.

Power Jack

Power jacks and their attachments are used to align (line up) damaged panels and frames that are out of alignment due to impact or, sometimes, normal wear. Fig. 1-29 shows a good power jack and attachments that would be used to repair serious body or frame damage.

Frame Straightener

There are many basic types of frame straighteners. Smaller units are often bought by low-volume body shops, whereas a larger shop

Fig. 1-28. Good wrecker equipment is usually owned by only larger body shops. Smaller shops may "farm out" wreck pulling to a larger shop or garage.

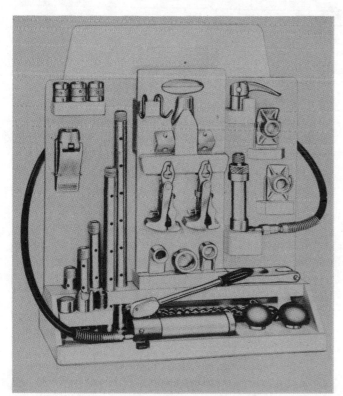

Fig. 1-29. A strong power jack and a good assortment of jack attachments are necessary for complete body work. (Courtesy of Snap-On Tools.)

would buy some type of large, permanent frame straightener.

All types of frame straighteners are used to align and straighten frames that are out of alignment because of collision damage. A common, portable frame straightener and attachments are shown in Fig. 1-30.

Oxy-Acetylene Welder

An oxy-acetylene welder is a very necessary tool in every auto body shop. The oxy-acetylene welder and its many attachments (Fig. 1-31) are used for heating, shrinking, welding, leading, brazing, and soldering metal.

Arc Welder

An arc welder may be needed by many body shops, especially those shops that do a good deal of frame damage repair. The arc welder is able to weld thick metal (such as the car frame) quickly, and with less heat loss and distortion than welding done with oxy-acetylene.

A common body shop arc welder unit is shown in Fig. 1-32. This unit can weld with up to 225 amperes, which is enough current for almost every body shop need.

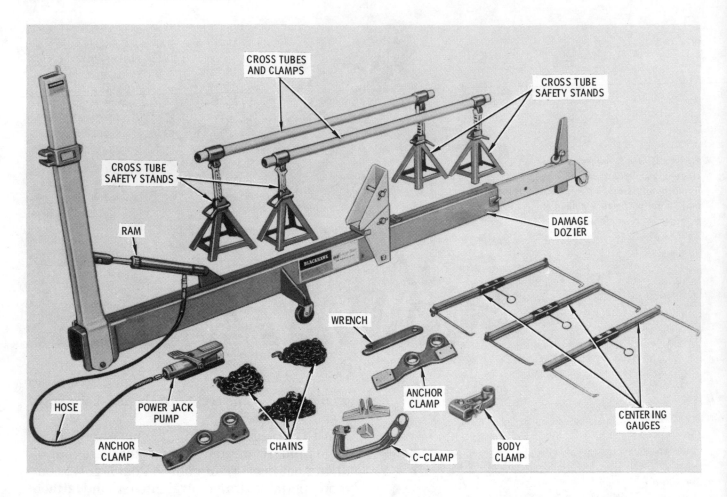

Fig. 1-30. A medium-size, portable frame straightener. (Courtesy, Blackhawk Division of Applied Power Industries.)

Creeper

A creeper is a tool that allows the body man to roll around under the car on his back. The four rollers on a creeper will automatically roll in whatever direction the creeper is pushed.

Fig. 1-33 shows a workman rolling under a car for a better look at the body damage underneath. Because a creeper rolls so easily, it must not be left lying flat on the floor. If it is left lying flat and someone steps on it, the creeper will roll out from under the person, probably causing a bad fall.

Safety (Jack) Stands

Safety (jack) stands are used to hold the car in position after it has been jacked up. They are used for the *safety* of the workman while he is under the vehicle.

When jack stands are used properly, the vehicle is first jacked up. Then, the jack stands are placed in a safe position under the vehicle. See Fig. 1-34. These help keep the car from falling if the jack should slip, leak down, or if the vehicle looses its balance on the jack.

The jack should be taken out from under the vehicle after the vehicle has been safely placed on the jack stands. This allows the jack to be used for other work and allows the car to be properly supported on stands.

Other Shop Tools

There are many shop tools and equipment that the shop owner must furnish. Some of these will be discussed in the unit on power tools. Others will be discussed in their own units.

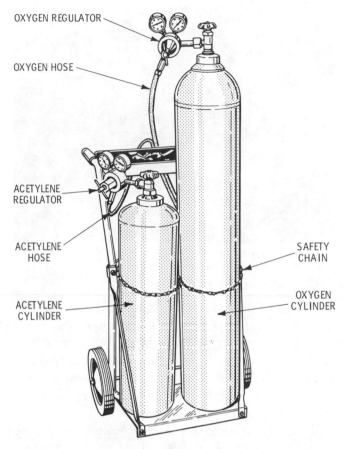

OXYGEN REGULATOR

OXYGEN HOSE

ACETYLENE
REGULATOR

ACETYLENE
HOSE

ACETYLENE
CYLINDER

SAFETY
CHAIN

OXYGEN
CYLINDER

Fig. 1-31. The oxy-acetylene welder is one of the most necessary tools in an auto body shop.

OFFICE EQUIPMENT

To run any body shop, a separate office area is needed. This will allow the shop owner or manager to have a place to conduct all the business part of the body shop. Usually, the office area is away from the shop area, so that the office can be cleaner than the shop.

The office usually has file cabinets, a desk and chair, an adding machine, a typewriter, and other small items such as a stapler. Larger office equipment may be purchased as the body shop's business grows.

File Cabinets

The center for business records is almost always a file cabinet, as in Fig. 1-35. The cabinet should contain folders with one folder for each customer, creditor, manufacturer, etc. The file contents are arranged in order of their dates. Folders are always filed alphabetically.

Fig. 1-32. A well-equipped body shop will usually have an arc welder. This unit is large enough for almost any body shop job. (Courtesy of Lincoln Electric Company.)

Cardboard guides may be used to divide the folders in each of the file cabinet drawers.

Estimates made on customers' cars are usually good for 30 days. The estimates should be kept on file for that time. This is one of the important jobs of the file cabinet and a good office system.

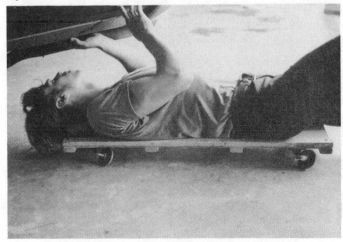

Fig. 1-33. A creeper is used to roll under the car.

Fig. 1-34. Firm safety (jack) stands should be in place before working under a car. (Courtesy, Blackhawk Division of Applied Power Industries.)

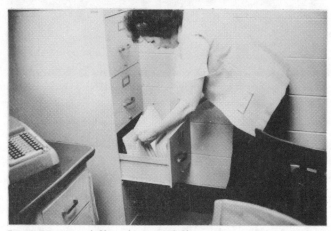

Fig. 1-35. A good file cabinet and file system are important for a successful body shop.

Fig. 1-36. An office desk and chair will be needed to sit down while figuring estimates, paying bills, and many other jobs.

Fig. 1-37. A good adding machine is necessary for any body shop.

Desk and Chair

The size or style of desk depends on the size of shop business. A small business will need only one desk, whereas a large business could use two or more. A desk that is not easily damaged, such as the metal desk shown in Fig. 1-36, is most suitable for a body repair shop office.

The desk should be large enough for ample working space. The desk chair should be one that will be comfortable when working at the desk. The chair may also be used when using the typewriter.

Adding Machine

The adding machine, Fig. 1-37, is a very important tool in the office of an automobile body

Fig. 1-38. Using a typewriter will help the business create a good impression.

Fig. 1-39. A body shop must have a telephone to handle orders and questions.

Fig. 1-40. A shop's office library should contain all the latest paint and body shop literature for quick, easy, and *clean* reference.

shop. It is used to total the estimates of damaged vehicles, when billing, and for banking, payroll, and other adding machine jobs.

Typewriter

The typewriter is not a necessity, especially in a small office. However, business letters, billing and other correspondence, when neatly typed, will create a good impression for the business. See Fig. 1-38.

Telephone

An auto body shop needs to make many telephone calls, both local and long distance. A large repair shop should employ an efficient person who is familiar with the business and can handle all the shop's telephone calls. See Fig. 1-39. A pleasant tone and intelligent answer can help establish a new shop's business.

Office Library

All offices will need a small auto body library. This should include damage report price manuals, text books, paint color guide manuals, service manuals from the automobile manufacturing companies, and other literature. Fig. 1-40 shows a small library that is typical of many auto body repair shops.

Estimating and Insurance

A successful auto body shop will need to make estimates of the cost to repair the damage on different vehicles. Estimates will range from large wrecks to small dents, and all repainting jobs.

If possible, it is a good idea to have only *one* person make all the estimates. The person making the estimates should know how to *sell* all the body shop's many services to private car owners. Also, he will have insurance appraisers (adjusters) to deal with. The appraiser is the insurance company representative who estimates damage and authorizes (ok's) the insurance company's payment.

Estimate—The estimate is a *cost* value of the damage done and, also, the price needed to repair the damaged vehicle. The estimate is completed as an itemized list that shows the cost of repairing the damage on the vehicle. A typical estimate is shown in Fig. 2-1.

The estimate is sometimes known as a *damage appraisal* by the insurance company. By either name, the estimate or appraisal becomes a *commitment* (or a binding bid with respect to the repairman's honesty) by both the shop's estimator and the insurance company or customer.

This chapter explains the correct procedure (plan) to follow when making an estimate. Included are the estimate costs involved, problems encountered, determining the type of insurance claim (if insurance is involved), and the party who will pay for the vehicle's repair.

ESTIMATING IN GENERAL

Actually, an estimator makes *two* estimates, so to speak. The *first* estimate is only made up of mental notes made when looking over the damage; a *visual* estimate. The person making the estimate walks around the damaged car and generally looks it over. While he does this, he is making mental notes, as in Fig. 2-2.

The *second* report is the actual written estimate itself. This report lists each item and operation (work) needed for repair. This will include parts, labor, refinishing, body shop materials, *sublet* repair costs, and other costs, if any. (Sublet repair refers to work such as wrecker use, car storage, radiator repair, bumper repair, and other work that will be sent or charged to another shop. Sending out sublet work is also called "farming out" the work.)

The shop estimator in Fig. 2-3 is working on the *written* estimate. The estimate may show the cost of five or more items: parts, labor, sublet repairs, materials, and refinishing. At least two copies of the estimate should be made. One copy of the estimate should be filed in the body shop office and the other copy given to the car owner or to the insurance company representative, depending on who asked for the estimate.

WOLFE BODY SHOP

PHONE 852-4129

55 So. Adams

BODY AND FENDER REPAIRS • EXPERT REFINISHING

NAME _Howard Thomas_

ADDRESS _321 Boulevard Motif_

Brownsburg, Ohio

$5.00 Pd.
for Estimate
S.W.

DATE _1-18-76_

PHONE _852-7310_

DATE WANTED _1-30-76_

REPAIR	REPLACE	YEAR-MODEL-COLOR _74 Must_	MAKE OF CAR _Ford_	BODY TYPE _Runabout_	LICENSE NO. _32B169_	SERIAL NO. _4556H267130_	MFG. PAINT NO. _3B_	MILEAGE _17,737_		
					SUBLET WORK	PARTS AND MATERIALS	LABOR	REFINISHING		
	✓	Front Bumper Assembly				271 65	18 00			
	✓	Front Valence Assembly				16 55	5 00			
	✓	Front Body Grille Panel				79 20	20 00			
	✓	Left Front Fender				70 55	22 00			
	✓	LF Fender Side Mldg & Light				12 05	5 00			
	✓	LF Headlight Assy Complete				27 35	5 00			
	✓	LF Wheel				59 45	5 00			
	✓	LF Tire (Goodyear CPSR 9/32 Remain.)				71 62	4 00			
✓		LF Fender Inner Panel					24 00			
	✓	Left Door Skin				150 35	25 00			
	✓	Left Quarter Panel				109 25	130 00			
	✓	Left Quarter Post Assy				17 90	32 00			
✓		Left Quarter Inner Panel					24 00			
	✓	Left Sill Plate				3 15	2 50			
	✓	Left Door Lock Assembly				20 65	4 00			
✓		Hood (and Align Hinges)					24 00			
		Shop Materials				45 00				
		Paint as Repaired						140 00		
		Align Front Wheels			15 50					
		Storage: 19 days @ $2 per day			38 00					
		Towing (Dolly Req'd)			35 00					
		SUB TOTALS			88 50	954 72	349 50	140 00		

THIS ESTIMATE IS BASED ON OUR INSPECTION AND DOES NOT COVER ADDITIONAL PARTS OR LABOR WHICH MAY BE REQUIRED AFTER THE WORK HAS BEEN STARTED. AFTER THE WORK HAS STARTED, WORN OR DAMAGED PARTS WHICH ARE NOT EVIDENT ON FIRST INSPECTION MAY BE DISCOVERED. NATURALLY THIS ESTIMATE CANNOT COVER SUCH CONTINGENCIES. PARTS PRICES SUBJECT TO CHANGE WITHOUT NOTICE. THIS ESTIMATE IS FOR IMMEDIATE ACCEPTANCE.

TOTAL	1532 72
SALES TAX	38 19
GRAND TOTAL	1570 91

THIS WORK AUTHORIZED BY _____

ESTIMATE SHEET AND REPAIR ORDER

A–70501

Fig. 2-1. A typical estimate should contain many items. (Courtesy of Wolfe Body Shop.)

Fig. 2-2. The *first* estimate is actually a mental estimate. Here, the estimator looks over the job to get an idea of how much work will be involved.

An *insurance report* (the insurance company's copy of the estimate) becomes a firm bid for doing the work during a certain length of time. Usually, it is a good idea to keep an insurance report on record for 30 days.

Damage Report—In some parts of the country, the estimate is often called a *damage report*. This is simply a different word for the estimate. The term damage report may be used today because customers may often associate the word *free* with the word estimate. Usually, body shops in most locations can no longer afford to make free estimates.

In many parts of the country, a damage report (estimate) will still be free *if* the body

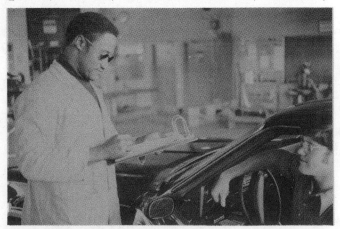

Fig. 2-3. The *second* estimate is actually writing up the report of the parts and work necessary to repair the damage.

shop making the report is allowed to repair the vehicle. However, if the report is made for an insurance company or for a car owner who simply wants to know how much the repair will cost, the cost of the damage report must reflect the extent of the collision. The extent of the collision, of course, determines the amount of paperwork needed to make the report.

WRITING UP THE ESTIMATE

Writing up the damage report (estimate) is serious business. The estimator must be able to tell the customer whether the extent of the damage *and* the cost of repair will justify the car being repaired. The appraiser (estimator) should know what the value of the vehicle was *before* the accident. Of course, he must keep in mind that the car will have to be repaired to the condition it was in before the accident.

Analyzing (Looking Over) the Accident

A thorough observation is important before writing up the actual estimate. The estimator must determine what happened and how much the vehicle was damaged. In Fig. 2-2, the estimator is making an analysis of a wreck.

The estimator must study the damage *thoroughly*, to determine how serious the damage is *before* making the written estimate. This time is well spent because it will help keep the appraiser from overlooking hidden damaged parts.

Determining the Car's Value

Sometimes, an appraiser may spend valuable time estimating the cost of collision repair and *then* find that the repair cost exceeds the value of the vehicle. To be sure that this does not happen, the estimator needs to know about how much money the car is worth. This will help decide whether the car will be declared a *total loss*, often simply called a "total." Whether a wrecked car is declared a "total" must be determined by comparing *three* cash values, as follows.

Market Value—the *first* cash value to consider is the *market value*. The market value of the car is the car's average *wholesale* price, as shown in Fig. 2-4. The *retail* price is the customer's price when he buys the car from a business such as a used-car dealer or the used car lot of a new car dealer. *Wholesale* price, on the other hand, is the price that the businessman, such as a used-car dealer, pays for the car. This might be at an automobile dealers' auction or the money allowed for a car taken in trade with a customer.

Of course, for the dealer to make a profit, he must sell at a retail price that is *higher* than the wholesale price. The dealer often determines his retail price by referring to published booklets of car values. The groups who publish the booklets make surveys to determine the average retail prices. These same books are used by body shop estimators and insurance

adjusters to determine the car's wholesale market value.

Repair Cost—The *second* cash value to consider is the *repair cost*. This is the total value of *all* the costs needed to make up the cost of the repair job. This cost is listed on the *total* estimate, including such items as towing fees, storage fees, paint work, labor, parts, and everything that determines the total cost of the repair to be made. All of these costs are used to make the estimate. Then, the total is carefully added to the salvage value of the car, explained next.

Salvage Value—The *third* cash value to consider is the *salvage value*.

When a car is "totally" wrecked, it is not really *totally* wrecked, since some parts on the car can still be used. In some cases, this often includes the drive shaft, engine, transmission, body parts not damaged in the wreck, etc. These good parts can still be sold as used parts, and so they *do* have a cash value. These salvage parts cause a badly wrecked automobile to have some cash value, even though the car may look worthless. The car in Fig. 2-5, for example, still has many good parts even though it is badly wrecked.

The salvage value, of course, is nowhere near what the car's market value was before the accident. For example, if the car's normal market value, in good condition, is $1,000, it might have a salvage value of only $200 when badly wrecked. Then, if the repair cost *plus*

AMERICAN MOTORS 1974-73 [1]

Av'g. Trd-In	Ins. Sym.	BODY TYPE	Model	Av'g. Loan	Av'g. Retail	Av'g. Trd-In	Ins. Sym.	BODY TYPE	Model	Av'g. Loan	Av'g. Retail
		MILEAGE CATEGORY: AMERICAN MOTORS						**MATADOR BROUGHAM—6**			
						2525	4	Cpe 2D	16-9	2275	3150
		Gremlin-1 American-1 Rebel-II						**MATADOR—V8**			
		Hornet-I Javelin-II Marlin-II				2475	4	Sed 4D	15-7	2250	3075
		Rambler-I AMX-II Ambassador-II				2550	4	Cpe 2D	16-7	2300	3175
		Matador-II				2750	5	Sta Wgn 2S	18-7	2475	3375
								MATADOR BROUGHAM—V8			
		1974 GREMLIN—6—AT				2625	4	Cpe 2D	16-9	2375	3250
1950	3	Sed 4P	46-5	1775	2525			**MATADOR "X"—VR**			
		GREMLIN—8—AT				2725	5	Cpe 2D	16-8	2475	3350
1950	4	Sed 2D 4P	46-5	1775	2525						
								225 Add Fact Air Condition		225	300
		25 Add Power Steering		25	50			75 Add Tape Deck		75	100
		150 Add Fact Air Condition		150	200			75 Add AM/FM Stereo		75	100
		125 Add "X" Pkg.		125	150			50 Add Vinyl Top		50	75
		50 Add Levi C Trim Pkg		50	75			100 Add 3 Seat Sta. Wgn.		100	125
		Deduct Manual Trans.						50 Add Lug. Rack S/W		50	75
		1974 HORNET—6—AT—P3						225 Deduct Manual Trans.		225	225
2075	4	Sed 4D	05-7	1875	2650			125 Deduct Convent Steer		125	125
2050	3	Sed 2D	06-7	1850	2625						
2200	4	Sed H'back	03-7	2000	2800			**1974 AMBASSADOR—AT—PS—AC**			
2350	4	Sportabout	08 7	2125	2950	2800	5	Sed 4D	85-7	2525	3425
		HORNET—V8—AT—PS				3100	5	Sta Wgn 2S	88-7	2800	3775
2075	4	Sed 4D	05-7	1875	2650						
2050	4	Sed 2D	06-/	1850	2625			50 Add Vinyl Top		50	75
2200	4	Sed H'back	03-7	2000	2800			100 Add 3 Seat Sta. Wgn.		100	125
2350	4	Sportabout	08-7	2125	2950			75 Add AM/FM Stereo		75	100
								75 Add Tape Deck		75	100
		175 Add Fact Air Condition		175	225			75 Add Power Windows		75	100
		50 Add Vinyl Top		50	75						
		75 Add Spt. D/L Pkg.		75	100			**1973 GREMLIN—6—AT**			
		50 Add Levi C Trim Pkg.		50	75	1575	3	Sed 2D 4P	46-5	1425	2125
		100 Add "X" Pkg.		100	125			**GREMLIN—V8—AT**			
		25 Add Lug. Rack Wgn.		25	50	1575	3	Sed 2D 4P	46-5	1425	2125
		125 Deduct Manual Trans.		125	125						
		75 Deduct Convent. Steer.		75	75			25 Add Power Steering		25	50
		1974 JAVELIN—AT—PS						125 Add Fact Air Condition		125	150
		JAVELIN—6						75 Add "X" Pkg.		75	100
2400	4	H'dtop 2D	79-7	2175	3000			Deduct Manual Trans			
		JAVELIN—V8						**1973 HORNET—6—AT—PS**			
2500	4	H'dtop 2D	79-7	2250	3100	1725	3	Sed 4D	05-7	1575	2275
		JAVELIN AMX—V8				1700	3	Sed 2D	06-7	1550	2250
2625	5	H'dtop 2D	79-8	2375	3250	1850	4	Sed H'back	03-7	1675	2425
						1975	4	Sportabout	08-7	1800	2550
		225 Add Fact Air Condition		225	300			**HORNET—V8—AT—PS**			
		75 Add Tape Deck		75	100	1725	4	Sed 4D	05-7	1575	2275
		75 Add AM/FM Stereo		75	100	1700	3	Sed 2D	06-7	1550	2250
		75 Add Vinyl Top		75	100	1850	4	Sed H'back	03-7	1675	2425
		225 Deduct 3 Spd. Trans.		225	225	1975	4	Sportabout	08-7	1800	2550
		125 Deduct 4 Spd. Trans.		125	125						
		125 Deduct Convent. Steer.		125	125			150 Add Fact Air Condition		150	200
		1974 MATADOR—AT—PS						25 Add Vinyl Top		25	50
		MATADOR—6						50 Add Spt D/L Pk.		50	75
2375	4	Sed 4D	15-7	2150	2975			25 Add Lug. Rack Wgn.		25	50
2450	4	Cpe 2D	16-7	2225	3050			100 Deduct Manual Trans.		100	100
2650	4	Sta Wgn 2S	18-7	2400	3275			75 Deduct Convent. Steer.		75	75
		DEDUCT FOR HIGH MILEAGE									
E		**CENTRAL EDITION**									

Fig. 2-4. Automobile prices are listed for the dealer's and estimator's use in booklets published by various groups. (Courtesy of National Automobile Dealers Used Car Guide Co.)

Fig. 2-5. A badly wrecked car always has some good parts still on it. The total value of these parts is called the car's *salvage value*.

the salvage value total *more* than the wholesale market price, the car will probably be declared a total loss.

If the car is badly wrecked, it must always be determined if the car is going to be repaired or declared a "total." Writing a very detailed estimate on a "totalled" car would then be a waste of time. The experienced shop owner or estimator should immediately consider this possibility when estimating collision claims, to determine if the car is worth repairing.

Obtaining Preliminary Information

A first step in making out the estimate is to obtain (ask, determine) the *preliminary* information. This will include items such as who owns the car, who will pay the bill, how much is to be repaired, whether the car owner wants the car repaired all over or spot repaired, whether new or used parts are to be installed, etc. Then, the estimator must determine whether the car is worth repairing, as discussed earlier. The estimator can then begin writing the damage report (estimate).

Basic Estimating Procedure

When writing up an estimate, start at one specific place and estimate the cost of parts, labor, and refinishing on each panel. Go from the outside of the car inward on each damaged panel, as in Fig. 2-6. Be certain to include the *full amount* of the damage. Move to the next panel and estimate it in the same manner, continuing all the way around the car. Include the

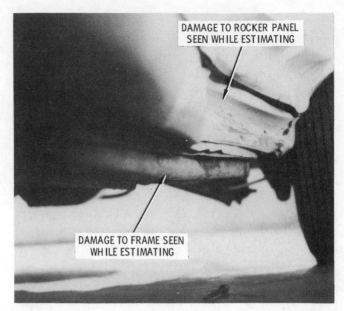

Fig. 2-7. Frame damage is serious and may not be easily seen while estimating. Always look very carefully for frame damage.

top and the frame, if necessary. Note any mechanical repairs needed, such as suspension or brake damage.

Frame Damage—Figs. 2-7 and 2-8 show an example of frame damage. When estimating frame damage, first identify the damaged frame area: for example; the left side rail, center section. In other words, to correctly estimate frame damage, list the *name* and *location* of each section of the frame that is damaged. Estimating

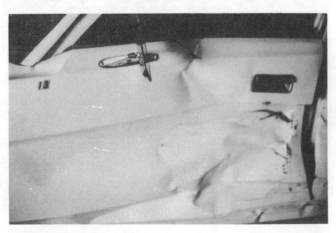

Fig. 2-6. When estimating, thoroughly estimate *all* the damage to *each* part, and the parts to which any damaged parts are attached.

Fig. 2-8. After the car is taken apart for repair, the frame damage may be more easily seen.

REAR DOOR, Cont'd.

MOULDINGS & TRIM, Cont'd.

Moulding, S/W (w/Decal)			
4. Upper	4489098-9	.2	2.75
5. Lower	4489100-1	.2	4.98
6. Decal, Wood Overlay	8122829	#1.0	26.45
(#Time is w/Mouldings Removed & After Painting)			
Cover, Upper Vinyl*	3669520-1	.3	1.69
(*Order by Trim Code From Dealer)			

HARDWARE

Latch	3614158-9	.6	10.03
Striker, Lock	3657930	.2	1.91
Handle, Outside	3602070-1	.6	8.97
Base, Outside Handle	3602132-3		4.31
Handle, Inside	3601340		2.41
Control, Remote R/L	3602056		3.02
Bellcrank, Door Locking w/Cable	3601056-7		3.08
Hinge, Upper	3574770-1	#.4	4.48
Hinge, Lower	3591190-1	#.4	7.84
(#R&R Both .6)			
Weatherstrip, Sedan	3616172-3	.5	10.76
Station Wagon	3574578-9	.5	11.94

DOOR GLASS & PARTS

Glass (Glass Co.)	Use	(Car Mfr.)		Use
Sedan				
Clear NAGS D4401-2	Glass	3615844-5	1.0	Glass
Tinted		3615846-7		
Station Wagon	Price			Price
Clear NAGS D3705-6		3575006-7	1.0	
Tinted	List	3575008-9		List
Frame, Door Window				
Sedan		3646050-1	1.0	24.09
Station Wagon		3646054-5	1.0	24.49
Channel, Glass Slide				
Sedan R/L		3616170	.4	5.71
Station Wagon R/L		3576155	.4	3.98
Weatherstrip, at Belt				
Outer Sedan		3651510-1	#.2	3.53
S/W		3651512-3	#.2	3.10
Inner Sedan		3651520-1	#.2	1.84
S/W		3651526	#.2	1.79
(#Time is w/Glass Removed)				
Sealer, Bottom Channel R/L		3576152		.75
Channel, Glass Lowering		3576146-7		3.31
Guide, Glass Channel R/L		3576358		.75
Regulator, Manual		3609088-9	#.6	14.17
Electric		4484260-1	#.7	27.51
(#exc. w/Glass Removed, Manual .2, Electric .3)				
Motor, Regulator R/L		3661224		39.10
Drive, Electric Regulator R/L		4484914		10.64
L/H		4484915		13.44
Handle, Regulator		3602986	.2	2.97

ROOF

Refinish	3.5
R&R Headliner	
Sedan, exc.	1.6
w/Electric Lifts	2.0
H.T.	.8
Roof Time Includes R&R	
Trim & Glass	
Rail Time Is w/Roof Removed	
Add to Roof R&R	
w/Vinyl Cover	6.5

Exc. STATION WAGON

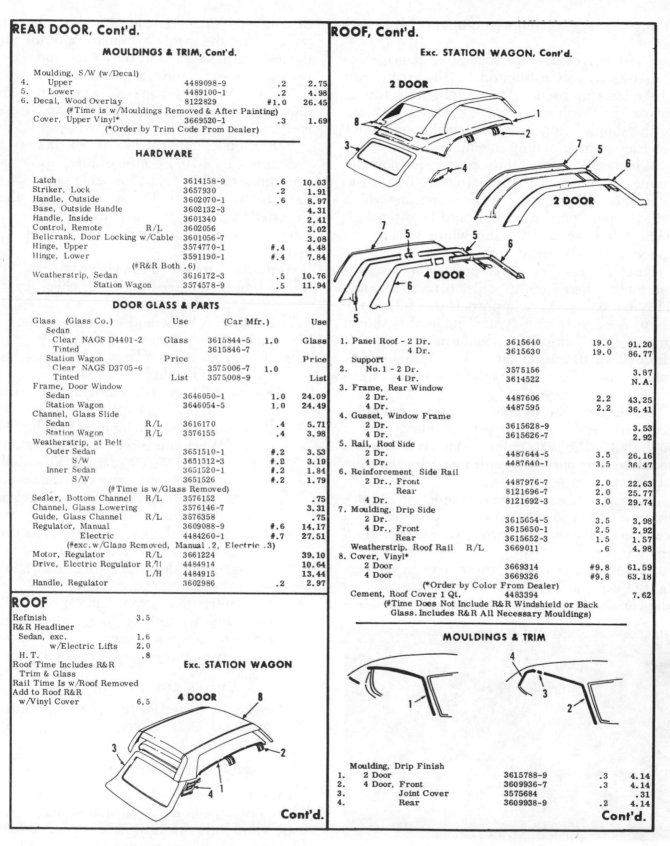

ROOF, Cont'd.

Exc. STATION WAGON, Cont'd.

1. Panel Roof - 2 Dr.		3615640	19.0	91.20
4 Dr.		3615630	19.0	86.77
Support				
2. No. 1 - 2 Dr.		3575156		3.87
4 Dr.		3614522		N.A.
3. Frame, Rear Window				
2 Dr.		4487606	2.2	43.25
4 Dr.		4487595	2.2	36.41
4. Gusset, Window Frame				
2 Dr.		3615628-9		3.53
4 Dr.		3615626-7		2.92
5. Rail, Roof Side				
2 Dr.		4487644-5	3.5	26.16
4 Dr.		4487640-1	3.5	36.47
6. Reinforcement, Side Rail				
2 Dr., Front		4487976-7	2.0	22.63
Rear		8121696-7	2.0	25.77
4 Dr.		8121692-3	3.0	29.74
7. Moulding, Drip Side				
2 Dr.		3615654-5	3.5	3.98
4 Dr., Front		3615650-1	2.5	2.92
Rear		3615652-3	1.5	1.57
Weatherstrip, Roof Rail R/L		3669011	.6	4.98
8. Cover, Vinyl*				
2 Door		3669314	#9.8	61.59
4 Door		3669326	#9.8	63.18
(*Order by Color From Dealer)				
Cement, Roof Cover 1 Qt.		4483394		7.62

(#Time Does Not Include R&R Windshield or Back
Glass. Includes R&R All Necessary Mouldings)

MOULDINGS & TRIM

Moulding, Drip Finish				
1. 2 Door		3615788-9	.3	4.14
2. 4 Door, Front		3609936-7	.3	4.14
3. Joint Cover		3575684		.31
4. Rear		3609938-9	.2	4.14

Cont'd.

Fig. 2-9. A typical page from a collision parts manual. These manuals show both the cost of the part and the labor time needed to replace the part. (Courtesy of Mitchell Manuals, Inc.)

frame damage is more thoroughly discussed later.

The labor charge for the frame damage estimate is usually estimated by the complexity of the hook-up required to straighten the frame, instead of the hours involved. This is because of the shop's heavy cost (financial investment) for frame straightening machinery.

When estimating, it must be decided how the frame repair charge will be made. Either the type of hook-up needed or the labor time which will be spent on the work should be estimated. This will have to be done while visually inspecting the damaged areas.

Parts Prices—The parts prices for the estimate are taken from a collision parts manual. This manual is a very important tool for a body shop. A page from a typical manual is shown in Fig. 2-9. Using the collision parts manual is thoroughly discussed later. For accurate estimates, never guess or take someone's word about parts prices.

To simplify the estimate, the cost of refinish material needed (paint, primer, filler, etc.) is included in the *parts* column. This is done since material and parts are both taxed by the sales tax in most states.

Unseen Damage—When completing an estimate, always take a second look at the damaged vehicle to be sure that you have included *all* the damage.

Sometimes, of course, there may be damage on the car that cannot or will not be seen until the car is taken apart. In these cases, the parts

Fig. 2-10. Bad collisions may cause damage that will not be found until the car is taken apart.

that *might* be damaged are listed on the estimate. Then, the words *left open* are written on the estimate instead of the parts and labor prices. This tells the car owner or insurance company that the shop will not know how much it will cost to fix the parts until the car is taken apart and checked.

For example, note the heavy side damage to the car in Fig. 2-10. Because of this impact, the transmission, driveshaft, or differential may have been damaged. Those parts would then be listed on the estimate and the words *left open* written in the price column of the estimate.

Finishing Up—When the estimate is finished up, the important steps to double-check are:

1. Be sure to know and *write down* the vehicle owner's *name*.
2. Be sure to know *who* will be responsible for *paying the bill*.
3. Find out if there is a *deductible* clause on an insurance claim estimate. Many collision insurance policies have a deductible clause. When this is the case, the customer pays the first $50.00 or $100.00 and the insurance company pays the remaining part of the bill. Be sure that the customer knows about this.
4. Determine if the car is *worth* repairing. That is, whether the total repair cost plus the salvage value is less than the wholesale value of the car.
5. Remember that some damage cannot be seen. Be sure to have those listed on the estimate as unestimated until further study. Use the term *left open* on those areas.
6. Carefully check all the numbers and addition on the estimate to be sure that the mathematics is correct.

USING COLLISION PARTS MANUALS

Collision *parts manuals* are also known as "collision *estimators*," "collision *damage manuals*," and other terms. They are available from several different book companies. These manuals contain several types of information.

They are very valuable sources of information. A good body shop manager or his estimator *must* have these on hand to make accurate estimates.

The collision parts manual gives both the parts and labor prices for installing new parts or panels. For this reason, an estimator must know how to use the collision parts manual to find the *price* of the new parts and amount of *time* needed to install the parts. Of course, the estimator will have to charge more for labor if it will be necessary to align (straighten) an opening after the damaged panel has been removed.

Body and Parts Information

The collision parts manual begins with information used to identify the model and make of the complete car. Fig. 2-11 shows a typical *model identification page*. This is necessary for the estimator to know the model *number* of the car.

In each case, the model and make identification pages are followed by identification of almost every part of the entire car, from the front bumper of the vehicle to the back bumper. Each part is listed with typical pictures of the assemblies. A list follows the pictures, showing the part numbers, hours needed to install, and the retail price of the part. Fig. 2-12 is a typical page from one such part number manual.

Labor Conversion Table

On the collision parts manual pages, the labor figures are given only in *time*, not *cost*. This is because labor charges per hour are different from one shop to another.

When the estimate is written, all the labor should be put down on the estimate in *hours*. Then, the total hours can be multiplied by the shop's charge per hour to get the actual *total* labor cost for the entire estimate.

To save the estimator time, each collision parts manual book contains a *labor conversion table*. In the table, the labor charge (per hour) is computed from 0.1 hour to 50 hours. Labor rates from $3.50 per hour to $15.00 per hour may be used in some manuals, as shown in Figs. 2-13 and 2-14.

Using the Table—As an example of how to use the table, note that if the shop's labor rate is $5.50 an hour, and if the labor total is 4.2 hours, the charge for labor is $23.10. See Fig. 2-13. The table provides quick, accurate results when figuring labor charges, and it saves the time of multiplying or using a computer.

USING MICROFILM ESTIMATORS

The auto body teacher in Fig. 2-15 is explaining a *microfilm estimator*. Many body shop managers are replacing collision parts manuals with this machine and its films. The microfilm is a miniature manual and contains the same information. The information contained in collision parts manuals can be purchased on microfilm, and the film can be "shown" on the microfilm estimator itself. A microfilm estimator is shown in Fig. 2-16, while one of the thin microfilm "cards" is shown in Fig. 2-17.

Microfilm estimators are much easier to use than the thicker, bulkier collision parts manuals. Microfilm estimators speed up the time it takes to make an estimate on a damaged vehicle. They can cut the time involved by as much as 50 per cent.

When the damage involves one or two parts, the microfilm estimator can be used to price the job while the customer looks on. Thus, the customer can see for himself how much the parts cost, and the labor time needed to install the parts.

How it Works—Basically, a microfilm estimator works like any film projector. That is, the picture on the microfilm is first magnified and then projected onto the machine's lighted screen. The microfilm estimator uses 4″ × 6″ strips of *microfilm* and a 4″ × 8″ picture *selection card*.

Microfilm

Each microfilm strip contains about 100 pictures of body parts. Fig. 2-17 shows a microfilm strip. The car's make is indicated by the strip of color used across the top of the microfilm. Different car manufacturers have different color strips. This helps the estimator be able to quickly select the correct film for any late-

1973

PINTO

62B   2 Door Sedan
64B   3 Door Sedan (Run About)
73B   2 Door Station Wagon

MAVERICK

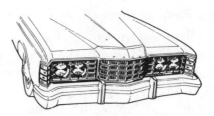

54A   4 Door Sedan
62D   Grabber 2 Door Sedan
62A   2 Door Sedan

TORINO

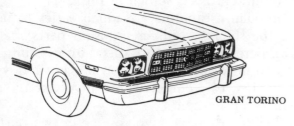

TORINO

GRAN TORINO

53B   4 Door Pillared Hardtop
53D   Gran Torino 4 Door Pillared Hardtop
63R   Gran Torino Sport 2 Door Hardtop (Fastback)
65B   2 Door Hardtop (Formal Roof)
65D   Gran Torino 2 Door Hardtop (Formal Roof)
65R   Gran Torino Sport 2 Door Hardtop (Formal Roof)
71B   4 Door Station Wagon
71D   Gran Torino Station Wagon
71K   Gran Torino Squire Station Wagon
97D   500 Ranchero
97R   GT Ranchero
97K   Squire Ranchero

FORD

53D   Custom 500 4 Door Pillared Hardtop
53F   Galaxie 500 4 Door Pillared Hardtop
53H   LTD 4 Door Pillared Hardtop
53K   LTD Brougham 4 Door Pillared Hardtop
57F   Galaxie 500 4 Door Hardtop
57H   LTD 4 Door Hardtop
57K   LTD Brougham 4 Door Hardtop
65D   Custom 500 2 Door Hardtop
65F   Galaxie 500 2 Door Hardtop
65H   LTD 2 Door Hardtop
65K   LTD Brougham 2 Door Hardtop
71D   4 Door Custom 500 Ranch Wagon
71F   4 Door Country Sedan
71H   4 Door Country Squire

MUSTANG

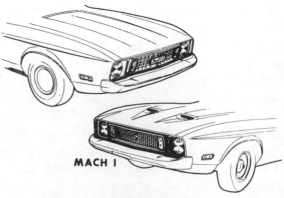

MACH I

63D   2 Door Hardtop (Fastback)
63R   Mach I 2 Door Hardtop (Fastback)
65D   2 Door Hardtop
65F   Grande 2 Door Hardtop
76D   Convertible

THUNDERBIRD

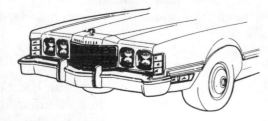

65K   2 Door Hardtop

Fig. 2-11. Typical model identification page. (Courtesy of Mitchell Manuals, Inc.)

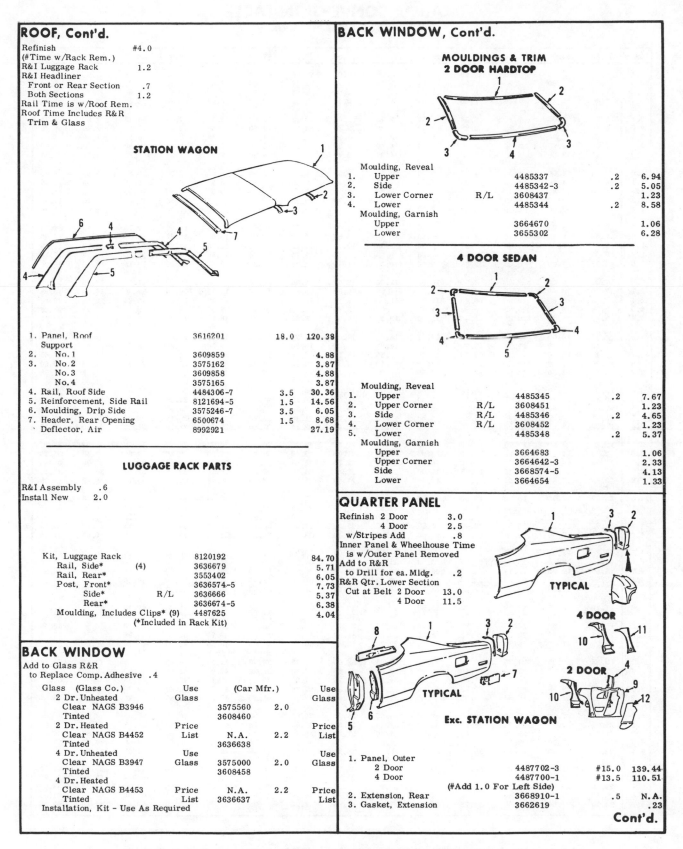

ROOF, Cont'd.

Refinish	#4.0	
(#Time w/Rack Rem.)		
R&I Luggage Rack	1.2	
R&I Headliner		
Front or Rear Section	.7	
Both Sections	1.2	

Rail Time is w/Roof Rem.
Roof Time Includes R&R
  Trim & Glass

STATION WAGON

1.	Panel, Roof	3616201	18.0 120.38
	Support		
2.	No.1	3609859	4.88
3.	No.2	3575162	3.87
	No.3	3609858	4.88
	No.4	3575165	3.87
4.	Rail, Roof Side	4484306-7	3.5 30.36
5.	Reinforcement, Side Rail	8121694-5	1.5 14.56
6.	Moulding, Drip Side	3575246-7	3.5 6.05
7.	Header, Rear Opening	6500674	1.5 8.68
	Deflector, Air	8992921	27.19

LUGGAGE RACK PARTS

R&I Assembly	.6	
Install New	2.0	

Kit, Luggage Rack		8120192	84.70
Rail, Side*	(4)	3636679	5.71
Rail, Rear*		3553402	6.05
Post, Front*		3636574-5	7.73
Side*	R/L	3636666	5.37
Rear*		3636674-5	6.38
Moulding, Includes Clips* (9)		4487625	4.04
	(*Included in Rack Kit)		

BACK WINDOW

Add to Glass R&R
to Replace Comp. Adhesive .4

Glass (Glass Co.)	Use	(Car Mfr.)		Use
2 Dr. Unheated	Glass			Glass
Clear NAGS B3946		3575560	2.0	
Tinted		3608460		
2 Dr. Heated	Price			Price
Clear NAGS B4452	List	N.A.	2.2	List
Tinted		3636638		
4 Dr. Unheated	Use			Use
Clear NAGS B3947	Glass	3575000	2.0	Glass
Tinted		3608458		
4 Dr. Heated				
Clear NAGS B4453	Price	N.A.	2.2	Price
Tinted	List	3636637		List

Installation, Kit - Use As Required

BACK WINDOW, Cont'd.

MOULDINGS & TRIM
2 DOOR HARDTOP

Moulding, Reveal					
1.	Upper		4485337	.2	6.94
2.	Side		4485342-3	.2	5.05
3.	Lower Corner	R/L	3608437		1.23
4.	Lower		4485344	.2	8.58
Moulding, Garnish					
	Upper		3664670		1.06
	Lower		3655302		6.28

4 DOOR SEDAN

Moulding, Reveal					
1.	Upper		4485345	.2	7.67
2.	Upper Corner	R/L	3608451		1.23
3.	Side	R/L	4485346	.2	4.65
4.	Lower Corner	R/L	3608452		1.23
5.	Lower		4485348	.2	5.37
Moulding, Garnish					
	Upper		3664683		1.06
	Upper Corner		3664642-3		2.33
	Side		3668574-5		4.13
	Lower		3664654		1.33

QUARTER PANEL

Refinish 2 Door	3.0	
4 Door	2.5	
w/Stripes Add	.8	

Inner Panel & Wheelhouse Time
is w/Outer Panel Removed
Add to R&R
  to Drill for ea. Mldg. .2
R&R Qtr. Lower Section
  Cut at Belt 2 Door 13.0
            4 Door 11.5

1.	Panel, Outer		
	2 Door	4487702-3	#15.0 139.44
	4 Door	4487700-1	#13.5 110.51
	(#Add 1.0 For Left Side)		
2.	Extension, Rear	3668910-1	.5 N.A.
3.	Gasket, Extension	3662619	.23

Cont'd.

Fig. 2-12. Typical part number and labor guide page. (Courtesy of Mitchell Manuals, Inc.)

LABOR CONVERSION TABLE
LABOR RATES PER HOUR

Hours	$3.50	$4.00	$4.50	$4.75	$5.00	$5.50	$6.00	$6.50	$7.00	$7.50	$8.00	$8.50	$9.00	$9.50
0.1	.35	.40	.45	.48	.50	.55	.60	.65	.70	.75	.80	.85	.90	.95
0.2	.70	.80	.90	.95	1.00	1.10	1.20	1.30	1.40	1.50	1.60	1.70	1.80	1.90
0.3	1.05	1.20	1.35	1.43	1.50	1.65	1.80	1.95	2.10	2.25	2.40	2.55	2.70	2.85
0.4	1.40	1.60	1.80	1.90	2.00	2.20	2.40	2.60	2.80	3.00	3.20	3.40	3.60	3.80
0.5	1.75	2.00	2.25	2.38	2.50	2.75	3.00	3.25	3.50	3.75	4.00	4.25	4.50	4.75
0.6	2.10	2.40	2.70	2.85	3.00	3.30	3.60	3.90	4.20	4.50	4.80	5.10	5.40	5.70
0.7	2.45	2.80	3.15	3.33	3.50	3.85	4.20	4.55	4.90	5.25	5.60	5.95	6.30	6.65
0.8	2.80	3.20	3.60	3.80	4.00	4.40	4.80	5.20	5.60	6.00	6.40	6.80	7.20	7.60
0.9	3.15	3.60	4.05	4.28	4.50	4.95	5.40	5.85	6.30	6.75	7.20	7.65	8.10	8.55
1.0	3.50	4.00	4.50	4.75	5.00	5.50	6.00	6.50	7.00	7.50	8.00	8.50	9.00	9.50
1.1	3.85	4.40	4.95	5.23	5.50	6.05	6.60	7.15	7.70	8.25	8.80	9.35	9.90	10.45
1.2	4.20	4.80	5.40	5.70	6.00	6.60	7.20	7.80	8.40	9.00	9.60	10.20	10.80	11.40
1.3	4.55	5.20	5.85	6.18	6.50	7.15	7.80	8.45	9.10	9.75	10.40	11.05	11.70	12.35
1.4	4.90	5.60	6.30	6.65	7.00	7.70	8.40	9.10	9.80	10.50	11.20	11.90	12.60	13.30
1.5	5.25	6.00	6.75	7.13	7.50	8.25	9.00	9.75	10.50	11.25	12.00	12.75	13.50	14.25
1.6	5.60	6.40	7.20	7.60	8.00	8.80	9.60	10.40	11.20	12.00	12.80	13.60	14.40	15.20
1.7	5.95	6.80	7.65	8.08	8.50	9.35	10.20	11.05	11.90	12.75	13.60	14.45	15.30	16.15
1.8	6.30	7.20	8.10	8.55	9.00	9.90	10.80	11.70	12.60	13.50	14.40	15.30	16.20	17.10
1.9	6.65	7.60	8.55	9.08	9.50	10.45	11.40	12.35	13.30	14.25	15.20	16.15	17.10	18.05
2.0	7.00	8.00	9.00	9.50	10.00	11.00	12.00	13.00	14.00	15.00	16.00	17.00	18.00	19.00
2.1	7.35	8.40	9.45	9.98	10.50	11.55	12.60	13.65	14.70	15.75	16.80	17.85	18.90	19.95
2.2	7.70	8.80	9.90	10.45	11.00	12.10	13.20	14.30	15.40	16.50	17.60	18.70	19.80	20.90
2.3	8.05	9.20	10.35	10.93	11.50	12.65	13.80	14.95	16.10	17.25	18.40	19.55	20.70	21.85
2.4	8.40	9.60	10.80	11.40	12.00	13.20	14.40	15.60	16.80	18.00	19.20	20.40	21.60	22.80
2.5	8.75	10.00	11.25	11.88	12.50	13.75	15.00	16.25	17.50	18.75	20.00	21.25	22.50	23.75
2.6	9.10	10.40	11.70	12.35	13.00	14.30	15.60	16.90	18.20	19.50	20.80	22.10	23.40	24.70
2.7	9.45	10.80	12.15	12.83	13.50	14.85	16.20	17.55	18.90	20.25	21.60	22.95	24.30	25.65
2.8	9.80	11.20	12.60	13.30	14.00	15.40	16.80	18.20	19.60	21.00	22.40	23.80	25.20	26.60
2.9	10.15	11.60	13.05	13.78	14.50	15.95	17.40	18.85	20.30	21.75	23.20	24.65	26.10	27.55
3.0	10.50	12.00	13.50	14.25	15.00	16.50	18.00	19.50	21.00	22.50	24.00	25.50	27.00	28.50
3.1	10.85	12.40	13.95	14.73	15.50	17.05	18.60	20.15	21.70	23.25	24.80	26.35	27.90	29.45
3.2	11.20	12.80	14.40	15.20	16.00	17.60	19.20	20.80	22.40	24.00	25.60	27.20	28.80	30.40
3.3	11.55	13.20	14.85	15.68	16.50	18.15	19.80	21.45	23.10	24.75	26.40	28.05	29.70	31.35
3.4	11.90	13.60	15.30	16.15	17.00	18.70	20.40	22.10	23.80	25.50	27.20	28.90	30.60	32.30
3.5	12.25	14.00	15.75	16.63	17.50	19.25	21.00	22.75	24.50	26.25	28.00	29.75	31.50	33.25
3.6	12.60	14.40	16.20	17.10	18.00	19.80	21.60	23.40	25.20	27.00	28.80	30.60	32.40	34.20
3.7	12.95	14.80	16.65	17.58	18.50	20.35	22.20	24.05	25.90	27.75	29.60	31.45	33.30	35.15
3.8	13.30	15.20	17.10	18.05	19.00	20.90	22.80	24.70	26.60	28.50	30.40	32.30	34.20	36.10
3.9	13.65	15.60	17.55	18.53	19.50	21.45	23.40	25.35	27.30	29.25	31.20	33.15	35.10	37.05
4.0	14.00	16.00	18.00	19.00	20.00	22.00	24.00	26.00	28.00	30.00	32.00	34.00	36.00	38.00
4.1	14.35	16.40	18.45	19.48	20.50	22.55	24.60	26.65	28.70	30.75	32.80	34.85	36.90	38.95
4.2	14.70	16.80	18.90	19.95	21.00	23.10	25.20	27.30	29.40	31.50	33.60	35.70	37.80	39.90
4.3	15.05	17.20	19.35	20.43	21.50	23.65	25.80	27.95	30.10	32.25	34.40	36.55	38.70	40.85
4.4	15.40	17.60	19.80	20.90	22.00	24.20	26.40	28.60	30.80	33.00	35.20	37.40	39.60	41.80
4.5	15.75	18.00	20.25	21.38	22.50	24.75	27.00	29.25	31.50	33.75	36.00	38.25	40.50	42.75
4.6	16.10	18.40	20.70	21.85	23.00	25.30	27.60	29.90	32.20	34.50	36.80	39.10	41.40	43.70
4.7	16.45	18.80	21.15	23.33	23.50	25.85	28.20	30.55	32.90	35.25	37.60	39.95	42.30	44.65
4.8	16.80	19.20	21.60	22.80	24.00	26.40	28.80	31.20	33.60	36.00	38.40	40.80	43.20	45.60
4.9	17.15	19.60	22.05	23.28	24.50	26.95	29.40	31.85	34.30	36.75	39.20	41.65	44.10	46.55
5.0	17.50	20.00	22.50	23.75	25.00	27.50	30.00	32.50	35.00	37.50	40.00	42.50	45.00	47.50
5.1	17.85	20.40	22.95	24.23	25.50	28.05	30.60	33.15	35.70	38.25	40.80	43.35	45.90	48.45
5.2	18.20	20.80	23.40	24.70	26.00	28.60	31.20	33.80	36.40	39.00	41.60	44.20	46.80	49.40
5.3	18.55	21.20	23.85	25.18	26.50	29.15	31.80	34.45	37.10	39.75	42.40	45.05	47.70	50.35
5.4	18.90	21.60	24.30	25.65	27.00	29.70	32.40	35.10	37.80	40.50	43.20	45.90	48.60	51.30
5.5	19.25	22.00	24.75	26.13	27.50	30.25	33.00	35.75	38.50	41.25	44.00	46.75	49.50	52.25
5.6	19.60	22.40	25.20	26.60	28.00	30.80	33.60	36.40	39.20	42.00	44.80	47.60	50.40	53.20
5.7	19.95	22.80	25.65	27.08	28.50	31.35	34.20	37.05	39.90	42.75	45.60	48.45	51.30	54.15
5.8	20.30	23.20	26.10	27.55	29.00	31.90	34.80	37.70	40.60	43.50	46.40	49.30	52.20	55.10
5.9	20.65	23.60	26.55	28.03	29.50	32.45	35.40	38.35	41.30	44.25	47.20	50.15	53.10	56.05
6.0	21.00	24.00	27.00	28.50	30.00	33.00	36.00	39.00	42.00	45.00	48.00	51.00	54.00	57.00
6.1	21.35	24.40	27.45	28.98	30.50	33.55	36.60	39.65	42.70	45.75	48.80	51.85	54.90	57.95
6.2	21.70	24.80	27.90	29.45	31.00	34.10	37.20	40.30	43.40	46.50	49.60	52.70	55.80	58.90
6.3	22.05	25.20	28.35	29.93	31.50	34.65	37.80	40.95	44.10	47.25	50.40	53.55	56.70	59.85
6.4	22.40	25.60	28.80	30.40	32.00	35.20	38.40	41.60	44.80	48.00	51.20	54.40	57.60	60.80
6.5	22.75	26.00	29.25	30.88	32.50	35.75	39.00	42.25	45.50	48.75	52.00	55.25	58.50	61.75
6.6	23.10	26.40	29.70	31.35	33.00	36.30	39.60	42.90	46.20	49.50	52.80	56.10	59.40	62.70
6.7	23.45	26.80	30.15	31.83	33.50	36.85	40.20	43.55	46.90	50.25	53.60	56.95	60.30	63.65
6.8	23.80	27.20	30.60	32.30	34.00	37.40	40.80	44.20	47.60	51.00	54.40	57.80	61.20	64.60
6.9	24.15	27.60	31.05	32.78	34.50	37.95	41.40	44.85	48.30	51.75	55.20	58.65	62.10	65.55

Fig. 2-13. Labor conversion table for shorter jobs at lower hourly rates. (Courtesy of Mitchell Manuals, Inc.)

LABOR CONVERSION TABLE

LABOR RATES PER HOUR

Hours	$10.00	$10.50	$11.00	$11.50	$12.00	$12.50	$13.00	$13.50	$14.00	$14.50	$15.00
7.0	70.00	73.50	77.00	80.50	84.00	87.50	91.00	94.50	98.00	101.50	105.00
7.1	71.00	74.55	78.10	81.65	85.20	88.75	92.30	95.85	99.40	102.95	106.50
7.2	72.00	75.60	79.20	82.80	86.40	90.00	93.60	97.20	100.80	104.40	108.00
7.3	73.00	76.65	80.30	83.95	87.60	91.25	94.90	98.55	102.20	105.85	109.50
7.4	74.00	77.70	81.40	85.10	88.80	92.50	96.20	99.90	103.60	107.30	111.00
7.5	75.00	78.75	82.50	86.25	90.00	93.75	97.50	101.25	105.00	108.75	112.50
7.6	76.00	79.80	83.60	87.40	91.20	95.00	98.80	102.60	106.40	110.20	114.00
7.7	77.00	80.85	84.70	88.55	92.40	96.25	100.10	103.95	107.80	111.65	115.50
7.8	78.00	81.90	85.80	89.70	93.60	97.50	101.40	105.30	109.20	113.10	117.00
7.9	79.00	82.95	86.90	90.85	94.80	98.75	102.70	106.65	110.60	114.55	118.50
8.0	80.00	84.00	88.00	92.00	96.00	100.00	104.00	108.00	112.00	116.00	120.00
8.1	81.00	85.05	89.10	93.15	97.20	101.25	105.30	109.35	113.40	117.45	121.50
8.2	82.00	86.10	90.20	94.30	98.40	102.50	106.60	110.70	114.80	118.90	123.00
8.3	83.00	87.15	91.30	95.45	99.60	103.75	107.90	112.05	116.20	120.35	124.50
8.4	84.00	88.20	92.40	96.60	100.80	105.00	109.20	113.40	117.60	121.80	126.00
8.5	85.00	89.25	93.50	97.75	102.00	106.25	110.50	114.75	119.00	123.25	127.50
8.6	86.00	90.30	94.60	98.90	103.20	107.50	111.80	116.10	120.40	124.70	129.00
8.7	87.00	91.35	95.70	100.05	104.40	108.75	113.10	117.45	121.80	126.15	130.50
8.8	88.00	92.40	96.80	101.20	105.60	110.00	114.40	118.80	123.20	127.60	132.00
8.9	89.00	93.45	97.90	102.35	106.80	111.25	115.70	120.15	124.60	129.05	133.50
9.0	90.00	94.50	99.00	103.50	108.00	112.50	117.00	121.50	126.00	130.50	135.00
9.1	91.00	95.55	100.10	104.65	109.20	113.75	118.30	122.85	127.40	131.95	136.50
9.2	92.00	96.60	101.20	105.80	110.40	115.00	119.60	124.20	128.80	133.40	138.00
9.3	93.00	97.65	102.30	106.95	111.60	116.25	120.90	125.55	130.20	134.85	139.50
9.4	94.00	98.70	103.40	108.10	112.80	117.50	122.20	126.90	131.60	136.30	141.00
9.5	95.00	99.75	104.50	109.25	114.00	118.75	123.50	128.25	133.00	317.75	142.50
9.6	96.00	100.80	105.60	110.40	115.20	120.00	124.80	129.60	134.40	139.20	144.00
9.7	97.00	101.85	106.70	111.55	116.40	121.25	126.10	130.95	135.80	140.65	145.50
9.8	98.00	102.90	107.80	112.70	117.60	122.50	127.40	132.30	137.20	142.10	147.00
9.9	99.00	103.95	108.90	113.85	118.80	123.75	128.70	133.65	138.60	143.55	148.50
10.0	100.00	105.00	110.00	115.00	120.00	125.00	130.00	135.00	140.00	145.00	150.00
10.5	105.00	110.25	115.50	120.75	126.00	131.25	136.50	141.75	147.00	152.25	157.50
11.0	110.00	115.50	121.00	126.50	132.00	137.50	143.00	148.50	154.00	159.50	165.00
11.5	115.00	120.75	126.50	132.25	138.00	143.75	149.50	155.25	161.00	166.75	172.50
12.0	120.00	126.00	132.00	138.00	144.00	150.00	156.00	162.00	168.00	174.00	180.00
12.5	125.00	131.25	137.50	143.75	150.00	156.25	162.50	168.75	175.00	181.25	187.50
13.0	130.00	136.50	143.00	149.50	156.00	162.50	169.00	175.50	182.00	188.50	195.00
13.5	135.00	141.75	148.50	155.25	162.00	168.75	175.50	182.25	189.00	195.75	202.50
14.0	140.00	147.00	154.00	161.00	168.00	175.00	182.00	189.00	196.00	203.00	210.00
14.5	145.00	152.25	159.50	166.75	174.00	181.25	188.50	195.75	203.00	210.25	217.50
15.0	150.00	157.50	165.00	172.50	180.00	187.50	195.00	202.50	210.00	217.50	225.00
16.0	160.00	168.00	176.00	184.00	192.00	200.00	208.00	216.00	224.00	232.00	240.00
17.0	170.00	178.50	187.00	195.50	204.00	212.50	221.00	229.50	238.00	246.50	255.00
18.0	180.00	189.00	198.00	207.00	216.00	225.00	234.00	243.00	252.00	261.00	270.00
19.0	190.00	199.50	209.00	218.50	228.00	237.50	247.00	256.50	266.00	275.50	285.00
20.0	200.00	210.00	220.00	230.00	240.00	250.00	260.00	270.00	280.00	290.00	300.00
25.0	250.00	262.50	275.00	287.50	300.00	312.50	325.00	337.50	350.00	362.50	375.00
30.0	300.00	315.00	330.00	345.00	360.00	375.00	390.00	405.00	420.00	435.00	450.00
35.0	350.00	367.50	385.00	402.50	420.00	437.50	455.00	472.50	490.00	507.50	525.00
40.0	400.00	420.00	440.00	460.00	480.00	500.00	520.00	540.00	560.00	580.00	600.00
45.0	450.00	472.50	495.00	517.50	540.00	562.50	585.00	607.50	630.00	652.50	675.00
50.0	500.00	525.00	550.00	575.00	600.00	625.00	650.00	675.00	700.00	725.00	750.00

Fig. 2-14. Labor conversion table for longer jobs at higher hourly rates. (Courtesy of Mitchell Manuals, Inc.)

Fig. 2-15. A teacher explains a microfilm estimator to a group of auto body students.

model car. The top part of the film also shows the year and make of the vehicle pictured on the film.

The microfilm strip is simply a miniature version of several collision parts manual pages.

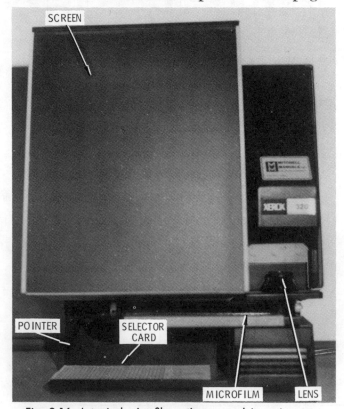

SCREEN

POINTER   SELECTOR CARD

MICROFILM   LENS

Fig. 2-16. A typical microfilm estimator and its major parts.

Each small square on the film pictures the information that would normally be shown on a *full page* of a collision parts manual. Of course, this makes the film too small to see directly. So, when the microfilm is used, it is placed in a holder where it can be projected ("blown up" and lighted) for viewing. The machine's *lens* enlarges the picture for screen viewing.

When the correct microfilm strip has been removed from the file, it is then placed on the *film holder* of the microfilm estimator. Fig. 2-18 shows a microfilm strip being placed in the film holder.

Picture Selection Card

Fig. 2-19 shows a *picture selection card*. The picture selection card measures $4'' \times 8''$ and contains coded references to the microfilm pictures. All of the references on one card are references to the *same* material pictured in the larger collision parts manual. To use the card, first slide the card onto the plate under the machine's pointer, as in Figs. 2-20 and 2-21.

The *pointer* is used to find the microfilm picture desired on the screen. When the microfilm and the picture selection card are both properly in place, the pointer can be moved to a coded section of the card by moving the film platform *under* the pointer. The viewing screen will

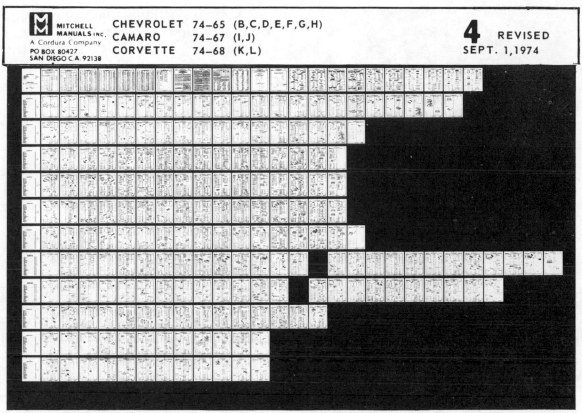

Fig. 2-17. Microfilm cards such as this are better known as *microfiche cards*. They are thin and transparent. (Courtesy of Mitchell Manuals, Inc.)

then picture the part of the *microfilm* that corresponds to the coded part of the *picture selection card*. Fig. 2-22 shows the type of information shown on one section of the picture selection card. Fig. 2-23 shows what the pointer looks like and where it is located on the microfilm estimator machine. Keep in mind that the estimator moves the pointer by moving the *film*

platform until the correct frame is found on the picture selection card.

Viewing Screen

The viewing screen is the place where the part numbers, the pictures and prices of the parts, and time needed to install the parts un-

Fig. 2-18. To use a microfilm estimator, the correct microfilm card must first be placed in the film holder.

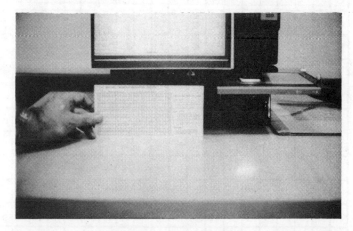

Fig. 2-19. To choose the correct square on the microfilm card, a picture selection card is used with a pointer on the **microfilm** estimator.

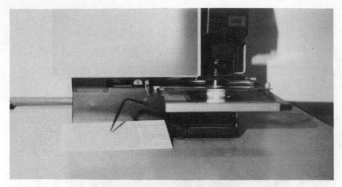

Fig. 2-20. Sliding the picture selection card onto the card platform under the pointer.

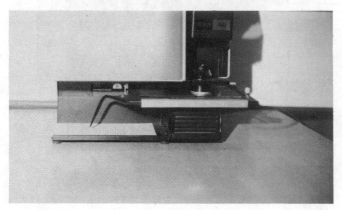

Fig. 2-21. The picture selection card and pointer in working position.

der normal conditions may be read. See Fig. 2-24. The viewing screen is 11" × 14" in size, actually *larger* than the same page of the collision parts manual! This makes the microfilm estimator easier to read than the collision parts manual.

TYPICAL ESTIMATES

Fig. 2-25 shows an example of an outer door panel (sometimes called a "skin") to be replaced. The inner door panel is also damaged,

Fig. 2-23. The pointer is used to select the correct number on the picture selection card.

OFF **MITCHELL MANUALS MICROFICHE SYSTEM** ON

← Move carrier LEFT   Move carrier RIGHT →

A	27	26	25	24	23	22	A	20	19	18	17	A	15	14	13	12	A	10	9	8	7	A	5	4	3	2	A
B							B					B					B					B					B
C	27	26	25	24	23	22	C	20	19	18	17	C	15	14	13	12	C	10	9	8	7	C	5	4	3	2	C
D							D					D					D					D					D
E	27	26	25	24	23	22	E	20	29	18	17	E	15	14	13	12	E	10	9	8	7	E	5	4	3	2	E
F							F					F					F					F					F
G	27	26	25	24	23	22	G	20	19	18	17	G	15	14	13	12	G	10	9	8	7	G	5	4	3	2	G
H							H					H					H					H					H
I	27	26	25	24	23	22	I	20	19	18	17	I	15	14	13	12	I	10	9	8	7	I	5	4	3	2	I
J							J					J					J					J					J
K	27	26	25	24	23	22	K	20	19	18	17	K	15	14	13	12	K	10	9	8	7	K	5	4	3	2	K
L							L					L					L					L					L

OPERATING INSTRUCTIONS

LOAD FILM

1. Pull carrier forward to open.
2. Place film to rear right hand side of carrier.
3. Push carrier in to operate.

VARI-OPTICS

(LOAD)

1. To increase image size, loosen Vari-Optic lock on rear of reader. Move Vari-Optic handle toward the rear of the reader until the desired magnification is attained. Tighten Vari-Optic lock.
2. To decrease magnification, reverse procedure.

TO FOCUS

Applying slight downward pressure, rotate ring on top of the lens until projected image is sharp.

Fig. 2-22. One section of a picture selection card. (Courtesy of Mitchell Manuals, Inc.)

Fig. 2-24. When the microfilm estimator is turned on and focused, the information is actually larger than it would be the same page of a collision parts manual.

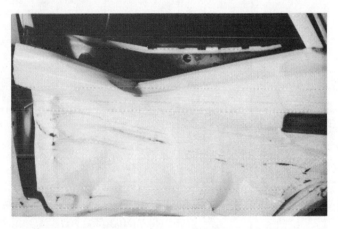

Fig. 2-25. Heavy collision damage requiring a new door outer panel.

so additional labor will be needed to straighten it. The estimate for this repair would then be written as shown in Fig. 2-26.

The price of the outer door panel and installation time is taken from the collision parts manual. The price of aligning the inner door panel must be estimated by the estimator. Collision parts manuals cannot tell the time needed to straighten the inner door panel damage because that depends on how serious the wreck was. This time, then, must be estimated by the estimator.

Actually, Fig. 2-25 is only part of the large wreck shown in Fig. 2-27. Fig. 2-28 shows a completed damage report (estimate) for the car in Fig. 2-27. This estimate is an example of the way in which an estimator or insurance appraiser might write up the estimate for that damage.

Fig. 2-29 shows a car with heavy damage to the left rear. Figs. 2-30 through 2-33 show the correct way to look over the vehicle damage before and while writing the estimate.

Fig. 2-29 shows the overall wreckage on the vehicle. The damaged left door panel and molding are shown in Fig. 2-30. Moving to the next panel, the left quarter lock panel can be seen in Fig. 2-31. Next, the left rear quarter panel and molding, shown in Fig. 2-29, are examined closely. Fig. 2-32 shows that the left quarter panel rear extension piece ("end cap") is missing. The rear bumper can be seen torn away in Fig. 2-33. Fig. 2-34 shows one correct way to write up the estimate needed to repair this damage.

Time Rule—Usually, the price of repair quoted on an estimate is only good for thirty (30) days. This is due to several reasons. After thirty days, for example, the damaged area rusts and deteriorates, meaning that it will cost more to repair.

Other factors will also cause a change in repair cost after thirty days. Changes in the prices of parts and labor rates may also change the estimate. Used parts, for example, may no longer be available.

Also, when estimating vehicles that have not been in an accident, but have normal wear damage such as rust-out, be careful of areas that have been damaged for long periods of time. These damaged areas can be very time-consuming when fixed thoroughly. The thirty-day limit should be stated on the estimate sheet, as shown at the bottom of the sample estimate sheets in this unit.

ESTIMATING FRAME DAMAGE

In many cases, *frame* damage is estimated differently from panel damage because the frame repair work may often be priced by the number of hook-ups. Each place a chain, clamp, or jack is placed on the frame to pull, push, or

EXPERT
BODY REPAIR
AUTO PAINTING
DU PONT
LUCITE · CENTARI · DULUX
AUTOMOTIVE
FINISHES

PHONE 852-4129

WOLFE BODY SHOP
55 So. Adams

BODY AND FENDER REPAIRS • EXPERT REFINISHING

NAME _John Bonecutter_   DATE _10/2/75_
ADDRESS _R.R.1_   PHONE _852-3371_
Box 793   DATE WANTED _10/7/75_

YEAR-MODEL-COLOR	MAKE OF CAR	BODY TYPE	LICENSE NO.	SERIAL NO.	MFG. PAINT NO.	MILEAGE
74 C-Ri 500	FORD	4S	32B 12	—		17230

REPAIR	REPLACE		SUBLET WORK	PARTS AND MATERIALS	LABOR	REFINISHING
✓		Outer door Panel		27 50	16 50	
	✓	Inner door Panel			22 00	
		Refinish as repaired				12 00
		Paint and Material		18 50		
		TOWING				
		SUB TOTALS	—	46 00	38 50	12 00

THIS ESTIMATE IS BASED ON OUR INSPECTION AND DOES NOT COVER ADDITIONAL PARTS OR LABOR WHICH MAY BE REQUIRED AFTER THE WORK HAS BEEN STARTED. AFTER THE WORK HAS STARTED, WORN OR DAMAGED PARTS WHICH ARE NOT EVIDENT ON FIRST INSPECTION MAY BE DISCOVERED. NATURALLY THIS ESTIMATE CANNOT COVER SUCH CONTINGENCIES. PARTS PRICES SUBJECT TO CHANGE WITHOUT NOTICE. THIS ESTIMATE IS FOR IMMEDIATE ACCEPTANCE.

TOTAL 96 50
4% SALES TAX 1 84
GRAND TOTAL 98 34

THIS WORK AUTHORIZED BY _John Bonecutter_

ESTIMATE SHEET AND REPAIR ORDER   A-70501

Fig. 2-26. Estimate written to repair the damage shown in Fig. 2-25. (Courtesy of Wolfe Body Shop.)

Fig. 2-27. A seriously damaged car such as this will require a longer estimate, carefully made out.

hold is called a *hook-up*. The price may vary from shop to shop and from city to city, depending on the type of frame equipment the shop owner has for his volume of business. In any case, the charge would still be based on the number of hook-ups.

A small body shop may have a *portable* frame straightener, like the one shown in Fig. 2-35. If so, the shop may charge less than would a larger shop. The larger shop may be equipped with a large *rack-type* frame straightener, as in Fig. 2-36. Generally speaking, a portable frame straightener can straighten almost any type of frame damage that can be straightened with a rack-type frame straightener. The difference is that the portable machine can usually straighten only *one* damaged area at a time.

A large rack-type frame straightener, on the other hand, is able to straighten several damaged areas at the same time, in one pull. Portable frame machines, however, are usually much slower and do not have as much power. In most cases, this is because a portable straightener has only one power jack. The rack-type frame machine may have up to six or eight power jacks, allowing many hook-ups (for six to eight pulls) to be made at one time.

Hourly Frame Rate

Some body-frame shops may prefer to make frame estimates by the *hour*, as for other work.

This type of frame estimate is usually priced by the hours of labor to be spent repairing each type of frame damage. For example, a frame that has *mash* damage, as in Fig. 2-37, would be estimated at so many hours for this type damage. (The different frame damage types, such as mash, are explained later in the book.)

Farming Out

If a body shop does not have a frame straightener, the frame damage is "left open" on the estimate. Then, the cost of repair is added to the estimate *after* the frame has been sent to a shop that *does* have a frame straightener. This practice is called *subcontracting*, or "farming out," the frame work.

When this is done, the frame shop bills the body shop for the frame work done to the car. Often, the frame shop will charge the body shop less than normal retail labor for the frame work. Then, the body shop can charge the retail labor price for the frame work. This allows the body shop to also make a small profit on the frame repair.

PARTS AVAILABILITY

Most body shop jobs will need new or good used parts to complete damage repairs. Small parts (moldings and light housings) or large parts (complete fenders) may be damaged beyond repair. When this happens, replacement parts must be found to properly repair the vehicle.

New Parts

When repairing cars less than about 5 years old, it is usually easier to repair the car with all brand new parts. New parts will usually still be available from the manufacturer. They can also be more easily installed and worked with, when compared to good used parts.

New parts, of course, will generally cost more money than will used parts. For this reason, the car owner or insurance company adjuster may want the car to be repaired with used parts.

Covington Appraisal Service

No 204

LEGAL PART OF ESTIMATION

Telephone 205-493-3709

Opp, Alabama 36467

OWNER: H. David Yates	DATE 6-7-19-	ID: 31Q1367 0106
APPRAISED FOR Acme Insurance Company		APPRAISER John Doe
MAKE Ford	YEAR 1973	BODY STYLE Delux	LIC. 23-3709	MILES 23,670

TYPE OF CLAIM — 3rd Party Claim

	PARTS	SERVICE	SUBLET
1 left rear quarter panel replaced	85.90	85 50	
1 replace left rear door shell	113.00	25 60	
1 replace center door post	32.00	24 60	
1 replace left front door	116.00	25 60	
1 replace left front door glass	26.00	— —	
1 replace rocker panel	24.25	18 60	
1 replace inside glass runner	4.50	— —	
Align inside door jam, left rear	—	12 50	
Align roof and drip rail	—	10 50	
Align front door post, left	—	12 50	
Align left front fender	—	12 50	
Align frame, back door area	—	85 00	
Align floor pan	—	17 00	
Align and adjust seat	—	12 60	
refinishing material	44.00	60 00	
Wrecker Charge			25 00
Transmission, differential, and drive shaft		(left open)	

SIGNATURE BELOW GUARANTEES REPAIRS AS ESTIMATED WHEN AUTHORIZED BY OWNER

REPAIR SHOP ACCEPTED BY	SERVICE HRS 57½ @ $7⁰⁰ PER HOUR	$ 402 50
City Body Shop, John Doe	NET ITEMS	$ 25 00
GOOD FOR 30 DAYS	PARTS LESS % $	$ 445 65
BY:	STATE TAX	$ 22 28
THIS IS NOT AN AUTHORIZATION FOR REPAIRS	TOTAL	$ 895 43

Fig. 2-28. The complete estimate for the damage shown on the car in Fig. 2-27. Parts and labor prices may vary slightly, depending on who is making the estimate and when it is made.

Fig. 2-29. Damage from the car having been hit in the left rear; checking the overall job before itemizing the repairs needed.

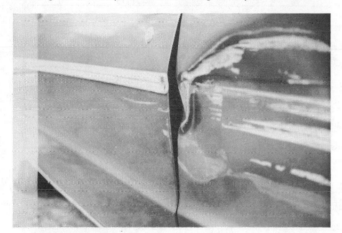

Fig. 2-30. Checking damage to the door panel and molding.

Fig. 2-31. Checking damage to the left quarter lock panel.

Used Parts

Used parts (parts from wrecking companies or junk yards) are sometimes used to repair damage. In this way, the good parts still on a "total" wreck may be used (salvaged) to re-

Fig. 2-32. Checking damage at the rear of the left quarter panel. Note that the extension piece is completely missing and that the bumper is seriously damaged.

Fig. 2-33. Checking the rear bumper damage.

pair another car. The value of those good used parts still on the car is what gives the car its *salvage value,* discussed earlier.

Salvage Yard Operations—When used parts are purchased from a large salvage yard, the good parts are usually removed from the wrecked vehicle *by* the salvage yard. Many times, the yard will also deliver the good used parts to the body shop.

Fig. 2-38 shows a group of "totalled" vehicles as received by the salvage yard. Larger salvage yards will often remove the good parts and bail up the remainder of the wreck as good business procedure. For example, if the wrecks in Fig. 2-38 were allowed to sit as they are, valuable storage space would be used to store parts that are no good.

Figs. 2-39 and 2-40 show good used parts being properly stored in a large salvage yard.

Covington Appraisal Service

Telephone 205-493-3709

Opp, Alabama 36467

OWNER: Opal Hill		DATE 6-10-1973	ID: 12L176422N	
APPRAISED FOR City Insurance Company			APPRAISER Jack Sparks	
MAKE Plymouth	YEAR 1972	BODY STYLE Fury	LIC. 23-3709	MILES 26724

TYPE OF CLAIM 1st party - $50.00 deductible	PARTS	SERVICE	SUBLET
Repair left door		10 00	
Replace left door molding	7.75	2 00	
Repair left quarter lock panel		8 00	
Replace left quarter panel	85.90	89 50	
Replace left quarter panel molding	9.40	NC	
Replace rear quarter panel extention	12.50	3 50	
Replace rear bumper face bar	72.00	7 60	
Paint material	17.00	30 00	
Undercoating for new quarter panel	3.15	NC	
Trunk spatter paint	3.15	7 00	

SIGNATURE BELOW GUARANTEES REPAIRS AS ESTIMATED WHEN AUTHORIZED BY OWNER

REPAIR SHOP City Repair Shop	ACCEPTED BY Leon	SERVICE HRS 19.7 @ $8.00 PER HOUR	$ 157 60
		NET ITEMS	$
		PARTS LESS % $	$ 210 85
THIS ESTIMATION GOOD FOR 30 DAYS		STATE TAX	$ 10 54
		TOTAL	$ 378 99

Fig. 2-34. The finished estimate for the car in Figs. 2-29 through 2-33.

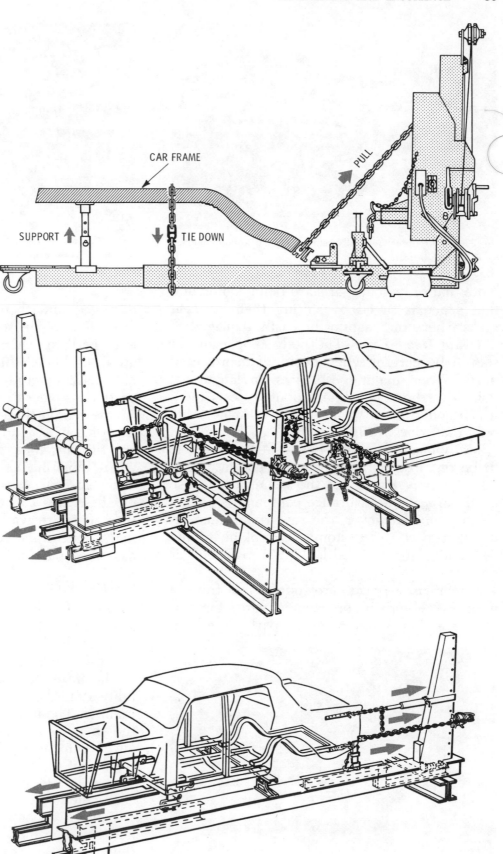

Fig. 2-35. A small, portable frame straightener. (Courtesy of Guy-Chart Systems.)

CAR FRAME

PULL

SUPPORT

TIE DOWN

Fig. 2-36. A larger, permanent, rack-type frame straightener. (Courtesy of Bear Manufacturing Company.)

Fig. 2-37. A rack-type frame straightener hooked up for correcting rear mash. (Courtesy of Bear Manufacturing Company.)

Fig. 2-38. A group of "totalled" vehicles waiting to be dismantled by a salvage yard.

Fig. 2-40. Good used front end assemblies being stored at a salvage yard. These assemblies are known as *doghouses* in the body shop trade.

Note that only good parts are being stored and that space is saved by storing them on neat racks where they cannot be easily damaged.

Using Used Parts—The body shop manager should be careful when deciding to use used parts. When making estimates on late-model vehicles (those less than about 5 years old), it is a good idea to write up the estimate using only the prices for *new* parts.

Many customers may not want their vehicle to be repaired with used parts. The insurance adjuster may try to get the repairman to use used parts if the insurance company is paying for the job. However, the repairman must remember that the customer is looking to the *repairman* for a good-looking repair on his vehicle.

When used parts are purchased from a wrecking company or salvage yard, there is always a chance that the used parts have been

Fig. 2-39. Good used doors being stored at a salvage yard.

damaged and then repaired, instead of just used. For this reason, the body shop manager must be sure, when the parts arrive, that they are in usable condition. He should inspect the used parts carefully before installing the parts on the customer's vehicle.

One reason that the wrecking company exists, of course, is to sell used parts for repairs. So, this resource should not be overlooked when repairing vehicles that are over about five years old. Most of the time, the damage on these cars can be repaired in less time if used parts are available. Sometimes, new parts may not be available for older models, in which case used parts *must* be located and installed.

Rechromed Bumpers

Many insurance adjusters want the body shop to install a rechromed bumper. This is a bumper that has been wrecked, straightened, and then rechromed.

The insurance company takes no responsibility for the condition of the rechromed bumper. The insurance adjuster may try to tell the shop owner or car owner that the insurance company will not pay for a brand new bumper if the car is over one or two years old. This policy is different for different insurance companies.

Usually, rechromed bumpers *look* as good and shiny as new when installed. However, the chrome may later begin to peel off, as shown in Fig. 2-41. If this happens within a

Fig. 2-41. The chromium plating has started to peel off this re-chromed bumper.

certain length of time, the shop owner can often get the rechroming shop to replace the peeling rechromed bumper, since it was a defective replacement part.

However, if the bumper needs to be replaced, there is still the question of who will pay the *labor* involved to replace the defective rechromed bumper. The body shop manager or estimator should look ahead *before* the rechromed bumper is installed, and be sure that the customer and insurance adjuster understand that they must pay for additional labor to put on a second rechromed bumper if the first one should fail. The shop owner cannot afford, under any conditions, to provide free labor to save the insurance company money.

Additional Parts Costs

There are other costs to be considered when the estimate is being written up. For example, are new parts available at the local dealership? Will the parts have to be ordered? If the parts are special ordered, will there be freight charges? Who will pay the freight charges if there are any? The shop owner cannot afford to pay for freight or long-distance telephone calls while looking for parts.

Often, there is a new-car dealership in the community, from which the parts can be ordered. Other times, the local salvage yard may have the parts. Then, the concern will be how much time is required to get the parts to the shop, and who will deliver or pick up the parts.

INSURANCE

Many auto body repairs are paid for, at least in part, by an insurance company. When an insurance claim (payment) is involved, the entire business of body repair becomes more complicated. This is because there are now *three* people involved in the auto repair; the body shop *estimator* or *owner*, the *car owner*, and the *insurance adjuster*.

Types of Insurance Claims

To complete the estimate, the estimator needs to know the type of insurance claim involved, as shown on the sample estimates. To do this, he needs to know the different types of insurance claims or repair situations. The estimator also needs to know how to deal with both insurance adjusters *and* customers about insurance repair matters. The estimator should understand *his* position as well as the rights of both the insurance company and the car owner.

There is no difference in the cost of the repair whether or not the job is covered by insurance. However, the written estimate should list *which* of the four following situations that the job falls into. Body men, shop owners, and shop estimators must know about these four situations.

1. No-insurance jobs.
2. Third-party claims.
3. First-party claims.
4. No-fault insurance claims.

No-Insurance Job—If the customer does not have insurance (or does not want to use insurance), the estimator deals directly with the customer. Then, of course, the estimator has to sell the job to get the job into the shop. The customer who is not using insurance pays the total charge directly to the body shop. A good example of a *no-insurance* job would be an overall paint job on a car five or six years old.

Third-Party Claims—A third-party claim happens when a vehicle is damaged by the driver of another vehicle and the damage is clearly that other driver's fault. Also, in a third party claim, the faulty driver may have *liability* insurance. Liability insurance pays for the damage that the faulty driver causes, whether he damages someone else's car, house, fencing, or other property.

The driver at fault *cannot* have his own vehicle repaired by his liability insurance. This is because liability insurance *only* covers damage to *other people's* property.

The car owner who is *not* at fault should not have to pay the cost of repairing his own car. That cost should be paid by the driver at fault, or by his liability insurance. Of course, the body shop manager must not get involved with who is at fault. In the end, the shop owner must see to it that the bill has been paid before the repaired car is returned, regardless of who is at fault.

First-Party Claim—A first-party insurance claim involves one of two kinds of damage: *collision* or *comprehensive. Collision* insurance is insurance the car owner has that will pay for fixing his car no matter who is at fault. If the car owner has collision damage and runs into a tree, the collision damage pays for fixing his car, even though it was his own fault. Most people have both *liability* insurance in case they damage *someone else's* vehicle and *collision* insurance in case they damage *their own* vehicle.

Comprehensive insurance pays for damage to the car due to vandalism, fire, theft, hail storms, or other damage while the car is normally standing still or not involved in a collision.

Sometimes, both collision and comprehensive insurance policies have a *deductible* clause. This clause (condition) states that the owner of the vehicle must pay the first $50 or $100, or another certain amount of the damage on each claim. The insurance company then pays the remainder.

No-Fault Claims—Another type of insurance that is becoming more common is *no-fault insurance.* No-fault insurance is not like most insurance plans. Most insurance plans require that the party who *is* negligent (careless, at fault) to pay for the injury and damage caused to the party who is *not* negligent.

Basically, though, *no-fault* insurance allows the injured person to collect his loss from his *own* insurance company, *no matter who is at fault.* The major feature of no-fault is that, in many cases, it will eliminate lawsuits between the motorists and insurance companies involved in an accident. This happens when the motorists cannot agree on who is to blame.

Basically, the advantages of no-fault insurance should include the following:

1. Prompt payment of all claims.
2. Payment for reasonable loss, but not *over-*payment.
3. Benefits for persons who would not have been compensated (paid for their loss) in the past.
4. Equalizing and lowering the cost of automobile insurance.

Many states are adopting no-fault insurance. This is due to both the insurance industry and the public recognizing the flaws (bad parts) of normal liability insurance, as discussed below.

Administration and court costs have often made liability insurance unable to provide quick and easy payment for the growing number of people injured and cars damaged in automobile accidents. Regular liability insurance uses about 58% of the money paid in to pay lawyer and court costs. This leaves only 42% of the money to actually compensate injured people and repair their cars. Also, in many cases, the delay while settling injury claims may take up to three years or longer.

No-fault insurance plans are promised to speed up payment for both injury and repair service. Claims should be settled more quickly, allowing the vehicle to be repaired almost immediately.

Dealing with Insurance Claims

As mentioned earlier, several parties are involved when dealing with insurance claims: the insurance adjuster, the customer, and the body shop estimator or manager. The body man must be able to deal with each person and treat everyone fairly, yet charge a fair price and make a fair profit. The body man should not allow himself to be threatened by an insurance adjuster, *nor* should he attack the insurance adjuster's viewpoint.

These ideas are explained in the following sections concerning repair shop responsibility for the customer's vehicle, the legal rights of the customer, fairness and honesty, the customer, and the insurance adjuster.

Repair Shop Responsibility—The vehicle's owner is a customer and deserves a first-class repair job, no matter who is paying for the repair. To make a good estimate, the estimator should always be fair to his shop, to his customer, and to the insurance company. Above all, he and the shop should *not* be ashamed to make a profit, since that is why the shop is in business. The labor rate that is established for his area of the country should be used.

When making out the estimate, keep in mind the following steps:

1. Know the value of the vehicle. Be sure that the cost of repair plus the salvage value does not exceed the vehicle's value.
2. Know the availability of parts.
3. Remember that the vehicle owner is, first of all, a customer.
4. Be sure that there is a clear understanding of who is going to pay the bill, and that the bill must be paid in full before the repaired car is released.

Insurance adjusters, too, are customers. However, they may not be interested in the quality of the repair, so long as the insured party is satisfied. The body man must beware of an insurance adjuster who is inexperienced or *only* trying to save his company money without caring about the customer or shop owner. Of course, it is his job to save his company's money, so a *compromise* may be needed. Illegal procedures and threats, of course, should not be tolerated by the body shop estimator or manager.

Bodyman's Position—When a question comes up about who is right and who is wrong, that is a job for a lawyer and not a bodyman. There is no need to argue or take sides with either a customer or an insurance company, because the shop must *only* be interested in the repairs being done correctly and the bill being paid

in full, *not* who pays the bill. In other words, let the customer and insurance company know that the shop's interest is in repairing the vehicle to preaccident condition (condition before being wrecked) and in collecting a reasonable price for the repair. *All* the costs of repairing the vehicle will have to be paid completely. In the end, the person who owns the vehicle is responsible for the bill being paid in full.

The Customer's Legal Rights—The vehicle *owner* is the repairman's customer. This customer has a right to expect the shop of his choice to check the repairs on the vehicle, regardless of where it is repaired. (The insurance adjuster may want the vehicle to be moved to another shop for repair.) The insurance adjuster may be notified by the customer that the customer's repairman will inspect the vehicle after the damage has been repaired, no matter where it is repaired. These repairs, then, will have to meet with everyone's approval before the vehicle is returned to the customer.

The car owner may demand from the insurance company that there be a time limit to repair the damage if the car is taken out of the shop in which the customer wanted his car to be repaired. After a reasonable period of time, the vehicle owner may demand that the insurance company provide him with a rental car of equal or better value and condition than his vehicle being repaired.

Fairness and Honesty—To be sure of making an estimate that is fair and honest to all concerned (insurance adjuster, customer, body shop), complete the itemized estimate *before* the insurance adjuster arrives. Whether an insurance adjuster is involved or not, the body shop's main interest should be in giving the customer a good job at a fair price.

For this reason, keep the following items in mind when writing up the damage report (estimate):

1. Can the parts on the car be repaired satisfactorily, or will they have to be replaced?
2. Are used parts available that will allow the repair to be made satisfactorily, or will new parts have to be used?

3. Will the customer accept used parts or the repair of his old parts?
4. Will the insurance company pay for new parts if the customer wants new parts?
5. Will the insurance company pay for new or used parts if the adjuster feels that the old parts can be repaired?

In the end, let the customer and insurance appraiser know that the shop's interest is to repair the vehicle to preaccident condition and to collect a reasonable price for repairing the damage as soon as the repair is completed.

When dealing with insurance adjusters, remember that they, too, are trying to do their job to earn a living. Treat them courteously, but be firm and correct. If the adjuster knows that a certain shop has a good reputation for doing quality work at a fair price, he will usually trust that shop. Then, the shop will have little trouble collecting the full and fair price for the repair work.

There should be a mutual understanding among the insurance company's adjuster, the vehicle's owner, and the body shop. When writing estimates and discussing work and prices, remember that there are usually three main concerns: the body shop's concern, the vehicle owner's concern, and the insurance company's concern. Usually, if everyone will be reasonable and considerate of the others, the vehicle can be fixed correctly, quickly, and at a fair price for all. In the end, this is in everyone's best interest.

Body Shop Jobs and Personnel

There are several different jobs in an auto body repair shop. For example, every shop has an *owner,* as is the dealer standing in front of his shop in Fig. 3-1. In a smaller independent shop, the shop owner will usually work on cars as well as run the shop.

Another important person in the body shop is the shop *manager,* or *foreman.* In very large shops, the manager and the foreman may be two different people. In most shops, however, the manager and the foreman are the same person. Fig. 3-2 shows a shop foreman directing a car into a working stall.

Other workers in the body shop include the *body men,* sometimes called *metal men,* who actually straighten and fill the metal parts of the car body. Fig. 3-3 shows a young metal man finishing a metal repair before primer paint is applied. The shop foreman is giving him some pointers on the job. In Fig. 3-4, another student is learning metal work from the older body man. When younger men are employed in the shops to learn the trade, they are called *apprentices. Specialty* men may be employed in the body shop. Examples of these men include *painters* and *frame men.* These workers specialize in only one area of the shop, such as painting or frame straightening.

SHOP OWNER

The shop's owner, of course, must be concerned with who runs the auto body shop.

Sometimes, after a few years as an auto body repairman, a worker may ask the shop owner about becoming the shop manager. Or, the worker may think about his own shop. Either way, *all* workers should have some knowledge of the shop owner's jobs in a body repair shop.

The average body shop may be small compared to the *service shop* of a large dealership (Fig. 3-5), where there are many departments. The owner of a large new-car dealership usually has a service *manager* or *foreman* to supervise all the service departments. Then, each de-

Fig. 3-1. Every body shop has a shop *owner.* At a new-car dealership, the body shop is a part of the owner's total dealership. (Courtesy of Grabber Manufacturing Company.)

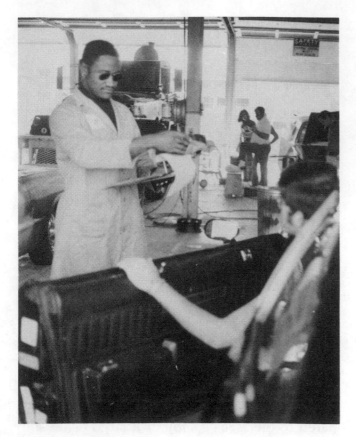

Fig. 3-2. One of the busiest men in the shop is the shop manager, or *foreman*.

Fig. 3-4. A younger apprentice learning from an experienced body man in the shop.

partment will have a *department foreman* to run that department.

The shop owner must be concerned with all areas of work in the shop. He must understand the work of the shop manager, the work of the body repairmen, and all the other work done in the shop and the office. Either the shop

owner or his foreman will be in charge of hiring and firing employees. He will also have to decide about promotions or raises for men in the shop. For all these reasons, he must know about training new bodymen, the employment outlook, wage scales, and other new ideas in the field of body repair work.

The shop owner or his foreman must also understand the work of the office workers, and must be able to supervise their work. He must also be concerned with safety in the shop, since he has a responsibility to his workers.

SHOP MANAGER

The job of managing any business is a highly skilled position. A body shop is not an easy

Fig. 3-5. The body repair department of a large new-car dealership. Here, the owner has a body shop *manager* to actually run the body shop.

Fig. 3-3. One job of the shop foreman is to help direct (teach) younger workers about the body shop's work.

business to operate. Keeping a body shop *clean*, for example, is a large problem. However, it *is* an important job, since people generally do not want to have their vehicle repaired in a dirty shop. A shop that does not keep clean will lose business in the long run.

A good display of tools and equipment is important, and the manager will have to help the body men keep the tools properly stored, as in Fig. 3-6. Good lighting will be another concern of the shop manager, for good work and for a place where the customer can relax while his vehicle is being appraised. Comfortable conditions will keep the customer feeling that his business will be appreciated; that the shop wants his job.

During the working day, the body shop manager will receive customers' wrecked vehicles and will decide into whose work stall or area the wrecked vehicle will be taken. He will also tell customers when their vehicles will be repaired and schedule work through the shop. The shop manager will also order parts needed for vehicle repair, except in a few large shops where there is an office worker to do this job.

Selling Repair Jobs

Collision repair is only one part of the auto body repair business. Painting, glass replacement, upholstery repair, vinyl top work, and other jobs are also profit-making business. Selling these repairs to the customers will take ability because this work is normally not covered by insurance. So, the shop manager will have to "sell" the customer these jobs.

When a car enters the shop for any work, a good manager will point out any visible damage on the car to the customer. Then, he can give the customer a price and recommendation for repairs, explaining what needs to be done and making the customer feel comfortable in the shop. Of course, customers want to feel that their vehicle will be in good hands if it is left in the shop for repairs. Because of this, a good manager will take the customer through the shop and show him what kind of work the shop does.

There are several typical jobs that the shop manager must be able to do to sell work successfully. These jobs include pricing work while the customer is waiting, providing interesting displays of the shop's work, and emphasizing the quality of a newly refinished car.

Pricing Work While the Customer Waits— Pricing work on a vehicle with the customer waiting is a difficult job. If he is in a hurry, the manager may overlook some damage. This, then, will make the estimate lower than it

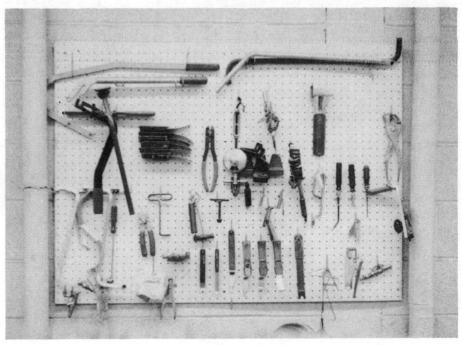

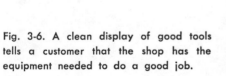

Fig. 3-6. A clean display of good tools tells a customer that the shop has the equipment needed to do a good job.

should be. On the other hand, of course, a customer always wants the best job possible for the money. Pricing work while the customer waits, then, must be done carefully and courteously.

Providing Work Displays—The shop manager should have some of the shop's quality work on display. Items such as cars being worked on (Fig. 3-7), pictures of wrecks before and after repairs, and a supply of quality material (name brand products, as in Fig. 3-8), that can be seen are all valuable. Then, if a customer comes in for a minor repair, the displays may make it easier for the shop manager to sell the customer on more complete repairs to all areas of the car needing attention, rather than repairing one simple damaged place.

Selling the Refinish Job—Most customers have pride in their automobiles. A customer can be shown that a newly refinished car will be more valuable and will look better overall than one that has been only partly repainted.

Fig. 3-9 shows a newly repainted car. This car was first brought in for only collision damage (see the Estimating Unit). Then, the customer was shown how little extra it would cost to have the car completely repainted at the same time. If possible, a completely refinished

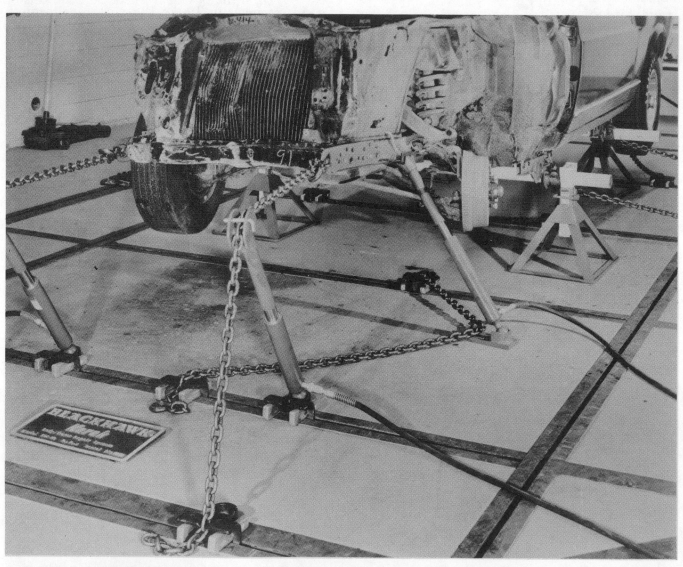

Fig. 3-7. The body shop manager should show customers that the shop has the equipment necessary to make good repairs. (Courtesy, Blackhawk Division of Applied Power Industries.)

Fig. 3-8. When customers are shown the shop, they will be impressed if the shop uses name-brand products and has clean working conditions. (Courtesy, Rinshed-Mason Products Division of Inmont Corporation.)

car may be on display to demonstrate the shop's quality workmanship.

Pointing Out Needed Work—A good shop manager will take a customer around the vehicle and point out all the areas that should be repaired. This gets the customer personally involved in the process of raising his vehicle's value. Then the customer can see the need for the other needed small repairs. Usually, customers will not be surprised at the total repair cost if all the areas needing repair are pointed out beforehand.

Pricing Repair Jobs

One of the shop manager's most important jobs is *estimating* (pricing repair jobs). The

Fig. 3-9. When this car came in for collision repair, the customer agreed to a new overall paint job.

shop manager must know good estimating and insurance practices, as discussed earlier, to do this job correctly.

Usually, the parts cost in the repair will be the same for each section of the country. The hourly *labor* rate charged is usually the same per hour, for all the cities in a certain area of the country. The shop manager must understand the prices in his area of the country. In the end, he will have to charge enough to make a fair profit from the repair on each vehicle.

Using Shop Manuals

Automobile companies print *shop manuals* each year on the different makes and models of their vehicles. See Figs. 3-10 and 3-11. These give important information about body styles and parts. Both shop managers and body men must know how to use the shop manuals. The manuals have many different types of information and are good reference books.

Types of Information—Shop manuals usually give several different types of information. This is very valuable to both the body man and the shop manager. Information may include:

1. Instructions on how to use the manual.
2. Model names and numbers. (Dart, Impala).
3. Body style names and numbers (2-door hardtop, station wagon).
4. Part identification names (Fig. 3-12).
5. Part identification numbers (Fig. 3-12).

Fig. 3-10. The body shop manager in a large shop will have to check on the shop's *library* to be sure that it is properly stocked with up-to-date shop manuals.

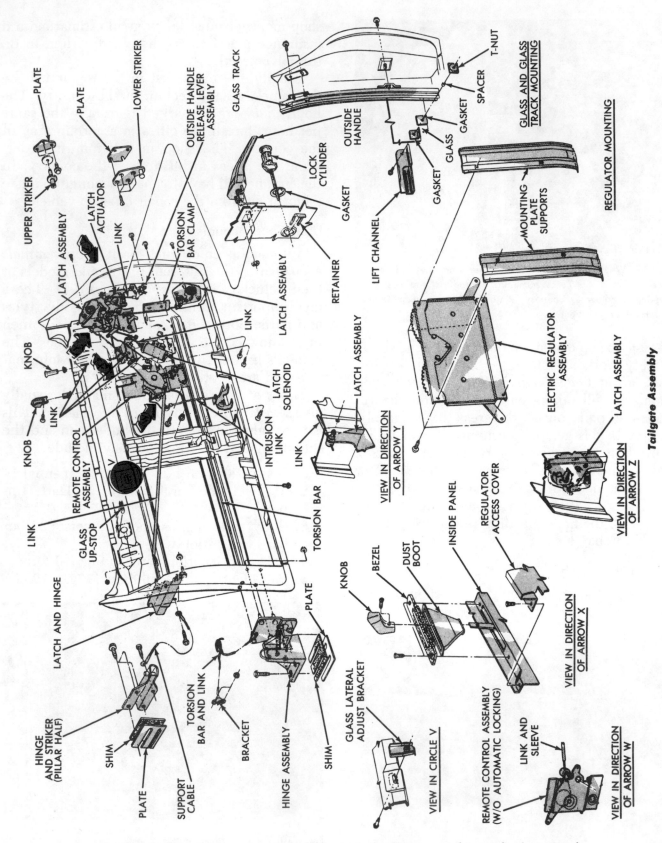

Fig. 3-11. Both the shop manager and the body men in the shop may need to use the shop manual to learn about assemblies such as this station wagon tailgate. (Courtesy of Chrysler Corporation.)

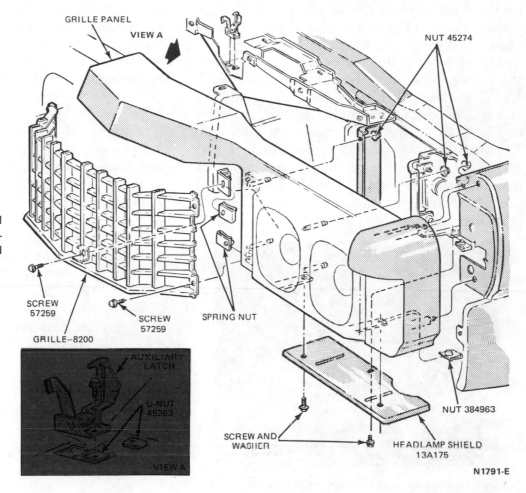

Fig. 3-12. A typical shop manual page with part names and reference numbers. (Courtesy of Ford Customer Service Division.)

Also included may be information on cutting keys and installing parts such as lock cylinders, door windows, windshields, and window regulators. It also tells about the types of paint the manufacturer used at the factory, what types of paints to use when refinishing, and problems the shop might have when refinishing.

Buying Shop Manuals—New-car shop manuals are available to all body shops. The shop manager should write to the manufacturing company about buying needed shop manuals. The shop may want to purchase manuals for more popular models.

Using Paint Manuals

The body shop manager and the shop's painter must also know how to use the *paint manual.* For accurate repaint work, the automobile has a body identification *plate,* as in Fig. 3-13. This plate gives all the information needed to identify the car body and the paint used on it by the manufacturer.

The identification plate may be located on either the *door jamb* (driver door opening) or

Fig. 3-13. Typical paint code *letters* on a body identification plate. (Courtesy of Refinish Division, DuPont Company.)

on the *cowl* (below the windshield under the hood). Fig. 3-14 shows a typical identification plate on the cowl.

The plate gives the model year of the car and the car's paint code letter, as circled in Fig. 3-13. Then, the same code letter (or number) can be looked up in the paint manual, as shown in Fig. 3-15. In the paint manual, a color *chip* (a small sample) of the paint used on the vehicle will also be found. Using the paint manual and the vehicle's body identification plate will be discussed more thoroughly in the section on automotive painting.

Fig. 3-14. Locating the body identification plate on a car's cowl. (Courtesy of Refinish Division, DuPont Company.)

BODY REPAIRMAN

The automobile body repairman is a skilled metal craftsman who repairs motor vehicles that are damaged by either collision or deterioration such as rust. The shop manager should be an experienced body repairman, because he must understand the work of the repairman to be a good shop manager.

A body repairman's work gives him great variety. Repairing each damaged vehicle presents a different problem, since no two vehicles are damaged in exactly the same way. Therefore, a good auto body man must have a broad knowledge of automobile construction and repair techniques and he must be able to best use that knowledge for each repair job.

Most body repairmen find their work challenging and take pride in being able to restore badly damaged automobiles. Body repairmen are expected to repair all types of vehicles, although most body men work on automobiles and small trucks. Some of them specialize in repairing large trucks, buses, or truck trailers.

Typical Work

A good, all-around body man will need to know how to use many tools and processes. He will need to use *power tools* of the trade, such as the disc grinder (Fig. 3-16) and the feather-edging sander (Fig. 3-17). A good knowledge of basic *hand tools* will be needed, as well as a knowledge of how to use *special* auto body tools. These will include the pick hammer being used in Fig. 3-18 and the slide hammer being used in Fig. 3-19.

Better body men will also know about jobs such as the glass replacement being done in Fig. 3-20. Good body men will also have a

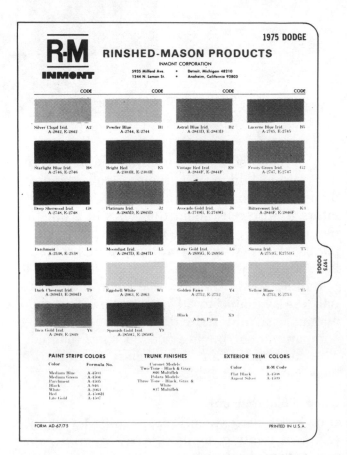

Fig. 3-15. A typical paint manual page contains color codes and paint chip samples. (Courtesy, Rinshed-Mason Products Division of Inmont Corporation.)

Fig. 3-16. A body man often uses the large disc grinder.

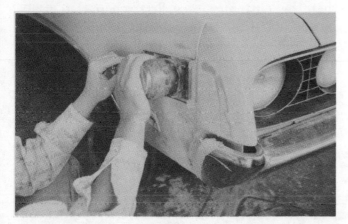

Fig. 3-17. For smaller areas and finer work, a body man must know how to use a *featheredging sander*.

Fig. 3-18. An important tool for a skilled body man is a pick hammer.

Fig. 3-19. For removing large creases, a slide hammer will often be used.

Fig. 3-20. A body man will need a basic knowledge of automobile glass work. Here, a body man is preparing a rear window opening for window replacement.

Fig. 3-21. A good knowledge of oxy-acetylene torch work will be needed by an all-around body man. Here, a piece of an old body is being removed.

knowledge of oxy-acetylene welding, brazing, and heat-treating, as being used in Fig. 3-21, and a good background of information about automotive painting. The more a body man knows about *all* the types of work in the shop, the better he can be paid and the better are his chances for a promotion.

SPECIALTY MEN

Large body shops may have one or more *specialty* men. These men are body men who have extra training or experience in one area. Usually, they do most of the shop's work that needs to be done in that area. There are two main types of specialty men: *frame men* and *painters.*

Frame Men

Repairing and straightening frames is a serious job in the body shop. It requires a good deal of skill. A specialty man who only works on frames, a *frame man,* will usually work on only serious wrecks. It will be his job to see to it that the car's frame is straight, so that the other parts will fit correctly and the car will drive out properly.

The frame man in Fig. 3-22 is straightening out a small bend in the frame behind the left front wheel. If this was not done correctly, the car's front wheels could not be properly aligned.

Painter

A good painter will always be a very valuable employee in any body shop. The painter applies the last work done to the car, the work that the customer sees first when the car is picked up. If the paint looks good and matches well, the customer will be more satisfied with all the other work. For these reasons, then, the painter has a very important job. Skilled auto painters are usually in high demand.

Fig. 3-22. A frame man has a serious and important *specialty job* in an auto body shop. (Courtesy, Blackhawk Division of Applied Power Industries.)

Today's painter is faced with an even more challenging job than in the past. In Fig. 3-23, for example, a rubber/plastic body front panel is being painted. This may need different products and techniques to be painted properly; the shop painter must keep up-to-date on these new products and techniques.

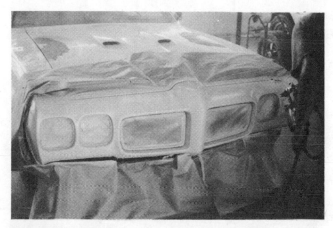

Fig. 3-23. A growing challenge for painters is the correct job of painting rubber and/or plastic parts.

Fig. 3-25. As painting becomes more involved, using clean equipment and thorough mixing of the paint products becomes more important.

Fig. 3-24. A good painter must have the ability to match and restore very thin *pin stripes*.

Fig. 3-26. To properly finish new lacquer paint, a painter must know how to *compound* the new paint.

In Fig. 3-24, a painter is applying a thin paint stripe (known as a *pin stripe*) to the car. All of the painter's jobs require that he know a good deal about paint products and how to mix them (Fig. 3-25), and that he know how to properly compound a new finish to full lustre, as is being done in Fig. 3-26.

GETTING STARTED IN AUTO BODY REPAIR WORK

Young people who are interested in becoming auto body shop employees should be in good physical condition and should have good eye-hand coordination. Although a high school diploma may not always be a requirement for getting an entry job, it is an advantage to have a high school diploma. Many employers believe that the diploma says that a person is able to "finish a job." Some high schools, of course, offer courses in body repair. These may be taken for high school credit toward graduation.

Learning About Auto Body Work

Most auto body repairmen learn the trade while working full or part-time in a body shop. This is called "on-the-job" experience. Before working by themselves to make repairs, a new body repairman would receive instructions from the other body men, or the shop's foreman or owner. Working with others, the new employee can then see which parts are to be repaired and which are to be replaced. Also, he will learn to estimate the amount of time the repairs should take, thus giving himself an idea of how fast to work.

Learning "on-the-job" has many advantages. However, the new person must be careful to watch and listen to the older man from whom he is learning. For example, the new painter in Fig. 3-27 is carefully watching the shop's painter adjust the paint gun air line pressure before painting. In Fig. 3-28, a younger worker is being shown how to reinstall a repaired fender.

Fig. 3-28. A new body man receives instruction on how to reinstall a front fender that was removed for repair.

Helper Apprenticeship Program—In some shops, repairmen are assisted by helpers who are in *apprenticeship training*. An *apprentice* is a person learning a trade while working at the trade.

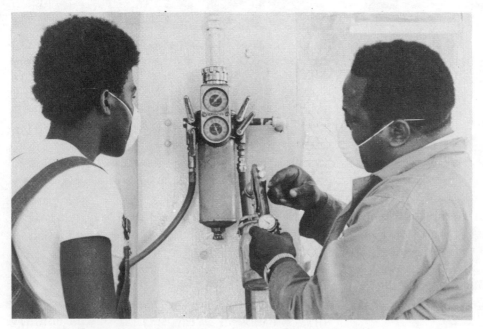

Fig. 3-27. A new painter watches an experienced painter adjust the air line pressure to the paint gun.

Young workers in this type of program usually start as helpers and pick up the skills of the trade by watching and learning from experienced workers. Helpers begin by working with body repairmen, doing such jobs as removing damaged parts, installing repaired parts, and sanding repaired surfaces before painting. Then, they gradually learn how to remove small dents and make minor repairs. After some time, they can then progress to more difficult body work jobs as they gain experience.

Generally, about three to four years of this type of on-the-job apprenticeship training is necessary before a helper becomes a fully qualified auto body repairman.

Formal Apprenticeship Program—Most workers who become auto body repairmen pick up the skills of the trade informally, as on-the-job apprenticeship helpers. However, many training authorities in schools and industry recommend that the learner complete a two- to three-year *formal* apprenticeship program in a vocational trade or high school. For many new workers, formal apprenticeship programs are the best way to learn the auto body trade and work into the auto body shop business.

Formal programs include *both* on-the-job training *and* related classroom teaching. By using this type of program, the student learns the practical skill of working on vehicles from the vocational school, *plus* the technical skill gained by textbook study in the classroom. The vocational school program is the quicker way to become a body repairman. Usually, it requires about two to three years to complete, instead of the three to four years of the "helper," on-the-job program.

Trade School Program—Many large high schools, trade schools, vocational schools, and junior colleges offer body shop courses. By taking these courses, students can learn basic, and some advanced, work of auto body repair. At the same time, credit is being earned toward a diploma. This type of program and courses are definite advantages for students who want to go into the auto body repair business after graduating from school. It provides them with career training while in school.

Keeping Up-to-Date

The auto body repair business is one of the most challenging jobs in the auto industry. Because of this, there is always a need for experienced body men to continue learning. The automobile industry is constantly making changes and advances on newer automobiles, adding to the need for more education. A well-trained repairman must keep up with these changes and new ideas. Even after he has finished an informal on-the-job program or a formal vocational school and apprenticeship program, a good body man will need to return to some type of learning from time to time. Often, major product companies will offer free or low-cost training sessions for body men using their products. Good body men realize the need for this extra training and normally take advantage of it.

ADVANTAGES OF BODY SHOP WORK

There are several advantages about making a living as an auto body repairman. For example, one of the main advantages is that almost all the work is done inside, out of the weather. Also, most body work is done in the daytime, leaving evenings and weekends free. The demand for *good* auto body repairmen is nearly always very high, sometimes even higher in some parts of the country.

Many shop employers (shop owners and managers) provide holiday and vacation pay. Others may pay additional benefits such as life, health, and accident insurance. Some employers will also contribute to retirement plans.

Body repairmen in some shops are furnished with laundered uniforms, as in Fig. 3-2. These may be rented and the cleaning paid by the shop owner, free of charge to the body repairman himself. Finally, of course, the courses needed to stay up-to-date are often given free to body men by product companies such as paint and equipment manufacturers.

Employment Outlook

Good auto body repairmen will have a choice of good jobs in every section of the country.

About half of the country's body men work in the eight states with the largest number of automobiles: California, New York, Pennsylvania, Ohio, Texas, Illinois, Michigan, and New Jersey. Also, these states will usually offer higher average wages.

The need for new auto body repairmen is expected to increase in the future. Thousands of job openings will then become available each year, as a result of employment growth. Jobs will also open up as some body repairmen retire or transfer to other lines of work.

The number of body men needed, however, is expected to increase *mainly* because of the increasing number of motor vehicles damaged in traffic accidents. The total number of wrecks is expected to continue increasing as the number of motor vehicles in use grows. New and improved highways, driver training courses, added safety features on new vehicles, and stricter law enforcement may slow down the *rate* of increase, but the total number of wrecks will probably continue to rise.

The favorable job openings due to the rising number of motor vehicle accidents may be somewhat offset, though, by the increasing efficiency of body repair practices. For example, the more common practice of replacing (rather than repairing) damaged parts, using plastics to fill dents, and improved tools, will allow body men to complete repair jobs in less time, benefiting both the body man and consumer.

Pay Scale

When deciding how much to charge customers for labor, the shops in any given area work together to set the hourly rate for their city or county. Insurance companies may help decide the hourly rate by stating the maximum that they will pay. The National Automobile Dealers Association (NADA) may be asked to help determine what hourly rate should be charged in a certain area.

Once a shop owner or manager knows how much he can charge for labor, he can then decide how much to pay the body men working in the shop. Of course, he will pay the workers less than he charges because the body shop has to make a profit *and* pay for large tools, the

building, insurance, and utilities (lights, heat, water, etc.).

Generally speaking, a body repairman may work from 37-1/2 to 48 hours per week, depending on his job and where he works. There are three basic ways in which a body repairman may be paid by the shop owner or manager:

1. Straight Commission (Percentage).
2. Salary Plus Small Commission.
3. Straight Salary or Wage.

Straight Commission—Some shops pay workers a *straight commission*. In this method, the body man is paid a *percentage* (part) of the total labor cost charged on each repair job that he completes. This is usually about 50% of the total labor cost charged to the customer. Under this method, the repairman's earnings depend on how much work he is assigned *and* how fast he completes it.

Salary Plus Small Commission—Some repairmen are paid a weekly salary, plus a smaller commission on each job completed. In this arrangement, the repairman knows he is getting paid something even if the shop is empty. Of course, he will also want to finish several jobs to earn the extra commission.

Straight Salary or Wage—Body repairmen employed by trucking companies, taxi companies, bus lines, and other organizations that repair their own vehicles are usually paid an hourly rate (wage). Or, they may be paid a *salary* (so much per week no matter how many hours are worked).

BODY SHOP OFFICE WORKERS

A final, and interesting, job to consider in auto body work is a job in the body shop *office*. Effective office workers use common sense and clear thinking. A body shop office is adapted to the needs of the shop and all its workers.

A thorough office worker makes clear notes (Fig. 3-29), checks bills, money and bank statements (Fig. 3-30), and files estimates, letters, and receipts (Fig. 3-31).

Ordering Parts—One of the office worker's important jobs is ordering, receiving, and pay-

Fig. 3-29. An office worker will have to take notes on many parts of the shop's operation.

Fig. 3-30. An adding machine must *always* be used when an office worker checks bills and bank statements.

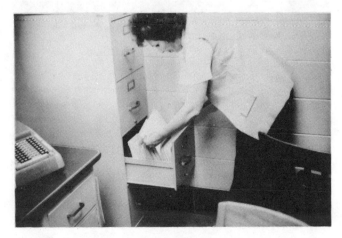

Fig. 3-31. One of an office worker's most important jobs is keeping all the shop's many written records filed correctly.

Fig. 3-32. Calling to order parts from the parts store, new car dealer, or salvage yard.

ing for parts, tools, and equipment needed by the shop to do business. This may be done by the office worker, the shop manager, or in some cases, the shop owner.

Ordering parts begins by telephoning the parts store, new car dealer, or salvage yard. When the call is made, Fig. 3-32, the parts should be clearly listed to the order-taker. If possible, part numbers from the collision manuals should be used.

Receiving Parts—Most parts houses employ a truck driver and delivery truck, Fig. 3-33, to deliver ordered parts to businesses such as body shops.

When the delivery man arrives, he will bring the parts into the shop's office and present the bill for the parts. See Fig. 3-34. The office

Fig. 3-33. Most parts stores employ a driver and delivery truck to deliver the ordered parts.

Fig. 3-34. When the parts are delivered, the driver will present the bill to the shop manager or office worker.

Fig. 3-35. If a shop pays for parts when they are received, the parts driver is given a check (right) and he returns the *paid* parts bill (left) to the shop manager or office worker.

worker or manager should compare the items on the bill with the items in the box, to be sure that everything listed has been delivered.

Paying for the Parts—When the parts are re-received and checked against the bill, they may be paid in one of two ways.

In the *first* method, the body shop has an account with the parts store. In this case, the shop office worker or manager signs his name at the bottom of the bill. Then, the shop is charged for *all* the signed bills at the end of the month, in one total amount. This saves the trouble of paying for each bill when the parts are delivered. The signature on the bill, of course, indicates that the shop *did* receive the parts.

The *second* method of paying for the parts is when the parts store driver is paid for the parts when he delivers them. In this case, Fig. 3-35, a check is given to the parts store driver when he presents the bill. The driver should always be paid with a check, *not* cash, because the check serves as the body shop's proof of having paid the bill.

When the parts house driver arrives with the parts and the bill, the items on the bill are checked to be sure that everything on the bill

has been delivered. Then, a check can be written for the amount on the bill. See Fig 3-36. Note that in Fig. 3-36, the check *number* and *amount* are entered on the check *register* to the left of the check itself.

Finally, the correct check is given to the driver, Fig. 3-35, and the shop office worker or manager receives the bill. The driver should write **PAID** and the check number on the bill before turning the bill over to the shop.

Fig. 3-36. For accurate records, a body shop should always pay for parts with a check.

Charging Parts to a Job—The office worker should then make sure that all the parts and materials bought are charged to the proper vehicle. The charge on the vehicle repair will be the *retail* price, giving the shop a fair and reasonable profit.

Types of Office Workers

Small businesses and body shops may not have a regular office worker. In these cases, the owner or manager takes care of day-to-day office work himself. He then hires an accountant or bookkeeper with an office somewhere locally to figure the books each month. The accountant may keep books for several other small businesses, too.

A larger body shop business may have a full-time bookkeeper and office worker. A very large body shop may have two or more full-time office workers. One of these would then be a full-time bookkeeper.

Bookkeeper—Whether full-time or part-time, every small business, and especially a body shop, needs a *bookkeeper*. The bookkeeper will know simple tax and accounting laws and know when certain taxes are due. He will know what reports need to be made and to whom and when they are due. A set of properly-kept books will tell the shop owner exactly what his profit or loss is for a certain period of time. In a small business, the bookkeeper can help make the system very simple.

One important job of the bookkeeper is keeping the *bank account* up-to-date. Handling the bank account involves:

1. Making Deposits.
2. Writing Checks and Paying Bills.
3. Checking Bank Statements.

When *making deposits*, all deposit slips for putting money in the bank are made in *duplicate* (two copies). One copy is for the bank teller, the other is to be kept on file in the body shop office. Deposits should be entered on the *stub* of the check book (left side, Fig. 3-36) to account for all deposits.

When *paying bills*, all bills should be paid as soon as possible, and always by check. If payment is ever made in cash, a receipt for the cash *must* be received and kept.

When *checking the bank statement*, the bookkeeper looks at checks written by the body shop that have been returned from the bank. Each check is then compared with its stub in the check book. See Fig. 3-36. The deposits entered on the check book stubs should also be compared with the deposits listed on the bank statement. The bank statement and the check book must agree on all accounts. If not, all entries must be double-checked carefully until the error is found.

Unit 4

Wholesale Auto Body Repairs

Most work done by an auto body shop is done for regular customers off the street. That is, normal collision and body repair work for the general public. This type of work is known as *retail* body repair work. This work makes up most of a shop's business and is normally the more profitable work.

Many body shops also do work for used car dealers and the used car departments of new car dealers. Because a used car dealer wants to sell cars for profit, a body shop will need to have a low-cost program for these customers. Quick and low-cost repairs on used cars being made ready for resale is known as *wholesale* body repair work.

To make money on lower-cost *wholesale* work, the shop owner or manager will need to know how to make used cars look good enough to sell while keeping the shop's cost down. This is done by using common short cuts to make the car look good for a short time. Then, the shop will not have to spend too much time and material on the job.

WHOLESALE REPAIR METHODS

There are many techniques and materials used to make low-cost, wholesale, auto body repairs. Materials including aluminum tape (also known as *bonding strip*), screen wire, and plastic filler are commonly used. Repair-

men doing wholesale work will need to know how to use all of these materials.

Polyester plastic body filler, Fig. 4-1, is the most popular low-cost material. It is used to complete and smooth the patch work done with other materials. It is also used to fill small damaged areas in the metal. Using plastic filler saves time because the repairman does not have to hammer, dolly, and file the metal as much when plastic filler will be used to level the dented metal to its original contour (shape).

Wholesale Repair Caution

In this unit, the methods outlined are to be used for the *wholesale* body repair trade, as discussed above. Generally speaking, wholesale repair methods do not last as long as do good retail repairs. When retail customers ask for low-cost wholesale repairs because they are going to sell their car, the shop owner or manager must explain to them that such repairs are only temporary. If the car owner plans to drive his car for some time, the shop owner or manager should recommend more thorough, retail, repairs.

WHOLESALE RUST REPAIR

Rusted places on any vehicle usually make the vehicle unattractive. Rusted panels defi-

Fig. 4-1. Polyester body filler (plastic) with the creme hardener needed to make the material hard. (Courtesy of The Martin-Senour Company.)

nitely lower the vehicle's resale value. Most used-car dealers, and especially used-car buyers, want their cars to be in good condition, without any rust areas on the outside, under the hood, or in the trunk. For these reasons, quick and inexpensive rust repair is an important wholesale repair job for most body shops.

Fig. 4-2 shows a typical rusted area that causes the vehicle's value to be lower than if the rust was not there. To bring the vehicle's value back up, the rusted area will have to be repaired. There are certain steps to follow and certain materials to be used to make wholesale rust repairs on a car to be resold.

Surface Rust

The underneath and lower side areas of a car body are those most likely to be damaged by rust. Road debris such as rocks or stones may break or chip the paint and cause the un-

protected metal to rust on the surface. The rocker panels (the panels under the doors), the doors themselves, the lower parts of the quarter panels, and the lower rear corners of the front fenders are commonly damaged this way. Wherever this type of rust appears, it is known as *surface rust*. See Fig. 4-3.

Rust-Out

The more serious type of rust is *rust-out*. For example, the rusted-out section on the lower part of a panel, Fig. 4-2, is very common. Here, moisture, dirt, and salt get inside the panel and cannot get out, causing the back side of the

Fig. 4-2. Typical, serious, rust damage.

Fig. 4-3. Surface rust occurs when the paint's protective surface is broken.

panel to start rusting. In time, the rust eats completely *through* the metal and the damage first appears as bubbles under the paint. Finally, it rusts *out* from the inside, completely through the metal and paint, as in Fig. 4-2. Quick, wholesale repair of this damage may often be necessary when a shop repairs used cars.

There are two basic types of *rust-out; internal* and *external.* Internal rust-out is by far the most common, and is the type described above. External rust-out is very rare, and usually happens only after the paint has been broken and the surface rust has been allowed to continue for several years.

Internal Rust-Out—The panel in Fig. 4-2 is damaged by *internal rust-out*. This is the result of moisture getting inside the trunk near the body seams. To stop this rust, both the moisture getting inside the trunk *and* the rust-out will have to be stopped. The rust on the inside of the trunk (internal rust-out) will need to be repaired.

A common wholesale repair for this type of internal rust-out is to cover the rusted area with some type of filler and then repaint the panel, without treating the rust. Although this method is often used for used cars, it is not recommended for first-class retail customer work. The low-cost repair, using plastic filler, will not correct or stop the cause of rust. The rust will soon work its way around the plastic filler and then through the new paint. This may rust back through in less than 3 months.

External Rust-Out—When rust-out is beginning from the outside, it is known as *external,* and it starts out as surface rust. A good sanding and refinishing is usually enough for a quick, wholesale, low-cost repair. However, if the rust is not treated, the panel will start rusting through the new paint soon after being refinished.

For this reason, the rust must be treated with a good *metal conditioner* during a first-class retail repair. This product will usually help control the surface rust, preventing a quick break-through in the new paint. The product in Fig. 4-4 is one brand of metal conditioner used to help control rust.

Fig. 4-4. One brand of *metal conditioner.*

Repairing Rusted Areas

On any repair job, the first step is to analyze the repair to be made. Looking over the job closely will help determine what has to be done. This analysis will give the repairman a "road map" procedure to follow, a step-by-step plan. The plan can then be used to successfully repair the rusted area. The analysis is usually a visual inspection. During the analysis, you must decide what *type* of rust damage there is; either *surface rust* or *rust-out.*

Repairing Surface Rust—If the problem is *surface rust,* there will be no holes in the metal and only brown discoloration where the metal is rusted.

On wholesale, quick, repair jobs, surface rust is repaired by first grinding off the existing rust. Then, the area is lightly sanded and heavily primed with primer-surfacer.

When the primer-surfacer is thoroughly dry, it is wet-sanded smooth to prepare the area for final painting. Then, the color coat is applied and, if necessary, rubbed out.

Repairing Rust-Out—If the problem is a *rusted-out* panel, as in Fig. 4-2, the damage is more serious. Holes will be eaten completely through the metal and there may be a large area (hole) that will have to be covered before the plastic filler is used to level the surface. Depending on how large the holes are and on the job quality needed, there are three common methods used to make quick, *wholesale* repairs on rusted-out vehicles:

1. Repairing the rusted-out area by patching it with *aluminum tape.* Then, covering the tape with plastic filler.
2. Repairing the rusted-out area by using plastic filler over *wire screen.* The wire screen is used to cover large holes in the panel. The wire screen may or may not be attached to the metal panel.
3. Repairing the rusted-out area by simply filling the hole *and* leveling the area's surface with *plastic filler.*

There is a fourth, and preferred, method of repairing rusted-out panels. This is done by repairing the rusted-out panel by patching the panel with a sheet metal patch. Then, the patch is covered with plastic filler. The sheet metal patch may be welded, brazed, or riveted into place, with brazing preferred for strength and less possibility of heat distortion. Carefully fitted and brazed, the sheet metal patch is the best method to *thoroughly* repair rust-out damage. Properly done, this repair will last for years. However, this method is rarely used for low-cost wholesale repairs, due to the additional time and material needed.

When beginning to repair a rusted-out area, first analyze the damaged area to decide what repair method to use. Then, remove all the parts that might be in the way or that might be hiding more rust. These would include stainless steel moldings, molding clips, or other parts, as necessary.

The reason for removing parts and moldings from a rusted panel is so that *all* of the rust on the panel can be repaired. If a molding or part has rust underneath it that is not also repaired, the rust will soon creep out from under the piece and cause further damage. During low-cost repairs, of course, extra moldings or parts may not be removed on a very quick job. This is a difference between first-class retail repairs and low-cost wholesale repairs.

Fig. 4-5 shows a rusted-out area after the molding and trim have been removed. Then, the next step is to grind the rusted-out area to remove any paint and surface rust, as in Fig. 4-6. Here, it is important to make sure that all the surface rust spots are removed with the disk sander (or wire brush). The old paint must also be removed from around the rusted-out area at the same time.

Fig. 4-5. Rusted-out panel where parts have been removed and some grinding has been done.

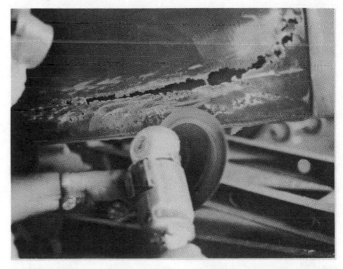

Fig. 4-6. Grinding paint and surface rust from the rusted-out area.

All the rusted metal will need to be sanded and made bright and shiny to help give the plastic a firm surface on which to grip. The area may be ground off (cut) with a 16-grit, 9″ sanding disk. This sanding disk is fast and will leave large sand scratches, giving a good "bite" for either the plastic filler or, when used, aluminum tape. Fig. 4-6 also shows a body man grinding off the paint with a disk sander.

After the metal has been prepared by grinding, the next step in a wholesale, quick, rust-out repair job will be to depress the area around the rusted-out holes. This is done with a body hammer, by pounding in on the edge of the rusted area. See Fig. 4-7. This will provide a good area for the filler material (aluminum tape, screen wire, or plastic).

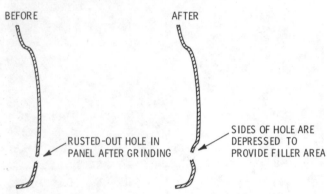

Fig. 4-7. After grinding the rusted area, the edges of the rust hole are depressed with a hammer.

When the area around the hole has been depressed, the hole is ready to be patched with plastic filler alone, aluminum tape and plastic filler, or screen wire and plastic filler. Fig. 4-8

shows a panel that has been prepared for filling before the plastic has been added.

Using Aluminum Tape and Plastic—Using aluminum tape and plastic is one of the fastest ways of completing low-cost repairs on a rusted-out panel. Aluminum tape may be used on large rusted-out panels *only* for wholesale-quality, quick, low-cost repairs. It is not as permanent nor as long-lasting as are higher-quality, more expensive repairs.

Aluminum tape is a tape-like product made by several different auto supply companies. The tape has an aluminum surface about 2″ wide (although it can be bought in wider widths), and it is sold on rolls about 15 yards long. The product has an adhesive (sticky) backing that sticks to the bare metal when applied, as shown in Fig. 4-9. Aluminum tape is inexpensive to buy, easy to use, and is reliable for at least several months, allowing the car to be sold.

To apply aluminum tape, the rusted-out area is first prepared for repair (patching), as discussed earlier. Then, the aluminum tape may be placed over the rusted-out area. The tape should be placed over the damaged area *and* about 1″ beyond the edge of the rust-out.

Press the tape down tightly, as shown in Fig. 4-9. Use a tool that has no sharp edges, such as the back side of a pocket knife. The rounded edge of the pocket knife can be used

Fig. 4-8. Rusted-out area prepared for filler.

Fig. 4-9. Aluminum tape being used to cover the holes in a rusted-out panel.

to *firmly* press down the aluminum tape. This is an important step, since the aluminum tape has an adhesive backing that must stick firmly and tightly to the metal panel.

If more than one thickness of tape is needed, another layer may be used. The first layer of tape, though, should be sanded or scuffed to roughen up the surface before a new layer of tape is applied. In Fig. 4-10, a second layer of aluminum tape is being applied.

Fig. 4-10. Applying a second layer of aluminum tape.

When the aluminum tape has been firmly applied to the metal, *all* of the tape must be covered with plastic filler, as in Fig. 4-11. Plas-

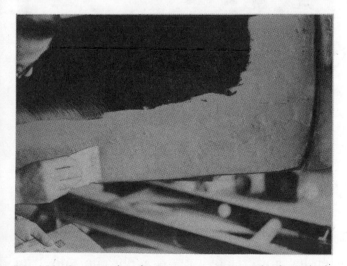

Fig. 4-11. Covering the aluminum tape repair with plastic body filler.

tic filler goes through a curing process that creates heat, helping cement the aluminum tape to the metal.

When the aluminum tape and plastic filler repair has cured, it may be smoothed to the original contour of the metal. The repair then becomes a good-looking, low-cost repair. The repair will last long enough to satisfy wholesale customers such as used-car dealers.

Using Screen Wire and Plastic—After the rusted-out area is prepared for patching, the area can be filled and repaired with screen wire and plastic. With this method, a screen wire is placed over or in the rusted-out hole. The screen wire is then trimmed to fit the hole with a small overlap under the metal.

The screen may then be cemented to the metal or simply fitted in place under the edges of the hole. When cement is used, the cement (clear resin) will hold the screen in place. Then, the plastic body filler may be applied and allowed to harden. After the plastic has been smoothed off, the area will be ready for refinishing.

Using a Sheet Metal Patch and Plastic—The procedures just outlined are the most common types of quick, low-cost, wholesale rust-out repairs. They are used to prepare a car for resale. If the rust-out repair is to last for some time, or if the rusted-out hole is very large, a *sheet metal patch* may be used to fill the hole and strengthen the panel.

In this method, the rusted-out area to be patched is thoroughly prepared, as usual, before being patched with the sheet metal plate. The panel to be patched and the sheet metal patch are then cut for a close fit with a 1" overlap. See Fig. 4-12. The metal patch is then placed over the opening and may be riveted, welded, or brazed in place.

When riveting the metal patch, the rivets should be placed about 3/4" apart. The rivets will then pull the new panel up against the panel being repaired, as in Fig. 4-13. The panels, then riveted together, are roughed up with a disk sander and then filled with plastic. When the plastic has hardened, it may be smoothed off. The repaired panel is then prepared for refinishing.

Fig. 4-12. Cutting and sizing a sheet metal patch to repair a rusted-out section.

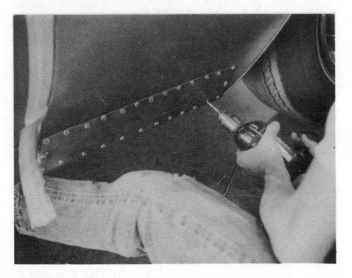

Fig. 4-13. Drilling holes to rivet the sheet metal patch to the panel being repaired.

WHOLESALE SHEET METAL REPAIR

Many times, automobiles are sold or traded in due to minor collision damage being on the car. Body shops doing wholesale repairs will be called on to quickly and inexpensively repair sheet metal that has been damaged in minor collisions. Such damage, while not serious, *does* reduce the car's resale value.

One of the commonly-damaged panels needing wholesale repairs will be the vehicle's fenders and rear quarter panels. Since the two front fenders are outside panels, and since they are on the front of the car, they are in an easily-damaged place. Quick, wholesale fender

repair will then be easy if the proper steps are taken.

Completing a wholesale, low-cost repair on the damaged fender in Fig. 4-14, for example, will take the knowledge of a trained repairman. The following sections will explain the steps to be taken to complete a quick, wholesale repair of the damaged fender shown in Fig. 4-14.

Fender Alignment

This step must be completed *before* the paint is sanded off with the sander. Fender alignment (straightening) will bring the dented fender back to the approximate contour (shape) of the original fender. (Curves or crowns on panels are known as the *contour*.)

Preparing for Straightening—Before straightening, the fender is first properly cleaned. Any chrome trim and any other parts in the way of repairing the damaged panel are first removed.

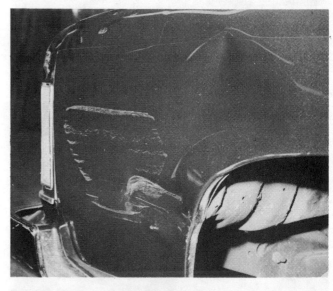

Fig. 4-14. Typical collision damage on the front fender of a used car.

All the parts and material needed to complete the job are then ordered. In Fig. 4-15, the tools needed for the repair have been placed in the working area. With the correct parts, tools, and material on hand, the fender may be quickly repaired as follows.

Power Jack Aligning—After cleaning the fender and removing extra chrome and trim parts, place the *power jack* under the fender.

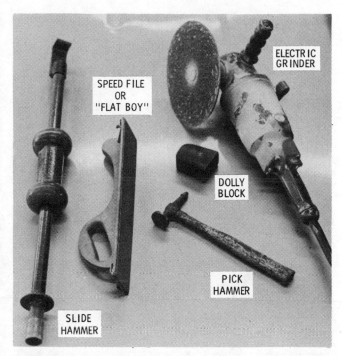

Fig. 4-15. Before beginning the fender repair, it is a good idea to have all the correct tools in the working area.

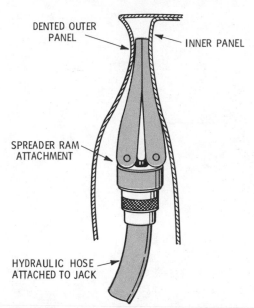

Fig. 4-17. The wedge ram attachment is one of the more useful tools used with the portable hydraulic jack.

See Figs. 4-16 and 4-17. Use the jack attachment known as a *wedge ram* under the fender. Fig. 4-17 shows the wedge ram attachment positioned under the fender. By using the wedge ram attachment, the damage can be moved back out into alignment without stretching the metal too much. The wedge ram has a spreading action that pushes the dent out, aligning the damaged metal.

Using the Vacuum Cup—Another tool used to help align metal is the *vacuum cup*, shown in Fig. 4-18. This tool is a large suction cup. It is pressed tightly against the damaged area

Fig. 4-16. The first step in the fender repair will be aligning the fender with the portable hydraulic jack.

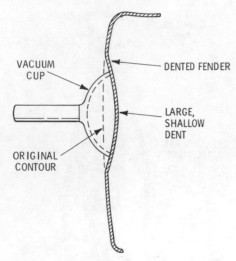

Fig. 4-18. A large vacuum cup may be used to pull out large, shallow dents.

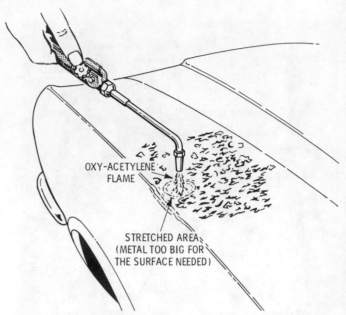

Fig. 4-19. To shrink metal, heat is first applied to the stretched area with an oxy-acetylene torch.

of the fender, pressing the air out of the cup and creating a vacuum. With the vacuum cup stuck tightly to the damaged area, some of the dented area can be pulled back to the original contour.

Shrinking the Stretched Metal

All the metal that was *stretched* in the collision will need to be shrunk. Usually, very little shrinking is done on low-cost, wholesale repairs. This is because shrinking requires talent and the use of a torch. Shrinking is discussed more thoroughly in a later unit.

To quickly shrink metal in a low-cost repair, heat will have to be applied with an oxy-acetylene torch. Then, quickly quenching the metal (cooling it with water) will help to bring the metal back to the original contour. Fig. 4-19 shows heat being applied to the stretched area. The stretched metal should be heated to a cherry red spot, as seen in Fig. 4-20.

After heating the stretched metal to a cherry red, lightly tap the spot with a smooth-face hammer. See Fig. 4-21. The stretched metal will draw up a little (become smaller) each time it is heated, tapped, and cooled. (The shrinking process is discussed in detail in a later unit.)

Finally, the damaged fender is brought back to its original shape by using a combination of the power jack, the vacuum cup, and the torch heat. Fig. 4-22 shows the fender after align-

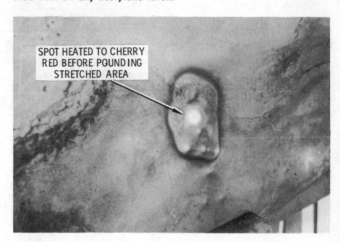

Fig. 4-20. Before pounding, the metal should be heated to a small, cherry-red spot.

ment and heat work, ready for final grinding and filling.

Disk Sanding

After the damaged area has been aligned, the *disk sander* is used to remove the paint from the damaged area. This will allow the filler to be applied to *bare* metal. Fillers will not properly stick (adhere) to painted surfaces. In Fig. 4-23 the paint is being removed from the damaged fender with the grinder. The disk sander (grinder) is removing paint in the area that had been stretched and was shrunk in the previous step.

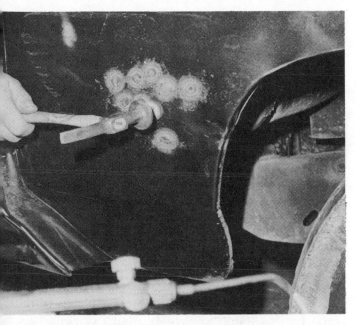

Fig. 4-21. Immediately, while the metal is heated to a cherry-red spot, the spot is pounded flat with a smooth-face hammer.

Fig. 4-23. Before applying plastic filler to completely level the area, the disk sander must be used to completely grind off any remaining paint.

Fig. 4-24 shows how the disk sander leaves the metal clean and bare, ready for applying plastic filler.

Using Plastic Filler

Mixing and applying plastic filler is a job that can be easily learned. When using the filler, the plastic is first mixed on a piece of cardboard, wood, or flat sheet metal scrap. A small portion of the mixed plastic is then placed on a *spreader* (a flat rubber or plastic piece about 2″-4″ long and 2″-3″ wide). Then, the mixture is applied to the prepared area with the spreader.

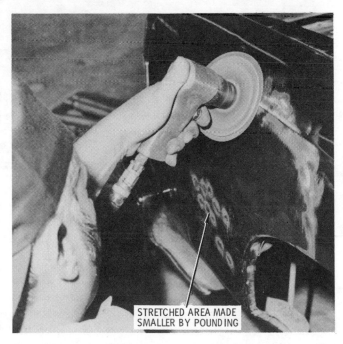

STRETCHED AREA MADE SMALLER BY POUNDING

Fig. 4-22. After several applications of heating and pounding down, the metal is much closer to the original shape.

Fig. 4-24. The completed metal straightening repair, ready for plastic filler.

Mixing Plastic Filler—To properly mix plastic filler, first take the plastic out of the can with a clean putty knife. Place the material on a piece of clean cardboard or other mixing board. Add a small amount of hardener, as shown in Fig. 4-25 and as recommended by the plastic and

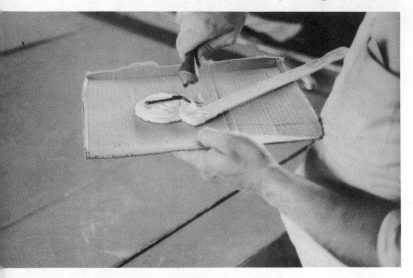

Fig. 4-25. Only a small amount of hardener should be added to plastic filler. Adding too much hardener will cause problems after the plastic hardens.

hardener manufacturer. Mix the plastic and hardener together as shown in Fig. 4-26.

The plastic should be stirred, not whipped. Whipping will cause air to get into the plastic. Then, when the plastic hardens, small holes called *pin holes* will appear as air pockets on

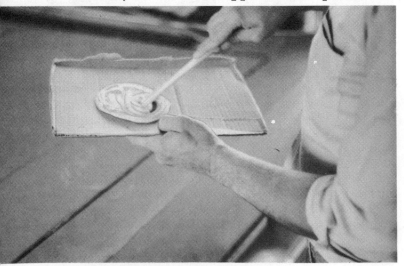

Fig. 4-26. The plastic filler and hardener must be *thoroughly* mixed.

the surface of the dried plastic. These pin holes will have to be filled with more plastic or with putty after the damaged area has been primed. Putty and primers are studied in a later unit.

Applying Plastic Filler—Before applying the mixed plastic filler to the metal, the metal must be clean and dry. Plastic should not be applied more than 1/4″ thick, even for wholesale-quality repair work. If the plastic is spread more than 1/4″ thick, it may crack in a few months. However, for wholesale-quality repairs, plastic *is* sometimes spread thicker than 1/4″, to get the repair made for less cost. Although this will get the job done, it is not quality work.

Fig. 4-27 shows how a wide plastic spreader is used to apply the mixed filler material. The mixed plastic filler should be applied and smoothed as much as possible with the plastic spreader.

Fig. 4-27. Appyling the plastic filler with a firm plastic spreader.

Grading Plastic Filler— When the plastic just *begins* to cure (harden), grade the material with a grading *file* (sometimes called a "cheese grader"). See Fig. 4-28. To grade the plastic filler, pull or push the file over the surface of the hardening plastic. Notice how the plastic is coming through the file in Fig. 4-28. The file is shaping the plastic's surface to the contour of the original metal. Grading the plastic while

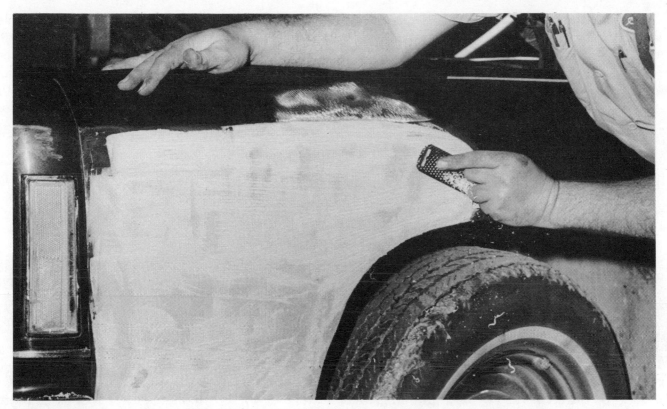

Fig. 4-28. Before the plastic is fully hard, it may be graded off with a grading tool, sometimes called a *cheese grader*.

it is setting up is another step in reducing the sanding needed to repair the damaged area.

Filing Plastic Filler—When the plastic filler has hardened (cured), the *speed file* may be used to further smooth the surface. See Fig. 4-29. Also referred to as a "flat boy," this tool is moved back and forth over the hardened

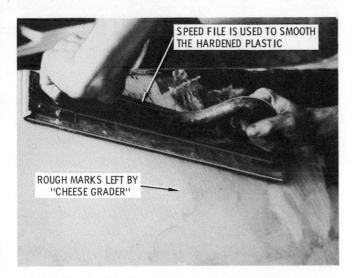

SPEED FILE IS USED TO SMOOTH THE HARDENED PLASTIC

ROUGH MARKS LEFT BY "CHEESE GRADER"

Fig. 4-29. A long, flat speed file is used only after the plastic has thoroughly hardened.

plastic. This smooths the plastic as it takes out the graded file marks left in the plastic by the earlier grading.

When using the speed file, rough paper of 40-grit should first be clipped in the file. This will be for the first use of the file. Then, after the grade marks have been removed, 80-grit paper may be used to further smooth the surface and prepare it for hand sanding with finer papers.

Wholesale Repair Refinishing

The steps discussed up to this point have been used to repair the damaged metal enough for a wholesale-quality repair. Paint work will follow, so that it will be difficult to tell that the fender has been damaged.

To refinish the panel, the first step in refinishing is to primer-surface the metal-and-plastic surface. Primer-surfacing, sanding the primer-surfacer, and refinishing the panel are discussed in later units. Usually, for a wholesale repair, the complete panel will be refinished with enamel paint.

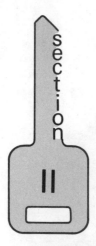

Body Working Tools

Unit 5

Hand Tools

A body man will often need to remove and replace damaged parts on automobiles. To do this, *tools* are used to tighten and loosen the nuts or bolts that hold the parts in place. Other tools will be used to hold parts for cutting, welding, or other work. For example, Figs. 5-1 through 5-4 show a body man using different tools to remove a deck lid. The tools that can be used to remove the deck lid are shown in Fig. 5-5.

Each individual hand tool is usually used for only one or two different jobs. Because of this, different tools are made for different jobs. Gen-erally speaking, any one tool should not be used for a job if another tool could do the job easier or more safely.

Personal Tools—Most body men have a "feel" for their own personal tools. For this reason, a fellow worker's tools may not feel as comfort-able to a body man as would one of his own tools. For this reason, most good body men do not abuse their tools by using them incorrectly.

Tools should always be kept clean and prop-erly stored. Most hand tools will last for years if they are good tools and if they are taken care of properly. Fig. 5-6 shows a good selec-tion of personal hand tools. An experienced body man may have this complete a set,

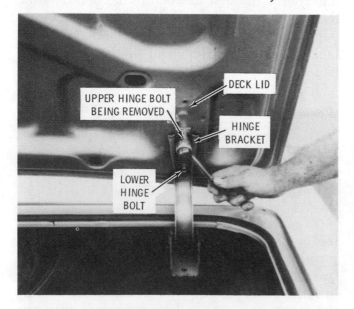

Fig. 5-1. Removing a deck lid bolt with *socket* and *ratchet handle* hand tools.

Fig. 5-2. Removing a deck lid bolt with *socket*, *extension*, and *ratchet handle* hand tools.

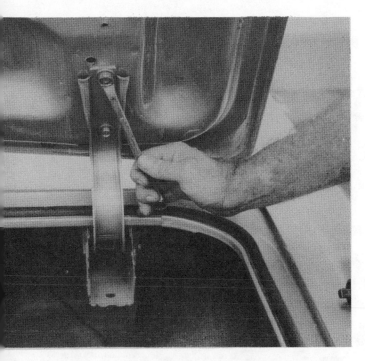

Fig. 5-3. Removing a deck lid bolt with a *box-end* wrench.

whereas a new employee probably would not have quite as many tools. Of course, a body man must expect to replace worn out tools before they become dangerous to use. Tools that are out-of-date (no longer used) should be sold or stored out of the way.

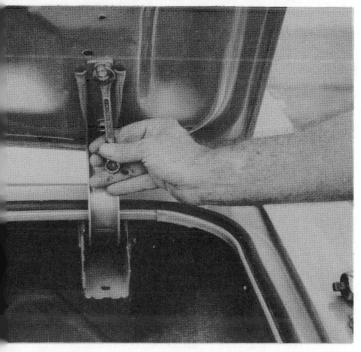

Fig. 5-4. Removing a deck lid bolt with an *open-end* wrench.

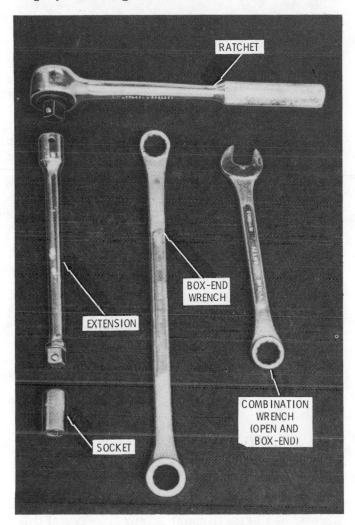An auto body man is normally expected to supply his own basic hand tools. Fig. 5-7, for example, shows a new body man arriving at work, carrying his own personal tools. These are his personal property and he will take these tools with him as he leaves one place of employment to go to another.

Fig. 5-5. Any one of several *hand tools* may be used for a simple job such as the bolt being removed in Figs. 5-1 through 5-4.

Shop Tools—The shop owner is expected to furnish larger or more expensive tools. These will include large hand tools such as the vise, post and body jacks, tap and die set, wheel wrench, and other tools that are too large or expensive for each individual body man to furnish. In Fig. 5-8, the body man is using the post jack to straighten a damaged door.

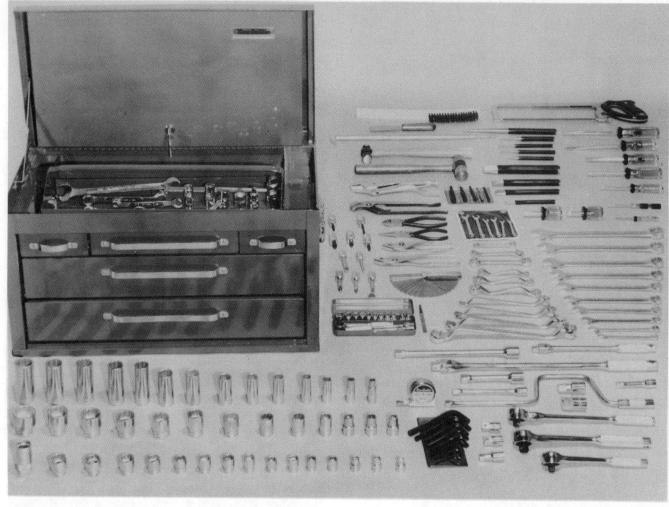

Fig. 5-6. A good set of personal hand tools. (Courtesy, Hand Tools Division of Litton Industrial Products.)

PERSONAL HAND TOOLS

A good body man owns many different types of personal hand tools. He will own tools from several basic groups, such as wrenches, screwdrivers, or pliers. In each group are several different types of tools in that group, such as *open-end* wrenches, *box-end* wrenches, or *combination* wrenches. In each group of tools are tools of many different sizes and shapes. A new worker will need several different types of tools for each basic group.

Wrenches

There are many different types of wrenches. Even so, any wrench is used to grip and then turn the head on a nut or bolt. The word *wrench* means to *twist* or *turn.*

The overall *length* of a wrench depends on the size of the nut or bolt on which it will be used. See Fig. 5-9. Longer wrenches have larger *sizes* (openings) on the end. The extra length gives the worker more *leverage* on larger nuts or bolts, which are usually harder to turn and need to be tightened more when installed.

Wrenches are designed for the special job of turning nuts or bolts, and should only be used for the job. Using the right tool at the right time will produce higher quality work with fewer damaged parts or injuries to the body man.

Wrench Size—The *size* of any wrench is the size of the opening on one end of the wrench. For example, the open-end wrench shown in Fig. 5-9 has a ⁹⁄₁₆-inch opening, so the opening will fit snugly on a ⁹⁄₁₆-inch nut or bolt head.

This is the way in which a wrench size is determined; by the size of nut or bolt that it fits.

Actually, a wrench size will always have to be just slightly larger than the nut or bolt head on which it fits, because it would not fit on the nut or bolt head if it were *exactly* the same size as the nut or bolt head.

Open-End Wrenches—A full set of open-end wrenches will be found in the tool boxes of all good body men. These tools are called *open-end* wrenches because they are open at *both* ends, as in Fig. 5-9. Open-end wrenches will fit both square head (4-corner) and hex-head (6-corner) nuts or bolt heads.

The main jobs for open-end wrenches include holding a nut so that a bolt can be removed from the nut, or holding the bolt when the nut is to be removed. Fig. 5-10 shows how an open-end wrench holds a common bolt.

The main advantage of an open-end wrench is that it can be used where a wrench cannot be lowered over the top of a nut, such as when a nut is on a long shaft. The main *dis*advantage of an open-end wrench is that it grips only *two* points of the nut or bolt head. If too much pressure is applied, there is a danger that the

wrench will "round off" the corners on the nut or bolt. This will damage the nut or bolt head, and, usually, also damage the worker's hands.

Fig. 5-7. When a new body man goes to work in a shop full time, he is expected to arrive with his own hand tools.

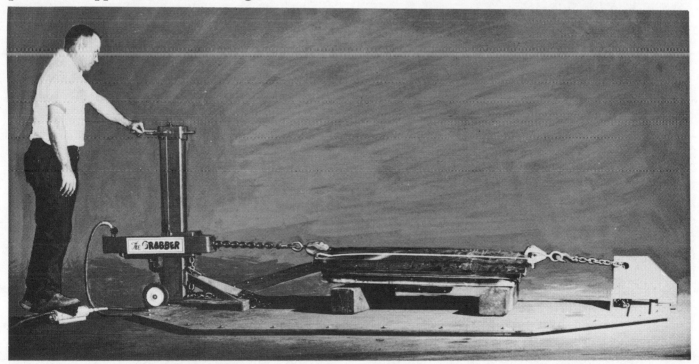

Fig. 5-8. Using a post jack, part of the *shop's* equipment, to straighten a door. (Courtesy of Grabber Manufacturing Company.)

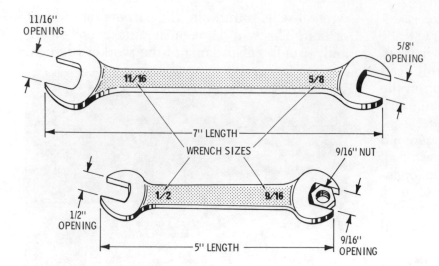

Fig. 5-9. A wrench *size* is the size of nut or bolt that the wrench will correctly fit.

Most sets of open-end wrenches include sizes of ⁷⁄₁₆-inch through 1-inch. Special larger or smaller sizes may be purchased for the times when they are needed. The normal number of wrenches in a complete set is from six to fifteen, depending on the cost of the set. Fig. 5-11 shows several different sets of open-end wrenches. A new body man should include a set of *metric-size* wrenches when purchasing new tools. These will be used to work on newer cars and on foreign makes.

Box-End Wrenches— These wrenches are very common to the auto repair trade. *Box-end wrenches* are named for their boxed (enclosed) ends. These ends "box-in" a nut or bolt head, as shown in Fig. 5-12.

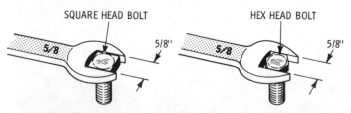

Fig. 5-10. An open-end wrench grips any *two* sides of a nut or bolt.

Box-end wrenches have either 6-point or 12-point openings on the ends. *Points* are the number of openings into which the nut or bolt may go. Note that in Fig. 5-13, only 6 of the 12 points are being used to grip the bolt head. The 12-point box-end wrench is easier to use because of the twelve positions in which it

may be placed on the nut. Note the 12-point wrenches in Figs. 5-14A, B, and E.

Box-end wrenches also come in 8-point and 6-point styles. Eight-point wrenches are not too popular because they fit only square-head bolts and nuts. The 6-point style, however, has the strongest grip, because its sides are larger and stronger. The stronger sides allow less chance of slipping off or rounding the nut. Fig. 5-15 shows a group of several box-end wrench sets.

Each box end of the wrench is offset (the head is lower than the handle). See Figs. 5-12 and 5-14. In this way, the worker's hand is *above* the surface or any object that might be in the way near the nut or bolt being turned. Note that the wrenches in Fig. 5-14 are not offset the same amount.

The main advantage of a box-end wrench is that the box-end has complete contact with all six points on the bolt head. This *completely* encloses (surrounds and grips) the bolt head or nut, allowing less chance of the wrench slipping on the bolt head or nut. With all six points of contact, the box-end wrench will not easily cut off the corners of the bolt head or nut. See Fig. 5-13. This makes the box-end wrench the safest wrench to use.

The main *dis*advantage of a box-end wrench is that there must be room for the box end to go *over* the top of the screw head. Also, a smaller disadvantage is that the box-end wrench will have to be lifted off the nut and

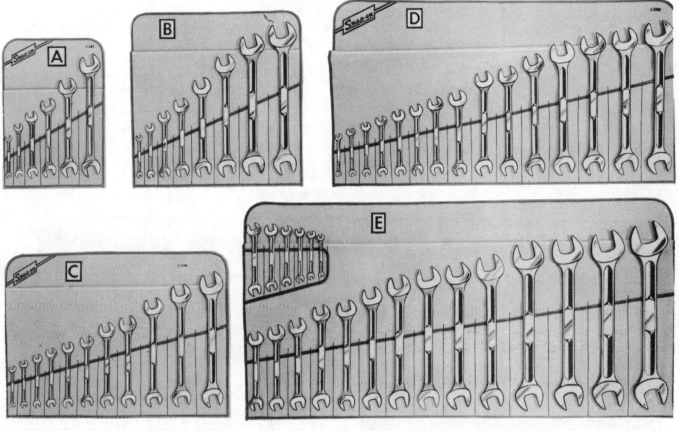

Fig. 5-11. Several common sets of open-end wrenches. (Courtesy of Snap-On Tools.)

put into a new position each time a pull is made.

Box-end wrenches come in sets of from six to fifteen wrenches per set (Fig. 5-15). The more common sets include sizes from 7/16-inch to 1-inch. Box-end wrenches can also be purchased in smaller or larger sizes, as necessary.

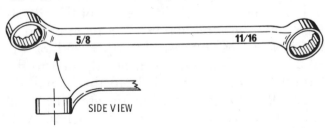

Fig. 5-12. A common box-end wrench has a different size on each of its' two ends.

Combination Wrenches— These wrenches have an *open-end* on one end of the wrench and a *box-end* on the other end of the wrench. See Fig. 5-16. Therefore, these tools are known

as *combination* wrenches. Either end of the wrench fits the *same size* bolt head or nut.

Combination wrenches are used for the same purposes as are open-end and box-end wrenches, and they can be bought in the same sizes. A combination wrench *set* is usually bought in addition to open-end and box-end wrenches. Combination wrenches should not be bought in place of open-end and box-end wrenches, because more than one wrench of

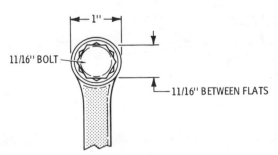

Fig. 5-13. The size of a box-end wrench is the distance across the flats.

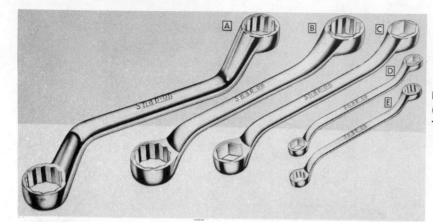

Fig. 5-14. Box-end wrenches come in either 12-point (A,B,E) or 6-point (C,D) styles. (Courtesy of Snap-On Tools.)

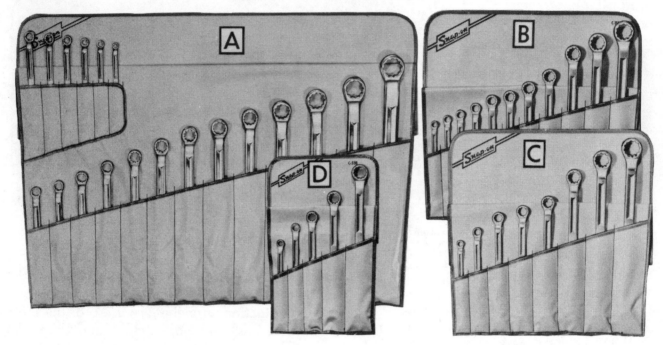

Fig. 5-15. Several sets of common 12-point box-end wrenches. (Courtesy of Snap-On Tools.)

the same size may be needed when holding a bolt and removing a nut of the same size.

Adjustable Wrench— This tool has an adjustable screw that allows the open end of the wrench to be adjusted to different sizes of nuts or bolts. See Fig. 5-17. At one end of the adjustment, an *adjustable wrench* can be adjusted to the closed position. At the *other* end of the adjustment, the wrench can be adjusted to the largest size of nut or bolt head that it will fit. Generally, *longer* adjustable wrenches will open wider than will shorter wrenches. A 4-inch adjustable wrench, for example, may be adjusted to a maximum opening of about one-half inch. A 15-inch adjustable, though, might be adjusted to a maximum opening of 1¾-inches.

Adjustable wrenches are handy because they can be easily adjusted to fit different sizes of

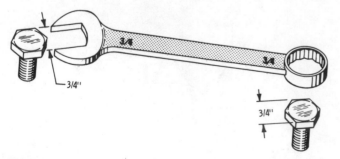

Fig. 5-16. A combination wrench is a box on one end and open on the other. The size is the same on either end.

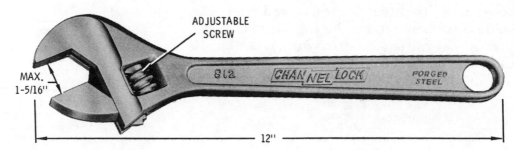
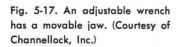

Fig. 5-17. An adjustable wrench has a movable jaw. (Courtesy of Channellock, Inc.)

ADJUSTABLE SCREW

MAX. 1-5/16"

12"

nuts or bolts. This is their main *advantage*. Their main *disadvantage* is that they have the same contact as do open-end wrenches. That is, an adjustable wrench has only *two* points of contact on the nut or bolt, allowing the wrench to slip under heavy pressure. Also, as the wrench becomes worn, the adjusting screw is less able to hold the movable jaw in correct alignment. For these reasons, adjustable wrenches should *not* be used when other wrenches are available.

Adjustable wrenches usually come in sets of three: 6-, 8-, and 12-inch lengths. They may also be bought individually. Smaller and larger sizes are available.

Pipe Wrench— This tool, like an adjustable wrench, has movable jaws. The pipe wrench also has very strong gripping power. It is used mainly on pipes, not on auto bodies, and from this use the wrench gets its name. Pipe wrenches can be bought in many different lengths; Fig. 5-18 shows a typical pipe wrench.

Pipe wrenches have an advantage over open-end wrenches and box-end wrenches because they can grip and hold objects that are round, such as pipes or *studs* (screws without a head). They can be used for several smaller jobs in a body shop, so a body man may want to have an average-size (10-inch) pipe wrench in his

tool box. However, this tool is usually thought of as a pipe fitter's tool because of its wide use in that trade.

Socket Set

A socket wrench set is a collection of tools that may be *interchanged* (connected in different ways). The basic parts of the set are the *sockets* themselves. They fit over a bolt head or nut and are used to loosen or tighten it. They are shaped inside like a box-end wrench, only with a closed top over the box-end. In the closed top is a square hole into which a tool may be placed. See Fig. 5-19.

The basic socket wrench, when put together, is made of two parts: 1. The Handle, of which there are several types (ratchet handle, "power handle," etc.), and; 2. The Socket itself. One handle is made to fit several sizes of sockets

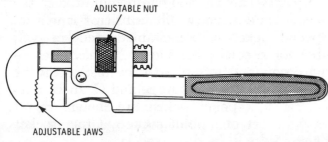

ADJUSTABLE NUT

ADJUSTABLE JAWS

Fig. 5-18. Like an adjustable wrench, a pipe wrench has movable jaws. However, a pipe wrench can also be used to grip *round* objects.

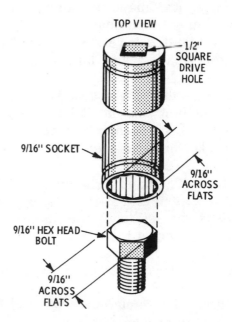

TOP VIEW

1/2" SQUARE DRIVE HOLE

9/16" SOCKET

9/16" ACROSS FLATS

9/16" HEX HEAD BOLT

9/16" ACROSS FLATS

Fig. 5-19. The size of a socket is the width of a nut or bolt that the socket will fit.

because of its drive size, discussed later. Fig. 5-20 shows how the handle lug fits in a socket. Notice that the square *drive lug* on the handle and the square hole in the socket are the same size—in this case, ½-inch.

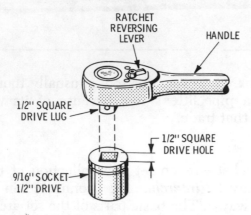

Fig. 5-20. A basic socket wrench is made up of one socket and a drive handle. They must be of the same drive size.

The part of a socket that fits over the nut or bolt head is usually not the same size as the drive. In this case (Fig. 5-20) *this* part of the socket is ⁹⁄₁₆-inch. Note that the ⁹⁄₁₆-inch hole is set down, into the socket. This helps keep the socket from easily slipping off the nut or bolt head.

A common socket set has many attachments, some allowing the socket to turn in either direction. Sockets are made in many sizes and depths, and may be purchased in small or large sets. Sockets and drive sizes are available to fit both the smallest and largest nut or bolt head.

Socket Size—The *size* of a socket is the same as the nut or bolt size on which it is used. A ½-inch socket fits a ½-inch bolt head or nut; a ⁹⁄₁₆-inch socket fits a ⁹⁄₁₆-inch bolt head or nut, etc. See Fig. 5-19.

Drive Size—The handle shown in Fig. 5-21A has what is known as a ½-inch *drive size*. The drive size is the *width* of the square peg or square hole on socket tools. The handle in Fig. 5-21B has a ⅜-inch drive. These are the two most common drive sizes used by auto body men.

Other drive sizes include ¼-, ¾-, and 1-inch. Most body men also have a small ¼-inch drive socket set. This is used for work on small parts

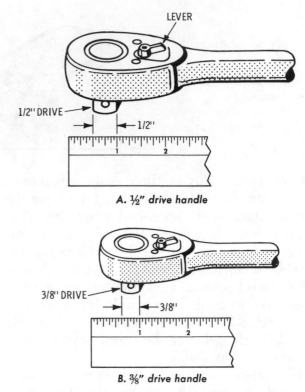

Fig. 5-21. Sockets and drive parts can be classified according to *drive size*. This is the width of square peg or hole in the socket set part.

or interior trim. The larger ¾-inch and 1-inch drive sets are usually used only by truck and heavy equipment mechanics.

Socket Points—The socket itself is a small, round cylinder. The *inside* of the small cylinder is made with 6, 8, or 12 *points,* as shown in Fig. 5-22.

The three sockets in Fig. 5-22 will all fit the same size bolt head or nut. However, the 8-point socket will only fit a ⅞-inch square-head nut or bolt, whereas the 6- or 12-point sockets will fit only 6-sided (hex-head) nuts or bolts that are ⅞-inch across.

Sockets can be bought in almost any size needed, and in many different shapes and sizes. Special sockets have been made and are available for special jobs. Fig. 5-23 shows several more common sets of sockets. Notice the 12-point sockets in Figs. A, B, and C. In Figs. D, E, and F, 6-point sockets are shown. Fig. L shows a set of 8-point sockets. Other sockets illustrated will be discussed later.

Socket Depth—Many sockets are longer (deeper) than others of the same size. This

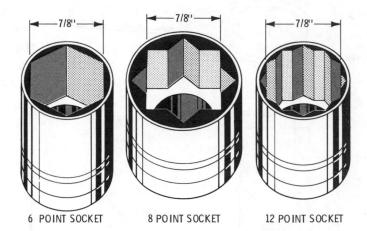

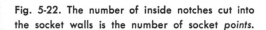

Fig. 5-22. The number of inside notches cut into the socket walls is the number of socket *points*.

6 POINT SOCKET   8 POINT SOCKET   12 POINT SOCKET

allows the deeper socket to go down over a long bolt to reach a nut, as in Fig. 5-24. These long sockets are called *deep-well* sockets.

Deep-well sockets are used for removing nuts or bolts in hard-to-reach places. Spark plugs, many bumper bolts, and nuts that screw far down on bolts (Fig. 5-24) are all examples. The extra depth gives the socket the clearance necessary to remove or tighten the nut. For normal socket jobs, standard-depth (shorter) sockets are sturdier and cost less than the same

size in a deep-well. Fig. 5-23 shows a number of different deep and short sockets.

A common socket set has sockets of different *depths*, as can be seen in Figs. 5-23, 5-24, and 5-25. The depths may range from ⅞-inch deep in smaller drive sets (¼-, ⅜-inch drive) to 3¼-inches deep in the larger drive sets (¾-, 1-inch drive). As usual, sockets can also be bought in special sizes of longer lengths.

Socket Tools—Most socket sets have many tools or attachments. Generally speaking, these

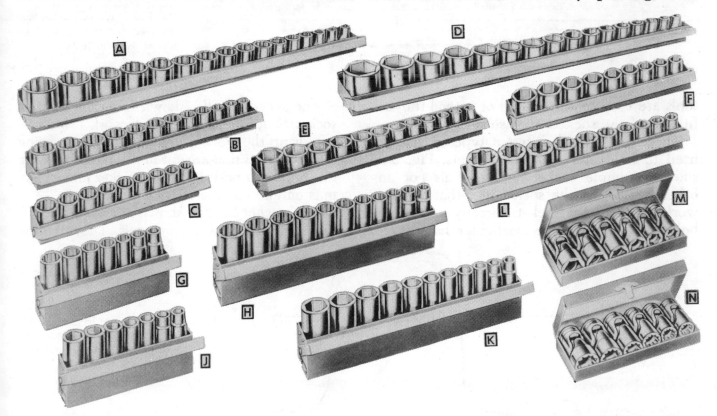

Fig. 5-23. Common sets of sockets. (Courtesy of Snap-On Tools.)

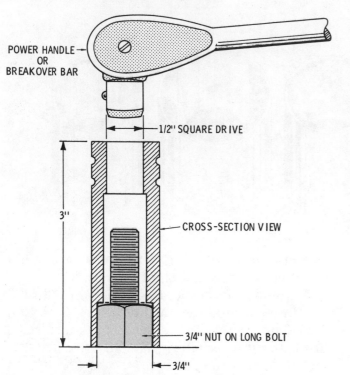

POWER HANDLE
OR
BREAKOVER BAR

1/2" SQUARE DRIVE

3"

CROSS-SECTION VIEW

3/4" NUT ON LONG BOLT

3/4"

Fig. 5-24. A deep-well socket must be used to remove a nut that is far down on the bolt threads.

gives speed in removing nuts by "breaking over" so that the drive lug is straight in front of the handle. For this reason, this handle is sometimes known as a *breaker bar*. Another common name for this handle is a *power handle*.

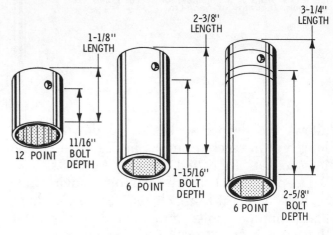

1-1/8"
LENGTH

2-3/8"
LENGTH

3-1/4"
LENGTH

12 POINT

11/16"
BOLT
DEPTH

6 POINT

1-15/16"
BOLT
DEPTH

6 POINT

2-5/8"
BOLT
DEPTH

Fig. 5-25. The same size socket (1") may be purchased in different socket *depths*.

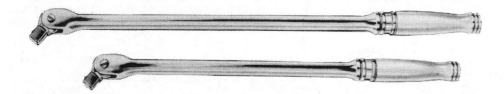

Fig. 5-26. A common socket handle used to turn sockets. (Courtesy of Snap-On Tools.)

tools are used to either hold or extend the usefulness of the sockets themselves.

There are several different types of handles used to hold and turn the sockets. Fig. 5-26 shows a simple socket handle. This (or any other handle) is the socket tool that allows a worker to turn the socket, thereby turning the bolt head or nut. This particular handle also

The *speed handle,* shown in Fig. 5-27, is a socket handle used for quick work. This tool speeds up the work of removing and replacing bolts and nuts that are out in the open. By using this tool with both hands, a worker may speed nuts on and off in a hurry.

The *ratchet handles* shown in Figs. 5-28B, C, D, and E are time-saving tools. They are the

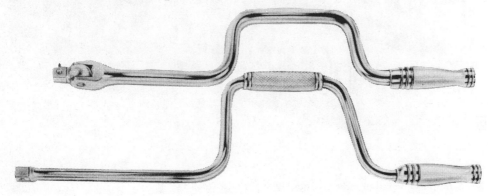

Fig. 5-27. Speed handles, used to quickly remove or tighten the bolt or nut in a socket. (Courtesy of Snap-On Tools.)

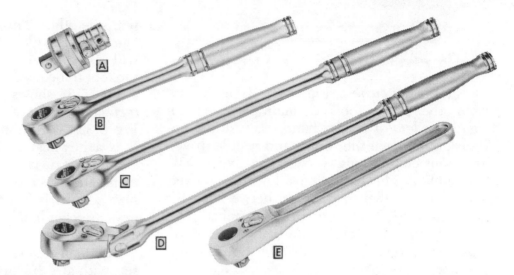

Fig. 5-28. Common ratchet handle tools. (Courtesy of Snap-On Tools.)

most commonly-used socket tools. The handle drive rests on a ratchet wheel, allowing the handle to back up without taking the socket off the nut. By flipping a small lever on the back of the ratchet, the ratchet direction may be reversed. The ratchet is a strong, useful, and handy socket tool. With proper care, it can last many years.

The *ratchet adapter* (Fig. 5-28A) is a ratchet converter. That is, it can be put on any socket handle that is not ratcheted, such as the handle in Fig. 5-26. These handles would then be converted to ratchet handles, able to move back and forth without being lifted off the nut and put back for each turn.

A *universal joint* (Fig. 5-29) is one of the biggest time-savers that can be purchased. This handy tool can be placed on the end of a handle or extension, as necessary, to work *around* parts of the car that are in the way. It works to reach nuts or bolts that have to be removed at an angle, as in Fig. 5-30.

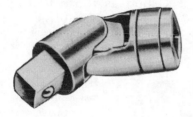

Fig. 5-29. A universal joint can be one of the handiest socket tools to own. (Courtesy of Snap-On Tools.)

Fig. 5-30. Using a universal joint with an extension to loosen a hard-to-reach bolt.

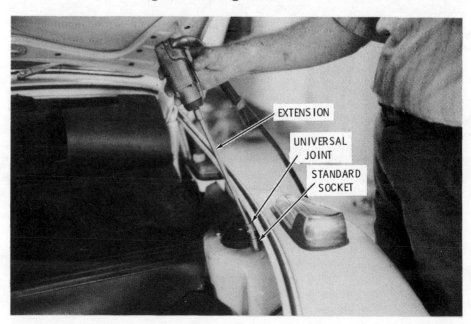

EXTENSION

UNIVERSAL JOINT

STANDARD SOCKET

Fig. 5-31. An extension is used to get the socket into tight places.

A simple *extension*, Fig. 5-31, is used between other socket tools. Its main purpose is to extend the *length* of the handle by adding an extension between the socket and handle drive. Extensions come in many sizes, usually from 1- to 36-inches. The extension allows the socket to be placed down in holes or between parts, places that could not normally be reached. On any extension, a ratchet or other handle may be placed on one end and a socket fastened on the other.

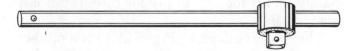

Fig. 5-32. A slide bar is sometimes known as a T-handle.

A simpler socket tool handle is a *slide bar,* or T-handle. This tool, Fig. 5-32, is used to grasp the socket from both sides, allowing the worker to push with one hand while pulling with the other. This allows smooth, even leverage on both sides of the nut or bolt. The bar will also slide all the way to one end, allowing the tool to be used as a regular handle.

Fig. 5-33 shows a group of *screwdriver attachments* that are very helpful in a body shop. Fig. 5-33A is a Phillips screwdriver attachment, B is a hex-head (or Allen-head) screwdriver attachment, C is a standard screwdriver attachment, and D is a special tool known as a *clutch-type* screwdriver attachment. Any of these allows a socket handle to be used for extra leverage on a stubborn screw.

Common Sets—Fig. 5-34 shows several socket sets with attachments. Fig. 34A shows the most complete set, including (from front to back), a short extension, a ratchet, a slide bar, a breaker bar, a long extension, a plastic handle, a universal joint, and several sockets. Note that each of the three sets includes several 6-point sockets. Fig. 5-34A and C show sets that include three 8-point sockets.

Socket sets such as those in Fig. 5-34 can usually be purchased in any of the four common drive sizes; ¼-, ⅜-, ½-, or ¾-inch. Sets of

Fig. 5-33. Socket screwdriver attachments are used to put extra leverage on stubborn screws by using a socket handle. (Courtesy of Snap-On Tools.)

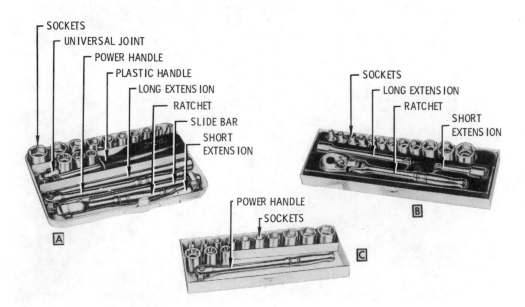

Fig. 5-34. A beginning body man would want to have at least one or two small socket sets similar to these. (Courtesy of Snap-On Tools.)

these four drive sizes and their common uses are discussed in the following sections.

Quarter-Inch Drive Set—The ¼-inch drive socket set, also known as the "midget set," is the smallest set of socket tools made. These sets usually have sockets to fit the smallest nuts used on auto bodies, and up to about ½-inch. Good ¼-inch drive sets include a ratchet handle, a universal joint, and several extensions.

Using a ¼-inch drive set is limited to small, easy-to-remove nuts and bolts. If two much pressure is used to loosen larger-sized bolts and nuts (⁷⁄₁₆-inch to ½-inch), the ratchet mechanism may break. If a ⁷⁄₁₆-inch or ½-inch bolt head or nut does not turn easily with ¼-inch drive socket tools, use a larger drive socket set.

Three-Eighths-Inch Set—This set has a ⅜-inch square drive, as was shown earlier. A good ⅜-inch drive set is the most commonly-used set in an auto body repair shop. The sockets in this set fit almost all auto body sheet metal panel bolts and nuts.

A common ⅜-inch drive set has sockets ranging in size from ⅜-inch through ¾-inch. Usually included is a breaker bar, a speed handle, a ratchet, extensions, and a slide bar. This drive size set can be bought with 6-, 8-, and 12-point sockets. Deep well sockets, universal joints, and many other accessories may be included.

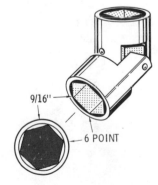

Fig. 5-35. When a universal joint and socket are built together, the tool is known as a flexocket.

9/16"

6 POINT

Flexockets, Fig. 5-35, are usually available in only ⅜-inch drive. These very handy and special sockets are used in the same way as are universal joints. A universal joint is a *drive* attachment, however, whereas the flexocket is a *socket* attachment. Generally speaking, flexockets are available in the same sizes as are standard sockets. However, ⅜-inch drive flexockets are limited to nuts and bolts of sizes up to ¾-inch.

Half-Inch Drive Set—This is a heavier set than the ⅜-inch drive. It is used for heavy work such as removing bumpers, front suspension parts, and other heavy jobs.

Socket sets of ½-inch drive usually include socket sizes from ⁷⁄₁₆-inch to 1¼-inch. These sizes make the ½-inch drive set very useful for heavier automobile repair. The set usually also includes several handles, a slide bar, extensions, and a universal joint. Sometimes, flexockets are available in ½-inch drive. Half-inch drive sets will usually not include sockets to fit nuts or bolt heads smaller than ⁷⁄₁₆-inch.

Three-Quarter-Inch Drive Set—This heavy-duty socket set is not often used for auto body work. Because of this, it is not practical for each body man in the shop to purchase his own ¾-inch drive set. This set is discussed later in the unit, in the section on tools furnished by the shop.

Screwdrivers

Most body men usually have several sets of *screwdrivers*. These tools are used to loosen and tighten screws. They are called screwdrivers because they drive (push) different kinds of screws. Like wrenches and most other tools, they come in many sizes and designs.

Each type and size of screwdriver is made for a certain type and size of screw. A screwdriver's *size* is the length of the *blade*, or handle. A group of common round-blade screwdrivers is shown in Fig. 5-36. The smallest of these screwdrivers (the stubby) is a 1½-inch size because its blade is 1½-inches long. The largest of the round blade screwdrivers pictured is an 8-inch size, because its blade is 8 inches long.

Standard-Tip Screwdriver—A common screwdriver used in almost all auto repair work is a *standard-tip*, shown in Figs. 5-36 and 5-37. Standard-tip screwdrivers may range in size from as short as a 1½-inch blade to a 20- or 24-inch blade.

A set of standard-tip screwdrivers that a new body man should choose would be the type with *insulated* handles. These will help

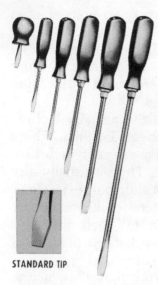

Fig. 5-36. A good selection of standard-tip screwdrivers is necessary for auto body work. These have a round shank. (Courtesy of Snap-On Tools.)

STANDARD TIP

Fig. 5-38. Phillips screwdrivers. (Courtesy of Snap-On Tools.)

PHILLIPS TIP

prevent electrical-shock if the tool accidentally comes in contact with the vehicle's battery or electrical wiring. Many new body men begin work with a set of six standard-tip screwdrivers and then add more later.

The main advantage of standard-tip screwdrivers is that they fit all slotted screws: sheet metal screws, wood screws, self tapping screws, and many others. If used properly, the standard tip screwdriver is safe. The disadvantage of this tool is that it may be incorrectly used as a chisel. Also, some workmen do not keep their standard-tip screwdrivers properly sharpened.

Phillips Screwdrivers—This type of screwdriver is very common to auto body repair. These screwdrivers usually come in sets including 4 to 6 screwdrivers, in length from 4 to 8

inches. Fig. 5-38 shows a typical set of Phillips screwdrivers.

Phillips screwdrivers are used many times a day in an auto body repair shop. This is because Phillips-head screws are used a good deal on modern automobile bodies. The main advantage of a Phillips-head screw is the screw's appearance. In any position, a Phillips-head screw is generally better looking than a standard screw. This is why so many Phillips head screws are used on modern auto bodies.

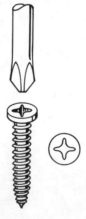

Fig. 5-39. A Phillips screwdriver has four "teeth" to fit the head of a Phillips-head screw.

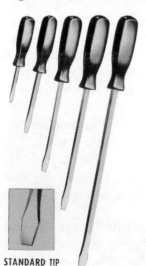

Fig. 5-37. Some auto repairmen prefer screwdrivers like these, with a *square* shank.

STANDARD TIP

A Phillips-tip screwdriver meets *four* sides in the screw head, as shown in Fig. 5-39. When enough pressure is applied, this helps make the screw back off or tighten easier. As with standard-tip screwdrivers, the screwdriver handle should be insulated to help prevent electrical shock if the screwdriver comes in contact with the battery or wire terminals.

*Dis*advantages of Phillips-tip screwdrivers include the fact that they can only be used on Phillips-head screws. Also, Phillips screwdrivers tend to wear out quicker than other screwdrivers. Sometimes, a Phillips screwdriver has worn out quickly because it was used as a punch. This is an incorrect and unsafe way to use a Phillips screwdriver.

Fig. 5-42. Screws with a Reed and Prince head are best removed with a Reed and Prince screwdriver.

Fig. 5-40. Clutch-type screwdrivers are used on clutch-tip screws. (Courtesy of Snap-On Tools.)

CLUTCH-TYPE TIP

Clutch-Type Screwdriver — This unusual screwdriver is also known as a *"clutch head."* Like a Phillips-tip, the clutch-type also has four sides for applying pressure. See Fig. 5-40. They also come in sizes of 4 to 8 inches long.

Clutch-type screwdrivers have limited use because not many vehicles use a clutch-type screw. They are used more frequently on General Motors trucks than on any other vehicle.

Reed and Prince Screwdriver — The screwdriver shown in Fig. 5-41 is a *Reed and Prince* screwdriver. This type screwdriver is normally sold in lengths from 4 to 8 inches.

Reed and Prince screwdrivers should not be confused with *Phillips* screwdrivers. There is a good deal of difference in the screw slots of the two types of screws *and* in the screwdriver points. See Figs. 5-38 and 5-42. Compare the tips closely and note that each screwdriver tip fits a different type of screw. Reed and Prince screwdrivers have a more definite point on the tip whereas Phillips screwdrivers are more blunt on the tip.

Tape Measure

One handy tool frequently used in the body shop is a *tape measure* also known as a "steel tape." A good steel tape such as the one shown in Fig. 5-43 is used for making measurements when cutting or aligning damaged panels or aligning frames. Smaller jobs include checking door window openings and measuring for many other jobs in the shop.

Fig. 5-41. A typical selection of Reed and Prince screwdrivers. (Courtesy of Snap-On Tools.)

REED & PRINCE

Fig. 5-43. A tape measure is necessary for many jobs in a body shop. (Courtesy of Snap-On Tools.)

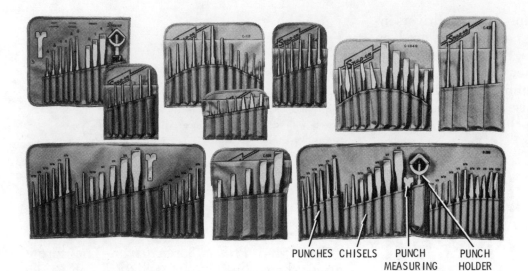

PUNCHES CHISELS PUNCH   PUNCH
                  MEASURING HOLDER
                  GAUGE

Fig. 5-44. Common punch and chisel sets. (Courtesy of Snap-On Tools.)

Punch and Chisel Set

Many times, auto body men need to cut or punch holes in metal panels or other parts. Other times holes need to be aligned to assemble body parts. All of these jobs are done with tools from a good *punch and chisel set*. Several typical sets are shown in Fig. 5-44.

Punches—These tools have rounded points. *Punches* come in sizes from about 4 to 20 inches long, depending on the use for which they were designed. Some of the more standard punch sizes are shown in Fig. 5-44.

Some punch sets include a measuring gauge and a holder. The measuring gauge is used to measure the *angle* on the punch tip. The holder is used to hold the punch or chisel while it is being driven with a hammer. This lessens the possibility of the body man damaging his hands while using the punch and holder.

During metal straightening work, the punch may be used to raise small dents that would be hard to reach with a pick hammer. Another use for the tool is to punch holes in panels for sheet metal screws or for pulling out dents. Finally, another use for punches is to align holes by pulling them to the same spot. This allows bolts to be inserted, holding the panels together and in alignment.

Chisels—The main use for these tools is to *cut* metal. Several common chisels are included in the sets shown in Fig. 5-44.

A good, sharp chisel will cut easily and smoothly, allowing clean cuts to be made on metal parts. The main use for a chisel is to cut metal when removing a metal panel. Other common uses include breaking weld joints and cutting off screws, rivets, or rusted parts.

Chisels comes in all sizes, from about 4 to 18 inches long, and in many different shapes. Most chisel and punch sets also include a measuring gauge and holder.

Pliers

Pliers come in many different sizes and shapes. All body repairmen need several sets of good *pliers* for gripping, cutting, holding, and many other jobs in the shop. Fig. 5-45 through 5-50 show several of the many different kinds of pliers.

Interlocking-Grip Pliers—These pliers, Fig. 5-45, have a tight gripping action in their jaws. *Interlocking-grip* pliers have long handles, allowing the worker a strong grip on the tool and

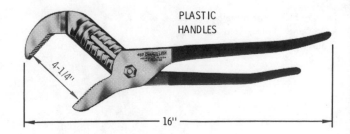

PLASTIC HANDLES

4-1/4"

16"

Fig. 5-45. Interlocking-Grip Pliers. (Courtesy of Channellock, Inc.)

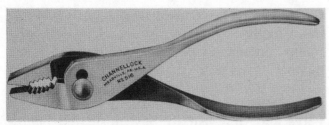

Fig. 5-46. Simple combination pliers. (Courtesy of Channellock, Inc.)

the object in the tool's jaws. They are basically used for holding and turning large nuts, bolts, and round pieces. These pliers are also known as Channellock® pliers, a brand name. Older auto mechanics and tradesmen may refer to these as "water pump" pliers, because they were used to tighten water pump seals on older-model cars.

Below the jaws of this tool are adjustable, interlocking channels, from which the tool gets its name. These channels allow the pliers to fit both large and small parts, by changing channels and, therefore, changing the jaw size. They have the advantage of being fast and easy to use. Since the jaws are offset, they can reach many hard-to-get-to places. These pliers usually come in sizes from about 6 to 14 inches long. A *dis*advantage is that these pliers have a tendency to round off the corners of bolts and

nuts. For this reason, they should not be used for this job when wrenches are available.

Combination Pliers—These are the most common plier tool. *Combination* pliers are so named because of the fact that they have both *notched* and *flat* jaws. See Fig. 5-46. These jaws allow the pliers to grip either round or flat work. These pliers are the most frequently used, general-purpose pliers in a body man's tool box. They have long handles to allow good leverage and they have a movable center bolt to change the jaw size. Combination pliers usually come in a number of lengths from 6 inches on up.

Many brands of combination pliers can also be used to cut wire. For this reason, combination pliers may sometimes be referred to as *wire pliers*. The wire-cutting part of the pliers is under the gripping jaws and above the adjusting bolt in the center of the pliers.

Midget Pliers—These pliers get their name from the fact that they are very small. *Midget pliers*, Fig. 5-47, are used for very close work in limited space. This would include work on switches, gauges, and other instrument panel work.

Like combination pliers, midget pliers have a movable center to adjust the jaws for different-sized bolts and nuts. They also have fairly long handles for good leverage. The main dis-

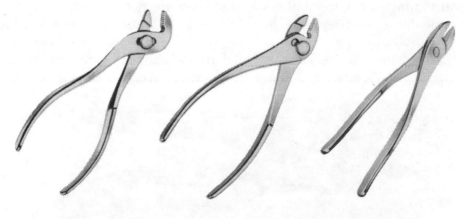

Fig. 5-47. Midget pliers are used on small parts and in limited working space. (Courtesy of Snap-On Tools.)

Fig. 5-48. Battery pliers are used to remove battery bolts and terminals on many batteries. (Courtesy of Channellock, Inc.)

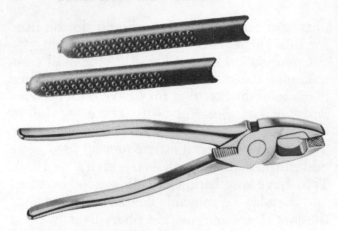

Fig. 5-49. Lineman pliers are used mostly by electricians. (Courtesy of Snap-On Tools.)

advantage of midget pliers is that they are small and must be used with caution. If there is room enough, it is better to use larger pliers than the midget models.

Battery Pliers—These special pliers, shown in Fig. 5-48, are very useful. The long handles on *battery pliers* give a body man good leverage on nuts or bolts. Basically, battery pliers are used to remove the nut on battery cable bolts. Corrosion from battery acid may have caused the nut to corrode so that it can on longer be removed with a wrench.

Battery pliers usually come in only one or two sizes, from about 6 to 10 inches long. A disadvantage of battery pliers is that they are not adjustable, so they only fit a few sizes of nuts and bolts.

Lineman Pliers—These special pliers, shown in Fig. 5-49, are used more in electrical work

than in auto body work. *Lineman pliers* are more likely to be used by an electrician or a power lineman, which is how they got their name.

These pliers also have a wire-cutting edge. They can easily cut the insulation off electrical wires and they usually have insulated handle grips to help guard against the workman getting a shock from electrical wires. A disadvantage of these pliers is that their best work is done on electrical equipment.

Locking-Jaw Pliers—Pliers like those shown in Figs. 5-50 through 53 are widely used in the auto body repair trade. These pliers have a spring-type locking mechanism to lock the jaws in position. When *locking-jaw* pliers are locked on an object, they continue to hold firmly *after* they are released; this explains their name. Locking-jaw pliers are available in various lengths from 6 to 12 inches. Special models are also available and are discussed later.

Standard locking-jaw pliers are useful for many types of work. They have double-action lock jaws, will grip almost any shape, and will normally not slip. These pliers will work in close quarters and at any angle. These tools are often used as a substitute for a vise, a clamp, or a pipe wrench. Standard locking-jaw pliers have either straight jaws (Fig. 5-50) or curved jaws (Fig. 5-51).

Special locking-jaw pliers are available to hold panels together for brazing or welding. Shown in Fig. 5-52, these pliers allow both hands to be free for welding or brazing. The

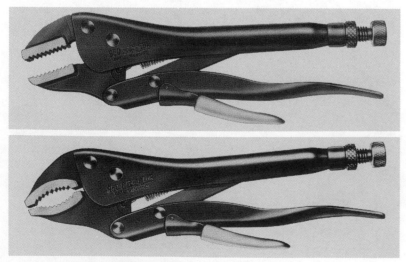

Fig. 5-50. The most common type of locking-jaw pliers are the standard, straight-jaw type shown here. (Courtesy of Channellock, Inc.)

Fig. 5-51. The second type of standard locking-jaw pliers are those with curved jaws. (Courtesy of Channellock, Inc.)

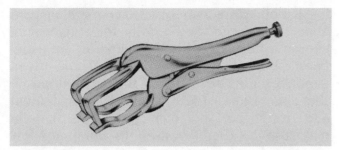

Fig. 5-52. These special locking-jaws pliers are used to hold panels together for welding or brazing. (Courtesy of Snap-On Tools.)

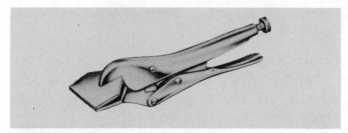

Fig. 5-53. Special locking-jaw pliers with wide, flat jaws are used for bending. (Courtesy of Snap-On Tools.)

special "reach over" top jaw can go over the top of seams or panel flanges, making the tool more useful.

Another special locking-jaw plier is the *bending tool* shown in Fig. 5-53. This tool has wide jaws that make it ideal for the bending and shaping that may be necessary during sheet metal work. These tools are also useful for upholstery work because the material can be pulled and stretched without damage.

Brushes and Scrapers

In a body shop, *brushes* (Fig. 5-54) are used for cleaning off rust and old paint. Qualities of good brushes include stiffness, durability, and long life. The group of brushes in Fig. 5-54 include wire brushes and bristle (hair) brushes.

The main uses of *scrapers* in a body shop are to remove paint and cements. Fig. 5-55 shows a group of scrapers commonly used in the auto body trade. Wide scrapers are some-

Fig. 5-54. Various types of brushes are used to clean rust and other material from auto body parts. (Courtesy of Snap-On Tools.)

Fig. 5-55. Scrapers may be used to remove paint and cements from auto body surfaces. (Courtesy of Snap-On Tools.)

times used to spread plastic or other resin-base materials.

Scratch Awl

Similar to an ice pick, but stronger, is a *scratch awl*. See Fig. 5-56. In a modern body shop, this is a much-used tool.

Fig. 5-56. A scratch awl. (Courtesy of Snap-On Tools.)

Scratch awls have two main jobs: 1. To scratch (mark) metal for cutting, drilling, or fastening, and; 2. To pierce holes in thin metal. In the second job, it is used instead of a drill because it is much faster than a drill for rough holes. Awls are made with a sharp point that can pierce metal easily. For heavier jobs, it can also be *driven* through thin metal with a light tap from a hammer. As with all cutting tools, awls must be kept sharp to be safe and effective.

Dolly Block

These small, heavy tools are one of the more basic auto body tools. *Dolly blocks* are small, simple tools. Each block has many curves and angles. See Fig. 5-57. Different dolly blocks are easy to identify by their shapes, such as (left to right in Fig. 5-57); toe, heel, general-purpose, and anvil.

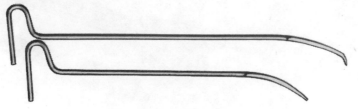

All dollies are mainly used *under* damaged areas. When choosing a dolly for a given job, choose a dolly that fits the shape of the panel *before* the panel was damaged. Then, use a hammer on the open side of the metal, opposite the dolly block. Light hammering will align and "rough out" the damaged metal. A dolly may also be used by itself to bump up low spots.

While a hammer would be used to bump *down* high crowns (outward dents), dolly blocks would be used *beneath* the panel to force the panel *up,* toward its original curve or contour. For the most part, dollies are used as back up tools for hammers. Dollies come in many sizes and shapes. A set of the four most common dollies is usually enough for a beginning body man.

Pry Bars

Another common metal-working tool is a *pry bar,* two of which are shown in Fig. 5-58. Pry bars are available in different lengths

Fig. 5-57. Common body *dollies.* Left to right: Toe, Heel, General-Purpose, Anvil. (Courtesy of Snap-On Tools.)

(sizes) and shapes. Most tool companies offer pry bars already included in a set of body tools. Or, of course, they may be purchased separately as needed.

When repairing doors, a pry bar may be slipped (or punched) through drain holes along the bottom edge of the door. If the holes are not near the damage, other holes may be made. Then, small dents and creases in the out-

Fig. 5-58. Pry bars. (Courtesy of Snap-On Tools.)

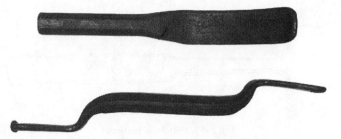

Fig. 5-59. Body shop *spoons*, used for many different jobs.

man cannot get to an area with a hammer or dolly. Two common spoons are shown in Fig. 5-59. Spoons come in many sizes and shapes.

Spoons are stronger and thicker than are pry bars. Spoons may also be used to pick up low spots when there is not enough room to use a hammer. They can be used as alignment tools in hard-to-reach places. When they are used this way, the visible end is bumped with a hammer to align an inside panel.

Spring hammering is also done with a spoon. Here, the spoon is placed against a crown or ridge near a dent or gouge. See Fig. 5-60. The spoon is then hammered to evenly flatten the high ridge down to its proper position.

side door panel can be pried out from inside the door, sometimes without removing trim or window parts.

Body Spoon

The most common use of a *body spoon* is to reach into hard-to-get-to places such as the insides of doors, deck (trunk) lids, and hoods. Like pry bars, spoons are used when the repair-

Hammers

Good *hammers* are one of the main tools in an auto body repair shop. A group of general

Fig. 5-60. Using a spoon to lower a high ridge.

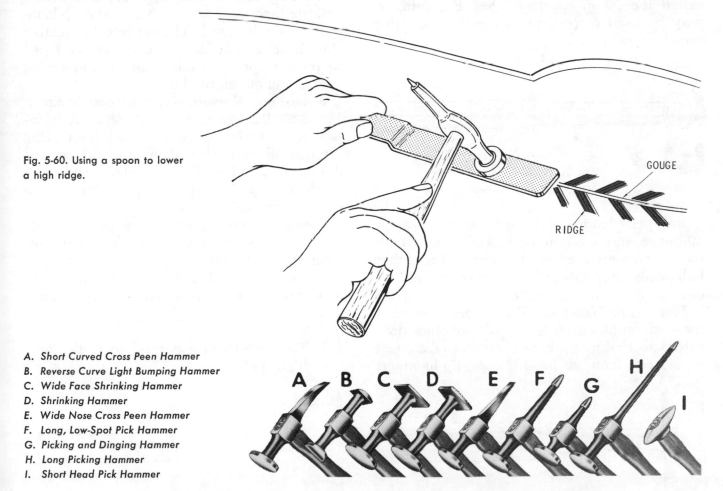

A. *Short Curved Cross Peen Hammer*
B. *Reverse Curve Light Bumping Hammer*
C. *Wide Face Shrinking Hammer*
D. *Shrinking Hammer*
E. *Wide Nose Cross Peen Hammer*
F. *Long, Low-Spot Pick Hammer*
G. *Picking and Dinging Hammer*
H. *Long Picking Hammer*
I. *Short Head Pick Hammer*

Fig. 5-61. Body shop hammers are made in many different shapes for different body shop jobs. (Courtesy of Snap-On Tools.)

body shop hammers is shown in Fig. 5-61. Some hammers are used for aligning or roughing out damaged metal. Other hammers are used for shaping and more carefully smoothing the metal after it has been roughed out.

The *size* of any hammer is the *weight* of the hammer *head* only. The length or weight of the hammer handle has nothing to do with the hammer's *size*. For this reason, a 16-ounce ball peen hammer has a head that weighs 16 ounces *before* the handle is installed.

There are special hammers that do not have metal heads. Instead, they have rubber or plastic heads. These hammers are used when the part being worked on would be damaged by a metal head. Several basic types of body shop hammers are discussed below.

Ball Peen Hammer—This is a general-purpose hammer. The *ball peen* hammer is also called the "shop hammer." See Fig. 5-62. It may be used to rough out metal or to drive punches and chisels.

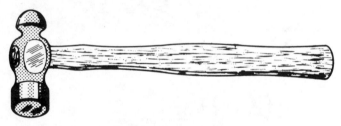

Fig. 5-62. Ball Peen Hammer.

Ball peen hammers come in several sizes. A 40-ounce and a 30-ounce ball peen are those most commonly used in a body shop. Like other ball peens, they have a flat, finished face on one end and a round face on the other end.

Plastic-Tip Hammer—This hammer is used for work on precision-finish parts or other delicate parts that might have their finish damaged by a metal hammer head. *Plastic-tip* hammers

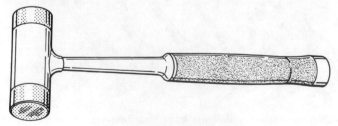

Fig. 5-63. Plastic-Tip Hammer.

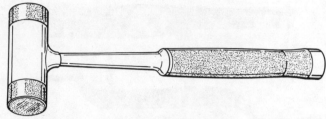

Fig. 5-64. Soft-Face Hammer.

are usually used more on mechanical parts than on body parts. The tough plastic tip will withstand a good deal of pounding without seriously marring the face. Many better plastic-tip hammers have tips that are easily replaced when necessary. See Fig. 5-63.

Soft-Face Hammer—This hammer usually has tips of hard *leather*. See Fig. 5-64. Soft-face hammers are used for working metal parts such as chrome trim without marring or damaging them. They may be used on parts that are more delicate than those on which a plastic-tip hammer would be used. The replaceable leather tips on better soft-face hammers are designed to resist chipping, flaking, and mushrooming (spreading out on the face).

Brass-Face Hammer—This special hammer, Fig. 5-65, has two faces of soft *brass*. A *brass-face* hammer is especially suited for driving mechanical parts that should not be scarred during installation. In body shop work, this would be especially true for parts involved in front suspension and alignment.

Pick Hammers— These are some of a body man's most-used hammers. *Pick* hammers have a flat, smooth face on one end and a sharp point on the opposite end. See Figs. 5- 61 and 66. In good body work, a pick hammer has 3 main jobs:

1. The smooth face is used to work down high spots.

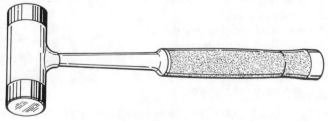

Fig. 5-65. Brass-Face Hammer.

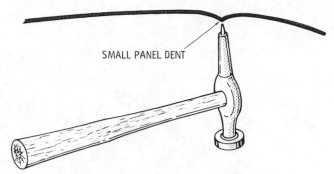

SMALL PANEL DENT

A. Using the pointed end to pick up small dents.

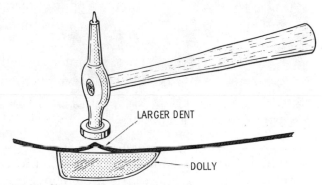

LARGER DENT

DOLLY

B. Using the smooth face and dolly to work down larger dents.

Fig. 5-66. Common uses for a bodyman's *pick hammer.*

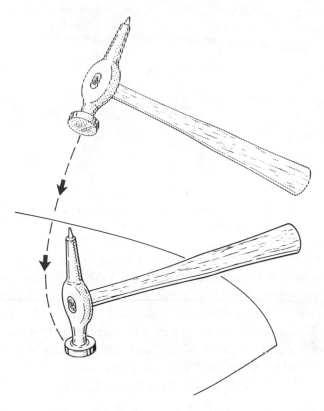

Fig. 5-67. The "spring" of the sheet metal will actually rebound the hammer for another tap.

2. The smooth face is used to work metal down on the dolly.
3. The sharp, pointed end is used to pick up small dents.

When using a pick hammer, be careful when using the sharp end. The sharp, pointed end can build up a great deal of pressure and may damage the metal if not used carefully. Only light, small blows should be used, and then only on small dents. Pick hammers can easily punch holes in the body sheetmetal.

When the damage has been roughed out to the correct *general* contour, the process known as hammering and dollying begins. A dolly is placed under the damaged area and the hammer's smooth face is used to work down the high spots, as in Fig. 5-66B.

A pick hammer should *not* be used to strike heavy blows. Instead, a pick hammer should be held *loosely* in one hand. Then, as the hammer lightly strikes the metal, it will automatically spring back into position for another blow, as in Fig. 5-67. The metal's "spring" makes the

hammer bounce back, off the surface being worked. The bodyman must guide the hammer's direction as it springs back.

Then, using the dolly, the low place is bumped on the underside, bringing the low place up and smoothing out the damaged area. The dolly brings the metal *up*, whereas the pick hammer works the high places *down*. Together, they work as shown in Figs. 5-66 and 67.

The *sharp* end of the pick hammer is used to lift up the tiny low spots left by the dolly *underneath* the surface. Here, the dolly is held on the *outside* of the panel, close to the dent, to back up the sharp end of the hammer, as shown in Fig. 5-68. This keeps the metal from coming too far upward.

Slide Hammer—The newest member of the hammer family is the *slide* hammer, also known as the "snatch hammer." A typical slide hammer is shown in Fig. 5-69. This modern tool is one of the more popular hammers in a body shop.

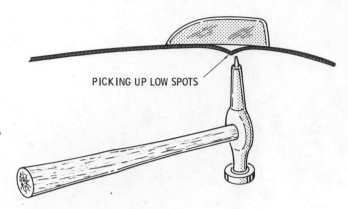

PICKING UP LOW SPOTS

Fig. 5-68. Using the sharp end of a pick hammer to pick up small dents left by the dolly on the underside.

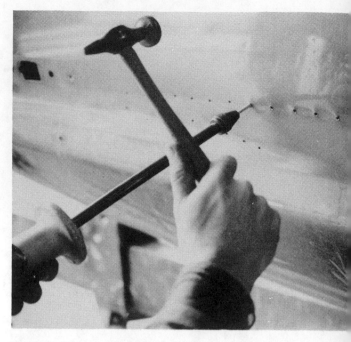

Fig. 5-70. Using a slide hammer with a pick hammer to pull out and level a long gouge in a panel.

A slide hammer is used opposite the way in which a pick hammer is used. With a slide hammer, the metal is *pulled* up instead of being *bumped* up. This may need to be done, for example, on newer types of body construction, especially cars with unitized bodies. These construction methods do not allow as much room for body men to get underneath or behind the panels.

To repair panels such as this with a slide hammer, a hole is first punched or drilled in the metal. (An awl or drill may be used to make the hole.) Then, a large sheet metal screw is screwed into the hole. A screw-holding attachment is *then* screwed onto the end of the slide hammer, as in Fig. 5-69. Attachments are made to fit almost any size metal screw. With the screw in place, pulling on the screw will pull out on the metal. This will allow the bodyman to pull the metal back into position, as shown in Fig. 5-70. Actually, there are *two* methods

by which the slide hammer may hold onto the sheetmetal screw. These are shown in Fig. 5-71. In the *first* method, the slide hammer attachment has a slot that fits under the screw head. This is shown in Figs. 5-69 and 5-71A. With this attachment, the screw is first screwed into the damaged panel, using a screwdriver. Then, the slide hammer is used to pull out the screw and, therefore, pull out the metal.

In the *second* method, the sheetmetal screw is actually *attached* to the slide hammer. This is shown, cutaway, in Fig. 5-71B. With this design, the sheetmetal screw is first put in position on the end of the slide hammer body. A "tooth" on the body end keeps the screw from

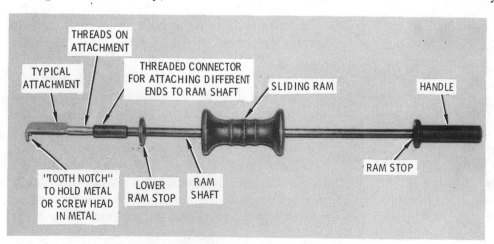

THREADS ON ATTACHMENT

TYPICAL ATTACHMENT

THREADED CONNECTOR FOR ATTACHING DIFFERENT ENDS TO RAM SHAFT

SLIDING RAM

HANDLE

"TOOTH NOTCH" TO HOLD METAL OR SCREW HEAD IN METAL

LOWER RAM STOP

RAM SHAFT

RAM STOP

Fig. 5-69. Slide hammer and parts. (Courtesy of Snap-On Tools.)

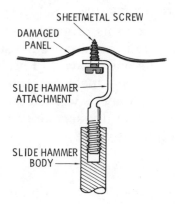

A. *Slide hammer attachment goes around the screw head from one side.*

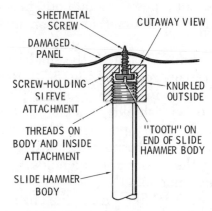

B. *Slide hammer attachment completely surrounds the screw head, becoming a screwdriver as well as a slide hammer.*

Fig. 5-71. How the slide hammer holds onto the sheet metal screw.

turning. Then, a screw-holding *sleeve attachment* is screwed *over* the sheetmetal screw threads, *onto* the end of the slide hammer body. This attachment completely surrounds the screw head and holds it tightly on the end (and the tooth) of the slide hammer body.

While either method will work, the second method (Fig. 5-71B) has a disadvantage in that the screw must be installed on the slide hammer *before* being screwed into the damaged panel. Then, the slide hammer becomes a large screwdriver, to turn the screw into the damaged panel before pulling. See Fig. 5-70.

After the metal has been pulled back into place by either type of slide hammer attachment, the damaged area is levelled. Usually, polyester plastic body filler is used to fill the screw holes and low places. Plastic may be used because the body panel's back side cannot be easily reached for hammering and dollying.

Pull rods—Smaller slide hammers, without the sliding weight, might be known as *pull rods*. See Fig. 5-72. Pull rods are actually another group of "hammers used in reverse." They are used to pull instead of push.

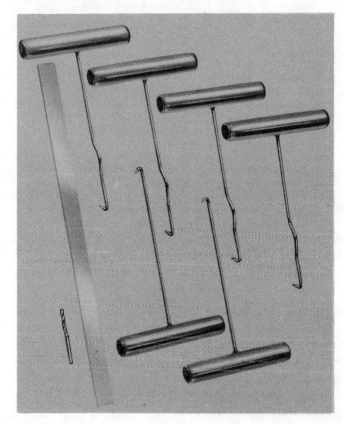

Fig. 5-72. Pull rod tool kit. Includes pull rods, straightedge, and drill bit. (Courtesy of Snap-On Tools.)

Pull rods are used for lighter work (more shallow dents)than are heavier slide hammers. Usually, one pull rod is used at a time, as in Fig. 5-73. A hole must be drilled or punched in

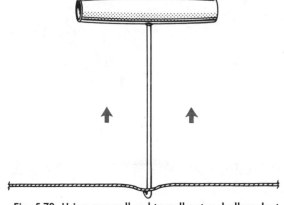

Fig. 5-73. Using one pull rod to pull out a shallow dent.

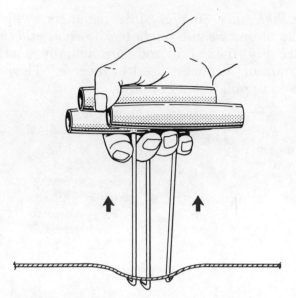

Fig. 5-74. Using several pull rods to pull a larger dent.

the metal to use a pull rod. Later, the hole will have to be filled with body solder or plastic.

An advantage of pull rods is that several rods can be used at the same time, as in Figs. 5-74 and 75. To do this, several holes should be drilled or punched in large damaged areas. Several pull rods can then be placed in the holes and a large section of damage pulled out at one time. To more easily repair creases, the high crown around the outer edge of the low place can be worked down with a pick hammer while the rods are pulled. This is being

done in Fig. 5-75. This helps the metal to straighten back to its original position.

Whenever pull rods are used, a straight edge tool such as the one shown in Fig. 5-72 may be used to see if the metal contour is correct. Then, the metal may be worked down or pulled up to level. Generally speaking, pull rods are used for only light work.

Files

For many years, metal *body files* have been used by the repairman to smooth metal. Figs. 5-76 and 5-77 illustrate major metal body files. The different types of metal body files are used for different contours (slopes) on metal body panels.

Reveal File—This file is the smallest file used in body repair work. See Fig. 5-76. *Reveal files* are used to file in closely rounded places, such as around windshields, backlights (rear windows) and wheel openings. Blades for reveal files can be purchased in almost any *shape*. However, the blades and the holders, of course, are all the same length.

When a reveal file is used, the cutting is done on the pulling stroke. If the file is pushed, as is a body file, it may bounce, producing a rough cut. Properly used, however, reveal files can help a body man produce good, very detailed, work.

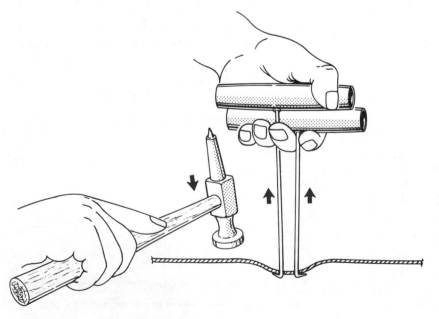

Fig. 5-75. A high crown around a crease may be worked down with a hammer while pulling a dent out with pull rods.

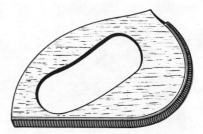

Fig. 5-76. A small reveal file has short, curved file surfaces.

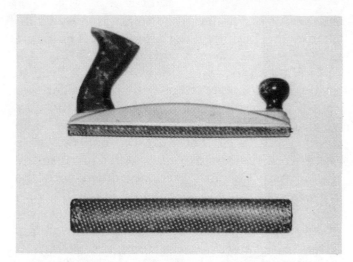

Fig. 5-78. *Surform* file and file holder. (Courtesy of Stanley Tools.)

Body File—This tool is also known as a metal file or metal-body file. See Fig. 5-77. *Body files* are used to work down very small high places after the damaged area has been aligned and dollied to almost exactly the right contour. Moving the file back and forth cuts the high spots off the metal. Then, a pick hammer and dolly may again be used to raise the low spots, making the metal smooth.

Blades for a body file come in three basic shapes: curved, round, and straight. Straight-shaped files can be *flexed* to fit the contour of the metal when using a holder with a turnbuckle screw. See Fig. 5-77. By turning the turnbuckle right or left, the holding plate of the flexible file holder can be flexed. This forces the file to also flex. Flexible file holders may be used for filing both concave (curved in) and convex (curved out) metal. The turnbuckle may also be readjusted for straight cutting.

Surform File—This special file has many nicknames, also being known as a cheese grader, cabbage grader, cabbage cutter, grading file, etc. All of these names refer to the *Surform* file tool shown in Fig. 5-78. The name

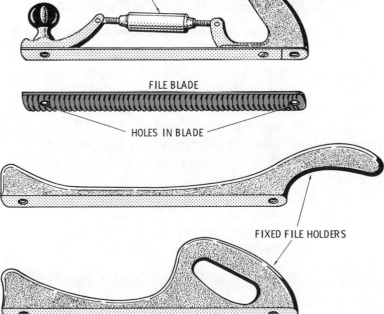

Fig. 5-77. Body files have several different types of holders.

FLEXIBLE FILE HOLDER
TURNBUCKLE SCREW
FILE BLADE
HOLES IN BLADE
FIXED FILE HOLDERS

Surform is the name given to the tool by its inventor, the Stanley Tool Company. The name comes from two words, *surface* and *form*.

In body shop work, a *Surform* tool is used to grade plastic body filler when the filler becomes semihard. At that time, the plastic may be graded off with the *Surform* tool, as is being done in Fig. 5-79. The *Surform* tool speeds up body work done with plastic filler because the plastic may be partly worked down with the *Surform* before it is completely cured. This reduces the body man's waiting time because the plastic can be worked sooner after applying. After using the *Surform* tool, the surface is smoother than when the plastic was first applied. When the plastic has completely cured, it can then be sanded smoother with a fine speed file, discussed below.

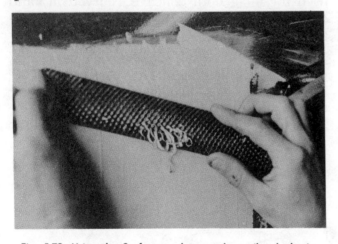

Fig. 5-79. Using the *Surform* tool to grade semihard plastic.

The *Surform* tool cannot be used effectively on fully cured (hardened) plastic. This is because the hardness of the cured plastic will quickly wear the cutting edge off of the *Surform* blade. When the plastic is fully hardened, it may be sanded with a speed file and then prepared for refinishing.

Speed File—This tool is used to hold strips of sandpaper *flat*, for smooth, even surface preparation. For this reason, the tool is sometimes known as a "flat boy." A typical *speed file* is shown in Fig. 5-80.

Normally, a speed file is used *after* the *Surform* tool has been used. (The speed file must be used after the plastic has fully hardened.)

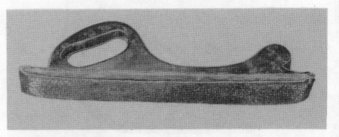

Fig. 5-80. A speed file, or "flat-boy," is used to hold strips of coarse, dry sandpaper.

The tool is first wrapped with sandpaper and then used to further smooth the plastic filler.

These tools are usually made of wood, with a hard fiber backing plate to hold the sandpaper flat. Speed files are about 17 inches long and 2¾ inches wide. First #40 and then #80 sandpapers are used with the file to smooth the plastic for final preparation. The advantages of a speed file are that it is fairly *long*, increasing sanding speed, and that it is *flat*, allowing flat surfaces such as doors and hoods to be sanded without waves or uneven areas.

Door Handle Tools

This tool is used by repairmen for interior door trim work. The *door handle tool* is used on almost all automobiles to remove the inside door and window handles or cranks. Door handle tools are also known as "clip tools" or "clip pullers." See Fig. 5-81.

Door handles and window regulator handles are usually held in place by wire spring clips that are shaped like a horseshoe. These clips fit over the window regulator or door handle shaft inside the door. The clips hold the handles to the shaft, forcing the handle to press up against the door panel upholstery for a good fit.

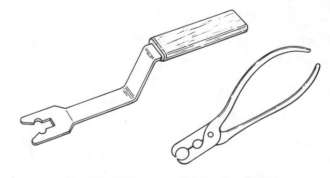

Fig. 5-81. Different types of door handle tools.

Some door handle tools pull the clip out, whereas others push the clip out. Either way, repairmen need this tool to properly work on automobile doors.

Upholstery Tool

This tool, shown in Fig. 5-82, is most often used in a trim (upholstery) shop. Auto body repairmen doing trim work will find an *upholstery tool* to be a handy tool.

Fig. 5-82. A common upholstery tool is needed for good, easy interior trim work.

An upholstery tool is used for removing the trim pad (upholstery) on door and quarter panels inside the car. The fork end of the tool is offset to allow the worker to pry up, removing upholstery tacks, nails and spring clips. This is needed for the special spring clips that hold the upholstery (trim) in place on the door, since these clips are very different from door handle clips.

Metal Snips

Many times, panels or metal pieces need to be trimmed or fitted in a body shop. *Metal snips* of different types may be used for these metal-cutting jobs. The main purpose of snips (shown in Figs. 5-83 through 85) is to cut *thin* metal. Bodymen may need to use the snips to cut metal into new shapes for patching holes from damage or rust-out. There are several types of snips available, discussed here. Most body repairmen keep at least one pair of metal snips in their portable tool box.

Panel Cutters—These special snips may be used to cut either straight or curved lines on existing *panels* of the car. They cut through body steel easily and they leave a clean, sharp edge on the metals. The sharp edge is especially important when a section of panel is being re-

Fig. 5-83. Panel cutters. (Courtesy of Snap-On Tools.)

moved and another section is to be installed. *Panel cutters* are shown in Fig. 5-83.

Metal Cutters—These cutters are used to cut hard metals, such as stainless steel. *Metal cutters* have a narrow body that allows the cut metal to pass freely over the snips. The blades have *serrated* (a raised grid pattern) cutting edges for easy cutting. Metal cutters are shown in Fig. 5-84.

Fig. 5-84. Metal cutters. (Courtesy of Snap-On Tools.)

Tin Snips—These snips are among the more common snips in use. *Tin snips* can cut straight, circular, or irregular shapes. The blades are shaped so as to draw the metal into the jaws. The jaws have great leverage for easy cutting into heavy steel. Fig. 5-85 shows a typical set of tin snips.

Fig. 5-85. Tin snips. (Courtesy of Snap-On Tools.)

Eye Protection Tools

For safe and comfortable working, a workman must keep his eyes protected at all times. Either safety or welding goggles *must* be used when working with certain hand tools, all power tools, or welding. Goggles may be purchased in many different styles and shapes. Some are held in place by frame horns that fit behind the worker's ears; other have elastic bands to be fitted around the worker's head.

Safety Goggles—*Clear* goggles, Fig. 5-86, are used on jobs that do not require welding or heat. These *safety goggles* are light-weight and made with a wide, clear plastic rim for wearing comfort. They have a wide, distortion-free field of vision. They may be used for eye protection from flying particles, such as those from a grinder, sander, hammer and chisel, etc.

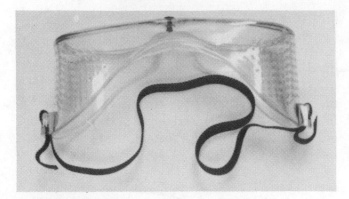

Fig. 5-86. Clear safety glasses for body shop work not requiring a torch.

Welding Goggles—These goggles, Fig. 5-87, are used when welding, brazing, and cutting with an oxy-acetylene torch. Welding with the dark shades in *welding goggles* protects eyes from *both* harmful particles and harmful rays of bright light.

Lenses for welding goggles may be bought in several shades from light to dark. The lightest (most clear) lenses are number 1 and the darkest lenses normally used for oxy-acetylene work are number 8. The final choice of lens should depend on the type of welding being done. Normal oxy-acetylene welding and brazing requires a number 4 or 5 lens, whereas gas cutting normally requires a number 5 or 6 lens. Usually, a number 5 lens will be enough protection for oxy-acetylene work in a body shop.

Rivet Gun

This handy tool is used to fasten two pieces of metal together when only one side of the

Fig. 5-87. Shaded welding goggles for body shop work with an oxy-acetylene torch.

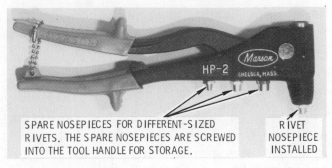

SPARE NOSEPIECES FOR DIFFERENT-SIZED RIVETS. THE SPARE NOSEPIECES ARE SCREWED INTO THE TOOL HANDLE FOR STORAGE.   RIVET NOSEPIECE INSTALLED

Fig. 5-88. Pop-rivet gun with different-size nosepieces. (Courtesy of Marson Corporation.)

joint is *accessible*. (This means that only one side of the joint is "open" for working; the other side is closed off or boxed in and cannot be reached.) The *rivet gun*, Fig. 5-88, is also known as a "riveter," or a "pop-rivet gun." The rivets used with this tool are the small metal pins shown in Fig. 5-89.

To use this tool, a hole is first drilled through *both* pieces of metal in the joint. The hole must be the size of the rivet being used and must go completely through both pieces along the joint's edge.

When the hole has been drilled, the proper size *rivet* (Fig. 5-89) and the proper size *nosepiece* for that rivet (Fig. 5-88) must be selected. A different nosepiece is used for each *diameter* of rivet. Finally, the rivet is inserted point first into the rivet gun, as in Fig. 5-90. The blunt, ball-shaped end of the rivet sticks out of the nosepiece.

When the blunt end of the rivet is put in the hole through the joint, the rivet gun pulls the rivet *through* the rivet's own long shank. By pulling the rivet through its shank, the rivet head spreads out the shank on the *underside* of the joint. When the shank and head are spread out under the joint, the two pieces of metal are firmly held together. Then, the rivet gun pops the rivet off on the outside, at the circular shoulder.

Pocket Knife

Most body men work with a good *pocket knife* available. This tool is always helpful for a number of jobs when repair work is being done. It is especially useful for cutting masking tape, cleaning in close places, and remov-

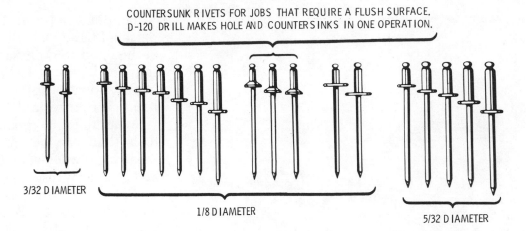

COUNTERSUNK RIVETS FOR JOBS THAT REQUIRE A FLUSH SURFACE.
D-120 DRILL MAKES HOLE AND COUNTERSINKS IN ONE OPERATION.

3/32 DIAMETER

1/8 DIAMETER

5/32 DIAMETER

Fig. 5-89. Rivets to use with a rivet gun are available in many sizes. (Courtesy of Marson Corporation.)

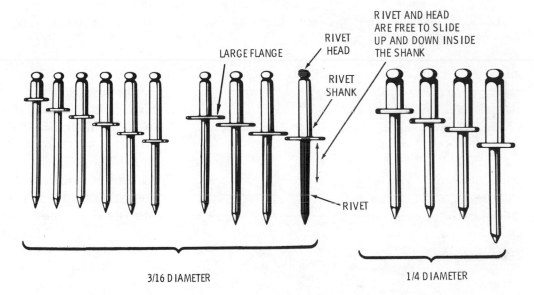

RIVET AND HEAD
ARE FREE TO SLIDE
UP AND DOWN INSIDE
THE SHANK

LARGE FLANGE

RIVET HEAD

RIVET SHANK

RIVET

3/16 DIAMETER

1/4 DIAMETER

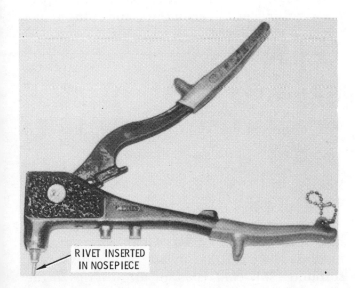

RIVET INSERTED IN NOSEPIECE

Fig. 5-90. The sharp, pointed end of a pop-rivet is pushed into the nosepiece of a rivet gun. (Courtesy of Marson Corporation.)

ing excess plastic filler from body seams and joints. Fig. 5-91 shows a typical pocket knife.

Tool Chest

A strong tool box, or *tool chest*, is very important, since a repairman needs to have his tools with him during working hours. A portable tool box is very desirable because the box can be moved around closer to different jobs.

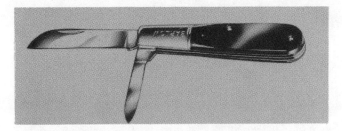

Fig. 5-91. Pocket knife. (Courtesy of Snap-On Tools.)

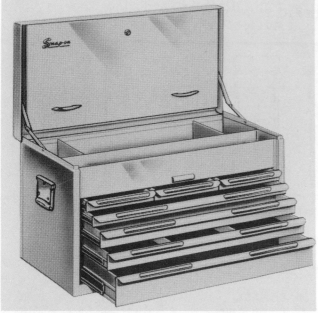

A. Portable, hand-carried tool chest.

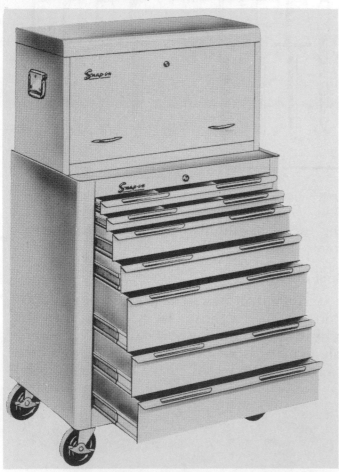

B. Cabinet-type tool chest on rollers, with a portable unit on top. This combination is sometimes known as a rollaway unit.

Fig. 5-92. A good, strong tool box should be purchased for safe, clean tool storage. (Courtesy of Snap-On Tools.)

A tool box will be stocked with all the worker's personal hand tools that are needed to do most of the hand work in day-to-day jobs. Fig. 5-92A shows a hand-carried portable tool chest. Fig. 5-92B shows a cabinet-type tool chest with the hand-carried portable chest sitting on top of it.

Sometimes, a repairman may want more tools than can be carried around easily. For repairmen who want to buy more tools than are ordinarily used in the average shop, two tool boxes or chests might be needed to store all the tools. Of course, a new bodyman should keep in mind that it is usually not a good idea to purchase seldom-used tools. These may be furnished by the shop owner.

SHOP TOOLS

The shop owner is usually expected to furnish the more special, expensive, or heavy tools used by all the workers in the shop. The exact selection of these tools may vary from shop to shop. They usually include large vises, thread-cutting tools, cleaning and washing supplies, and other tools for very heavy work. Shop tools furnished by the shop are usually stored in a supply room. In larger shops, these tools may be checked out when needed to do special jobs. In smaller shops, the tools may simply be left in one area for use by all the employees.

Generally speaking, repairmen can expect the shop owner to provide the following tools:

1. Shop Vise.
2. Tap and Die Set.
3. Auto Washing Materials.
4. Rim (Lug) Wrench.
5. ¾-inch Drive Socket Set.
6. Other heavy shop *equipment*, discussed later.

Vise

This tool, Fig. 5-93, is for most general automotive service work where pieces need to be held for working. The usual shop vise is medium duty and has metal, diamond-shaped, serrated (saw-cut) jaws for a firm grip on the material being held. Most vises have a swivel base so that the vise and jaws may be turned.

Fig. 5-93. Medium-duty bench vise.

The vise is usually bolted to a heavy table and used by all the workmen in the shop.

Tap and Die Set

This tool is used to make threads for nuts and bolts to be used as fasteners. A tap and die set may also be used to repair damaged threads on nuts, bolts, or *studs* (threaded fasteners made as a part of a larger body piece.) The good-quality *tap and die set* shown in Fig. 5-94 may be used for most of the tap-and-die needs in a body shop. This set can straighten or make threads on nuts, bolts, and parts with diameters as large as ½ inch.

Washing Materials

Vehicles need to be *washed* in a body shop, both before and after their repair. To do this correctly, body *washing materials* are needed.

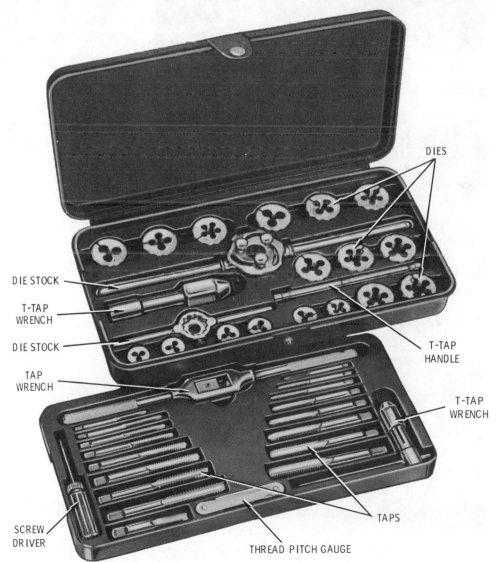

Fig. 5-94. Tap and Die Set. (Courtesy of Snap-On Tools.)

DIES

DIE STOCK

T-TAP WRENCH

DIE STOCK

TAP WRENCH

SCREW DRIVER

THREAD PITCH GAUGE

TAPS

T-TAP WRENCH

T-TAP HANDLE

Fig. 5-95. An auto body washing brush.

These are normally provided by the shop. The person hired to wash cars may not have any tools of his own at the shop.

An auto body *washing brush*, shown in Fig. 5-95, is used for fast, thorough washing of

Fig. 5-96. Using a washing brush.

vehicles for repair. See Fig. 5-96. Good brushes are filled with long, soft, nylon and horsehair bristles. Plenty of soap and water must be used when washing cars with a washing brush.

Fig. 5-97. Using a washing mitt.

Fig. 5-98. An auto body washing mitt.

Fig. 5-97 shows a washman washing a car with a *washing mitt*. Washing mitts are made of different materials and construction. The good, soft mitt shown in Fig. 5-98 is a shag, cloth type. Washing mitts are used to wash the vehicle as are washing brushes. A mitt, however, can get into closer places than can a brush. This would include areas around door handles, bumper ends, etc.

Rim Wrench

These tools are most often used to remove wheel lugs (nuts or bolts holding the wheels in place). Four-way *rim (lug) wrenches* have the four most-often used sizes of hex openings for wheel lugs. See Fig. 5-99. The cross shank

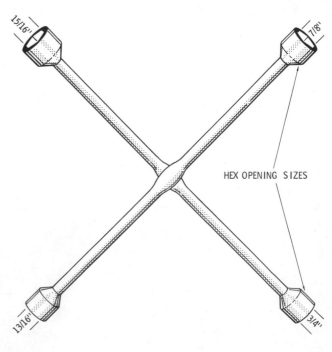

HEX OPENING SIZES

Fig. 5-99. Rim (lug) wrench.

of the wrench is usually about ⅝-inch diameter for extra strength. The hex sockets are fairly deep for long bolts.

Three-Quarter-Inch Drive

A ¾-inch drive socket set is used for very heavy shop work. Each body man will usually *not* have enough uses for this set for him to buy one. However, many shop owners will want to have this large set on hand for use during some frame work and heavy jobs such as work on large trucks.

Most of these large sets come with socket sizes of ¾-inch through 2⅜-inch. The set usually includes a strong power handle (breaker bar), ratchet, and several extensions. This set is too heavy for daily use in the shop on jobs such as panel removal or replacement. Its use is limited to very large bolts and nuts. Because these sets are rugged, they can take a good deal of punishment.

Unit 6

Power Tools and Shop Equipment

To make a profit in the auto body business, a shop needs to have a number of power tools and pieces of shop equipment. This will include the jacks, wrenches, drills, spray painters, sanders, and other types of power tools and equipment in use every day. Although power tools are necessary for top working speed, it *is* possible for a shop to operate without a large number of power tools. However, jobs will be turned out much slower without power tools.

Fig. 6-1 shows a typical group of hand-held shop power tools. Power tools are tools that use either *air* or *electricity* as a source of power. The *air*-powered tools are also known as *pneumatic* (new-*ma*-tick) *tools*. These tools are powered with compressed air.

The main reason that power tools are used in a modern shop is to increase the shop's working *speed*, to enable the shop to finish jobs quicker. Most auto body repair jobs, of course, are "sold" by contract bid. Therefore, the *time* involved is one of the main factors on the cost estimate to repair the damage on an automobile. Labor costs when no power tools will be used are usually *higher* because it will take *longer* to do the same job. If a shop wants to compete favorably for new business, purchasing power tools will be one of the shop's best investments.

Power tools and good shop equipment *are* expensive. However, most shop owners find that they pay for themselves and return much more profit in a short time. The power tools and equipment discussed in this unit include power jacks, air-powered tools, and electric-powered tools.

POWER JACKS

Several different types of jacks are used in an auto body shop. Some of them are used for raising or lowering vehicles, or to move a vehicle when it cannot be driven. When a vehicle has been raised with a *power jack*, the vehicle must be placed on safety (jack) stands. See Fig. 6-2.

Elsewhere in the shop, repairmen will use *body jacks* for aligning panels. Body jacks are smaller than large power jacks and are used for lighter work. However, body jacks are available with many different accessories. See Fig. 6-3. These accessories, plus the jack's small size, allow it to do many different types of work.

Another type of jack, and a large one, is the *frame-and-panel straightener*. This large tool may be either stationary or portable. It has many attachments that are used for good leverage while bending or pulling. Fig. 6-4 shows a typical *stationary* (stays in one place) frame-and-panel straightener. Note that the jack part of this tool is much larger than are other jacks. Fig. 6-5 shows one company's line of jacks and a few of the areas on a vehicle where each of them might be used.

110

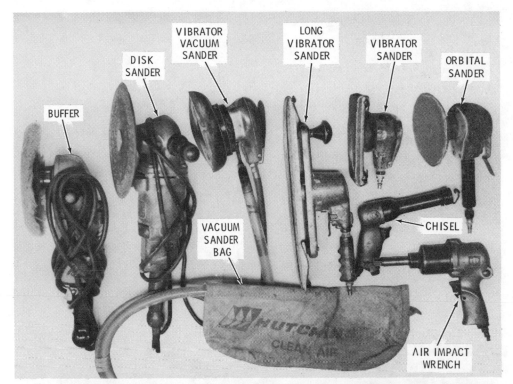

Fig. 6-1. A typical selection of hand-held power tools.

Fig. 6-2. Using a power jack to raise a car for frame straightening work. (Courtesy, Blackhawk Division of Applied Power Industries.)

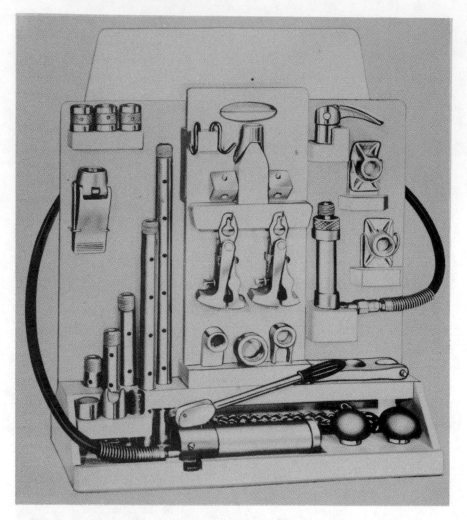

Fig. 6-3. A useful body jack with many attachments. (Courtesy of Snap-On Tools.)

How Jacks Are Powered—Hydraulic is a word used to describe how a power jack develops its power. *Hydraulic* means that the jack uses an oil-like fluid (hydraulic jack fluid) to develop pressure for pushing or pulling.

On simple jacks, the worker pumps on a handle to build up the fluid pressure. On *power* jacks, however, a small motor develops the pressure needed to force the hydraulic fluid into the jack.

Power jacks, therefore, are known as either "electricity over hydraulic" or "air over hydraulic." *Air* or *electricity* over hydraulic means that either an air- or electric-powered motor is used to force the hydraulic fluid into the jack cylinder. The jack cylinder then causes the jack to push or pull when a button is pushed or a lever is turned. In Fig. 6-2, for example, note that only thumb pressure is needed on the hydraulic jack lever to raise the car.

Frame and Panel Straighteners

Frame and panel straighteners, also known as frame and panel pullers or jacks, are usually the largest and most expensive power tools in a repair shop. There are many sizes of frame and panel pullers. However, all of them are either *portable* (Fig. 6-6) or *stationary* (Fig. 6-7).

Most frame and panel straighteners are *portable*. They have many attachments for pulling, pushing, and holding a panel to straighten or align the metal. Portable units are usually lower in cost than are stationary units. However, they cannot make as many pulls at one time as can more expensive, stationary units, Fig. 6-8 shows a portable frame and panel jack with attachments. Fig. 6-9 shows how the jack ram parts of the frame and panel puller are assembled.

Fig. 6-4. Stationary frame and panel straightener. (Courtesy, Blackhawk Division of Applied Power Industries.)

Stationary frame straighteners, on the other hand, can pull and push in several directions at one time, as in Fig. 6-7. This is done by multiple hook-ups. This means that the frame straightener is attached to several different points on the vehicle at the same time, allowing more than one pull to be made.

The main *dis*advantage of a stationary frame straightener is its cost. Generally speaking, it is too expensive for shops that do not specialize in frame straightening. This is the reason that most shops use only a *portable* frame straightener, even though the portable can usually make only one push or pull at a time.

Hook-Ups—Repairmen need an understanding of how to make *hook-ups* for repairing frame or body damage with a frame and panel straightener. Fig. 6-10 shows how the frame straightener is hooked up to pull and align the front section of a vehicle's frame. On another vehicle, the frame and panel straightener is being used to align the damaged quarter panel in Fig. 6-11. More information on frame and panel hook-ups is outlined in later units.

Body Jacks

Body jacks may be used with a frame straightener, as in Fig. 6-5, or they may be used

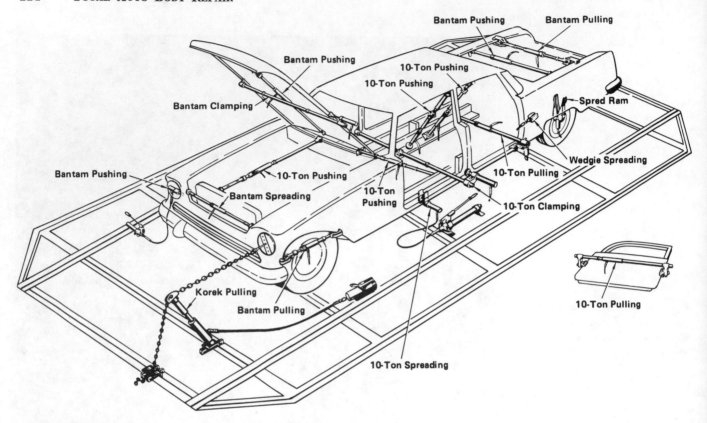

Fig. 6-5. With attachments, power jacks may be used on different places on the vehicle. (Courtesy, Blackhawk Division of Applied Power Industries.)

by themselves, as on the door being repaired off the car in Fig. 6-5. Hydraulic body jacks are one of the most-often used power tools in body shops today. Although a body jack is a simple tool, a body man must have some knowledge of how it works.

As a useful source of power, a body jack can be used for an almost unlimited number of jobs. The basic jack and several jack tools (Fig. 6-12) may be hooked up to a number of different attachments (Fig. 6-13). They can then be used to push or pull to align body panels, for example, as in Fig. 6-5. The assembled tool can be made long or short. Power can be applied to either or both ends of the jack at the same time.

No matter how many accessories the jack has, the *basic* body jack itself normally has three major parts: 1. the *pump*; 2. the *hose*; and 3. the *ram*.

The Pump—Fig. 6-14 shows the *pump* section of a body jack. The pump acts as a power source for the whole jack assembly. It is also

a reservoir for the hydraulic fluid that is pumped through the hydraulic hose into the ram.

Hydraulic pressure is applied (sent out) to the ram section by first opening a fluid control valve. Then, raising and lowering the pump handle causes the fluid to pass through the hose *from* the pump reservoir *to* the ram section.

A small valve at the end of the pump is used to control the flow of the hydraulic fluid in or out of the pump. This is known as a *fluid control valve*. See Fig. 6-12. To allow fluid to go out to the ram section, the valve must be turned fully *clockwise*. Then, raising and lowering the pump handle will push fluid into the ram.

To *release* the pressure and allow the fluid to return to the pump reservoir, the fluid valve must be turned *counterclockwise*. When this is done, most body jack rams will pull back automatically. If the ram does not return automatically, the pump handle must be raised and lowered to help the ram section move inward.

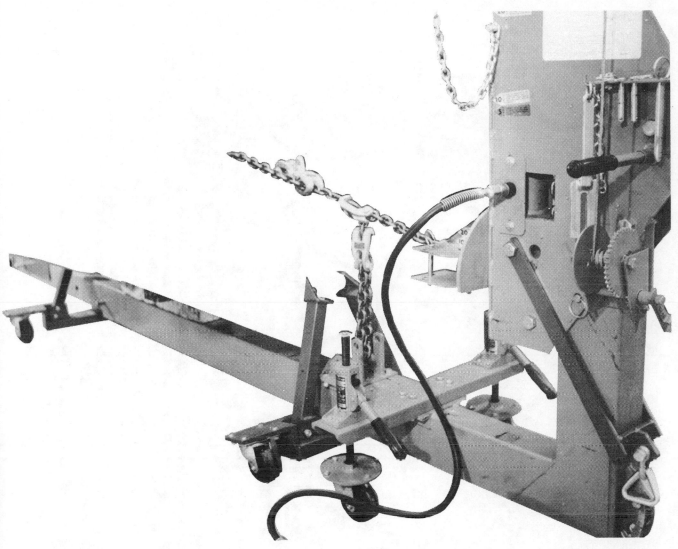

Fig. 6-6. Portable frame straighteners are usually moved around on small, hard rubber wheels. (Courtesy of Guy-Chart Systems.)

Fig. 6-7. A stationary (fixed) frame straightener is fastened to the floor and cannot be moved. (Courtesy of Bear Manufacturing Company.)

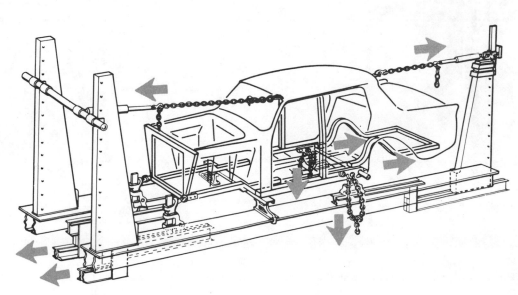

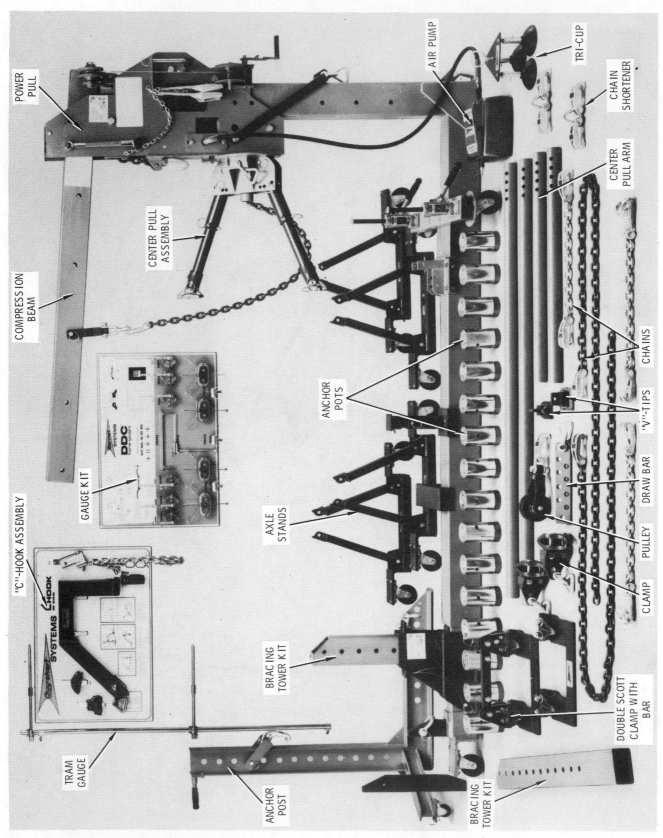

Fig. 6-8. A portable frame straightener with many attachments. (Courtesy of Guy-Chart Systems.)

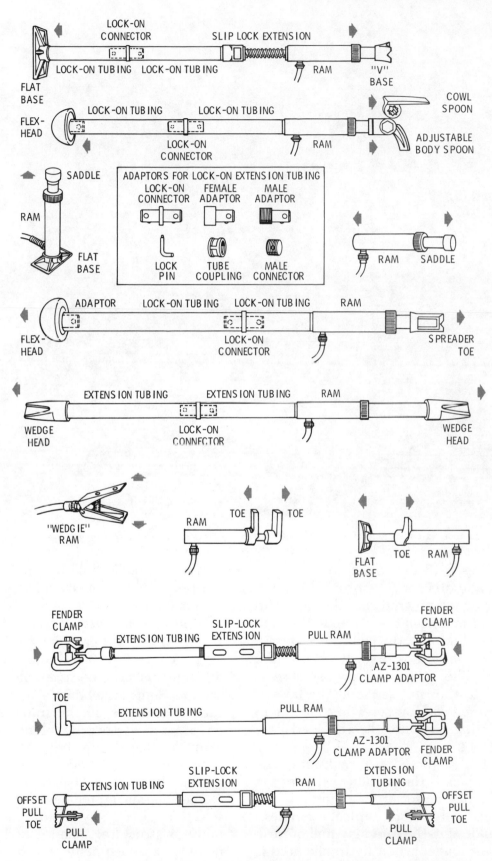

Fig. 6-9. Assembling the jack ram and attachments for different jobs. (Courtesy, Blackhawk Division of Applied Power Industries.)

Fig. 6-10. Hooking up a fixed straightener for a front pull. (Courtesy, Blackhawk Division of Applied Power Industries.)

The Hose—Fig. 6-15 shows a body jack *hose*. The hose is made of strong, reinforced rubber. It must be designed to transmit the powerful hydraulic fluid force *from* the pump *to* the ram.

When assembling a body jack for a certain job, one end of the hose is first attached to the *pump* section. The other end of the hose is then attached to the *ram* section. The hose is attached at either end by screwing the pump or ram connecting *nut* onto the threaded hose connection *fitting*.

The Ram—Fig. 6-16 shows a jack *ram*. The ram part of the jack is the section that does the actual work. It may be set up in almost any position. (See Fig. 6-5 for many typical examples.) Depending on design, the ram may pull or push by making itself longer when hydraulic fluid is pumped into it. The ram also acts as a reservoir

for the hydraulic fluid and returns the fluid to the pump when the control valve on the pump is opened.

Ram Attachments—Most of the attachments shown in Fig. 6-3 can be joined directly to the ram section. Fig. 6-9 shows how many major attachments may be assembled onto the ram section. Some attachments are used to hold the ram at an angle on the frame straightener or on a panel. Other attachments are used to clamp and hold onto body panels for pushing or pulling. Still others are used to straighten or align body panel structure parts.

Special ram attachments are designed and sold to fit almost any contour on an automobile body or structure. Using a body jack and the many jack attachments will be fully discussed in later units of the book.

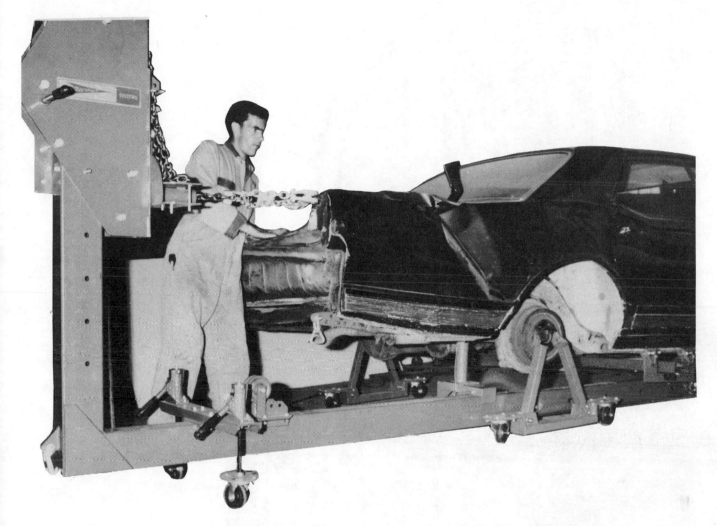

Fig. 6-11. Using one hook-up on a portable straightener to align a quarter panel. (Courtesy of Guy-Chart Systems.)

Floor Jacks

Often, vehicles need to be *elevated* (raised off the floor) so that certain areas can be seen or reached. Hydraulic *floor jacks* are designed to pick up the vehicle for these jobs. See Figs. 6-17 and 6-18. They can be used under bumpers or major suspension parts, or under frame or unitized body side rails. (These are located behind the rocker panel on the vehicle's side.) See Fig 6-17. Floor jacks have wheels so that the vehicle can be moved while on the jack and so that the jack may be easily moved about the shop. After raising a vehicle, of course, always be sure to put safety stands (jack stands) under the car before working on it.

Manual Floor Jack—Most repair shops have at least one *manual floor jack,* as in Fig. 6-17.

These jacks have a hydraulic pump that is pumped by moving the jack handle up and down. When the jack handle is raised to its highest position, the hydraulic piston moves in back of the fluid chamber. Then, when the jack handle is pushed down, the hydraulic piston forces the fluid forward in the jack cylinder. This moves the jack *pad* up a few inches, thus raising the vehicle. Pumping and jacking is then repeated until the vehicle is raised.

Air Floor Jack—An *air* floor jack is usually designed to raise vehicles by placing the jack under the bumper or side frame rail. Then, the vehicle may be raised to the desired height. This jack, as was the manual floor jack in Fig. 6-17, is sometimes used under the frame rail or unitized body reinforcing rail behind the rocker panel on the vehicle's side.

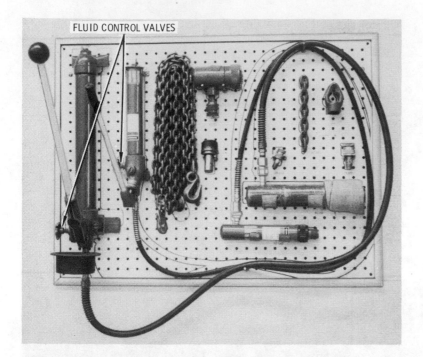

FLUID CONTROL VALVES

Fig. 6-12. Basic body jack parts.

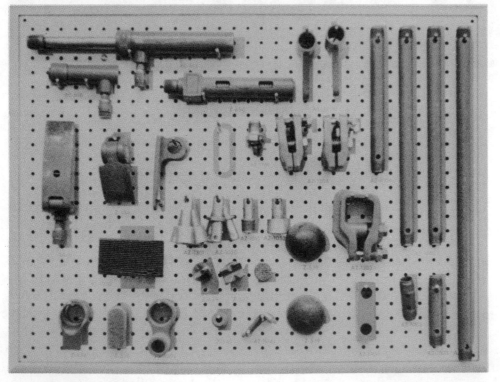

Fig. 6-13. Special body jack *tools* to be used with the basic body jack ram and parts.

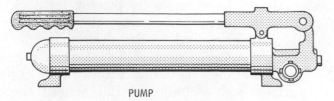

PUMP

Fig. 6-14. Body jack pump.

Air floor jacks are usually *pneumatic* pieces of equipment. This means that the jack is operated with *compressed air*. The compressed air to the jack is controlled by an air valve on the jack. When the air valve lever is moved in one direction, it forces air into the hydraulic chamber. The force of the air pressure is then used to raise the vehicle. Note the air valve lever on the top of the jack in Fig. 6-18. When the air valve lever is moved in the opposite direction, the jack lowers the vehicle to the floor by releasing the air pressure in the hydraulic chamber.

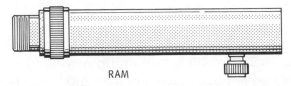
RAM
Fig. 6-16. Body jack ram.

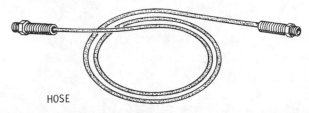
HOSE
Fig. 6-15. Body jack hose.

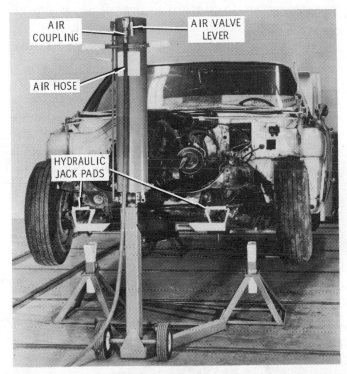
Fig. 6-18. A floor bumper jack, air operated. (Courtesy, Blackhawk Division of Applied Power Industries.)

Fig. 6-17. A common hydraulic floor jack, manually operated.

Fig. 6-19. A typical air compressor.

AIR SUPPLY EQUIPMENT

Air-powered tools and equipment used in an auto body repair shop need a good supply of clean, dry, *compressed air*. The shop's *air compressor* is an important piece of shop equipment for this reason. It compresses the air and then stores it, under great pressure, in its storage tank. See Fig. 6-19.

Compressed air is then piped from the compressor's storage tank to one or more *separator-regulators* in the shop. Here, it is cleaned even further and the pressure is regulated for the air-powered tool being used. Finally, the air is transferred by a rubber hose *from* the separator-regulator *to* the tools and equipment, as in Fig. 6-20.

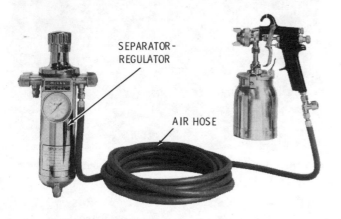

Fig. 6-20. An air separator-regulator, air hose, and paint gun. (Courtesy of Binks Manufacturing Company.)

Air compressors and separator-regulators are very important pieces of equipment in an auto body shop. The shop owner and all employees must know something about air compressors, especially how to care for them. For this reason, air supply equipment is discussed in greater detail in a separate unit of the book.

AIR-POWERED TOOLS

Air-powered tools operate with *compressed air* as the power source. The compressed air, of course, is supplied from the air compressor through pipes and the separator-regulator. More common air-powered tools include paint *spray guns* (Fig. 6-21), air *wrenches* (Fig. 6-

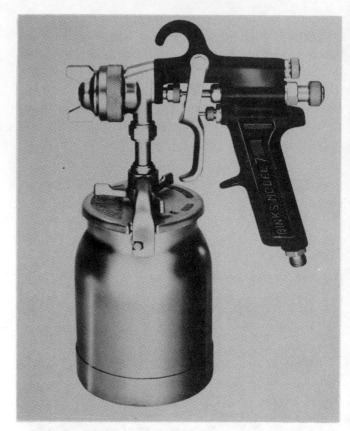

Fig. 6-21. A common suction-type paint spray gun. (Courtesy of Binks Manufacturing Company.)

22), air *chisels* (Fig. 6-23), air *sanders* (Fig. 6-24), and air *drills*.

Paint spray guns are used for almost all the shop's refinishing, whereas air wrenches are

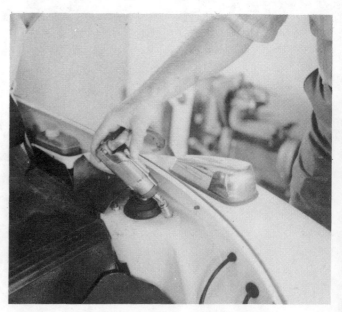

Fig. 6-22. Using a ⅜"-drive, air-powered impact wrench.

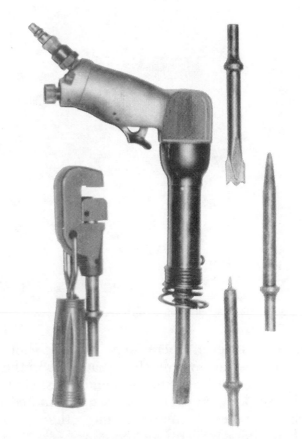

Fig. 6-23. An air chisel and common attachments.

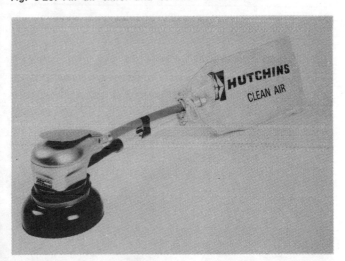

Fig. 6-24. An air sander. (Courtesy of Hutchins Manufacturing Company.)

used to quickly loosen and tighten bolts and nuts. Air chisels are used to cut flanges, or punch sheet metal parts. Repaired metal or plastic filler surfaces are sanded by using air-powered sanders. Holes may be drilled for repair work by using an air drill. Each of these tools and their use is discussed in detail below.

Paint Spray Gun

Probably the most-used of the air-powered tools in many body shops are the *paint spray guns*. These tools are one of the most efficient air-powered tools. Paint spray guns are used in almost all body repair shops, since almost all shops do refinishing work.

There are *two* basic types of spray guns. The two types are the *pressure pot* type, shown in Fig. 6-25, and the *suction cup* type, shown earlier in Fig. 6-21. The suction cup type is the easier gun to move from one place to another. Therefore, suction cup spray guns are normally used in most auto body repair shops.

Because paint spray guns are air-operated (air-powered) tools, they need a good supply of clean, dry air. For one spray gun, the air is first piped from the air compressor to the separator-regulator. Next, a flexible, reinforced rubber hose takes the air pressure *from* the separator-regulator *to* the spray gun, as was shown in Fig. 6-20. One-quart capacity, suction cup spray guns are the type used in most repair shops. These guns need a hose with an *inside* diameter of $\frac{5}{16}$ inch. The hose is usually about 50 feet long.

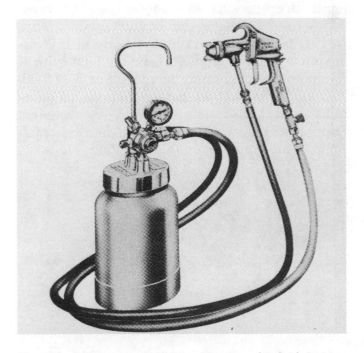

Fig. 6-25. A pressure pot spray gun. (Courtesy of Refinish Division, DuPont Company.)

Suction cup paint guns are portable, easy to handle, lightweight, and durable. Good guns will last for many years if they receive proper care. Using a paint spray gun, along with a full description of its parts, is discussed in a later unit on painting equipment.

Air Impact Wrench

One important tool for quick work is an *impact wrench*. This tool uses an impact (pounding) motion to loosen or tighten nuts or bolts. Impact wrenches may be powered with an electric motor or an air-powered motor. The most common impact wrenches used in a body shop are the *air* impact wrenches discussed here.

Air impact wrenches can be bought in different sizes, just as any other socket-holding tool. See Figs. 6-26 and 6-27. Air impact wrenches have different sets of sockets for each drive size. A ⅜-inch drive air impact wrench might have sockets ranging in size from ⅜ inch to ¾ inch. A ½-inch drive air impact wrench might have socket sizes from ⁷⁄₁₆ inch to 1¼ inch.

As with other socket tools, air impact wrenches may be equipped with universal joints, deep sockets, extensions, or other accessories used to make the wrench more useful. In Fig. 6-28, for example, the body man is using an extension and a universal joint with a ⅜-inch drive air impact wrench. See Fig. 6-28.

Good air impact wrenches are built for durability and high-speed work. When fasteners (nuts and bolts) are located in hard-to-reach

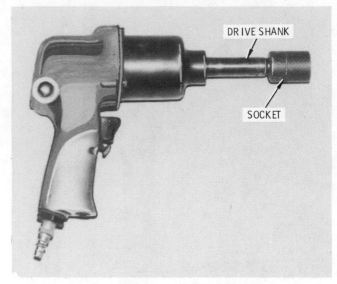

Fig. 6-27. Larger ½"-drive air impact wrench.

places, however, there may not be enough room to use an air wrench in that area. In these cases, it is necessary to use hand tools. Generally speaking, impact wrenches are limited to use on wheels, bumpers, and other places where there is plenty of room.

Air Chisel

Fig. 6-29 shows an air-powered *chisel* and replaceable chisel attachments. An air chisel is used for many different cutting and punching jobs in a body shop. Removing damaged panels and trimming replacement panels to the proper

Fig. 6-26. Smaller ⅜"-drive air impact wrench.

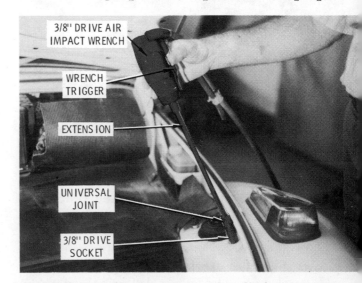

Fig. 6-28. Using socket accessories to make a ⅜"-drive air impact wrench more useful.

Fig. 6-29. An air-powered chisel and attachments. (Courtesy of Snap-On Tools.)

size are two common jobs. See Fig. 6-30. Power chisels are also used to make fast, smooth jobs of cutting spot welds for sheet metal repair. Finally, an air chisel may be used to make patches for repairing holes in panels and fenders.

Disk Sander

A common air-powered body shop tool is a *disk sander*. See Fig. 6-31. This tool uses the compressed air to rotate a disk. Different types of sandpaper are cemented to the disk. The disk part of the sander has a revolving clockwise motion. The disk backing plate and sanding disks can be bought in large or small sizes. Two of the different sizes and types of sanding disks are shown with the sander in Fig. 6-31.

Good disk sanders are rugged tools light in weight and easily handled. They may be found

in any well-equipped body repair shop. They are used for lightly preparing and sanding smaller areas of damaged surfaces. This further prepares the surface for final hand sanding.

Fig. 6-31. An air-powered disk sander and sanding disks.

With finer-grit sanding disks, this tool is used for *featheredging* a broken (scratched) finish. For this reason, the disk sander is often known as a *featheredger*.

Vibrator Sanders

Another common air-powered sander is a *vibrator sander*. These sanders usually come in two sizes. In Fig. 6-32 are the two different sizes of vibrator sanders that are normally available. These sanders are sometimes called *oscillating* or *orbital* sanders. In some body

Fig. 6-30. Using an air chisel to trim a replacement panel.

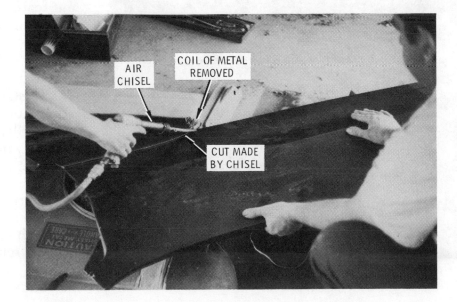

AIR CHISEL

COIL OF METAL REMOVED

CUT MADE BY CHISEL

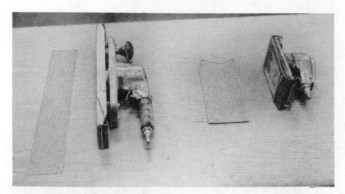

Fig. 6-32. The two basic sizes of vibrator sanders and the sandpaper size used on each.

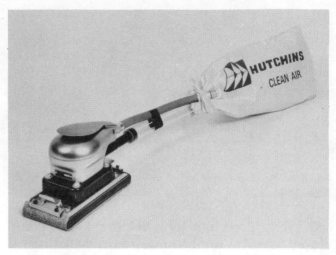

Fig. 6-34. A smaller vacuum vibrator sander. (Courtesy of Hutchins Manufacturing Company.)

shops, the smaller vibrator sander is known as a "vibrator" or "jitterbug."

By whatever name, this tool's main job is to quickly and evenly level old paint or plastic filler for a smooth, *even* finish. Usually, a 40-grit paper is first used in the vibrator. When only the rough 40-grit paper is used, the metal must be heavily primed after using the sander. However, good 80-grit papers are available to be used after the 40-grit has broken down a rough surface. When the finer 80-grit paper is used the metal does not have to be as heavily primed before further finishing.

Vacuum Vibrators—Figs. 6-33 and 34 show special types of vibrators known as *vacuum vibrators*. In Fig. 6-33 is a larger-size vacuum vibrator, whereas in Fig. 6-34 is a smaller vi-

Fig. 6-33. A larger, high quality, vacuum vibrator. (Courtesy of Hutchins Manufacturing Company.)

brator sander. These vacuum vibrators are the same tool and do the same jobs as do regular vibrator sanders.

On *vacuum* vibrator sanders, however, a special vacuum cleaner and a vacuum bag are added to the tool. When the sander is being used, the sanding dust is blown through a tube (into the vacuum bag) by the vacuum cleaner in the sander itself. The sanding dust, then, cannot escape through the fiber of the bag. This "vacuum cleaner" system cuts down on the dust and dirt in the shop air. This helps the shop turn out better, "cleaner" paint jobs. Also, the repairmen in the shop do not have to breathe the sanding dust. This is a very important feature, especially for the body man operating the sander.

Rotary Sander

A final type of air-powered sander is a *rotary sander,* shown in Fig. 6-35. In Fig. 6-36, a rotary sander is being used to work down the plastic filler on a fender. This sander is usually used to work down plastic filler. Regular 8" × 11" sheet sandpaper may be used on the round cylinder of a rotary sander. Usually, only a coarse-grit paper is used (such as 60- or 80-grit), since rotary sanders are most often used for rough sanding. A surface worked down with a rotary sander will need additional work and priming to smooth the sand scratches left by the rotary sander.

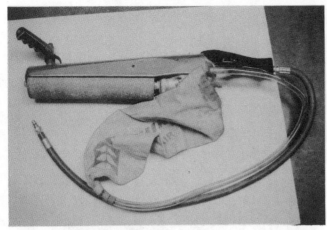

Fig. 6-35. A common rotary sander. Here, the sanding grit is mounted on a round drum.

Fig. 6-37. An air drill.

1 inch needs to be drilled, a hole cutter should be used. These are sometimes known as *hole saws*. Several hole cutter combinations are shown in Fig. 6-40.

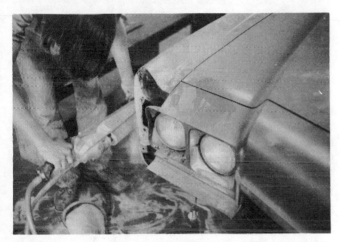

Fig. 6-36. Using a rotary sander to work down plastic filler on the side of a fender.

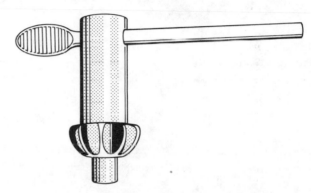

Fig. 6-38. A drill chuck *key*, as would be used in the chuck of either an air drill or an electric drill.

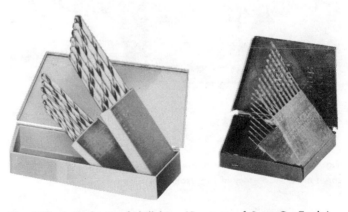

Fig. 6-39. Typical sets of drill bits. (Courtesy of Snap-On Tools.)

Air Drill

Fig. 6-37 shows an *air drill*. This tool does the same jobs as does a *common* electric drill, but uses compressed air for power instead of electricity. Like an electric drill, an air drill is used to drill holes in metal panels being repaired. On the end of the drill is a drill *chuck* that holds the drill bit firmly in place.

Chuck Key—The chuck *key* is a small tool used to loosen or tighten the drill *chuck*. This is necessary when installing or removing a drill bit from the chuck. Fig. 6-38 shows a drill chuck key.

Drill Bits—Fig. 6-39 shows several sets of drill *bits*. Drill bits are usually available in sizes of from ⅟₃₂ inch to 1 inch. If a hole larger than

Drill Brushes—Either air or electric drills may also be used to clean away rust and paint. Wire brush attachments are available for these jobs. Fig. 6-41 shows some of the more common wire brushes and attachments that may be used on a power drill.

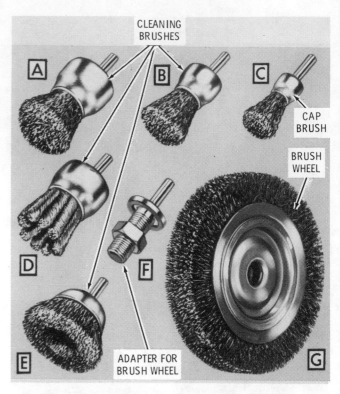

Fig. 6-41. Common brushes and attachments used with either electric or air drills. A, B, D, and E are drill brushes; C is a cap brush; F is an adapter to use a bench grinder brush in a drill; G is a bench grinder brush. (Courtesy of Snap-On Tools.)

most the same tools and do the same jobs as do air-powered tools. However, they use electricity as a power source instead of compressed air.

Some tools are normally available with only electric power. These tools include bench grinders, vacuum cleaners, paint shakers, polishing machines (polishers) and drill presses. These "electric only" tools are described below.

Fig. 6-40. Hole cutters are used to cut large holes (over 1") in sheet metal. (Courtesy of Ingersoll-Rand Company.)

ELECTRIC TOOLS

Impact wrenches, power sanders, and power drills just described as air-powered tools can also be powered by *electric* motors instead of air. For example, Fig. 6-42 shows two common *electric drills*. Fig. 6-43 shows an *electric disk sander* being used. These electric tools are al-

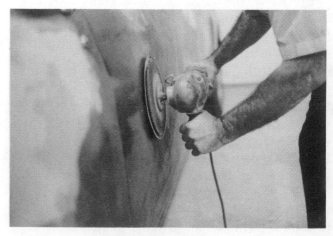

Fig. 6-43. Using an electric disk sander.

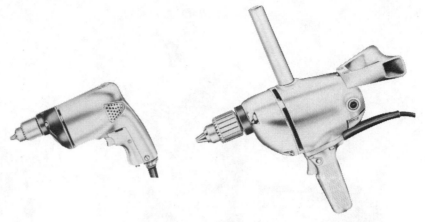

Fig. 6-42. The more common electric tools in a shop.

Bench Grinder

Fig. 6-44 shows a common shop *bench grinder*. This electric power tool is usually bolted to one of the shop's work benches. It may be used to sharpen (or "dress") tools that frequently need repair, such as drill bits, screwdriver blades, and chisels. Often, a wire brush wheel will be attached to one end of the grinder for buffing. Bench grinders can be purchased in several different sizes.

Fig. 6-44. A shop bench grinder. (Courtesy of Snap-On Tools.)

Vacuum Cleaner

All paint and body shops need a good vacuum cleaner, such as the one in Fig. 6-45. A vacuum cleaner should be one of the first tools used when a vehicle is to be refinished. The vehicle should be thoroughly vacuumed and washed *before* it is prepared for painting. This will help reduce the chance of dirt getting into the paint job.

Vacuum cleaners may be purchased in almost any size. Most paint and body shops have a vacuum cleaner with a 1- or 2-horsepower motor and a 20- or 30-gallon dust tank. Good vacuum cleaners have a 10- to 12-foot hose. Many attachments are available for reaching into all the hard-to-reach areas that are inside vehicle interiors or trunks.

Fig. 6-45. A large shop vacuum cleaner.

Paint Shakers

For good paint work, it is very important that the paint be properly and completely *mixed*. While the shop's painter might do this by stirring the paint, stirring is a boring and very time-consuming job. A better mixing job will be done faster if the shop has a good *paint shaker*. Fig. 6-46 shows a large shaker, as might be used in a fairly large body shop.

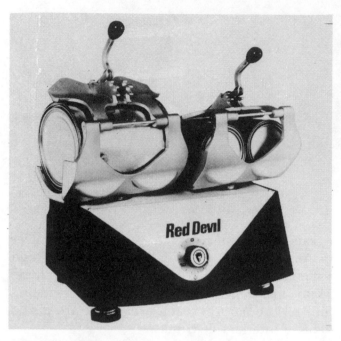

Fig. 6-46. A large paint shaker. (Courtesy of Ditzler Automotive Finishes Division.)

Fig. 6-47. A "one-can" body shop paint shaker.

In all cases, paint shakers are designed to hold and shake the entire closed can of paint.

Polishing Machine

This tool is also known as a *polisher*, Fig. 6-48. By either name, a polishing machine or polisher is a tool used to polish and "buff up" the topcoat. The tool is used on old paint to restore

Many newer vehicles are painted at the factory with *metallic* paint topcoats. Metallic paint actually contains tiny particles (pieces) of

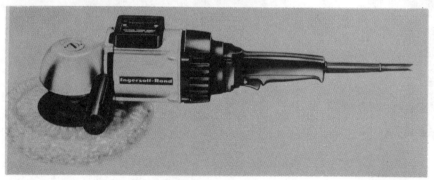

Fig. 6-48. An electric polisher. Using this tool correctly requires a good deal of skill and experience. (Courtesy of Ingersoll-Rand Company.)

metal. Usually, this metal is aluminum. These pieces are flakes of aluminum that are heavier than the paint itself. Because of this, they settle to the bottom. For this reason, using this paint will require very thorough stirring or mixing. Usually, the mixing is best done by some type of paint shaker.

The paint shaker in Fig. 6-46 is a larger model. This type may be used by large paint-mixing businesses such as parts houses selling a large volume of paint, as well as by large body shops. The smaller shaker in Fig. 6-47 is the "one-can" type used by most body shops.

Fig. 6-49. Compounding a new lacquer finish.

the paint lustre (shine). It is *also* used to "cut" new lacquer paint with rubbing compound to bring up the paint's correct color and lustre. In Fig. 6-49, a painter is compounding new lacquer paint. New *enamel* paint, of course, must not be compounded or it will ruin the finish.

Drill Press

An electric drill that is permanently mounted in a rigid frame with a platform for drilling is known as a *drill press*. Drill presses are used in larger body shops for many different drilling jobs, such as making holes in thin sheet metal repair pieces. These tools are built so that the electric motor and the drill are held on top of a pipe-like stand. See Fig. 6-50. A square-shaped plate (platform) is attached to the stand and it may be adjusted up or down. The platform is used to hold and support the material being drilled.

Fig. 6-50. A larger body shop may be equipped with a drill press.

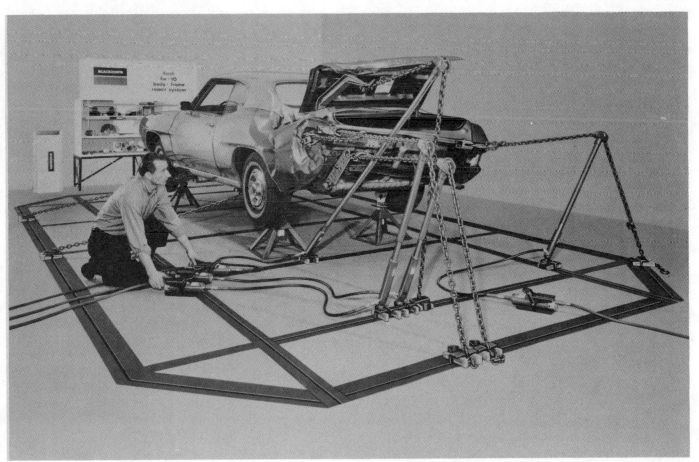

(Courtesy, Blackhawk Division of Applied Power Industries.)

Air Supply Equipment

All auto body shops must have a good supply of clean and dry *compressed air*. This can be supplied by a good air compressor, one that is large enough to supply several pieces of equipment at the same time. Many body shops have more than one air compressor. Fig. 7-1 shows a typical air compressor as might be used in a smaller shop. In Fig. 7-2 is a gang of three air compressors. A setup such as Fig. 7-2 would be required in a large body shop.

To be used in the shop, the compressed air must be cleaned and then delivered to the air-powered tools throughout the shop. From the air compressor, the *air lines* take the air to the different work stations in the shop. Air lines are steel pipes used to transport the compressed air. A shop will usually have a large system of air lines running to different work stations. A simple air line is shown in Fig. 7-3.

When the air lines have the air piped to the work stations, the air must be cleaned and its pressure regulated before it passes through flexible hoses to the air tools. This cleaning and regulating is done with pieces of air supply equipment known as *separator-regulators*. High-pressure air goes in the separator regulator directly from the air line. Hoses or couplers for hoses then take the air from the separator-regulator to the air tools. Fig. 7-4 shows a typical separator-regulator with couplings for the hoses.

Finally, of course, *air hoses* take the air (cleaned and at the correct pressure) to the air-powered tools. Air hoses must be strong, reinforced, and flexible. Fig. 7-5 shows an air hose from separator-regulator being connected to a paint gun. Quick-change fittings are being used; these are discussed later in the unit.

Testing the Air Supply—One way to test for an ample air supply is to leave the paint gun

Fig. 7-1. A medium-size air compressor, as would be used in a smaller body shop. (Courtesy of Ingersoll-Rand Company.)

Fig. 7-2. A large, three-compressor air supply system, as would be required by a large body shop. (Courtesy of Binks Manufacturing Company.)

hose open, releasing compressed air. If the air compressor builds up enough pressure to shut off even though the paint hose is open, there will be enough compressed air to operate an average-size body shop. The average shop will need a 7- to 10-ton compressor to furnish enough air.

AIR

Air is a mixture of oxygen, nitrogen and other gases. Body repairmen use air for much of the work done in an auto body shop. Oxy-acetylene welding, for instance, uses oxygen that is found in the air. Auto body repair shops have many

tools that require air for power, cleaning, or applying paint.

To be able to use air, it must first be controlled and *compressed*. It is compressed by the shop's air *compressor*. Then, the air is piped through an air line to the separator-regulator. Here, it is cleaned and its pressure is regulated before being released into the air hose. Through the air hoses, finally, travels the air supply needed by the tools and equipment in the shop.

HOW AIR IS COMPRESSED

To compress air, the air compressor draws air in and packs (compresses) it into a small

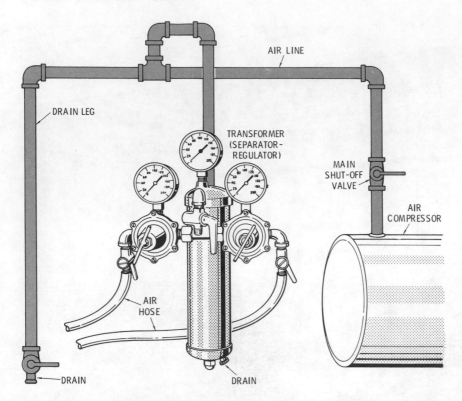

DRAIN LEG

TRANSFORMER
(SEPARATOR-
REGULATOR)

AIR LINE

MAIN
SHUT-OFF
VALVE

AIR
COMPRESSOR

Fig. 7-3. A simple air line system.

AIR
HOSE

DRAIN

DRAIN

Fig. 7-4. A smaller separator-regulator.

Fig. 7-5. Air hose being used to take air from the regulator to the paint gun.

Fig. 7-6. The air compressor unit is the actual pump that compresses the air. The fins on a compressor help to cool the unit.

Fig. 7-7. Usually, the largest part of an air compressor is the storage tank.

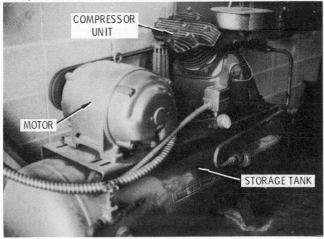

COMPRESSOR UNIT

MOTOR

STORAGE TANK

Fig. 7-8. The three basic parts of an air compressor.

area. The compressor does this by first pulling the air into the compressor unit and then forcing it out, into the storage tank. Fig. 7-6 shows the air compressor unit, whereas Fig. 7-7 shows the pump mounted on top of the storage tank.

The compressed air in the storage tank is stored under very great pressure. Under pressure, the air is held in the storage tank until an air outlet somewhere in the shop is opened to let the air escape.

Air Compressor Parts

A shop air compressor has three main parts:

1. The Motor
2. The Compressor Unit
3. The Storage Tank

See Fig. 7-8. Most compressor set-ups have a shut-off valve on the air line system, as shown in Fig. 7-9. This valve is used to shut off the

SHUT-OFF VALVE

Fig. 7-9. An air shut-off valve is installed on the compressor to shut off all the air to the shop if repairs need to be made to the shop's air line system.

Fig. 7-10. Typical electric motor used to power a medium-size shop air compressor.

air supply to the shop's air line system. This holds the air in the storage tank, allowing air line repairs to be made elsewhere in the shop.

Compressor Motor—The air compressor's *motor* may be either electric or gasoline. Most repair shops use a compressor with an *electric* motor. See Fig. 7-10. The compressor motor rotates the compressor pulley and flywheel through a "V-belt" drive. See Fig. 7-11.

When the motor turns the flywheel, the crankshaft is turned since the flywheel is mounted on the crankshaft. The crankshaft, then, moves the compressor unit's pistons.

Compressor Unit—The basic part of an air compressor is the compressor unit itself. This

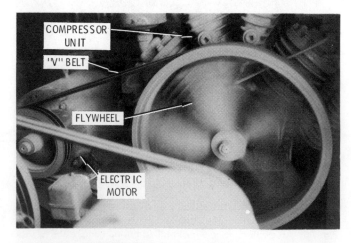

Fig. 7-11. A "V-belt" drive connects the electric motor to the V-belt groove in the outside of the compressor unit's flywheel.

is the part that takes in and compresses the air. See Fig. 7-12.

In the compressor unit, a piston (or pistons) is attached to the crankshaft, for example, as in a small lawnmower engine. When running, the piston is pulled *down* the compressor cylinder by the crankshaft. At the same time, an air inlet check valve opens and allows air from the air cleaner to enter the cylinder.

Then, as the crankshaft revolves, the piston is pushed back *up* in the cylinder. This causes the air intake check valve to close, keeping the air from going back out the intake.

When the piston goes back up the cylinder, it forces the air in the cylinder *out*. The air leaves the cylinder through an air *exhaust* valve. When the air leaves, it goes through a short pipe into the compressor storage tank. A check valve keeps the air from coming back out of the storage tank and into the compressor unit.

Most body shop compressor units have two or more pistons that work at the same time and are attached to the same crankshaft. If the air is pumped from one cylinder into the next cylinder and *then* into the storage tank, the compressor is known as a *two-stage* air compressor. Otherwise, both cylinders pump air directly into the storage tank.

Compressor Lubrication—An air compressor unit has several moving parts. The crankshaft, pistons, connecting rods and other moving

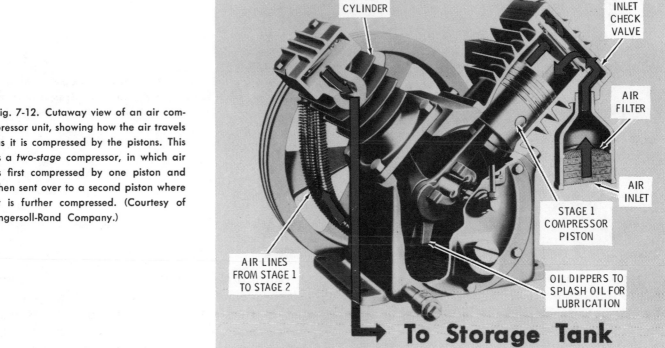

Fig. 7-12. Cutaway view of an air compressor unit, showing how the air travels as it is compressed by the pistons. This is a *two-stage* compressor, in which air is first compressed by one piston and then sent over to a second piston where it is further compressed. (Courtesy of Ingersoll-Rand Company.)

parts must be lubricated. This lubrication is the job of the compressor unit's *lubricating system*. The lubricating "system" usually consists of dippers on the connecting rods. See Fig. 7-12. As the crankshaft turns, these dip into the oil and splash it onto the parts inside the unit.

The compressor unit must have the correct amount of oil in it for long compressor life. For this reason, compressor units may have an oil level gauge inside a glass window, showing

the oil level, as in Fig. 7-13. The oil level on the glass should be on the **FULL** mark. If not, oil should be added until the full mark is reached. [Not all compressor units have a sight glass. Some have a plug to be removed (Fig. 7-14) and others have an auto engine-type oil dipstick.]

Fig. 7-13. Checking the compressor oil through an oil gauge window.

Fig. 7-14. On most compressors, engine oil is added through a pipe plug hole.

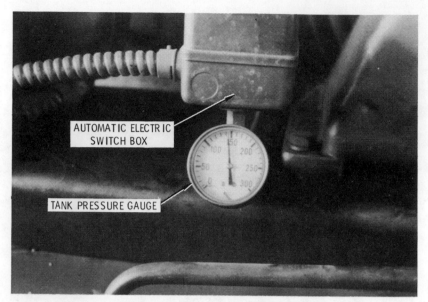

AUTOMATIC ELECTRIC SWITCH BOX

TANK PRESSURE GAUGE

Fig. 7-15. A pressure gauge shows how much air is in the tank, whereas an automatic switch box shuts off the electric motor when a certain amount of air has been pumped into the tank.

Generally speaking, 20- or 30-weight motor oil should be used in the compressor unit. However, most compressors have a tag on them describing what oil to use. Oil can then be added by removing the oil cap and pouring the oil into the opening. In Fig. 7-14 is the oil cap for adding oil on one compressor.

Storage Tank—The air compressor's *storage tank* holds the highly compressed air until it is needed. The storage tank on an average body shop air compressor holds from 60 to 80 gallons.

On most storage tanks is a *gauge* like the one shown in Fig. 7-16. The gauge shows the pressure of the air in the tank. An average body shop needs about 150 pounds of pressure (psi; *pounds* per *square inch*) to operate the shop's air tools and equipment.

Also on the compressor tank is an automatic electric *switch box*. In Fig. 7-15 is the switch box containing the automatic switch. As air is used from the tank, the air pressure in the tank drops. When the air pressure drops to a pre-set

pressure, the automatic switch starts the compressor's electric motor. This builds up pressure in the tank to replace the air that was used. When the air pressure is built up enough, the switch turns the electric motor off. This on-off procedure goes on automatically, day after day, so that the compressor tank always has enough air for the shop.

Draining the Tank—When air is compressed, it becomes hotter; it develops heat. This is why air compressor units have fins on them, to help cool the unit from the heat of the compressed air.

When the warm, newly-compressed air arrives in the storage tank, the air begins to cool. When it cools, moisture in the air *condenses* and forms water droplets inside the storage tank. (This is much the same as morning *dew* on grass; formed when water condenses from cool night air.)

The air compressor's storage tank, then, should be drained *each day* to remove the

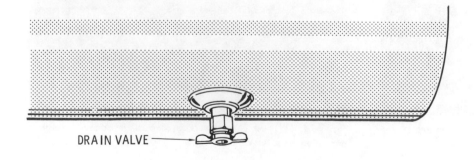

DRAIN VALVE

Fig. 7-16. A drain valve or drain plug is usually located at the bottom and at one end of the compressor's storage tank.

condensed water. If the water is not removed: it takes up space that could be used to store compressed air; it causes the inside of the tank to rust; and it may get into air-powered tools and cause trouble. Worst of all, the water may get into the air going to a paint spray gun, causing severe painting problems. When the air compressor's tank is drained daily, these problems are eliminated.

Compressor storage tanks usually have a drain valve like the one shown in Fig. 7-16. The drain valve can be opened by turning it easily. When the drain valve is opened, the air pressure in the tank forces the water out the valve.

AIR LINES

Fig. 7-3 illustrated a system of *air lines*. Air lines are the *metal pipes* that take the air from the compressor storage tank to one or more separator-regulators. Air lines are usually made of galvanized pipe to resist rust.

Air Line Moisture—The air line system should begin with a connection *above* the possible water level of the compressor storage tank. The reason for taking the air out above the possible water level is to keep as much moisture (water) out of the air lines as is possible. If the air line were attached to the *bottom* of the storage tank, water could be forced into the lines, separator-regulators, and air tools. Note that the outlet lines in Fig. 7-3 are attached to the *top* of the main line. This is done to further guard against moisture getting into the air outlet lines.

The air line pipes will then run to any number of transformers (separator-regulators) to clean the air and regulate its pressure. The number of separator-regulators used in a shop depends on how many air-powered pieces of equipment are in use. A separator-regulator may have up to *four* different outlets for air hoses leading to equipment. See Fig. 7-17. Therefore, only one separator-regulator would be needed for each four pieces of equipment when this type of unit is used.

If more than one separator-regulator unit is used, a separate pipe must run from the main air line to each unit. Usually, the main air line and the outlet lines will either go through the center of the shop or will go around the shop's inside wall. Either system allows tools and equipment to be easily used in different areas of the shop.

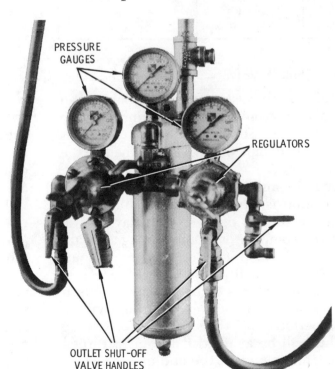

Fig. 7-17. A separator-regulator with four outlets.

PRESSURE GAUGES

REGULATORS

OUTLET SHUT-OFF VALVE HANDLES

Main Line Size

The main air line from the air compressor to the separator-regulator outlets should be larger than the air outlet lines. For example, if the main air line coming from the air compressor is 1½-inch diameter, the air outlet line coming off this main air line should be about ¾-inch diameter. By supplying compressed air in this way, enough pressure is left in the main line at all times no matter how many tools are connected to the air supply.

In all cases, the main line should be large enough to carry all the air needed by the shop equipment being used. Also, the main line should be larger in diameter if it must run longer distances from the air compressor. See the recommendations in Table 7-1.

Table 7-1. Recommended Air Line Diameters

Compressor Horsepower	Main Air Line Length (Feet)	Recommended Main Air Line Diameter (Inches)
1½– 2	under 50	½
1½– 2	50–200	¾
3– 5	under 200	¾
3– 5	200–400	1
5–10	under 400	1½
5–10	over 400	2

Main Line Shutoff Valve

In all air supply systems, there should be an air shut-off valve on the main air line, close to the storage tank. See Fig. 7-3 and 7-9. This valve is used to shut off the air at the storage tank.

Keeping the air shut off at the storage tank when the shop is closed insures a full tank of air when the shop is opened each day. It also prevents the compressor from running all night should a leak develop. (Air equipment and outlets in the shop normally have very small leaks.) If the air compressor is turned on in the morning and the storage tank is empty, there will be a waiting period while the storage tank is being filled. This will be avoided if the air is turned off at the storage tank at the end of each working day.

Air Line Drain Leg

An air line *drain leg* should be placed somewhere in the main air line, as in Fig. 7-3. The purpose of a drain leg is to collect moisture from the main air line. As moisture collects in the main air line, air pressure forces the moisture into the drain leg. The drain leg is usually connected to the main line near the end of the line. This allows the moisture to collect in the drain leg from all along the main system. Then, the moisture can be drained from the drain leg by *first* emptying the air tank and *then* opening the drain leg cap or valve. Together, the drain leg system helps keep much of the moisture from entering any of the separator-regulators in the system.

SEPARATOR-REGULATORS

Fig. 7-18 shows a common air system separator-regulator. Separator-regulators are also sometimes known as *transformers*. However, this is not exactly correct. An air *transformer* can only reduce and control the air pressure, whereas a separator-regulator does that *and* cleans the air, as well. It might be said, then, that a transformer is *part* of a separator-regulator. In fact, the transformer would be the *regulator* part of a complete separator-regulator assembly.

By whatever name, this piece of equipment is still another filter for the air coming from the storage tank. Ordinary compressed air from the main line may contain small amounts of oil, dirt, and water. The air separator-regulator changes this contaminated air to the cleaner air needed for shop use.

The separator-regulator, of course, does more than just clean the air. Actually, it has *two* jobs. The *first* job, discussed above, is to separate water, dirt, and oil from the air; to clean the air. The *second* job is to regulate the air pressure to a constant, lower pressure. In this way, the separator-regulator changes (regulates) the high air presseure to a steady, lower pressure. This is the same as an electrical transformer that changes a high electrical voltage to a lower voltage.

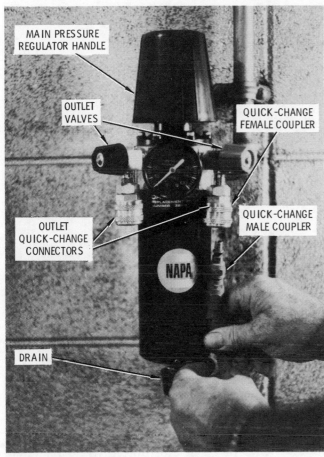

Fig. 7-18. A simple separator-regulator that delivers air to two hoses.

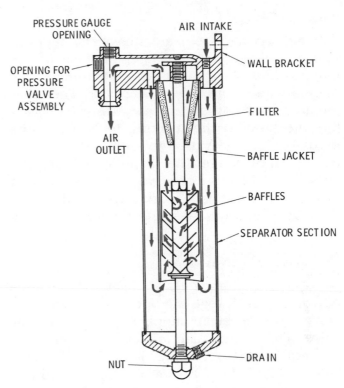

Fig. 7-19. The inside of a separator section of a separator-regulator.

Cleaning the Air

Air pressure of about 150 to 160 pounds per square inch (psi) is built up by the air compressor and stored in the air compressor storage tank. Air pressure forces the air through the main and secondary air lines and into the separator-regulator. Of course, the air pressure is still 150 to 160 psi.

As the air enters the separator-regulator, it is forced down the sides of the separator section, as shown by the arrows in Fig. 7-19. As the air travels down the sides of the regulator section, it strikes baffling plates (*baffles*) on the sides of the baffle jacket. See Fig. 7-19. The baffles cause the air to be deflected (thrown) against the sides of the baffle jacket. This causes the moisture to "fall out" of the air and drip down to the bottom of the separator section. Here, it can be drained through a drain plug or valve.

As the air is forced up through the baffles, it loses most of its moisture. Then, the air passes through a rockwool *filter* that cleans remaining moisture, dirt, and oil from the air. The rockwool filter is near the top of the separator chamber. Here, clean, dry air enters the regulator section of the separator-regulator.

Regulating the Air Pressure

As the clean air goes into the regulator section, it passes by a *diaphragm* that controls the air flow. The diaphragm is controlled by a regulator valve *handle*. See Figs. 7-17 and 7-18.

As the valve handle (Fig. 7-17) or cap (Fig. 7-18) is turned inward (tightened), the regulator diaphragm is pushed away from its seat. This allows the compressed air to more easily pass through the regulator to the outlet air pressure gauge(s) and the air outlet(s). As the adjustment is turned further inward, more air can pass through the pressure regulator. This allows more air to go through the regulator, increasing the pressure supplied to the pressure gauge(s) and air tool(s).

Pressure Gauges

Some separator-regulators have *two* types of pressure gauges, as in Fig. 7-17. One of the gauges shows how much air pressure is in the main air line from the storage tank. The other gauge shows how much air ·pressure is going out the hose to the working tools. Once the regulator handle is used to set a certain psi on the pressure gauge, the diaphragm keeps the air flow *at* that pressure while the air tool is being used. For this to work correctly, the pressure must be adjusted *while the tool is turned on.*

Hose Shut-off Valves

Most separator-regulators have a hose shut-off valve at each regulated pressure outlet. This valve turns off the air supply to the hose at that valve. This reduces any air leakage from tools and equipment not being used. The air regulator in Fig. 7-17, for example, has four outlets and four shut-off valves.

Quick-Change Adapters

Many separator-regulators have the air hoses screwed directly into the regulator outlet. This is not convenient for easily changing air hoses or fittings in the shop. To make changing the air hoses easier, *quick-change* adapters are used.

Fig. 7-20 shows an air hose being attached to a paint gun by using a quick-change adapter. Quick-change adapters makes it easy to change the air hose quickly from one air tool to another. By using these adapters throughout the shop, the slower process of changing air lines with a wrench is avoided.

Adapter Parts—Quick-change adapters are made in two parts: the male part and the female part. See Fig. 7-18. The *female* part is screwed in place on the separator-regulator outlet with a wrench. It stays there on the outlet all the time. A valve in the female part keeps the air from escaping when there is nothing attached to it.

The *male* part of the coupler is screwed onto the *air hose* and left there all the time. When the two parts are then snapped together, the air

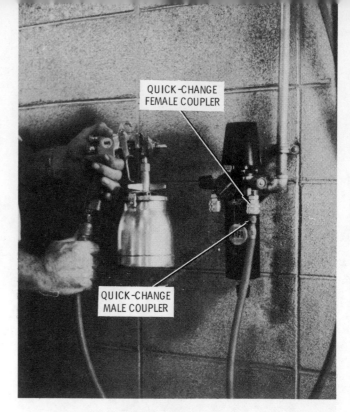

Fig. 7-20. Basic parts of a quick-change adapter.

can pass through the adapter, allowing the air to flow freely to the end of the air hose. When the hose needs to be connected or disconnected, it can be quickly snapped on or off.

Attached to the *other* end of the air hose is *another* female adapter part. This allows an air tool or other piece of equipment to be attached as shown in Fig. 7-21. All tools and equipment that use air should have *male* adapter parts permanently screwed in the tool air inlet ports. Then, the tools and air hoses can be quickly put together or taken apart. Using quick-change adapters throughout the shop saves time and their cost is low.

AIR HOSES

To transfer the air *from* the regulators *to* the tools require a very strong, flexible hose. This job is handled by the shop's *air hoses.*

Air hoses are made of a special rubber and are heavily reinforced with fabric. They are specially coated inside to help prevent air leakage. Air hose inside diameter should be no smaller than $5/16$-inch. Air hoses are available in different lengths, coatings, and diameters. Although air hoses come in many lengths, most shop air hoses are either 50 or 75 feet long.

A special paint room hose should be used in the shop's paint booth. Paint room hose is dif-

ferent from other air hoses, and is made for use only on paint guns. It does not loose as much pressure between the regulator and the paint gun because it is designed and made with better materials to do a more thorough job of holding the air.

Air hoses should be properly cared for. They must be protected from cuts, oil, and grease. Shop employees should be careful not to drive cars over the shop hoses. Also, air hoses should not be used to "pull" attached air tools across the shop floor. This weakens the hose walls and connections. Finally, air hoses should be neatly coiled for storage at the end of the working day.

Fig. 7-21. Using a quick-change adapter on a paint gun air hose connection.

(Courtesy of Binks Manufacturing Company.)

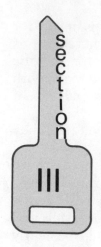
Body Shop Materials

Unit 8

Body Fillers

The process of completely working the metal to remove *all* the dents and make it smooth enough for painting is very difficult. Even the best "metal man" will need to spend a good deal of time to work out all the damage. Even so, working out all the damage *is* possible. Many times, though, it is very difficult and time-consuming. Because of this, it is usually a good deal easier, and less costly, to use a *filler* on top of the damaged metal.

Body *fillers*, then, will smooth the metal to its final contour without the metal underneath having to be "perfect." This will allow the repair to be completed much easier and faster. Also, the cost of the filler material will still be much less than the additional labor cost would be to smooth the panel without using filler.

Body fillers may also be used to fill dents that cannot be removed with bumping hammers and dollies. Fig. 8-1, for example, shows such a dent, where the panel is boxed in so that the dent cannot be easily worked from the back side. Fig. 8-2 shows what metal is on the back side of the damaged door panel in Fig. 8-1. Note that the door cannot be worked from the inside of the panel because the panel is boxed in with inner panels. When panels are boxed in, as in Figs. 8-1 and 8-2, they will mostly have to be worked from the outside. In Fig. 8-3 is another such panel, being worked from the outside before using a filler.

TYPES OF FILLERS

There are three basic types of *body fillers* in use today. The most common filler is *plastic* body filler. There are many plastic fillers on the market, such as the one in Fig. 8-4. Other common fillers are *fiberglass* fillers. Shown in Fig. 8-5, fiberglass fillers may be used on either fiberglass or metal bodies, as discussed later.

For many years, the most common auto body filler was body *solder*. Body solder is a soft metal and is a mixture of lead and tin. It is applied to the panel with heat from a torch; the torch melting the solder stick and causing the stick to flow out over the body surface being repaired. See Fig. 8-6. Body solder, sometimes

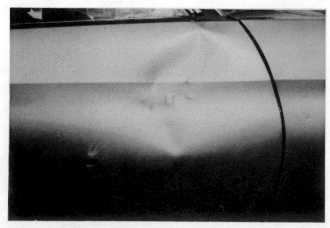

Fig. 8-1. A damaged door panel in which body filler will be needed for a complete repair.

Fig. 8-2. Boxed-in back structure of the door shown in Fig. 8-1. Because this structure is boxed in, access to the back of the dent is limited.

Fig. 8-4. Typical plastic body filler. (Courtesy of Ditzler Automotive Finishes Division.)

simply known as "lead," requires more skill and time to use than does plastic filler. For this reason, plastic filler is today more commonly used in most body repair shops.

Either plastic or fiberglass filler may be used on both metal and fiberglass bodies. Body *solder*, of course, must not be used on fiberglass bodies. Any filler product should be mixed with the manufacturer's products and recommendations. The instructions for mixing and using most products are written on the material's package.

PLASTIC FILLER

Different types of plastic fillers have become some of the most-used materials in modern auto body shops. Almost all damaged metal

Fig. 8-3. Because panel access is limited, a slide hammer is being used here to pull out a crease. Then, body filler will be used for final repair.

will need some plastic to complete the repair. Good brands of plastic filler are easy to mix, spread smoothly, are easy to work down, and hold up well during use.

The two most common types of plastic are *polyester* plastic and *metal* plastic. See Figs. 8-7 and 8-8. Both polyester plastic and metal plastic are used widely throughout the automobile body repair trade.

Polyester Plastic—Polyester plastic contains resin and magnesium silicate. This product must be mixed with a hardener before it is used. The *resin* is the binder that holds the mixture in solution and binds it to the surface on which it is used.

Unfortunately, resin is a gummy substance and is extremely difficult to file or sand. Therefore, the resin must be mixed with magnesium silicate so that the product is easy to sand or file. The hardener is the curing agent which causes the material to undergo a chemical reaction, drying and hardening the material. Polyester plastic is the most common auto body plastic filler. Fig. 8-4 shows a common polyester plastic auto body filler, whereas Fig. 8-7 shows another common brand with its cream hardener.

Metal Plastic—Metal plastic is made of resin and ground aluminum particles, mixed together to form a paste. Before it is used, the hardener must be added to make the product cure (harden), as with polyester plastic filler.

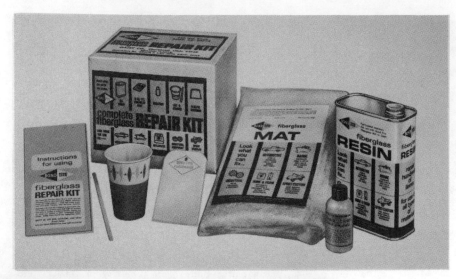

Fig. 8-5. The typical parts of a fiberglass filler kit. (Courtesy of Oatey Co.)

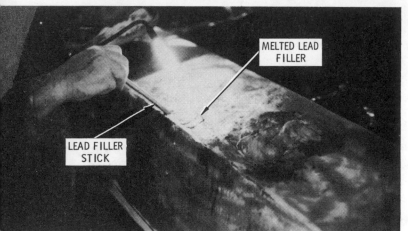

MELTED LEAD FILLER

LEAD FILLER STICK

Fig. 8-6. Using lead body filler, also known as *body solder*. The solder is in stick form and must be melted down by a torch.

Fig. 8-7. Another common polyester body plastic and the creme hardener used with this plastic. (Courtesy of The Martin-Senour Company.)

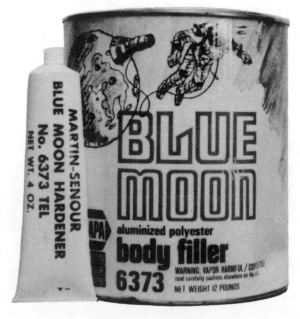

Fig. 8-8. A brand of aluminized plastic filler, sometimes known as *metal plastic,* and the hardener used with this product.

Metal plastic filler is sometimes referred to as metal *mender* and often costs more than polyester plastic fillers. Metal plastic fillers, Fig. 8-8, are often stronger than polyester plastic fillers and have other desirable characteristics to offset their additional cost on high-quality work.

Advantages of Plastic Fillers

Generally speaking, plastics are quick and easy to use and have good adhesion (stick well) to clean base metal. When properly prepared, paint primer-surfacers adhere well to plastic fillers.

Plastics are smooth, easy to apply, and will cure fast, forming a hard finish that may be sanded and painted as if it were metal. Plastic fillers are low in cost. When using plastic fillers, damage can be repaired fast and the job will last for years if all the materials are properly used.

Disadvantages of Plastic Fillers

The greatest disadvantage of plastic fillers are that if they are applied more than ¼-inch thick, the repair is likely to crack within a few months. Plastic filler will not adhere well to metal if the metal surface is not rough ground. Smooth metal and old paint are bad surfaces on which to apply plastic filler.

When plastic is sanded, it creates dust and dirt in the repair shop. This plastic dust is a shop problem and must be carefully controlled. Uncontrolled plastic dust will easily float in the air, causing breathing problems and collecting on other vehicles in the shop. Worst of all, the plastic dust may sift through paint booth filters and get into fresh paint, causing "dirty paint."

When to Use Plastic Filler

Plastic filler may be (and is) used on almost every damaged area. This includes dents, rusted-out areas, and the broken edges of panels. Plastic filler's adaptability, wide range of use, and ease of application are the reasons for its popularity. Plastic filler will harden correctly and does not crack if properly applied. It can be used to level out large, *shallow* areas

of metal damage that putty and primer-surfacer cannot fill properly.

Generally speaking, areas that may be repaired with plastic fillers include:

1. Body sections that cannot be fully worked with metal working tools such as a hammer and dolly.
2. Sections that cannot be completely restored to the original contour by working from the inside of the panel.
3. Panel holes or tears.
4. Sections weakened or damaged by rust-out.
5. Areas that have been patched by welding, or over seams where entire replacement panels have been fastened on. For example, the panel that was replaced in Fig. 8-13.

Also, when a panel cannot be bumped or aligned from its back side, the damage will then have to be repaired from the front side. To do this, the dent first must have holes made in it, using an awl and a hammer or a drill.

Then, after the holes are made in the dent, a *slide hammer* is used to pull the dent out. This was shown earlier in Fig. 8-3. After pulling with the slide hammer, the surface of the damage will still be slightly rough and uneven *and* the holes will still be present. To repair this, the metal is then cleaned and plastic filler is smoothed over the damage area, shaping it to the original contour of the metal.

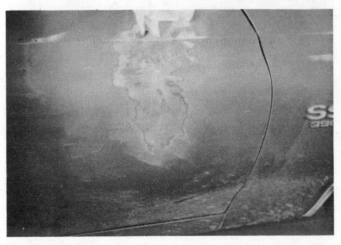

Fig. 8-9. The panel in Fig. 8-1, now metal-worked and ground for plastic filler.

Using Plastic Filler

Polyester plastic filler is more widely used on sheet metal such as the panel to be repaired in Figs. 8-1 and 8-9. When mixed with hardener, the product mixes to a thick, mud-like paste that may then be easily spread over the uneven surface of a bare sheet metal panel. The body man in Fig. 8-10 is about to spread polyester plastic on the prepared metal panel. Fig. 8-11 shows the plastic having been spread on another panel to finish levelling a dented area. Polyester plastic is sometimes referred to as "mud," "bondo," or any of several nicknames.

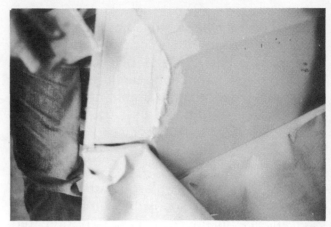

Fig. 8-11. Plastic filler, having been applied to a panel repair, before rough grading.

Fig. 8-10. Appyling the plastic filler with a firm plastic spreader.

Metal plastic, on the other hand, is used to more permanently repair *rusted* metal, like the metal in Fig. 8-12. The aluminum in the filler helps keep the metal from weakening further due to the rust damage.

Metal plastic is stronger than polyester plastic and can therefore be used to build up the edges of sheet metal that would be likely to break off. Metal plastic is not as economical to use as is polyester plastic. It may cost a little more than polyester plastic, but has definite strength and durability advantages.

The following text outlines a plan to use when applying plastic fillers. The procedure holds true whether polyester plastic or metal plastic fillers are being used.

Surface Preparation—To use a plastic filler successfully, *the surface area of the damage or low spot must be carefully prepared.* First, dirt and road grime must be removed from the area, using soap and water.

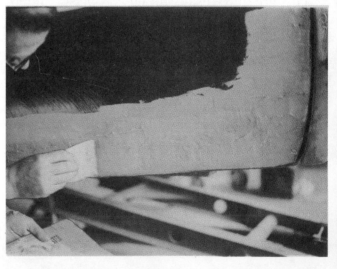

Fig. 8-12. Repairing a rusted-out section with metal plastic filler.

After washing with soap and water, the area then must be cleaned with grease and wax remover. This remover cleans off any tar, wax, silicone, and other contaminants not completely removed by soap and water.

The old paint and minor surface rust is then ground off the damaged area with #16 open-coat grinding disk. This rough-cutting disk

Fig. 8-13. Plastic filler being used to cover the seam for a partial panel replacement.

gives the surface a rough area on which the plastic may grip and adhere to the metal. See Fig. 8-14. The plastic needs a rough area for good holding power.

Fig. 8-14. Before using plastic filler, the area to be repaired must be cleaned and then sanded with a #16 open-coat sanding disk. (Courtesy of Ditzler Automotive Finishes Division.)

After the old paint is ground away, the bare metal must be cleaned with metal conditioner to prevent rusting. Fig. 8-15 shows an area being cleaned with metal conditioner. The metal conditioner must be immediately wiped off with a clean rag, as shown in Fig. 8-16. The damaged area has then been correctly prepared for the plastic filler.

Preparing Plastic Filler—Before *preparing the material,* always read carefully any instructions on the container. No two plastic filler products are exactly the same. For this reason, it is very important to rely on the manufac-

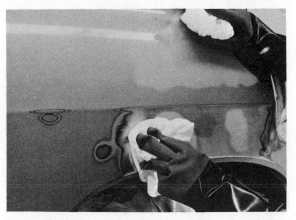

Fig. 8-15. Applying metal conditioner to a bare metal surface. (Courtesy of Refinish Division, DuPont Company.)

turer's instructions to mix and use a product correctly.

When removing the plastic from the can, scoop out the amount needed for the repair and place it on a clean, smooth, mixing plate See Fig. 8-17. The plastic may be dipped out of the can with a paint paddle, such as the one shown in Fig. 8-18.

Next, the hardener is added. For best results, buy and use the hardener recommended by the plastic's manufacturer. Add *only* the amount of hardener needed to make the plastic dry as fast as is desired. Either the can of plastic or the tube of hardener will have directions on how much hardener to use for the product. If the plastic has too much hardener added, the plastic will cure before it can be applied and smoothed. It will also tend to *pinhole* as it cures.

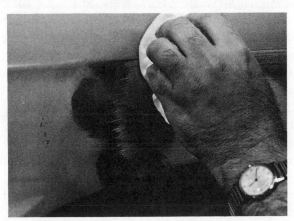

Fig. 8-16. Wiping off the wet metal conditioner. This must be done immediately after the conditioner is wiped on. (Courtesy of Refinish Division, DuPont Company.)

Fig. 8-17. Mixing plastic filler and hardener on a clean, dry mixing plate. (Courtesy of Ditzler Automotive Finishes Division.)

Fig. 8-19. Mixing the plastic filler.

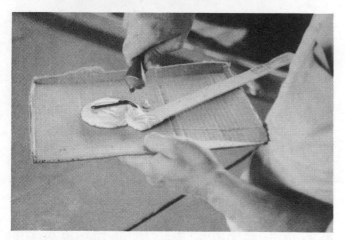

Fig. 8-18. Adding hardener to the plastic removed from the can. Note the *paint paddle* used to remove the plastic from the can.

Using the paint paddle or other stirring device, *mix* the plastic and hardener thoroughly. Mix the hardener and plastic until the mixture becomes a smooth, creamy paste that is all one color with no streaks. See Fig. 8-19. The mixture must *not* be whipped. If the plastic mixture is whipped, air will be whipped into the plastic, causing air bubbles. Later, when the plastic has hardened, the air bubbles will cause the plastic surface to have small *pinholes* that will need additional filling. By stirring (instead of whipping) the plastic filler mixture, air will be worked out of the plastic. Also, be careful not to let any hardener get into the large can of plastic filler, since this will cause lumps in the unused plastic.

Applying Plastic Filler—When *applying* the plastic, it must always be applied immediately after mixing. This is because it begins hard-

ening very rapidly after it has been mixed with hardener. A plastic spreader like the one in Fig. 8-20 should be used to apply a smooth, even stroke of plastic filler to the entire damage area.

The flatter the plastic spreader is held, the thicker a layer of plastic will be built up on

Fig. 8-20. Applying mixed filler with a plastic spreader. (Courtesy of Ditzler Automotive Finishes Division.)

the surface being repaired. If the spreader is held more straight up, a thinner coat of plastic will be applied. Plastic should *never* be applied so that the repaired area is built up with plastic over ¼-inch thick. If the plastic is built up over ¼-inch, it will likely crack after the repair is a few months old.

Smooth the plastic as much as possible while it is soft. Allow it to dry until it is semicured (beginning to harden and not sticky) before beginning to shape the repaired area to the desired contour, as in Fig. 8-21.

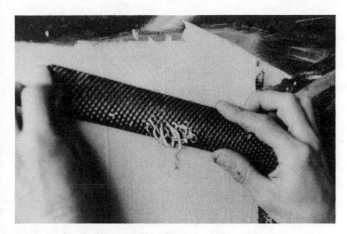

Fig. 8-21. Shaping the plastic filler while it is hardening.

FIBERGLASS FILLER

Fig. 8-22 shows a fiberglass filler repair kit. A common repair kit will normally contain a quart of resin, a tube of hardener, a 4-foot-square piece of fiberglass matting material, a mixing cup, a paddle to mix the resin and hardener, and a plastic spreader. Fiberglass repair kits are designed for body shop use and include written instructions. One **CAUTION** always applies when repairing with fiberglass: **USE RUBBER GLOVES.**

Fiberglass filler is used in two parts: 1. Fiberglass epoxy resin and hardener, and; 2. Fiberglass reinforcing matting. Epoxy resin is a thick syrup which is mixed with hardener to become a firm binder. This mixture is used on the fiberglass matting included in the kit. The matting used may be either the loosely-woven, straw-

like type shown in Fig. 8-22, or the closely-woven fabric type shown in Fig. 8-23. Both types of matting are woven from fiberglass yarn.

When the materials are used, the resin and hardener mixture is applied to the matting and the matting is then placed over the damage. Then, a polyester plastic filler made especially

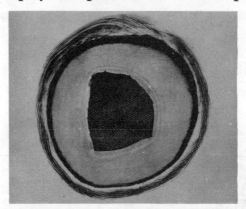

Fig. 8-23. Fabric-type fiberglass matting. (Courtesy of Ditzler Automotive Finishes Division.)

for use on fiberglass is used over the matting. The *plastic* filler is easier to smooth and sands more easily than does fiberglass filler.

Advantages of Fiberglass Filler

Fiberglass filler is quick and easy to use for making many body repairs. Pound for pound, it may be built up to be stronger than steel. It will not rust or dent. Fiberglass repairs may be primed, sanded, and painted like any other type of repair.

Fig. 8-22. The typical parts of a fiberglass filler kit. (Courtesy of Oatey Co.)

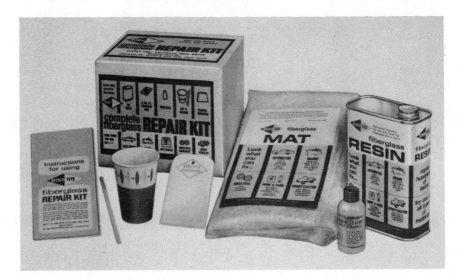

Fiberglass filler is durable and is easy to mix and apply to damaged areas. Filler kits can be bought in large or small sizes. These kits are excellent for repairing complete fiberglass bodies (such as Corvettes) or fiberglass parts on steel bodies, such as the fiberglass front panel shown in Fig. 8-24. Metal bodies may also be repaired with fiberglass filler kits.

Fig. 8-24. A cracked fiberglass nosepiece on the front of a steel body.

There are many auto body repair jobs that can be repaired with fiberglass. It may be used on tears, cracks, gouges, dents or rust-outs. Either fiberglass or metal body parts may be repaired with fiberglass. The following sections outline a step-by-step procedure for repairing the rusted-out metal body section in Fig. 8-25.

In the snowbelt, there is a good market for fiberglass repair work on snowmobiles. Procedures for repairing damaged snowmobile bod-

Fig. 8-25. A common, large rust-out hole that may be repaired with fiberglass matting.

ies are the same as for repairing fiberglass automobile bodies.

Disadvantages of Fiberglass Filler

The main disadvantage of fiberglass filler kits is that many auto body repairmen do not understand how to properly use these materials for auto body repair work. This is because the material and procedures are not often used and are relatively new to the auto body repair industry. Some repairmen will not work on damaged fiberglass bodies because they are not experienced in fiberglass repair. This makes the fiberglass repair market even better for new bodymen who are willing to learn fiberglass repair.

Fiberglass matting or resin will sometimes cause skin irritation if rubber gloves are not used. Also, fiberglass filler may be difficult to sand and work due to its gummy, varnish-like properties. Usually, it is also necessary to use a plastic filler coat over fiberglass repair sections.

Using Fiberglass Filler to Repair Rust-Out

Most of the sheet metal on auto bodies is thin. If this metal is exposed and allowed to rust for a few months, the metal will have rust holes eaten through it. Fig. 8-25 shows this type of rust damage that has eaten through the metal. This type of rust-out damage can be filled with fiber matting and resin, using a good fiberglass repair kit as outlined below.

Cleaning and Sanding—The area to be repaired should first be cleaned with grease and wax remover to remove the contaminants from the paint and metal. Then, the area must be rough-sanded (ground) with a disk grinder to remove the surface rust and expose the bare metal around the edges of the hole. Fig. 8-26 shows the area having been ground 2-3 in. beyond the damaged area. This allows the fiberglass material to adhere to the rough base metal edges.

Depressing the Damaged Area—A hammer is then used to tap down the damaged area so that the entire area forms a depression, or "rut." The fiberglass material will then be able to fill the depression and be built-up until the repair is even with the rest of the panel.

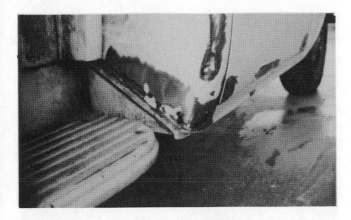

Fig. 8-26. The area in Fig. 8-25 prepared for a fiberglass mat repair.

Cutting Fiberglass Matting—The fiberglass matting is then trimmed to fit the area being repaired. This step is being done in Fig. 8-27. The material should be cut about 2 in. larger than the damaged area. This 2 in. allows the material to have plenty of undamaged metal on which to hold.

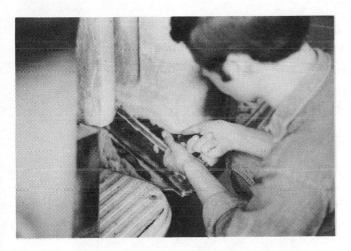

Fig. 8-27. Using a knife to cut the fiberglass mat to size.

Mixing Fiberglass Resin—A container, usually a waxpaper cup, is used to mix the resin for the matting. Usually, about 4 ounces of resin mix is needed for each square foot (12 in. × 12 in.) of fiberglass matting. The hardener is then added to the resin in the cup, as recommended by the kit manufacturer. The resin and hardener are then mixed together in the cup.

Each 4 ounces of resin will usually need about 30 drops of hardner, although all manufacturers have their own specific directions for

mixing their products. Most manufacturers use the formula of one tube of hardener to one quart of resin. This is a general rule that can be remembered easily. In any case, *heat* or *fire* must not get near the fiberglass resin since it is highly explosive.

Applying the Matting—After the resin is mixed, place the already-cut fiberglass matting on a plastic bag or plastic wrapping. This is done because the matting will not stick to the plastic after the resin has been poured or spread on the matting.

Next, lightly coat the matting by brushing resin on the mat. Finally, apply the mat to the damaged area, as is being done in Fig. 8-28. Rubber gloves *should* be used. Allow the 2-inch overlap so that the matting has plenty of metal on which to cling.

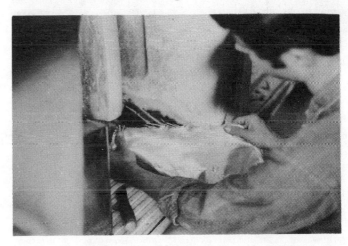

Fig. 8-28. Applying the matting to the hole being repaired.

Saturating the Matting—Using a plastic spreader, saturate (soak) the attached matting with the resin mixture. Spread the resin *evenly* over the entire matting, as is being done in Fig. 8-29. If a second or third layer is needed, they can be placed over the first layer. The more layers of material that are used, the stronger is the repair.

Removing Air Bubbles—Air bubbles will sometimes form under the resin or fiberglass mat. To remove these air bubbles, press the material with the spreader, working from the center and pressing toward the outside. See Fig. 8-30. The air bubbles will easily move out from under the material.

Fig. 8-29. Applying the fiberglass resin mixture to the mat in place over the hole.

Fig. 8-31. Using polyester plastic body filler to smooth the top of the repair.

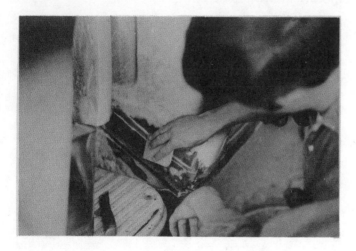

Fig. 8-30. Smoothing out the air bubbles from the liquid resin on the mat.

Allow the resin and matting to dry on the damage area. Then, the matting may be trimmed if it is too wide at any part.

Applying Plastic Filler—After the fiberglass mat and resin filler cures (usually about 15 minutes), it may then be covered with polyester plastic filler. This step is being done in Fig. 8-31. Polyester plastic filler is used over the fiberglass because the plastic is easier to sand and smooth. For the best possible results on fiberglass work, be sure to use a plastic filler specifically designed for use on fiberglass. As it hardens, the plastic is worked down and finished as usual.

Using Fiberglass Filler to Repair Damaged Fiberglass

The same fiberglass kit materials are needed to repair a damaged fiberglass body part as to repair damaged sheet metal body parts with fiberglass. However, the *procedure* differs slightly because of the differences between fiberglass and metal body parts.

Damage in a fiberglass body cannot be "worked" with tools before applying fillers because fiberglass parts do not bend or "give" as do metal parts. For that reason, damage on a fiberglass body cannot be tapped down. This creates the problem of the repair possibly being *above* the normal area of the panel. To solve this problem, the fiberglass matting must be applied on the *inside* of the damaged panel and then built-up from the *inside* to the *outside*. This is done so that the completed repair will not extend above the rest of the panel.

Repairing Holes in Fiberglass Panels—The following procedure is used to repair *holes* in fiberglass panels. Note that this procedure is similar to repairing rust-out holes on a metal body *except* that repairing a fiberglass body does not include depressing the damage area.

Repair work on *holes* in fiberglass panels, then, is done from the *inside* of the panel to the *outside*, as follows.

1. Thoroughly clean the surface around the damaged area with grease and wax re-

mover. Also, clean the reverse side (inside) of the area. See Fig. 8-32.

2. Remove any loose fiberglass from the damaged area, as in Fig. 8-33.

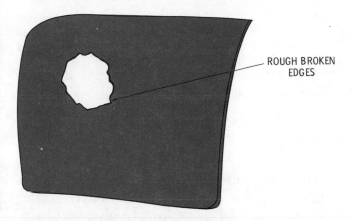

Fig. 8-32. A fiberglass panel with a hole broken through it.

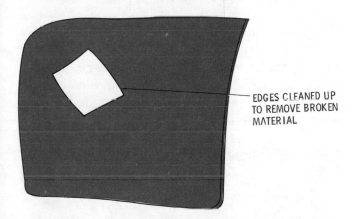

Fig. 8-33. Loose damaged material, having been removed, gives the hole a more uniform appearance.

3. Grind or sand off the paint and primer to expose the base fiberglass material 2-3 in. beyond the damaged area. Grind or sand both the *outside* and *inside* surfaces if at all possible. Bevel the edges of the hole as in Fig. 8-34.

4. Cut two repair pieces of fiberglass mat material. One piece should be about 2 in. larger than the hole on all sides. This piece will be used on the *inside* of the panel. The *other* piece should be cut to fit just barely *within* the damage area. The two pieces of matting will thereby fit together so that the repair area is level with the rest of the panel.

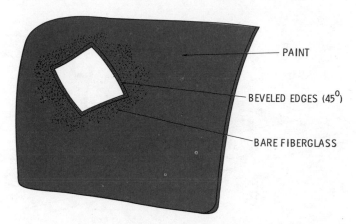

Fig. 8-34. When prepared for the fiberglass mat repair, the edges of the damage are beveled to about 45° and the area is cleaned of paint for good adhesion.

5. Mix the resin with the hardener, following the manufacturer's directions in the kit.

6. Lay a sheet of plastic on the workbench. See Fig. 8-35. (Plastic bags such as those used by dry cleaners are handy for this job.)

7. Lay the two fiberglass mats on the plastic and pour the mixed resin onto them. See Fig. 8-35.

8. Using the spatula, work the resin back and forth on the mats until they are *thoroughly* saturated (soaked) with the mixture.

9. Lay the *larger* mat on the *inside* of the panel. Work it well into place, squeezing the resin through the mat to help the mat stick to the panel. Work out any air bubbles, using the spatula.

10. Place the *smaller* mat *on* the larger piece and *within* the damage area. Work the smaller mat into place.

11. Allow the mats and resin/hardener material to harden in place, making up the base of the repair.

12. Apply polyester plastic filler over the hardened area to smooth out the entire surface.

13. Allow time for the filler to harden. Then, sand the area smooth and featheredge it for painting. This will allow the completed repair to be level with the rest of the panel, as in Fig. 8-36.

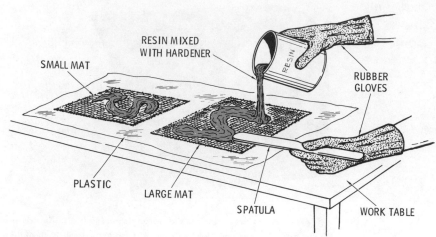

Fig. 8-35. The cut sections of fiberglass mat are saturated with a resin/hardener mixture before being placed on the section being repaired.

Repairing Cracks in Fiberglass Panels— Cracks, Figs. 8-37 and 38, may develop in fiberglass panels. When the *back* side of the damaged panel can be reached, the proper procedure after cleaning is to grind or sand the *back* side of the damaged panel for about 8-10 in. on either side of the crack.

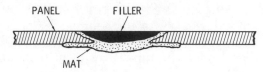

Fig. 8-36. Completed fiberglass repair, level with the original surface.

Then, saturate a piece of matting as outlined before and roll this piece of matting over the *back* side of the crack. Sometimes, it is wise to use a double layer of matting. This will reinforce the area to help prevent further cracking. At this point, however, a crack is still present on the *outside* of the panel.

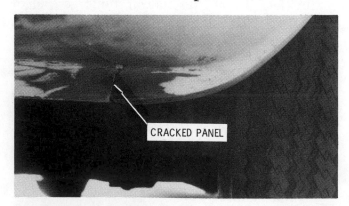

Fig. 8-37. A stress crack in a fiberglass panel under a front bumper.

To repair this outer crack, bevel the crack's edges and fill it with resin mixture. After the resin hardens, a coating of polyester plastic filler may be applied over the resin to make the final surface of the repair.

When a crack is present but the back side of the panel *cannot* be reached, a different procedure must be used. Fig. 8-38 shows a lower body panel with this type of damage. In Fig. 8-39, the broken panel has been riveted back in place and the area has been cleaned of dirt and paint.

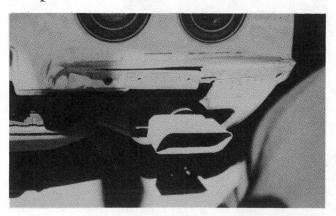

Fig. 8-38. A damaged lower body panel on a fiberglass-body car.

Next, resin/hardener-saturated fiberglass matting is placed on the *outside* of the damaged area, as is being done in Fig. 8-40. Fig. 8-41 shows the area after the fiberglass repair has been sanded and before the area is given a coat of primer-surfacer.

On short, *minor* cracks or splits due to impact, a very fast repair can be made by simply grinding the edges of the crack at about a 20°

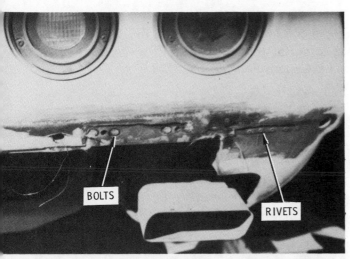

Fig. 8-39. Damaged panel having been repaired with riveted reinforcing material.

angle. Then, the cracked area may be filled with a resin/hardener mixture. Allow this mixture to harden and then sand about 1 in. beyond the cracked area with course sandpaper. Finally, apply and smooth a coat of plastic filler before painting.

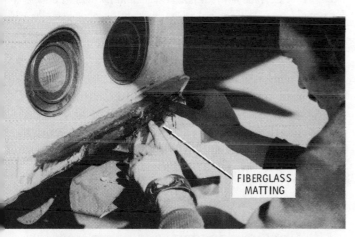

Fig. 8-40. Applying fiberglass matting to the repaired area.

Fig. 8-41. Completed repair area, ready for primer-surfacer.

Repairing Shattered Fiberglass Panels—Often all of the pieces from a wreck can be salvaged and put back together like a jigsaw puzzle. This forms a basic panel which may then be repaired. Fiberglass filler is ideally suited for this type of repair. The procedure below should be used.

1. Working from the back side, remove the dirt from all the pieces and from the edges of the main structure.
2. Find any piece that mates to the main structure.
3. Clamp the piece into place on the main structure with gripping pliers or C-clamps.
4. Smear a coating of resin/hardener mixture on both the main structure and the piece, building a resin "bridge" over the crack.
5. Repeat this process with each one of the pieces until all of the broken fragments have been glued together. This will form one rough, basic structure. *Overall*, however, it will be properly shaped, as in Fig. 8-42.
6. Next, quickly check this assembly for *rigidity*. It will usually need more resin to reinforce the back side of the panel. In any case, most of the broken edges will be visible on the outside of this area.

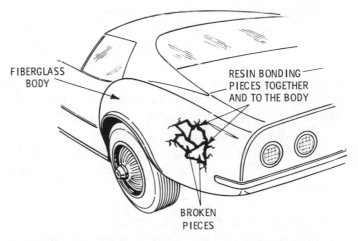

Fig. 8-42. A reconstructed fiberglass body panel. Although the area may *look* the same as the original, it is not as strong. This is because hardened fiberglass resin is not as strong as are the fibers in a good fiberglass panel.

7. With a rough disc, grind the whole outer surface, removing all the high points and corners. This will leave a thin, weak shell, held together only with resin but no fiberglass fibers.

8. A complete rebuild is now possible by using fiberglass matting. Pieces about one foot square, saturated with resin, should be laid on the *back* side of the thin shell. This is best done by *shingling* the area (overlapping the pieces). Do not try to work with pieces that are too large. Air bubbles should be carefully removed as the sheets of matting are laid in place.

9. Finally, after all the pieces of fiberglass have been positioned and have dried, apply a coating of plastic filler on the outside of the panel. Then, the area may be smoothed and prepared for painting.

Connecting Two Fiberglass Panels—Some plastic companies manufacture a special adhesive product for bonding together two fiberglass panels. This product is used to join two fiberglass panels that are made to overlap.

Generally speaking, fiberglass panels purchased from the manufacturer are made with a *lip* designed to go over or under the panel to which the panel joins. This panel *joint* must then be bonded together so that a permanent repair is made. These special fiberglass adhesives, usually paste-like products, are applied to both surfaces of the joint to make the repair.

It is important that the mating surfaces are rough and clean. If necessary, use rough sandpaper on the joint parts before applying the adhesive. When the two panels are joined with the adhesive in place, clamp them together until the adhesive hardens.

Making a Fiberglass Core—When a whole section of fiberglass is missing and there are curves in the missing section, it would be very difficult to lay fiberglass mat across the hole and properly reshape the area.

This would be true, for example, on the nose of a fender. In a case such as this, a body man may make one of two choices: either a new section can be purchased, or a *mold core* can

be made. The following steps are the procedure that would be used to make a *mold core*. A left rear fender section of a Corvette is used as an example. See Fig. 8-43.

Fig. 8-43. A Corvette left rear fender section to be used as a mold for a *mold core*. This original section will not be damaged when it is used as a mold.

1. Find an undamaged fender on another car. It will not be damaged during the process. The car may be found at a used car lot, a junk yard, or anywhere where it may be used for an hour or so.

2. Mark off an area on the fender with a strip of masking tape. Make the area slightly *larger* than the damaged area on the body being repaired.

3. Using masking tape and paper from this line outward, cover the outer areas to protect them from any spill.

4. Using paste floor wax, smear the section of the fender being used as a mold. Leave a wet coat of wax all over the surface. (Sometimes, it is possible to simply lay a piece of plastic cellophane wrap over the area being used as a mold.) See Fig. 8-44.

5. The surface is now ready to be used as a mold for making a new section to replace a damaged one on another car.

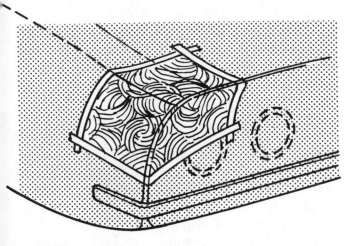

Fig. 8-44. Area prepared and protected for use as a mold.

6. Use a special mold-making veil (pronounced "vale," a thin layer of mat). Cut from the veil a number of small pieces ranging from 2″ × 4″ to 4″ × 6″.
7. Mix the resin and hardener according to directions.
8. Lay the small pieces of cut veil on a cellophane sheet and use a spatula to spread the resin/hardener mixture on the veil pieces. Pick up the small pieces with the spatula and lay them on the waxed surface. Use smaller pieces of veil on the edges and around difficult curves. In all cases use only *one* layer of veil. See Fig. 8-45.
9. To force the veil into curves and around corners, use a small, inexpensive paint brush. Wet the paint brush in the resin and push the material into place with

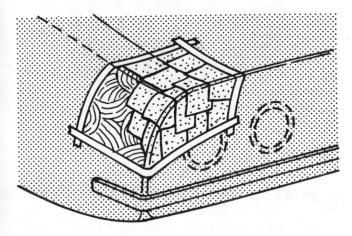

Fig. 8-45. Laying strips of *veil* on the waxed surface.

the end of the bristles. Do *not* brush back and forth. See Fig. 8-46.
10. Continue laying small pieces of fiberglass veil on the waxed surface until the *entire* surface has been covered with only one layer. The layers should be slightly overlapped and shingled, similar to the roof shingles on a house. See Fig. 8-45.

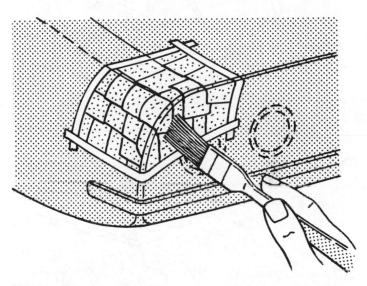

Fig. 8-46. Using a paint brush to force the veil down, making the exact contour.

11. After the whole surface has been covered with the layer of veil, allow the new "shell" to harden at least an hour.
12. After the shell has thoroughly hardened (cured), gently work the piece away from the original panel. See Fig. 8-47. This shell will then be an excellent reproduction of this section of the panel. Of course, it will be slightly larger than the original area.
13. Now, the wax which was protecting the paint finish may be removed and the panel polished.
14. Place the shell under the damaged panel and align it with the damaged area on the vehicle. See Fig. 8-48.
15. Cement the shell into place with the fiberglass adhesive discussed earlier. Then allow the shell and panel to cure.
16. The remaining steps will now be the same as for any other fiberglass repair.

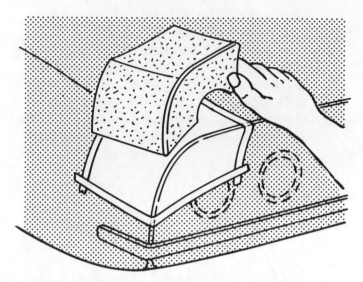

Fig. 8-47. Removing the completed "shell."

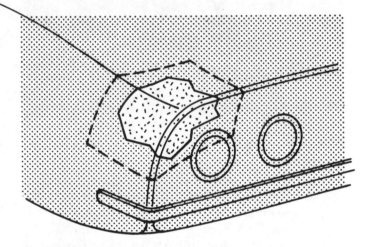

Fig. 8-48. When the new "shell" is in place behind the damaged area, the repair may be completed as would any other fiberglass repair.

The surface must be built up to the original thickness with fiberglass mat.

17. First, grind back the edge of the original fender to a long taper, being careful not to damage the shell underneath. Then lay the fiberglass mat, soaked in resin/hardener, on the taper and around and over the entire inner shell.

18. After the fiberglass mat hardens, it may be levelled with a coating of plastic filler and then prepared for painting.

The operation discussed above will not usually take more than 2 hours. The cost of an entirely new panel section will be saved. Also, the time needed to get parts from the factory will be saved, allowing the repair to be done faster and at a lower cost.

BODY SOLDER

Body solder is also known as body *lead*. By either name, this body filler is a product made from *lead* and *tin*. Usually, "body lead" is made in 12-inch sticks about ½" in diameter. The sticks weigh about ½-pound each.

In Fig. 8-49 is a common stick of body solder. Also in Fig. 8-49 is a roll of *acid core solder*. This product is used to clean a panel during the body solder ("leading") process. This process is explained later in the unit.

Fig. 8-49. A common stick of auto body solder and a roll of acid core solder to be used during preparation.

Advantages of Body Solder

Body solder is a good filler since it is made of metal, as is the panel on which it is used. Body solder is hard and will not mar easily. It will adhere (stick) well to properly prepared steel. When body solder is properly cleaned, it may be painted with regular automobile paint. Body solder will not crack, is very stable, and will last as long as the panel on which it is put.

Disadvantages of Body Solder

Body solder is still used in many body shops even though it has generally been outdated by other materials used for commercial work. For high-priced custom body work, however, many people do prefer that body solder be used as a filler. In these cases, the customer is often willing to pay a higher price if body solder will be used.

Body solder is expensive and using it as a filler is slow and messy. Generally speaking, the use of body solder is becoming obsolete. Other fillers such as fiberglass and polyester plastic are more commonly used today.

Types of Solder

Body solder containing 80% lead and 20% tin content is the best solder to use. This is known as *80-20 solder*. Some body solder, however, has 70% lead and 30% tin. This is known as *70-30 solder* and is cheaper than 80-20. The more lead there is in the solder, the more expensive it will be.

Using Body Solder

When an area is filled with body solder, several different pieces of equipment and tools must be used. These should be placed in the work area as in Fig. 8-50.

The *tools* included will be an oxy-acetylene torch equipped with a soldering tip; a fire extinguisher; and a disc grinder with a #16- or #24-grit grinding disc and a #80-grit featheredging disc. Also needed will be a wooden soldering paddle, a body file, and several clean rags. The *materials* needed will include several sticks of body solder, a roll of acid core solder, and a can of lacquer thinner.

At this time, the work area should be cleared of all flammables, since extreme heat will be used and anything that will burn will be a fire hazard. Then, when all the tools and materials are ready, body *soldering* may be done.

Using the Heating Torch—An oxy-acetylene welding outfit must be used to heat and melt body solder. Setting up and operating oxy-acetylene welding equipment is outlined in later units. Many times, an oxy-acetylene welding torch is referred to as a *leading torch* when it is used to heat and melt body solder (lead).

Fig. 8-51 shows the heating tip used to melt body solder. This style of heating tip (for soldering) has a large flame opening at the end. This heating tip is also known as a *soldering tip* and is attached to the torch chamber by screwing the threaded collar on *only* hand tight. See Fig. 8-51.

The *flame* used to solder is a large flame. A soldering flame is a low-temperature flame

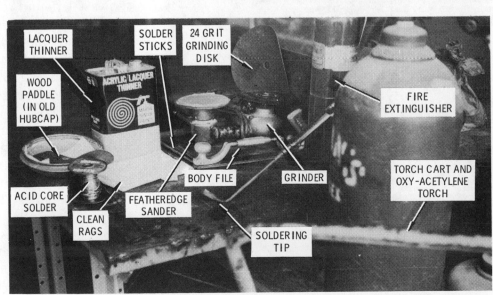

Fig. 8-50. The tools and equipment needed for body soldering.

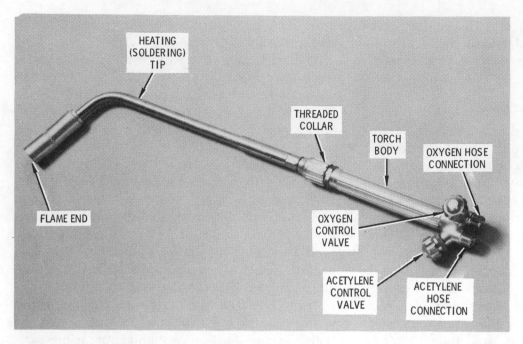

HEATING (SOLDERING) TIP

THREADED COLLAR

TORCH BODY

OXYGEN HOSE CONNECTION

FLAME END

OXYGEN CONTROL VALVE

ACETYLENE CONTROL VALVE

ACETYLENE HOSE CONNECTION

Fig. 8-51. A soldering tip attached to the torch body for auto body soldering work. (Courtesy of Harris Calorific Division.)

when compared to the high temperature needed for welding. A flame of about 800°F can be used to melt body solder. Adjusting the torch valves for different flames is discussed in the oxy-acetylene welding unit.

Cleaning the Area for Soldering—Before good body soldering may be done, the metal must be *cleaned* and *ground* as for any other type of filler. Fig. 8-52 shows a damaged panel being ground with a disk grinder. All the paint must be ground off the panel and the metal

must be made bright and shiny for the tinning process discussed next.

Tinning—After the damaged area is ground, the area must be *tinned* with either acid core solder or tinning compound. *Tinning* prepares the metal so that the solder may easily grip the metal. *Tinning compound*, a powdery mixture of solder and acid, is more often used to tin larger areas that will be filled with body solder.

Acid core solder is usually used to tin smaller damaged areas for spot repair filling. Acid core solder comes in different-sized rolls. Fig. 8-50 shows a 1-pound roll of acid core solder for use on this repair.

The body man in Fig. 8-53 is tinning the metal for body soldering by applying acid core solder to the area. Either tinning compound and acid core solder could be used for this job. Both materials are used in the same way. Their purpose is to clean the metal and provide a surface on which the solder will stick (adhere). Body solder will not adhere to the metal if the tinning process is not properly done.

To tin a panel, the panel is first heated with a torch. Then, the tinning material (acid core solder or tinning compound) is melted onto the hot metal by the torch soldering tip, as in Fig. 8-53. While molten, the hot tinning material is wiped with a rag to spread it over the

Fig. 8-52. Grinding a damaged panel to prepare for body soldering.

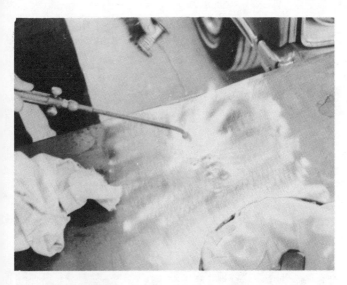

Fig. 8-53. Tinning the area with acid-core solder.

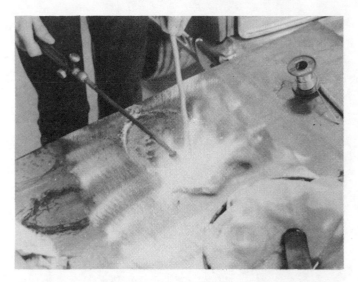

Fig. 8-55. Melting the hot solder on the tinned panel.

entire damaged area. See Fig. 8-54. When the metal is tinned, it will be a dull silver color.

Soldering Procedure—To melt the body solder itself onto the tinned surface, hold the torch tip at a 45° angle to the solder, as in Fig. 8-55. Place the solder on a low area of the damaged panel. Heat both the metal and the solder. When the solder is properly molten, it will stick on the hot metal. The solder will melt quickly on the hot metal at between 700° and 800° F.

Fig. 8-54. Wiping across the panel with a clean rag to spread the tinning material.

Heat about ¾-in. of the body solder stick at one time, and then push it in against the hot metal. This will cause the hot solder to flow out and stick to the metal. Repeat this procedure several times. After several inches of solder has been melted on the damaged

area, use the wooden paddle to spread the hot solder evenly across the damage. See Fig. 8-56.

Smoothing the Solder—Body solder is softer than body steel. When it is cold, solder will be harder than plastic but softer than steel. Because of this, body solder must be worked down and leveled with a *metal* body file, as in Fig. 8-57.

When the repaired area has been smoothed and leveled, the edges may be featheredged with fine sandpaper. Finally the area is then ready for *neutralizing*.

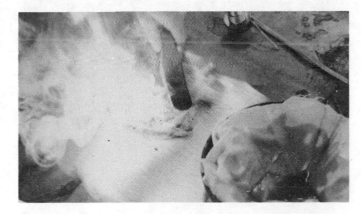

Fig. 8-56. Using a wooden paddle to spread the hot, molten body solder.

Neutralizing the Solder—The tinning agent (either acid core solder or tinning compound) contains *acid*. Acid is an enemy of paint and will attack either the paint topcoat or primer-surfacer. When body solder is melted on the

Fig. 8-57. Smoothing body solder with a metal body file.

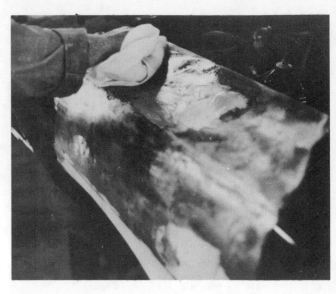

Fig. 8-58. Using lacquer thinner to neutralize the acid in the tinning material.

damaged area, the tinning agent becomes hot. This heat causes the acid to mix with the body solder. Therefore, after the body solder is hard and smooth, acid will still be present on the surface of the repaired area. Before the area is painted, the acid must be made harmless. This is called *neutralizing* the acid.

If the acid is not neutralized, the paint finish will peel off soon after the damage has been repainted. One of the easier ways to neutralize the acid is by cleaning the area with lacquer thinner. This is being done in Fig. 8-58. However, the lacquer thinner must *not* get on the paint around the repair area since it will damage the other paint. The lacquer thinner should be allowed to evaporate. Then, the primer-surfacer and paint topcoats may be applied.

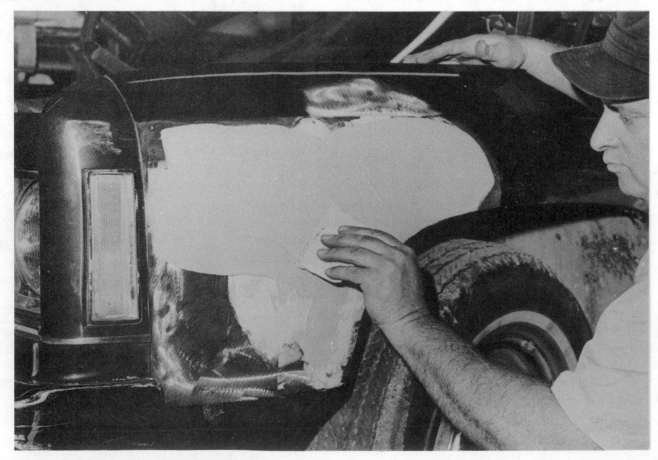

Body Abrasives

In body shop work, it is often necessary to remove material from a body or panel surface. This material may be old paint, rust, or excess body filler. To remove this material, tools with body shop *abrasives* are used.

The word *abrasive* refers to a substance that is used to cut material off a surface. Abrasives used in a body shop should be chosen with the same care that is used to choose other tools and equipment. Different types of repair jobs, and different steps on the *same* repair job, will require different types of abrasives.

For example, *grinding disks* (Fig. 9-1) are used to remove paint or rust from a panel to be repaired. *Sandpaper*, on the other hand, is normally used for finer jobs such as preparing the surface of bare metal or primer-surfacer.

Fig. 9-2 shows several sheets of sandpaper. Finally, *cutting* (rubbing) compound is used to clean old finishes and rub out new lacquer paint. See Fig. 9-3.

When choosing an abrasive for a given repair or procedure, the user must know a good deal about the different types of abrasives. This is because there are so many types and classifications of abrasives. This unit will discuss these types in detail.

GRINDING DISKS

Grinding disks are used for quick, rough jobs such as grinding off paint and rust. For grinding disks to perform these jobs, they must have a hard, rugged surface, or *grit*. Notice the coarse texture of the #24-grit grinding disks that were shown in Fig. 9-1.

Fig. 9-1. Grinding disks. (Courtesy of The Norton Company.)

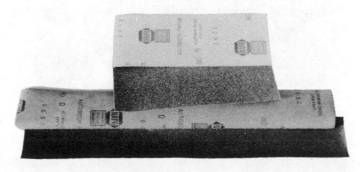

Fig. 9-2. Sandpaper strips for use in a "jitterbug" or a speed file.

Fig. 9-3. Cutting (rubbing) compound.

Almost all grinding disks are *round*. Large disks are used on a disk sander or on a large body grinder. Smaller disks are used on a power drill. (Note that grinding disks should not be confused with *sandpaper* disks. Sandpaper disks have a finer, less durable grit and have softer backing material.)

Disk Sizes—Grinding disks are available in sizes from 3 to 9 inches in diameter. The most common disks are the 7-inch and 9-inch sizes shown in Fig. 9-4. Some grinding disks have

Fig. 9-4. The two most common disk sizes: 7-inch and 9-inch.

either ½-inch or ⅞-inch center holes. The center hole is used to fasten the disk (and the backing plate, discussed next) to the grinder. This is done by using a special screw and spacer, as shown in Fig. 9-5. Other disks are not attached in this way. Instead, they are *glued* onto the grinder's backing plate.

Disk Backing Plate—Because grinding disks are thin and easily bent, they must have a *backing plate* (or *pad*) to provide stiffness for the turning disk. The plate must be the same size as the grinding disk with which it is used. Fig. 9-6, for example, shows a 9-inch backing pad that would be used with a 9-inch disk.

Some small grinding disks (3-inch diameter or smaller) do not need backing plates. These disks have a stud on the back, as shown on the back of the disc in Fig. 9-7. The stud will fit down into the drill chuck so that the chuck may be tightened onto the stud.

Other small disks are mounted on small *backing pads*. The backing pads themselves have a stud to fit into the drill chuck. Fig. 9-8 shows this backing pad with a stud for use in a drill chuck. Generally speaking, smaller disks are used with a power drill to grind in close places.

Disk Cutter—Many repair shops buy grinding disks in only the 9-inch size. Then, after the outer edge of the 9-inch disk has been worn off by use on a 9-inch grinder pad, a *disk cutter* is used to cut the disk down to fit a 7-inch backing pad. This saves the cost of buying new 7-inch disks for the shop's 7-inch grinders. When

Fig. 9-5. Three different sizes of backing pads with the center spacer and screw that would be used with each. (Courtesy of 3M Company, Automotive Division.)

Fig. 9-6. A backing pad that would screw onto a grinder's *spindle* and used with 9-inch grinding disks. (Courtesy of 3M Company, Automotive Division.)

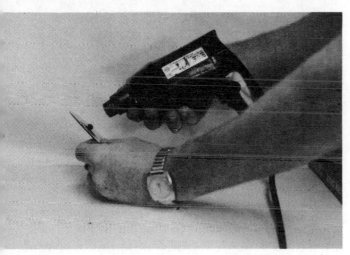

Fig. 9-7. A small, 3-inch sanding disk with a built-in stud for use in a power drill.

Fig. 9-8. A molded backing pad for small discs without a stud. To use those discs, they would be glued onto the other side of this small pad.

Fig. 9-9. A disc cutter. This tool is used to cut off the outer (worn) edge of a grinding disc. (Courtesy of Plymouth Products Corp.)

the 7-inch disk is worn down on the edges, it may then be cut to fit a 5-inch backing pad.

Fig. 9-9 shows a 9-inch disk being cut with a disk cutter. The disk cutter is operated by turning the handle and feeding the disc around the cutter. See Fig. 9-9. This money-saving piece of shop equipment may be used to cut a disk to fit most any size of backing plate.

How Grinding Disks Are Made

Grinding disks are made by attaching a rough *grit* (the cutting material) to a glue-covered *backing*. The grit must first be *sized;* then, it may be fastened to a glue-covered backing by one of several different *bonding* processes.

Disk Grit—The *cutting* part of a disk is the *grit*, also known as the *grain*. There are two types of disk grits: *man-made* grit and *natural* grit.

Man-made grits are either the *aluminum oxide type* or *silicon carbide* type. Aluminum oxide grit is the most widely-used grit in automobile repair work. Fig. 9-10 shows an aluminum oxide "rock" before it is crushed into grit.

Natural grits include embra, garnet, and flint. All of these are natural minerals mined from the earth. These natural minerals are very hard and are more often used for grinding very hard surfaces. In Fig. 9-11 is a mound of ungraded garnet grit.

Fig. 9-10. Aluminum oxide before crushing. (Courtesy of The Norton Company.)

Fig. 9-11. Natural garnet grit before grading. (Courtesy of The Norton Company.)

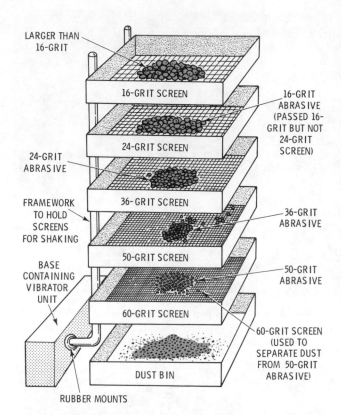

Fig. 9-12. A set of screens on vibrating racks are used to separate the grits of different sizes.

Grit Sizes—There are four basic *grades* (sizes of grit) that are used to make grinding disks. These are: 16-grit, 24-grit, 36-grit, and 50-grit. The coarsest grade is 16-grit, whereas 50-grit is the finest grade.

To grade and sort the sizes of grit, a pile of crushed grit material is placed in the top hopper of a grading machine. See Fig. 9-12. When the racks are vibrated, the grit falls down through the holes in the hopper screens.

As the grit falls down through the hopper screens, each lower screen has smaller openings. This allows the larger grit to be filtered out and the smaller grit to fall onto the next screen. For example, the top screen, with 16 holes per square inch, will filter out any grit *larger* than 16-grit. This allows the 16-grit grains to fall to the next lower screen, which has 24 holes per square inch. Since the 16-grit size cannot pass through the 24-grit screen, the

16-grit grains collect on top of the 24-grit screen. This filtering process continues on down the grading machine's hoppers, until, finally, the finest grit size has been filtered out and only dust remains.

Bonding the Grit—All grit particles of a certain size must be glued to a paper or fiber backing with a *bonding* agent. To do this, a coat of resin binder is first applied to the backing. Then, the sized grit is applied to the resin-covered backing.

One of several methods may be used to apply the grit. Of these, the *electrostatic* method is the most popular. In this method, the grit is pulled onto the resin-covered backing by electrical force. The electrostatic method is used to space the grit evenly and to *orient* (position) the grit so that the grit's sharpest points stand up for good cutting. The electrostatic method will also firmly imbed (stick) the grit into the bonding material. See Fig. 9-13.

After the grit is stuck to the backing, the resin is allowed to dry. Then, another coat of resin is applied *on top,* to anchor the grit firmly to the backing material.

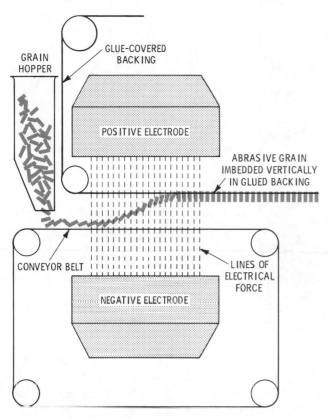

Fig. 9-13. The electrostatic process being used to apply grit to resin-covered backing material. (Courtesy of The Norton Company.)

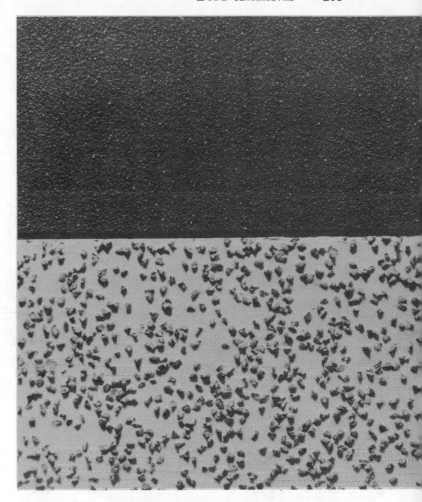

Fig. 9-14. Closed-coat surface (top) and open-coat surface (bottom). (Courtesy of The Norton Company.)

Disk Coats

The *coat* of a disk refers to how close together the pieces of grit are positioned. There are only two basic coat types: *open-coat* and *closed-coat.* The difference between the two is shown in Fig. 9-14. Closed-coat disks are made by allowing the backing and resin to be *completely* covered with grit. Open-coat disks, on the other hand, have abrasive grit material covering only about 60% of the backing surface.

The main reason for using a *closed-coat* disk instead of the same grit in an open-coat is to produce a slightly smoother cut. Since the entire surface area is covered with abrasive grit, there is less chance of the disk digging into the panel. The *open-coat* design, on the other hand, will help keep the grinding disk from clogging or loading up with grinding residue (old paint and metal). Open-coat disks will allow the re-moved material to drop out through the spaces between the grit. This keeps the disk from loading or gumming up. It also helps keep the disk cool during fast, heavy cutting. Open-coat disks, therefore, will usually have faster cutting action and longer life than would the same grit in a closed-coat disk being used under the same conditions.

Using Grinding Disks

Grinding disks are normally used on a *disk grinder.* Hardback 16-grit and 24-grit grinding disks are those most often used. The grinder being used in Fig. 9-15 has a 9-inch backing pad and a 9-inch, 24-grit closed-coat disk.

Grinding disks are used for removing paint, preparing metal for filler, grinding off welds or rust, and rough-working plastic filler. Fig. 9-15 shows a sander and disk being used to prepare

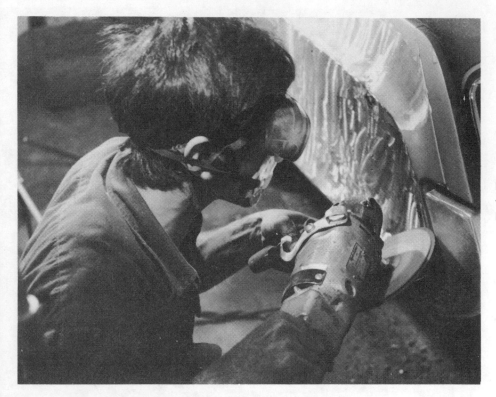

Fig. 9-15. Using a 24-grit disc to prepare a worked panel for body filler. (Courtesy of The Norton Company.)

rough metal for filler. Note that the repairman is using safety goggles and a dust mask for his own protection.

A 9-inch disk should *only* be used on disk sanders that produce less than 4000 RPM (revolutions per minute). A 7-inch grinding disk should only be used on grinders that produce less than 5500 RPM. When using a disk at a higher speed than is recommended, the grinder will heat up the surface of the metal being worked. This heat may cause the metal to warp, ruining any straightening that had been done to the metal. Also, too much speed may hurt the body man using the grinder. Part of the disk might break off at high speed, causing injury.

SANDPAPER

Sandpaper is a body shop material like a grinding disk. This is because both disks and sandpaper have grit, cement, and backing. Some sandpaper is made to be used for either *hand* sanding, *block* sanding, or *machine* sanding. Many sandpapers can be used either dry or with water (wet).

Originally, sandpaper is made in large sheets and is then cut into smaller sheets or disks of various sizes. Fig. 9-16 shows two sandpaper disks. The most common sandpaper disk sizes are 5-inch, 6-inch, and 8-inch. Disks are packed in boxes of 50 or 100 per box.

Fig. 9-16. Common sandpaper disks.

Sandpaper for auto body repair work is made with one of two types of grit materials: *silicon carbide* or *aluminum oxide*. Sandpaper that may be used wet or dry is made of silicon carbide. Sandpaper made of aluminum oxide must only be used *dry*. Fig. 9-17 shows an aluminum oxide sandpaper disk. The disk may be purchased with or without the center hole.

Grit Size

Fig. 9-18 shows a mound of graded abrasive grit *before* being applied to the paper backing. The grit size, of course, is the sandpaper's num-

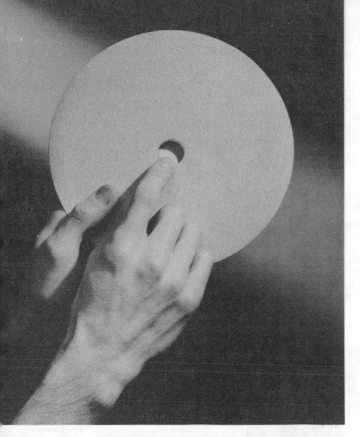

Fig. 9-17. An aluminum oxide sandpaper disk with a center hole for use on a large sander. Disks of this type are also available in smaller sizes and without the center hole. (Courtesy of The Norton Company.)

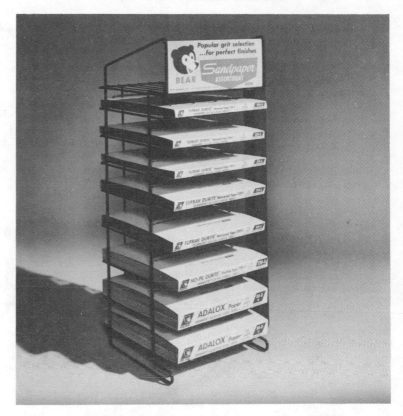

Fig. 9-19. A sandpaper selection rack stocked with some of the more popular auto body sandpapers. Note the grit sizes on the right side of the packages: 80, 220, 320, 400. Other grits are also available. (Courtesy of The Norton Company.)

ber. As with grinding disks, sandpaper grits are "riddled" through screens to determine the grit size. Then, the grit is applied to the paper backing.

Fig. 9-19 shows a display of several different grits of sandpaper in protective wrappers. There are many different grit sizes on the market; however, several basic grits are used in the auto repair business. The sandpaper grits most often used in auto body work range from a coarse 40-grit to the finest 600-grit.

Choosing a Grit Size—The grit size to use depends largely on the job. If sandpaper is

being used to rough-smooth plastic, as in Fig. 9-20, then a 40- or 80-grit paper would be used. An 80-grit paper would then be used on a speed file or rubber block for further smoothing or, with a disk sander, featheredging.

The most popular grits for final metal and plastic finishing are 150-grit and 220-grit. After using one of these two grits, the repaired area must be covered with primer-surfacer. This is

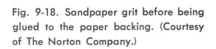

Fig. 9-18. Sandpaper grit before being glued to the paper backing. (Courtesy of The Norton Company.)

Fig. 9-20. Rough-smoothing plastic filler with 80-grit sandpaper mounted in a power sander. (Courtesy of The Norton Company.)

done to fill the sanding marks (sometimes called *sandscratches*) before the finish coat is applied.

Sanding old *enamel* paint is sometimes done for low-price work with 220-, 240-, and 280-grit sandpapers, if the paint does not need an undercoat before being refinished. To sand old enamel for quality work or old *lacquer* paint jobs that do not need an undercoat, 320- and 400-grit papers are used. Fine, 600-grit paper is used to sand fresh lacquer topcoats to help smooth and polish the topcoat before compounding.

Sandpaper Backing

Sandpaper grits may be cemented to different types of *backings*. The different backings are known as a sandpaper's weight. Different backing weights are chosen for different jobs due to their flexibility, or how they may be bent and twisted without breaking.

Sandpaper backings range from **A** weight to **E** weight. Note the weight labeling letters after the grit numbers on the packages in Fig. 9-19. **A** weight is the most flexible and will tear the easiest. If a tougher, more tear-resistant backing is needed, **C, D,** or **E** weights may be used.

Although they are stronger, they are also less flexible. **E** weight is usually the stiffest weight available.

Generally speaking, **A, B,** and **C** backings (weights) are more often used with finer grit papers. **D** and **E** backings, on the other hand, are more often used with coarse-grit papers. In Fig. 9-19, note that the top paper is a 400-A paper, whereas the bottom is an 80-D paper. The letter, of course, refers to the backing used.

Using Dry Sandpaper

Dry sandpaper is always used without water. This includes most rough-sanding work. For example, Fig. 9-21 shows a workman using a long vibrator-sander with 80-D dry sandpaper to smooth a plastic filler repair. This step could also be done with a hard rubber sanding *block* and dry, 80-D paper.

Dry sandpaper must not get wet because the cement used to hold the grit on dry sandpaper is animal glue. This glue, made from animal parts, should not be used with water because it will dissolve and allow the grit to come off the paper backing. Dry sandpaper is used for smoothing metal and plastic repairs and for sanding old finishes.

Fig. 9-21. Using 80-D dry sandpaper to work down a plastic filler repair. (Courtesy of The Norton Company.)

Although most dry sandpapers are coarse-grit, dry fine-grit papers are available. For example, Fig. 9-17 illustrates a dry, aluminum oxide sandpaper disk. This disk is a finer 220-grit, has a 6-inch diameter, and should be used on a disk sander with a ⅞-inch hole. A soft rubber backing pad, Fig. 9-22, is used with sandpaper disks.

Fine-grit dry sandpaper is also used in sheets as well as disks. Fig. 9-23 shows a repairman using dry, 220-grit sandpaper with a rubber sanding block to featheredge old paint and finish smoothing a plastic-filler repair. The rubber block can be used for either wet or dry sanding.

Using Wet Sandpaper

Wet sanding is usually done to a surface during final preparation before the color coat

Fig. 9-22. With dry sandpaper disks, a rubber backing pad such as this should be used. (Courtesy of 3M Company, Automotive Division.)

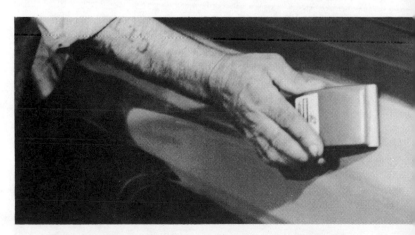

Fig. 9-23. Smoothing a plastic-filler repair and featheredging old paint with a sanding block and 220-grit dry sandpaper. (Courtesy of The Norton Company.)

is applied. Wet, "waterproof" sandpaper is made with silicon carbide grit and a resin binder. It is usually sold in fine grit sizes from 220 to 600.

Fig. 9-24, for example, shows a package of 220-grit waterproof sandpaper. Waterproof sandpaper is usually sold in packages of 50 sheets each. Each 50-sheet package is known

Fig. 9-24. Waterproof sandpaper is sold in "sleeves" of 50 sheets, as shown above. (Courtesy of The Norton Company.)

as a *sleeve* and each sheet in the sleeve is 9 × 11 inches in size. Normally, the sheets are cut and folded to get more use out of each sheet.

Waterproof sandpaper is usually used with water. See Fig. 9-25. Water acts as a *lubricant*

Fig. 9-25. Using waterproof paper with a sanding block to prepare primer-surfacer for a color coat.

for the sandpaper. It allows the paper to sand smoother by floating away the sanding dust, keeping the paper unclogged. Although waterproof paper may be used without water, this is not recommended. Without water, the paper is more likely to clog, causing a rougher surface.

CUTTING COMPOUND

Fig. 9-26 shows a shop-sized gallon can of cutting compound. This product may be known as *cutting* compound, *rubbing* compound, or simply *compound*. By whatever name, compound is a product used on the top coat (color

Fig. 9-26. Cutting (*rubbing*) compound.

coat) of a vehicle. The purpose of compound is to smooth and polish the topcoat by cutting off the high parts of the paint or removing the dull top film on an old finish. Compound is used on both new lacquer finishes and on any type of old finish that has aged and become dull due to exposure to rain, sun, and chemicals.

Types of Compound—There are several different types of compound available. These are graded according to the abrasive coarseness in the compound. Terms such as *hand-cut, fast-cut,* and *polish* are used to describe the qualities of different compounds. Many are used with water, the compound and water being mixed together before being used on the finish. Some compounds should not be used on enamel. In any case, the manufacturer's recommendations and directions must be used for the particular *line* (brand name) of compounds being used in a given shop.

How Compound Is Made—Cutting compound grit is made from *volcanic pumice,* a

Fig. 9-27. Compounding by hand.

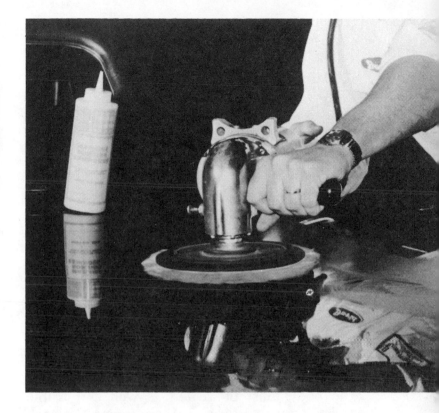

Fig. 9-28. The shine on this finish indicates that this paint man knows how to properly compound paint for a high gloss. (Courtesy of 3M Company, Automotive Division.)

type of natural glass. The pumice is first ground to a fine, dust-like grit. Then, the grit is added to the compound paste.

Using Compound

When compound is rubbed on paint, it cuts off the rough and dull top of the color, leaving a smooth and glossy topcoat. Fig. 9-27 shows a workman using compound by hand. The pumice used in hand cutting compound is coarser than the pumice used in machine cutting compound.

Most compounding done in a body shop is done by *machine*. Fig. 9-28 shows a polishing machine as it was positioned to machine compound the restored old finish in the picture. Machine compounding, or *wheeling*, is a job requiring experience, practice, and talent. The step-by-step procedure for using compound, both hand and machine, are fully explained in the later unit on paint rub-out and restoration.

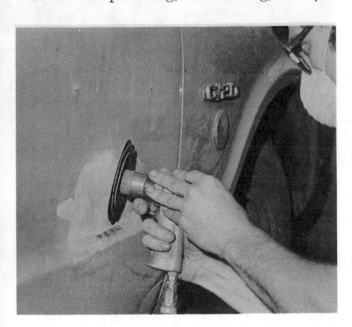

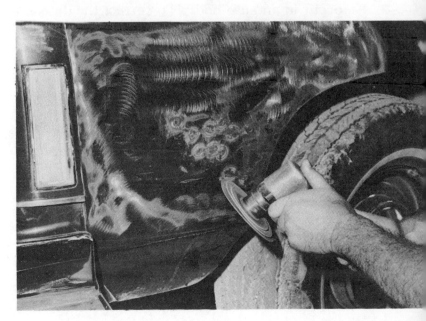

Body Leaks and Sealers

An automobile body must be built up of many different parts and panels. It must also be built to be waterproof, dustproof, and, to a degree, soundproof. Every outside panel of the body must be sealed as well as possible to keep out moisture, dust, and noise. For each space or joint between two pieces of metal, or between metal and other materials such as glass, there is a special sealer for that joint. Because there are many different types of joints, several different types of adhesives and sealers will be required in auto body work.

This unit will show different ways to check for, and correct, water or dust leaks that may occur in an auto body. To *correct* the different types of leaks, a repairman must know about different body sealer products. These will include *seam sealer*, *rubber seal*, *caulking compound*, and *undercoating*.

Spot-welded panels, for example, are sealed with a soft, flexible *seam sealer* that will correctly seal the panel joint for many years. Fig. 10-1 shows a tube of seam sealer being applied along a body seam to seal it against dust and water leaks. Seam sealers are usually used where two panels are spot welded together.

Rubber seal is used around door jams and trunk lid openings where the joint will be opened and closed. *Caulking compound* is normally used to stop water leaks around windshields or other *stationary* glass. The workman in Fig. 10-2 is using caulking compound to stop

a windshield leak. Sometimes, a small leak will develop in a window glass that is otherwise satisfactory. This type of small leak may often be stopped with a clear, liquid windshield sealer. This product is being used in Fig. 10-3.

Undercoating is used to seal the underside of an automobile body. In Fig. 10-4, an aerosol (pressurized) can of undercoating is being sprayed on a new underbody welded seam.

Fig. 10-1. Sealing a body seam against leaks with a *seam sealer*. (Courtesy of 3M Company, Automotive Division.)

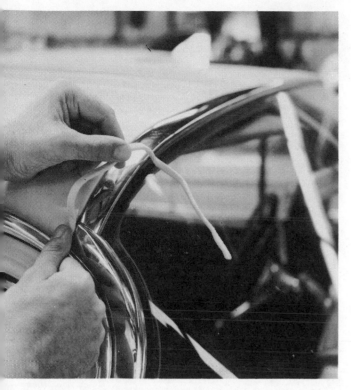

Fig. 10-2. Using caulking compound to seal a windshield leak. (Courtesy of 3M Company, Automotive Division.)

This will protect the seam and seal it from water and dust leaks. Undercoating also helps to deaden road noise, making the car quieter.

BODY LEAKS

Body leaks such as air, water, and dust, can be irritating problems for both the vehicle's

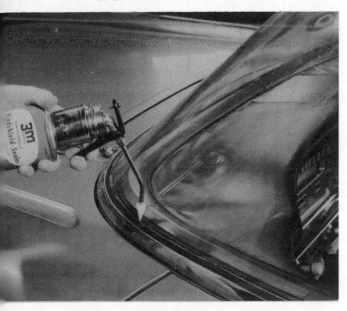

Fig. 10-3. Using windshield sealer to stop a small leak. (Courtesy of 3M Company, Automotive Division.)

owner and a service shop. Both new and used car dealers are generally given the responsibility of stopping any body leaks in the cars they have sold. The dealer's auto body shop or an independent shop will likely be called on to correct these problems.

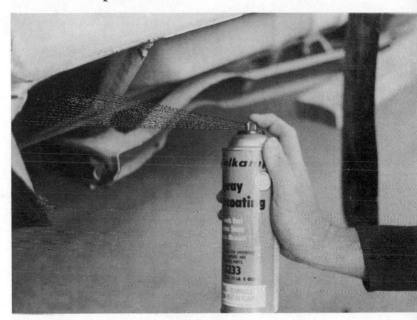

Fig. 10-4. Sealing and protecting an underbody seam with spray undercoating.

Often, water or dust leaks can cause serious damage if they are not found and corrected soon after they begin. Because of this, body men need to know when and where to look for these leaks and how to stop them quickly and easily.

LEAK TESTS

Several basic tests may be used to find common body leaks. When a body leak is found, it may be assumed that either air, dust, or water could leak in at that point.

Testing for body leaks should be done carefully so that no leaks are missed. A leak cannot be stopped unless it is *first* determined exactly where the leak occurs. For this reason, there are several basic tests used to find body leaks. These include the water test, chalk test, powder test, paper test, light test, and, finally, the air test. More than one test may need to be used to find the source of a difficult leak.

Water Test

When testing with water, the test should always begin at the *bottom* of the panel or area being tested. The water hose is then moved up the panel slowly, as shown in Fig. 10-5. A gentle stream of water should be used, and only one section should be tested at a time.

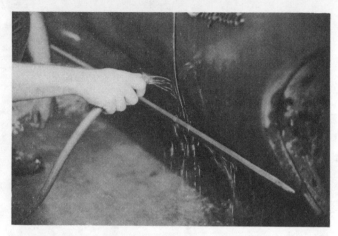

Fig. 10-5. Using low-pressure water to test for water leaks. If high-pressure water was used, it would splash all over and make it more difficult to locate the leak.

When making the *water test*, have a helper check from the inside and mark any places where even the slightest dampness comes through. The water test may be used to find water and dust leaks around the edges of doors, glasses, and trunk lids.

Chalk Test

The *chalk test* is used mainly at the rubber seals around the door and deck lid openings. All that is needed for this test is a stick of white chalk.

To make the test, first rub the chalk along the rubber seal, as is being done in Fig. 10-6. Then close the deck lid or door. Open the door or deck lid and check to see where the chalk has not been touched. If the chalk has not been touched, dust and water could enter the opening at that point.

Powder Test

The *powder test*, like the chalk test, is used along the rubber seals on door and trunk lid openings. To make this test, talcum powder

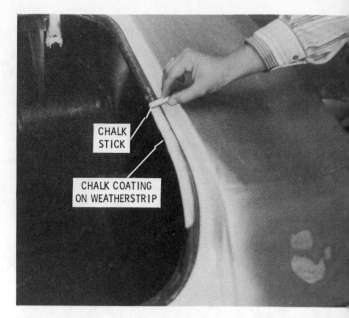

CHALK STICK

CHALK COATING ON WEATHERSTRIP

Fig. 10-6. Coating the weatherstrip with chalk before making water and dust leak tests.

(or other light powder) and a common rubber syringe (bottle pump) are needed.

First, put the powder in the rubber syringe. Close the car door or deck lid and use the syringe to pump the powder in the rubber seal area between the two metal panels. See Fig. 10-7. Then, *very slowly* open the deck lid or

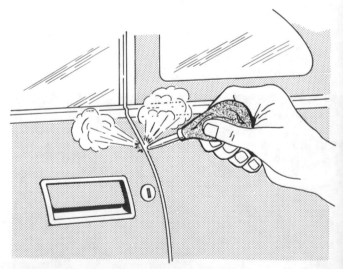

Fig. 10-7. To make the powder test, powder is blown into the closed joint with a syringe.

door so as not to disturb the powder. Look carefully to see if the powder line is broken anywhere that the powder went all the way *under* or around the rubber seal. Wherever this has happened, the rubber seal is not sealing correctly and a leak is probably present.

Paper Test

The *paper test* is used to see if the rubber seal around a door, deck lid, or window seals tight enough. To make the test, use a piece of paper about the size and shape of a dollar bill.

Place the paper strip in the joint against the rubber seal and hold it in place while closing the door, window, or deck lid. See Fig. 10-8. Then, slowly pull the paper out. If the rubber seal is tight enough, the paper will have a good drag when pulled out of the closed joint. If the paper pulls out easily (or falls out), the rubber seal is not sealing tight enough. Either the joint needs adjusting or the seal needs to be replaced.

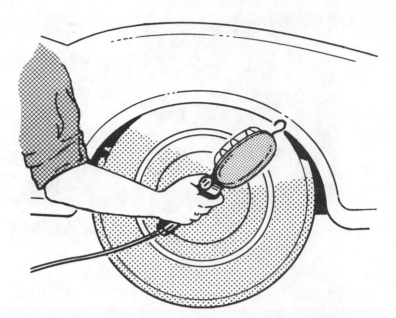

Fig. 10-9. Positioning a trouble light before going inside the trunk to check for leaks.

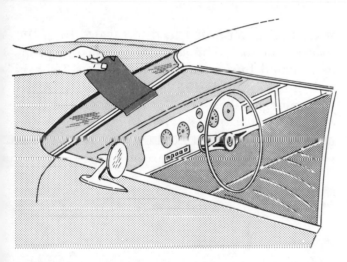

Fig. 10-8. To test for tight seals and joints, the *paper test* may be used.

Light Test

The *light test* is easy to make. To make the test, you must use a bright flashlight or shop trouble light.

First, place the light where the leak is suspected, as in Fig. 10-9. Leave the light in place and then check for light on the *other* side of the area; for example, inside the trunk. When the light shows through, a leak is present and water and dust will probably enter.

Air Test

The *air test* is also known as the "sonic test." This test, along with the paper test, is often used for checking high-speed wind noises (air leaks) as well as water and dust leaks. However, moisture and dust can enter wherever air can enter. The air (sonic) test is especially helpful when trying to locate small leaks around windows and doors.

To make the air test, first close the vehicle tightly. Then turn the heater blower on to the "high" position. This will pressurize the inside of the vehicle, since air will be trying to get out. With the blower on, get out of the vehicle and check for escaping air by feeling along the vents, doors, and openings. When a leak is found, mark it with masking tape or chalk. Then, continue checking until the entire car has been checked. Often, there is more than one leak.

SOURCES OF BODY LEAKS

There are two major types of body leaks: *dust* and *water*. Any body *air* leak may also let in dust and water, depending on where the air leak is located.

Generally speaking, water and dust leaks are more common in certain body areas. Fig. 10-10 shows where each type of leak usually happens most frequently. In the upper part of a vehicle, water leaks are more common. Dust leaks, on

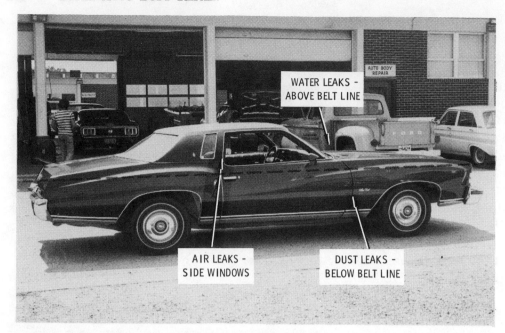

WATER LEAKS -
ABOVE BELT LINE

AIR LEAKS -
SIDE WINDOWS

DUST LEAKS -
BELOW BELT LINE

Fig. 10-10. Areas where different types of leaks usually occur.

the other hand, are more often located around the bottom (lower section) of the vehicle's body.

Upper Body Leaks

Leaks that cause owners the most problems are normally in the windshield and back glass areas, around the upper doors, and around the deck lid opening. Since these upper parts of the vehicle are more exposed to rain, water leaks are more likely to happen in this area.

Upper Door Glass Leaks—The various joints in the upper part of the door may leak if the area is not properly fitted. These areas include where the door and door glass meet or where the door glass and the roof meet. Fig. 10-11 shows a typical door glass leak.

There are four major causes of water leaks above the belt line in the upper door glass area. These include:

1. Doors that are not properly fitted.
2. Sealer that does not cover the seams or joints around the nearby metal panels.
3. Space around the glass due to improper adjustment.
4. Damaged weather stripping.

Drip Rail Leaks—The drip rail is the *uppermost* place that is likely to leak. It is very susceptible to leaks because the roof panel and the drip rail are spot-welded together, forming a

seam that is supposed to drain water from the sides of the roof. This seam, then, must be properly sealed to prevent leaks. Fig. 10-12 shows a drip rail being tested for leaks.

The drip rail is usually welded to the door opening *pillow plate*. The pillow plate is the metal body part that is above the door and is

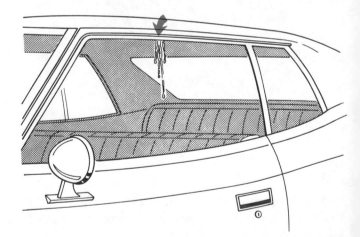

Fig. 10-11. Typical upper door glass leak.

part of the door jamb. The drip rail runs from the front of the roof to the rear, keeping water that runs off the roof from dripping on passengers when they enter or leave the vehicle. It catches the water and channels it to either the front or rear of the vehicle.

At times, a leak may occur between the drip rail and the pillow plate over the door. The pil-

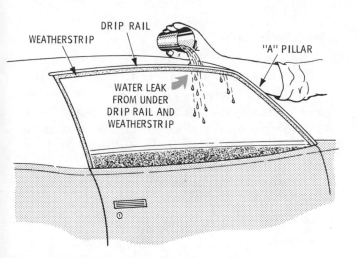

Fig. 10-12. Testing a drip rail seam for leaks.

Fig. 10-13. Sealing small leaks along the drip rail.

low plate and the drip rail are spot welded about every ¾-inch along the sides of the roof. If there is a break anywhere in the sealer used in this seam, a leak can occur. If this happens, water draining along the rail cannot get out of the pillow plate. Then, the water will be transferred to either the front (at the windshield pillow post) or back, behind the quarter panel.

When moisture appears on the floor mat near the front of the front door or at the rear of the back door, a thorough check of the drip rail seam must be made. Water may leak in at the middle of the drip rail seam and travel along the pillow plate *inside* the body, yet above the door opening. This may cause the leak to appear at the front, middle, or rear door jam post, or back in the quarter panel area. This will then appear as a leak in the area where the floor is wet.

To seal holes along the drip rail, check closely along the rail to find the opening causing the leak. Remember, the opening may be at some distance from where the moisture appears in the car. Then, seal the opening with a clear sealer or with seam sealer the same color of the car. This will eliminate the need for repainting the area around the hole. Fig. 10-13 shows a drip rail hole being sealed with seam sealer.

Stationary Glass Leaks—Most modern windshields (front glass) or backlights (rear glass) are held in place with a gum-like sealer. They usually have a finishing (reveal) molding around the edge of the glass for appearance. These moldings are held in place with spring-type clips. The clips are often held in place with metal nails or sheet metal screws. Water can then leak in around these fasteners if they are not properly sealed. For this reason, fasteners should be sealed with caulking compound when they are installed. The compound should be placed on the fastener *before* it is driven or screwed into place.

To check for windshield leaks, first run water along the *bottom* of the windshield, as in Fig. 10-14. Have a helper inside looking for leaks. If the leak does not appear, slowly run the water *up* each side of the windshield (the pillow rails) and then *across* the top of the windshield until the leak is discovered.

When the leak appears, mark the spot and finish checking the entire windshield. Go completely around the windshield or glass area,

Fig. 10-14. When checking a windshield for leaks, always start at the bottom, work *up* the sides, and then across the top.

because there is often more than one leak. Finally, repair any leaks found as follows:

1. Place a protective cover over the working area in front of and behind the windshield.
2. Remove all the moldings and the wiper blade arms. Use a molding removal tool, Fig. 10-15. Fig. 10-16 shows how this tool is used.

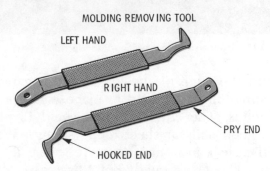

Fig. 10-15. Types of window molding removal tools.

3. Using soap and water, clean around the area where the leak is marked. Clean well beyond the leak area.
4. Trim away any old cement and sealer around the leak.
5. Reseal the complete area with windshield sealer or caulking compound.
6. Check the repair with water *before* replacing the moldings and wiper blades.
7. Replace the moldings and wiper blade arms.
8. Clean the entire work area as needed.

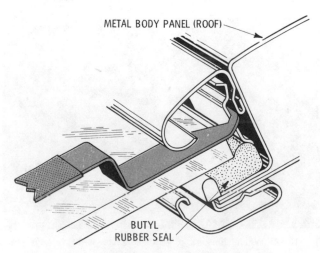

Fig. 10-16. Using a window molding removal tool.

Lower Body Leaks

The lower body section of a vehicle, below the belt line, is more subject to *dust* leaks than is the upper section. This is because the vehicle's wheels stir up dust from dusty roads. As a vehicle moves along, it creates a *vacuum*. This vacuum will then help pull any dust and water into the vehicle.

The lower sections where leaks are most frequently found include the:

1. Underbody Welded Seams.
2. Trunk (Deck Lid) Joints.
3. Quarter Panel Joints.
4. Moldings.
5. Lower Door Openings.

Underbody Seam Leaks—There are several seams in a vehicle's underbody area. Fig. 10-17, for example, shows the location of three seams on a typical vehicle.

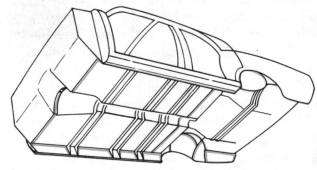

Fig. 10-17. Typical locations of different underbody seams.

The most common cause of underbody seam leaks is an open place in one of the seams shown in Fig. 10-17. When the body is involved in a collision or an object strikes the underbody, sealer can be knocked off a seam. This may cause dust and moisture leaks at the seam. Carefully *looking* at the seams will reveal the area where sealer is missing.

To repair underbody leaks, first examine the underbody carefully to locate the leak. Then, clean the area with a wire brush. When the basic dirt, broken sealer and undercoat have been removed, clean the area with a cleaning solvent such as lacquer thinner. Finally, replace the seam sealer with the caulking gun and then undercoat the area.

Trunk Leaks—Trunk leaks happen most often from rust-out in the area directly under the rear glass. Here, moisture gets trapped under the reveal molding at the edge of the rear glass and stays there until the metal under the molding rusts through. Fig. 10-18 shows a rusted-through area beneath a rear glass reveal molding. This hole, of course, causes water to leak into the trunk.

Fig. 10-18. When water is trapped under the rear glass molding edge, it may rust holes through the bottom of the rear window. This will allow water to enter the trunk.

When moisture or dust appears in the trunk of a vehicle, climb in the trunk and check the area along the bottom of the rear window. If water or dust is entering here, rust or dust will appear on the *underside* of the panel. Repairing this type of damage is discussed in the chapter on rust-out.

There are several other places where dust and water may leak into the trunk: around the taillights, the wheel housing *flanges* (the area where the inside wheel housing panel and the quarter panel meet), the rubber deck lid seals, and around any molding screws or clip holes. Fig. 10-19 shows several of these likely trunk leak locations. Fig. 10-20 shows a twisted rubber seal which could cause a leak in the trunk. This could be easily repaired by cementing the seal in place with trim or rubber cement.

Fig. 10-19. Areas where other trunk leaks may occur.

Quarter Panel Joint Leaks—Quarter panel leaks are usually found in one of two places:

1. At the seam where the quarter panel and wheel housing panel are spot welded together and sealed, or;

Fig. 10-20. A rubber seal that has become twisted over a period of time. This may cause a trunk leak.

2. At the lower seam where the quarter panel and floor pan are welded together.

Fig. 10-21 shows a repairman testing for leaks at the seam where the quarter panel and floor pan are welded together. To stop any quarter panel joint leaks in this area, clean and reseal the opening with seam sealer and undercoat.

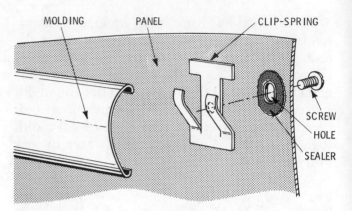

Fig. 10-22. Sealer must be used around the screw holes that are needed to install molding clips.

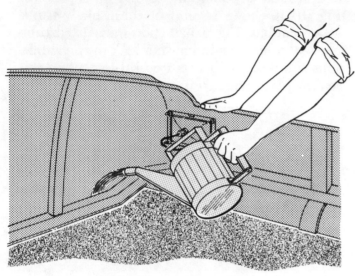

Fig. 10-21. Pouring water in a quarter panel joint to test for leaks. Some drainage here is OK, excessive leaks and holes are not. (Courtesy of Ford Customer Service Division.)

Molding Leaks—Almost all vehicles have some moldings. All moldings are attached with some type of clip. If the *holes* that the clip-springs or screws go through are not properly sealed with caulking compound, water and dust may enter the car body around the spring or screw.

To repair molding leaks, reseal the clip-spring, screw, or screw hole with caulking compound. Fig. 10-22 shows how a molding leak may be stopped by resealing the screw hole for the clip-spring screw. See Fig. 10-22.

Door Opening Leaks—There are many places around a door where water and dust may leak into any vehicle. To check for leaks at a door opening, use the water test shown earlier in Fig. 10-5. Start at the bottom of the door, as with a window test. Then work up each side and, finally, check the top edge of the door. Then, check the window glass as well as the door. Have a helper inside the vehicle looking

for any water leaks. When leaks appear, mark the spot and continue checking the entire door.

When the water test is completed, check the rubber seal (weatherstrip) to see if it is cracked, cut, worn, or twisted anywhere near the leak. If it is twisted or sagging, it should be recemented with weatherstrip adhesive. See Fig. 10-23. If the weatherstrip is damaged, replace the entire piece of weatherstrip with new material. Finally, if repairing the weatherstrip placement or condition does not stop the leak, the door or window must be realigned. This type of repair is discussed in the units on body panel aligning and on glass work.

Using Undercoating—Undercoating sealer is a thick, black, oily material. It is usually applied on only the *outside* of the underbody. It is used to seal underbody parts such as the wheel housing, flooring, frame, and the outside of the gas tank. Undercoating is useful because it pro-

Fig. 10-23. Cementing a rubber molding to the backside of a door frame to repair an upper door leak.

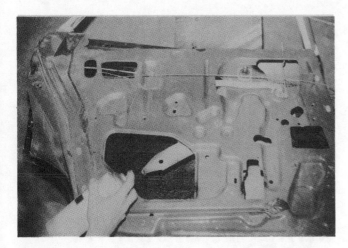

Fig. 10-24. Undercoating the inside of a replacement door to protect against rust and to help deaden noise.

high-quality product that will stay flexible and not crack over long periods of time. Undercoat should be applied on small repair areas such as places in the underbody where repairs were made or seam sealer was applied to repair a leak. Using an aerosol (spray) can of undercoat is the easiest method for undercoating these small repair areas.

Undercoating is also used during certain replacement panel repairs. For example, when a quarter panel is replaced, the underside of the quarter panel and the wheel housing should be given a thorough coat of undercoating. Welded joints on replacement panels should be sealed with undercoating after seam sealer has been applied to the joint. This will help prevent rust and deaden road noises on the part.

Replacement door panels (Fig. 10-24) are sprayed on the inside with undercoat to deaden the metal's sound. This is done so that the door will close with a secure "thunk" and sound tight.

vides insulation that helps keep moisture and noise from underneath the car. It also helps seal the seam joints on the underbody parts.

To properly undercoat a vehicle or replacement parts, the undercoating material must be applied *evenly*. The undercoat itself must be a

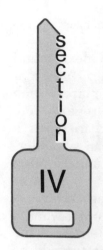
Using Heat to Work Metal

Unit 11

Oxy-Acetylene Welding Equipment

Many times, auto body repairs will need *heat* to be completed. Heat will be needed to soften a vehicle's metal for welding, bending, and many other jobs that may be necessary. To supply the high heat needed for these jobs, *welding equipment* is used.

The type of welding equipment most frequently used in an auto body shop is known as *oxy-acetylene* welding. This welding process creates heat from an *acetylene* flame burning in pure *oxygen*. A typical body shop oxy-acetylene welding outfit is shown in Fig. 11-1. Common jobs using the acetylene welding process include welding or brazing two pieces of thin sheet metal, Fig. 11-2, and cutting body panels for removal, Fig. 11-3.

The oxygen and acetylene gases used for the oxy-acetylene process are compressed and stored in tall, round tanks called *cylinders*. The gases are held under great pressure in these tanks, the hoses, and other parts of the system. Oxy-acetylene welding tanks and equipment are designed to contain these high-pressure gases so that they can be used under safe, controlled conditions.

Safety—Even though welding equipment today is very safe, body men *must* keep in mind that very high heat and very hot flames will be present during *any* oxy-acetylene welding process. Also, there is always the possibility of gas leaks when setting up and using oxy-acetylene equipment. The combination of heat, flames,

and leaks is dangerous and may cause an explosion or a fire. For this reason, body men should be especially careful when checking the connections of all welding equipment and all the time the equipment is in use. A fire extin-

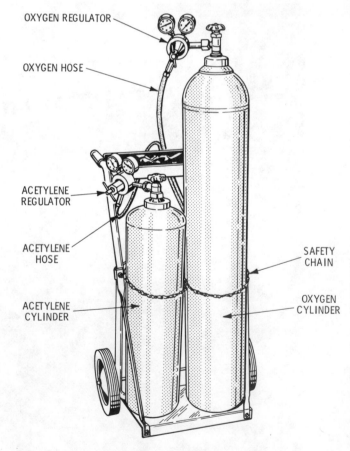

Fig. 11-1. A typical oxy-acetylene welding outfit.

Fig. 11-2. Welding thin sheet metal parts with an oxy-acetylene torch. (Courtesy of Harris Calorific Division.)

guisher, Fig. 11-4, should be "standard equipment" on or near every welding cart.

This unit will describe the different pieces of equipment needed for oxy-acetylene welding and cutting. Also discussed will be how the equipment should be set up for safe operation. Later units will discuss the correct operation

Fig. 11-3. Cutting an auto body panel with an oxy-acetylene cutting torch.

Fig. 11-4. A safe welding cart will have a fire extinguisher installed on the cart.

and procedures for using the equipment set up in this unit.

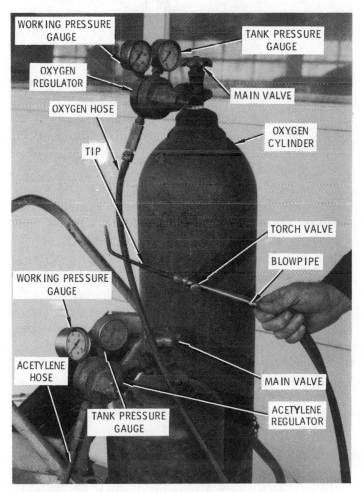

Fig. 11-5. Parts of a basic oxy-acetylene welding outfit.

Fig. 11-5 shows the 5 major parts of a basic oxy-acetylene welding outfit:

1. The oxygen and acetylene cylinders.
2. The portable carrier cart.
3. The regulators.
4. The hoses.
5. The torch blowpipe and tip.

These major parts must be examined and set up carefully, using *all* the necessary safety precautions, before the equipment may be used. The following sections explain the *function* of each major part, any *accessory equipment* used with the part, and the correct *procedure* to set up the equipment using each of the parts.

GAS CYLINDERS

Fig. 11-6 shows a typical *oxygen* cylinder. When the cylinder is full, the inside walls may be holding over 2000 pounds (1 ton) of pressure per square inch (psi). Oxygen cylinders are made of thick, high-carbon steel; a government standard. Oxygen cylinders are painted either yellow or green for easy identification.

In Fig. 11-7 is a typical *acetylene* cylinder. This cylinder must be especially designed to store a liquid known as *acetone*. The liquid acetone gives off acetylene gas.

The acetylene gas pressure inside the cylinder may be as high as 250 psi (pounds per square inch). Acetylene cylinders are not hollow, as are oxygen cylinders. Instead, acetylene cylinders are filled with *porous* (contains holes) materials such as asbestos or charcoal in a wet, cement-like mixture. When the cylinder is made, the cylinder is *baked* with these materials inside. This baking causes the materials to form a porous, sponge-like mass.

When acetylene cylinders are filled, the acetone already inside the "empty" cylinders is saturated with the acetylene. The acetone absorbs the acetylene gas and keeps it stable. This helps prevent any high-pressure pockets of acetylene from forming in the tank. Acetylene cylinders should always be stored upright to help avoid any unequal pressure distribution.

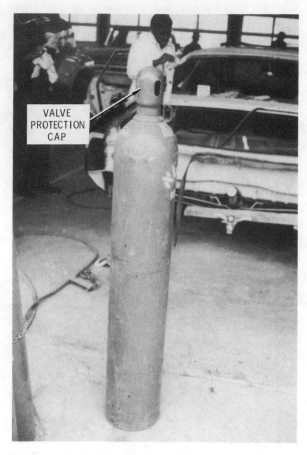

Fig. 11-6. An oxygen cylinder with the valve cap installed.

Acetylene cylinders have one or more *safety valves* on the ends, one is usually near the main valve, Figs. 11-8 and 9. These valves are installed in case fire, upset, or other trouble should cause the cylinder pressure inside the cylinder to go too high. In that case, the valves will automatically open to release the gas.

Acetylene cylinders are usually painted either red or black, with black the more common color. Both oxygen and acetylene cylinders should be firmly chained or otherwise attached to a portable carrier cart, discussed later, when they are to be moved.

Valve Protection Caps

Both oxygen and acetylene cylinders are made with safety caps to protect the cylinder valves on top of the cylinders when the cylinders are stored or shipped. These caps, Figs. 11-6, 7, and 8, will help protect the cylinder valve from breakage if the cylinder falls over. Valve protection safety caps must not be re-

Fig. 11-7. An acetylene cylinder with the valve cap installed.

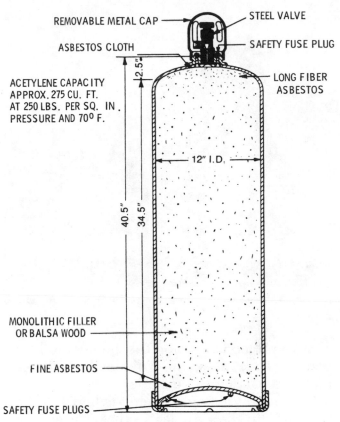

Fig. 11-8. Cutaway view of an acetylene cylinder.

moved before the cylinder is safely chained to a portable carrier cart. Fig. 11-10 shows a body man unscrewing a cap before attaching a regulator.

Carrier Cart

Fig. 11-1 showed an oxy-acetylene outfit mounted on, and chained to, a carrier cart. The carrier cart is a type of two-wheel *truck*. The cart is used to move the cylinders, welding equipment, and tools from place to place in the shop.

A typical cart is made up of a metal frame, a safety chain, two wheels, and an axle for the wheels. A safety chain on the welding cart (Fig. 11-11) is used to hold the cylinders securely on the cart. The chain must be safety fastened *all* the time. The chain may be fastened by slots, hooks, or nuts and bolts. In Fig. 11-12, a body man is chaining a replacement cylinder to the welding cart.

Changing Cylinders

When a cylinder on the cart is empty, it must be replaced. To do this, first be sure to fasten

Fig. 11-9. A typical acetylene cylinder safety valve, also known as a *fuse plug*.

Fig. 11-10. Removing the valve protection (safety) cap from a gas cylinder.

a valve protection cap on the cylinder to be replaced. Then, move the cylinder from the cart after unchaining the cylinder.

To move the replacement cylinder toward the cart, tip the cylinder so that it is on edge,

SLOTS TO HOLD CHAIN ENDS TO THE CART

Fig. 11-11. Many times, *slots* are used to hold the chain ends to the cart frame.

Fig. 11-12. Chaining a replacement tank to the cart.

as in Fig. 11-13. Then, carefully roll the cylinder to the welding cart. Finally, attach the chain around the cylinder to the cart frame.

Caution must always be used when moving a cylinder. Sudden movements might cause friction and a spark that could ignite the gas from a leaking acetylene cylinder. On the other hand, sudden pressure release (such as from a broken-off valve) can turn the oxygen cylinder into an uncontrolled missile. With so much pressure in an oxygen cylinder, it can break through concrete walls and cause injury and death if the valve is broken off.

Fig. 11-13. The correct method of rolling a gas cylinder from one place to another.

Clearing the Cylinder Valve

After the cylinder has been installed on the welding cart, fasten the safety chain. When the tank is securely held with the chain, the cap may now be removed. To remove the cap, simply unscrew it in a counterclockwise direction.

After the cap is removed, the cylinder valve may be "cracked" to blow out any dust or dirt in the valve opening and threads where the regulator will be attached. To "crack" the valve, grasp the cylinder valve handle, as is being done in Fig. 11-14. Quickly open and close the valve. This is done by first turning the handle counter-clockwise, and then clockwise until it is closed.

"Cracking" the valve is done to allow the escaping gas to blow any dirt out of the valve opening. Dirt or other foreign matter might get into the regulator and later cause serious damage or trouble. After clearing the valve openings, the regulators may be attached.

Fig. 11-14. "Cracking" the cylinder valve.

REGULATORS

Figs. 11-15 and 11-16 shows the *regulators* used in oxy-acetylene welding. One regulator (Fig. 11-15) is used for the *oxygen* cylinder gas, whereas a different regulator (Fig. 11-16) is used for the acetylene cylinder gas. Oxygen regulators may be color-coded *green* for easy identification. Acetylene regulators, on the other hand, are often color coded *red*.

Regulators control the *pressure* of the welding gases leaving the cylinders and going through the hoses to the welding torch. As the regulator adjusting handle is turned (Fig. 11-17), the *outlet* pressure gauge shows the gas pressure of the gas leaving the regulator. The readings are given in psi; *p*ounds per *s*quare *i*nch. (Actual pressure adjustment is explained in later units.)

The regulator *inlet* pressure gauges, Figs. 11-15 and 16, register how much total gas pressure still remains in the tank. Whenever the tank valve is opened, gas pressure will pass through the valve to the regulator. Then, the regulator inlet pressure gauge will report how much gas is left in the tank.

Installing Regulators

Each regulator is designed for use with either the oxygen or acetylene tank *only*. They are *not* interchangeable. The threads on the regulator connections and the cylinder outlets are designed so that the regulators cannot be accidentally connected to the wrong cylinder. This has been done as follows and is the standard for all manufacturers of welding equipment.

Oxygen Regulator—The threads on the connecting nut of an *oxygen* regulator are *right-hand* threads. These threads will fit the right-hand threads on the oxygen cylinder's outlet valve. Fig. 11-18 shows how to install and tighten the oxygen regulator. Use an open-end wrench and tighten the nut *clockwise*. Before the nut is completely tight, turn the regulator assembly so that the gauges are easy to read. Then, tighten the nut to a snug fit.

Acetylene Regulator—The threads on the acetylene regulator nut and the acetylene cylinder valve are *left-hand*, or "reverse," threads. The acetylene regulator should be connected, positioned, and tightened as was the oxygen valve, using an open-end wrench. However, the acetylene connections must be tightened in a *counter-clockwise* motion.

NOTE

Do not use oil or grease to lubricate regulator connection threads. These products

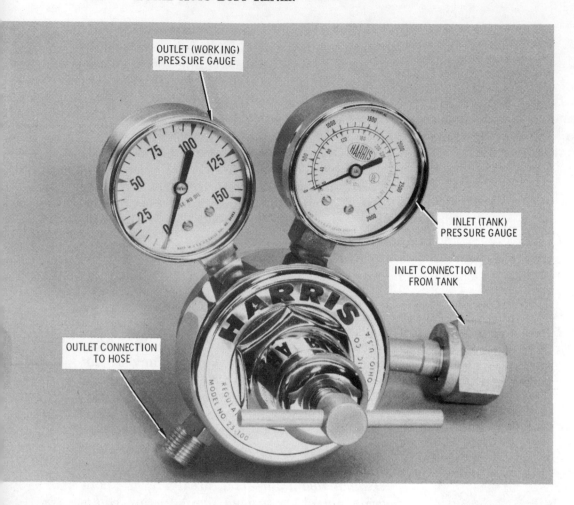

OUTLET (WORKING)
PRESSURE GAUGE

INLET (TANK)
PRESSURE GAUGE

INLET CONNECTION
FROM TANK

OUTLET CONNECTION
TO HOSE

Fig. 11-15. Oxygen regulator and gauges. (Courtesy of Harris Calorific Division.)

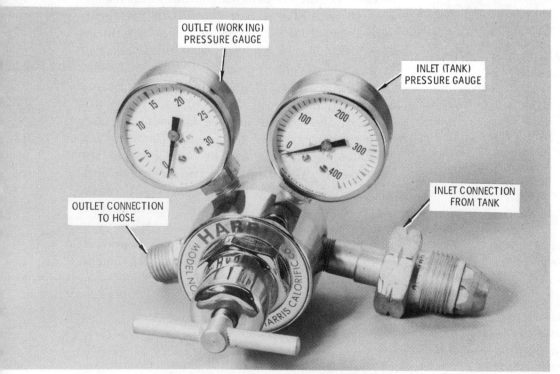

OUTLET (WORKING)
PRESSURE GAUGE

INLET (TANK)
PRESSURE GAUGE

INLET CONNECTION
FROM TANK

OUTLET CONNECTION
TO HOSE

Fig. 11-16. Acetylene regulator and gauges. (Courtesy of Harris Calorific Division.)

Fig. 11-17. Turning the regulator adjusting handle to regulate the outlet gas pressure to the hose and torch.

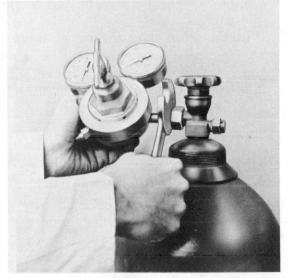

Fig. 11-18. Attaching the regulators. Here, the oxygen regulator is being installed. (Courtesy of Victor Equipment Co.)

could become highly explosive when combined with pure oxygen. This could cause an explosion when the torch is in use. No parts of an entire oxy-acetylene outfit should ever be lubricated.

HOSES

After the regulators are attached, the *hoses* may then be connected to the regulators, as

shown in Figs. 11-19 and 20. First, attach the *green* hose to the *oxygen* cylinder and tighten the hose connection snugly with an open-end wrench. See Fig. 11-20. Then, attach the other end of the green oxygen hose to the welding blowpipe and tighten it.

Fig. 11-19. Attaching the oxygen hose to the oxygen regulator outlet.

Fig. 11-20. Tightening the oxygen hose on the regulator outlet.

Repeat the above procedure to attach the *red* acetylene hose to the *acetylene* connection on the torch body. Remember that the acetylene hose connections and threads are left-hand, or "reverse." Finally, check both the oxygen and acetylene connections at the blowpipe to be certain that they are tight. See Fig. 11-21.

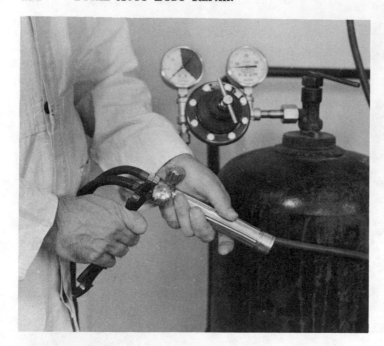

Fig. 11-21. Tightening the hose connections at the torch body, or *blowpipe*. (Courtesy of Victor Equipment Company.)

Purging the Hoses

After the regulators and hoses are connected, they need to be purged (cleaned out). To do this, the tank valves and regulators are opened up briefly to clear any dirt out of the regulators and hoses. Both the oxygen and acetylene regulator and hose assemblies are blown out (purged) in the same way.

To properly open the valves and regulators and purge the assemblies, follow these directions separately for each cylinder:

1. Loosen the regulator pressure valve by turning the valve handle *counter-clockwise* until it is loose and easy to turn. See Fig. 11-7. Doing this helps protect the regulator from possible damage when the cylinder valve is opened.
2. Open the cylinder valve. See Fig. 11-22. This allows the gas to leave the cylinder and enter the regulator. This will cause the cylinder pressure gauge to rise, indicating how much gas is in the tank. Open the *oxygen* cylinder valve *all the way*, but open the *acetylene* cylinder valve only ½ turn.
3. With the cylinder valve opened, *tighten* the regulator pressure valve on each tank by turning the valve handle *clockwise* until gas begins coming out of the hose.

4. With gas coming out of the hose, turn the *torch valve* off. This will shut off the gas flow from the end of the torch or blowpipe.
5. With the torch valve turned off, there will be gas pressure throughout the system. Use a mixture of soapy water over all the regulator and hose connections to check

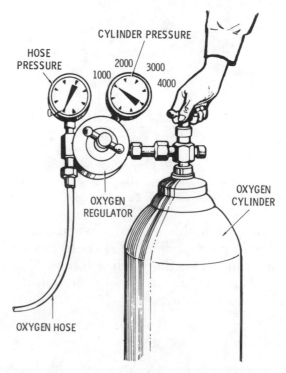

Fig. 11-22. Opening the cylinder valve to purge the hose.

for leaks. See Fig. 11-23. If any leaks are present, they will cause bubbles in the soapy solution. Then, reopen the torch valves.

6. Turn off the gas at the *cylinder* valve. This will cause gas to stop flowing through the regulator and hose.
7. Repeat step #1. Should any gas leak out of the cylinder valve, this will prevent it from flowing out through the regulator and hose.

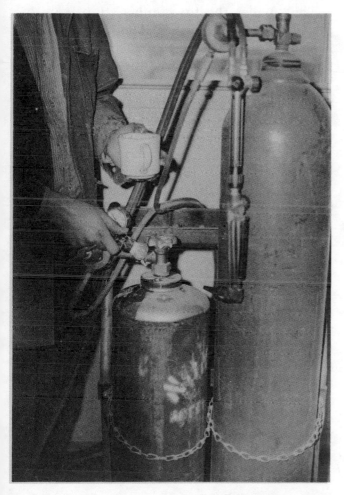

Fig. 11-23. Testing the gas connections for leaks by using a soapy mixture.

NOTE

Do not allow *acetylene* gas to escape into the air in an area where there is any danger of *fire*. Check the area carefully before testing or blowing out the equipment.

TORCH BLOWPIPES

To properly *mix* the oxygen and acetylene gases, a chamber is needed. This mixing takes place in a torch *blowpipe*.

Basically, oxy-acetylene equipment uses two types of torch blowpipes: *welding* blowpipes and *cutting* blowpipes. Figs. 11-24 and 25 show these two pieces of equipment. Welding torch blowpipes and tips are used for welding metal parts, whereas cutting torch blowpipes and tips are used to cut metal.

Torch blowpipes are normally made of copper, special steels, or aluminum. They are lightweight and often have ridges to keep the blowpipe from turning in the worker's hand. Either type of torch blowpipe is attached to its hose in the same way.

Both torch blowpipes have three main parts: the oxygen and acetylene control valves, the mixing chamber, and the tip. Figs. 11-24 and 25 show the location of these parts on each torch. In addition, a *cutting* torch will have a cutting oxygen control valve, discussed later.

The *control valves* are used to control the amounts of oxygen and acetylene that go from the hoses into the blowpipe's *mixing chamber*. The gases leave the mixing chamber as a mixture and then exit the torch at the *tip*, where they are burned in a high-temperature flame.

Either type of torch blowpipe may be used with one of several different tips. Figs. 11-26 and 27 show two typical *tip sets*. Welding torch tips, Fig. 11-26, are known as *welding* tips. Cutting torch tips, Fig. 11-27, are known as *cutting tips*. Detailed information on using the tips is given in later units.

Installing the Torch Blowpipes

Each torch blowpipe has two threaded inlets where both the hoses are attached. See Fig. 11-24. The *oxygen* hose fits the inlet with "normal" *right-hand* threads, whereas the *acetylene* hose fits the inlet threads that are "reverse" *left-hand*. Some torches have the letters "oxy" and "acet" stamped or cast near the inlets to help identify each inlet. Other models may have the inlet connections color-coded green (oxygen) and red (acetylene).

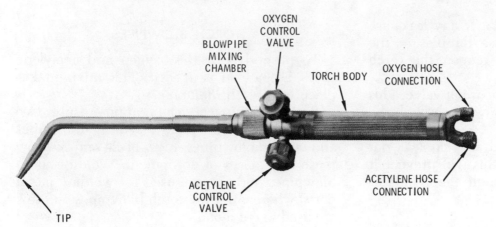

OXYGEN
CONTROL
VALVE
BLOWPIPE
MIXING
CHAMBER
TORCH BODY
OXYGEN HOSE
CONNECTION
ACETYLENE
CONTROL
VALVE
ACETYLENE HOSE
CONNECTION
TIP

Fig. 11-24. A typical welding torch, blowpipe, and tip assembly. (Courtesy of Harris Calorific Division.)

To install the torch blowpipe assemblies, tighten each hose connection onto the correct inlet. See Fig. 11-21. Use an open-end wrench to tighten the connections to a snug fit. The oxygen hose connection must be tightened *clockwise*, whereas the acetylene connection must be tightened *counter-clockwise*.

WELDING TIPS

When a new welding outfit is purchased, there are usually several tips included. These will include *welding tips* (Fig. 11-26), a *cutting attachment* (Fig. 11-28), and *cutting tips* (Fig. 11-27). Cutting tips may be used with either cutting attachments (Fig. 11-28) or standard cutting torches (Fig. 11-25). Torch tips and cutting attachments screw onto the torch blowpipe *hand tight only*.

Tip Size

Welding tips used for all work in a body shop are sized #1 through #8. The numbers normally used in the shop for welding thinner body sheet metal are #1, #2, and #3.

The smaller the tip number, the smaller is the tip opening, or *orifice*. The size of the orifice determines the size of the welding flame and the amount of heat that the flame produces.

Table 11-1 shows how the thickness of the metal being welded determines the welding tip size and the regulator gauge pressures needed. Metal thickness may also be denoted (described) by its *gauge number*. The *larger* the gauge number, the *thinner* the metal. For example, 16-gauge metal is about ⅟₁₆-inch thick. The regulator gauge pressures in the table show the amount of oxygen and acetylene pressure that is needed at the torch.

WELDING ACCESSORIES

To properly, safely, and successfully weld, several different *welding accessories* are needed. These will include the tools used to properly light and clean the torch. These tools are shown in Fig. 11-29. Additional tools and accessories will be needed to safely use the equipment and reduce the chance of injury while welding.

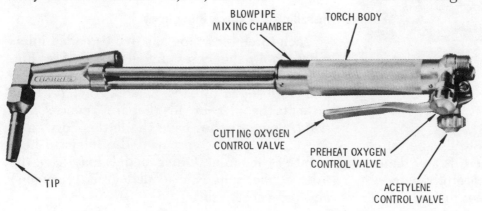

BLOWPIPE
MIXING CHAMBER
TORCH BODY
CUTTING OXYGEN
CONTROL VALVE
PREHEAT OXYGEN
CONTROL VALVE
ACETYLENE
CONTROL VALVE
TIP

Fig. 11-25. A typical cutting torch assembly. (Courtesy of Harris Calorific Division.)

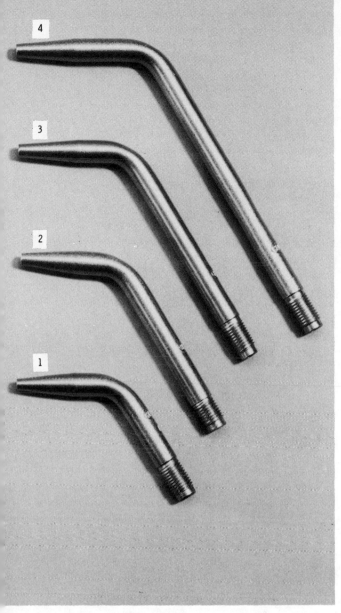

Fig. 11-26. Typical welding tips and their sizes. (Courtesy of Harris Calorific Division.)

Torch Lighter

In Fig. 11-29 is a torch *lighter* or *striker*. This striker is equipped so that the striker *flints* may be replaced. The flints (Fig. 11-29) are used

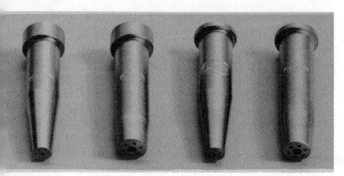

Fig. 11-27. Typical cutting torch tips. (Courtesy of Harris Calorific Division.)

to create the spark for lighting the torch. To light the torch, the lighter has a *cup* under the striker bar. This cup traps acetylene from the torch when the torch acetylene valve is opened. See Fig. 11-30. Squeezing the striker handle then causes a spark, easily lighting the acetylene gas.

NOTE

Matches and cigarette lighters should not be used to light an oxy-acetylene torch. If the torch is lit with these open flames, it can easily cause badly burned hands.

Tip Cleaners

Tip cleaners are used when a welding tip becomes dirty or contaminated, causing a poor welding flame. Most sets of tip cleaners have

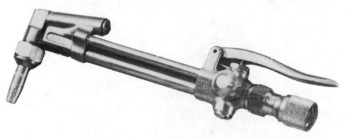

Fig. 11-28. A typical cutting attachment. This unit fits onto a standard welding torch body after the welding torch tip has been removed. (Courtesy of Harris Calorific Division.)

a *file* to smooth and shape worn or damaged welding tips. In Fig. 11-29 are two sets of slightly different tip cleaners and a file among the other tools.

Some tip cleaners have grooved surfaces, whereas others are made of two pieces of twisted wire. Tip cleaners are moved up and down the tip to scrape away soot or dirt, as in Fig. 11-31. A different size tip cleaner should be used for each size of welding tip. Using too large or small a tip cleaner could fail to clean the tip properly or damage the tip.

Frequently using tip cleaners is a safety precaution. If a tip becomes partly blocked by dirt or soot, it can cause a problem known as *flashback*. This happens when the flame backs up, *inside* the torch or tip. This can cause a dangerous explosion.

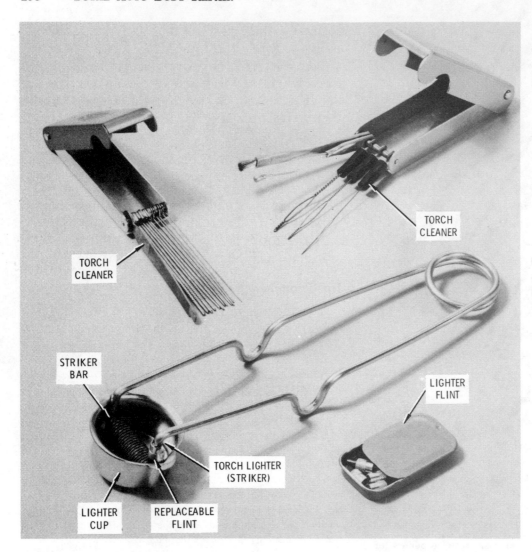

TORCH CLEANER

TORCH CLEANER

STRIKER BAR

LIGHTER FLINT

TORCH LIGHTER (STRIKER)

LIGHTER CUP

REPLACEABLE FLINT

Fig. 11-29. Tools used to light and clean the torch. (Courtesy of Harris Calorific Division.)

Table 11-1. Guide to Oxygen and Acetylene Pressures for Different Welding Jobs.

Tip No.	Thickness of Metal (inches)	Thickness of Metal (gauge)	Oxygen & Acetylene Pressure (psi)	Acetylene Flow (cu ft/hr)	Oxygen Flow (cu ft/hr)
00	$\frac{1}{64}$	28	1	0.1	0.1
0	$\frac{1}{32}$	22	1	0.4	0.4
1	$\frac{1}{16}$	16	1	1	1.1
2	$\frac{3}{32}$	13	2	2	2.2
3	$\frac{1}{8}$	11	3	8	8.8
4	$\frac{3}{16}$		4	17	18
5	$\frac{1}{4}$		5	25	27
6	$\frac{5}{16}$		6	34	37
7	$\frac{3}{8}$		7	43	47
8	$\frac{1}{2}$		8	52	57
9	$\frac{5}{8}$		9	59	64
10	$\frac{3}{4}$ up		10	67	73

1. Pressures and consumptions shown are approximately correct for both separable tips with appropriate mixers and for tip-mixer assemblies.
2. Gas pressures should be increased slightly for hose lengths greater than 25 feet.

Courtesy of Canadian Liquid Air

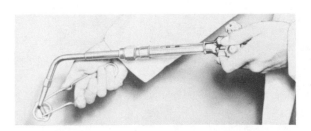

Fig. 11-30. Opening the torch acetylene valve to fill the striker cap with acetylene gas. (Courtesy of Victor Equipment Co.)

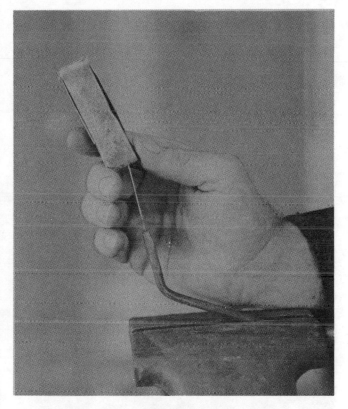

Fig. 11-31. Cleaning a torch tip. The tip cleaner must always be inserted *straight* into the tip and not moved on an angle.

Fig. 11-32. A safe welder uses welding gloves and goggles during a cutting job. (Courtesy of Harris Calorific Division.)

Safety Precautions

Safety is very important in the welding area. Safety precautions must always be followed when setting up a welding torch. Leaks, for example, can be a special problem around the acetylene regulator connections and hoses.

There are several pieces of safety equipment that should always be used during welding and cutting. *Safety goggles* and *leather gloves* (Fig. 11-32) protect a worker using the torch. Torch *lighters,* discussed above, provide a safe method to light the torch. Tip *cleaners,* also discussed earlier, keep the torch tip clean and free of dirt or soot. Finally, a good *fire extinguisher* will help control any trouble that might happen while using the torch.

Safety Goggles—Tinted *safety goggles,* like those being used in Fig. 11-32, should *always* be used when either welding or cutting. This is because the torch gives off ultraviolet rays that can cause eye damage. Goggle types and shade numbers are discussed in the Tool and Equipment units.

Gloves—Leather *gloves* should be used when working with a torch, especially during cutting. Sparks from molten metal can cause serious burns and gloves will help prevent these. Also, gloves will help prevent burns should you accidentally touch hot metal after welding or cutting. Safety equipment used in welding includes tinted safety goggles, gloves, torch lighters, and tip cleaners. Properly using this equipment helps prevent welding hazards and possible explosions.

Unit 12

Oxy-Acetylene Welding and Cutting

Welding is the process of joining two pieces of metal by applying heat and, sometimes, pressure. A common welding job on a mild steel frame is being done in Fig. 12-1. Oxy-acetylene welding is also known as *gas welding,* and, in some areas, *torch welding.* By whatever name, oxy-acetylene welding equipment may be moved from place to place easily, and, because of its flexible hoses, can reach almost any position.

Oxy-acetylene equipment may be used to weld, heat, and cut metal. Fig. 12-1 shows a welder using an oxy-acetylene torch to *weld* two pieces of metal, whereas Fig. 12-2 shows an oxy-acetylene cutting torch being used to *cut* metal. The main purpose of an oxy-acetylene welder in a *body* shop, though, is to weld and cut *thin* sheet metal that could not be easily welded with an arc welder. Oxy-acetylene welding equipment will be economical, safe, and do a good job on most metals *if* properly used. Its simplicity makes it easy to learn and not very expensive to use.

OXY-ACETYLENE WELDING PRINCIPLES

Auto body men must be good welders of thin sheet metal. Welding heat will melt thin sheet metal fast. If this heat is not carefully controlled, the metal will warp and cause extra work for the body man. [Generally speaking, it is harder to control the heat and keep the metal from warping on *low-crown* metal (panels with low or slight curves) than on *high-crown* metal. For example, door panels, quarter panels, and lower fender parts may be problem-causing, low-crown sheet metal areas. When welding on these panels, warpage will be harder to control.]

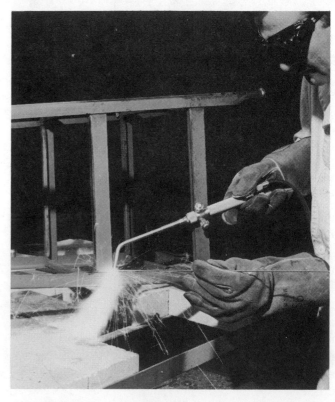

Fig. 12-1. An oxy-actylene outfit being used to weld metal. (Courtesy of Harris Calorific Division.)

200

Fig. 12-2. Using a cutting torch on mild steel framework. (Courtesy of Harris Calorific Division.)

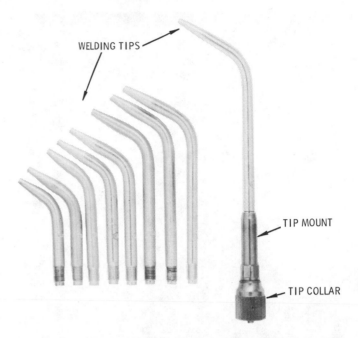

Fig. 12-3. Different welding tips are needed for different welding jobs. (Courtesy of Harris Calorific Division.)

Fig. 12-4. A common ⅛-inch welding rod.

To practice oxy-acetylene welding, the *thickness* of the metal being welded must be taken into account. The metal thickness will partly determine the tip and filler rod sizes needed. The gas pressures needed for practice are also determined by the thickness of the metal.

Tip Size—Most body shop welding is done on thin metal, so the torch welding tip and welding rod must be small. A #1, #2, or #3 tip is used for most auto body panel repair. Fig. 12-3 shows several sizes of welding tips and Fig. 12-4 shows a ⅛-inch welding rod. For most auto body work, the welding rod sizes normally used are ¹⁄₁₆-inch and ⅛-inch diameters. Tip and gas pressure recommendations for common metal thicknesses were shown in Table 11-1.

Regulator Settings—Generally speaking, the regulator handles and gauges on the oxygen and acetylene regulators should be adjusted to read the same pressures during common welding jobs, as in Table 11-1. The regulator pressure is set by turning the valve handle, as discussed earlier. Most of the light sheet metal welded in a body shop may be welded with 5 psi from each regulator.

There are exceptions to all rules. Welding is a skill that is handed down from one person to another or is learned by "trial and error." Not all good welders will use the same tip size and regulator pressures on the same thickness of metal. However, most better welders (or those trained in technical schools) will often use the recommendations shown in Table 11-1.

Lighting the Torch

The correct procedure for lighting the torch should always be followed. Common "shortcut" methods may be unsafe and should never be used. Setting up and lighting the torch will be quick, easy, and *safe* if the following directions are followed.

First, be sure the equipment is set up properly, as outlined earlier and shown in Fig. 12-5. Then, select the proper tip for the metal thickness being used and install the tip. Finally, open the oxygen and acetylene cylinder valves

Fig. 12-5. A properly set up welding outfit, ready to weld.

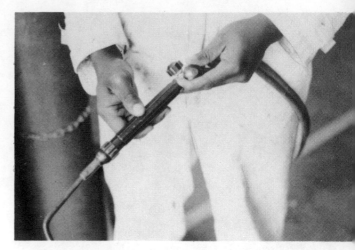

Fig. 12-6. Open the acetylene control valve slightly before lighting the torch.

and set the correct pressure readings on the regulator gauges.

Welding Goggles—Be sure to *put on welding goggles* before lighting the torch. Place the goggles over your forehead so they may be easily pulled down over your eyes when the torch is lit and welding is being done.

With goggles in place, open the torch acetylene valve from ⅛ to ¼ turn, as in Fig. 12-6. Then, hold the torch tip in the striker while making a spark by squeezing the striker. See Fig. 12-7. Be sure to use a friction lighter (striker) to light the torch, *not* a match or cigarette lighter. Lighting the torch can be dangerous if the proper tool is not used.

When the acetylene lights, it will burn with a bright, bushy-orange flame. This flame, Fig. 12-8, *looks* violent but is actually not hot enough for welding. To properly adjust this flame, first open the acetylene valve slightly until the flame "jumps" off the end of the tip

(Fig. 12-8), leaving an air gap. Then, *close* the acetylene valve slightly until the flame *just returns* to the tip, as in Fig. 12-9.

Next, *slowly* open the oxygen valve until the acetylene flame starts to "calm down," becoming smaller *and* hotter. Finally, the orange acetylene flame will become part of the sharply defined, intense blue inner cone of the *neutral flame*. See Fig. 12-10.

Flame Properties

A *neutral* oxy-acetylene welding flame may be used on almost all types of metal. It should not be used, however, for bright metal parts such as door handles, aluminum trim, or chrome bumpers. Because of the neutral flame's wide use, one of the more important steps in welding is correctly adjusting the control valves for a neutral flame.

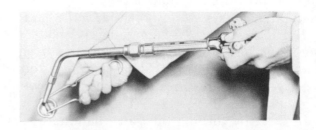

Fig. 12-7. Squeeze the striker (lighter) to light the pure acetylene coming out of the tip. (Courtesy of Victor Equipment Co.)

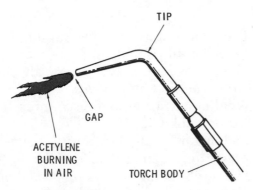

Fig. 12-8. Opening the acetylene valve too far will cause the flame to "jump" off the end of the tip.

Neutral Flame—The common *neutral* flame gets its name from the fact that it does *not* change the chemical composition of the metal melted. That is, it does not add either carbon or oxygen to the molten metal.

With the neutral flame, then, the *form* of the metal is changed from a solid to a liquid, but the chemical makeup stays the same. This is because the correct amounts of oxygen and acetylene are being burned in the neutral flame and there is no "extra" carbon (acetylene) or oxygen to enter the molten metal.

A correctly adjusted neutral flame will cause the metal to melt quickly so that the pieces of metal may be properly welded together. When the flame is too cool (too much acetylene), it will put unburned carbon into the molten metal. When this happens, the molten metal is *carbonized,* sometimes called carburized, and the metal pieces will not weld together properly. On the other hand, if there is too much *oxygen* in the flame, it will "oxidize" the metal.

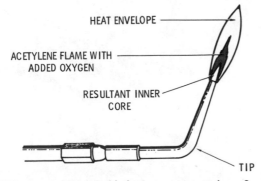

Fig. 12-9. As oxygen is added to a pure acetylene flame, the orange acetylene flame will begin to disappear into the bright blue inner cone of an oxy-acetylene flame.

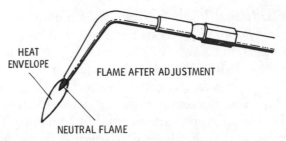

Fig. 12-10. As the oxygen valve is further opened, the acetylene flame completely disappears into the bright inner cone of the neutral flame shown here.

This may cause the weld to crack in the center because the weld metal will be too hard when it cools.

The *length* of the neutral flame's cone is measured and known as **X** length. For this reason, it is known as an **X** flame. The **X** neutral flame is easily identified. It does not have any acetylene feather on the inner flame, as shown in Fig. 12-10. It also has a smooth, round head on its inner flame and is fairly quiet when compared with the hissing sound of the oxidizing flame discussed later.

Other torch flames can be measured by comparing them with the neutral flame. The neutral flame, of course, is when the inner flame (or *cone*) is rounded as shown in Fig. 12-10. An *oxidizing* flame is present when more oxygen is added to a neutral flame and the inner cone becomes pointed and shorter, as in Fig. 12-11. An oxidizing flame is shorter than a neutral flame and produces a hissing sound not heard with a good neutral flame.

When *acetylene* is added to a neutral flame, it becomes a *carbonizing* flame. A carbonizing flame is present when a flame "feather" appears between the cone and the outer flame, as in Fig. 12-9. This feather indicates that excess acetylene is causing too much carbon in the flame. The feather varies from 2 to 3 times as long (**2X** or **3X**) as the inner cone.

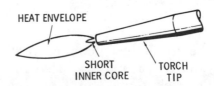

Fig. 12-11. An oxidizing flame is shorter than a neutral flame and will produce a hissing sound.

Oxidizing Flame—Fig. 12-11 shows an *oxidizing flame*. This is not a good welding flame. An oxidizing flame has too much oxygen in the flame, causing chemical changes in the molten metal as excess oxygen is added to the molten metal. This excess oxygen causes the puddle to boil, flame, and spark, making welding dangerous and difficult. An oxidizing flame has a violent hissing sound.

An oxidizing flame weakens the weld area by oxidizing the edges of the metal being welded. Many times, welding with an oxidizing flame may leave a hairline crack in the metal when the weld cools. Sometimes, a close inspection with a magnifying glass will show the small crack.

An oxidizing flame *does* have some good uses. For example, if thin sheet metal needs to be cut, an oxidizing flame may be used to cut the thin metal. This saves the time needed to change to a cutting tip. However, this type of cutting is not recommended for cutting thick metal or for a long cutting job.

Carbonizing Flame—Fig. 12-9 shows what a *carbonizing* flame looks like. This flame is also known as a *carburizing* flame and a *reducing* flame. By whatever name, this flame is produced when there is too much acetylene in the flame's mixture. This acetylene deposits excess carbon in the melted metal. This type of flame makes welding difficult because the flame is not as hot as is a neutral flame and, therefore, will not melt the metal as easily.

A carbonizing flame *is* used for some oxy-acetylene jobs. When brazing or soldering, for example, a slightly carbonizing flame may be used. When *brazing*, a flame with a feather 1 or 2 times (1X or 2X) longer than the neutral cone is used, depending on the thickness of the metal. Soldering is often done with a flame feather 3 times (3X) as long as the neutral flame cone.

Safety Review

When the torch has been properly set up and safely started, it may be used for practice welding. Practicing oxy-acetylene welding will be safe if at least six basic safety rules are followed. These include:

1. The connections of a welding outfit must never be lubricated.
2. The acetylene valve must always be turned *on first* and *off last*.
3. Welding must be done in an area free of fire or smoke.
4. Welding or torch work must be done with *goggles* protecting your eyes.
5. The torch should always be turned off immediately when it is not being used.
6. When you are finished welding, the cylinder valves must be closed.

BASIC OXY-ACETYLENE WELDING

After lighting the torch, the first step in any welding operation is to make a puddle of molten metal. Then, the torch may be used to melt puddles of molten metal across a piece of flat steel, known as *running the bead*. This is the most basic type of welding practice and is being done in Fig. 12-12.

When running the bead has been done successfully, welding *rod* can be added to the puddle for further practice. Welding rod is needed to give the weld bead the buildup necessary for a strong weld. This was being done earlier in Fig. 12-1. Fig. 12-13 shows the torch and rod positions necessary for practicing welding while adding welding rod.

Often, practice panels being welded need to be *tack welded* before practice. See Fig. 12-14.

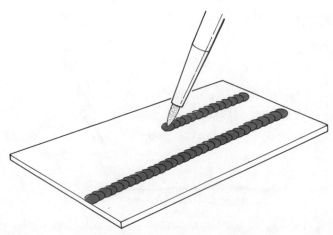

Fig. 12-12. The first, and easiest, form of practicing welds is known as *running the bead*, being practiced above.

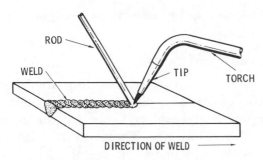

Fig. 12-13. Welding practice with a welding rod.

This is done *first* so that the practice pieces will remain in place while the bead is run.

Practice Flame—A *neutral flame* must always be used when practice welding, either with or without using added welding rod. A neutral flame will help keep the molten metal from

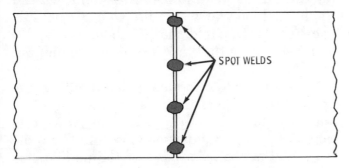

Fig. 12-14. To hold the practice pieces in position, they may be *tack welded* as shown.

popping and throwing hot metal during practice. During practice, the *tip* should be held in a position where the hot metal will not be blocking the tip. See Fig. 12-13. (The *carbonizing* flame is used for the brazing explained in another unit.)

Bead Running

The easiest oxy-acetylene welding technique to practice is known as *bead running*. The first step toward bead running is to be able to make and recognize a molten metal *puddle*. The puddle is the molten metal formed when the torch flame has melted the metal. Then, to practice, you must *guide* the puddle in the direction in which the metal is to be welded or the bead is to be run.

To form a puddle, hold the neutral flame *cone* about ⅟₁₆- to ¼-inch from the metal until the metal is melted and a bright orange puddle

is seen. Then, use a circular motion and slowly move up the panel to melt new metal. This will form beads of solid metal as the torch passes by, as shown in Fig. 12-12. This movement causes the molten metal to "run" in a straight line of beads, and is therefore known as bead running.

Adding Welding Rod—A very important part of bead running is adding *welding rod* to the bead. To do this, first form the puddle of molten metal as usual. Then, move the torch in a circular pattern over the puddle while slowly adding and melting filler rod. Tilt the torch back to about 45° above the metal being welded. The rod should be held in the opposite direction at about the same angle. See Fig. 12-15. (Although oxy-acetylene welding may be done without a rod, this may leave low and weak places in the bead being run.)

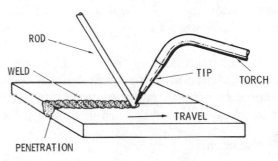

Fig. 12-15. Adding filler metal from a welding rod to the puddle.

Welding Two Pieces—When practice welding together *two* pieces of metal, there should be a space between the two pieces about as wide as the filler rod being used. See Fig. 12-16. For example, if a ⅟₁₆-inch rod is being used, there should be a ⅟₁₆-inch space (gap) between the two pieces of metal.

Troubles—During practice, if the torch pops and cracks even though the flame is neutral, *both* the oxygen and the acetylene valves should be opened more. This is because the flame is too cool, causing trouble when trying to melt the metal. When this happens, you may be tempted to push the cone too far into the molten metal. This will cause a pop, throwing molten metal out from the weld in a small explosion. This condition can cause a serious torch problem known as *flashback*.

A *flashback* happens when the flame "backs up" into the mixing chamber of the torch. There, the flame actually begins to burn *inside* the torch, instead of at the tip. This is very dangerous. When a flashback happens, the torch must be shut off *immediately*. This will

Fig. 12-16. When using a filler rod, thicker metals should be spaced as far apart along the joint as the filler rod is wide.

keep the tip from getting too hot. Tips are made of brass and become very hot quickly. Also, it will keep the flame from backing up into the hoses and possibly causing a serious explosion.

Torch Movement

When simple *bead running* with a filler rod has been mastered, additional practice will include different welding jobs and more experience in *torch movement*. When the metal has been melted and a puddle formed, for example, move the torch from side to side approximately ⅛-inch at a time to weld thin body sheet metal. Make the torch curve around the end of the weld and filler rod as it goes from side to side, similar to the letter **C**. While moving the flame from side to side, move forward along the weld line very slowly. Be sure that the *sides* of the weld bead overlap the sides of the panels being welded.

Some welders move the torch in a circular motion, rather than in a side-to-side, C-shape motion. The circular motion is also a good technique. Practice both methods of torch movement to determine the one that is best for you. If a method is comfortable and you are able to

make good welds with it, it is a good method for you to use.

Welding With Filler Rod

To practice fusing (welding together two pieces of metal), first have all the needed equipment and materials nearby, including the correct welding rod. Then, position and properly space the pieces of metal to be welded. Tack weld the pieces to prevent them from spreading apart while welding. Space the "tacks" about one inch apart.

With the pieces positioned and tacked, start welding from the left side of the tacked pieces. Bring the torch almost straight down on the end of the joint, heating the metal to form a puddle. As the puddle begins to form, tilt the torch back in the weld direction about 45°. See Fig. 12-13. Hold the tip about 1⁄16- to ¼-inch away from the work just after forming the puddle.

With the puddle formed, place the filler rod at the *front* edge of the puddle at about a 45° angle to the metal. Keep the flame in a position so that the puddle remains hot. The molten metal at the front edge of the puddle can be used to melt the filler rod.

Move the torch tip and filler rod back and forth so that the molten puddle and filler rod are together used to build up a weld bead down the weld joint. Remember to move the torch tip in a slightly curved, C-shape motion, as discussed earlier. Of course, the torch must be moved slightly backwards and the filler rod moved down a little each time the tip goes back and forth across the molten puddle. The filler rod must be moved down as it melts into the joint.

Puddle Control—To control the puddle heat so that the molten metal does not melt down *through* the panel, raise or lower the tip as needed. When the molten metal in the puddle gets too hot, raise the tip.

The puddle heat is also controlled by the *angle* at which the tip is tilted. Tilt the torch *backwards* (toward the metal) to keep the hot metal from melting holes in the panel. Tilting the torch backwards also helps keep the puddle molten while welding.

After a practice welding job is completed, check the *back* side of the weld to make sure of good penetration. Fig. 12-17 shows the back side of a partially-completed weld. Notice that there is an open area in the joint where the weld is yet to be made.

Fig. 12-17. A partially-completed weld, as seen from the back side.

Welding Without Filler Rod

Two pieces of metal may also be welded together *without* using a filler rod. A weld that is made without filler rod can be neat, clean, solid, and strong. Welding without a rod can be as easy as welding with a rod. To do this, first position the two pieces of metal by overlapping the edges on which the weld will be made. Fig. 12-18 shows how this should be done. The overlap should be at least the width

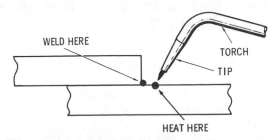

Fig. 12-18. Directing the flame heat toward the larger base part will help both the thick base and the thinner edge of the top piece melt at about the same time.

of a welding rod since the overlapped area takes the place of the welding rod.

After overlapping the two pieces, tack weld them in position. (If you are left-handed, it will probably be easier to work from right to left.) When forming a puddle for the tack welding, aim the torch more toward the bottom piece of metal, as in Fig. 12-18. This is done because the wide bottom piece of metal is harder to melt than is the edge of the top piece. Thus, the torch should be aimed to equalize the melting time needed for both pieces of metal.

Procedure—When making a weld without welding rod, bring the neutral flame about ⅟₁₆- to ¼-inch from the joint to form *most* of the puddle on the bottom piece. Hold the torch at approximately the angle shown in Fig. 12-18. When the puddle begins forming, move the torch back and forth across the edge of the top piece of metal to fuse it with the molten lower piece. Keep in mind that the thin edge of the upper piece will melt quicker than the thicker surface of the lower piece. For this reason, the torch must generally be pointed at the lower piece during most of this weld.

WELDING POSITIONS

Auto body repairmen must be able to weld metal in several *positions*. The four basic welding positions include: *flat, horizontal, vertical,* and, *overhead*. When you have mastered the processes of bead running and simple welds, you will have little problem welding in the different weld positions.

Flat Weld—A *flat* weld is made whenever the torch tip is pointed *downward* during welding. See Fig. 12-13. Flat welding is almost always used when a panel is being repaired *off* the vehicle. Flat welding is usually the easiest weld position to learn.

Horizontal Weld—The *horizontal* position is the weld position that will be used more on the *side* of an auto body. Some horizontal welding must be done during almost all panel replacements. For horizontal welding, the torch and rod are pointed *up*, to control the puddle and keep it from running down. See Fig. 12-19.

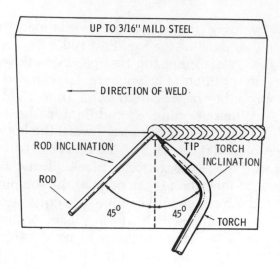

Fig. 12-19. Positioning the torch and rod for *horizontal* position welding.

Fig. 12-21. Positioning the torch and rod for *overhead* welding.

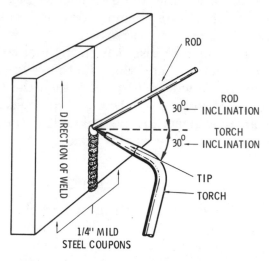

Fig. 12-20. Welding panels in the *vertical* position.

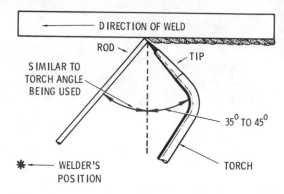

Fig. 12-22. The correct angles for the torch tip and rod during overhead welding practice.

Vertical Weld—Vertical welding, Fig. 12-20, is done up and down on a panel. Nearly all panel installations, especially on the sides of a vehicle, will require *some* vertical welding. Although this type of weld is not difficult to make, it does require slightly different techniques. First, welding is normally done from the bottom to the top. Secondly, the torch and filler rod are held closer together, with the torch on the bottom. See Fig. 12-20 for the different angles to be used when welding in the *vertical* position.

*Overhead Weld—*Making good welds in the *overhead* weld position, Fig. 12-21, is one of the hardest welding jobs to do. Also, the area

being welded is often in a difficult place to reach. A danger during overhead welding is that the welder's body is often in a position where *burns* could be suffered due to sparks or molten metal dripping from the weld puddle. For this reason, always position yourself to *one side* of the immediate weld puddle. Notice the correct angles for the torch tip and filler rod in Fig. 12-22.

TYPES OF WELD JOINTS

When two pieces of metal are to be welded together, they must first be positioned next to each other. *How* they are positioned for welding makes up the *weld joint*. After the weld has been made, the finished part then has one type of *weld joint* under the weld.

There are five basic types of weld joints shown in Figs. 12-23 through 28. These include:

1. Butt Welds, Fig. 12-23.
2. Lap Welds, Fig. 12-24.
3. Edge Welds, Fig. 12-25.
4. Tee Welds, Fig. 12-27.
5. Corner Welds, Fig. 12-28.

Auto body repairmen need to know how to make and weld the type of joint needed for a specific job. Usually, body replacement panels are made to be welded in place with one type of welded joint. At other times, replacement panels are made with an offset flange that requires a special weld.

Butt Weld

A *butt weld* joint is made by placing two pieces of metal side by side, with or without a gap. A typical *butt joint* is shown in Fig. 12-23. Most holes or tears in body panels are butt welded.

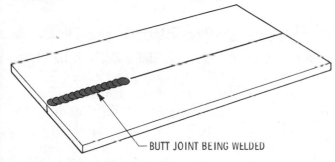

Fig. 12-23. Butt weld joint.

Any time metal cracks are being repaired, a butt weld is usually used. To do this, the two sides of the tear or crack are lined up side by side and then butt welded. When butt welds are made, the bead should be built up very little. The outside edges of the bead should be melted back into the sides of pieces being welded togther. Then, the back side of the completed weld must be checked, if possible, to make sure of complete weld penetration.

Lap Weld

A *lap weld* joint has been made when two pieces of metal overlap each other, as in Fig. 12-24. A lap weld joint is often used on outer replacement panels.

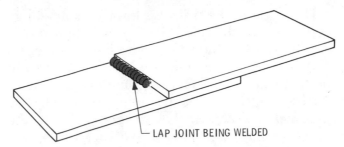

Fig. 12-24. Lap weld joint

When making a lap weld, first tack weld the two pieces of overlapping metal. Then run the weld bead along both sides of the lap to complete the weld. When welded like this on both sides, a lap weld joint is stronger than a butt weld joint. The additional strength comes from the fact that *two* welds have been made.

Edge Weld

Fig. 12-25 shows how two pieces of metal are positioned for making an *edge weld* joint. This weld joint makes a fairly strong weld. The two L-shaped flanges often make this weld joint stronger than a butt weld.

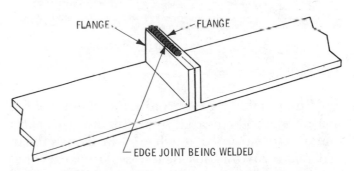

Fig. 12-25. Edge weld joint.

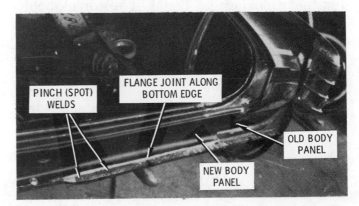

Fig. 12-26. A lower back panel that has been spot welded along the flange. (Courtesy of Lenco Automotive Equipment Division.)

This type of weld is also known as a "flange weld" or "pinch weld." It is used often during auto body manufacturing, where it is known as a *pinch weld*. The name *pinch weld* comes from the fact that, at the factory, the two flanges are pinched togther with the points of an electric *spot welder*. This makes a spot weld at the pinch, joining the flanges. See Fig. 12-26.

Tee Weld

Tee weld joints are not often used in auto body repair. Fig. 12-27 shows how two pieces of metal are positioned in a tee joint. The end of one piece of metal is placed against the side of another piece of metal. This welded joint can be very strong if it is welded on both sides of the tee.

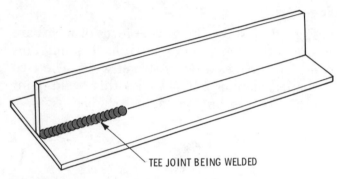

Fig. 12-27. Tee weld joint.

When making a tee weld joint, there is more metal area to be heated by the flame. This extra metal area absorbs much of the flame's heat. To make up for this heat loss, use a tip that is one size larger than would normally be used for that thickness of metal. The torch should be positioned evenly between the two panels, and possibly be held up for a slight amount of extra heat on the bottom panel.

Corner Weld

A *corner weld* joint has been made when two pieces of metal are positioned at right angles to each other and will be welded on the edge of the corner formed by the pieces. Fig. 12-28 shows how two pieces of metal would be positioned for this type of weld joint. This type of weld is often done without using a fiiller rod on many jobs.

Corner weld points are fairly easy to make. However, the torch flame must be handled carefully so as not to overheat the corner edge of the intersecting panels. If the corner edge becomes too hot, the puddle will burn through the corner and hot metal will drip through to the underside of the joint. To avoid this problem, raise the flame slightly when moving back and forth over the corner edge.

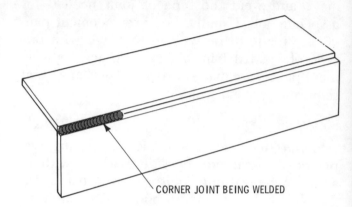

Fig. 12-28. Corner weld joint.

OXY-ACETYLENE CUTTING PRINCIPLES

Some type of oxy-acetylene *cutting* has been done ever since the welding torch was first invented. The earliest cutting torches were no more than a pipe clamped along the side of a normal welding tip. When the metal became hot enough to melt, more oxygen would be added through this outside pipe. This extra oxygen would then cause a hole to be burned in the metal.

Although cutting torches or cutting attachments are still used to supply extra oxygen to the flame, their design has advanced along with all other welding tools. Fig. 12-2 showed a welder using a modern cutting attachment to cut mild steel. Fig. 12-29 shows a cutting attachment and the torch blowpipe with which it would be used.

Setting Up for Cutting

Setting up the welding equipment for cutting is similar to setting up the equipment for welding. The cylinders, regulators, hoses, and the torch body are all set up as usual. There are two major changes, though, as noted below.

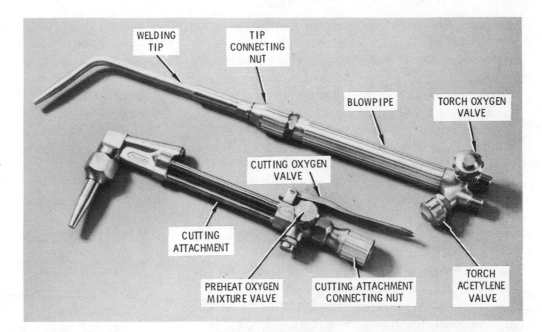

Fig. 12-29. A welding torch, welding tip, and cutting attachment. (Courtesy of Harris Calorific Division.)

First, a *cutting attachment* must be fastened (Fig. 12-29) to the torch instead of a welding tip. This attachment is fastened to the torch blowpipe as is a welding tip. The cutting attachment should be positioned on the torch so that the cutting oxygen valve handle is *between* the torch oxygen and acetylene valves.

Second, the oxygen regulator must be adjusted to 25 psi for the type of cutting done in a body shop. This extra oxygen is needed because a good deal of oxygen will be released when the cutting oxygen lever is depressed. Adjust the oxygen regulator with the *torch* oxygen valve and the *cutting* oxygen valve all the way *open*. See Fig. 12-29 to locate the different valves. (When the torch oxygen valve is opened, no oxygen will escape unless *either* the *preheat* oxygen valve *or* the *cutting* oxygen valve is opened.)

Safety Checks—After setting up the equipment for cutting, remember to make *all* the usual safety checks. Use soapy water to test for leaks, as was discussed earlier. Check to be sure that the cutting equipment, and the job, are away from any oil, grease, paint, or other flammable materials.

At all times, be sure to notice the direction in which the cutting torch is being pointed. When cutting near a vehicle's *gas tank, remove the tank* and place it a safe distance from the

Fig. 12-30. Common welding goggles, as would be used over unprotected eyes. (Courtesy of American Optical Corp.)

Fig. 12-31. Welding goggles with a large frame. These may be used over standard eyeglasses. (Courtesy of American Optical Corp.)

cutting area. Also note where the torch *hoses* are. A serious fire could start if the hoses were cut by sparks or metal from the cutting job. Overall, a cutting torch must be used with extreme caution since the flame and sparks are hotter than those of a welding torch.

When cutting, always wear *dark* tinted safety goggles to prevent eye injury. Figs. 12-30 and 31 show the types of safety goggles that would work well for protection from cutting rays. Also, double-check to be sure that there is a *fire extinguisher* in the work area. Note the extinguisher on the back of the welding outfit shown earlier in Fig. 12-5.

Final Preparation—Place some soapstone in the work area if *unpainted* metal is to be cut. This is used for marking the direction in which the cut will be made. Soapstone marks will show up easily on bare steel, as in Fig. 12-32. Either a scratch awl (Fig. 12-33) or a soapstone may be used for marking the cut line on *painted* metal.

Before beginning the cutting operation, position the metal at a convenient working height.

This could be on a metal table or on metal stands. Then, draw a cut line on the metal in the direction to be cut. Use soapstone for marking unpainted metal, or a scratch awl for marking painted metal. Double check to be certain that flammables and the hoses are safely out of danger. Lighting the torch is the next step.

Lighting the Cutting Torch

When all the equipment is set up in the cutting area, the torch is ready to be lit. To light the torch, follow these steps *in order*. Refer to Fig. 12-34 as needed.

1. Open the torch oxygen valve all the way.
2. Depress the cutting oxygen lever to release oxygen. With the lever depressed, check to see that the outlet gauge pressure on the oxygen regulator is 25 psi. Adjust the regulator if necessary.
3. Release the cutting oxygen lever.
4. Open the torch acetylene valve about ⅛ turn.

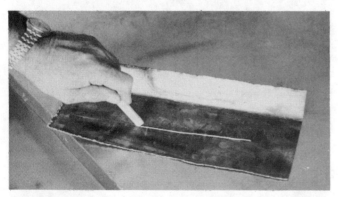

Fig. 12-32. Using a soapstone stick to mark a cut line on bare metal.

Fig. 12-33. Using a scratch awl to mark a cut line on painted metal.

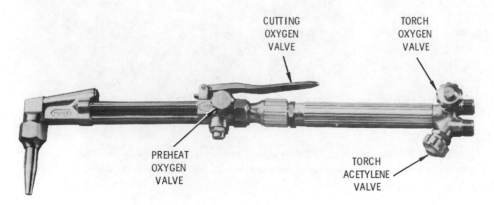

CUTTING OXYGEN VALVE

TORCH OXYGEN VALVE

PREHEAT OXYGEN VALVE

TORCH ACETYLENE VALVE

Fig. 12-34. A torch with a cutting attachment connected. (Courtesy of Harris Calorific Division.)

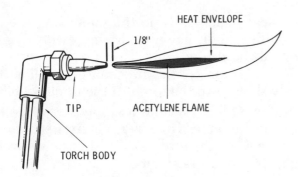

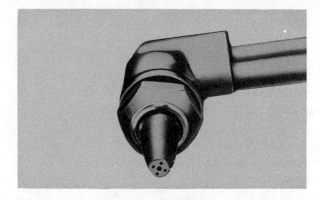

Fig. 12-35. The first step for adjusting the preheat flame is to adjust the pure acetylene flame until it just "jumps" off the tip. Then, close the acelylene valve until the flame just *returns* to the tip.

Fig. 12-36. Neutral preheat flames come from the outside holes of a cutting tip. Only pure cutting oxygen comes from the center hole, and only when the cutting oxygen lever is depressed. (Courtesy of Union Carbide Canada Ltd.)

5. Use the striker to light the acetylene at the cutting tip.

6. Open the torch acetylene valve until the acetylene flame "jumps" from the tip. See Fig. 12-35.

7. Close the acetylene valve until the flame just returns to the tip.

8. Open the *preheat oxygen valve* on the side of the cutting attachment (Fig. 12-34) to form neutral flames with the acetylene.

9. Adjust the *torch acetylene valve* as required to get good, long neutral preheat flames. The preheat flames will be made up of *several* neutral cones. If any cones are shorter or different-looking, shut the torch off and clean the preheat holes after the torch has cooled.

10. When the preheat flames have been adjusted to be neutral flames, press down on the *oxygen cutting lever* to be certain that the extra oxygen is coming out with the preheat flames.

Preheating

The end of a cutting tip has several small holes that surround a larger center hole. See Fig. 12-36. During operation, these outside holes each have an oxy-acetylene neutral preheating flame. The larger inside hole, however, is *only* used for the *cutting oxygen* needed after the metal has been preheated. When preheating the metal, therefore, the cutting oxygen control handle is not used.

The first step to actually cutting with an oxy-acetylene cutting torch is to *preheat* the area to be cut. To preheat the metal, place the neutral flame tip on the edge of one side of the metal to be cut. Be sure to preheat *on* the cut line marked earlier. Preheat a point on the edge of the metal until it becomes cherry red and just begins to melt, as shown in Fig. 12-37.

Cutting

After preheating the cut starting point (Fig. 12-37), the metal may then be cut with the

Fig. 12-37. Preheating the metal to a bright cherry red, using *only* the preheating flames. (Courtesy of Victor Equipment Co.)

cutting oxygen. To do this, the cutting oxygen control handle is used to supply the extra burst of oxygen needed for cutting. This extra oxygen leaves the tip through the tip's center hole.

To actually make the cut, push down the cutting oxygen handle, as is being done in Fig. 12-2. Then, *slowly* move the torch along the line to be cut, holding the neutral preheat flames just above the metal surface. Move the torch only as fast as a clean, distinct cut can be made. This will take practice. *Flashback*, discussed earlier, is usually not a problem while cutting. If flashback occurs, however, first close the oxygen valve and then close the acetylene valve.

SHUTTING DOWN

Whether a welding tip or a cutting attachment is being used, the torch must be shut down when work is complete. With either a cutting attachment or a welding tip, the torch is basically shut down in the same way. A cutting attachment, however, has an extra oxygen valve to be turned off.

Below is the correct procedure to follow to safely shut down the torch. If the torch is being shut down for a few minutes, only steps #1 and #2 need be done. However, all six steps must be done when the torch will be shut down overnight or for several hours.

1. Close the torch acetylene valve.
2. Close the torch oxygen valve. On the *cutting* attachment, close the preheat oxygen valve.
3. Close the acetylene cylinder valve.
4. Close the oxygen cylinder valve.
5. Release the pressure against the regulator valves on each regulator by turning the regulator handles counter-clockwise.
6. Open both the acetylene and oxygen torch valves to let the remaining pressure off the regulator gauges.

Brazing and Heat Shrinking

The oxy-acetylene processes of *brazing* and *heat shrinking* have much in common. For example, an oxy-acetylene torch is used for both types of work. The same regulator gauge settings may be used for either process. Both processes may accurately be described as *low-temperature* welding processes. Both brazing and heat shrinking are done without using the extreme heat that must be used for welding. Whether brazing or heat shrinking, the base metal being repaired is worked *without* melting any part of it.

Brazing—Oxy-acetylene *brazing* is a joining process done with brass rods. During brazing, these rods are used to form the puddle and run the bead. By doing this, the panels being joined are not actually melted, but are held together by the melted brass rods. The melted brass does not actually go all the way through the base metal.

Heat Shrinking—Oxy-acetylene *heat shrinking* is the process of shrinking stretched metal back to a smaller size by using the oxy-acetylene flame. When sheet metal is damaged, caved in, or gouged, it is often *stretched* out of shape. Fig. 13-1 shows a damaged area of this type. This type of damage can be brought closer to the metal's original contour by using an oxy-acetylene flame to heat and shrink the damaged area.

BRAZING PRINCIPLES

Oxy-acetylene *brazing*, like oxy-acetylene welding, uses the heat of an oxy-acetylene flame to fuse together two pieces of metal. During brazing, however, a lower-melting-point metal is added to make the joint. Brazing is often used in body shops to replace quarter panels, door outer panels ("skins"), and other auto body panels.

During brazing, the oxy-acetylene torch and tip first heat the base metal. Then, the brass

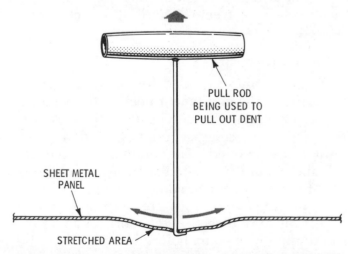

Fig. 13-1. When metal is dented in, it is usually stretched. When it is pulled out, the stretched area must be shrunk back down to its original size.

215

filler rod is melted and drawn into the joint by the metal's heat. The brass seeps into the base metal's *pores*, allowing the two pieces of metal to be held together strongly when the liquid brass cools and again becomes solid.

Advantages of Brazing

The main advantage of brazing is that it allows metal to be joined at a lower temperature than welding. When properly applied, brazing will firmly join pieces of almost any type of metal. When panels are joined by brazing, there is less danger of the base metal warping. This is because the brass melts and the joint is made at a low temperature. Thus, the panels being joined are subjected to less heat than if they were welded.

Another advantage of brazing is that the oxy-acetylene carbonizing flame, rather than the neutral flame, may be used. The carbonizing flame is slightly cooler than a neutral flame. Therefore, it will require less oxygen than would a neutral flame. In addition to requiring less oxygen than welding, brazing is also a *faster* process because less time is required to get the base material up to brazing temperature.

Oxy-acetylene brazing is often used for joining "soft" metals such as copper or brass. Extreme heats should not be used on these metals since they will melt easily. Brazing is also used to repair and join *cast iron*. Cast iron will crack easily under extreme heat if it is not evenly heated.

Brazing Equipment

The equipment needed for brazing is about the same as the equipment needed for welding. For brazing, an oxy-acetylene torch, brass filler rods, welding goggles, gloves, and a torch lighter are needed. The brass rods used for brazing should be coated with *flux*, a cleaning agent necessary for brazing. See Fig. 13-2.

If *uncoated* brass rods are used, a container of *flux* must be placed in the work area and the rod dipped in the flux before brazing. Fig. 13-3 shows a container of flux and the coated and uncoated portion of a brass rod. When the brass rod is heated, it may be pushed into the can of

Fig. 13-2. Brazing rods coated with flux.

flux. This causes the flux to stick to the brass rod. Flux is later discussed in detail.

Brazing Tip Size

In brazing, as in welding, the thickness of the metal being brazed determines the tip and brazing rod sizes and the regulator gauge pressures needed. Generally speaking, the sizes and pressures given earlier for welding may also be used for brazing. Many body men, however, prefer to use a tip size one number larger than

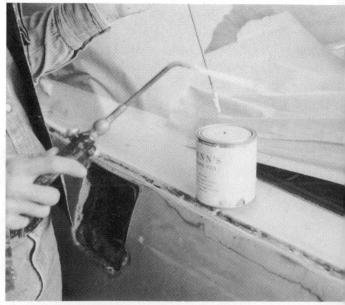

Fig. 13-3. Uncoated brazing rod with flux from a can of flux on one end of the rod.

would be the size used for *welding* metal of the same thickness.

For most oxy-acetylene brazing on outer body sheet metal, gauge pressures of five to six psi each may be used with $\frac{1}{16}$-inch diameter brazing rod and a #2 or #3 welding tip. For thicker metal (unibody subframes, for example), $\frac{1}{8}$-inch diameter rod and a #3 or #4 tip should be used. Slightly additional gas pressures may be needed for a larger tip.

Brazing Flame

During welding, of course, the oxy-acetylene flame to use was the neutral flame. The flame to use for *brazing*, however, is a slightly *carbonizing*, or "reducing," flame. The torch oxygen valve does not have to be opened as much for a carbonizing flame as it does for the neutral flame. This is because less oxygen and, possibly, slightly less acetylene are needed for a carbonizing flame.

The carbonizing flame, discussed earlier in the welding section, can be recognized by its flame "feather" positioned just above the neutral flame cone. See Fig. 13-4. The flame feather should be about one or two times longer (1X or 2X) than the neutral flame cone, depending on the thickness of the metal.

When brazing, the torch should be held about twice as far from the work as when welding. This is because the molten brass may be blown away by the flame if the torch tip is held too close. Usually, a distance of about $\frac{1}{4}$ inch is far enough from the surface for good brazing.

Fig. 13-4. A carbonizing flame has an inner flame twice as long (2X) or three times as long (3X) as a neutral flame cone.

Brazing Rods

There are two types of rods used for brazing: brass rods *coated* with flux and those that are *not coated* with flux. Flux-coated rods are easily identified because they are much thicker than would be the same diameter of rod not coated with flux. Also, flux-coated rods may have different colors, whereas uncoated rods are brass (yellow-gold) colored. Plain, uncoated brass rods must be coated with flux when the brazing process is begun.

Flux Purpose—The flux, either in a can or on a rod, is very necessary for good brazing and has several purposes. Flux is used to *clean* the metal to be brazed, thus helping assure better adhesion by the melted brass. Flux also helps prevent the brass rod from *oxidizing*, allowing the brass to flow freely onto the base metal.

BRAZING THIN METAL

Thin sheet metal (up to $\frac{1}{8}$-inch thick) is not normally brazed in the same way as is thicker metal. Thin metal, such as auto body sheet metal, may usually be brazed as shown in Fig. 13-5. It may also be brazed in a butt weld joint, as in Fig. 13-6. Thin metals can normally be brazed by making one pass over the joint. This pass will usually leave a layer of brass from $\frac{1}{16}$- to $\frac{1}{8}$-inch thick. Brazing thicker metal will require a different procedure.

Preparation

Brass will only adhere properly to metal that is *clean*. Therefore, before actually brazing, the metal to be brazed should be cleaned. Soap and water or enamel reducer may be used. The metal should be scrubbed clean with a wire

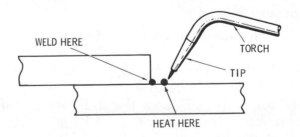

Fig. 13-5. A lap joint, sometimes used to braze thin metal.

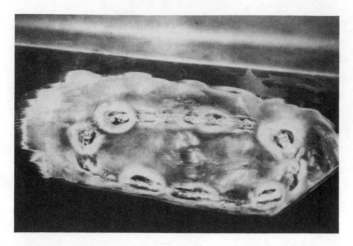

Fig. 13-6. Brazed joints may always be identified because the filler metal will be a bright yellow-gold color instead of the darker gray color of the filler metal in a welded joint.

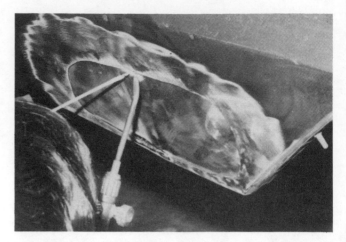

Fig. 13-7. The correct angle for feeding a brazing rod into a joint being brazed.

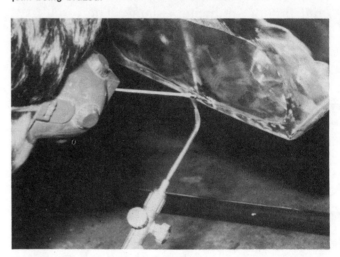

Fig. 13-8. Forming a brazing puddle.

brush. Some body men skip this step, but it *should* be done to insure good adhesion by the brass.

If an uncoated brass rod is being used, the rod must first be coated with flux each time as it is used. To coat the rod, use the torch to heat about 1½ inches of the end of the rod each time. Push the heated end of the rod into the can of flux, as was shown earlier in Fig. 13-3. The heated rod end will then pick up a coating of flux. The rod, with flux, is then ready for use.

Forming the Puddle

To actually begin brazing, move the torch back and forth across the metal joint to be brazed, heating a short space to *just* a dull red color, *no* more. Next, position the rod at about a 45° angle to the heated metal, as in Fig. 13-7. Then, melt the flux-coated part of the rod onto the hot metal to form a brass puddle. See Fig. 13-8.

Running the Bead

Before running a brass bead along the joint, tack weld (or braze) the panels or pieces being joined. Place the "tacks" about 1 inch apart, as in Fig. 13-9. Be sure to follow the same procedure for each tack: *coat* the rod with flux if it is uncoated, *heat* the metal, and then *melt* the rod on the hot metal. Each tack weld should be about ¼-inch long.

When actually running the bead to make a brazed joint, the temperature of the puddle is controlled by raising and lowering the torch tip. Normally, the torch tip is held at about a 45° angle to the metal's surface and about ¼ inch away from the puddle, as in Fig. 13-10. The flame heat is used to direct the puddle flow as desired by first heating a given area of the joint. For good brazing, use the same back-and-forth torch movement as is used for welding.

During brazing, the puddle and the procedure move much faster than during welding. The brass bead will also spread a little wider than does a steel weld bead, as was shown in Fig. 13-6. If the brazing bead is made a little higher than the two pieces being brazed, the bead may later be ground off level if desired.

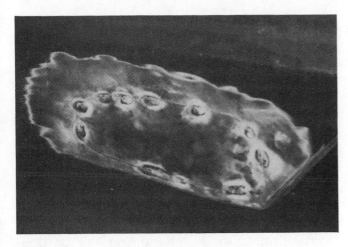

Fig. 13-9. Tack welds on a joint to be brazed.

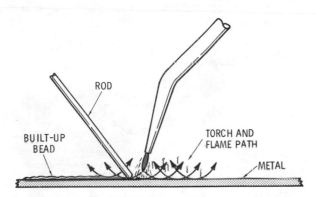

Fig. 13-10. Similar to welding, an up-and-down, back-and-forth torch technique is used for brazing.

BRAZING THICK METAL

Metal over ⅛-inch thick, such as cast iron, requires that a different brazing procedure be used. Thick metal should not be overlapped as may be done with thin metal. Instead, thick metal should have the edges ground back to a slight angle so that they form a V when butted together. See Fig. 13-11. This grinding may be done with a disk grinder.

After preparing the pieces and placing them side by side so that the V shape is formed, the pieces may be brazed. The brazing procedure is almost the same as when brazing thin sheet metal. When heating the V to a dull red, be careful to not overheat the *top* edges of the V. Several passes will usually be needed since one layer of brass is not normally enough to fill the V.

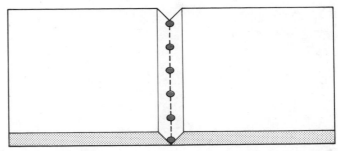

Fig. 13-11. Thicker metal should have the sides ground back to form a "V" at the joint.

On the *first* pass, the bead should be made so that it is *convex* (humped), as in Fig. 13-12. The bead of the *second* pass should almost fill the V and will be only slightly convex, as shown in Fig. 12-13. The *third* and final pass should overfill the V so that the bead is made a little

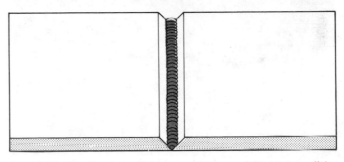

Fig. 13-12. The first braze pass on a thick-metal butt joint will be convex (humped).

higher than the level of the base metal. See Fig. 13-14. Then, if a smooth surface is desired, the final bead may be ground smooth with a grinder, as in Fig. 13-15.

TYPICAL BRAZING JOB

Because brazing causes less heat distortion than welding, brazing is often used when re-

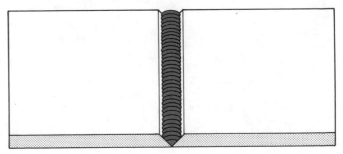

Fig. 13-13. The second pass on a thick-metal butt joint will be only slightly convex and will almost fill the "V".

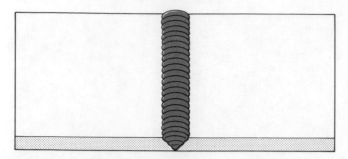

Fig. 13-14. The final pass on a thick-metal butt joint will overfill the "V".

Fig. 13-15. Grinding down the convex "hump" of a filled butt weld joint on a thick-metal brazing job. (Courtesy of The Norton Company.)

placing the thin outer sheet metal panels of automobiles. By *brazing* replacement panels in place, there is less chance that the repair will be warped, which would require a good deal

Fig. 13-16. A typical quarter panel that is damaged beyond repair. A replacement panel must be installed.

of additional body work before refinishing. Brazing skill is one of the most important skills a body man may have.

A typical body shop panel replacement done with brazing is shown in Figs. 13-16 through 13-23. In this series, the severely damaged quarter panel in Fig. 13-16 is replaced with a salvage panel from a wrecking yard (Fig. 13-17). In Fig. 13-18, the car has been brought into the shop, opened up, placed on jack stands, and has had the rear bumper removed for the repair. In Fig. 13-19, the replacement panel has been trimmed for installation on this particular car. (When a wrecking yard removes a used part from a car, they will not always cut it off the wrecked car exactly as needed for the car being repaired.)

Fig. 13-17. A replacement quarter panel as received from a salvage yard. This is a used part, removed from a wrecked vehicle that had not been damaged in this area.

In Fig. 13-20, the damaged quarter panel section has been cut away. This is best done with an air chisel, since it will leave a clean, sharp edge for brazing. After the panel is removed, the edges must be cleaned and the weatherstripping laid aside before brazing.

Fig. 13-18. The damaged car has been moved inside, jacked up, and the rear bumper has been removed.

Fig. 13-19. The replacement panel is trimmed to correctly fit the edges of the body where the old section will be removed.

Fig. 13-21. The replacement panel is spot-brazed in position.

Fig. 13-20. The damaged panel has been removed.

Fig. 13-22. The rear seam of the repair has been brazed. The black soot on the rear area is from the excess acetylene in the carbonizing flame used for brazing. The area will have to be thoroughly cleaned and levelled before it is refinished.

The first step toward installing the replacement panel is to hold it in position and *spot braze* it in place. This has been done in Fig. 13-21. Note also in Fig. 13-21 that the lower roof panel and upper quarter panel part have had the paint ground off with a disk grinder in preparation for the final, sturdy brazing along that seam.

When the panel is properly held in position with spot brazing, it may be completely brazed in position with brazing along the new seams. This is shown in Figs. 13-22 and 13-23. In Fig. 13-22, the rear section of the replacement panel has been brazed to the car's rear tail piece. In Fig. 13-23, the panel has been partially brazed to the lower roof panel. Following these steps, the brazing repair will have to be levelled and filled with body filler before the panel is refinished.

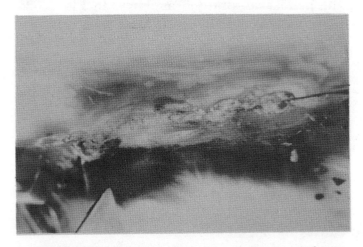

Fig. 13-23. The brazed joint where the replacement panel joins the lower section of the roof.

HEAT SHRINKING

Heat shrinking is an important part of repairing damaged metal. "Shrinking" will be necessary when the metal has been stretched out of shape due to the impact of a collision. If the metal is not "shrunk," completely repairing the panel will be difficult. This is because the repaired area will be "wavy" when the stretched metal is forced to fit the smaller original shape.

All metal has a certain amount of "give" and will normally return to its original contour after a *light* blow. However, when metal is struck with a blow which causes it to *exceed* the limits of its "give," it is stretched out of shape. For example, this would happen when an object hits a panel and causes a deep gouge or dent in the metal, causing it to permanently bend and stretch.

Another way to understand stretch is to look at a panel in cross-section before and after it is hit. For example, notice the edge of the door panel in Fig. 13-24. The outside edge of the door panel on this car is 16 inches wide, measured from Point **A** to Point **B**.

In Fig. 13-25, however, the door panel in Fig. 13-24 has been *hit* at Point **C**. When the panel was hit at Point **C**, the metal was pushed in and stretched. Notice that the distance from point **A** to Point **C** is 9¼ inches and the distance from Point **B** to Point **C** is 7¼ inches. This adds up to 16½ inches, or ½ inch more than when the panel was straight, as it was in Fig. 13-24. This means that *when the panel was hit at Point **C**, it was pushed in and stretched ½-inch.*

Normally, stretch as severe as in Fig. 13-25 would require installing a new door outer panel, or *skin*. However, if the panel was to be repaired, an oxy-acetylene torch would have to be used to *heat shrink* the damaged metal back to near the 16-inch width that it was originally.

Heat Distortion—To successfully shrink body sheet metal, a body man must understand the effect that *heat* has on sheet metal. Briefly, *heat* causes the metal to *expand*. Then, as the metal cools, it shrinks. This is caused by the movement of the molecules in the metal as it is

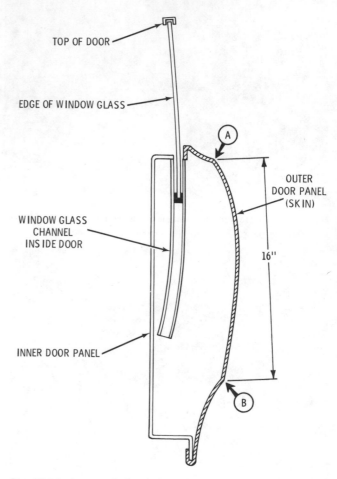

Fig. 13-24. A normal door, showing the outer door panel (the *skin*) before being hit.

heated and when it cools. The more extreme the heat, the more expansion will take place. If the metal is quickly cooled, it will contract (shrink) even more than when it cools slowly.

The effect of heat on metal can best be understood by noticing how it changes a flat piece of sheet metal. If the torch is used to heat a flat (not damaged) piece of metal in one spot, the metal will first expand, as in Fig. 13-26. Then, as the metal cools, it will contract slightly, as in Fig. 13-27. These complete changes in the metal's contour are caused by heating and cooling. As the metal is heated, its molecules expand *toward* the heat, since the molecules nearest the heat are getting hotter and becoming larger than those underneath. As the metal cools, its molecules contract, reducing their size and causing the bulge to shrink.

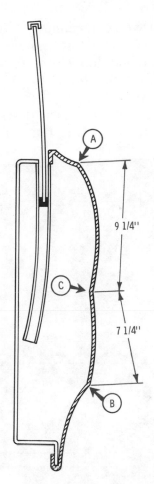

Fig. 13-25. The same door panel as in Fig. 13-24. Here, the skin has now been hit at Point C. This has *stretched* the skin.

Warpage—The *degree* of expansion and contraction (how much will take place) is controlled by the *amount* of heat applied and the *size* of the area heated. The *hotter* the area is heated, the more the panel expands and contracts (warps). The *larger* the heated area, the greater the resulting warpage to the area.

Low-crowned metal (no sharp bends) or slightly curved metal is more easily warped by heat. If too much heat is applied to the area, the panel will quickly become wavy and irregular in contour. However, the amount of panel warpage can be controlled through practice in handling a torch while heat shrinking.

The warpage which takes place during heat shrinking may be partially controlled by noting the *size* of the area heated and the *amount* of heat applied to that area. Also, there are several methods used to speed up the shrinking process. These include using a bumping hammer and dolly, and quickly cooling the heated area by using water-soaked rags or sponges.

Shrinking Procedure

To properly heat shrink metal, be prepared to work *quickly* during the process. To do this, have on hand all the materials needed before beginning to heat the metal. Materials on hand should include an oxy-acetylene torch, a fire extinguisher, a bumping hammer and dolly, and a bucket of water with rags or sponges in the water. Usually, a #2 welding tip is used for heat shrinking thin auto body sheet metal.

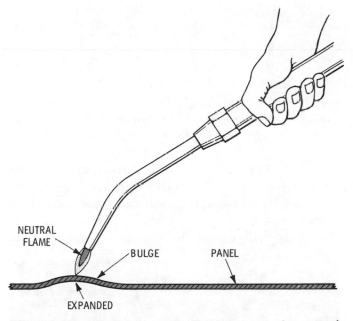

Fig. 13-26. Heating a flat metal panel causes the panel to expand at the spot where it is heated.

Fig. 13-27. When the metal is allowed to cool slowly, it will return to a slightly contracted shape.

Heating the Area—To heat the stretched area properly, first bring the oxy-acetylene torch to a *neutral* flame. Keep the inner cone of the flame about ½ inch from the surface of the metal, as in Fig. 13-28. Normally, only a small area is heated at a time; usually no larger than the size of a dime. Sometimes, the damaged area may have an oblong (elongated) shape.

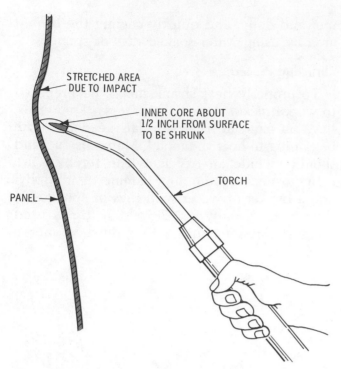

Fig. 13-28. Heating the metal to a cherry-red color with the inner cone about ½-inch from the stretched metal.

In these cases, it is often convenient to heat only a narrow strip of the damaged area.

Heat the first spot to be shrunk to a hot, cherry-red color, as has been done in Fig. 13-29. This will cause the damaged area to ex-

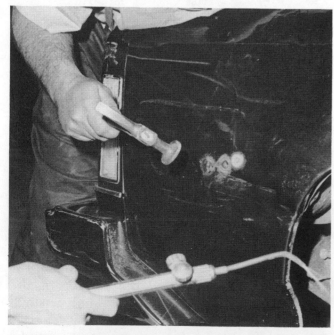

Fig. 13-29. Using a hammer to work down the expanded, dimesized, hot spot on the area being shrunk.

pand outward, forming a slight bulge. Take care not to overheat the metal or allow the cone to come too close to the metal. (This could cause the torch to burn a hole in the metal.) After the metal is heated cherry-red, use a hammer to knock down and shape the hot metal, as is being done in Fig. 13-30.

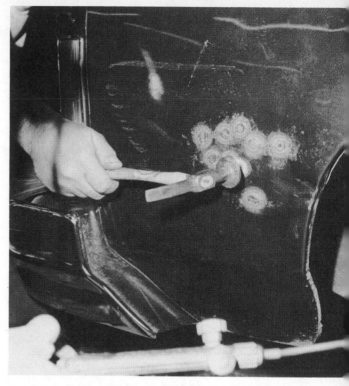

Fig. 13-30. Working down the expanded metal with only a hammer.

Using the Hammer and Dolly—A bumping hammer and dolly are normally used to speed up and help the shrinking process after the metal has been heated. Since the heated metal is soft, it can easily be worked down into shape as it begins cooling.

To do this, use the open face of the bumping hammer to strike two light blows on the heated spot as soon as the metal is hot. Next, place a dolly (shaped similar to the original contour) on the backside of the damaged area. Finally, flatten or shape the metal by working it against the dolly with the hammer, as is being done in Fig. 13-31. *Be careful* when doing this, as the metal being worked is *hot*.

Using Water—When the damaged area cannot be reached on the back side, a hammer may

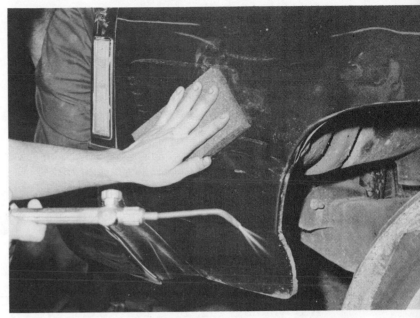

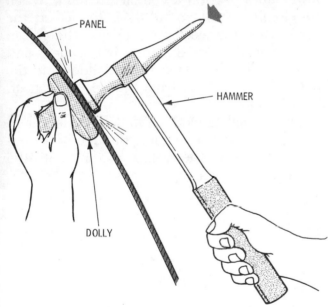

Fig. 13-31. Working down the expanded metal with a hammer and dolly to correctly reshape the hot metal.

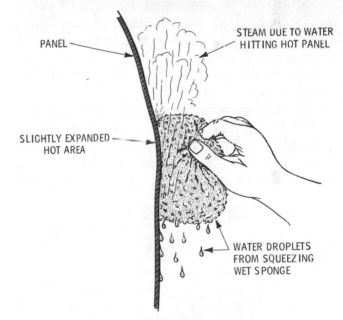

Fig. 13-32. Using a wet sponge to quickly shrink the expanded metal. This process will cause a hissing sound and steam will rise from the panel as the water quickly boils and turns to steam when it hits the hot panel.

be used without a dolly for some work. However, in this case, *water* may also be used to speed up the shrinking process. This is done by wiping a wet sponge or wet rags across the heated area, causing it to cool faster. Fig. 13-32 shows how this is done. The amount of shrinkage is more difficult to control when water is used. Also, care must be taken to avoid getting burned while holding the wet sponge or wet rags against the hot panel.

Practice—The ability to properly shrink metal takes a good deal of *practice*. The ability to work *quickly* is important because the metal must be worked while it is *hot* for the best results. After the metal is worked down close to its original size, it may then be smoothed, filed, and filled as necessary before refinishing.

Arc Welding

Arc welding, Fig. 14-1, is a welding process that uses *electric current* as a source of power and heat. For this reason, arc welding is also known as *electric* welding. Basically, arc welding uses two electric cables and an *electrode* (an electric welding rod) to direct the flow of electricity, as in Fig. 14-2.

Fig. 14-3 shows a common arc welding electrode. Electrodes are coated with different types of *flux* to provide the chemical cleaning and protection necessary for the arc as it makes the weld. The weld is formed at the arc (Fig. 14-4)

because of the fact that electricity flows through power lines to form a complete circuit. When the circuit is broken, an *arc* is formed at the break when the electricity "jumps" the gap in the circuit. Because the arc is hot, it melts and joins together the metals being welded *and* the metal that is melting from the electrode itself. See Fig. 14-4.

All arc welders work on the above-described principle of electricity going through heavy cables and causing the weld by arcing onto the surface of the metal(s) being welded. The elec-

Fig. 14-1. Common arc welding procedure.

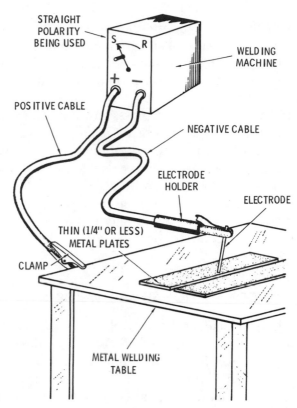

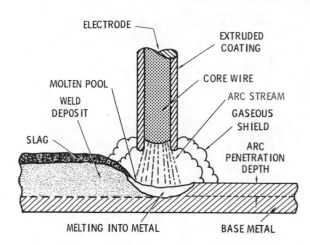

Fig. 14-4. The actual welding arc in an arc-welding circuit.

this set-up is used to provide a path for the electricity.

Fig. 14-2. A simple arc welding set-up. Note that the wires, the work table, and the work itself are all metal. This is necessary to complete the arc welding circuit, since electricity must flow through *all* those parts.

tricity used to create the arc comes *from* the welding machine, *through* the electrode, *across* the arc, and then *through* the metal to the ground cable. Here, it completes the circuit by returning, through the ground cable, to the welding machine. A typical machine is shown in Fig. 14-5.

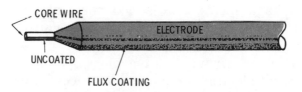

Fig. 14-3. A typical metal electrode with a thick flux coating.

Although some of the newer electric welding machines operate in a more complicated manner, all of them operate on basically the same principle. They all have lead (electrode) cables to provide the current to the electrode holder, and they all have a ground (work) cable to complete the circuit by returning the electricity to the machine. Fig. 14-2 shows how

Fig. 14-5. A common shop arc welding machine. (Courtesy of Lincoln Electric Company.)

ARC WELDER USES

Some types of smaller arc welding machines may be used for light sheet metal welding, such as body shop work. However, most machines are used effectively on heavier gauges of metal, such as the framework job being done in Fig. 14-6. This is because arc welding machines have the current (and, therefore, the heat) needed to weld heavy metal. Also, the metal

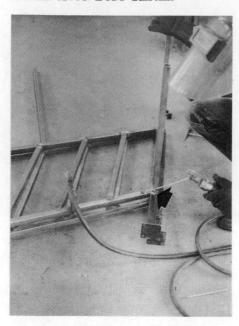

Fig. 14-6. Preparing to arc weld heavy steel framework.

provides the type of surface that will readily conduct the heavy electric current flow of an arc welding machine.

Until recently, arc welding was not often used in auto body repair shops because most thin auto body sheet metal could be warped by the heat of a heavy-current arc welding machine. However, new and specially-designed arc welding machines are now being used more often in the auto body field. Recent developments in arc welding machines have produced machines that can be used to easily weld overlapping panels of thin sheet metal.

Arc welding machines are often used to weld the heavy-gauge metal used to make automobile *frames*. This may be required when a frame has been damaged and straightening it, or the original damage, broke one or more of the frame's factory arc welds. Arc welding may also be used to make permanent changes or additions to the frame. These would include, for example, adding a heavy-duty trailer hitch.

Types of Electric (Arc) Welders

There are three basic types of electric welders that may be used in an auto body shop:

1. Conventional Arc Welders.
2. Spot Welders.
3. Panel Spotters.

Up to this point, *conventional arc welders* are the type that have been discussed. When arc or electric welding is discussed, it is usually discussed concerning conventional arc welders and the principle on which they operate.

In the body shop business, however, the electric welding processes of *spot welding* and *panel spotting* are quite important. For this reason, these processes are discussed in detail later in the unit. In any case, to be able to use electric welding correctly, body men need to know how to select the type of welding equipment and the materials needed to best complete the job to be done.

CONVENTIONAL ARC WELDERS

There are several types of *conventional arc welders*. Most of them (Figs. 14-5, 7, and 8) are known as *transformer machines* and may be operated from 220-volt electric power lines. On the other hand, portable *gasoline-powered* welding machines, like gasoline-powered air compressors, can be operated where there is no other electric power. These machines, Figs. 14-9 and 14-10, have an electric generator powered by a gasoline engine.

Transformer Machines

The most commonly-used arc welders are those that operate only from the shop's electric power lines. These machines, known as *transformer machines,* are shown in Figs. 14-5, 14-7, and 14-8. Their output sizes include 180, 225, and 250 amperes. This is the amount of current that they are able to put out, since current is measured in amperes, or *amps.*

Transformer welding machines operate from 220-volt electric lines. The differences between the machines are their size and the maximum amperage that they are able to produce. For example, 180- or 225-amp machines are satisfactory for welding any gauge metal found on a modern auto body or frame. Although a 250-amp welder can produce faster welds due to its higher amperage, it is more often used in industries such as construction. Here, much heavier metal pieces are welded than are found in an automobile.

Fig. 14-7. A portable, 225-amp transformer arc welding machine. (Courtesy of Lincoln Electric Company.)

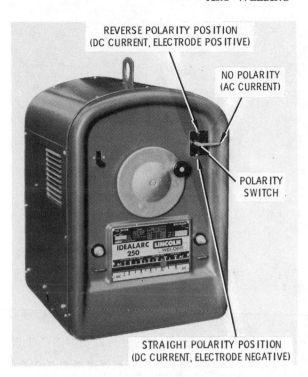

Fig. 14-8. A fixed, 250-amp transformer arc welding machine. (Courtesy of Lincoln Electric Company.)

Portable Machines

Portable, gasoline-powered welding machines get their name from the fact that they can be operated anywhere to which they can be moved. Basically, these machines are operated as are any other conventional arc welders. The difference is that they generate their own electricity from a gasoline-engine-powered generator. Figs. 14-9 and 14-10 show two common portable machines. Note that the machine in Fig. 14-10 has a second amperage control for *fine adjustment* of the amperage supply. This is used to more carefully adjust the "rough" amperage selection of the first dial.

Welding Equipment

Both types of conventional welding machines use the same pieces of welding equipment (attachments and supplies). This equipment includes supply cables and electrode holders, ground cables and clamps, welding helmets, electrodes, and gloves. See Fig. 14-11. *An arc welding helmet must always be worn while*

using an arc welder. The welding arc is much brighter than an oxy-acetylene welding flame, so proper eye protection is a "must" while arc welding. A good supply of electrodes should be kept on hand since the electrodes burn down as they form weld metal. Electrodes should be discarded when they are burned down to a 1- or 1½-inch length.

Fig. 14-9. A small, gasoline-powered generator welding machine. (Courtesy of Lincoln Electric Company.)

Fig. 14-10. A larger, gasoline-powered generator welding machine. (Courtesy of Lincoln Electric Company.)

Types of Electrodes—There are many different kinds of electrodes. Each electrode manufacturing company color-codes the electrodes according to several factors. These include the base metal on which the electrode should be used, the type of flux coating on the electrode, the welding position in which the electrode should be used, and other factors.

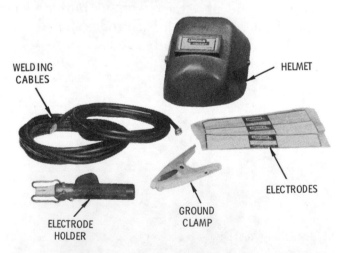

WELDING CABLES

HELMET

ELECTRODE HOLDER

GROUND CLAMP

ELECTRODES

Fig. 14-11. Welding equipment needed for arc welding. (Courtesy of Lincoln Electric Company.)

To be sure of using the right electrode for the job, read a manufacturer's color-coding chart. As shown in Table 14-1, these charts list the applications and color-code dots for various electrodes. These are industry standards.

Using Conventional Machines

Transformer welding machines are simple to operate. Generally speaking, the controls include an off-on switch, a control for setting the amperage, a *polarity* selector (on DC machines), and two lead terminals. One of the terminals is used for connecting the supply (output) cable to the machine. The supply cable is also known as the *electrode* cable; Fig. 14-8. The other terminal is used for connecting the ground (work) cable to the machine. The ground cable clamps directly onto the metal being welded (the work) so that the electricity can be returned to the machine, completing the circuit needed for welding.

Polarity—On an automobile battery, you may have noticed that the battery connections are marked + and −, or *plus* (positive) and *minus* (negative). This is because an automobile has a direct current, or *DC*, electrical system. When an electrical system (or circuit) is DC, one of the connections in the circuit must be positive and the other negative.

Electricity in a home or shop, though, is known as *AC*, or *alternating current*. AC has no positive or negative connections, just so long as the circuit is *complete* (has an unbroken path for the electricity to follow). Most of the smaller transformer welding machines, such as the machine in Fig. 14-7, put out only AC current, so polarity is no problem.

Larger machines, however, such as in Fig. 14-8, have a *polarity switch*. This allows the welder to choose the polarity he needs if an electrode (Table 14-1) or a certain position calls for a certain polarity. These larger machines have *rectifiers* inside, to change the incoming AC to DC for welding. For this reason, these machines are more properly known as transformer/rectifier welding machines.

Most body shop welding may be done with AC current, using the type of welder shown in Fig. 14-7. With this type of machine, there is no polarity to worry about. If a machine with a *polarity selector* (Fig. 14-8) is being used, the selector should be set on AC unless the electrode or job application recommends DC straight or DC reverse polarity. When a ma-

Table 14-1. Popular Arc Welding Electrodes and Their Common Uses

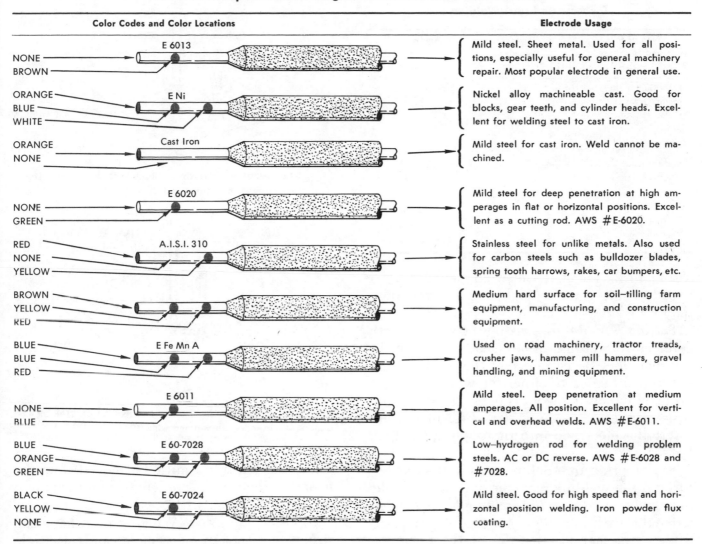

Color Codes and Color Locations	Electrode Usage
NONE / BROWN — E 6013	Mild steel. Sheet metal. Used for all positions, especially useful for general machinery repair. Most popular electrode in general use.
ORANGE / BLUE / WHITE — E Ni	Nickel alloy machineable cast. Good for blocks, gear teeth, and cylinder heads. Excellent for welding steel to cast iron.
ORANGE / NONE — Cast Iron	Mild steel for cast iron. Weld cannot be machined.
NONE / GREEN — E 6020	Mild steel for deep penetration at high amperages in flat or horizontal positions. Excellent as a cutting rod. AWS #E-6020.
RED / NONE / YELLOW — A.I.S.I. 310	Stainless steel for unlike metals. Also used for carbon steels such as bulldozer blades, spring tooth harrows, rakes, car bumpers, etc.
BROWN / YELLOW / RED	Medium hard surface for soil–tilling farm equipment, manufacturing, and construction equipment.
BLUE / BLUE / RED — E Fe Mn A	Used on road machinery, tractor treads, crusher jaws, hammer mill hammers, gravel handling, and mining equipment.
NONE / BLUE — E 6011	Mild steel. Deep penetration at medium amperages. All position. Excellent for vertical and overhead welds. AWS #E-6011.
BLUE / ORANGE / GREEN — E 60-7028	Low–hydrogen rod for welding problem steels. AC or DC reverse. AWS #E-6028 and #7028.
BLACK / YELLOW / NONE — E 60-7024	Mild steel. Good for high speed flat and horizontal position welding. Iron powder flux coating.

chine is set on DC *straight* polarity, the welding cable to the electrode holder must be the *negative* cable. For DC *reverse* polarity, the welding cable to the electrode holder must be the *positive* cable.

To use a conventional arc welder successfully, a body man must know how to strike an arc with the electrode and then how to use the arc to make a molten puddle for arc welding. The same type of welded joints made with an oxy-acetylene welder can also be made with an arc welder. However, these welds are made slightly differently when arc welding is used. For example, the metal may not be spaced in the same way, and the electrode may not be held at the same angle as would an oxy-acety-

lene torch. The following material explains how to correctly use conventional arc welders for body shop arc welding jobs.

Selecting Amperage and Electrode—To make good arc welds, the proper diameter electrode must be selected for the metal thickness being welded *and* the correct amperage must be used for that diameter electrode. Table 14-2 shows the recommended amperages and electrode diameters for common arc welding jobs in an auto body shop.

Tables 14-1 and 14-2 should be used together to determine the correct electrode number, diameter, and amperage to use for a certain job. When practicing, it is a good idea to start with the *lowest* recommended amperage shown in

Table 14-2. Amperage and Electrode Specifications for Auto Body Arc Welding

Type of Metal and Thickness (inches)	Electrode Diameter (inches)	Amperage Range (amperes)
Light Gauge Sheet Metal (Outer sheet metal, etc., up to 7/64-inch thick.)	1/16	10-30
	5/64	25-45
	3/32	40-70
Thin Mild Steel (Inner body structure, etc., 7/64- to 3/16-inch thick.)	1/8	50-130
	5/32	90-180
	3/16	130-230
Thick Mild Steel (Frames, etc., 3/16- to 5/16-inch thick.)	1/8	60-120
	5/32	90-160
	3/16	120-200
	1/4	190-300

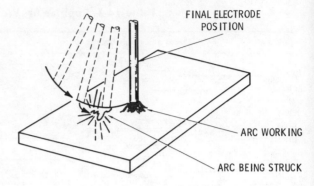

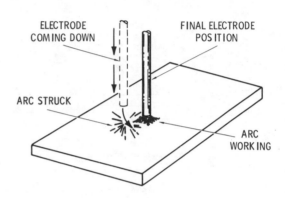

Fig. 14-12. Using the "scratch" method to strike the arc. This is most often used when welding with AC.

Fig. 14-13. Using the "tap" method to strike the arc. This method is more often used when welding with DC.

Table 14-2. Then, if the weld penetration or speed is not great enough, higher amperages may be used.

Setting Up—Before striking the arc, correctly connect the welding cables (leads) to the welding machine. Be certain that the ground cable is firmly attached to either the work or a metal table on which the work is being done. Finally, squeeze the electrode holder (Fig. 14-11) and insert the electrode into the open jaws of the holder.

Striking the Arc—Before striking the arc, first turn on the welding machine, put on the welding gloves, and *lower the welding helmet.* Then, strike the arc by scratching or touching the electrode to the metal so that the arc is formed. See Figs. 14-12 and 14-13.

Once the arc is working, the electrode must be held at the correct distance from the base metal so that the arc can be maintained. If the electrode is held too far away from the base metal, the arc will be broken. On the other hand, if the electrode is held too close, the electrode may become welded to the work! When this happens, the electrode holder can usually be twisted to free the electrode from the work surface.

Maintaining the correct arc length will require practice. Usually, however, an arc length of 1/16- to 1/4-inch is used for body shop arc welding, depending on the electrode diameter. See Fig. 14-14. This arc length should be maintained during the entire length of the weld.

Thus, the electrode must be moved down to maintain the correct arc length as it melts into the weld. See Fig. 14-15.

Running the Bead—When the arc has been struck, the molten base metal and electrode metal may be used to form a bead across the joint or work surface. Fig. 14-16 shows how the electrode should be held to do this. For the arc to properly melt the base metal, the electrode should be held at an angle of about 15° back toward the direction of travel, as shown in Fig. 14-16.

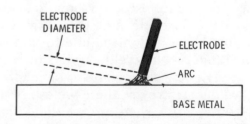

Fig. 14-14. After the arc is struck, the arc length should be about equal to the electrode diameter; about 1/16-inch to 1/4-inch for most body shop arc welding jobs.

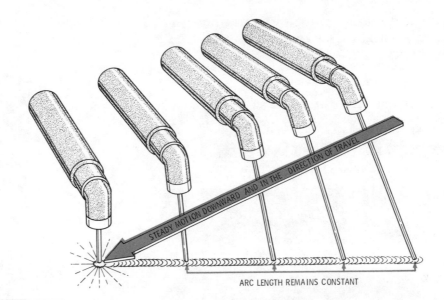

Fig. 14-15. As the electrode melts down, the holder must be moved down to keep the arc at the correct length.

STEADY MOTION DOWNWARD AND IN THE DIRECTION OF TRAVEL

ARC LENGTH REMAINS CONSTANT

If you are right-handed, hold the electrode holder in your right hand and use your left hand to help steady the right. Using *both* hands on the electrode holder gives better control over the electrode movement. If you are left-handed, reverse the hand positions. In either case, hold your elbows in close to your body for added balance and control.

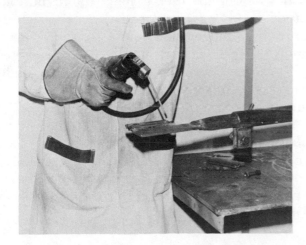

Fig. 14-16. The correct electrode angle for arc welding practice.

As the arc burns and melts the electrode, a puddle of molten metal is formed. This puddle will become solid, forming the bead, as the hot arc and melting electrode move forward along the weld line. When welding is done at the proper forward speed, the bead ridge where the puddle becomes solid will be about ⅜-inch behind the arc and electrode. As you weld,

then, *watch the puddle carefully* to be certain that the weld bead is forming evenly along the weld line for the speed being used.

Move the electrode and direct the arc at an even, steady speed while watching the weld bead solidify. Be sure to also maintain the proper arc gap and electrode angle with the work. Usually, only a forward motion is needed for bead practice. Avoid moving the electrode backward, sideways, or up and down. Correctly moving the electrode forward while lowering it as it melts will provide a strong, even weld.

The welds in Fig. 14-17 show examples of common weld defects. While practicing, these welds should be used for comparison. Also, notice the example of a *good* weld shown in Fig. 14-17. Arc welding skill is best learned by continued *practice*. For this reason, do not become discouraged if your first few arc welds have a poor appearance. Continue practicing the basic steps until you are able to properly control and direct the weld.

Arc Weld Joints

The five basic types of weld joints used in arc welding are the same as those used for oxy-acetylene welding. These include the butt, lap, tee, edge, and corner weld joints discussed in the oxy-acetylene units. When thin sheet metal is arc welded, a lap joint is most often used.

Metal plates to be arc welded should first be *tack* welded to keep them from spreading apart

WELDING CURRENT TOO LOW

WELDING CURRENT TOO HIGH

ARC TOO LONG (VOLTAGE TOO HIGH)

WELDING SPEED TOO FAST

WELDING SPEED TOO SLOW

PROPER CURRENT VOLTAGE & SPEED

Fig. 14-17. Practice welds and probable causes of the defects shown. (Courtesy of Hobart Brothers Company.)

while welding. When making a butt joint arc weld, be careful not to space the metal too far apart. Generally, a space of about 1/16-inch should be used between *thin* sheet metal pieces, and a space of about 1/8-inch between heavier pieces. Proper spacing provides good penetration and helps avoid melting away the edges of the metal.

SPOT WELDERS

Fig. 14-18 shows an electric *spot welder*. This handy body shop tool operates somewhat differently from the conventional arc welders just discussed. Spot welders do not have an amperage *dial* like those of conventional arc welders. Instead, spot welders have plug-in

Fig. 14-18. A typical body shop *spot welder*.

holes for either *low, medium,* or *high* amperage connections to the supply cable. See Fig. 14-18.

Spot welders are used to make round, button-shaped welds on over-lapping panels such as the lighter-gauge steel used for auto body panels. A spot welder may be used in almost any position. The tool is easy to use, light weight, and quickly welds panels with a minimum of warpage or distortion.

A limitation of spot welders is that they must *only* be used to weld lap joints or flange joints. See Figs. 14-19 and 14-20. This is because a spot welder depends on the electrical resistance between two pieces of metal to melt the pieces of metal together at that "spot."

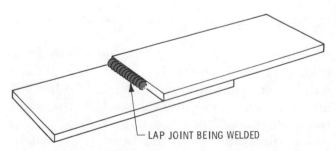

LAP JOINT BEING WELDED

Fig. 14-19. A lap joint, one of the two basic joints that may be welded with a spot welder.

Fig. 14-20. A *flange* (edge) joint, the second basic joint that may be welded with an arc welder. (Courtesy of Lenco Automotive Equipment Division.)

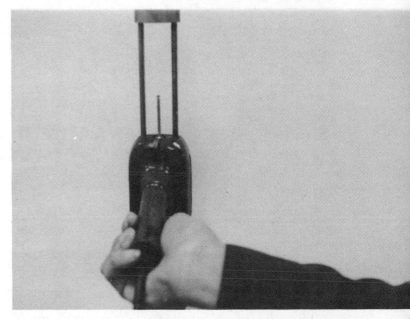

Fig. 14-22. The electrode is normally withdrawn and protected in the area between the guide rods.

Equipment—The lead cable from the spot welder has an electrode *gun* on the opposite end, as shown in Fig. 14-21. The welding electrode itself is positioned *between* the two guide rods of the gun. See Fig. 14-22. A "burn time" adjustment *knob* on the back of the gun is used to control the amount of time that the arc will "burn" on one spot weld. This refers to how long (how many seconds) the welder will pass electricity through the joint being spot welded.

Spot Welder Operation

To practice operating a spot welder, first connect the gun lead cable to the *low* amperage connection. If this setting does not provide a good, strong weld, the two higher amperages may be tried later. By starting out on the low setting, however, there is little danger of burning through the metal or otherwise damaging it while learning how to spot weld.

Next, insert the electrode into the nose of the gun. Then, turn the "burn time" adjustment on the back of the gun to a low (short burn) setting. Again, this is done to avoid damage to the work while practicing. If needed, the timer can be turned up later. Finally, clamp the return (ground) cable to the base metal near the weld area. See Fig. 14-23.

Procedure—To make a weld, position the gun so that the round, circle-shaped end of the gun's nose is firmly against the "spot" to be welded. The nose *must* make good contact with the base metal. (During spot welding, the gun is *not* held away from the metal while making the weld. This is a major difference between spot welding and conventional arc welding.)

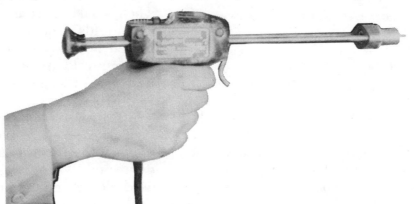

Fig. 14-21. A spot welder gun.

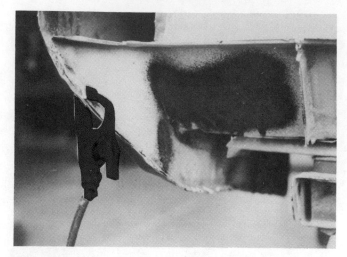

Fig. 14-23. The return cable clamped to the base metal. This is also known as the *ground cable*. On the spot welder in Fig. 14-18, it is known as the *work lead*.

With the nose firmly in place, push *down* on the gun, as in Fig. 14-24. This is done so that the guide rods in the nose retract. When they retract (go out the back of the gun), they allow the electrode to come into contact with the metal at the spot to be welded.

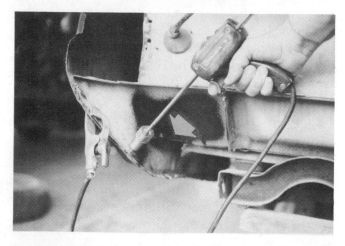

Fig. 14-24. Pushing down on the gun until the electrode contacts the base metal.

When the electrode has made contact, pull the trigger to form the arc. See Fig. 14-25. (This allows the electrode to supply electrical current for the weld.) This current melts the base metal within the round nose tip. Then, when the current is turned off by the timer, the metal solidifies to form the weld.

There is no need to worry about releasing the trigger because the gun automatically shuts

Fig. 14-25. Pulling the trigger causes electric current to pass through the electrode, making the arc weld at the "spot" being welded.

off (stopping the arc) when the timer "says" that the spot weld is completed. Of course, the weld timer is controlled by the timer knob that is usually on the back of the gun.

Technique—To install a panel, use the spot welder to *first* tack weld the overlapping panels. Then, make the required number of actual *spot* welds. The actual spot welds should be placed about one inch apart along the overlapping weld area or joint. This will produce a neat line of small welds with little distortion. Fig. 14-26 shows a completed spot weld repair.

After several spot welds, the electrode may be burned down enough so that it no longer touches the base metal when the gun nose is depressed. When this happens, discard the used electrode stub and place a new electrode in the gun nose.

Fig. 14-26. Small spot welds along the seam where a replacement panel has been installed.

PANEL SPOTTERS

Panel spotters, like electric spot welders, are special arc-welding machines used for spot welding in a body shop. Panel spotters are also used only on flange or lap joints or two pieces of metal that are closely clamped together. Panel spotters have an advantage in that they always make *two* spot welds at the same time. This allows the shop's work to be done faster. Fig. 14-27 shows a common body shop panel spotter.

A typical panel spotter has an automatic timer built into the amperage control. The amperage control may run from 0 to 100 amps. Each electrical cable of the panel spotter actually does two jobs. It *first* acts as a supply cord and *then* acts as a return cable for the electricity supplied by the *other* cable. At the end of *both* cables, then, is an electrode used to supply electricity for the spot welding process. These electrodes have special tips that do not melt into the spot weld. Normally, they are used for several months before being replaced.

Panel Spotter Operation

To use a panel spotter, first turn the control dial to the correct amperage and time selection for the job being welded. The correct time and amperage may vary according to the manufacturer's recommendations for the type of job being done. For this reason, *refer to the manufacturer's instructions and recommendations* for the brand of panel spotter being used.

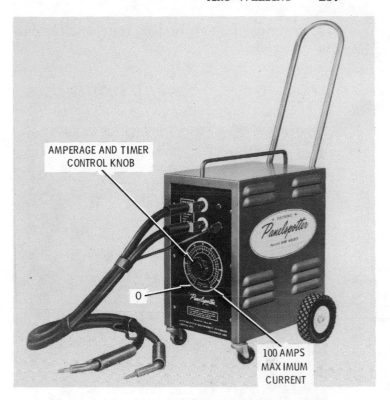

AMPERAGE AND TIMER CONTROL KNOB

0

100 AMPS MAXIMUM CURRENT

Fig. 14-27. A common panel spotter machine. This machine makes two spot welds at one time. (Courtesy of Lenco Automotive Equipment Division.)

With the adjustments made correctly, turn the machine on and place the two electrode "guns" on the areas where the *two* spot welds are to be made. See Fig. 14-28. Then, pull the control handle button on one electrode handle, turning on the current. The panel spotter machine will then produce two automatically-time-controlled spot welds. Examine the welds

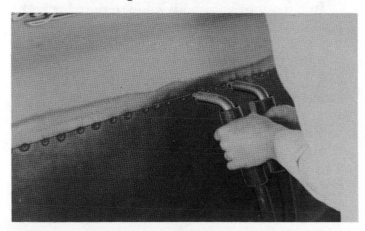

Fig. 14-28. Positioning the electrode guns to make additional spot welds on a replacement panel. (Courtesy of Lenco Automotive Equipment Division.)

to determine if more or less time and/or current is needed.

SPOT WELDER AND PANEL SPOTTER USES

Fig. 14-29. A small replacement panel that has been spot welded in place to repair a rusted-out area. (Courtesy of Lenco Automotive Equipment Division.)

In a modern auto body shop, either (or both) a spot welder and a panel spotter may be used to quickly spot weld clamped, overlapping panels with flange or lap joints. These machines are especially useful for quickly replacing or repairing panels damaged by rust or collision. For example, Fig. 14-29 shows a small, spot-welded patch on a panel that was rusted out. This type of spot-weld patchwork is especially useful on rusted out panels or those that have been torn in a collision.

Larger panel repairs may also be made quickly with a panel spotter. For example, Fig. 14-30 shows serious quarter panel damage that can easily be repaired with *either* a spot welder or a panel spotter.

To replace the damaged panel in Fig. 14-30, the panel would first be ground off along the line where the cut is to be made. This is done so that there will be a clean, roughed-up metal surface to which the spot welds and filler may adhere. When the metal has been ground off, the cut line may be marked with a heavy lead pencil or other marking tool. Then, the panel is cut along the cut line with a power chisel. The panel in Fig. 14-30 was cut about two inches below the high crown peak at the upper part of the panel. Fig. 14-31 shows the panel after the damaged area has been cut away.

The *new* panel area to be overlapped and spot welded must then be lightly ground with a disk grinder. This is done to remove the factory

Fig. 14-30. A badly damaged quarter panel. Notice the buckling and damage *in front* of the wheel as well as to the rear. This panel will have to be replaced. (Courtesy of Lenco Automotive Equipment Division.)

primer paint, preparing the surface for spot welds and filler. The new panel is then positioned so that it overlaps the cut-off edge of the old panel. Finally, Fig. 14-28 showed how the panel spotter would be used to spot weld the two panels. Fig. 14-32 shows the newly-spotted replacement panel before being filled, levelled, and refinished.

Fig. 14-31. The damaged panel in Fig. 14-30 has been removed with a panel-cutting power chisel. (Courtesy of Lenco Automotive Equipment Division.)

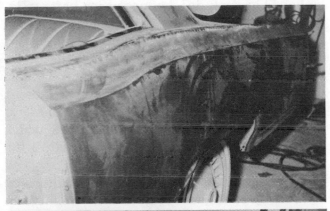

Fig. 14-32. A new quarter panel that has been spot welded in position. (Courtesy of Lenco Automotive Equipment Division.)

SPOT WELDER/PANEL SPOTTER ADVANTAGES

Spot welders and panel spotters used for fastening thin sheet metal are not as likely to buck or warp the metal as much as would the flame of an oxy-acetylene torch. This is because the heat from the actual weld itself is concentrated in a small area. These small electric welders are also less of a fire hazard than are oxy-acetylene welders, especially around fuel tanks and upholstery.

These machines normally cause fewer metal sparks and less molten metal in the shop than would conventional arc welders or oxy-acetylene welders. This is helped by having the weld automatically time controlled, so that the surrounding metal gets no hotter than is absolutely necessary.

SPOT WELDER/PANEL SPOTTER DISADVANTAGES

A major *disadvantage* of spot welders and panel spotters is that they cannot be used to fill large holes, tears, or gaps. Generally speaking, even *conventional arc welders* should not be used on openings more than ⅛-inch wide. This is because the high arc temperature may *burn away* the edges of a large opening, making it even larger. For this reason, care must be taken to leave an opening of *less than* ⅛ inch when two pieces of metal are to be electrically welded.

Another disadvantage of spot welders and panel spotters is that the electrode holders ("guns") must be held more or less *straight up* from the base metal for the best welds. Oxy-acetylene welders, of course, can also be used at different angles to the base metal. This allows a body man doing oxy-acetylene welding to have more control over heating the metal and moving the torch. Finally, oxy-acetylene equipment can be used to *heat* metal without welding it.

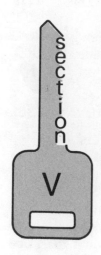
Major Repairs

Unit 15

Auto Body Construction

An automobile must be designed and put together so that it is able to do several jobs at once. For example, it must provide protection for its passengers, be fairly leak-proof, and be able to withstand the pressure of minor impacts. See Fig. 15-1. As the average person places more demands on his automobile each year, high-quality design, construction, and durability of the product become more necessary.

A comfortable, properly-designed automobile will give a smooth, tight ride, and will be relatively free of wind noises, road noises, and water leaks. To do these jobs over a long period of time, an auto body must be strong, yet flexible. It must be able to "give" with road shock without being damaged.

Basic Parts—There are two basic parts of an automobile: the *frame* and the *body*. The frame is the *foundation* of the vehicle. It provides the basic part to which all the other parts are attached. This includes the suspension parts (Fig. 15-2), the steering parts, and large parts such as the engine, transmission and differential.

The second basic part of the car, the *body*, is also attached to the frame. The body is built up, around, and over the frame in different panel sections, as shown in Fig. 15-3. These panels work together to seal out wind, water and noise, and to provide a protective cover for the engine, passengers, and luggage.

For an auto body to provide the qualities of comfort, strength, flexibility, and durability, its parts must be designed and assembled so that

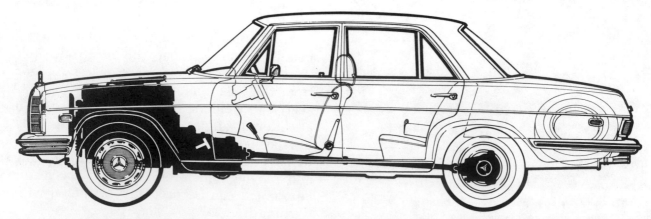

Fig. 15-1. An automobile must be a strong, integrated design that is able to do many jobs for a long period of time. (Courtesy of Road & Track Magazine.)

Fig. 15-2. Some part of the car's *frame* must be designed to support the front suspension parts.

they work *together*. Each individual part must do its own job and *also* coordinate with the other parts. Otherwise, the work of one of the parts might eliminate or work against a feature provided by another part. The frame, for example, must provide a strong foundation for the car and also help provide a smooth ride with the suspension system.

The information in this unit will explain, in detail, the jobs of the frame and the body parts of modern auto body construction. Major frame and body design is discussed along with their relative strengths and weaknesses. Finally, the various *parts* of these frame and body assemblies are explained.

FRAME

All vehicles must have some type of *frame* to act as the foundation of the vehicle. The underbody parts such as the front and rear suspensions must be attached to the steel beams or box sections of the frame. The vehicle's "drive train" or "running gear" must also be attached to the frame. These parts include all the parts needed to turn the wheels and move the ve-

hicle forward, such as the engine, transmission, driveshaft, etc. See Fig. 15-3. The body, with its riding compartment, is also fitted onto the frame.

Since the body (and the drive train and suspension parts) of a vehicle are attached to the frame, the *frame* is the most important part of the vehicle. The frame must provide the support and strength needed by the parts attached to it. If the frame parts are designed to go around the outside of the underbody, the frame's metal barrier will act as a safety guard for the body section of the vehicle. The frame must be strong enough to keep the other parts of the car in alignment. It must secure them so that they can withstand the forces and twisting action during all types of driving and minor impacts.

Basic Types—Since the early automobile, there have been many design changes and developments in frame sections and frame designs. Generally speaking, these changes have all centered around the development of *two basic types of frames*. These are known as the *conventional* frame (Fig. 15-4) and the *unitized body-frame* (Fig. 15-5).

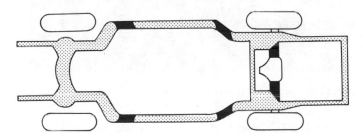

Fig. 15-4. A conventional frame from a late-model Chevelle.

Conventional Frame

Fig. 15-6 shows a typical *conventional* frame from under a late-model vehicle. Like others, this conventional frame is built of strong steel.

Fig. 15-3. An automobile *body* must be built up from and around the frame of a modern automobile.

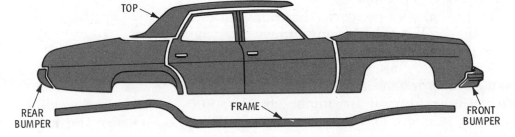

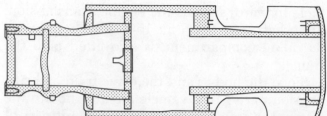

Fig. 15-5. A common frame design used with a unitized body-frame.

Not all frames are designed like the typical frame in Fig. 15-6. For example, Fig. 15-7 shows the designs used for other types of conventional frames.

Fig. 15-6. A typical conventional frame.

Conventional frames are normally built much like a bridge. They usually have two strong, heavy beams that run the full length of the vehicle. These are known as *side rails*. Several *crossmembers* hold the side rails in place and *parallel* (equally spaced) to each other. There are usually four or more crossmembers. See Fig. 15-8.

The body and other major parts of the vehicle are normally *bolted* to the frame. In this way, the body's riding compartment and the other major parts of the vehicle are supported by the frame. Basically, the earliest conventional frame designs and the latest designs are fairly similar, except for minor changes. For example, side rails and crossmembers were first

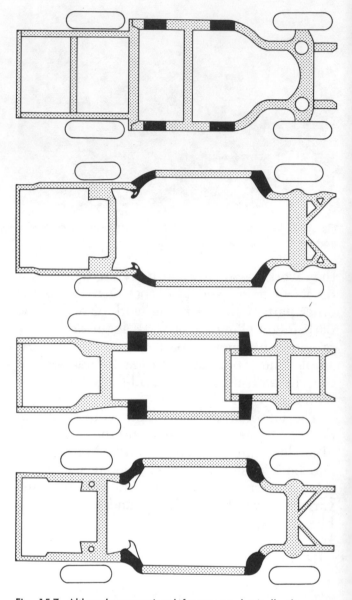

Fig. 15-7. Although conventional frames are basically the same, certain parts of each design may vary from one manufacturer to another.

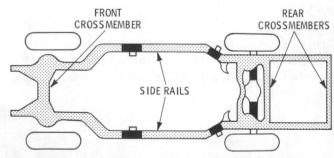

Fig. 15-8. The basic parts of a conventional frame.

joined to the side rails by being *riveted*. Now, they may be joined to the crossmembers by riveting, welding, or bolting them in place. For example, note that the crossmember in Fig. 15-9 is *bolted* to the side rail. The most basic change in conventional frame design, however, has been in the *shape* of the side rails and cross-members.

Early Frames—On the first conventional frame designs, the frame side rails were fairly simple, flat steel beams. Crossmembers were either made of flat pieces or were shaped from so-called *channel iron*. Channel iron crossmembers are often still used in today's designs, such as the channel iron crossmember shown in Fig. 15-10. The channel iron design gives the metal a U shape, like a channel. This is the reason for the name *channel iron*.

Fig. 15-10. A rear frame crossmember made of channel iron.

Fig. 15-9. A typical crossmember that is bolted to the side rail.

However, as automobile manufacturers began to build faster vehicles, better roads were built. Also, the public began to purchase and drive more and more automobiles. As speeds and the vehicle population increased, more cars came into use and there were more collisions and upsets. Because of these factors, the need and demand for safer vehicle designs and stronger frames were met in several ways. For example, manufacturers began to make both bodies and frames of thinner, yet stronger, more flexible, steel. Also, the shape of the *side rails* went through several changes.

Late Frame Designs—First, the side rail's shape was changed from a flat beam shape to an "I-beam" shape. See Fig. 15-11. This was done by simply welding flat "ends" to the top and bottom of the standard flat beam.

Many side rails were then changed from an I-beam to an angle-iron shape. See Fig. 15-12. Later, the channel iron shape that was first used for crossmembers was adapted to side rail design. Figs. 15-10 and 15-13 show the channel iron design.

Current Frame Design—Finally, the shape of the side rail was changed to a *box* shape. This was done by welding two channel iron pieces together to form a box section, as in Fig. 15-14. This side rail design has four flat sides to make up a box-like shape. This is the type of side rail commonly used in current frame designs. The crossmembers used with this box-like side rail have either a channel iron or box shape.

This type of frame design provides a strong, safe frame. Although it is strong, it is also *flex-*

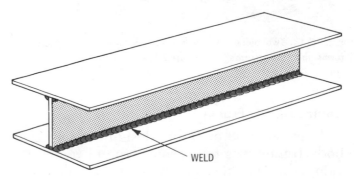

Fig. 15-11. I-beam iron.

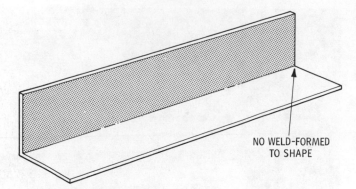

Fig. 15-12. Angle iron.

ible. It may give on impact, thereby absorbing much of the shock of a collision. This makes the vehicle safer for the passengers inside.

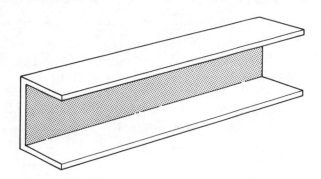

Fig. 15-13. Simple channel iron.

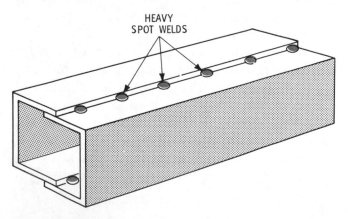

HEAVY SPOT WELDS

Fig. 15-14. Two pieces of channel iron spot welded together. This forms the "box frame" often used for the side rails in modern frame design.

Unitized Body-Frame

A newer type of frame design, the unitized body-frame, was the second type of frame developed. It has the same purpose and does the same jobs as a conventional frame. However,

the unitized body-frame *design* and *principle* are different because the body and frame are one piece. See Fig. 15-15.

Fig. 15-16 shows the underside of several different unitized body-frame designs. When unitized body-frame vehicles were first designed, the frame section was in some ways similar to that of conventional frame vehicles. The side rails extended down the entire length of the vehicle's sides, as in the unitized design shown in Fig. 15-17. The difference was that the body floor panels were *welded* to the frame. Conventional frame design, of course, had the body floor panels *bolted* to the frame.

Thus, the body panels and frame sections of a unitized body-frame design *are joined together as one unit*. As far as construction is concerned, the body and frame should be thought of as *one piece*, rather than as two separate parts. This idea is the reason for the name *unitized* or *unit* body-frame. The frame and body are designed and built as one unit.

Fig. 15-15. A common unitized body-frame design. (Courtesy of Autobody and The Reconditioned Car.)

Fig. 15-16 also shows how some of the later unitized body-frame designs differ from conventional frame designs. Note that many unitized body-frame designs do not have side rails down the full length of the body-frame. However, the body panels and frame sections are still welded together as one unit. Thus, some of the body panels are heavily built and reinforced to replace the side rail sections of a conventional frame.

Advantages—An important advantage of unitized body-frame vehicles is that they tend to be more tightly constructed because the

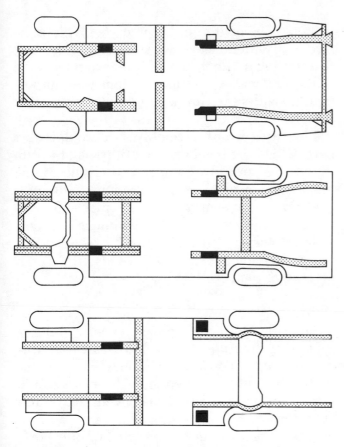

Fig. 15-16. Common underbody views of several unitized body-frame designs.

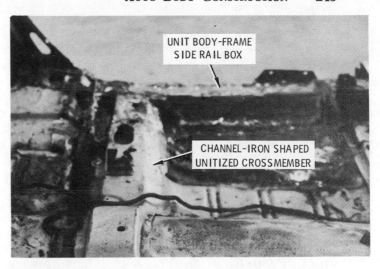

Fig. 15-18. Parts of the floor pan on a typical, unitized body-frame design.

major parts are all welded together. This construction design helps prevent squeaks, rattles, and water and dust leaks. Most unitized body-frame parts, then, are made of thinner steel than are the frame sections of conventional frame vehicles, and most of the frame section panels are made with a box-like construction. This makes the body-frame stronger but more flexible. See Fig. 15-18.

Disadvantages—A major disadvantage of u-nitized body-frames is that when one frame section is damaged, the frame sections attached to

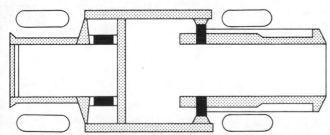

Fig. 15-17. A type of body-frame unitized design that uses welded side rails in its construction.

that section are usually also damaged. This means that the repair cost to the customer will be higher for this type of construction and that the vehicle may be harder to work on than one with conventional frame construction.

Floor—The actual *floor* part of a unitized body-frame is made of heavier metal than that of a body designed to be installed on a conventional frame. The floor is usually made up of a strong layer of sheet metal and reinforced with several crossbars (crossmembers). These cross-bars and the large metal floor stamping are welded together so that the floor section becomes several strong box sections. These welded box-like sections make the floor very strong but difficult to realign if it becomes seriously damaged.

The *floor* of a unitized vehicle, then, plays a major role in the alignment of the entire unit. If the floor has been buckled or damaged in an accident, the appraiser must add extra time and labor charges to align the floor structure when an estimate is made.

Additional strength is sometimes built into the floor by welding metal strips inside the box-shaped crossbars or side rail boxes. These metal strips usually run from one corner of the box to the other. These reinforcing strips are another reason for the name *reinforced channel* used to describe these parts. See Fig. 15-19.

Stub Frame—Some unitized body-frame designs appear to have side rails extending down

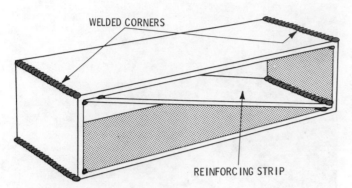

Fig. 15-19. When a reinforcing strip is welded inside a box channel, the box channel becomes much stronger.

the full length of the vehicle, when viewed from under the hood. This is actually not the case. Instead, this is a so-called "stub frame" design, shown in Fig. 15-20. Stub frames are widely used throughout the automobile industry, usually on smaller cars.

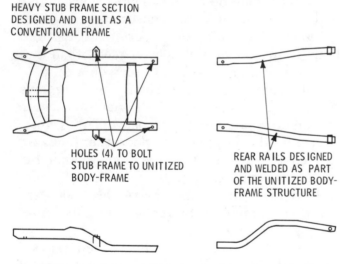

Fig. 15-20. A stub frame is bolted to the front of a unitized body-frame.

In a unitized body-frame *stub frame* design, the stub frame looks and is built just like a conventional frame. However, this "frame" does not extend under the complete vehicle. Rather, the stub frame stops under the car at about the front seat. Several bolts hold the front stub frame to the reinforced floor of the unitized body-frame making up the rear section of the automobile.

With a stub frame design, then, the side rails *do not* extend along the entire length of the

vehicle. The center and rear parts of the unitized body-frame have *no* side rails. The floor section takes the place of the extended side rails. This makes the floor section very important, as with other unitized body-frame section designs.

The stub frame assembly is a replaceable part. When the front or side rail parts of a stub frame are severely damaged, the stub frame may be replaced. The floor section of the unitized body-frame may also be replaced if it is damaged so severely that realignment is impossible. However, it usually *can* be realigned. If the floor is damaged *that* severely, the car is probably "totalled."

Torque Boxes

An important design development leading to smother riding and longer life was the *torque box* concept. Torque boxes may be adapted (used) on either conventional frames *or* unitized body-frames. A typical conventional frame with torque boxes is shown in Fig. 15-21. A unitized body-frame design with torque boxes is illustrated in Fig. 15-22.

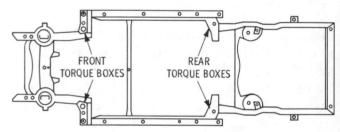

Fig. 15-21. Torque boxes on the corners under the passenger compartment of a conventional frame design. The torque boxes are part of the frame itself.

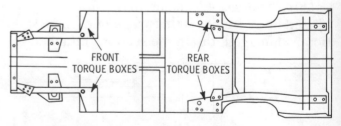

Fig. 15-22. Torque boxes on the corners under the passenger compartment of a unitized body-frame.

In a torque box design, the passenger compartment section of the frame is *wider* than either the front or rear sections *and* it is *box-*

shaped. The corners of this box are attached to the front and rear sections of the frame or unitized body-frame with *torque boxes.* The torque boxes actually twist to absorb the shock of bumps or rough roads while the car is moving along. The torque boxes also absorb much of the impact of a collision.

Simply, *torque* is a twisting or turning force. The purpose of torque *boxes* is to allow the front and rear sections of the frame to move up and down (twist) to absorb road shocks or impacts. See Fig. 15-23. Therefore, torque boxes *twist* to help keep the rough ride or shock in the front and rear sections of the automobile. This helps keep the shocks and jolts from reaching the passenger compartment.

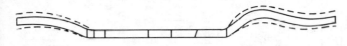

Fig. 15-23. A torque box operates by allowing the front and rear sections of the frame or unitized body-frame to actually twist (go up and down) with the suspension. Because the twist (up-and-down motion) is very small, it cannot be seen as the car moves along.

By 1965, most conventional and unitized body-frames had been equipped with some type of torque box design. Most of today's unitized body-frame automobiles have torque boxes in their construction. Torque boxes are so specialized that automotive engineers often use a computer to determine (figure out) where, exactly, the torque boxes should be and how they should be made. If the torque boxes become misaligned or damaged, the vehicle's steering and riding comfort may be seriously affected.

Frame Alignment

Automobile frames are constructed from strong steel. They must hold the vehicle and its parts in alignment over many types of driving conditions and for a long time. For these reasons, it is very important that the frame be in correct *alignment* if the car is to drive out and ride properly. Frames are designed and built with identification points for correctly measuring and checking the frame alignment. When a vehicle has been involved in an accident or may otherwise be misaligned, the checking points on the frame are used to be sure of the frame's correct alignment. Fig. 15-24 shows the location of one frame's reference points used for measurements when checking alignment.

Frame alignment is a *very* important part of total auto body repair. This is because if the frame is misaligned, the vehicle's body will also be misaligned. Frame misalignment will affect the appearance, the ride, and the handling of the vehicle. It can also cause greatly increased tire wear. The increased friction caused by frame misalignment may cause greater fuel consumption, since the engine will have to work harder to move the car. The procedure for checking and adjusting frame alignment is discussed in other units.

BODY

Vehicle bodies either fit or *form* the top of the vehicle's *frame.* There are several different jobs that *any* vehicle body must be able to do. It must provide a solid foundation for the passenger seats, glass, instrument panel, doors, and all the other body parts. It must protect passengers, luggage, and the engine from the weather. The body must be designed, therefore, with enough luggage, passenger, and engine space.

Main Sections

All automobile bodies have three main sections. These are "broken down" in Fig. 15-25:

1. The Front End Assembly.
2. The Passenger Section.
3. The Rear Section.

The different sections of an auto body are often given short "nicknames" by auto body repair men and auto body designers. For example, notice the used automobile front end assembly on top of the salvage yard delivery truck in Fig. 15-26. This part will be used to repair an automobile that has heavy front end damage. Then, look at the part from the *backside* in Fig. 15-27. This *front end* assembly is sometimes called a *doghouse,* because of the way it looks when it is taken off an automobile. It is made

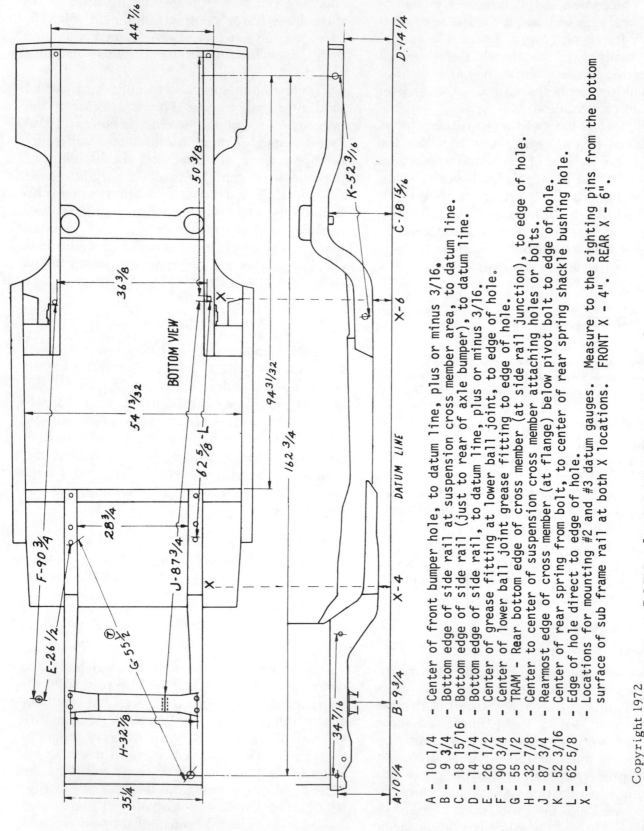

44 7/16

50 3/8

D-14 1/4

K-52 3/16

C-18 15/16

X-6

36 3/8

BOTTOM VIEW

94 31/32

54 13/32

162 3/4

62 5/8 - L

DATUM LINE

28 3/4

F-90 3/4

J-87 3/4

X-4

E-26 1/2

G-55 1/2

B-9 3/4

H-32 7/8

34 7/16

A-10 1/4

35 1/4

A - 10 1/4   - Center of front bumper hole, to datum line, plus or minus 3/16.
B - 9 3/4   - Bottom edge of side rail at suspension cross member area, to datum line.
C - 18 15/16 - Bottom edge of side rail (just to rear of axle bumper), to datum line.
D - 14 1/4   - Bottom edge of side rail, to datum line, plus or minus 3/16.
E - 26 1/2   - Center of grease fitting at lower ball joint, to edge of hole.
F - 90 3/4   - Center of lower ball joint grease fitting to edge of hole.
G - 55 1/2   - TRAM - Rear bottom edge of cross member (at side rail junction), to edge of hole.
H - 32 7/8   - Center to center of suspension cross member attaching holes or bolts.
J - 87 3/4   - Rearmost edge of cross member (at flange) below pivot bolt to edge of hole.
K - 52 3/16   - Center of rear spring from bolt, to center of rear spring shackle bushing hole.
L - 62 5/8   - Edge of hole direct to edge of hole.
X -   - Locations for mounting #2 and #3 datum gauges.   Measure to the sighting pins from the bottom
                surface of sub frame rail at both X locations.   FRONT X - 4". REAR X - 6".

Javelin   110 W.B.
Javelin AMX   110 W.B.

1972 American Motors - Javelin

Copyright 1972
by Harry M. Depew

Fig. 15-24. Typical frame dimensions for a unitized body-frame automobile. (Courtesy of Tru-Way Company.)

Fig. 15-25. An automobile body is made up of three main sections.

BACK SECTION
(REAR CLIP)

FRONT END ASSEMBLY
(DOGHOUSE)

PASSENGER SECTION
(GREENHOUSE)

up of the hood, the two front fenders and inner fenders, the grille, the radiator support framework, and other trim and small parts.

The *passenger* section in the center is often called the *greenhouse* because of the large amount of *glass* in the section. This section is made up of the roof panels, window glasses, cowl and instrument panels, floor pan, door frames, doors, and other major parts. Usually, the center section of an automobile is not replaced as part of a collision damage repair. If the collision was so bad that the center section was damaged beyond repair, the car is undoubtedly "totalled."

Fig. 15-26. A used doghouse being delivered from a salvage yard.

Finally, the back or *rear section* is usually referred to as the *rear clip*. When a rear section is badly damaged, it cannot be unbolted as easily and cleanly as can a doghouse. The rear section must be *cut off* the passenger section, usually with a cutting torch or power chisel. When this is done, the rear section appears to have

been "clipped" from the passenger section. This is why a removed rear section may be known as a rear clip, or simply *clip*. The back section (clip) includes the upper extension panel, deck lid, lower extension panel, quarter panels, trunk floor, and other trim and rear body parts.

Fig. 15-27. The rear view of a used doghouse.

Body Types

There are two basic types of bodies, just as there were two basic types of frames. The two *body* types are the *conventional* body and the *unitized* body-frame. Both types do the same jobs and have basically the same parts. However, they are different in certain design features and the method in which they are attached to the frame. Because of this, different body designs provide two different ways of handling the same problems, or doing the same jobs.

Conventional Body—A vehicle built and designed with a *conventional body* is designed so that the entire body is *bolted* to the frame. Conventional bodies are not as strong as are unitized body-frames because conventional bodies need a strong, separate frame underneath for much of their strength and tightness. The body sections alone do not have as much safety support for the passengers as do the sections of a unitized body-frame.

In conventional body construction, the body sections and parts are either bolted or welded to each other. Then, the entire body assembly is bolted to the conventional frame discussed earlier. In early automobile designs, the body was not designed to be as strong as the frame. In many recent designs, however, the body is designed to be quite strong and the frame is designed to be less rigid and more flexible than early designs. With this type of design, a flexible conventional frame (often with torque boxes) is used under a strong body so that the body and frame may flex together to provide a smooth, tight ride.

Unitized Body-Frame—The *unitized body-frame* is actually the same large piece as was discussed earlier under the *frame* topic. A unitized body-frame vehicle is a vehicle in which the body and the frame are designed, built and welded as one single piece of construction. A unitized body-frame is a reinforced shell (or welded group of boxes) to which the running gear and suspension are attached. Certain parts

of the unitized body-frame structure are used to support and align the running gear and suspension parts. Thus, the unitized body-frame structure must provide support and alignment points for the vehicle.

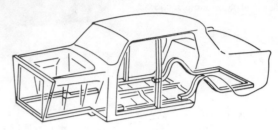

Fig. 15-28. A common structure of a unitized body-frame design. (Courtesy of Bear Manufacturing Company.)

Unitized body-frames are designed and assembled to provide their own strength. The structural member parts reinforce each other so that many adjoining box sections are formed. Fig. 15-28 shows how the *entire* vehicle is welded together from several box sections. The box section idea is particularly true in the floor section, as shown in Figs. 15-16, 17, 18, and 28. The heavy and important floor section has several support assemblies, many of which are sheet metal pieces spot welded into box sections.

Bumper Assemblies

Since the 1920's, most automobiles have had front and rear bumpers as standard equipment. Most present-day bumpers, like the one shown in Fig. 16-1, are made of bright, shiny, chrome-plated spring steel. There are also spring steel bumpers that are not chrome plated. These bumpers are simply painted, such as the bumper in Fig. 16-2.

Finally, some of the latest bumper designs are not made of steel. Instead, they are made of a special rubber called *urethane*. This urethane is molded around a steel core and the core is then attached to the car's frame. Because the urethane has no special color of its own, it may be colored the same as the car's body, or "body color." A typical urethane front bumper is shown on the Corvette in Fig. 16-3.

Fig. 16-1. A chrome-plated front bumper, also known as a *face bar*.

Fig. 16-2. A painted front bumper (face bar).

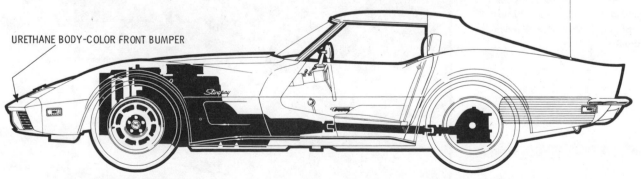

URETHANE BODY-COLOR FRONT BUMPER

Fig. 16-3. The newest type of front bumper is a urethane, body-color bumper. (Courtesy of Road & Track Magazine.)

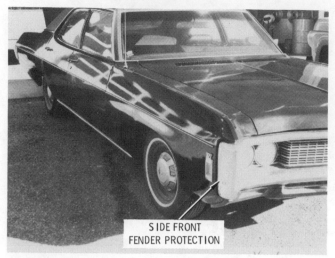

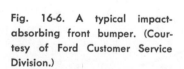

Fig. 16-4. A front bumper that wraps around and protects the front fender.

Fig. 16-5. A rear bumper that wraps around and protects the rear quarter panel.

Any type of bumper is very important in auto body design, and is usually an expensive item. The bumpers provide the vehicle's only protection for both the front and rear panels of the vehicle, since they extend across both the front and rear.

Bumpers on many vehicles also protect *side* areas of both the front fenders and rear quarter panels. These bumpers curve around the lower parts of the front fenders (Fig. 16-4) and quarter panels (Fig. 16-5). These extensions along the fenders and quarter panels provide additional protection for the sides of the vehicle.

Bumper Types—There are two general types of bumpers in use today. These may be described as *fixed* and *impact absorbing*. Most automobiles manufactured since 1972 have at least an impact absorbing *front* bumper. Most automobiles built since 1973 also have an impact-absorbing *rear* bumper. Impact-absorbing bumpers better protect the vehicle and its passengers from injury. Fig. 16-6 shows an impact-absorbing bumper. Before 1972, automobiles

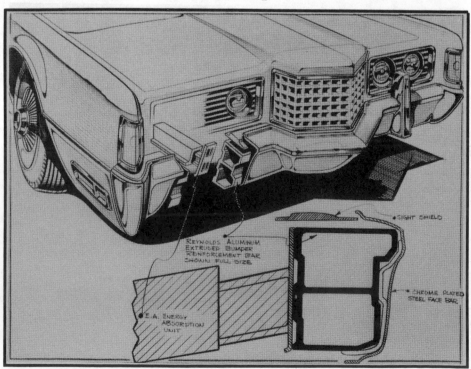

Fig. 16-6. A typical impact-absorbing front bumper. (Courtesy of Ford Customer Service Division.)

were usually protected with a fixed bumper such as the one shown in Fig. 16-7.

FIXED BUMPERS

Fixed bumpers are made from strong spring steel. They are attached to the vehicle's frame with one or more *brackets* on either side. See Fig. 16-7. These brackets are also made of very strong reinforced steel. The face bar and brackets have just enough spring or "give" to allow them to be pushed in slightly and to then move back in place. This spring-like action protects the vehicle's body and also absorbs some of the shock that would otherwise reach the passenger compartment. Of course, it does not do this job very well when compared to better, impact-absorbing bumpers.

Fixed Bumper Parts

Fixed automobile bumpers have several basic parts: a front or rear *face bar, bumper bolts,* and, sometimes, *bumper guards.* Bumper *brackets* are used to attach the bumper to the *frame* of the automobile.

Front Face Bar—The front bumper *face bar* on most cars is hard spring steel that is plated with the bright metal *chromium.* The front bumper is protection for the front end parts of the body. The front face bar is also an accent molding which helps beautify the front of the automobile. Fig. 16-7, for example, shows a front bumper face bar from an automobile with a fixed front bumper.

Rear Face Bar—Rear bumper face bars are made like front bumper face bars. They are made of the same steel and, usually, are also plated with chromium. They serve as the rear accent panel for the vehicle and help protect it during very minor rear end collisions.

Bumper Guards—Fig. 16-8 shows a face bar with *bumper guards* attached. Bumper guards have the same job as does the face bar. The main job of bumper guards is to protect the ends of the vehicle from other bumpers riding up, over the vehicle's bumper. However, bumper guards are also used to accent the appearance of the face bar and the grilles or panels in back of the bar.

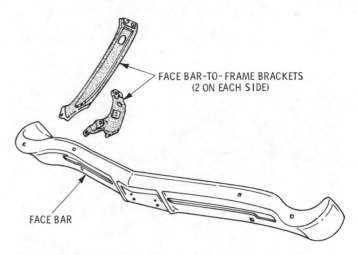

Fig. 16-7. A typical fixed front bumper.

Fig. 16-8. A face bar equipped with bumper guards.

Bumper Bolts—Bumper bolts are used to fasten the face bars to the *frame brackets.* These bolts normally have a square shoulder just under the head of the bolt, as in Figs. 16-9 and 10. This square shoulder fits into the square hole in the face bar, as shown in Fig. 16-10. A flat washer, lock washer, and nut hold the bolt in place from backside of the frame bracket, in back of the face bar. Most face bars have from two to eight bumper bolts. Chrome-plated heads or stainless steel "caps" on the bumper bolt heads add to the appearance of the face bar.

Bumper Brackets—In Fig. 16-7 are common bumper *brackets.* Bumper brackets are used to connect the face bar to the vehicle's frame.

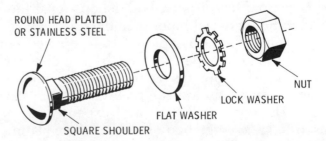

Fig. 16-9. A bumper bolt, washers, and nuts, as would be used to hold a face bar to its frame brackets.

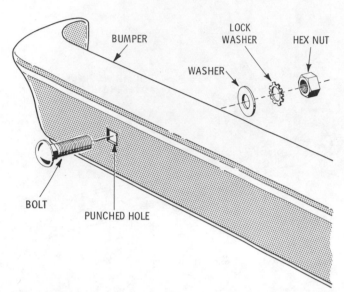

Fig. 16-10. The square shoulder of a bumper bolt is designed to fit in a square hole in the face bar. This keeps the bolt from turning as the nut is tightened.

The brackets are attached to the face bar with the bumper *bolts* mentioned earlier. Then, the brackets are bolted to the outer ends of the vehicle's frame. The brackets hold the face bars firmly in place on the frame.

Fixed Bumper Repairs

There are several repairs that need to be made to fixed bumpers during most auto body work. These commonly include *repairing* the bumpers, *replacing* the bumpers, and *adjusting* the bumpers. A complete body repair may be criticized if the bumpers are not properly aligned and adjusted.

Repairing Chrome-Plated Bumpers—Most chrome-plate bumpers that are damaged cannot be repaired in a body shop. This is because a damaged chrome surface cannot be ground smooth and filled as can a painted surface. For this reason, few, if any, body shops repair and rechrome plated bumper face bars.

Chrome plating is applied to a repaired (or new) metal bumper surface by an electrical process. This process is used by automobile manufacturers and in the rechroming industry, but it is too complicated and expensive to be used in an average body shop. Chrome plating, therefore, is not normally replaced by a body repair shop.

For a shop to "repair" damaged chrome bumpers, then, the damaged bumpers are usually exchanged for rechromed bumpers. Rechrome repair shops specialize in picking up damaged chrome bumpers that can be repaired. Then, workers at the rechrome shop reshape and rechrome the damaged bumpers so that they may be used again.

Fig. 16-11 shows a damaged, chrome-plated rear bumper face bar. It has been pulled away from the side of the car. Although the damage looks bad, this bumper may be straightened, rechromed, and used again. Fig. 16-12 shows the same bumper after it has been reshaped and rechromed. [Some damaged chrome bumpers are so badly bent up that they cannot be properly repaired. Most rechrome shops do not attempt to repair badly damaged bumpers, although many shops may splice (weld together) the good halves of two bumpers that were each badly damaged on one end.]

Insurance appraisers or wholesale customers often want a wrecked bumper to be replaced with a rechromed bumper. This is because a "rechrome" is usually cheaper than a new bumper. However, a rechrome bumper *is* a used and repaired bumper, so it should *only* be installed with the permission *and understanding* of the vehicle's owner. The customer must understand, from the shop manager, that the shop cannot guarantee a rechromed bumper. This is because rechromed bumpers will sometimes have the plating start to peel off. This causes the bumper to rust. See Fig. 16-13.

Fig. 16-11. A rear face bar that was badly bent in a collision along the side of the car.

Fig. 16-12. The same car and bumper as in Fig. 16-11. The bumper has been straightened, rechromed, and installed on the repaired car.

When this happens, the customer must understand that he will have to pay a *labor* charge to install another rechrome bumper, even if the rechrome shop guarantees the bumper itself.

Fig. 16-13. A rechromed bumper from which the chromium metal plating has started to peel.

Repairing Painted Bumpers—Painted bumper face bars are those that are not chrome plated. Instead, they are painted with enamel paint. Painted bumpers are used on almost all *trucks*. Earlier, Fig. 16-2 illustrated a painted bumper from a small truck. This type of bumper can be repaired in much the same way as are other metal parts.

Painted bumpers may be reshaped and aligned with power jacks. They can then be ground smooth and filled with body filler as necessary. Painted bumpers may then be prepared and repainted in the same way as are body panels.

Replacing Bumpers—When a vehicle has been involved in a front or rear collision, one or both bumpers usually need to be replaced. Whether a new, a rechrome, or a repainted bumper is installed, the procedure is basically the same. To replace a bumper, then, follow the procedure below:

1. Plan to remove the bumper face bar *and* brackets, together, from the frame.
2. Roll under the car and disconnect any light wires or attachments running to the bumper, such as the rear license plate light.
3. Remove the bumper bracket nuts and bolts *at the frame*. Rust penetrant may be needed to help break the bolts loose if they are large and rusty.
4. Have a helper hold the bumper while you remove the last two bolts.
5. With the helper, remove the complete bumper assembly (face bar, guards, light assemblies, and frame brackets) from the car.
6. Place the bumper face down on a convenient work surface. See Fig. 16-14.
7. Check the slotted bolt holes on the vehicle's *frame*. See Fig. 16-15. Be sure that they are not badly torn or stretched. If so, the vehicle may have additional frame damage.
8. Set the replacement bumper next to the old bumper.
9. Transfer all the brackets and lights from the old bumper to the replacement.
10. If the vehicle has bumper *guards*, Fig. 16-16, be certain that they are installed correctly. First, install the guard's rubber strip, if so equipped, as in Fig. 16-17. Then, install the guard on the bumper, Fig. 16-18.
11. With a helper, install the complete bumper on the vehicle's frame. *Leave the frame bolts loose* to allow for adjustment.
12. Connect any light wires running to lights in the bumper assembly.
13. Adjust the bumper for a correct, even fit. This is discussed next.

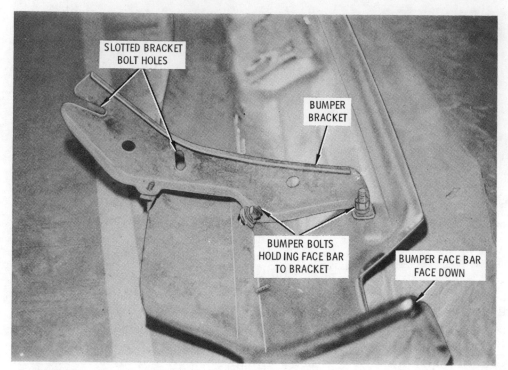

SLOTTED BRACKET
BOLT HOLES

BUMPER
BRACKET

BUMPER BOLTS
HOLDING FACE BAR
TO BRACKET

BUMPER FACE BAR
FACE DOWN

Fig. 16-14. A bumper assembly removed from the car and positioned for disassembly.

Adjusting Bumpers—To allow the bumper to closely and correctly fit the contour of the car, the bumper and its brackets can be adjusted up, down, in, and out. This adjustment is possible because of the slotted holes in the end section of the frame to which the brackets are attached.

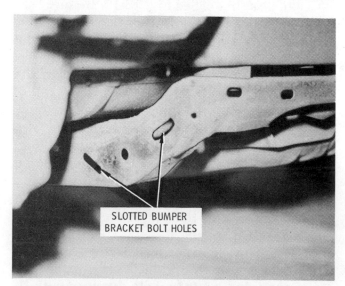

SLOTTED BUMPER
BRACKET BOLT HOLES

Fig. 16-15. Slotted bolt holes in the frame allow the bumper assembly to be adjusted by changing the bolt locations.

These slots allow most bumpers to be adjusted as much as one inch up and forward or down and inward. The slotted holes on both the

frame and brackets are covered with large flat washers to hold the parts in tight alignment when the frame-to-bracket bolts are tightened.

To adjust a bumper, have at least one, and preferably two, helpers to hold the bumper in position while you tighten the bolts at the frame from under the car. Tighten the bolts just slightly and then roll out from under the car. Check the bumper alignment at the corners and across the top edge of the bumper. Be certain that the distances are *equal* all the way across and around the bumper. If necessary, loosen the frame bolts slightly and realign the bumper.

Fig. 16-16. Replacing a bumper guard on a bumper assembly.

Fig. 16-17. Replacing the rubber strip on the front of the bumper guard.

Finally, tighten the frame bolts very tightly. Then, check the operation of any lights in the bumper to be sure that they are working correctly.

Fig. 16-18. Fastening the assembled bumper guard to the bumper face bar.

IMPACT-ABSORBING BUMPERS

Since the early 1970's, most automobiles built in the United States are equipped with bumpers that will withstand much more shock than will fixed bumpers. These bumper assemblies have many parts and are known as *impact-absorbing* bumpers. Generally speaking, impact-absorbing bumpers are able to withstand impact with a flat barrier at 5-mph in the front and 2½-mph in the rear, without being damaged. These bumpers are designed to withstand these impacts without damage to the vehicle's lighting, exhaust, fuel, cooling, and the hood and deck lid latching systems. This was done to

provide better protection for both the vehicle *and* its passengers.

Impact-absorbing bumpers, then, are able to absorb low-speed impacts without damage to either the vehicle or its passengers. Also, impact-absorbing bumpers *absorb* minor impacts and are then able to return to their original position without being damaged. Because of these design requirements, many new parts and new technology were needed to produce impact-absorbing bumpers. For example, Fig. 16-19 shows a typical breakdown of an impact-absorbing bumper assembly. A basic feature of most impact-absorbing bumper systems is the use of energy (impact) absorbing hydraulic cylinders to which the bumper assembly is mounted. Fig. 16-20 shows a common hydraulic cylinder absorber unit.

Fig. 16-20. Energy (impact) absorber unit. This unit replaces the conventional frame brackets in the bumper assembly. (Courtesy of Fisher Body Division.)

Other Systems—Some impact absorbing bumper systems are completely different than those used on most larger, late-model passenger cars. In this second design, a "metal deformation" (deforming, bending) technique is used to absorb the impact. Also, the bumper face bar *surface* is actually a "body color" urethane pad covering a steel bumper bar. The pad looks like part of the body because it fits up close *to* the body and is the same color *as* the body. This system is shown in Fig. 16-21.

After an impact at up to 5 mph, the urethane pad comes back out to its original shape with little or no *visible* evidence of the bump. However, the steel impact bar, the two energy-absorbing bolts, and the two end brackets *must* be replaced, since they will have been per-

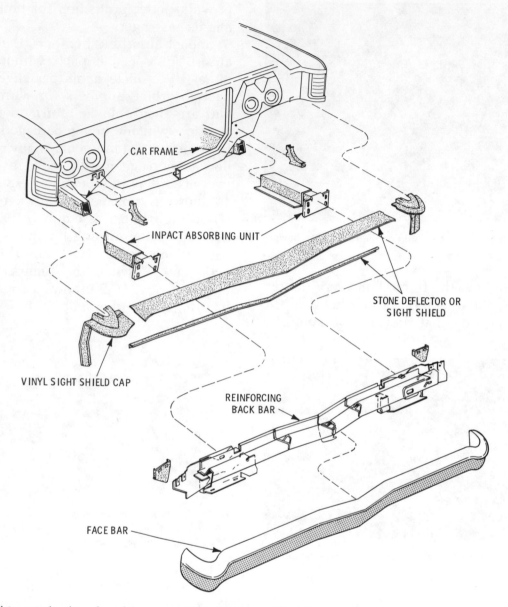

CAR FRAME

INPACT ABSORBING UNIT

STONE DEFLECTOR OR SIGHT SHIELD

VINYL SIGHT SHIELD CAP

REINFORCING BACK BAR

FACE BAR

Fig. 16-19. Typical impact-absorbing front bumper assembly. (Courtesy of Ford Customer Service Division.)

manently damaged (deformed) by the impact. See Fig. 16-21.

The advantages of this system are lower initial cost and lighter weight. Of course, it is more expensive to *repair* this system because the parts mentioned above must be replaced after *each* impact at up to 5 mph. In a standard impact-absorbing system, no parts are damaged by impacts below 5 mph.

Impact-Absorbing System Parts

Impact-absorbing bumper systems usually have more parts than fixed bumper systems. Al-though many of the parts have similar jobs, the parts of an impact-absorbing system are generally heavier, stronger, and more expensive than comparable parts of a fixed bumper system.

Face Bar—An impact-absorbing bumper *face bar* is much like a fixed bumper face bar. It is usually chrome plated and has the same types of curves and shapes as does a fixed bumper bar. Both types of face bars also have the same types of bumper guards. Painted impact-absorbing face bars can be repaired and repainted in the same way as can painted fixed face bars.

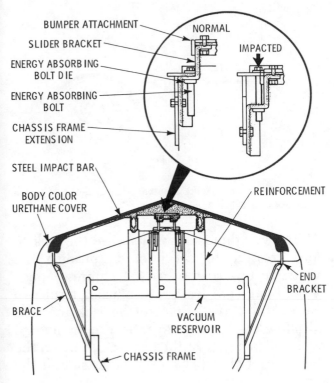

Fig. 16-21. A metal deformation impact-absorbing system. In this system, several parts are permanently damaged with each impact and those parts must then be replaced. (Courtesy of Fisher Body Division.)

Chrome-plated impact-absorbing face bars can also be repaired and rechromed as described earlier.

There are several differences between fixed and impact-absorbing face bars. One of the big differences is that impact-absorbing face bars are mounted about three to four inches away from the sheet metal parts of the vehicle. This is true for both front and rear face bars. This distance allows the bumper assembly to move in, absorbing impact, without damaging the vehicle's sheet metal.

Two other differences include the *weight* of the face bar and the method by which it is attached to the frame. Face bars on impact-absorbing bumper systems tend to be made of thicker and heavier steel. Because of this, the face bar usually weighs a good deal more than the face bar of a fixed bumper system. Impact-absorbing face bars (and back bars, discussed next) are attached to the frame with absorber units (Figs. 16-19 and 16-20) instead of fixed frame brackets.

Back Bar—Impact-absorbing bumper systems have strong, heavy *back bars* just in back of the face bar. The face bar is bolted to the back and the back bar is then bolted to the impact-absorber units. Notice the heavy back bar in Fig. 16-19 and how it is mounted to the vehicle's frame in Fig. 16-22.

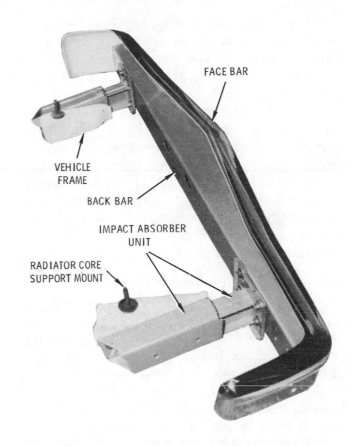

Fig. 16-22. Impact-absorbing bumper system, as mounted on the vehicle's frame. (Courtesy of Ford Customer Service Division.)

Normal bumper bolts hold the face bar to the back bar. Many bumper bolts are often used because the face bar and back bar must be securely fastened together to act as one unit. Note the row of bumper bolts used on the impact-absorbing face bar shown earlier in Fig. 16-1. Large bolts then hold the back bar to the impact-absorber units.

Impact Absorbers—The reinforcing back bars of impact-absorbing bumper systems are attached to the impact absorbers themselves. The impact absorbers fit onto the frame horns as shown in Fig. 16-19.

Like other automotive parts, the design and shape of the impact absorbers is not exactly the same from one manufacturer to another. Manufacturers generally use either *round* impact absorbers (Fig. 16-20) or *square* impact absorbers (Figs. 16-6 and 16-22). No matter what their shape, all impact absorbers do basically the same job.

When an impact occurs, the impact-absorbing bumper assembly is pushed back, *into* the impact absorbers. The absorbers act like shock absorbers, cushioning the blow inside the absorber unit so that the frame does not have to absorb or feel the impact. Then, the impact absorber pushes the bumper back out, into its normal position. Thus, low-speed (under 5 mph) impacts are absorbed without damaging the vehicle's body parts. (At speeds *over* 5 mph, the impact absorber units and other parts of the car will likely be permanently damaged and will require body shop work to repair and replace the damaged parts.)

Testing Impact-Absorbing Bumpers

Impact-absorbing bumper systems may be *tested* to see if they are in proper working condition. Testing the system involves separately compressing the impact absorber on each side of the car. The absorber must be compressed at least ⅜ inch. After this compression, the bumper must return to its normal position if the impact absorber is working correctly.

Procedure—To test the impact absorber system, the vehicle's ignition must be turned off, the transmission placed in *Park*, and the parking brake *firmly* set. Be sure that the car is first parked near a usable barrier. Any suitable barrier (either inside or outside a building) may be used. Good examples would include a pillar, a sturdy block wall, or a post. Then, locate a hydraulic or mechanical jack and place the jack in a horizontal (flat) position *between* the face bar and the barrier. See Fig. 16-23.

Align the jack so that it is in front of the impact absorber unit being tested. (Bumper jack slots under the bumper may be used to locate the absorbers.) Position the jack *squarely* with the bumper to avoid having it accidentally slip off to one side.

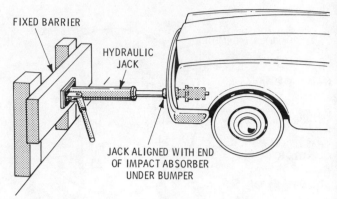

Fig. 16-23. Testing an impact absorber unit on one side of the car. (Courtesy of Fisher Body Division.)

With everything in position, use the jack to apply pressure to the bumper, pushing the bumper in toward the body. Compress (push in) the bumper at least ⅜ inch, using a ruler to measure the travel. Release the jack pressure and allow the bumper to return to its normal position. Then, repeat the test procedure on the other impact-absorber on the other side of the bumper.

If both impact absorbers return correctly, the bumper system is able to withstand low-speed impacts and return to its original position. If a unit fails to return to its original position, it should be replaced. (Driving into the post, walls or other barriers to perform this test is **NOT** recommended.)

Testing Collision Cases—A similar test may be used to check impact absorbers that have been removed to make repairs on a vehicle after a collision. In this case, the jack is again used to compress each absorber about ⅜ inch. However, *two* fixed barriers must be used. This is necessary so that both the absorber unit *and* the jack can be held firmly in position. To do this, one barrier is placed behind the jack and a second barrier is placed behind the impact absorber.

Make the test and observe whether the unit returns to its normal position after being compressed. If it does not return to its normal position, the impact absorber is damaged internally and must be replaced.

Replacing Impact-Absorbing Bumpers

When an impact-absorbing bumper has been damaged in a collision, certain precautions must be taken when working on the assembly. The precautions are necessary due to the fact that the absorber units are filled with either a gas or a liquid, or both. Impact absorbers can produce considerable force if they are bound up and suddenly released.

Generally speaking, removal and repair procedures for impact absorbing bumpers and fixed bumpers are similar. However, when working on an impact-absorbing bumper system, keep the following points in mind:

1. Do not apply heat to the impact-absorbers, either with a welding torch or other heat tools.
2. Do not attempt to weld or bend impact absorber units. If a unit does not work correctly, it must be replaced.
3. When only *one* impact absorber is being removed, support that end of the bumper so that the bumper will not fall when the one absorber is removed.

Bound-Up Absorbers—When a vehicle with *round* impact absorbers has been involved in a bad collision, one or both absorbers may have been pushed back and bent, causing them to stick (bind up) in the *compressed* position.

This is a dangerous situation, because if the pressure holding the absorber compressed is suddenly released, the absorber may shoot forward causing injury or damage in the area.

To handle this problem and disassemble the damaged car without being injured, follow these directions:

1. Wear safety goggles.
2. Stand clear of the bumper at all times.
3. Attach a chain or cable to the bumper to restrain (keep) the bumper from flying forward if the tension is suddenly released.
4. *Relieve* the pressure in the absorber by drilling a small hole in the front part of the absorber, near the bumper back bar.
5. With the pressure relieved, remove and discard the damaged impact absorber unit.

Adjusting Impact-Absorbing Bumpers

Like fixed bumpers, impact-absorbing bumpers will also need to be properly adjusted for good fit and appearance when collision damage has been repaired. To adjust impact-absorbing bumper assemblies, slotted holes are usually

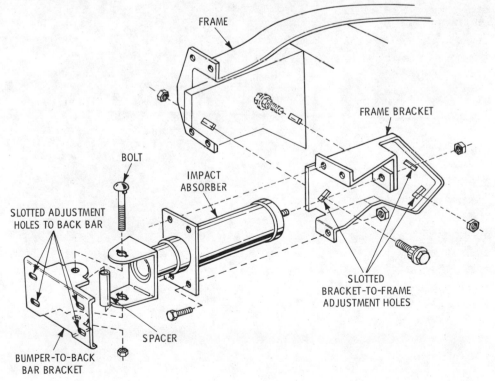

Fig. 16-24. Adjusting an impact-absorbing bumper assembly may be done by having slotted adjustment holes at the back bar and frame brackets.

provided in the rear of the back bar where it bolts to the absorber bracket *and* at the absorber-to-frame bracket. See Fig. 16-24.

Side-to-side face bar adjustments are normally made at the slotted holes in the bumper-to-back bar bracket (Fig. 16-24). Up and down and/or in and out adjustments are usually made back at the frame, similar to the adjustments made on a fixed bumper assembly. The exact adjustments and slots will vary from car to car, but the procedure is very similar to the procedure outlined earlier for adjusting fixed bumpers. Since impact-absorbing bumper assemblies are quite heavy, two helpers will probably be necessary to help hold the assembly while it is aligned and the bolts tightened.

(Courtesy of Guy-Chart Systems.)

Frame Straightening

Automobile *frames* are made in many different shapes and from different types of steel. *All* frames, though, must provide a firm and correctly aligned foundation for the vehicle. The frame must support the major parts such as the engine, the front and rear suspensions, and the body. Because the frame is heavy and important, expensive and accurate equipment (Fig. 17-1) is required to correctly straighten a frame should it become bent.

Frame Review—Figs. 17-2 and 17-3 review the basic types of frames: *conventional frames* and *unitized body-frames*. Conventional frames, of course, have the body *bolted* to the frame. Unitized body-frames, Fig. 17-3, have both the body and frame designed, welded, and built as one piece. The alignment and strength of either frame design is equally important.

Many late-model frame designs use *torque boxes* for a smooth ride. Fig. 17-4 shows the

Fig. 17-1. Positioning a damaged automobile on a permanent, "in the floor" frame alignment rack. (Courtesy, Blackhawk Division of Applied Power Industries.)

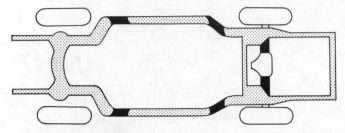

Fig. 17-2. Conventional frame construction, where the body and the frame are two separate parts.

common locations of torque boxes on torque-box-equipped frame designs. From a safety standpoint, frames with torque boxes may be safer because the frame's torque box area will absorb much of the impact of a front or rear collision. The torque box area will give, absorbing some of the impact.

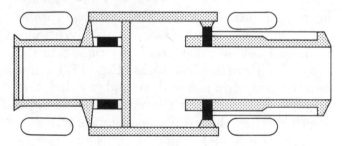

Fig. 17-3. Unitized body-frame construction, where the body and the frame are designed, built, and welded as one unit.

The "everyday" job of torque boxes, of course, is to help provide a smooth ride. If one wheel hits a bump, part of the shock transferred to the frame is absorbed by the torque box near that wheel. This reduces the shock transferred to the passenger compartment.

IMPORTANCE OF FRAME STRAIGHTENING

There is a good deal of profit and importance in the frame straightening work of a modern body shop. Considering the time saved and the customer satisfaction received, most frame straighteners will pay for themselves in a short time. Since the vehicle's tightness, panel fit, and driving accuracy depend on good frame alignment, frame work is a very important part of any larger auto body repair business.

Frame Man's Job—To get the best results, a body mechanic or special frame man must

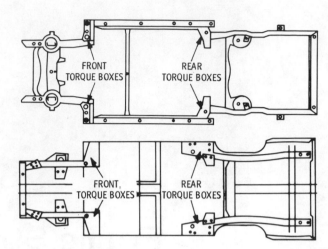

Fig. 17-4. Torque boxes may be designed into either conventional or unitized body-frame vehicles.

know the basic principles of frame straightening *and* the instructions on how to operate the unit being used in a given shop. He must know how to *disect* a frame (check it by sections) for a complete and accurate appraisal (idea) of what damage has been done to the frame. He must also be able to estimate the *cost* of repairing the damage. The repair man must have and know how to use a *specification book* to see how much damage is present and how far the frame is out of alignment. Finally, this specialist must know how to gauge (measure) a frame after repair, to be sure that all the measurements are within specification.

TYPES OF FRAME STRAIGHTENING EQUIPMENT

All but the smallest body shops are usually equipped with some type of *frame straightener*. Smaller shops normally have *portable* units priced from several hundred dollars on up, such as the unit in Fig. 17-5. Permanent *rack-type* frame straighteners, costing several thousand dollars, are normally used in large shops or frame specialty shops. A typical rack-type straightener (Fig. 17-6) is available with many different attachments.

Portable Units—Portable frame straightening units are profit-making pieces of equipment. They are especially useful in small shops that cannot afford big, expensive equipment. A main advantage of a portable unit over a larger, rack-

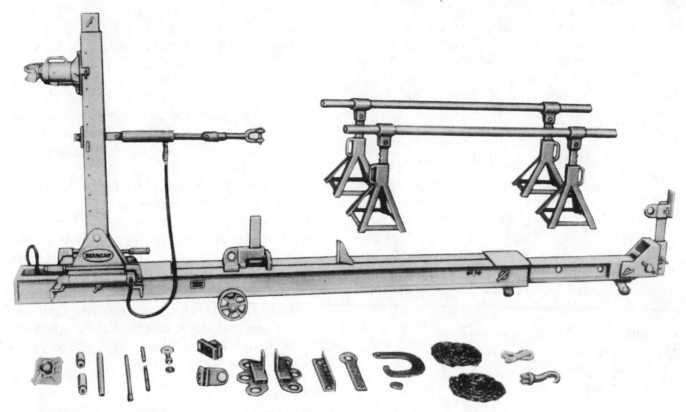

Fig. 17-5. A portable frame straightener. (Courtesy of Bear Manufacturing Company.)

type straightener is that the portable unit can be moved anywhere in the shop and then easily stored out of the way. Portable units are light, strong, and inexpensive. Small shops should have a good portable frame straightening unit.

Rack-Type Units—Heavy rack-type frame straighteners are stationary and more expensive than portable units. They are, however, the best frame straighteners to use from the standpoint of *speed.* The vehicle is either pulled or driven onto the rack and, then, *several* hook-ups may be made. By doing this, more than one damaged area can be pulled *at the same time,* a feature that is usually not available on most portable frame straightening units.

PREPARING FOR FRAME STRAIGHTENING

Getting the vehicle ready for frame straightening may be time-consuming and expensive. Vehicles in serious enough collisions to require frame straightening are often not able to be driven. Because of this, they must be towed or pushed around the shop and parking area. Sometimes, damaged panels may need to be removed *before* the frame may be straightened. This, of course, will require shop labor even before the frame straightening is done.

When a seriously wrecked vehicle is pulled to a shop's storage area, the wreck is usually left in storage (at a daily charge) until all the insurance work and legal action has been settled.

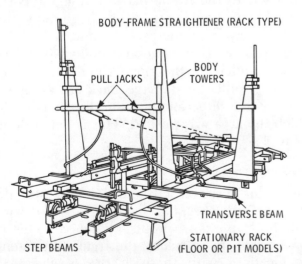

Fig. 17-6. A stationary, rack-type frame straightener. This type of unit is normally bolted to the floor and remains in one location. (Courtesy of Bear Manufacturing Company.)

Then, the vehicle is positioned in the frame straightening area (Fig. 17-1) or on the frame rack. When the vehicle is properly positioned on the frame rack, it may be measured and checked to see how much damage has been done.

ESTIMATING FRAME DAMAGE

There are four basic steps used to straighten a frame. These steps must be considered and followed when making an *estimate* of the cost to repair any frame damage. All four steps are important to correct frame straightening. Because of this, the time spent doing each step will affect the total cost of the frame repair. The four basic steps include:

1. Diagnosis
2. Preparation
3. Hook-Ups
4. Checking

Diagnosis

Making a *diagnosis* of frame damage includes *looking* at the damage and then using your eyes *and* the frame gauges to inspect the frame and see just how much damage has been done. This should include making a complete mental diagnosis of the damage and "thinking out" the method that will be used to straighten the damage. When making this diagnosis, try to answer the following questions to yourself:

1. How many parts will need to be removed?
2. How much time will the hook-ups take?
3. Will the frame need to be welded or heated during the repair?
4. How much time will the actual pulls require?
5. How much time will the *total* frame repair take?

Preparation

To prepare yourself for the frame repair on a given job, first know and understand the type of frame on which you are working. Next, find and arrange the materials needed. Put the needed tools and alignment equipment in the frame work area. Arrange all the charts and specification books for the vehicle frame to be repaired. For example, Fig. 17-7 shows a specification page for a conventional frame automobile. Fig. 17-8, on the other hand, shows a specification page for a unitized body-frame automobile. Fig. 17-9 shows one manufacturer's specification books *and* tools marketed for checking frame damage.

The next step toward preparation is to move the vehicle onto the frame rack. If the vehicle is badly damaged, of course, it may have to be towed or pushed into the frame repair area or onto the alignment rack. With the vehicle in the frame repair area, remove any sheet metal panels that are blocking easy access to the needed repair. In Fig. 17-1, for example, note that most of the damaged sheet metal (the "doghouse") has been removed to allow good access to the frame damage being repaired.

Hook-Ups

The process of actually repairing the frame damage is done by connecting frame holders, pushers, and pullers to various parts of the frame. Then, when these tools are jacked or pulled, the frame is straightened out to its original shape. Making these connections is known as *making the hook-ups.*

The hook-ups should be planned after locating the point of impact and determining what happened to the frame parts during the collision. Then, hooking-up and beginning the pull(s) may be done. (On a unitized body-frame vehicle, the frame and body panels are usually pulled at the same time.) Generally speaking, pull the damage back by applying pressure in a direction opposite the direction in which the area was pushed. This is being done in Fig. 17-10.

Checking

The final cost on a frame damage estimate must include *checking* the job to make sure that the frame is in proper alignment. This is done, again, by checking the frame alignment specifications with those in the specification book. Another minor cost will be repainting all the frame areas where heat and chains have

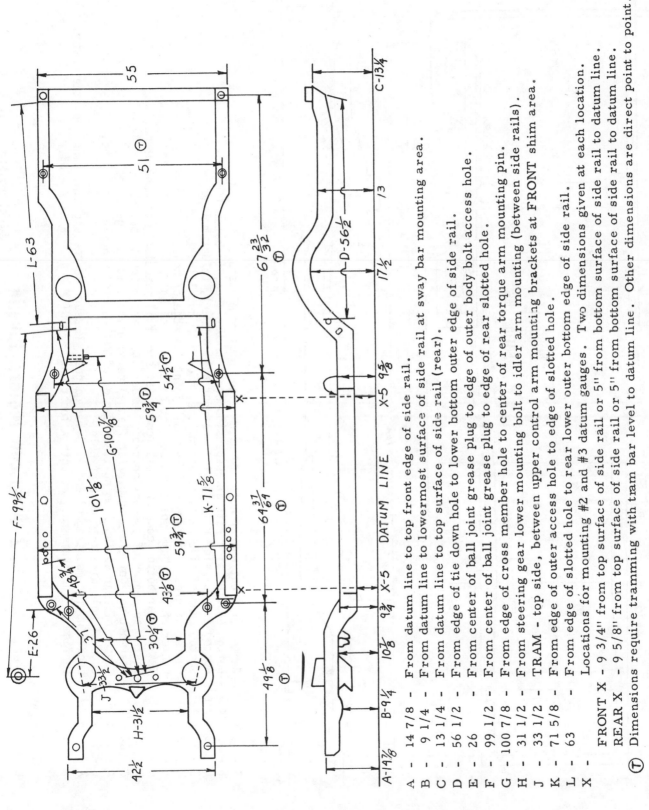

A - 14 7/8 - From datum line to top front edge of side rail.
B - 9 1/4 - From datum line to lowermost surface of side rail at sway bar mounting area.
C - 13 1/4 - From datum line to top surface of side rail (rear).
D - 56 1/2 - From edge of tie down hole to lower bottom outer edge of side rail.
E - 26 - From center of ball joint grease plug to edge of outer body bolt access hole.
F - 99 1/2 - From center of ball joint grease plug to edge of rear slotted hole.
G - 100 7/8 - From edge of cross member hole to center of rear torque arm mounting pin.
H - 31 1/2 - From steering gear lower mounting bolt to idler arm mounting (between side rails).
J - 33 1/2 - TRAM - top side, between upper control arm mounting brackets at FRONT shim area.
K - 71 5/8 - From edge of outer access hole to rear lower outer bottom edge of side rail.
L - 63 - From edge of slotted hole to rear lower outer bottom edge of slotted hole.
X - Locations for mounting #2 and #3 datum gauges. Two dimensions given at each location.

FRONT X - 9 3/4" from top surface of side rail or 5" from bottom surface of side rail to datum line.
REAR X - 9 5/8" from top surface of side rail or 5" from bottom surface of side rail to datum line.
(T) Dimensions require tramming with tram bar level to datum line. Other dimensions are direct point to point.

1972   **Buick Riviera**   122" W.B.

Copyright 1972
by Harry M. Depew

Fig. 17-7. Typical frame alignment specifications for a conventional frame automobile. (Courtesy of Tru-Way Company.)

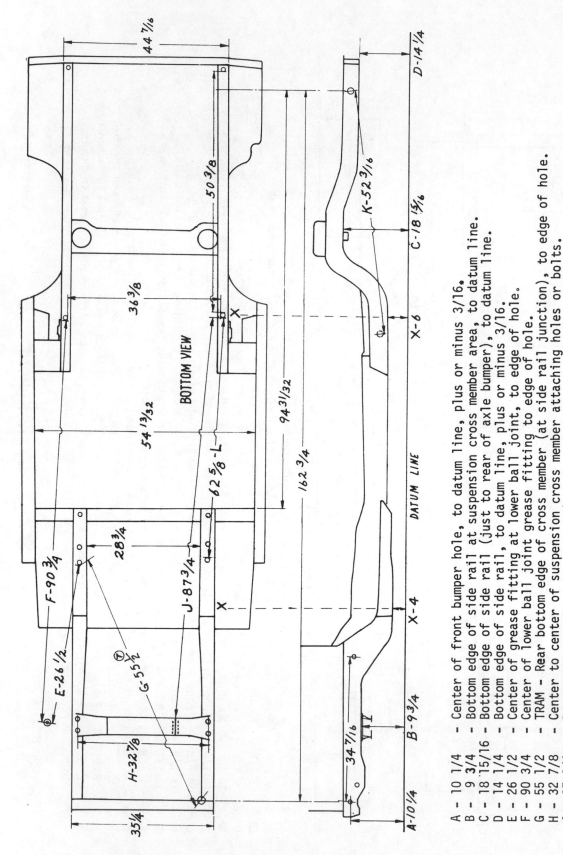

BOTTOM VIEW

DATUM LINE

A — 10 1/4   — Center of front bumper hole, to datum line, plus or minus 3/16.
B — 9 3/4   — Bottom edge of side rail at suspension cross member area, to datum line.
C — 18 15/16 — Bottom edge of side rail (just to rear of axle bumper), to datum line.
D — 14 1/4   — Bottom edge of side rail, to datum line, plus or minus 3/16.
E — 26 1/2   — Center of grease fitting at lower ball joint, to edge of hole.
F — 90 3/4   — Center of lower ball joint grease fitting to edge of hole.
G — 55 1/2   — TRAM - Rear bottom edge of cross member (at side rail junction), to edge of hole.
H — 32 7/8   — Center to center of suspension cross member attaching holes or bolts.
J — 87 3/4   — Rearmost edge of cross member (at flange) below pivot bolt to edge of hole.
K — 52 3/16 — Center of rear spring from bolt, to center of rear spring shackle bushing hole.
L — 62 5/8   — Edge of hole direct to edge of hole.
X —   — Locations for mounting #2 and #3 datum gauges.   Measure to the sighting pins from the bottom
               surface of sub frame rail at both X locations.   FRONT X - 4".   REAR X - 6".

Copyright 1972
by Harry M. Depew

1972 American Motors - Javelin

Javelin   110 W.B.
Javelin AMX   110 W.B.

Fig. 17-8. Typical frame alignment specifications for a unitized body-frame automobile. (Courtesy of Tru-Way Company.)

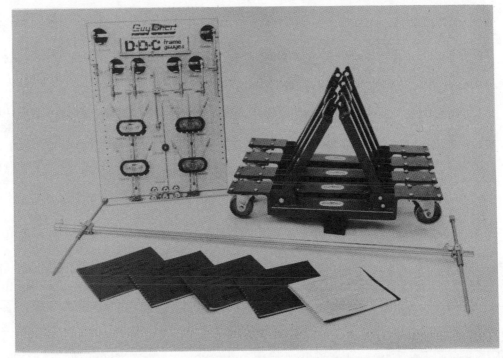

Fig. 17-9. Frame alignment checking tools and specification books. (Courtesy of Guy-Chart Systems.)

removed or damaged the paint. A paint brush with frame (chassis) paint and/or undercoat may be used to repaint the damaged frame areas.

Fig. 17-10. Straightening frame and body damage from a rear-end collision. The lower pull chain is connected to the frame while the upper chain is connected to a rear body inner panel. (Courtesy of Guy-Chart Systems.)

FRAME GAUGES

There are two main tools that must be used to straighten a frame: the *frame straightener*

itself and the *frame gauges*. The frame *straightener* is the large, heavy unit (discussed earlier) that actually bends the frame back into position. The frame *gauges*, on the other hand, do no bending or forcing; they report the frame's condition before, during, and after straightening. They are also used to help determine the location and extent of the frame damage.

To correctly repair frame damage, a frame man must know about each of the different frame gauges and how to use them. There are four basic types of frame gauges:

1. Self-Centering
2. Datum Line
3. Tracking
4. Tram

Each gauge has a certain frame location to gauge or measure. For example, self-centering gauges (also called *centering gauges*) always gauge the frame *side rails* to see if they are *level*. The tram gauge, on the other hand, may be used to check measurements above or below an object or obstruction (such as an engine), as shown in Fig. 17-11.

Self-Centering Gauges

Self-centering frame gauges are used to "find" the imaginary center line when checking

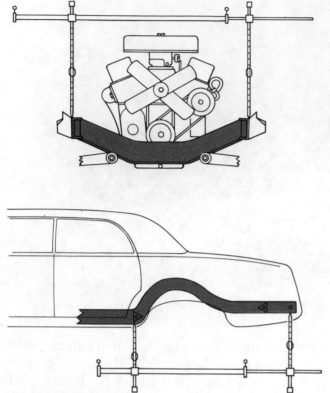

Fig. 17-11. Using a tram gauge to measure over an obstruction. (Courtesy of Guy-Chart Systems.)

to see if the frame side rails are parallel. Each *self-centering gauge* consists of two sliding crossbars that may be adjusted for almost any frame width. See Fig. 17-12. Each end of the gauge may have an adjustable *extension hanger* that can be adjusted to different heights and then tightened in that position to hold the gauge steady.

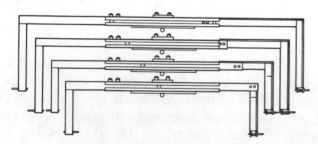

Fig. 17-12. Self-centering frame gauges. (Courtesy of Bear Manufacturing Company.)

The pin in the center of a "self-centering" gauge, between the two sides, is a *sighting pin*. The gauge is designed so that the sighting pin is kept *centered* at all times, thus the name *self-*

centering gauge. The pin is automatically kept in the center of the gauge between the two sides. When one side (leg) of the gauge is moved, the other side automatically moves the same distance in the opposite direction.

Using Self-Centering Gauges—To correctly gauge a frame with self-centering gauges, use at least three gauges at one time. Sometimes four gauges are used, as in Fig. 17-13. Hang the gauges in the same factory-formed holes on opposite sides of the frame side rails. Actually, any two points on the frame where the same mark or holes can be found on either side of the frame may be used to "hang" the centering gauges. A number of attachments are available (Fig. 17-14) to hang the centering gauges

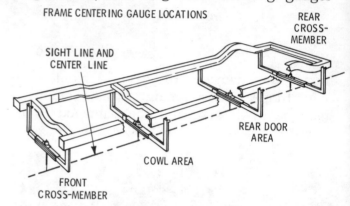

Fig. 17-13. Typical locations for frame centering gauges. At least three gauges must be used. (Courtesy of Bear Manufacturing Company.)

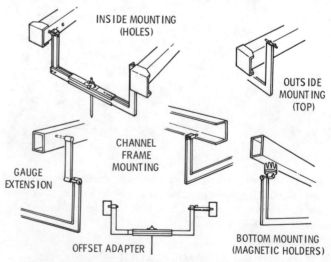

Fig. 17-14. Different mountings and extension accessories may be needed for attaching self-centering frame gauges. (Courtesy of Bear Manufacturing Company.)

where required even though the frame has no holes (or hard-to-reach holes) in the area to be checked.

When the gauges are in place, they are then checked to see if the frame side rails are parallel and if the frame is square and level. This is done by standing at the front or rear of the gauges and then sighting down the center pins and crossbars of the gauges to see if they line up properly. This is discussed in greater detail later in the unit.

Datum Line Gauges

Datum line gauges are used to measure the frame side rail by checking the specifications used to measure *down to* an imaginary line under the frame called the *datum line*. All of the frame's vertical (up and down) lines are measured from the frame to this imaginary datum line under the frame. All the *datum line gauges* will have to be level before the frame is in alignment.

Using Datum Line Gauges—Datum line gauges are normally used to sight down to the datum line. Like centering gauges, more than one datum line gauge must be used. The #1 gauge is always the first gauge looked at when sighting the datum line and is often mounted at the cowl area of the frame. It may be attached with magnets. The #2 gauge is normally side mounted on the frame in the rear door area. The #3 gauge, finally, may be mounted on the frame rails near the rear crossmember.

Datum line gauges are fairly simple. Certain models have two intersecting (cross) bars, which, when placed on the frame, become upside down. They may also have extensions to give the gauges length and swivel joints (Fig. 17-15) that allow the gauges to be moved at an angle that is closer to or farther away from the bottom of the frame. These models have a level on one end of the horizontal (cross) bar. When the gauges are set correctly and are aligned and level, the frame is square and correct.

Another type of datum line gauge is shown in Fig. 17-16. This gauge is combined with the self-centering gauge. When the centering pins

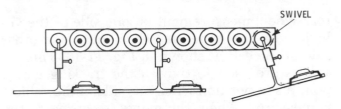

Fig. 17-15. Typical datum line gauges. (Courtesy of Bear Manufacturing Company.)

form a bullseye *and* when all the horizontal bars are level, as in Fig. 17-16, the frame datum line is correct.

Fig. 17-16. A "bullseye" type of combination datum line and self-centering gauge. (Courtesy, Blackhawk Division of Applied Power Industries.)

Tracking Gauges

Wheel *tracking gauges* show when the front and rear wheels are in alignment with each other. Fig. 17-17 shows a typical wheel tracking gauge. If the front and rear wheels are not in alignment, the vehicle will not drive out properly. For example, note the wheel tracking problem due to the bent frames in Fig. 17-18.

Using Tracking Gauges—Wheel tracking is measured by comparing the front-wheel-to-

WHEEL TRACKING GAUGE

Fig. 17-17. A typical wheel tracking gauge.

rear-wheel measurement on one side of the vehicle with the same measurement on the other side of the car, as shown in Fig. 17-18. Thumbscrews are used to tighten the tracking gauge pointers in position when one side of the vehicle is measured. Then, the gauge is carried to the other side of the vehicle to check the measurement on the other side. If the frame's wheel tracking is correct, the dimensions will be the same on both sides.

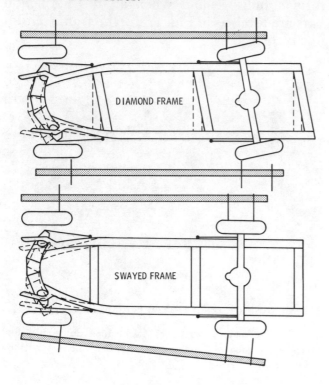

Fig. 17-18. Common types of frame damage that may be determined by using a wheel tracking gauge. (Courtesy, Blackhawk Division of Applied Power Industries.)

Tram Gauges

Fig. 17-19 shows one manufacturer's *tram gauge.* Basically, tram gauges are used to gauge (measure) above or below objects or obstructions such as the engine, transmission, or differential. See Fig. 17-11. Tram gauges are often used to check types of frame damage known as mash, diamond, or any other damage that would cause frame shortness. (These specific types of damage are explained later in the unit.)

Using Tram Gauges—To use a tram gauge, place the pointers in the manufacturer's specified frame holes, according to the frame align-

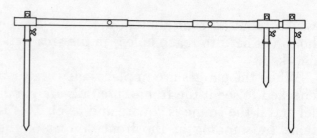

Fig. 17-19. Tram gauge. (Courtesy of Bear Manufacturing Company.)

ment charts. Then, use the gauge to measure from one side rail to another, or from one point to another on the same side rail. When the measurement has been made, compare the measurement with the specification on the frame alignment charts. If the specification is not the same as on the alignment charts, the frame is damaged and must be straightened.

INTRODUCTION TO FRAME STRAIGHTENING

The basics of frame diagnosis, straightening, and checking are the same as those that were practiced over thirty years ago. When analyzing frame damage, the repairman must still determine the location and the extent of the damage before repairs can be made. This analysis is best done by mentally "dividing" the vehicle's frame into *three sections:* front, center, and rear. These sections are shown on a conventional frame in Fig. 17-20 and on a unitized body-frame in Fig. 17-21. Each of these sections is bordered by what are known as *controlling points.*

Controlling Points

The controlling points on any frame structure are the areas at the *front crossmember, cowl,*

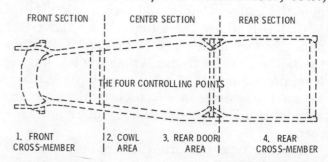

Fig. 17-20. The three sections and four controlling points of a conventional frame. (Courtesy of Bear Manufacturing Company.)

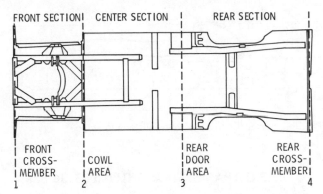

Fig. 17-21. The three sections and four controlling points of a unitized body-frame. (Courtesy of Bear Manufacturing Company.)

rear door, and *rear crossmember.* When estimating frame damage, then, the repairman must examine the controlling points and indicate on the appraisal sheet what section or sections are damaged. Inspecting frame damage by examining the controlling points will help the repairman to not overlook any damage *and* to quickly identify the location and extent of the damage.

Measuring Points

All vehicle frames that provide the foundation for a good-driving vehicle must be square and level. To *measure* the frame and determine if it is square and level, there must be measuring points built into the frame and specifications provided for the distances between the points.

The measuring points for dimensions may be made from side rail to side rail, from a hole in *a* crossmember to a side rail, from one point to another on the same side rail, or any of several other points, as called for on the specifications. The frame may be measured with a steel tape or a tram gauge, depending on the measurement location. Measurements involving *holes* are always taken from the *center* of the hole unless otherwise specified.

Not all specifications can be given between two points on the frame itself. For example, each *end* of the frame must be a certain distance from the ground and from the center of the car. To provide these specifications, the vehicle's manufacturer must use two *imaginary lines:* the *center line* and the *datum line.*

Center Line—The *first* specification line is the imaginary (cannot be seen) *center line* that runs down through the *center* of the frame from front to rear. This line determines the boundaries of the right and left sides of the frame. The imaginary center line may be seen by looking at either the top or bottom of the frame specifications. Notice the center line in the specifications shown in Fig. 17-22.

Datum Line—The *second* specification line is the imaginary *datum line.* It also runs lengthwise but is *under* the bottom of the frame. The datum line is an imaginary line *between* the frame and the shop floor. It runs the length of

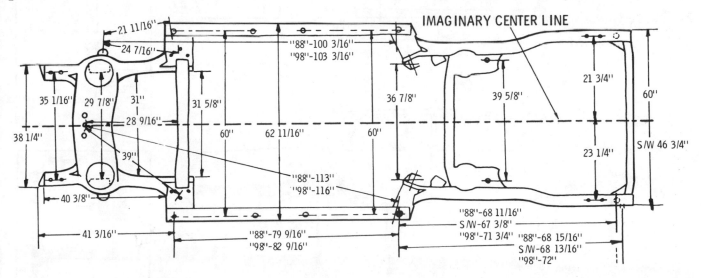

Fig. 17-22. The center line of the frame is an imaginary line down the center of the frame, "cutting" it in half. (Courtesy of Mitchell Manuals, Inc.)

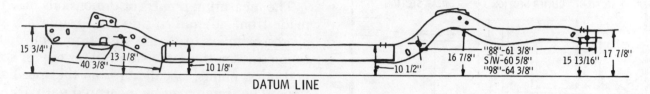

Fig. 17-23. The datum line runs the length of the frame *under* the frame. (Courtesy of Mitchell Manuals, Inc.)

the vehicle and measurements are made down *to* the datum line, as shown in Fig. 17-23. Arrows on specification drawings, such as Fig. 17-24, show where the datum line gauges should be placed on the frame. The datum line is normally checked by using the side rail and the gauges. When the frame is straight, the datum line measurements will be correct and the datum line will be straight. Then, the gauges may be viewed from either the front or rear of the vehicle and they will line up. That is, all the gauges will be at the same level, *which is the datum line,* as in Fig. 17-24.

BASIC FRAME STRAIGHTENING JOBS

The "key" to even the most difficult frame straightening job is to *completely analyze the frame damage in three major steps.* The *first* step to correctly diagnosing *all* the frame damage is to locate and describe the damage on each of the three sections of the frame. This requires a good knowledge of frame and automobile construction *and* a knowledge of how to use the shop's frame equipment (Fig. 17-25) and specification charts.

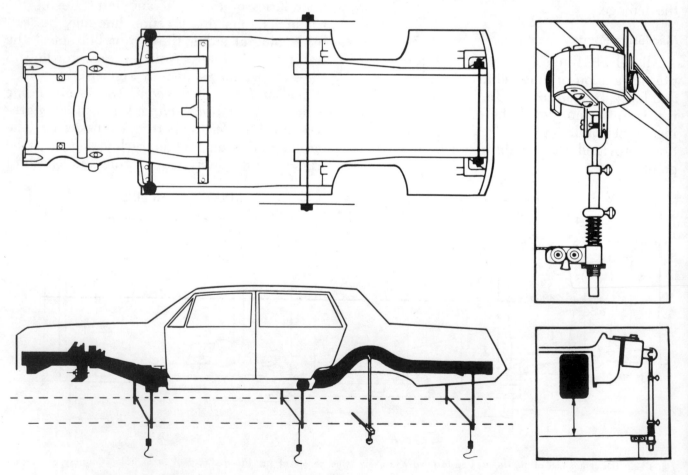

Fig. 17-24. Datum line gauges may be mounted in one of several positions. (Courtesy of Mitchell Manuals, Inc.)

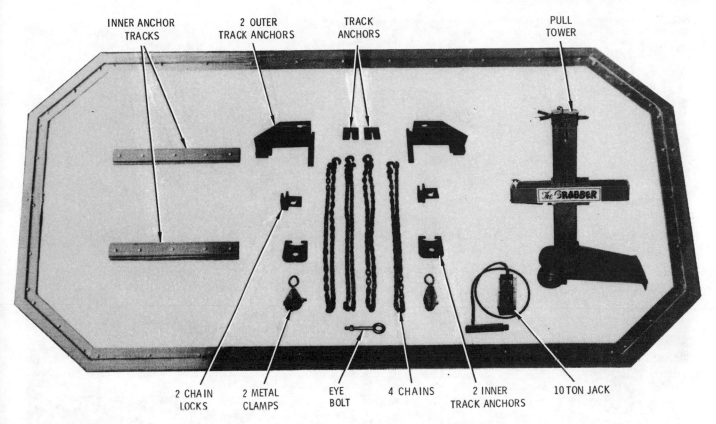

INNER ANCHOR TRACKS   2 OUTER TRACK ANCHORS   TRACK ANCHORS   PULL TOWER

2 CHAIN LOCKS   2 METAL CLAMPS   EYE BOLT   4 CHAINS   2 INNER TRACK ANCHORS   10 TON JACK

Fig. 17-25. Permanent frame alignment equipment. (Courtesy of Grabber Manufacturing Company.)

The *second* step is to *remove all the parts* that block access to the damaged section(s) of the frame. This has been done in Fig. 17-27. Finally, the *third* step is to *make the correct hook-up(s)* necessary to straighten the frame. This is also shown in Fig. 17-27.

To be able to straighten damaged frames, the body or frame man must be able to recognize and understand the different types of frame damage. Also, there is usually a pattern to collision damage. A repairman should learn the pattern and *in what order* damage is likely to happen as a vehicle is hit from the front, rear, or side. If this is learned, the repairman will have little trouble repairing frame damage.

Side Rail Damage

The first major frame damage that normally happens when a collision takes place is *side rail* damage. The three most common types of side rail damage on the *front* section of the side rail include *sidesway, mash,* and *sag.* In rear-end collisions, sag is usually present on only severe wrecks.

Sidesway—Sidesway damage is normally the first side rail damage to happen during either front or rear-end collisions. Fig. 17-26 shows typical front end sidesway. This type of damage may be found on both conventional frames and unitized body-frames that have been involved in major accidents.

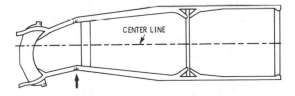

CENTER LINE

Fig. 17-26. Sidesway on the front section of a frame due to a front-end collision.

To check for sidesway, fasten self-centering gauges to the frame as usual. See Fig. 17-30. Then, look at the gauges from front to rear, as in Fig. 17-30. Notice that, in this case, the rings do not line up because the front ring is to one side of the two rear rings. This means that the left front of the car (the driver's side) was pushed to the left of the center line. This vehicle was

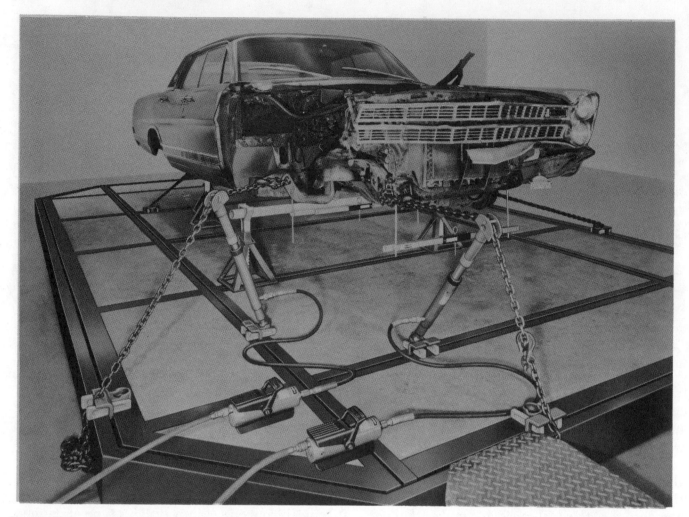

Fig. 17-27. An automobile that has been completely dismantled, set up, and "hooked up" for frame straightening. (Courtesy, Blackhawk Division of Applied Power Industries.)

hit on the right front side, pushing the frame to the left; a condition known as *front end sidesway*. Note that the horizontal bars are parallel (aligned) with each other, indicating that there is no up-and-down damage, or *sag*.

Rear sidesway, shown in Fig. 17-28, is misalignment of the *rear* section of the frame. This is similar to front sidesway except, of course, that the damage is done to the *rear* section of the frame's three sections. Rear sidesway would appear on the "bullseye" self-centering gauges similar to front sidesway, except that the rear bullseye would be out of alignment.

A *double* sidesway frame, Fig. 17-29, will have misalignment of *both* the front and rear frame sections, so that the sides of the frame will not be parallel. Double sidesway results from a severe impact in the *center* (body)

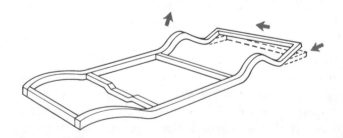

Fig. 17-28. Rear sidesway.

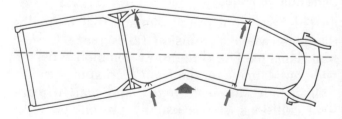

Fig. 17-29. Double sidesway on the frame's outer section.

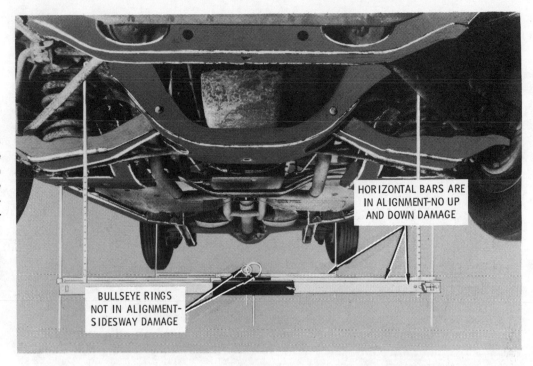

Fig. 17-30. Sidesway damage is indicated because the bullseye rings are not in alignment even though the horizontal bars are in alignment. (Courtesy, Blackhawk Division of Applied Power Industries.)

HORIZONTAL BARS ARE IN ALIGNMENT-NO UP AND DOWN DAMAGE

BULLSEYE RINGS NOT IN ALIGNMENT-SIDESWAY DAMAGE

frame section. The vehicle's entire frame (front, center and rear) is affected during double sidesway collision damage. The heavy arrow in Fig. 17-30 shows the *direction* of the impact that caused the damage. Smaller arrows in the figure point out buckles in the side rails.

Sidesway correction for unitized body-frame vehicles is made in the same way as for conventional frame vehicles, except as follows. The body panels at the *wheel areas* (the *wheelhouse panels*) must be corrected at the same time as is the lower frame when working on a body-frame vehicle. A damaged wheelhouse at the left front is being straightened on the unitized body-frame car being repaired in Fig. 17-33.

Fig. 17-31 shows how a *portable* frame straightener is used to repair sidesway damage on a conventional frame. The same portable frame machine may also be used to pull out sidesway damage on a unitized body-frame, as shown in Fig. 17-32. When straightening sidesway damage with a permanent *rack type* frame straightener, multiple hook-ups are used. For example, Fig. 17-34 shows a rack-type straightener being used to correct double sidesway.

Sag—Typical side rail *sag* may be damage to the frame at the cowl area, as shown in Fig. 17-35. Sag usually results from a heavy impact.

The impact causes the front of the frame to kick up, making the side rail appear to drop at the cowl. The actual amount of side rail buckling

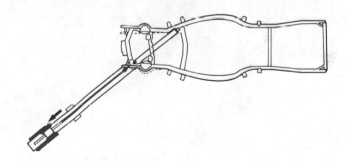

Fig. 17-31. Using a portable frame straightener to repair sidesway damage on a conventional frame. (Courtesy of Bear Manufacturing Company.)

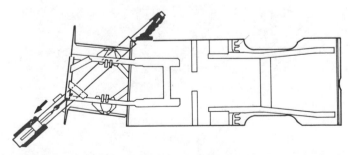

Fig. 17-32. Using a portable frame straightener to repair sidesway damage on a unitized body-frame. (Courtesy of Bear Manufacturing Company.)

Fig. 17-33. Straightening a bent wheelhouse panel and structure on a unitized body-frame car. (Courtesy of Grabber Manufacturing Company.)

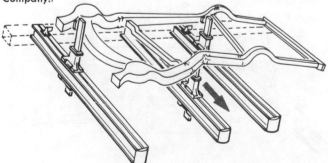

Fig. 17-34. Correcting double sidesway with a permanent, rack-type frame straightener. (Courtesy of Bear Manufacturing Company.)

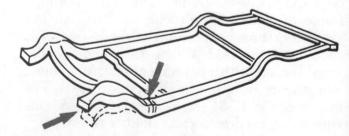

Fig. 17-35. Sag on the left front frame section due to a front-end collision. Notice the buckle at the cowl. (Courtesy of Bear Manufacturing Company.)

depends on the severity and the direction of the impact. Sag may occur on either or both sides of the car *and* on either the front or rear.

To check for sag on one side of the frame's *front* section, sight along the frame centering gauges from the front of the car. The sag will then appear *behind* the high point of the #1 gauge. See Fig. 17-36. To check the exact amount of sag damage, place two frame centering gauges at the controlling points on the front section and sight along the lower bars of the gauges, as in Fig. 17-36. Here, the sag is located on the right front side, behind the high corner of the front gauge.

To check for *rear* sag frame damage, first place one frame centering gauge at the rear door area of the frame. Then, locate the other gauge *ahead* of the mash area, near the rear axle housing. See Fig. 17-37. (Mash damage is discussed next.) Finally, sight along the lower bars of the gauges. Sag, then, is located on the frame rail behind the high corner of the #1 gauge shown in Fig. 17-37. (Notice that, when checking sag, the gauges are placed in *front* of any mash and sidesway damage on the frame's rear section; this will give a correct gauging of *only* the sag damage.)

The most serious type of sag is where *both* side rails have sag damage. Notice that, in Fig. 17-38, the center line pins are on center, indicating that the frame has no side damage. Also, although the horizontal bars are parallel to each other, the center gauge is *lower* than the other two gauges. This indicates that sag damage has occured equally, on both side rails, in the cowl area.

The gauges in Fig. 17-38 show that the #1 gauge is high *all the way across*. This means that the frame has sag on both the right and left sides. If, however, only one side had sag, only that side of the #1 gauge would be high.

Mash—Side rail *mash* is a buckle area located on the underside of the side rail. It may be directly behind the front crossmember, Fig. 17-39, known as *front mash*. Or, it may be located on the underside of the side rail directly over the rear axle housing. This is known as *rear mash*, Fig. 17-40.

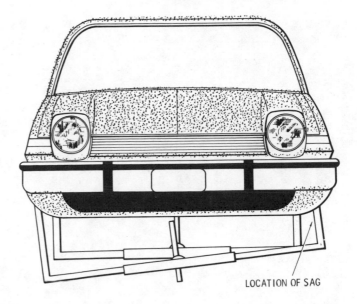

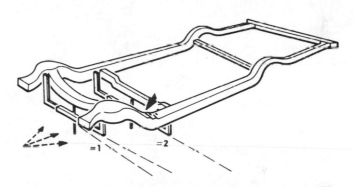

Fig. 17-36. Gauge hook-up to measure *front* sag. (Courtesy of Bear Manufacturing Company.)

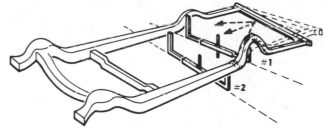

Fig. 17-37. Gauge hook-up to measure *rear* sag. (Courtesy of Bear Manufacturing Company.)

In either case, mash causes the frame side rail *length* to become shorter. Mash results from a heavy impact on one corner (end) of the frame side rail, causing it to "mash up" and shorten.

To check for mash misalignment, measure from a point on the side rail at the front crossmember to a point on the side rail back near

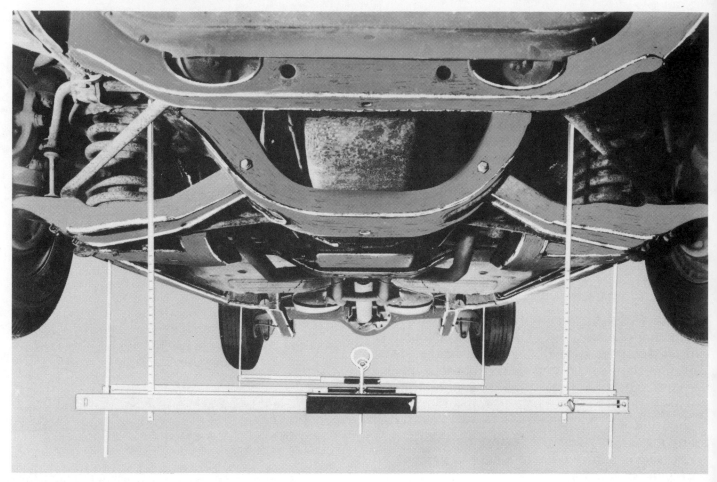

Fig. 17-38. Gauge hook-up showing sag on *both* front side rails. (Courtesy, Blackhawk Division of Applied Power Industries.)

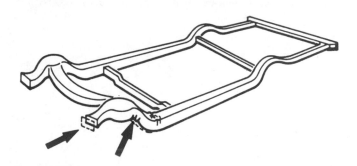

Fig. 17-39. Front side rail mash. (Courtesy of Bear Manufacturing Company.)

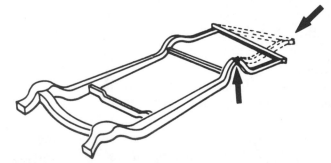

Fig. 17-40. Rear side rail mash. (Courtesy of Bear Manufacturing Company.)

the cowl. See Fig. 17-41. Compare the measurement to the same measurement on the opposite side rail *and* to the vehicle's frame specification chart.

To correct *mash* damage, either a permanent or a portable frame straightener may be used. In Fig. 17-42, for example, the frame man is hooking up for a straight mash pull using a permanent, rack-type straightener on a unitized body-frame automobile. In Fig. 17-43, another type of unitized body-frame is being repaired with a portable frame straightener. Here, the top hook is pulling to correct *sag* while the bottom hook is pulling to correct *mash*. This is an example of a portable straightener being able to make two pulls at one time.

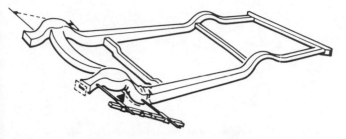

Fig. 17-41. Gauging mash on the front of the left side rail. (Courtesy of Bear Manufacturing Company.)

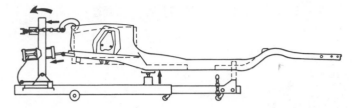

Fig. 17-43. Using a portable frame straightener to pull out both sag and mash damage at the same time. (Courtesy of Bear Manufacturing Company.)

Diamond

Another type of frame damage is known as *diamond*. Diamond damage affects the entire frame, not just the side rails. A diamond frame usually happens due to a heavy impact on one corner of the vehicle's frame. This impact is severe enough to push one side rail back, out of square with the opposite side rail and distorting the crossmembers. See Fig. 17-44.

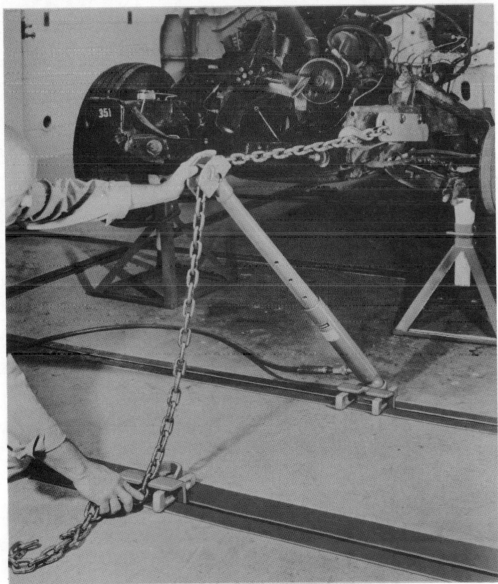

Fig. 17-42. Using a permanent frame straightener to pull out mash damage on the front frame section of a unitized body-frame automobile. (Courtesy, Blackhawk Division of Applied Power Industries.)

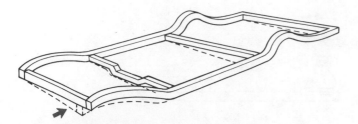

Fig. 17-44. Diamond damage on a frame as a result of a front end collision on the left side.

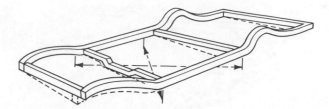

Fig. 17-45. Making the frame measurements that will show the diamond damage.

When diamond damage exists on a damaged frame, the diamond damage must be the *first* damage corrected. That is, the diamond damage would be repaired before any sag, mash, or other damage is repaired.

Checking for Diamond—To check for diamond damage, use a tape measure or tram gauge. Measure the center (body) section of the frame, between the cowl and rear door

areas. See Figs. 17-45 and 17-46. By measuring the frame at these points, the danger of measuring other frame damage is reduced.

When a frame has diamond damage, the center section by itself will look like a diamond. This will make one of the measurements *longer* than the other, indicating diamond damage. In Fig. 17-46, a tram gauge is being used to measure between two holes on the vehicle's frame. This measurement will be compared with the

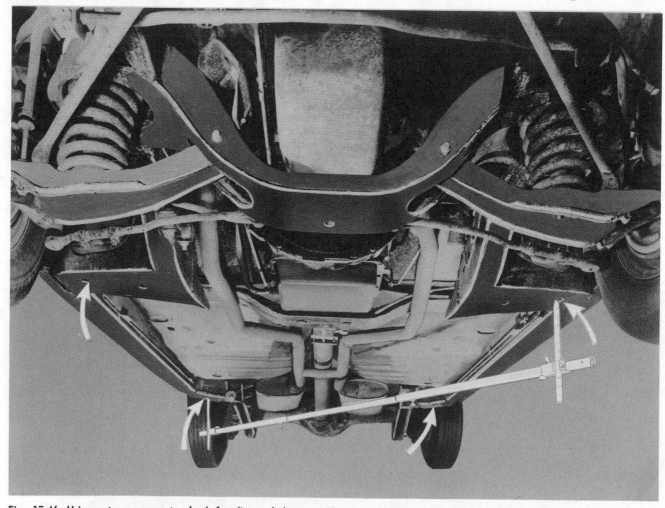

Fig. 17-46. Using a tram gauge to check for diamond damage. (Courtesy, Blackhawk Division of Applied Power Industries.)

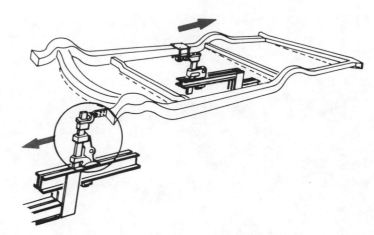

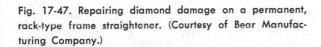

Fig. 17-47. Repairing diamond damage on a permanent, rack-type frame straightener. (Courtesy of Bear Manufacturing Company.)

measurement between the *other* two holes at the white arrows in Fig. 17-46. If the measurements are not the same, the frame has diamond damage.

Correcting Diamond—During frame repairs, remember that diamond is the first damage to correct. Stretch and pull hook-ups are usually used, securing one end of the frame and pulling on the other. Diamond correction may be made with either permanent (Fig. 17-47) or portable (Fig. 17-48) frame straighteners.

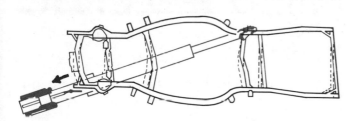

Fig. 17-48. Repairing diamond damage with a portable frame straightener. (Courtesy of Bear Manufacturing Company.)

Diamond has been corrected when the two diagonal (X) measurements at the frame's center section are equal. If the frame is "diamond" ½-inch, for example, pulling one side rail only ¼-inch will make the X measurement equal. As one side rail is pulled forward the other is forced backward.

Twist

Another type of *total* frame damage is known as *twist*. This is a serious type of frame damage. Twist damage is where the side rails are not on the same plane with each other. See Fig. 17-49. This is usually caused by running into a ditch

or by some other severe twisting action on the vehicle's frame and chassis parts.

Diagnosing Twist—When a frame is suspected of having twist, the vehicle may be put on the rack and the self-centering gauges then fastened to the frame. See Fig. 17-50. Notice that the self-centering gauge *center pins* show correct vertical and horizontal alignment since the "bullseyes" are OK.

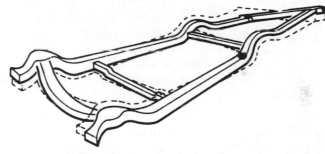

Fig. 17-49. Twist damage is likely to happen if a vehicle is run off the road into a ditch. (Courtesy of Bear Manufacturing Company.)

However, the position of the *horizontal* bars is not correct. Note that the horizontal bars are tilted; the left front and the right rear are both low. This shows that twist damage is present, since the frame is not level.

Correcting Twist—Twist has been corrected when both of the side rails are square and level. Either a permanent or a portable straightener may be used to repair twist damage. Fig. 17-51 shows an example of a rack-type (permanent) frame straightener being used to correct twist.

When a *portable* frame straightener is used to correct twist damage, a heavy *crossbeam* must be used. The crossbeam is mounted *on top*

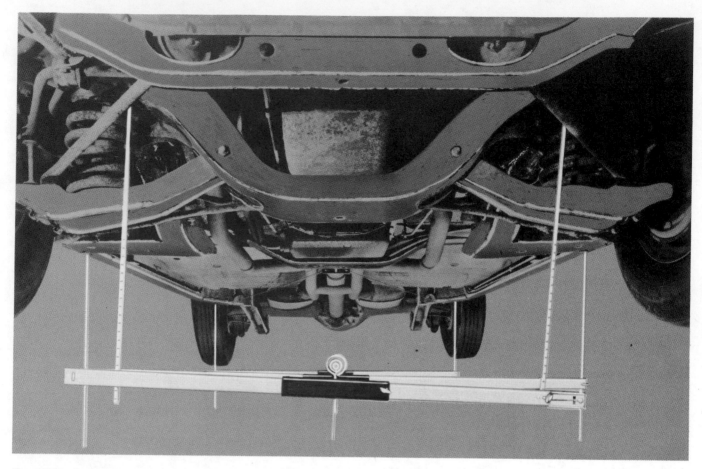

Fig. 17-50. Gauging twist with self-centering gauges. This frame has twist damage because the "bullseyes" are OK but the horizontal bars are not in alignment. (Courtesy, Blackhawk Division of Applied Power Industries.)

of the main beam. See Fig. 17-52. The crossbeam is then used to help correct the twist by holding the high points of the frame with chains. To make the repair, the frame straightener is positioned under the frame with the crossbeam in place. Then, the crossbeam is tied to the high points of the frame with chains. Equal pressure is then applied to the *low* end

of each side rail by hydraulic jacks on the main beam.

Frame Horn Damage

When a vehicle has been involved in a front-end collision, at least one of the frame *horns* may be damaged. This is the smallest type of frame damage. See Fig. 17-53. If the frame also

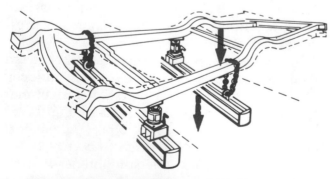

Fig. 17-51. Correcting twist damage on a rack-type frame straightener. (Courtesy of Bear Manufacturing Company.)

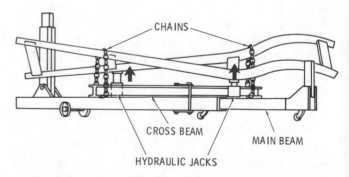

Fig. 17-52. Using a portable frame straightener to correct twist. (Courtesy of Bear Manufacturing Company.)

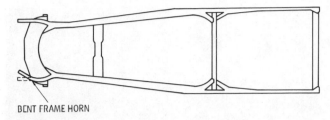

Fig. 17-53. A minor type of collision damage is a bent frame horn. (Courtesy of Bear Manufacturing Company.)

has other damage, straightening the frame horns is the final step in repairing the frame.

When the frame horn(s) are damaged, they may be straightened one at a time. This is done by using small hydraulic jacks, as in Fig. 17-54. To check for correct alignment, frame centering gauges, steel tape measurements, and the manufacturer's specifications may be used. If the frame horns are not properly straightened, it may not be possible to align the front bumper.

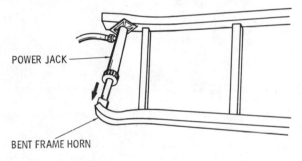

Fig. 17-54. Straightening a bent frame horn.

Crossmember Damage

One type of serious frame damage is *crossmember damage*. This damage, especially on the front crossmembers, can affect the safe driving and handling of the vehicle by causing it to pull or wander. Although cross member damage is rare, it must be detected and repaired if it is present.

The crossmember most often damaged in an accident is the *front* crossmember. This is because the engine applies heavy weight to either end of the crossmember. The engine is usually attached to both ends of the crossmember with a *motor mount*. In a roll-over accident, especially, the engine weight pushing and pulling on either end of the crossmember is likely to cause crossmember damage.

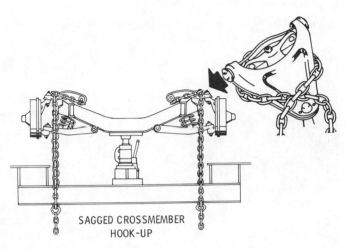

Fig. 17-55. Correcting crossmember sag. (Courtesy of Bear Manufacturing Company.)

Correcting Crossmember Damage—Crossmember damage may be corrected as shown in Fig. 17-55. This is done by using a heavy crossbeam, two chains, and a hydraulic jack. The chains are used to hold the ends of the crossmember to the crossbeam, while the hydraulic jack is used to apply pressure to the center of the crossmember.

To actually make the repair, use the hydraulic jack to apply pressure while holding each end of the crossmember in place. Check the repair with a tram gauge and compare the specifications to those on the frame dimension charts. The tram gauge can be placed either underneath or on top of the crossmember. Gauging should be done on each side of the crossmember, where the crossmember connects to the side rails; the tram gauge will be needed to measure over or under the engine.

CORRECT FRAME ALIGNMENT

When a frame is in correct alignment, all the frame centering gauges will line up. Notice how the frame centering gauges in Fig. 17-56 show that the understructure of this vehicle is in correct alignment. The horizontal bars are parallel to each other, indicating that the frame is level and has no twist. The round centerline pins form the correct "bullseye" target, indicating a perfect center line. Overall, the gauges report that the frame rails are in the proper posi-

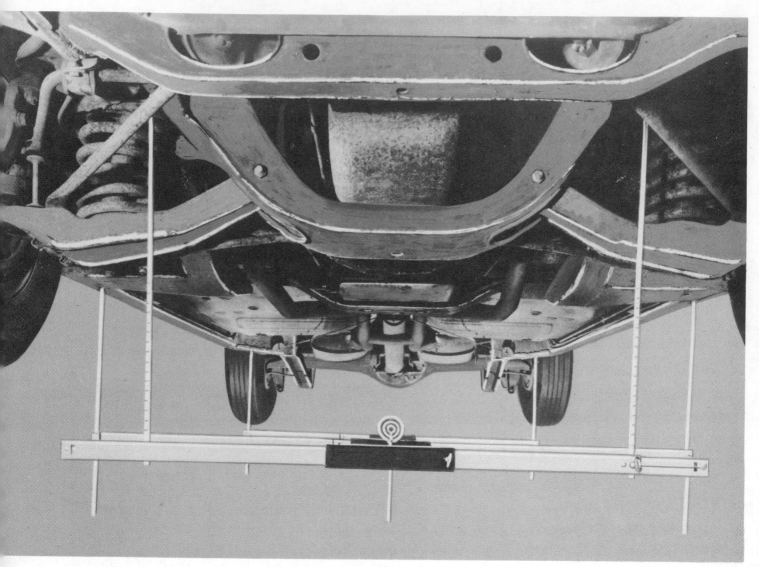

Fig. 17-56. When the frame is in correct alignment, all of the "bullseye" gauges will be properly centered, they will all be level, and they will all be parallel to each other. (Courtesy, Blackhawk Division of Applied Power Industries.)

tion, both horizontally and vertically. The frame has no sidesway, sag, or mash. The vehicle will drive out properly if all the chassis parts are also in good condition.

Major Body Repairs

The body of an automobile or small truck is made up of sections, as discussed earlier. These sections are built up from *groups* of panels that are fitted together to form the entire body assembly. This assembly (*and* the vehicle's frame) make up the entire vehicle.

The major body assembly includes everything except the bumpers, window glass, trim

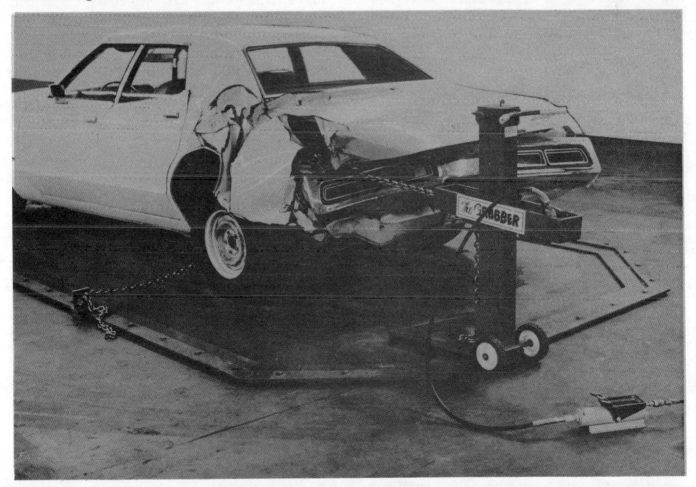

Fig. 18-1. Major body repairs will be required on this car after the frame has been straightened. Many inner panels are badly damaged, in addition to the outer panels that can already be seen. Here, a frame rack is being used to pull out the rear bumper so that it may be removed from the car. (Courtesy of Grabber Manufacturing Company.)

(door handles, moldings), and, of course, the vehicle's moving parts. Conventional construction, as discussed earlier, has the body assembly *bolted* to the frame. Unitized body-frame construction, on the other hand, has the body and frame assembly *welded* together except for the doors, front fenders, hood, deck lid, and bumpers.

When straightening major body structure damage, the repair must be made from the *inside* to the *outside*, not the other way around. On any vehicle, for example, the major body assembly and its inner and outer panels cannot be properly aligned if the *frame* section is not properly aligned *first*. Then, the *outer* panels cannot be correctly aligned until the *inner* panels are correctly aligned. Notice the *total* damage in Fig. 8-1. The outer panel damage cannot be corrected until the inner body panels have been straightened or replaced. Finally, even that cannot be done until the *frame* is repaired and aligned.

BASIC ALIGNING PRINCIPLES

When an automobile is badly wrecked, there is usually some type of frame damage that must be repaired *before* the inner and outer panel damage can be successfully repaired. For ex-

ample, the car in Fig. 18-1 will have frame damage, possibly a good deal of *mash* damage with a smaller amount of *sidesway*. These types of damage are discussed in another unit; they must be repaired first, before body panel repair and replacement can begin.

Techniques

To repair major body damage, either unitized body-frame or conventional frame construction, a body man may not have to begin at the same point on every job. Since straightening tools and major wrecks vary to a great degree, no specific procedure can be outlined for all jobs. However, the following generalizations hold true for straightening the two basic types of auto construction.

Conventional Construction—When repairing major damage on a car with *conventional* construction, the frame, inner panels, and outer panels can be pulled separately if the type of wreck and the equipment being used require that they be pulled separately. On the other hand, they can also be pulled at the same time by using *multiple hook-ups*, as is being done in Fig. 18-2. In Fig. 18-2, most of the chains are fastened to major body parts, although one chain is fastened to the car's frame. This "frame chain" will require more pull than the others,

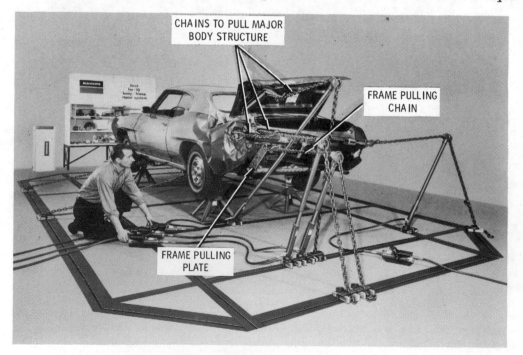

CHAINS TO PULL MAJOR BODY STRUCTURE

FRAME PULLING CHAIN

FRAME PULLING PLATE

Fig. 18-2. On large, permanent frame racks, several pulls may be made at one time. Here, this automobile is set up to receive several pulls and straighten *both* the major body structure *and* the frame at one time. (Courtesy, Blackhawk Division of Applied Power Industries.)

since the frame must be straightened just ahead of the major body parts *and* the frame is stronger, requiring more face to straighten it.

Unitized Body-Frame Construction—When repairing major damage on a car with *unitized* construction, any major parts *bolted* onto the welded structure may have to be removed if they block access (are in the way) to the major structure. They may need to be removed anyway if they need to be replaced due to serious damage. These include doors, front fenders, hood, deck lid, and bumpers. These parts can be repaired while they are off the vehicle. Or, if they are not too severely damaged, they can be bolted back onto the unitized body-frame after it has been straightened and repaired on the car.

Inner and Outer Panels

Usually, there is at least one *inner* panel for every outer panel. Inner panels may be made of either very strong or very thin sheetmetal, depending on their job. See Fig. 18-3. When an outer panel is badly damaged, the inner panel is normally damaged as well. The inner panel(s), then, will also require repair or replacement.

Most modern body structures have all the inner panels spot welded together wherever possible. The inner panels may *also* be spot welded to the outer panels, as in Fig. 18-3. Although this spot welding makes the auto body

stronger, it will be more difficult to repair than if it was all bolted together.

Seam Sealer—When the joint between an inner and outer panel is spot welded at the factory, *seam sealer* is used to seal the joint against air, water, or dust leaks. When an outer panel is replaced during major body repair, the outer panel must again be sealed to the inner panel. This is done with *seam sealer*, Fig. 18-4.

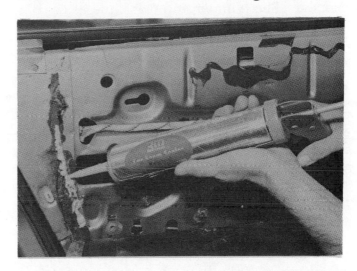

Fig. 18-4. Using seam sealer during an inner body panel repair. (Courtesy of 3M Company, Automotive Division.)

REPAIRING REAR DAMAGE— CONVENTIONAL FRAME

Figs. 18-1 and 18-5 show a badly damaged rear end section on an automobile with conven-

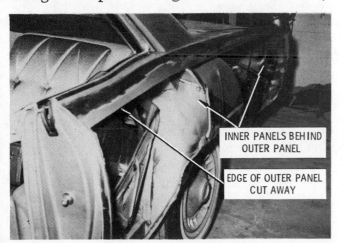

INNER PANELS BEHIND OUTER PANEL

EDGE OF OUTER PANEL CUT AWAY

Fig. 18-3. Behind most outer panels are one or more *inner* panels. When body damage is severe, the inner panels are also damaged. (Courtesy of Lenco Automotive Equipment Division.)

Fig. 18-5. Another view of the severe damage to the car in Fig. 18-1. (Courtesy of Grabber Manufacturing Company.)

tional frame construction. Close inspection will show that all the panels in the section are damaged. The rear bumper face bar and brackets are also damaged.

The body panel behind the bumper face bar is damaged. The outer and inner quarter panels are badly damaged. The deck lid is badly damaged. The rear floor is damaged, the frame is bent, the rear door is jammed, and there is roof damage. The bumper and many pieces of trim must be replaced. The alignment and repair of this car will take the knowledge of a skilled body man.

Basic Set-Up

Before this car (Fig. 18-5) may be repaired, it must be set up on the frame rack. In Fig. 18-6, the front of the car has been chained to the frame rack so that the car will not move backward when the pulls are made. The car must also be chained from the *sides* so that it cannot move sideways when the pulls are made.

Earlier, in Fig. 18-1, the first pull was set up to be made. Here, a hook has been put on the rear bumper to pull the bumper out. In Fig. 18-7, the first pull is being made. Since the rear bumper is already damaged, it does not hurt to damage it by pulling on it with the hook. This pull is made so that the body man can get to the bumper bolts and then remove the bumper.

Fig. 18-7. Making the first pull. This pull is not actually made to straighten the car. Instead, it is made so that the rear bumper may be removed. Before the pull was made, it was not possible to get at the bumper bolts to remove the bumper. (Courtesy of Grabber Manufacturing Company.)

This must be done before the frame and rear body panels may be straightened.

Repair Pulls

The repairman in Fig. 18-8 has removed the back bumper before making the actual repair pulls. Then, a *pinch clamp* is bolted to the rear edge of the car's frame. Finally, a *chain* hooks the pull tower to the frame to make the first pull.

In Fig. 18-9, the *second* hook-up has been made. Here, the pulling tower and jack are clamped onto the rear edge of the damaged quarter panel to make the second pull. This pull will help straighten out the inner quarter panel and the trunk floor. It will also relieve the pressure on the rear door opening and the roof.

When the two pulls in Figs. 18-8 and 18-9 have been made, the body man will have to check for additional frame damage. If the frame is now in alignment, the car is ready for final body straightening and panel replacements.

REPAIRING REAR DAMAGE— UNITIZED BODY-FRAME

When a unitized body-frame automobile has serious rear end damage, the entire structure is

Fig. 18-6. To keep the car from being pulled backwards, it must be chained to the frame rack. (Courtesy of Grabber Manufacturing Company.)

Fig. 18-8. The first *major* pull is made to the frame. (Courtesy of Grabber Manufacturing Company.)

Fig. 18-9. The second major pull is made to the edge of the quarter panel. (Courtesy of Grabber Manufacturing Company.)

pulled out at one time. For example, Figs. 8-10 through 8-13 show damage similar to that on the car in Figs. 8-5 through 8-9. The main difference is that the car in Figs. 8-10 through 8-13 has unitized body-frame construction. This makes the procedure slightly different.

First Pulls

To bring the lower quarter panel, trunk floor, and frame member back into alignment, *two* pinch clamps are used for the first pull. Fig. 18-10 shows the basic type of hook-up that is needed for the first pull on this job. Notice the *second* clamp that has been fastened to the pinchweld below the first. This is done to grasp the metal more firmly so that the pulling force will not tear the metal away from the rest of the structure. This hook-up will allow the first pull to straighten the quarter panel, the "frame," and the trunk floor.

In Fig. 18-11, the hook-up has been moved to the upper part of the rear quarter and back panels. Since there is no flange or pinchweld on which to clamp in this area, an "eyebolt" has been brazed into place. This provides a hook-up point for the pull tower chain. This hook-up is necessary to pull the buckle out from around the back glass and at the top edge of the deck lid opening.

Fig. 18-10. Using two clamps and a bar to make the first pull on the damaged left rear of a unitized body-frame car. (Courtesy of Grabber Manufacturing Company.)

TWO PINCH CLAMPS USED

BAR DISTRIBUTES PULL TO BOTH CLAMPS

Fig. 18-11. To pull out the top damage where there is no place on which to anchor the chain, an eyebolt is brazed in place. (Courtesy of Grabber Manufacturing Company.)

BRAZING TO BODY

EYEBOLT BRAZED TO REAR OF DAMAGED QUARTER PANEL

Fig. 18-12. Aligning the rear panel and straightening the trunk floor. Note that three pinchweld clamps are used to distribute the pull over a wide area. (Courtesy of Grabber Manufacturing Company.)

Fig. 18-13. Making a light side pull to align the wheel housing before removing the damaged quarter panel. (Courtesy of Grabber Manufacturing Company.)

Later Pulls

Fig. 18-12 shows where the hook-up has been moved to the body *rear extension panel*. This is done to align the trunk opening and help straighten the trunk floor. Note that *three* clamps and a metal bar are being used so that the chain applies equal pressure to a wider area.

In Fig. 18-13, the pull tower has been moved around to the side of the quarter panel. This hook-up has been made to align the wheel housing opening and the *inner* panels before the quarter panel is replaced. The quarter panel and rear bumper can then be replaced, since

they are too badly damaged to be repaired. Note, however, that the quarter panel *was* left on the car for the basic straightening operations.

REPLACING QUARTER PANELS

Although replacing a quarter panel is now a common major job, it takes both skill and knowledge. Most quarter panels on current automobiles are spot welded in place. A good body man must know how and where a panel is to be cut *and* how to cut it. Tools will be needed for removing the bumper, cutting the panel, fastening the new panel in place, and filling the seams.

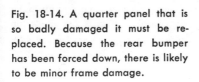

Fig. 18-14. A quarter panel that is so badly damaged it must be replaced. Because the rear bumper has been forced down, there is likely to be minor frame damage.

Typical Job—A badly damaged quarter panel is shown in Fig. 18-14. Since this damage is severe, the panel must be replaced. Note that the bumper has been pulled down, indicating that the damage may involve a bent frame. Minor damage may also include a bent trunk floor. The following procedure shows how to repair this damage.

Planning the Repair

To inspect for frame damage and begin this repair, the rear bumper must be removed. Fig. 18-15 shows that there has been slight frame damage. The inner panels and bent frame must be pulled back into alignment before the outer quarter panel is replaced.

Fig. 18-15. With the rear bumper removed, the minor frame damage may be seen.

Experience shows that this damaged quarter panel can best be repaired by rough aligning the area and *then* removing the damaged panel by cutting it off at the *belt line*. This is on the upper high crown of the fender. The cut will also be made along the row of spot welds at the bottom edge and front side of the panel. Cutting along these lines will make the job easier, since the undamaged areas above the beltline can be avoided and left intact.

Finally, the new panel will have to be trimmed to fit the cut-out repair area. The panel

replacement may be spot welded or brazed into place. Then, the repair seams are filled with body filler and worked down smooth. To complete the repair, the panel is primer-surfaced and refinished.

Bumper Removal and Rough Aligning

To make the repair, first remove the bumper before rough aligning. Since the bumper may be replaced, this will insure that it is not in the way and will not interfere with the hook-up or panel pulls. Then, use frame alignment tools and procedures to straighten the small frame damage. Make the hook-up with the panel puller and pull back on the damaged quarter panel to rough align it.

Removing the Old Panel

When the "roughing out" is done, the damaged quarter panel may be cut away. A power chisel should be used to cut the sheet metal because it will leave a clean edge for spot welding and finishing. Fig. 18-16 shows a power chisel with its blades and *flanging tool*. This tool is used to bend a *flange* (bent-over edge) on replacement panels so that they may easily be welded in place.

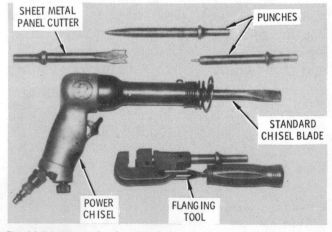

Fig. 18-16. Power chisel and tools for panel repair. The sheet metal panel cutter should be used to cut the smooth metal along the sides of the car.

The panel is trimmed as discussed earlier under *Planning the Repair*. Along the *bottom* edge of the panel, the panel must be broken loose from the spot welds holding the panel to the trunk floor. This is being done in Fig. 18-17.

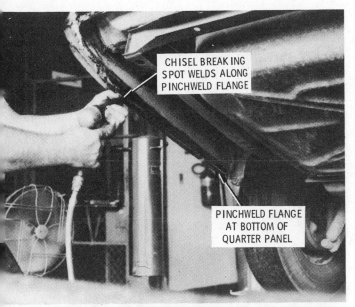

Fig. 18-17. Using a power chisel to break the spot welds holding the quarter panel to the trunk floor.

Fig. 18-18. The repair area after the old quarter panel has been removed.

Aligning—When the outer quarter panel is removed, the wheel house inner panel and brace are exposed. See Fig. 18-18. The cut edges and flanges may now be straightened as needed before attaching the new quarter panel. Also, on this car, note the slightly damaged trunk floor. This must be straightened before installing the new panel. The frame damage noted earlier may now be easily repaired.

Trimming the Replacement Panel

Not all of the old quarter panel was actually removed in Figs. 18-17 and 18-18. Note that the undamaged "dog leg" and upper edge of the old quarter panel were left in place. Because of this, the new quarter panel must be *trimmed* to fit the opening left by the old panel. See Fig. 18-19.

In Fig. 18-19, a power chisel is being used to trim the extra metal from the new quarter panel. The old panel may be used as a pattern to see where to cut the new panel and how much to cut. After the panel is trimmed, both the new panel edges and the edges on the car's opening should be ground with a coarse grinder, preparing the edges to be welded together.

Fastening the Replacement Panel

After the new panel is trimmed, it may be placed in the repaired opening. See Fig. 18-20.

Fig. 18-19. Trimming a new quarter panel to fit the prepared opening on this particular job.

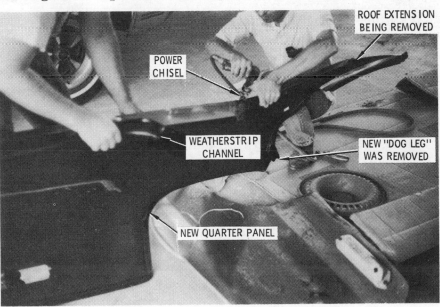

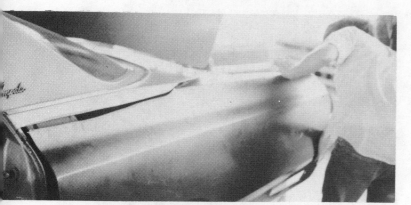

Fig. 18-20. Positioning the new quarter panel.

The new panel may need to be moved and shifted around until it is fitted in place. Then, the panel is clamped into place firmly and correctly, positioned for welding. This has been done in Fig. 18-21.

Fig. 18-21. The new panel, positioned and clamped in place, ready for welding.

Welding—When the panel is in position, either the panel spotter or brazing materials may be used to spot weld (or braze) the panel about every ¾-inch along the joint. See Fig. 18-22. This type of spot weld will do a good job of holding new panels without excessive heat distortion.

Along the *bottom* pinchweld flange, brazing may be preferred for a tight, strong, leakproof joint. In any case, the panel seams, especially the bottom seam, must be sealed after welding. The sealer shown earlier in Fig. 18-4 should be spread along the seams from inside the trunk.

Filling the Welded Seams

When the weld is completed, the welded area, old paint, and new primer at the seams are ground with a disk grinder. This will allow the area to be filled with body filler. In Fig. 18-23, *plastic* filler is being spread on the prepared weld area and seams. If the area was properly prepared, trimmed, and welded, only a thin layer of filler will be needed.

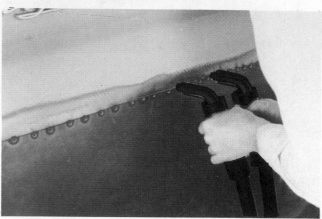

Fig. 18-22. Using a two-electrode panel spotter to install a new quarter panel. (Courtesy of Lenco Automotive Equipment Division.)

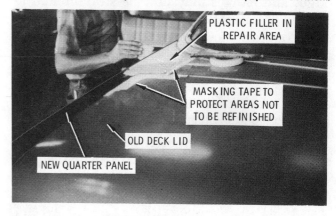

PLASTIC FILLER IN REPAIR AREA

MASKING TAPE TO PROTECT AREAS NOT TO BE REFINISHED

OLD DECK LID

NEW QUARTER PANEL

Fig. 18-23. Filling the repair area.

Refinishing

When the plastic filler has been worked down, both the repaired area *and* the factory primer are prepared for refinishing. To do this, the entire area is sanded with either #240 or, for a better finish, #320 sandpaper. Although water *may* be used on the factory primer, it is not a good idea to use water on fresh plastic repairs. This is because the plastic may absorb some of the water and later cause paint problems.

After the area is sanded, it may be primed by spraying with primer-surfacer, as in Fig. 18-24. Then, when the primer-surfacer is dry, the area

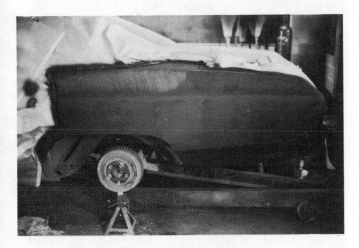

Fig. 18-24. The panel repair after the filler and new panel have been smoothed and then painted with primer-surfacer.

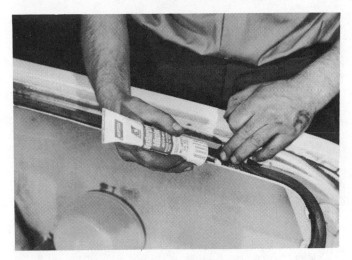

Fig. 18-26. Cementing the deck lid weatherstrip to the weatherstrip channel. (Courtesy of The Norton Company.)

may be sanded and prepared for refinishing as discussed in the painting units. Finally, the panel is refinished and, if necessary, rubbed out. The refinished quarter panel may be seen in Fig. 18-25.

Fig. 18-25. Using a floor jack to help align the heavy bumper. The repair has been painted and the new lacquer paint has been rubbed out, producing a smooth, factory-like quarter panel.

Bumper Alignment

In Fig. 18-25, the rear bumper is being reinstalled. Although the old rear bumper did have slight damage, this customer did not want the bumper replaced. A floor jack is being used to properly align the bumper.

Final Work

After the bumper is aligned, the quarter panel molding (shown later in Fig. 18-27) is

Fig. 18-27. With all the repair work done, the car is ready to be cleaned for delivery to the customer.

replaced. Because the deck lid rubber weatherstrip was damaged in the collision, it must be replaced. In Fig. 18-26, the new weatherstrip is being cemented into place with weatherstrip cement. Whenever a quarter panel is replaced on most late-model cars, the deck lid weatherstrip needs to be replaced or at least resealed. This is because the new quarter panel actually forms part of the weatherstrip channel. Notice the weatherstrip channel shown earlier on the new quarter panel in Fig. 18-19.

After the bumper, moldings, and weatherstrip are properly installed, the car should be cleaned up for delivery. The repair in Fig. 18-27 is now complete. As soon as the wheel cover is installed, the car will be washed and cleaned inside before being delivered to the customer.

SECTIONING QUARTER PANELS

Fig. 18-28. Only the rear section of this quarter panel is damaged. To analyze the job, the car is jacked up and safety jacks are put under the rear wheels.

REAR VALENCE
(A SHEET METAL PIECE
BELOW THE BUMPER)

Fig. 18-29. To begin the repair, the damaged rear bumper is removed. It will later be replaced with a rechromed bumper. The rear *valence*, attached below the bumper, is also removed. A new valence will later be installed.

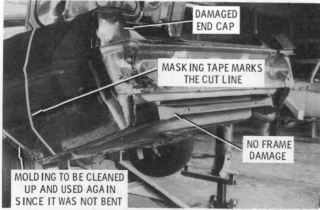

DAMAGED
END CAP

MASKING TAPE MARKS
THE CUT LINE

NO FRAME
DAMAGE

MOLDING TO BE CLEANED
UP AND USED AGAIN
SINCE IT WAS NOT BENT

Fig. 18-30. To remove all of the quarter panel damage, the body man making this repair decided to cut the quarter panel about 14" from the rear edge. The cut line is accurately marked with masking tape. The damaged *end cap* will be thrown away with the removed section.

Fig. 18-31. Cutting the spot welds at the bottom of the trunk-floor-to-quarter-panel seam. Next, the cut will be made down the side of the quarter panel at the masking tape cut line. Then, the panel will be cut off the body at the rear body panel, behind the bumper.

Fig. 18-32. Removing the damaged section from the car.

RUBBER WEATHERSTRIP
REMOVED FROM CHANNEL

EDGE OF WEATHERSTRIP
CHANNEL

REPAIRED PINCHWELD
FLANGE

Fig. 18-33. Since there was slight damage to the trunk floor in the pinchweld area, it had to be straightened with a hammer and dolly. Also, note that the weatherstrip was removed from the weatherstrip channel, since the channel was cut off with the old section.

Fig. 18-34. Installing the new rear section. This section was cut from a brand new quarter panel.

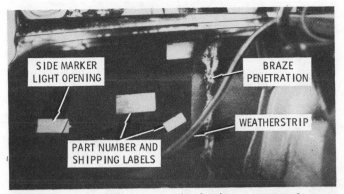

SIDE MARKER LIGHT OPENING

BRAZE PENETRATION

WEATHERSTRIP

PART NUMBER AND SHIPPING LABELS

Fig. 18-37. From inside the trunk, the braze penetration can be seen.

INNER EDGE AND WEATHERSTRIP CHANNEL WILL BE CLAMPED DOWN WHILE BRAZING

LOWER EDGE WILL BE CLAMPED TO PINCHWELD FLANGE FOR BRAZING

Fig. 18-35. Checking the fit and alignment of the new section. The "high" parts of the new section will need to be clamped down in position for brazing or spot welding.

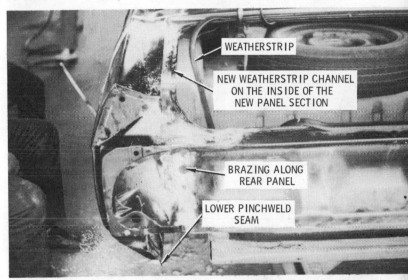

WEATHERSTRIP

NEW WEATHERSTRIP CHANNEL ON THE INSIDE OF THE NEW PANEL SECTION

BRAZING ALONG REAR PANEL

LOWER PINCHWELD SEAM

Fig. 18-38. Parts of the repair seen from the rear. Note that the new section must be *firmly* fastened to the car *all the way around* the repair.

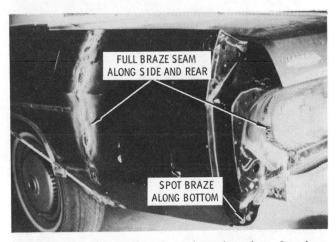

FULL BRAZE SEAM ALONG SIDE AND REAR

SPOT BRAZE ALONG BOTTOM

Fig. 18-36. The new panel section is brazed in place. Spot brazing was used along the bottom while seam brazing was done along the side, top, and rear seams. Electric spot welding could have been used instead.

Fig. 18-39. When the brazing has cooled, the repair is then ground along the top and sides. A #40 (or coarser) grit grinding disk should be used. This roughs up the joint and seam for plastic filler. Here, the first coat of plastic has been applied and the body man is using a *Surform* file to work down the rough top of the filler as it hardens.

Fig. 18-40. As the filler is worked down, a *straightedge* is used to check the repair area and make sure that it is as flat as it should be. When it has been worked down correctly, the entire area may be sanded and prepared for primer-surfacer.

GOOD USED END CAP

Fig. 18-41. The repair has been painted with primer-surfacer and the primer-surfacer has been wet-sanded to prepare it for the final (color) coat. A used end cap, now painted white since it is from another car, has been installed.

Often, it is quicker and easier to replace a damaged *section* of a quarter panel if the entire panel has not been damaged. However, if the section is large and contoured, the job will be estimated as if the entire panel is to be replaced. This is because an entirely new panel will have to be purchased even if only part of it will be used. The amount of damage to be cut away must be determined by the body man for the particular job being repaired.

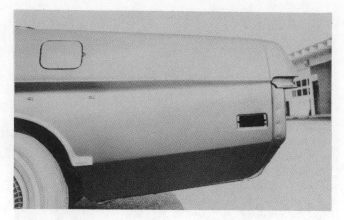

Fig. 18-42. The completed quarter panel section repair. Moldings, lights, and the bumper assembly must be installed to finish the job.

In the preceding series (Figs. 18-28 through 18-42), only a *section* of a quarter panel is replaced. In the quarter panel repair completed in Figs. 18-14 through 18-27, almost the entire quarter panel was replaced, by comparison. The quarter panel sectioning done in Figs. 18-28 through 18-42 will save a good deal of repair time and help maintain the body panel's original alignment and appearance in the areas that are not affected. Compare Figs. 18-14 through 18-27 with Figs. 18-28 through 18-42.

PATCHING QUARTER PANELS

The smallest *replacement* repair normally done to a quarter panel would be to *patch* the quarter panel. Here, even less of the panel is cut away than the sectioning process just

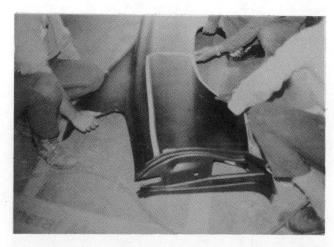

Fig. 18-43. Using masking tape to prepare a new quarter panel for cutting. When the cut is made around the tape, a "new" patch will be available to repair a damaged quarter panel.

Fig. 18-44. The patch prepared in Fig. 18-43 is being brazed in place on a quarter panel that has had heavy collision damage. To reduce heat distortion, only spot brazing is being done when making the repair.

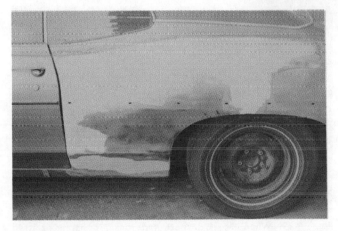

Fig. 18-45. Plastic filler has been smoothed over the seams and distortion of the panel patch. The panel is now ready to be refinished.

shown. Any repairs smaller than patching would not include installing part of a new quarter panel. Figs. 18-43, 44, and 45 show a typical quarter panel patch repair.

REPAIRING SIDE DAMAGE

When a vehicle is hit hard on the *side*, major body parts are often damaged seriously. When repairing this type of damage, more emphasis is placed on the *inner* panel areas. These are not normally replaced when they are damaged, whereas *outer* panels *are* normally replaced. Since the *inner* panels must be properly aligned before the *outer* panels will line up correctly, it is *very* important that the inner panels be straightened properly when they are repaired. The fit of the car's doors and windows will be poor if the inner panels and floor are not straightened correctly. Skill and the ability to "think out" the repair are needed to locate and repair inner body panel damage from a side collision.

Floor Damage

When a vehicle is hit hard in the side, the floor may be damaged or *buckled*. When the sides of the car and rocker panels are pulled back into place, most of the buckle will be removed. Then, the remaining buckle may be worked down with a hammer *while the puller is pulling on the side*. This pull will help the metal to straighten while it is hammered. Fig. 18-46 shows typical floor damage from a side collision. Figs. 18-47 and 18-48 show how this type of damage would be pulled out. Fig. 18-49 shows the completed repair on the floor.

Cowl Damage

The *cowl* of a vehicle (Fig. 18-50) is a very important part of the body assembly. The front door hinges are bolted or welded to the cowl and the windshield's lower edge is sealed to the top of the cowl. Door, windshield, and complete body alignment may be affected if the cowl is damaged.

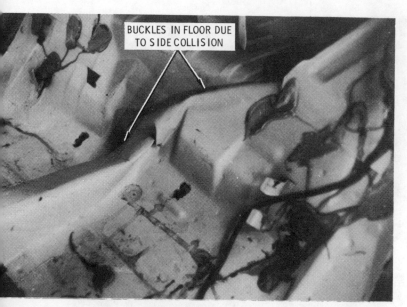

Fig. 18-46. Floor buckles due to a heavy side collision.

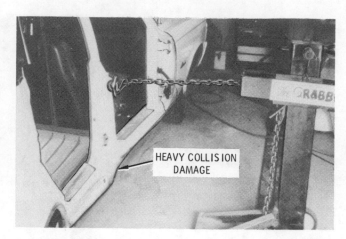

Fig. 18-48. After the lower end of the door post has been pulled, a clamp is moved higher on the post to pull the post out in the center. This procedure and the procedure in Fig. 18-47 are repeated until the rocker panel and the door post are brought back into alignment. (Courtesy of Grabber Manufacturing Company.)

Fig. 18-47. Using a puller to pull out the bottom of the door post, the rocker panel, and the floor.   (Courtesy of Grabber Manufacturing Company.)

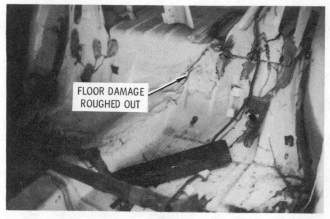

Fig. 18-49. When the door post and rocker panel have been straightened, the floor will have been pulled out to some extent. The floor should be worked out (hammered) while straightening the outer parts. The floor will not have to be worked out as smooth as the outer panels because the carpet and rear seat will cover the area.

Like other types of damage, cowl damage may be repaired in one or more of several different ways. Figs. 18-50 and 18-51 show two common hook-ups that may be used to pull out cowl damage. Cowl damage must be carefully repaired and checked for alignment after repair. If necessary, the door may need to be hung to check the alignment of the cowl area to which the door hinges are attached.

Extension Panel Damage

When an outer panel is severely damaged, the pressure from the impact may cause the

adjoining panel (the panel to which the damaged panel is attached) to also be damaged. For example, Figs. 18-52 and 18-53 show a quarter panel that is severely damaged. The adjoining panel was also buckled even though it was not hit. In this case, the panel that was also damaged is the *extension* panel below the back glass. The damage to this panel must be straightened as much as possible *before* the quarter panel itself is removed.

To repair the damaged extension panel, a metal plate is first *brazed* onto the damaged quarter panel. See Fig. 18-54. This is done be-

Fig. 18-50. Making two pulls at one time to align the cowl. Bolts are used to hold the chain attachments to the cowl. The bolts were installed from behind the cowl, under the dash. (Courtesy of Guy-Chart Systems.)

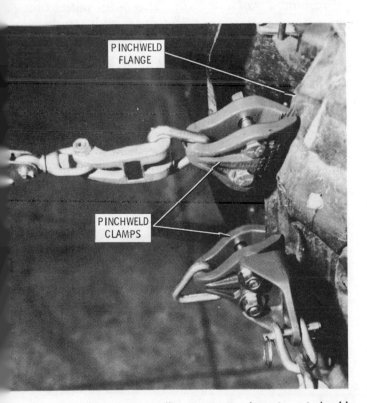

Fig. 18-51. Making two pulls at one time by using *pinchweld* clamps. Here, *bolts* through the clamps are used to hold the clamps to the pinchweld flanges. (Courtesy of Guy-Chart Systems.)

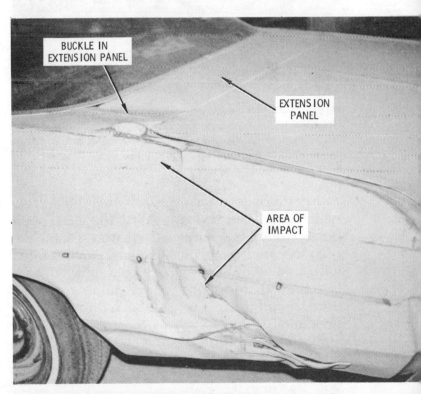

Fig. 18-52. When this quarter panel was hit very hard and pushed in, it buckled the extension panel to which the quarter panel is attached.

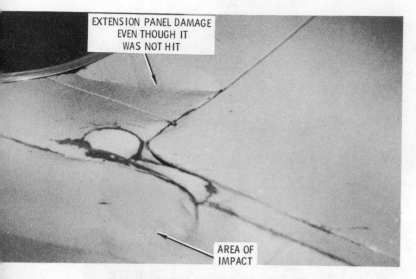

Fig. 18-53. Close-up view of the extension panel damage.

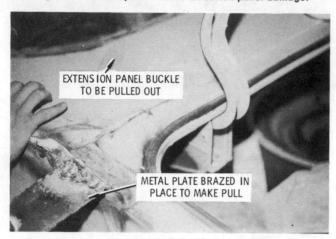

Fig. 18-54. To pull out the extension panel damage, a metal plate is brazed to the damaged quarter panel. The pull is then made *before* the quarter panel is removed. (Since the quarter panel will be replaced, there is no need to worry about damaging the quarter panel by brazing onto it.)

cause there is no flange or other area from which a pull can be made. With the metal plate brazed onto the damaged quarter panel, the quarter panel *and* extension panel can be pulled with a panel puller before the old quarter panel is removed. Most any panel puller could be used to pull the metal plate brazed to the quarter panel. *Clamps* such as those in Fig. 18-51 would be used to fasten the chain to the metal plate.

Door Damage

Almost all automobiles involved in a side collision will have *door* damage. Often, the

inner door panels are not damaged or have minor damage that may be easily straightened. For example, notice the door in Fig. 18-55. Here, there is slight damage to the door *jamb* (the side edges of the door and its opening on the car's body). When the *outer* door panel is removed, the door jamb will have to be aligned with a hammer and dolly.

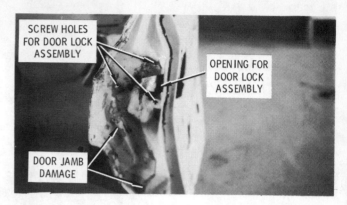

Fig. 18-55. The *door jamb* is the part of the door along the edges of the door. The door jamb is the opening on which the door *striker* is located.

Replacing a Door Skin—The outer panel of a door is also known in the auto body trade as the door skin, or simply *skin*. This is the part of the door that actually forms the outside of the door itself. Fig. 18-56 shows a new door skin.

Replacing outer door panels (skins) is one of the most common panel replacement jobs done in a body shop. Door skins are among the easier panels to replace. If the skin is damaged to a great extent, it is almost always replaced. When

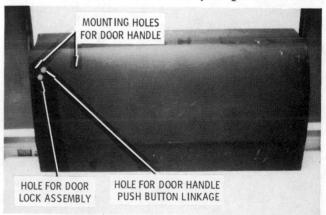

Fig. 18-56. A new *door skin* (outer door panel). The panel is shipped in factory primer, with holes already punched in it for the door lock parts.

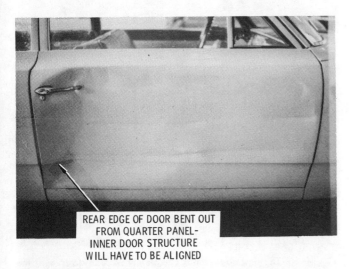

Fig. 18-57. Serious collision damage to an outer door panel (skin). This door skin will be replaced as shown in Figs. 18-58 through 18-69.

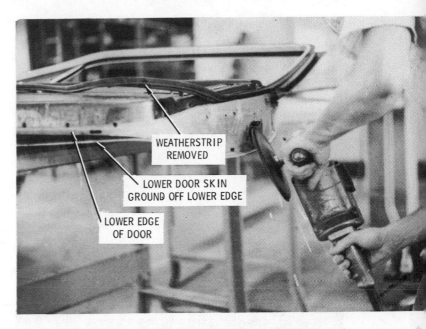

Fig. 18-60. Grinding off the edge of the old door skin. When the edge has been ground off *all the way around*, the skin may be removed.

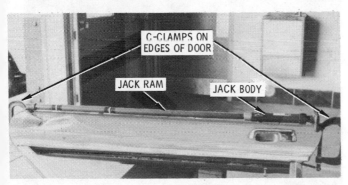

Fig. 18-58. If the inner door structure is bent, it should be straightened (aligned) by using a body jack *before* the door skin is removed. Here, a body jack is pressing against two C-clamps to stretch the door assembly out to its original length after being removed from the car.

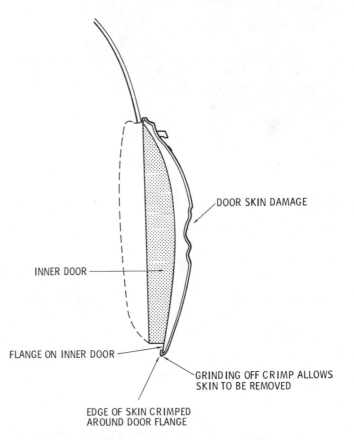

Fig. 18-61. Cutaway view of a door structure. Notice how the door skin *crimp* is folded around the inner door flange. When the crimp is ground away, there is nothing to hold the door skin in place, allowing the skin to be removed.

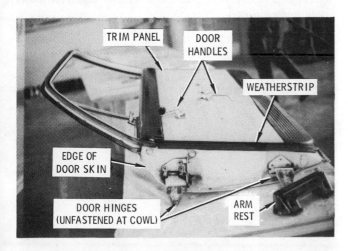

Fig. 18-59. After the door is stretched, it may be turned over. Then, the handles, the arm rest, and the weatherstrip may be removed before removing the door skin itself.

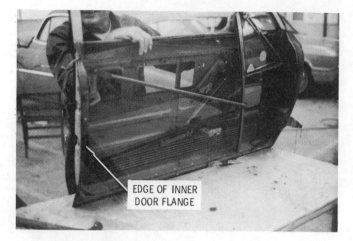

Fig. 18-62. The inner door structure after the skin has been removed. Where needed, a hammer and dolly should be used to straighten out the flange before the new skin is installed.

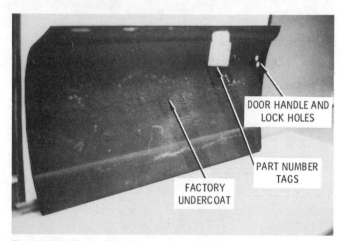

Fig. 18-63. The inside of the new replacement skin shown earlier in Fig. 18-56.

Fig. 18-64. Using a ball peen hammer to bend the *edge* of the new door skin over the *flange* of the inner door. (New skins are normally sold with the edge already bent at a 90° angle.)

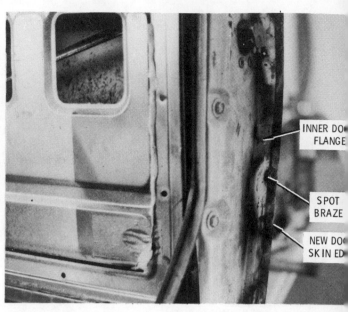

Fig. 18-65. The new door skin is completely worked down over the flange edge of the inner door. Then, spot brazing is done around the edge to hold the skin and inner door securely together.

Fig. 18-66. Working down the plastic filler that was used to repair slight warpage in the new skin. The heat from brazing or spot welding may slightly warp the outside of the new skin. Also, *some* filler is usually needed on the outside of most new panels due to factory dents.

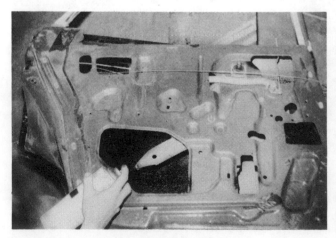

Fig. 18-67. Undercoating the inside of the new skin. This is done to seal the inside seams and to deaden noise.

Fig. 18-68. Using seam sealer to seal the *outside* edge of the new skin-to-door seam. This prevents water from creeping into the door around the edge of the door skin.

Fig. 18-70. The completed job, cleaned and ready for delivery. The door was repainted *before* it was installed on the car. By repainting the door while it is off the car, the edges, spot brazing, and seam sealer may all be painted at the same time, producing a neat, clean job.

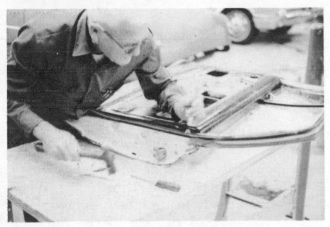

Fig. 18-69. When the outside of the door has been repaired, the weatherstrip may be reinstalled around the door. Then, the outer door handle and lock, and the trim panel, handles, and arm rest are replaced. (New seam sealer should be used to seal the *moisture cover* (water dam) on the inside of the door before the trim panel is installed.)

the labor charge to straighten a door skin amounts to three or four hours, it would prob-

ably be less expensive to replace the panel with a new skin.

Generally speaking, door skins are inexpensive and can be quickly installed when compared to an entirely new door. A new door skin gives the appearance of a new door. Also, the skin can often be installed without removing the inner working parts of the door or window glass. (However, the inside trim panel may need to be removed. The outer door handle is usually bolted to the door skin from the inside.)

Fig. 18-57 shows a badly damaged door. Since only the outer panel (skin) is damaged, a new skin will be installed. This will save the time required to work out this severe damage. Figs. 18-57 through 18-70 show the procedure to follow when replacing this typical door skin.

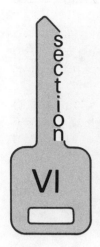

Minor Repairs

Unit 19

Basic Metal Straightening

Metal straightening is probably the most important part of total auto body repair. Metal straightening is also an *art*. A dented or damaged automobile panel cannot be measured as can a table or a chair needing repair. For this reason, a body shop *metal man* has to form a picture in his mind of what the panel looked like, how it was shaped, *before* it was damaged.

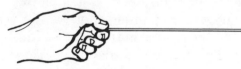

Fig. 19-1. A length of wire, like a metal panel, is straight before it is bent.

Then, he will be able to more easily restore the metal to its original shape.

The basic problems of metal straightening can be described by a comparison with a length of wire. If a length of wire (Fig. 19-1) is bent into a loop (Fig. 19-2), the wire's *elasticity*, or ability to regain its original shape, is lost. When an attempt is made to straighten the wire, the large curve in the wire cannot be removed completely. Fig. 19-3, for example, shows the curve in the wire after trying to straighten it.

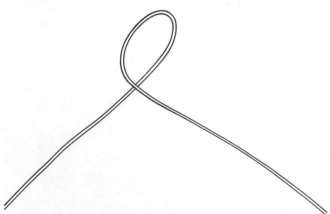

Fig. 19-2. When the wire is bent into a loop, it is stretched out of shape, beyond the limits of its *elasticity*. It cannot return to its original shape when it is released.

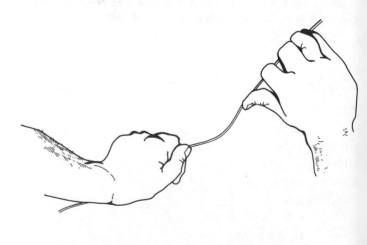

Fig. 19-3. When an attempt is made to force the wire back to its original shape, it is still unable to return completely. This is because a kink (stretched hump) remains in the wire after it is "straightened."

These problems exist when trying to straighten damaged metal.

BASIC STRAIGHTENING METHODS

To remove the curves or bends that make up the metal damage, the low spots have to be lifted up and the high spots worked down. On a given job, this may be done by one or more of the *seven basic methods* used to straighten metal. These include:

1. Aligning the metal with a *power jack.*
2. Working the metal with a *hammer* and *dolly.*
3. Pulling the metal with one or more *vacuum cups.*
4. Pulling the metal with *pull rods* or a *slide hammer.*
5. Shrinking stretched metal by using the *heat shrinking* process.
6. *Kinking* the metal to provide a surface for body filler.
7. Using *pry bars.*

All seven straightening methods may be used either separately or together on the same job. The method(s) used depend on many different factors on each individual job. These include the *amount* of damage, the *size* of the affected area, the *extent* to which the metal has been stretched, and how *accessible* the damage is (how easily it can be reached) from the front and back sides of the panel. After considering everything on any one job, a body man must select the best method or combination of methods to use for the damage being repaired on that job.

After the metal has been straightened, any small high places remaining on the outside of the damaged area may be filed down. The area may then be ground smooth and prepared for refinishing. If it is not completely leveled and shaped to the correct contour, the area may be filled with a body filler before being refinished.

A Word About Tools—All *tools*, especially hammers, dollies, and files, must be free of dirt, dents, or marks. Any dents or dirt on the face of a hammer or dolly will be transferred to the metal being worked. Also, for this same reason,

undercoating and mud must be scraped off the panel before straightening it. Use sandpaper to "dress" the faces of any hammers and dollies that are not smooth.

The *tools* a body man uses are very important, especially during straightening. The right tool is always the best tool for the job being done. Using the right tool is a good safety precaution *and* will help make sure that the job is done correctly. The tools used for a typical metal straightening job, for example, are shown in Fig. 19-4.

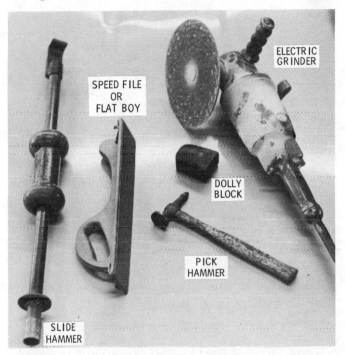

Fig. 19-4. Several of the tools needed for a correct metal straightening job.

Using a Power Jack

Normally, large damaged areas are aligned with a power jack. This is done by either *pushing* the dent out or by *pulling* on the panel using power jack attachments. Fig. 19-5 shows several common uses of a power jack.

Large power jacks (panel pullers) can also be used to stretch a panel when repairing collision damage. Figs. 19-6 through 19-8 show how this is done. The damaged panel is first clamped on each end with a pinchweld clamp to hold the jack attachments in place. Pressure is applied to the jack and, as the jack extends, the damaged panel is pulled and straightened.

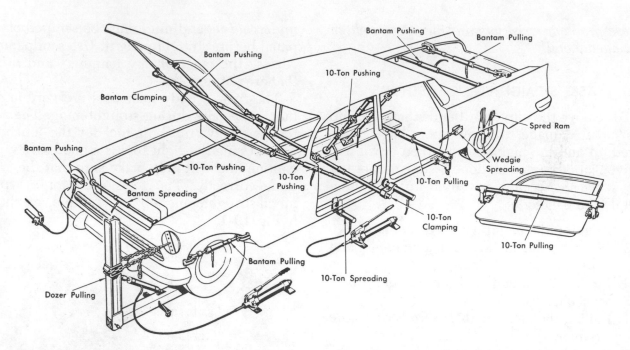

Fig. 19-5. Porta-Power combinations for basic body straightening set-ups. (Courtesy, Blackhawk Division of Applied Power Industries.)

Fig. 19-8 shows what the damaged panel in Fig. 19-6 looks like after it has been pulled. Note that it is not completely repaired. Additional body work and filling will be required, but the panel is now basically straight.

Hammer and Dolly Work

Metal work that is not severe is normally repaired with only a hammer and dolly. Also, a hammer and dolly are often used on any remaining high and low spots *after* a power jack or panel puller has been used. Hammer and dolly straightening may be done on small damaged areas that can be reached from both the inside and the outside of the panel.

To straighten damaged metal with a hammer and dolly, the basic procedure is to use a dolly *under* the damage and a hammer on *top* of the damage. The dolly is used to shape and support metal as the hammer works the metal. See Fig. 19-9.

By itself, a *dolly* may also be used to knock up low spots from under the damage, as shown in Fig. 19-10. This has to be done carefully so that the dolly does not lift the low spots too high. If the spots are lifted too high, a sander or a grinder may cut off the *top* of the high spot, leaving a hole in the metal. For these reasons, it takes a good amount of practice to repair damaged areas without leaving high and low spots. This takes time, patience, and experience in hammer and dolly work.

There are three basic hammer and dolly processes. These include hammering *on* the dolly, hammering *off* the dolly, and *picking*. Picking is done by either the dolly *or* the hammer in very small areas.

Fig. 19-6. Fastening a clamp to the door and skin of a pinchweld flange. This allows both the door structure *and* the skin to be pulled at the same time. (Courtesy of Grabber Manufacturing Company.)

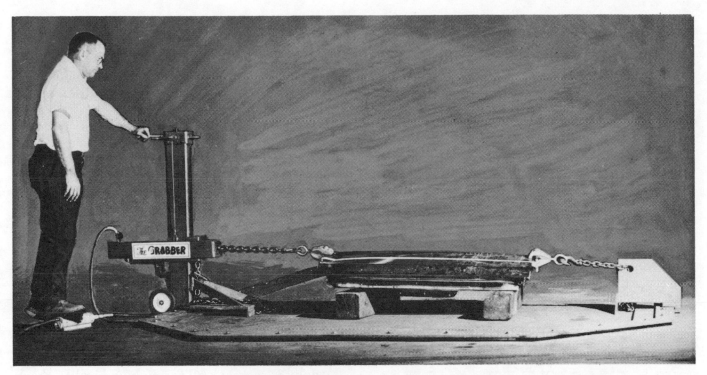

Fig. 19-7. Making the pull to straighten the door in Fig. 19-6. (Courtesy of Grabber Manufacturing Company.)

Fig. 19-8. Door repair after basic straightening has been done. (Courtesy of Grabber Manufacturing Company.)

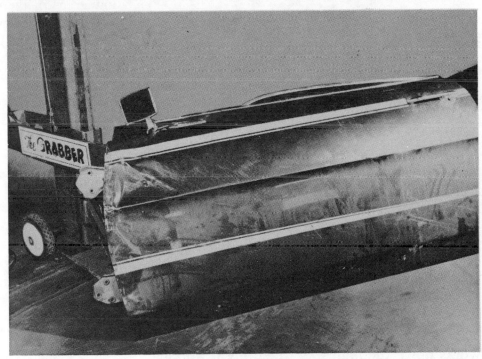

Hammering On the Dolly—To work down a high spot to the correct contour, first place a dolly *under* the high spot. The dolly should have the contour desired for the panel *after* it is repaired. Then, strike the high spot with a body hammer, as shown in Fig. 19-9. The strikes should be *light* and several should be used to *gradually* work the metal down slowly, moving the hammer and dolly around the area as needed.

Hammering Off the Dolly—Hammering *off* the dolly is done to remove a high spot and a bordering low spot at the same time. Fig. 19-11 shows how this is done. While the hammer

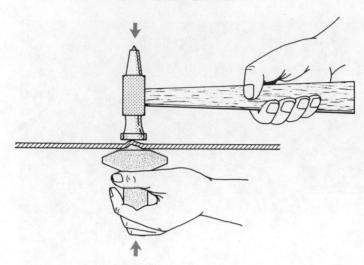

Fig. 19-9. Using a hammer and dolly to work out a small repair area.

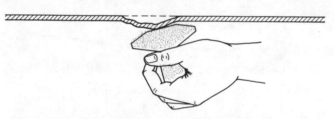

Fig. 19-10. Using a dolly alone to work up a low spot from the underside of a panel.

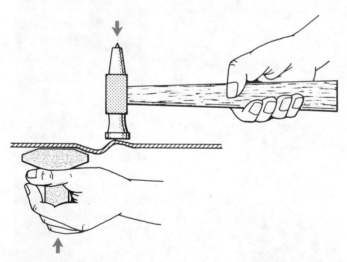

Fig. 19-11. Hammering off the dolly.

is being done. Fig. 19-12 shows how the picking end of a hammer can be used to level very small high or low spots left in the metal *after* using the hammer and dolly together on an area.

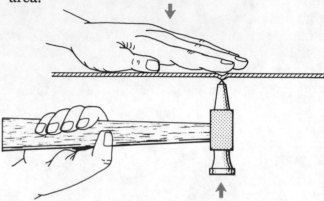

Fig. 19-12. *Picking,* used to work out very small dents or high spots.

Picking may also be done using only a dolly. A dolly is more useful for picking hard-to-reach low areas of the repair. Often, these areas cannot be reached with a hammer due to limited space under the panel. Fig. 19-13, for example,

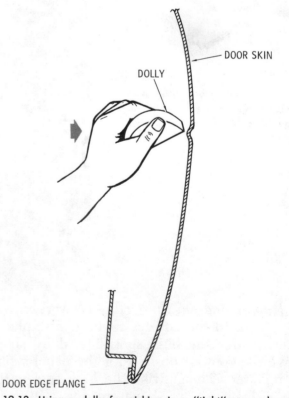

Fig. 19-13. Using a dolly for picking in a "tight" area where a hammer could not easily be used.

works down the high spot, the dolly is working up the low spot, so that both types of damage level off at about the same time. The pressure and "high" metal from the hammer blow is displaced (spread out) from the high spot to the low spot, causing the low spot to rise.

Picking—When *either* the hammer *or* the dolly is being used alone to work metal, *picking* shows how one corner of a dolly may be used to "pick up" low spots from inside the panel.

Pulling with Vacuum Cups

One or more *vacuum cups* may be used to pull out shallow, low-crown dents *where there is no buckled metal*. Fig. 19-14 shows how this is done on a simple job using one vacuum cup. Special plates are available with as many as *three* vacuum cups on one plate, allowing very large areas to be pulled. See Figs. 19-15 and 19-16.

Fig. 19-16. Using a large, three-cup hookup to pull out a damaged roof.

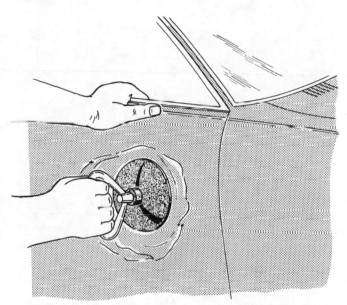

Fig. 19-14. Using one suction cup on a handle to pull out a large, *shallow* dent.

Fig. 19-15. A large vacuum plate using three suction cups on one pulling plate. (Courtesy of Guy-Chart Systems.)

To use any vacuum cup materials, the panel(s) being pulled *must* be clean and, preferably, *wet*. If possible, the panels should have paint on them and must not be sanded or

"roughed up" before using a vacuum cup. Finally, the cup itself will probably grip better if it is also wet.

To actually make a pull, first push *in* on the vacuum cup to push all the air out of the cup. Then, pull slowly out on the vacuum cup to pull out the dent. Although this is a very quick procedure, it is limited to use on low-crown dents. These are dents that have no sharp ridges around the outside edge of the damage.

Pulling with Pull Rods or Slide Hammers

Sometimes, a dent cannot be worked with a hammer and dolly because it cannot be reached from the back side. Also, the dent may be too deep or have edges that are too sharp to use a vacuum cup. In this case, a *pull rod* or a *slide hammer* can be used to "pull out" the dent. A major disadvantage of these pulling tools, of course, is that *holes* must be drilled in the panel being repaired.

Slide Hammer—To use a slide hammer, first drill a series of holes in the panel along the bot-

Fig. 19-17. A common slide hammer with a screw-like attachment to grip holes that are drilled in a panel to be pulled. (Courtesy of Guy-Chart Systems.)

SCREW-LIKE
FASTENER

SLIDE HAMMER
WEIGHT

SLIDE HAMMER
HANDLE

tom (deepest part) of the crease. Then, insert a sheetmetal screw, slightly larger than the drilled holes, into the end of the slide hammer. See Fig. 19-17. With the screw fastened on the slide hammer, turn the hammer handle *clockwise*, screwing the metal screw into the drilled hole. See Fig. 19-18. Then, pull out the dent by pulling out on the slide hammer.

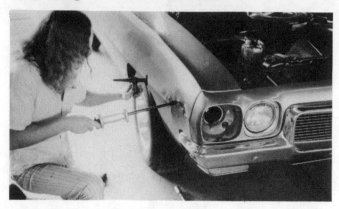

Fig. 19-18. Using a slide hammer to pull out a dent while using a body hammer to relieve the pressure at the high crown of the damage.

Note that the repairman in Fig. 19-18 is using a pick hammer to tap around the *outer* edge of the dent. This is done to help release the pressure causing the dent to stay in, so that the slide hammer can easily pull the metal out. If need be, the hammer *weight* may be slid back and forth to help pull the dent out if the dent is large or deep. See Fig. 19-19. In either case, when the dent is pulled out and the metal is

fairly well straightened, the repair area may be ground smooth and filled with body filler before being refinished.

Pull Rods—To use *pull rods,* Fig. 19-20, the area must be prepared as for using a slide hammer. Again, holes are drilled along the bottom of the crease. The holes should be slightly larger than the diameter of the pull rods. When the

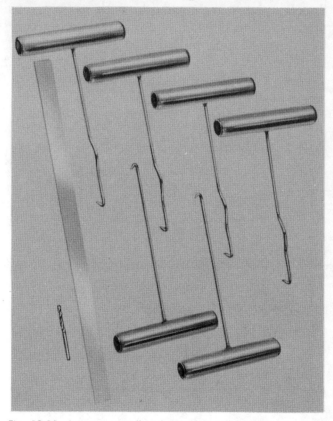

Fig. 19-20. A common pull rod set. The drill bit is used to drill the holes needed for the pull rods. The straightedge is used to judge the pulled area to determine when it has been made reasonably level. (Courtesy of Snap-on Tools.)

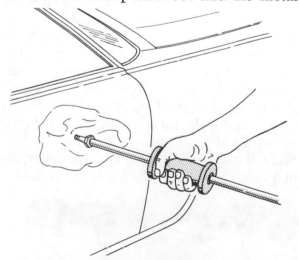

Fig. 19-19. Using the weight on a slide hammer to pull out a large, difficult dent. (Courtesy of Guy-Chart Systems.)

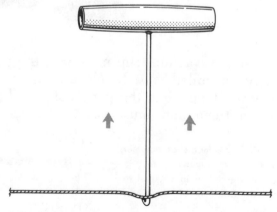

Fig. 19-21. Using one pull rod to make a simple pull.

holes have been drilled, the pull rods may then be used alone (Fig. 19-21 and 22) or with a pick hammer (Fig. 19-23). Pull rods are normally used on smaller, more shallow dents than is a slide hammer.

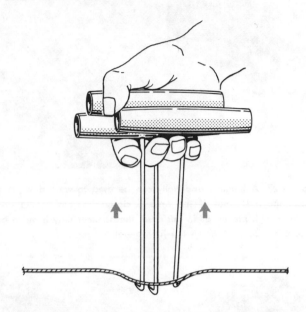

Fig. 19-22. Using more than one pull rod at the same time to pull out a larger area. If the pull rods and pull holes were spaced farther apart, both hands would have to be used to pull on the pull rods.

Heat Shrinking

When metal is damaged (dented) by an object, the metal will usually stretch. Many times, an experienced "metal man" can repair the damage without stretching the metal even more. This is one of the "secrets" of good metal straightening; be able to restore the damaged area without any further *stretching* of the metal.

However, if the metal is stretched too much either in the original accident or while straightening, the metal must be *shrunk*. This is done by *heat shrinking* and is necessary to shrink the metal so that it will occupy the same area on the panel as it did originally. Shrinking a stretched area is done, basically, by softening the area with heat and then applying either force to *flatten* the area or water to "shrink" the area.

Quenching (soaking) the hot metal with a wet sponge or rag is one of the better ways to shrink the stretched area back to its original shape. When hot metal is cooled faster than it would normally cool by itself, it will shrink. The faster it is cooled, the more it will shrink. Therefore, using a wet sponge or rag to cool hot sheet metal will cause the metal to shrink. See Fig. 19-24.

The basic theory and procedure for heat shrinking is discussed in the unit concerned with *Oxy-Acetylene Brazing and Heat Shrinking*. Figs. 19-25 through 19-28, however, review the basic procedure to use when working stretched metal with the heat shrinking process.

Fig. 19-23. Using a pick hammer with a pull rod. Here, the pick hammer helps to relieve the pressure around the edge of the damage while the pull rod pulls out the center.

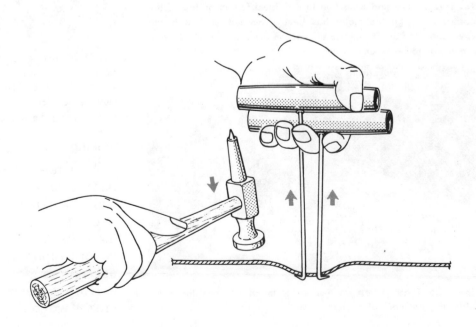

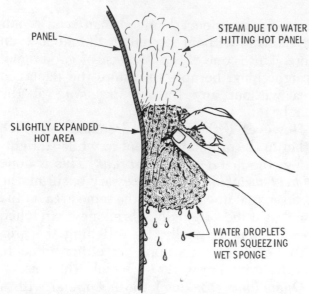

Fig. 19-24. Using a wet sponge to cool and shrink a stretched metal panel.

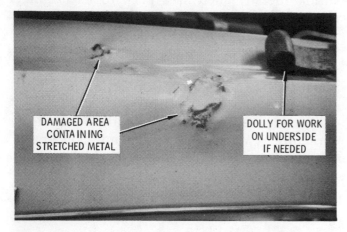

Fig. 19-25. Damaged area due to an object falling on top of the fender. Although the metal has been "roughed out," it is still wavy and not flat. This indicates that the area has stretched metal and needs to be shrunk.

Fig. 19-26. The first step when shrinking metal is to heat the metal fairly hot, *but not hot enough to melt.*

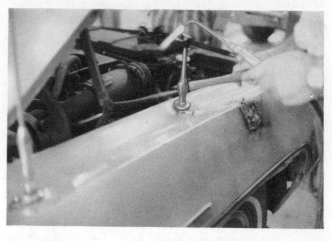

Fig. 19-27. A hammer and dolly can be used to work down and shape the hot metal. If the area is closed in from behind and contains high places, as in this case, the hammer may have to be used alone to work down the high metal.

Fig. 19-28. *Before* the metal has cooled after any hammer and dolly work, it may be qenched (soaked) with a wet rag or a sponge. This cools the metal quickly, causing it to shrink. This must be done *carefully* so as not to get burned on the hot metal while holding the wet sponge or rag.

Kinking

A metal-working process used *only* to prepare an area for filler is known as *kinking.* Basically, kinking is a method used to deal with stretched metal *without* actually shrinking the metal itself *or* straightening it. Actually, kinking is not supposed to return the metal to its original contour.

During kinking, the warped, wavy, stretched area is worked into a series of lowered kinks. A pick hammer is used to do this by tapping the metal with a scratch awl or "picking" metal against the edge of a dolly. See Fig. 19-29. Either the scratch awl or the pick hammer provides the sharp point necessary to make a small kink in the stretched area.

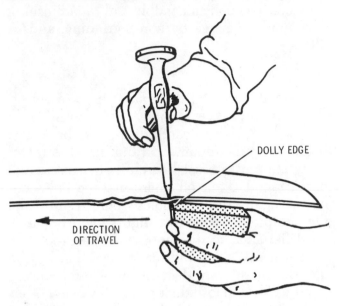

Fig. 19-29. This is the basic procedure used during *kinking*.

After the stretched area has been kinked several times, it will be slightly lower than the surface of the panel. Then, the stretched and kinked area is filled with body filler and prepared for refinishing. Kinking does not, of course, actually straighten the damaged metal.

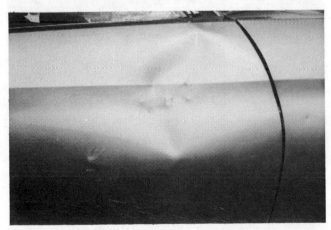

Fig. 19-30. Door panel damage. This is not bad enough to require a new door skin. A slide hammer or pull rod tools could be used to pull out the damage, but these would require drilling holes in the door. A better way to work out part of this damage would be to use a *pry bar*.

For this reason, kinking should not be considered for first-class body work. Only in an emergency or during wholesale-quality repairs should kinking be used.

Using Pry Bars

Many times, interior trim panels may be removed from *behind* a damaged area. When these panels are removed, a body man has *access* to the damage from behind. Then, *pry bars*

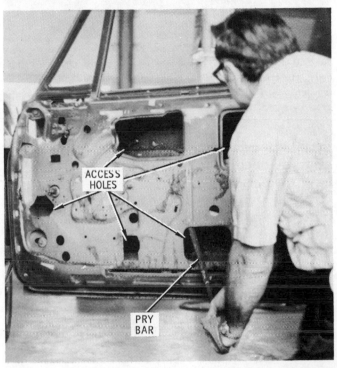

Fig. 19-31. From *inside* the door, the trim panel is first removed. This exposes the inner door with several different access holes. These may be *carefully* pried against to work out the outer door panel, as is being done here.

Fig. 19-32. Using the pry bar in a different access hole for a different angle against the back of the damage.

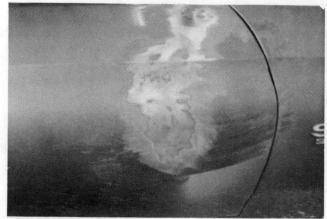

Fig. 19-33. After working with a pry bar, hammer and dolly work may be done to further smooth the smaller areas of the damage. Here, the door in Fig. 19-30 is shown after it was pried out, the smaller areas worked with a hammer and dolly, and the entire area then ground for filler.

may be used to pry out the damage. This will save the need to drill holes if a puller does not have to be used.

When using pry bars, care must be taken so that the metal is not pried out *too* far. This might stretch the metal and, in any case, will cause more work to be needed to complete the repair. Figs. 19-30 through 19-33 show a typical repair in which a pry bar may be used.

LEVELLING BEFORE REFINISHING

After the metal in a damaged area has been straightened, it must be *levelled* (made very level, flat) and worked very smooth before refinishing. Levelling may be done by one or more of the following processes:

1. Filing, Fig. 19-34.
2. Grinding, Fig. 19-35.
3. Filling, Fig. 19-36.

During these processes, *filing* removes any tiny high spots remaining on *the metal itself* after the area has been straightened. *Grinding* is used to remove damaged paint, knock off rough high places, and further prepare the area for refinishing. If the area is not completely level after any filing or grinding, the area can then be built up by *filling*. Any of the body fillers may be used before refinishing, depending on the job being done.

Generally speaking, the basic repair methods just discussed should be used as much as possible *before any filing, grinding, or filling is done. Filing, grinding, and filling are not substitutes for good sheet metal repair.* Good body work depends on *first* using the basic repair methods as much as possible and *then* finishing very minor damage by filing, grinding, and/or filling.

Filing

Basically, a metal *body file* is used to cut off (level) minute (very small) high spots. To do this, a body file is *carefully* moved back and forth across the repair, as in Fig. 19-34. A metal body file must be used carefully because if too much metal is cut off, there may be holes cut in the repair area. The holes would result if the file completely cut off a high spot. Also, care must be taken so that no metal is cut too *thin*. If the metal is cut and made very thin by the file, the metal may dent easily or flex, causing paint or filler to lose their grip. Like many other tools, then, a body file has a very limited *but very important* job.

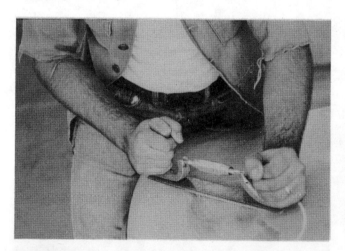

Fig. 19-34. Using a body file holder to file a repaired area when levelling the area.

Grinding

All sheet metal repairs normally leave heavy marks or scratches on the repair area. These marks are usually too deep to be filled and covered with primer-surfacer before the repair is refinished. Because of this, a disk grinder and grinding disk are used to remove the file marks, work marks, and any damaged paint in the area *before* body fillers are used.

If grinding is done with a *very fine* disk, further filling with body fillers may not be necessary. However, this is usually not the case. Instead, most grinding is done to level *and* roughen up the surface, preparing it for body filler. Figs. 19-35 and 19-37 show rough grinding disks being used to prepare a repaired surface for body fillers.

Filling

Generally speaking, *filling* the repair area with body filler is done *after* the area has been

Fig. 19-35. Using a body grinder to *grind* a repaired area when levelling the area.

Fig. 19-36. Using body filler to *fill* a repaired area when levelling the area. (Courtesy of The Norton Company.)

filed and then ground with a disk grinder. An area that needs filling may usually be filled with any of the body fillers; plastic, fiberglass, or lead. Basically, the types of areas needing filling are the places that cannot be completely worked out because they are in hard-to-reach places and/or places that cannot be worked from the back side.

Plastic filler, the filler most often used today, is first mixed and then applied, as in Fig. 19-36. As the plastic *begins* to harden, it may be grated with a *Surform* tool, as in Fig. 19-38. Then, it may be sanded with one or more of several sanding tools, such as the power sander being used in Fig. 19-39. Finally, the filled area is *feather-edged* with a sanding block and at least #240 sandpaper before being painted with primer-surface. Note that plastic *must always*

Fig. 19-37. Using a grinder and grinding disk to prepare a surface for body filler. (Courtesy of 3M Company, Automotive Division.)

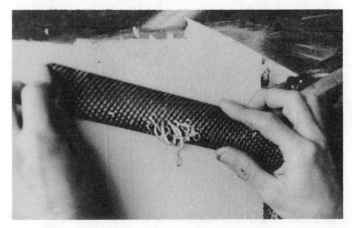

Fig. 19-38. When plastic filler has begun to harden, but is still not firm, it may be partially worked down with a *Surform* tool.

Fig. 19-39. When plastic filler has firmly hardened, it may be worked down with a number of abrasives and tools, such as the power file shown here. (Courtesy of The Norton Company.)

be applied less than ¼ inch thick. Coatings of plastic thicker than this, of course, tend to crack.

TYPICAL MINOR REPAIRS

Almost all minor sheet metal repairs may be made with one or more of the seven basic straightening methods, plus levelling, just discussed. When an auto body man, or *metal man*, has a good knowledge of these methods *and the ability to use them*, he will be a valuable em-

ployee in any body shop. For example, notice the quality of the repair being made in Figs. 19-40 through 19-43. Very shallow scratches (such as the damage in Fig. 19-40) require a good knowledge of levelling and refinishing practices so that the repaired panel does not have any waves in it suggesting that it has been repaired. See Figs. 19-40 through 19-43.

Fig. 19-40. Heavy scratches have produced a shallow dent along this door panel. Since the deepest part of the dent is less than ¼-inch deep, the repair may be made with body filler.

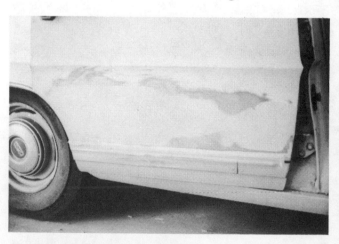

Fig. 19-41. Here, the area being repaired was ground back *well beyond* the actual bottom of the dent. This is done so that *all* the filler will be able to grip bare sheet metal. The plastic filler used was worked down and, finally, featheredged. Painting the panel with primer-surfacer will be done next. Then, the primer-surfacer will be wet-sanded with #320 sandpaper.

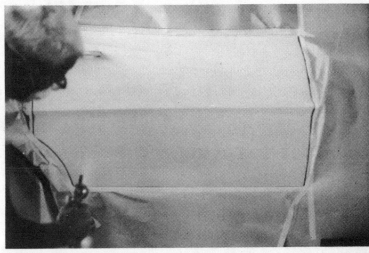

Fig. 19-42. Applying the top coat. Primer-surfacer and good featheredging under the top coat will help provide a nice, smooth repair.

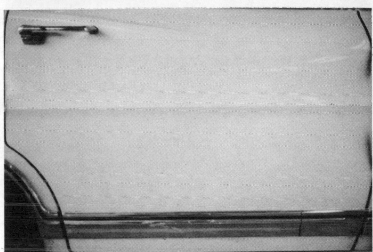

Fig. 19-43. The completed repair. Note that there are no waves where the dent was repaired. This is the final "test" of good auto body sheet metal work.

Fender or Quarter Panel Repair

Fender and quarter panel repairs are basically the same types of sheet metal repair. To decide whether to repair the damage, a body man must compare the amount of *time* needed to repair the panel with the cost of replacing the panel. If repairing the panel is quicker and more profitable, the panel must be straightened, levelled, and refinished.

Fig. 19-44 shows a damaged front fender. Analyzing the damage shows that it will be quicker and easier to repair the area than to replace the complete front fender. This fender damage, then, is repaired as shown in Figs. 19-44 through 19-62.

Door Repair

Making simple *door repairs* requires sheet metal straightening much like the work done to straighten fenders and quarter panels. Most outer door panels (skins) have large, low-crown sheet metal. Because the metal is low-crown (has few sharp bends), it may be more difficult to straighten than high-crown panels with sharp, easily seen edges.

Fig. 19-63, for example, shows a damaged outer door panel. After analyzing the repair, it is seen that the outer panel (skin) may be more easily repaired than replaced. Although a new skin may be easily and inexpensively installed, this damage can be straightened more profitably than installing a new skin.

In Fig. 19-63, the door has been damaged by being hit along the high crown (ridge) that runs the length of the door. This repair may be aligned and completed *without* putting holes in the door. Figs. 19-63 through 19-70 show how this repair would be made.

Fig. 19-44. A damaged front fender to be repaired. *Step 1:* Before beginning the repair, note *all* of the damage from the accident. This will include the slight damage to the end cap *and* the lower part of the fender, as well as the large dent.

Fig. 19-45. *Step 2:* Wash the area thoroughly with soap and water.

Fig. 19-46. *Step 3:* Clean the area thoroughly with precleaning solvent to remove tar, wax, and any chemicals on the finish. Follow the instructions printed on the product's label.

Fig. 19-47. *Step 4:* Decide on the metal straightening method to be used. Here, the sheet metal was not easily accessible from the back side, so it was decided to use a slide hammer to pull out the damage. The holes are being punched for the slide hammer's large screw. The holes could have been drilled, but drilling would take more time. Note that the holes (and, later, the pulls) are located along the *bottom* of the crease and the *top* of the original contour "break" along the center of the fender.

Fig. 19-48. *Step 5:* Use the metal straightening method(s) needed to straighten the damaged metal. Here, the slide hammer is being used to pull out the damage.

Fig. 19-49. *Step 5,* continued: Notice that the damage has already been pulled out reasonably straight at the top of the area.

Fig. 19-50. *Step 6:* Grind and, if necessary, file the repair area to prepare It for body filler.

Fig. 19-51. *Step 7:* Prepare the body filler. Here, plastic body filler will be used, so the filler and hardener are being thoroughly mixed.

MASKING TAPE TO PROTECT EDGES OF GOOD CHROME TRIM

Fig. 19-52. *Step 8:* Apply the body filler to the area. Spread the plastic evenly across the entire repair area. The plastic must be worked *into* the pull holes so that the plastic has a firm grip *on* the area and *in* the holes.

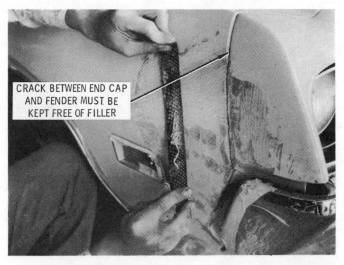

CRACK BETWEEN END CAP AND FENDER MUST BE KEPT FREE OF FILLER

Fig. 19-53. *Step 9:* Work down the body filler. Here, a *Surform* tool (cheese grader, cabbage cutter, etc.) is being used to work down the plastic as the plastic "sets up" (begins to harden). In this repair, note that there is a line (groove) between the fender and the end cap. This groove must be cleaned out so that filler cannot be seen in the crack. Most body men clean filler out of these cracks with a pocket knife.

Fig. 19-54. *Step 9,* continued: The plastic has been worked down with a *Surform* tool and has hardened. It is now ready for final levelling.

Fig. 19-55. *Step 9,* continued: Using a rotary sander to work down the filler. Dry #40 paper should be used.

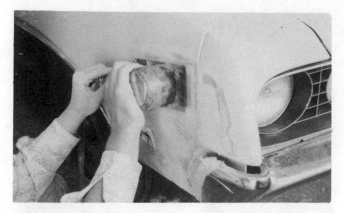

Fig. 19-56. *Step 9*, continued: Using an orbital sander ("jitterbug") to work down the filler. Dry #80 paper should be used on the jitterbug to smooth the scratches left by the #40 paper used earlier. After the jitterbug is used, the area should be finish-sanded (featheredged) with #150 or #240 dry sandpaper.

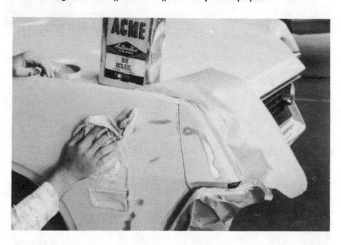

Fig. 19-57. *Step 10*: Clean the completely repaired and levelled area with enamel reducer. This includes body filler, bare metal, and featheredged old paint. Wipe off the enamel reducer *before* it dries.

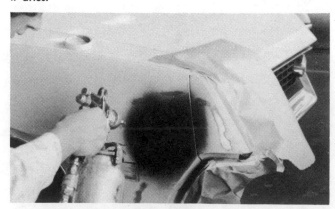

Fig. 19-58. *Step 11*: Apply primer-surfacer to the repaired area. In this case, the entire fender will not be painted, so only the repaired area will need primer-surfacer. Masking tape and paper protect the areas not to be refinished.

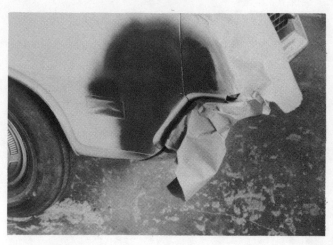

Fig. 19-59. *Step 12*: Allow the primer-surfacer to dry thoroughly before wet sanding.

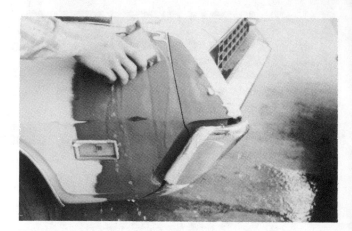

Fig. 19-60. *Step 13*: Wet-sand the primer-surfacer to prepare it for the top (color) coat. Use wet #400 sandpaper before quality enamel topcoats and all lacquer topcoats. Use wet #320 sandpaper before quicker enamel topcoats. In all cases, dry the area thoroughly and clean it with enamel reducer before applying the topcoat.

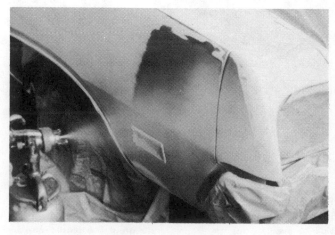

Fig. 19-61. *Step 14*: Apply the color topcoat. Follow the directions outlined in the painting units.

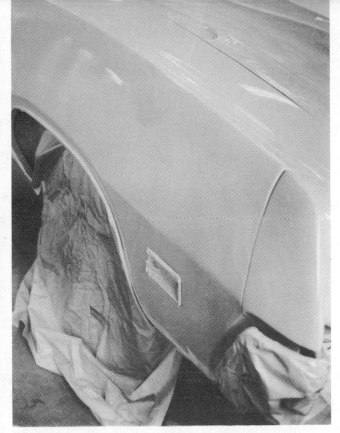

Fig. 19-62. *Step 15:* The completed job. The masking tape and paper must be removed and the car must be cleaned up before it is delivered to the customer.

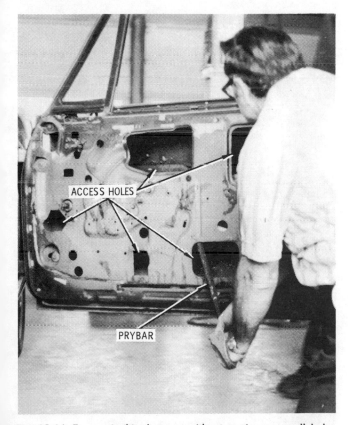

ACCESS HOLES

PRYBAR

Fig. 19-64. To repair this damage *without* putting any pull holes in the door skin, the damage may be worked out from the *back* side of the skin, as shown. The inside trim panel has been removed, exposing the access holes on the inside of the door. These holes are used to work the outer panel (skin) with a pry bar.

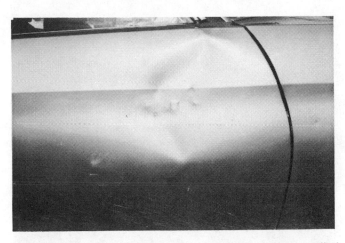

Fig. 19-63. Door skin damage. A new door skin could be installed to repair this damage. However, installing a new skin would be more costly than if this damage was repaired with the door still installed on the car.

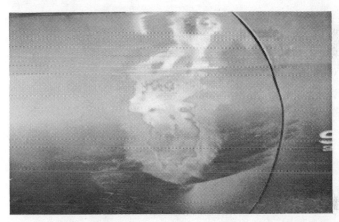

Fig. 19-65. The worked area, ground and prepared for body filler. Note that all the work was done from *inside* the door, behind the panel. This resulted in no holes having to be drilled in the panel. After the pry bar was used, a hammer and dolly were used to further straighten the panel.

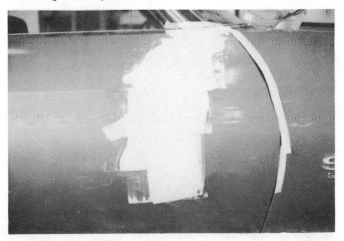

Fig. 19-66. Plastic filler applied over the straightened and prepared panel. The plastic is first worked down with a *Surform* tool and then with finer sandpapers.

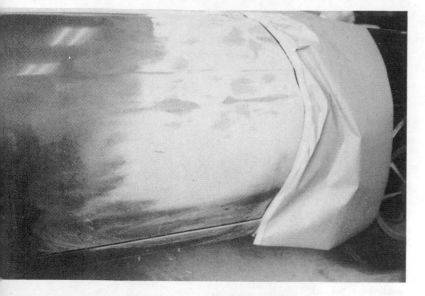

Fig. 19-67. Primer-surfacer applied to the completed repair. When the primer-surfacer was wet-sanded, several small nicks in the plastic filler were exposed.

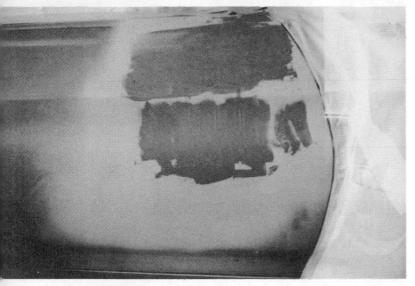

Fig. 19-68. Primer *putty* being used. This product is spread very, very thin on top of primer-surfacer to fill tiny nicks and imperfections in the primer-surfacer. The primer-surfacer *and* putty are then wet-sanded to prepare the surface for the color coat.

Fig. 19-69. Final preparation for the color coat. The primer-surfacer and putty were sanded with wet #400 sandpaper. This was done to provide extra smoothness, since the panel will be refinished with a lacquer topcoat.

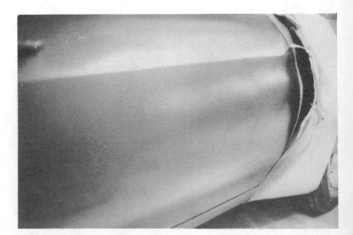

Fig. 19-70. The completed repair. Here, the paint does not have enough luster. This is because it is new *lacquer* paint. Before the car is delivered to the customer, the lacquer paint will have to be rubbed out (*compounded*) to full luster.

Body Panel Adjustments

Most of the panels that are bolted to an automobile or small truck body may be *adjusted* to fit their openings or adjoining panels. These "adjustable" bolt-on panels usually include the front fenders, the hood, the doors, the deck lid, and many small body parts. Each of these normally has at least two adjustment points. These points are used to position the panel or part either forward, backward, inward, or outward so that it is properly aligned. An auto body repairman must be able to align and adjust these panels or parts to fit properly.

There are two main reasons for having adjustable body parts: *appearance* and *tightness*. If body parts are not properly adjusted, the vehicle's *appearance* may suffer because of uneven gaps between parts. Paint may be chipped from adjoining parts because of too small a gap if they rub together as the vehicle moves along. On the other hand, body *tightness* may suffer if the parts are improperly adjusted. Loose panels may cause rattles, wind noises, and water leaks. For all of these reasons, then, properly adjusting new or repaired body parts is very important.

For example, notice the damaged fender in Fig. 20-1. This fender will have to be replaced, not repaired. When the new fender is installed, it must be adjusted to fit properly at the front, top, and rear. The new fender has been installed and properly adjusted in Fig. 20-2.

Fig. 20-1. A damaged fender to be replaced. The replacement fender must be aligned properly at the front, top, and rear edges.

GOOD FENDER REPAIR ALIGNMENT AT TOP, FRONT AND REAR

Fig. 20-2. The replacement fender installed on the car in Fig. 20-1. Note the good alignment at the front, top, and rear of the fender. This is a sign of quality auto body repair.

Fig. 20-3 shows common door alignment after a major repair. Note that the door is reasonably well centered in its opening. Proper door alignment is very important in auto body repair. Although a door must line up with many different panels (fender, quarter panel, roof, and rocker panel), customers will often judge body alignment quality by the look and fit of the car's *doors*.

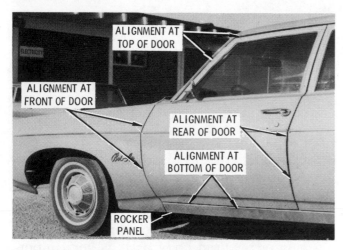

Fig. 20-3. Good door alignment is very important even though it may be difficult. A properly adjusted door will have reasonably equal gaps at the front, rear, top, and bottom.

HOW ADJUSTMENTS ARE MADE

All auto body panel and part adjustments are not made in the same way. Several different methods are used by automobile manufacturers and body men to make the adjustments necessary during auto body construction, assembly, and repair. Generally speaking, these methods include:

1. Slotted Holes
2. Caged Plates
3. Adjustable Stops
4. Shims
5. Bending

Each of these methods may be used alone or in combination to provide the adjustment and fit necessary on a given part or panel. *Which* method(s) to use depends on how the car was *designed* to be adjusted and what type of adjustment needs to be made. When all of the

adjustments have been made as much as possible and the part or panel *still* does not fit correctly, *bending* may be done to further align the part.

Slotted Holes

One of the most common methods of providing an adjustment for a part is to provide *slotted holes* for the bolts holding the part in place. See Fig. 20-4. These allow the part to be shifted around into position *before* the bolts are tightened. If the part is especially heavy, *two* workmen may be required; one to hold the part in the correct position and the other to tighten the bolt(s).

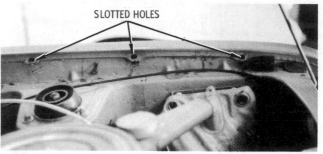

Fig. 20-4. Slotted holes allow a panel or a part to be moved slightly before the bolt going through the hole is tightened.

Slotted holes are usually larger than the heads of the bolts going through the holes. For this reason, large *flat washers* must be used under the *heads* of the bolts so that the bolt heads do not "pull through" the slotted holes. Also, the large washer allows the bolt to grip the metal all around the slotted hole, helping hold the panel or part and prevent it from slipping out of adjustment. See Fig. 20-5.

Caged Plates

Many times, especially on door hinges, slotted holes cannot be provided for up-and-down or in-and-out adjustments. For example, notice the small area around each hinge bolt in Fig. 20-6. Because this area is small, there is little room for slotted holes to be provided on the hinge. Also, slotted holes only provide for up-and-down *or* in-and-out adjustment, not both. If *both* adjustments were provided, the hole would be far too large for even a flat washer to cover *tightly*.

are *threaded* so that the door bolts or hinge bolts *screw directly into the caged plate itself.* To hold the plate in position when the bolts are removed, a thin sheetmetal *cage* is spot welded inside the door or door post after the plate is in position. Then, when the bolts are removed (or loosened for door or hinge adjustment), the plate *can* move inside the door or door post, but it *cannot* fall down inside the post. See Figs. 20-7 and 20-8.

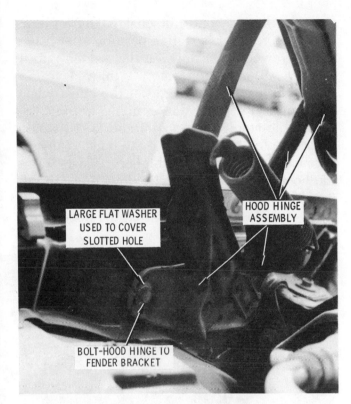

Fig. 20-5. Large flat washers are used under bolt heads when the bolt goes through a slotted hole.

To solve the above problems, then, *caged plates* are designed into the car's doors or door posts. Caged plates are heavy, thick pieces of metal into which *holes* are drilled. The holes

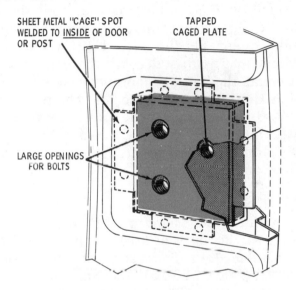

Fig. 20-7. Caged plates are usually located inside doors or door posts. They act like very large "nuts" into which the hinge bolts are screwed. The "cage" keeps the plate from falling down inside the door or post when the bolts are removed.

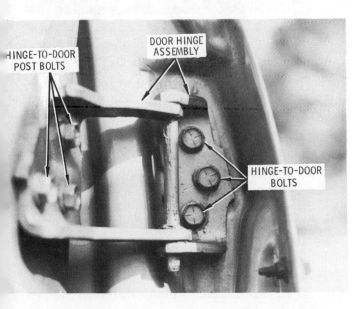

Fig. 20-6. There is little room for slotted holes under the hinge-to-door bolts on this door design. To adjust this door, a caged plate is provided behind the bolt location in the door.

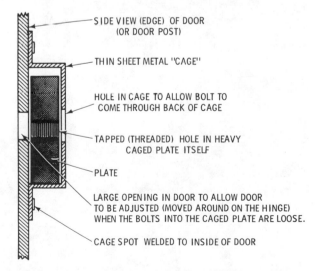

Fig. 20-8. A cutaway view of a caged plate. The sheet metal "cage" is spot welded to the inside of the door or door post, holding the thick plate nearly in position when the bolts are removed.

Caged plates are normally used in doors and door posts so that the door's hinges may be moved around on the door or post when the bolts are loosened. Extra-large holes in the *door,* for example, allow the hinge *and* the caged plate to move around together when the bolts are loosened. Then, when the door is adjusted, the bolts are tightened. Tightening the bolts squeezes the door's sheet metal *between* the hinge and the caged plate. Since the hinge and caged plate are squeezing the door's sheet metal, the door cannot move, thereby holding the adjustment. On the other hand, when the hinge and plate are squeezing the *door post's* sheet metal, the hinge cannot move on the post, holding the hinge in position on the post. In Fig. 20-6, for example, the bolts shown are screwed into caged plates. Of course, the cage plates cannot be seen because they are *inside* the door and door post.

Adjustable Stops

Many times, the *height* or *position* of a panel (usually the hood) is at least partly controlled by *adjustable stops.* These stops are large bolts (Figs. 20-9 and 20-10) that are threaded toward the bottom. The lower part of the bolt screws into a nut that is *welded* to the body or

framework. A second nut on top, the *locknut,* holds the adjustable stop in position after it has been screwed up or down in the welded nut.

After an adjustable stop is moved up or down, it changes the height of the panel when the panel is closed. For example, *raising* the adjustable stop in Figs. 20-9 and 20-10 would cause the left rear corner of the hood (the corner near the driver) to be higher (raised) when the hood is closed. Likewise, lowering the adjustable stop will cause the hood to be lower when it is closed, assuming that the hood hinge is adjusted down as well.

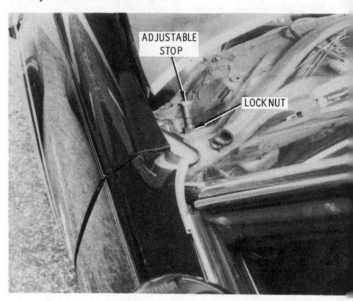

Fig. 20-10. Another view of the adjustable stop shown in Fig. 20-9.

Most adjustable stops have a *rubber cap* on top. This cap helps keep the stop from rattling against the underside of the hood on rough roads. Also, the cap helps prevent the stop from chipping the paint on the underside of the hood, which would cause rust. Most cars have at least two adjustable stops, one on each side of the hood at the front.

Shims

Small wedges of metal known as *shims* are often installed between two parts to make body alignment adjustments. These pieces of metal, Fig. 20-11, are made in many different shapes and widths. The purpose of any shim is to permanently change the *distance* between any two parts. This is done to move the parts farther

Fig. 20-9. Here, an adjustable stop is used to stabilize the hood height at the left rear corner. Most of the time, these stops are covered with a rubber cap.

apart or, when shims are removed, closer together.

Shims have a *mouth* that allows them to be slipped around bolts holding two parts together. See Fig. 20-11. Without the mouth, shims would be like washers and the bolt would have to be removed to add or remove shims. The mouth of the shim makes removing the bolt unnecessary, speeding up the job of adjusting body panels when adding or removing shims.

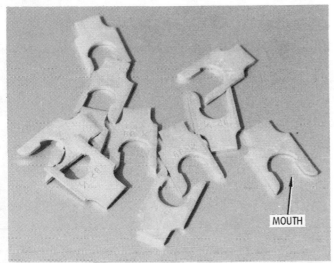

Fig. 20-11. *Shims*. The mouth of a shim allows it to be placed in position around a bolt without having to remove the bolt.

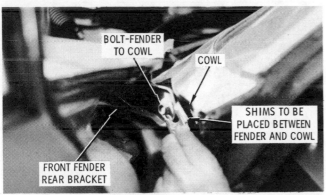

Fg. 20-12. A common location for shims is between the fender bracket and the cowl at the upper rear corners of front fenders.

Common uses of shims include making adjustments at fenders (Fig. 20-12) and deck lids (Fig. 20-13). In Fig. 20-12, the upper bolt at the front fender rear bracket was loosened, allowing shims to be placed *between* the fender bracket and the cowl. Then, when the fender bolt is tightened with the shims in place, the fender will be moved *out* at the upper rear corner. If the fender is out too far, the bolt may be loosened and one or more shims removed *or* thinner shims installed.

In Fig. 20-13, a deck lid will be adjusted by adding shims *between* the hinge and the deck lid. Adding shims will make the deck lid higher, whereas removing shims will make it lower. Usually, adding and removing shims is a "trial-and-error" procedure until the panel being adjusted is at the correct height. In all cases, however, shims are always positioned *around* the bolt and *between* two parts.

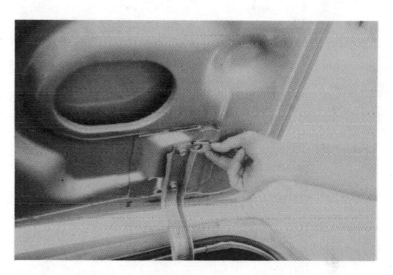

Fig. 20-13. Adjusting the deck lid height by adding a shim on top of one of the deck lid hinges.

Bending

A final method used to align body parts is by *bending* the parts. *Bending should only be done if the parts or panels cannot be aligned by any other method.* That is, if the adjustment cannot be made by any slotted holes, caged plates, adjustable stops, or by adding or removing shims.

However, bending is *not* necessarily a bad method of adjusting body panels. All automobile manufacturers use force to bend body panels into alignment during final inspection. It is not necessarily a sign of bad body work if a panel or part must be bent to bring it into alignment. Normal body adjustments only allow for a small amount of adjustment in, out, up, or down. If more serious adjustment is necessary, then, the panel or part may have to be *bent* to bring it into alignment.

Whenever a part or panel is to be bent into alignment, the following "rules of bending" should be kept in mind:

1. Be sure that the panel cannot be adjusted by any other means. Check to be certain that *all* the bolts were loose when the panel was being adjusted; one or two tight bolts may have prevented the panel from moving over its normal range of adjustment.
2. Use only large, soft objects for bending. These would include large blocks of *wood*, pry bars heavily padded with *rags*, etc.
3. If heavy *metal* tools are being used to bend a panel, *protect the panel* with heavy pads or blocks of wood so that the panel will not be damaged when pressure is applied.
4. Try to pry against surfaces that are not normally seen. For example, the edges of parts or the underside of doors. This way, if prying leaves any small marks on the panel, they will not be easily noticed.
5. Use jacks or prying tools to *gradually* and *evenly* apply pressure to the area. Using hammers to *hit* a panel is more likely to dent the panel than to actually bend it into alignment.

HOOD ADJUSTMENTS

A vehicle's *hood* is usually the largest adjustable panel on the vehicle. Also, because the hood is "up front" and easily noticed, it is very important that it be adjusted correctly. The hood must fit evenly along both fenders, the cowl, and at the front. This job may be done easily if the procedure is done in order.

Basically, the hood is held in place by the hood *hinges*. When the hood is open, usually only the hinges are supporting it. See Fig. 20-14. When the hood is closed, of course, it is also held in place by the hood latch assembly, Figs. 20-15 and 20-16. Finally, *adjustable stops* at the corners of the hood help position the hood so that it is level at the front and along the

Fig. 20-14. Basically, the *hinges* are the main support for the hood.

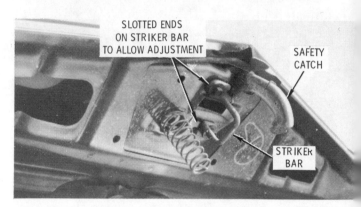

Fig. 20-15. At the front of the hood, the striker bar and safety catch support the hood and hold it closed when the hood is lowered.

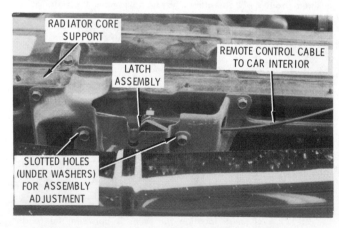

Fig. 20-16. The hood latch assembly is usually bolted to the radiator core support.

sides. These were shown earlier in Figs. 20-9 and 20-10.

Hood Hinges

The *bottom* of each hood hinge is usually attached to the cowl and/or the inner fender panel. See Fig. 20-17. Normally, either three or four bolts are used to hold the hinge in place on the body. The bolt holes in the hinge may be *slotted* so the hinge can be adjusted in place on the inner fender panel or cowl. These bolts will allow the hinge to be moved up or down, raising or lowering the hood when it is in the closed position.

The *top* of each hood hinge is bolted to the hood itself with two or more bolts. See Fig. 20-17. The upper hinge holes are also slotted, allowing the hood to be moved forward or backward on the hinges. Thus, the hood can be adjusted on the hinges so that it is positioned farther forward, toward the front of the car, or farther backward, toward the rear of the car.

When hood adjustments are made at the hinges, normally more than one person is required. The usual procedure is to install the hinges on the body and install the hood on the hinges, *not quite tightening all the bolts.* Then, lower the hood *slowly,* carefully watching to see that it does not bind or chip paint due to incorrect fit. With the hood lowered and the hinges not quite tight, shift the hood as required. Finally, *slowly* raise the hood so as to not disturb the hinge positions and then tighten all the hinge attaching bolts.

Hood Height Adjustment

On most hood designs, at least two and sometimes four *height adjustment screws* are used to hold the hood level with the panels around it. If one corner is lower than the other three corners, the adjusting screw under the low corner may be raised as necessary to make the hood fit level all the way around the opening. Most hood height adjustment screws are adjustable stops, as shown earlier in Figs. 20-9 and 20-10.

Raising or lowering the adjustable stops should be done to only *support* the hood once it is lowered. Moving the adjustable stops *must not be a substitute for correct hinge adjustment,* especially at the rear of the hood. If the hinge is too low and the stop is too high at the rear of the hood, it will cause the hood to bind when it

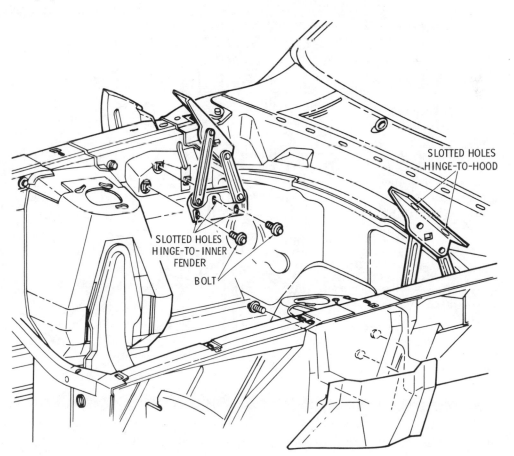

Fig. 20-17. Slotted holes on both "ends" of the hinge allow the hinge to be adjusted to the body and then allow the hood to be adjusted on the hinge. (Courtesy of Ford Customer Service Division.)

SLOTTED HOLES
HINGE-TO-HOOD

SLOTTED HOLES
HINGE-TO-INNER
FENDER

BOLT

is closed. This binding could permanently bend the hood, causing *more* work than was originally needed to align the hood!

At the front of the hood, the adjustable stops do control the height of the hood. However, the stops must work *with* the hood latch assembly, discussed next. Once the stops have been adjusted and the hood is level when closed, it must be noted how easily the hood closes and latches. If the hood must be slammed very hard to close even though it is level when closed, the latch assembly must be adjusted.

Hood Latch Adjustment

Almost all hoods today are held closed at the *front* with a *hood latch system*. All hood latch systems must have a latch assembly (Fig. 20-16) and a striker bar (Fig. 20-15). The latch assembly is normally bolted to the radiator core support. See Figs. 20-16 and 20-18. The latch assembly has a V-shaped opening in which the striker bar fits when the hood is closed. The

striker bar pushes down on the catch, tripping the catch so that it holds the striker bar, keeping the hood closed. When the hood is closed, the latch assembly on the front and the hinges at the rear hold the hood in place.

There are two basic types of *controls* for the latch assembly. These are the external (outside) hood release, Fig. 20-18, and the internal (inside the car) hood release, Fig. 20-16. The latch assembly itself is basically the same, whether controlled from inside or outside the car. All latch assemblies are also "backed up" by some type of *safety catch*, Fig. 20-15. This catch holds the hood almost completely closed if the regular latch assembly fails.

Repairing and adjusting hood latch assemblies and safety latches is serious business. If a car is turned out of the shop and the latch and/or safety catch fails, the hood could fly up and cause a serious accident. Whether the hood latch assembly has an internal or external control, then, it must be carefully adjusted as follows.

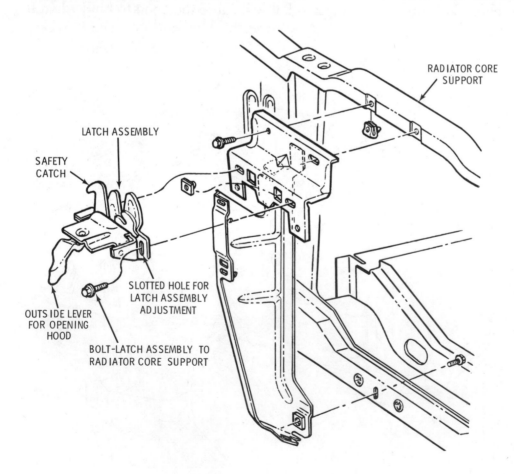

RADIATOR CORE SUPPORT

LATCH ASSEMBLY

SAFETY CATCH

SLOTTED HOLE FOR LATCH ASSEMBLY ADJUSTMENT

OUTSIDE LEVER FOR OPENING HOOD

BOLT-LATCH ASSEMBLY TO RADIATOR CORE SUPPORT

Fig. 20-18. A hood latch assembly with an outside (external) control. (Courtesy of Ford Customer Service Division.)

Adjustment—Basically, the hood latch has two adjustable parts: 1. the *striker bar screws* on the underside of the hood itself, and; 2. the *latch assembly screws* holding the latch assembly to the radiator core support. See Figs. 20-15, 16, and 18. To be certain that the hood is latching correctly, slowly lower the hood and watch the striker bar enter the "V" of the latch assembly. If the striker bar does not enter the "V" squarely *and the hood hinges are properly adjusted,* adjust either the striker bar *or* the latch assembly sideways until the bar squarely enters the latch.

The *last* hood adjustment to be made is the *height* of the latch assembly. This should be done *after* the hinges are adjusted, *after* the height adjustment stops have been adjusted, and *after* the striker bar and latch assembly have been adjusted to come together properly. In Figs. 20-16 and 20-18, note the bolts and slotted holes used to hold the latch assembly to the radiator core support. These will be used to change the *height* of the latch assembly.

To make the latch *height* adjustment, close the hood *after* the other adjustments have been made. If the hood will not latch or must be slammed down hard to latch, loosen the bolts and *raise* the latch assembly slightly. Retighten the bolts. Again, close the hood and note if it latches correctly.

If the hood does *not* latch tightly, you will be able to lift the hood slightly even though it is latched. When this is the case, loosen the latch assembly bolts and *lower* the latch assembly slightly. Then, close the hood and note if it latches correctly. Repeat any up-and-down adjustments until the hood closes easily *and* tightly. Finally, check the operation of the *safety catch* and bend it as required if it does not "catch" the hood correctly when the hood is slightly opened.

FRONT FENDER ADJUSTMENTS

The *front* section of most front fenders is attached to the radiator core support and/or to the grille. Along the sides of the engine compartment, the inner and outer fender panels are normally bolted together. See Figs. 20-19

and 20-20. Wherever these bolt locations are used, some type of fender alignment can usually be made.

However, the major fender alignment locations are the two or more bolts located on the cowl. See Figs. 20-21 and 20-22. On the upper cowl area there is usually a large bolt behind the door, as shown in Fig. 20-21. At the lower

Fig. 20-19. Oversize slotted holes are used to provide up and down and forward and backward adjustments.

Fig. 20-20. Bolt locations around a front fender.

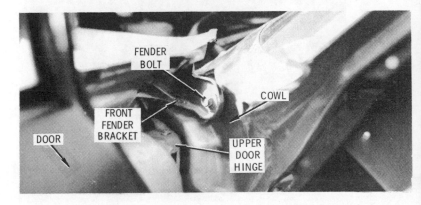

Fig. 20-21. Bolt location at the top rear of a front fender.

end of the fender, there is usually a fender bolt under the car or at the lower part of the cowl, in front of and below the door. See Fig. 20-22. These bolts can be loosened, allowing the fender to be moved in several directions. This is possible because the fender and its brackets have *oversize bolt holes* at these points. Also, *shims* can be removed or added at these locations for added adjustment. This was shown earlier in Fig. 20-12.

Many times, the hood adjustments just described and the fender adjustments described here must be made at the same time. After all the adjustments have been made, the gap between the fender and front door should be no more than ¼-inch. The gap between the fender and the hood should also be no more than ¼-inch. The gaps should be the same *all around* the sides and edges of the fender to provide uniform alignment and a good appearance. See Fig. 20-2.

Basic Adjustments

To correctly align a front fender, there are three basic adjustments that must be made. These include:

1. Up and Down
2. Forward and Backward
3. In and Out

Generally speaking, the first two adjustments are made at the same time *and* by moving the fender at the same bolt locations. Moving a fender in and out, however, may require different techniques and the use of *shims*.

First Two Adjustments—Normally, the first two adjustments (up and down, forward and backward) are made when the fender is installed. For example, the fender in Fig. 20-20 is being installed in Fig. 20-23. Note that the slotted holes in this fender (Fig. 20-20) will provide an allowance for up and down and forward and backward adjustment before the bolts are tightened.

Fig. 20-23. Installing a replacement front fender.

To move a fender up or down, first loosen all the bolts along the top, front, and in the cowl area (both upper and lower). Then, raise or lower the fender as desired. This can usually be done by hand. While holding the fender in position, have a helper retighten the bolts. To move the fender backward or forward, pressure may need to be applied with a power jack since forward and backward adjustment is limited on most fender designs.

Third Adjustment—To move a fender in or out, *shims* may need to be added or removed.

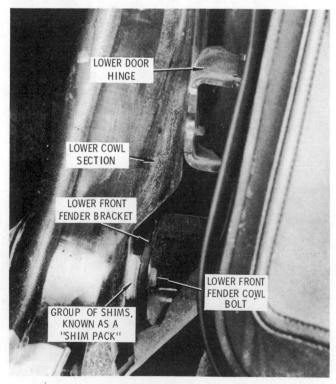

Fig. 20-22. Bolt location at the bottom rear of a front fender.

The shims will usually be placed between the outer fender bracket at the *upper* cowl area, as in Fig. 20-12. At the *lower* cowl area, the shims may be placed between the fender itself and the cowl.

To move the fender in, loosen the bolt(s) holding the fender to the top and/or bottom of the cowl. Then, *remove* shims as needed and retighten the bolt(s). This will pull the fender back in toward the cowl.

To move a fender *out*, first loosen the bolt(s) at the top and/or bottom and place more shims on top of the original ones. Or, install shims if there were none. Then, tighten the bolt(s) and check the new fender position.

DOOR ALIGNMENT

One of the most important, and often difficult, adjustment and alignment jobs in auto body repair is *door alignment*. Doors are made to fit openings in auto bodies. When a door fits the body opening properly, there is a gap of no more than ¼ inch all the way around the door. Note the reasonably uniform gap around the door assembly that was shown in Fig. 20-3.

Basically, the doors are held in place on the body with the door *hinges*. When the doors are closed, the door *latch assembly* holds the door closed and in position on the body. Both the hinges and the latch assembly on most cars may be adjusted to properly align and seal the door. The hinges fit on the front of the door and hold the door to either the *door post* or the *cowl*. The latch assembly does its job with a latch and striker, similar to the latch and striker bar on the hood but much stronger.

Door assemblies also have weatherstrip (rubber seals) like the one shown in Fig. 20-24. These seal out water, air, and dust, helping provide a clean, quiet ride. Weatherstrip must fit properly to do these jobs and not interfere with good door alignment. If weatherstrip is loose, it should be resealed. If it is damaged, it should be replaced.

Most doors also have one or more rubber *bumpers*, such as the lower bumper shown in Fig. 20-24. These help eliminate "metal-to-metal" contact and rattles when the door is

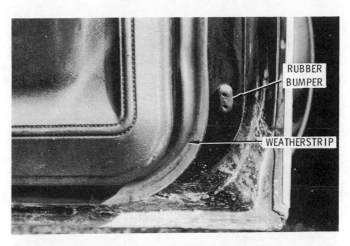

Fig. 20-24. All doors have some type of *weatherstrip* to prevent air and water leaks. Many doors also have rubber bumpers to help prevent rattles and to firmly position the door in the opening.

closed. These should be replaced if they are missing.

Door Hinges

The door *hinges* actually hold the doors to the vehicle's body assembly. Normally, the door hinges are *bolted* to the front of the door, as in Fig. 20-25. Some newer designs, however, have the hinges *welded* in place. Front door hinges are attached to the front edge of the door and to the sides of the upper cowl. See Fig. 20-26.

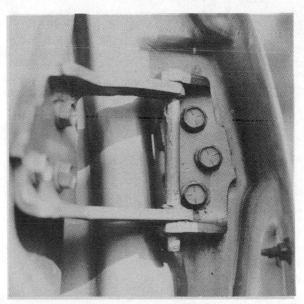

Fig. 20-25. The rear part of a door hinge is bolted to the front part of the door itself. The bolts pass through very large holes in the door and tighten into a caged plate inside the door.

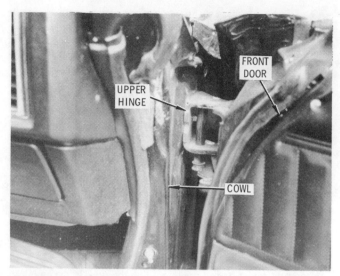

Fig. 20-26. At the *front* doors, the hinge assembly is bolted to the cowl.

If an automobile has *four* doors, the rear door hinges work the same as do the front door hinges. The difference is that the rear door hinges are attached to the center door post. See Fig. 20-27. Both front and rear door hinges are adjusted in the same way, as follows.

Fig. 20-27. At the *rear* doors, the hinge assembly is bolted to the door post. *Caged plates* inside the door post allow the hinge to be adjusted.

Hinge Adjustment—There are *two* basic hinge adjustments that may be made. The *front* part of each hinge (the part attached to the body) can be adjusted to move the door up or down in the door opening. See Fig. 20-27. The *rear* part of each hinge (the part attached to the door) can be adjusted to move the door in

or out in the door opening. See Fig. 20-25. In either case, loosening the door hinge bolts allows the *caged plate*, discussed earlier, to be moved around inside the cowl, the door post, or the door assembly. This depends on which adjustment is being made and, of course, which hinge bolts are loosened.

To move a door up or down, open the door and loosen the bolts on the *front* part of the hinges, the bolts holding the hinges to the cowl (front) or door post (rear). See Fig. 20-22. Do not loosen the bolts too much but *just enough* so the door can be moved when it is pulled up or pushed down. Then, push forward or pull backward, up or down, on the door and hinge, as needed. This forces each hinge and its bolts and caged plate to slide forward, backward, up, or down inside the cowl or door post. When the door is adjusted as required, *carefully* open the door so as not to disturb the position of the caged plates. Then, retighten the bolts and check the adjustment.

To adjust a door *in* or *out*, first open the door. Then, *slightly* loosen the bolts at the *rear* hinge sections; the bolts holding the hinges to the door. See Fig. 20-25. Next, move the door *in* or *out* as required. This lets the door slide in or out while the hinge, bolts, and caged plate stay in position. Since the bolts and caged plate are loose, the door's sheet metal can move around between the caged plate and the hinge.

When the door is moved in or out as desired, *carefully* open the door so as not to disturb the door position. Then, tighten the bolts at the rear of the hinge. Check the door alignment, then, with the door closed.

Door Check—One door hinge assembly, either upper or lower on each door, is usually equipped with a *door check*. This is used to hold the door open and in position each time the door is opened. A door hinge with a door check built in is normally adjusted as any other hinge. See Fig. 20-28.

Door checks do not normally need repair or replacement. They should be *oiled* regularly, however. The *roller* on each check will not "roll" with the door check *cam* unless it is oiled. If a door hinge with a door check is replaced, the check *spring* must be installed correctly.

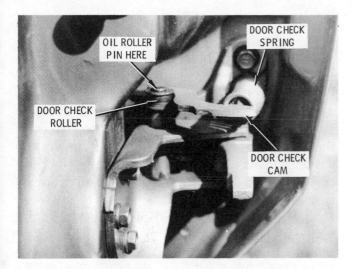

Fig. 20-28. A door check assembly as part of a lower door hinge.

Door Striker

The rear of a door must have some type of *lock assembly* to hold the door closed and, if necessary, locked. Fig. 20-29 shows a typical door lock assembly and door handle. The lock assembly holds the door tightly to the *door striker*. To adjust the rear of the door, adjust the door striker, discussed next.

There are two basic types of strikers, depending on the type of lock assembly used. The two types of strikers include striker *bolts* and striker *plates*. Either type of striker does the same job, although each striker must be used with its own type of latch assembly.

Striker Bolts—Striker *bolts* are made of a metal bolt and washer assembly that screws into a caged plate inside the door lock pillar. Many striker bolts have a ⁵⁄₁₆-inch *hex hole* in the center of the bolt's head, as in Fig. 20-30. To adjust a striker bolt, loosen the bolt head with the correct tool. Then, the bolt may be moved up, down, in, or out for adjustment. The caged plate, of course, moves with the bolt until the bolt is tightened again.

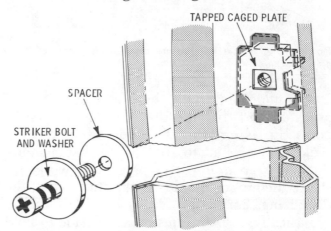

Fig. 20-30. A typical *striker bolt* assembly. (Courtesy of Fisher Body Division.)

Striker Plates—Striker *plates* are attached to the caged plate with several smaller *screws*, rather than by a large striker *bolt*. To adjust a striker *plate*, all the screws must be loosened slightly. Then, the striker plate screws, striker plate, and caged plate may be moved around on the door post as desired. See Fig. 20-31.

Adjusting—After the door hinges are correctly adjusted, the door striker may need to be adjusted. When the striker is properly adjusted, the door will close and latch *without being moved up or down by the latch and striker*. Striker *plates* may be adjusted so that the door latch drags *slightly* on the striker plate. However, at *no time should a door latch and striker move the door up more than* ¹⁄₁₆-inch when the door is closed. If this *does* happen and the hinges are properly adjusted, the striker needs to be adjusted.

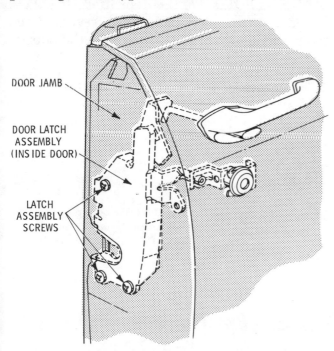

Fig. 20-29. A typical door latch assembly. Normally, the latch assembly itself is not adjustable. (Courtesy of Fisher Body Division.)

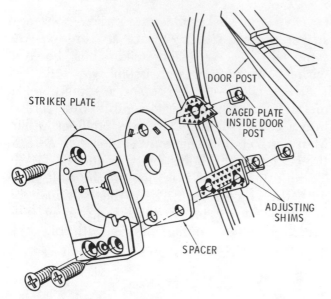

Fig. 20-31. A typical *striker plate* assembly. (Courtesy of Fisher Body Division.)

It is important, then, that the door hinges be adjusted and that the door fits in its opening correctly *before* the striker is adjusted. If a striker is adjusted to "pull up" a low-hanging door, it is an example of poor body work. Instead, the hinges should be adjusted so that the door hangs correctly.

Basically, striker adjustment is made to hold the door in or out, as required. Also, if the striker pulls the door up or down even though the hinges are adjusted correctly, the striker

must be adjusted so that it does not pull the door up or down.

To make the adjustment, simply loosen the striker bolt or striker plate screws slightly. Leave them tight enough so that light taps with a hammer are needed to move the bolt or plate. Then, use a small hammer to tap the striker in the direction(s) needed. This will move the striker and its caged plate. Try closing the door *carefully* so as to not move the striker from its new setting. Check the new striker position to see if the door closes and fits properly at the rear edge. Then, readjust or tighten the striker as required.

Door Locks

An important part of a door assembly is the *door lock*. Fig. 20-32 shows the basic parts of a door lock assembly. This assembly keeps the door closed and, when desired, locked. The assembly has 3 main parts:

1. The door lock assembly
2. The outside lock and handle
3. The inside remote control

Door Lock Assembly—The door lock assembly is installed *inside* the door itself. It is held in place on the door jamb with several large screws, as shown in Fig. 20-32. Both the outside

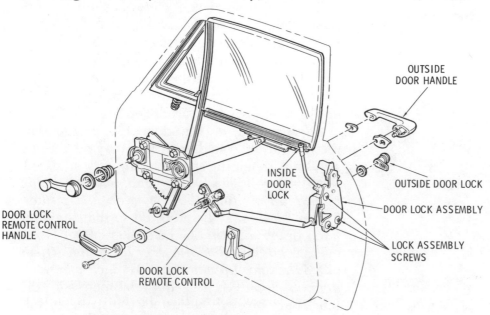

Fig. 20-32. The basic parts of a door lock assembly and controls. (Courtesy of Fisher Body Division.)

handle and the inside remote control work the door lock assembly.

Outside Lock and Handle—The *outside* lock and handle operate the lock assembly from outside the car. These include *push-button handles* (Fig. 20-33) and *pull handles* (Fig. 20-34). When either handle is engaged, the door lock assembly releases the striker bolt or striker plate, allowing the door to be opened.

Fig. 20-33. A push-button outside door handle.

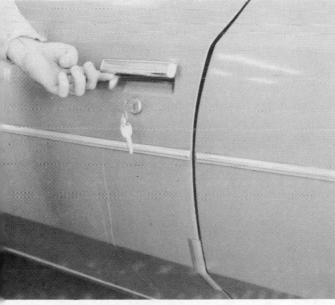

Fig. 20-34. A pull type outside door handle.

The outside lock *cylinder* is operated with a key. The correct key, inserted in the lock cylinder, may be turned to lock or unlock the door from the outside. Fig. 20-35 shows how the outside lock cylinder is connected to the door lock assembly.

Inside Remote Control—The inside remote control is normally some type of pull handle. It does the same job as the outside door handle; when it is pulled, it causes the door lock assembly to release the striker bolt or striker plate. This allows the door to be opened.

The inside *door lock* remote control is normally a small *knob* located on the top of the trim panel, directly below the window glass. The knob is attached to a connecting link, as shown in Fig. 20-32. When the knob is pushed down, the door is locked by the connecting link locking the door lock assembly.

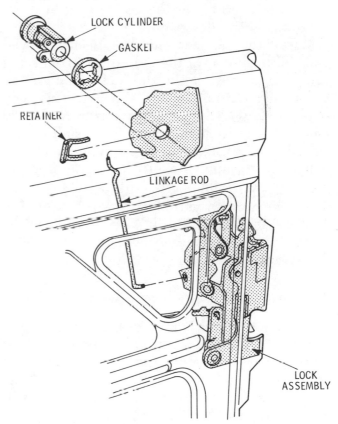

Fig. 20-35. Linkage connects the door lock assembly to the inner and outer door lock controls. (Courtesy of Chrysler Corporation.)

Replacing the Door Lock Assembly—If a door lock assembly is worn or has been damaged in an accident, it must be replaced. To do this, the door handle remote control and the door trim panel must first be removed. This is outlined in the Trim Work unit.

Then, to actually remove the lock assembly, first roll the window glass up and disconnect the remote control and door lock connecting links. Finally, remove the screws that hold the lock assembly to the inside of the door. Then, remove the lock assembly by pulling it out through one of the large *access holes* in the inner door panel. To install the new assembly, reverse the procedure.

Replacing the Door Lock Cylinder—To replace a lock cylinder, first remove the trim panel as outlined in the Trim Work unit. Place a pointed tool or screwdriver behind the retainer clip and pull the clip sideways, off the cylinder's shoulder. See Fig. 20-36. Then, disconnect the back end of the cylinder from the door lock assembly or the connecting link, depending on the design.

When the retainer clip has been removed and the back end of the cylinder disconnected from the lock assembly, the lock cylinder may be removed from outside the car. This may require turning the cylinder assembly slightly to remove it from the door. To install a new cylinder, or to install the old cylinder after a door repair, simply reverse the procedure. A few retainer designs are made so that the retainer may easily be removed from inside the door jamb. With these designs, it may not be necessary to remove the trim panel to remove the lock cylinder.

DECK LID ALIGNMENT

The deck (trunk) lid, like the hood, usually has two hinges and a support system to hold it up when it is open. Like the doors, the deck lid or its opening has a weatherstrip around the edge. The weatherstrip seals water and dust out of the trunk. The weatherstrip must fit properly around the opening or it can cause the deck lid to be out of alignment. If the weatherstrip is damaged or twisted, it must be resealed or replaced.

Most deck lids have three main adjustments for proper alignment:

1. Hinge Adjustment
2. Torsion Bar Adjustment
3. Lock Adjustment

A deck lid is properly adjusted when the gap all the way around the lid is no more than ¼

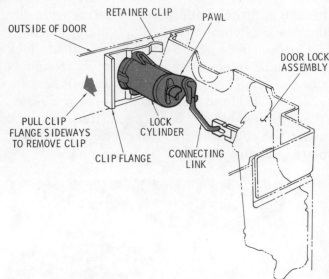

Fig. 20-36. To remove most outer door lock cylinders, the retainer clip must be pulled sideways. (Courtesy of Fisher Body Division.)

inch. Fig. 20-37 shows a properly fitted deck lid.

Hinge Adjustment

The front part of a deck lid (the part near the rear window) can be adjusted forward, backward, up, or down, as necessary, so that it fits flush with the other body panels. This is done by adjusting the deck lid at the *hinges*. A few deck lids have caged plates inside the lid, but most deck lid adjustments are made by slotted holes in the hinge arms and/or installing shims *between* the hinge arms and the deck lid. See Fig. 20-38.

To adjust a deck lid forward or backward, open the lid and slightly loosen the bolts hold-

Fig. 20-37. A properly fitted deck lid. The gap all the way around the lid is about ³⁄₁₆-inch.

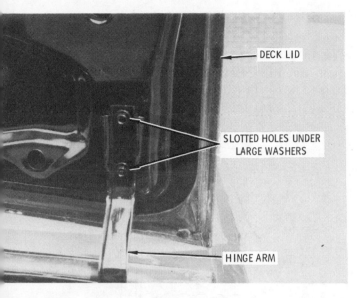

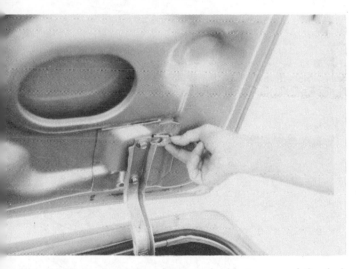

Fig. 20-38. Most deck lid adjustments are made where the deck lid is bolted to the hinge arms. Here, slotted holes, caged plates, and/or shims are used to adjust the entire deck lid forward or backward, and to adjust the front part of the deck lid up or down.

Fig. 20-39. Removing shims between the hinge arm and the deck lid will change the deck lid adjustment.

ing the lid to the hinge arms. See Fig. 20-38. Then, slide the deck lid into a new position, forward or backward, as desired. Carefully close the deck lid and check its alignment. When the alignment has been corrected, re-tighten the bolts.

To move the front part of the deck lid up or down, *shims* may be used. For example, to move the deck lid *down*, remove one or more shims from under the hinge arms. Note the shim being removed in Fig. 20-39. Then re-

tighten the bolts and check the new deck lid position. To *raise* the deck lid, *add* one or more shims between the hinge arms and the deck lid.

Torsion Bar Adjustment

Deck lid torsion bars, Fig. 20-40, hold the deck lid open when it is unlocked. This is because the bars are twisted when the hinges close with the deck lid. When the lid is unlocked, the bars can untwist, opening the hinges. This pressure holds the hinges open until the lid is pushed down, twisting the bars and putting them (and the deck lid) under tension until the deck lid is again opened.

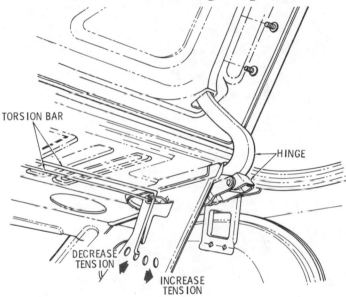

Fig. 20-40. Torsion bars are used on many deck lid designs to hold the lid open. The tension in the torsion bars can be adjusted by moving the bars to different holes.

Fig. 20-40 also shows how the torsion bars can be adjusted to increase or decrease their tension. Moving the adjusting end of each bar in or out gives the bar more or less tension, depending on the anchoring hole used. Both bars should be anchored in the same relative hole position on opposite sides of the trunk. Care must be used when moving the bars because they are usually in tension and can cause injury if they "get loose" while being moved.

Deck Lid Lock

Deck lid lock systems have two main parts; the lock assembly and the striker plate. The lock assembly is normally attached to the deck lid itself, as in Fig. 20-41. A lock cylinder, opened with a key, allows the lock to be opened from outside the trunk. The lock assembly may *also* be attached to the lower rear end panel, below the deck lid. This design is shown in Fig. 20-42.

the *lock assembly* is in the deck lid, the *striker plate* must be in the lower body panel, as in Fig. 20-43. On the other hand, of course, if the lock assembly is in the lower body panel, the striker plate must be in the deck lid. This design is shown in Fig. 20-44.

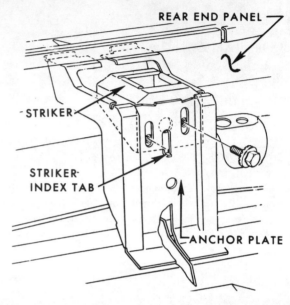

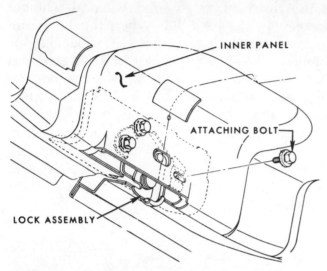

Fig. 20-41. Typical deck lid lock assembly mounted in the deck lid itself. Slotted holes allow the entire assembly to be adjusted. (Courtesy of Fisher Body Division.)

Fig. 20-43. Typical deck lid striker mounted in the lower rear body panel. Slotted holes allow the striker to be adjusted. (Courtesy of Fisher Body Division.)

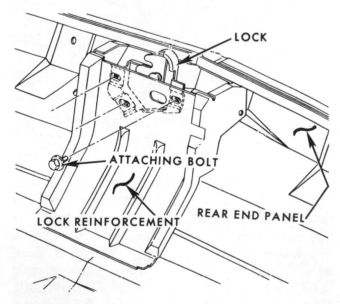

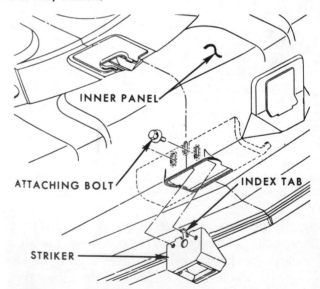

Fig. 20-42. Typical deck lid lock assembly mounted in the lower rear body panel under the deck lid opening. (Courtesy of Fisher Body Division.)

Fig. 20-44. Typical deck lid striker mounted in the deck lid itself. (Courtesy of Fisher Body Division.)

The striker plate, like the lock assembly, may be mounted in either the deck lid itself or below the deck lid in the lower body panel. When

When the deck lid is closed, the striker plate enters the lock assembly. This forces the lock catch to roll shut, automatically holding the striker down when the lock assembly closes.

Later, when the trunk key is used to turn the lock cylinder, the lock assembly releases the striker. The catch rolls loose, releasing the striker as the torsion bars pull the deck lid open.

Lock and Striker Adjustment—Normally, both the deck lid lock assembly and the striker may be adjusted. By adjusting them, the deck lid can usually be held evenly at the rear edge *and* be easily closed. However, lock and striker adjustments should *not* be used to move the deck lid right or left for alignment. Moving the deck lid right or left should be done at the hinges or by bending. Only after the deck lid is properly aligned side-to-side and front-to-back should the lock and striker be adjusted.

To adjust the lock and striker, slowly close the deck lid and watch the striker enter the lock. The striker should enter the lock squarely, *without* pulling the deck lid to one side. If the striker does not enter properly and tries to pull the deck lid to one side, loosen the bolts holding the lock assembly and/or the striker. Then, move the lock assembly and/or the striker right or left as much as needed. Again, slowly lower the deck lid to see if the striker enters the lock correctly. If so, retighten the bolts in their slotted bolt holes.

After the side-to-side adjustment is made, the rear edge of the deck lid may be adjusted either up or down. This is done moving the striker either up or down, as needed. To do this, open the deck lid and slightly loosen the bolts holding the striker. Move the striker up or down as desired. Retighten the bolts and then close the deck lid. Readjust if necessary. Take care not to change the side-to-side adjustment while doing this. Finally, recheck the entire deck lid adjustment for equal spacing and height.

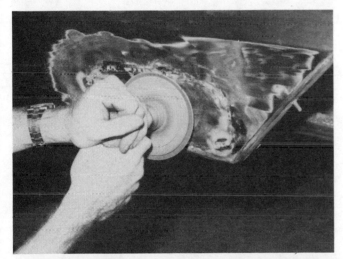

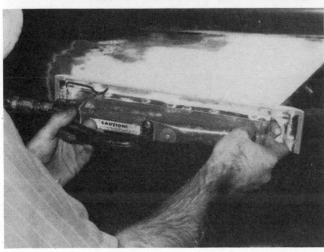

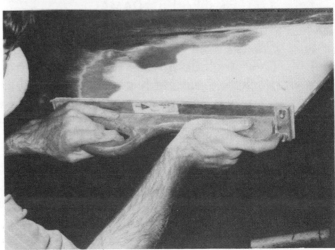

Unit 21

Repairing Rust Damage

Most automobile and small truck bodies will *rust* when moisture and chemicals penetrate the paint and come in contact with the bare metal. Rust is actually a *chemical reaction* known as *oxidation*. In this reaction, *oxygen* in the air, water or chemicals combines with *iron* in the metal to form *iron oxide*. Iron oxide is brown in color and is commonly known as *rust*, Fig. 21-1. Rust is harmful to any metal because it weakens the metal by turning the metal into flaky or powdery iron oxide (rust). If rust is not removed, it will usually "eat through" the metal within a few months, leaving a hole or holes. See Fig. 21-2.

TYPES OF RUST DAMAGE

Generally speaking, there are *two main types of rust damage* that may appear on an automobile. These include *surface rust* and *rust-out*. Rust-out, where holes are eaten through the body sheet metal, is also known as *cancer*. Although rust damage may begin anywhere paint is broken, most automobile rust damage begins along the lower body panels, as in Fig. 21-3. This is because the lower body panels are more likely to be damaged by stones, road chemicals, and water thrown up by the wheels. Often, these collect *behind* the panel to cause rust-out (cancer) in several years.

Fig. 21-1. Common surface rust. Surface rust appears as brown spots or areas on a panel and does *not* go all the way through the panel.

346

Some type of rust will usually begin anywhere that moisture and/or road chemicals (such as salt) come in contact with bare metal. This may be on either the outside *or* the inside of a panel. This means that rust can begin working *outside* the panel and work *inward* or it can begin *inside* the panel and work *outward*. Once rust begins, it will continue "eating away" the metal until it is stopped.

Surface Rust

Surface rust usually begins wherever paint has been *chipped*, is *flaking off*, or is *cracked*. When this happens, moisture and road chemicals can reach the bare metal under the paint, causing surface rust to begin. Metal-to-metal contact, for example, will cause surface rust by chipping the paint on the metal. This may happen when panels or trim are not properly aligned, allowing them to rub together and chip the paint.

When surface rust begins, it should be repaired as soon as possible. If it is not repaired soon enough, it will continue "eating" the metal around the area. Finally, the surface rust will become more severe and will eventually cause rust-out. This is what usually happens, for example, at the lower edge of rear window glass, as in Fig. 21-2.

Rust-Out

Rust-out damage results from moisture and/or chemicals (such as salt) reaching the bare metal. Then, when the rust is allowed to continue eating away the metal for several months, the metal is damaged with rust holes *through* the metal. Although several months is a short time period, it may often be enough time for rust-out to happen. This is because most body panels are fairly thin and rust can eat through them quickly.

There are two types of rust-out: 1. Rust-out caused by rust eating through the metal from the *outside* to the *inside*, and; 2. Rust-out caused by rust eating through the metal from the *inside* to the *outside*. Outside-to-inside rust-out, the first type, is caused by not repairing

surface rust soon enough. A good example of this is the rust-out under the back window in Fig. 21-2.

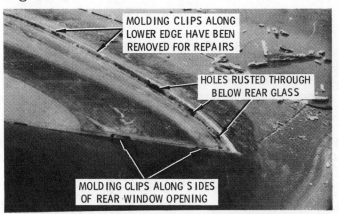

Fig. 21-2. Common rust holes *through* the metal.

Inside-to-outside rust-out, the second type, is the most common rust-out. It is usually caused by moisture and road chemicals getting inside a panel and staying there for some time. Fig. 21-3 shows bubbles on the paint near a rusty area. These bubbles indicate inside-to-outside rust-out. This is due to moisture coming through from *behind* the paint, causing a bubble. Areas like this should be carefully inspected for clogged drain holes or leaks at sealers.

Fig. 21-3. Lower body panels are those most likely to show rust damage. Here, both surface rust and rust-out are seen.

To *correctly* repair any type of rust damage, you must *locate and stop the cause of the rust*. Carefully inspecting inside-to-outside rust-out areas is especially necessary to locate and repair any sealer leaks or clogged drain holes. During all *good* rust repairs, any cancerous rust-out should be removed and the remaining area treated with *metal conditioner*.

METAL CONDITIONER

An important part of *good, lasting* rust repair is to treat cleaned, bare rusted metal with a good *metal conditioner*. This product must be used where either surface rust *or* rust-out is being repaired. If metal conditioner is not used, such as on a wholesale repair, the rust repair will not last as long; rust will more quickly re-appear. Fig. 21-4 shows one manufacturer's metal conditioner product.

Fig. 21-4. One manufacturer's *metal conditioner*.

Metal conditioner is an acid-like liquid that attacks the rust itself to help stop the rust from spreading further. Even though a good deal of rust is ground away during a repair, any re-maining rust edge or rust pit will continue to rust the metal *underneath* the completed repair if metal conditioner is not used. Then, the rust will eventually come out again because it was not treated. Using metal conditioner is impor-tant to help prevent the rust from coming back.

Using Metal Conditioner

Good brands of metal conditioner have complete instructions printed on the container. Be sure to *follow the instructions carefully and use the product exactly as directed*. Metal con-ditioner is a type of acid, so it is a good safety precaution to *wear rubber gloves and safety goggles* when using the product.

Generally speaking, metal conditioner is first mixed with water before being used. Then, it is scrubbed on the area being repaired, using steel wool or old (but clean) rags. Finally, the prod-uct *must be completely wiped off the area while it is wet*. Metal conditioner must *not* be allowed to dry on the surface.

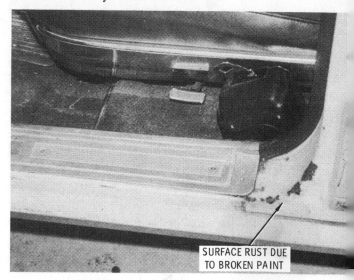

SURFACE RUST DUE TO BROKEN PAINT

Fig. 21-5. A typical panel with only surface rust damage. Here, small chips in the paint have allowed surface rust to begin.

REPAIRING SURFACE RUST DAMAGE

Normal surface rust begins as small blisters on the bare metal. These may be easily repaired by using the procedure shown in Figs. 21-5 through 21-15. Some surface rust is "deeper" than the blister stage. In these cases, the metal actually becomes *pitted*, although it is not rusted through. To repair this type of surface rust, the pitted areas must be filled with a body filler *after* the smaller rust pits have been ground away and any remaining pits have been treated with metal conditioner. The filling is done to restore the original contour of the panel.

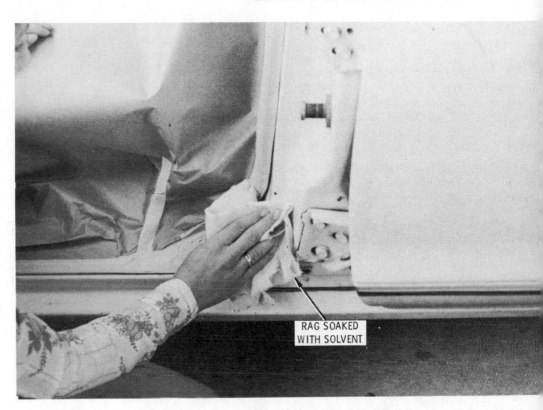

Fig. 21-6. *Step 1:* To repair surface rust damage, first clean the area with precleaning solvent.

RAG SOAKED WITH SOLVENT

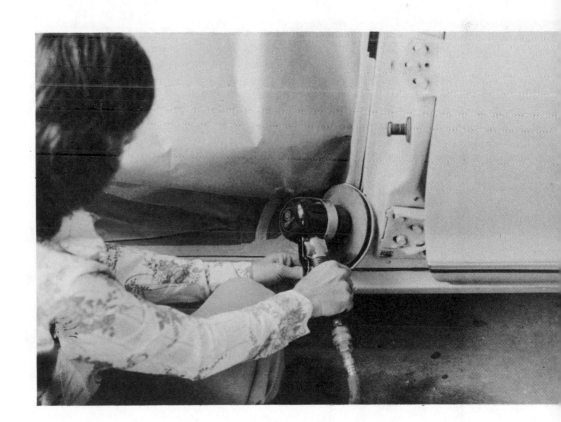

Fig. 21-7. *Step 2:* Use a disk grinder or featheredger to remove the paint and surface rust from the area.

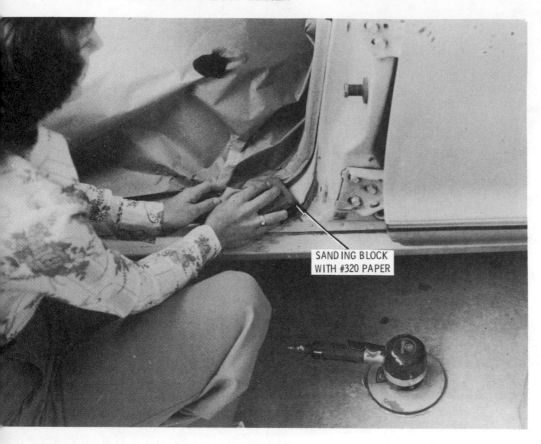

SANDING BLOCK
WITH #320 PAPER

Fig. 21-8. *Step 3:* Block-sand the repaired area with wet #320 paper. Carefully featheredge the broken paint all around the area.

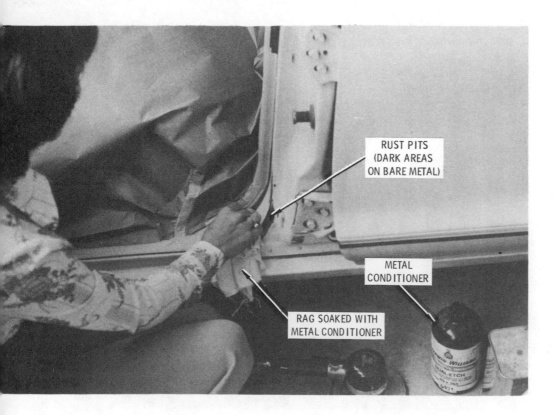

RUST PITS
(DARK AREAS
ON BARE METAL)

METAL
CONDITIONER

RAG SOAKED WITH
METAL CONDITIONER

Fig. 21-9. *Step 4:* Treat the bare metal, especially any small surface rust pits, with metal conditioner.

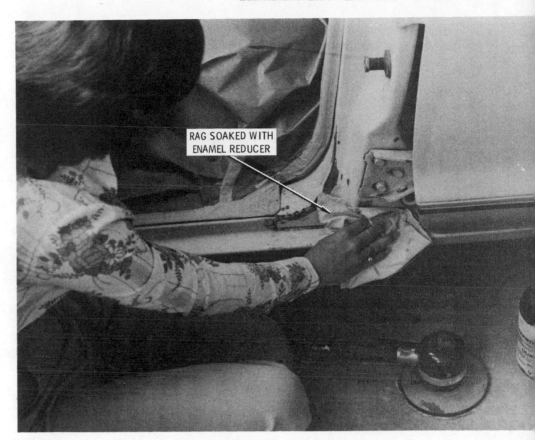

Fig. 21-10. *Step 5:* Wash the area with enamel reducer.

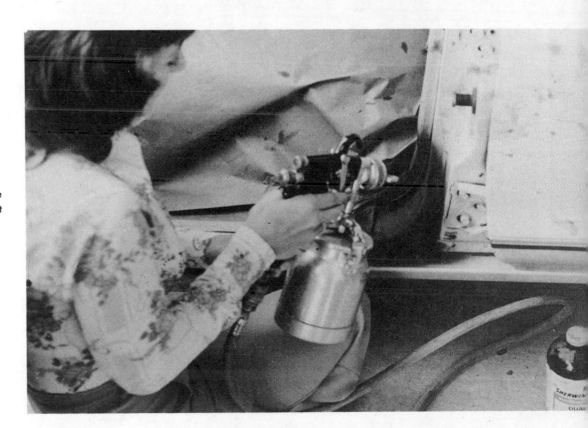

Fig. 21-11. *Step 6:* Paint the entire area with primer-surfacer. Allow it to dry.

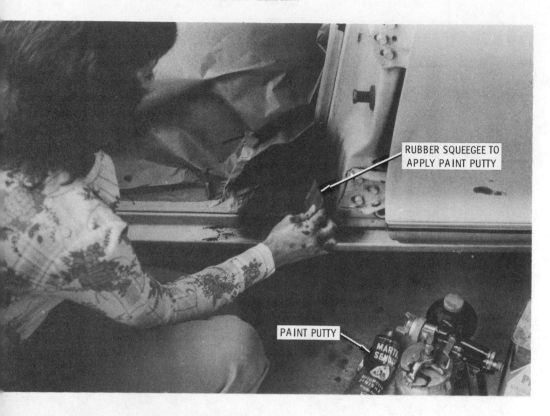

RUBBER SQUEEGEE TO
APPLY PAINT PUTTY

PAINT PUTTY

Fig. 21-12. *Step 7:* Use paint *putty* to fill any small imperfections, pits, or low spots in the primer-surfacer.

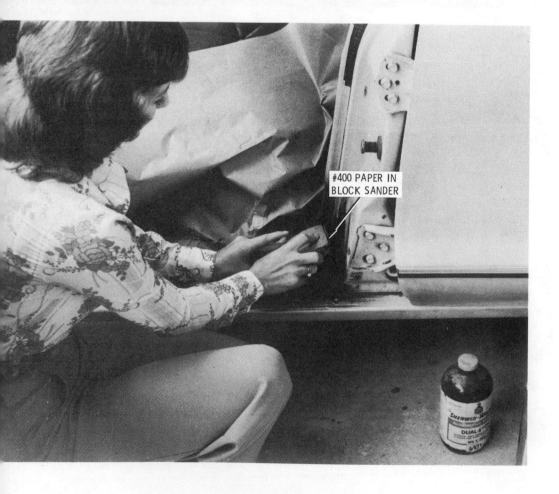

#400 PAPER IN
BLOCK SANDER

Fig. 21-13. *Step 8:* Block-sand the putty and primer-surfacer with #320 or #400 wet sandpaper. Feather-edge the area carefully, preparing it for the color topcoat.

Fig. 21-14. *Step 9*: Apply the color topcoat. Allow the topcoat to dry. Then, if it is a *lacquer* topcoat, compound the lacquer to full luster.

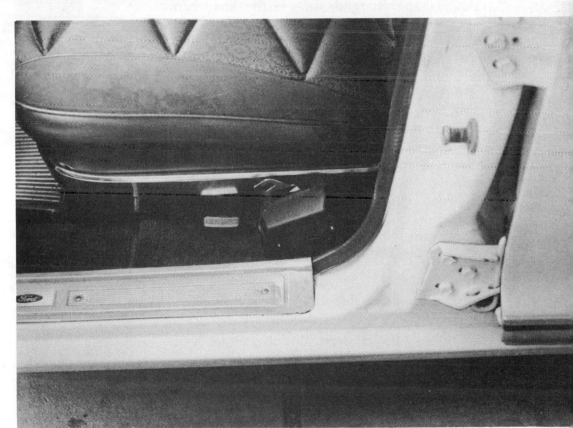

Fig. 21-15. The completed repair. Properly done, this job will prevent any surface rust from coming back for some time.

REPAIRING RUST-OUT DAMAGE

Rust-out damage is serious body damage. Where rust-out exists, the body's metal has been weakened. If only a few bubbles are present, there is likely to be a good deal more rust-out damage than can be seen. Grinding off the paint and metal in the area will likely reveal many more small rust-out holes. To repair rust-out damage *properly*, the panel must be repaired so that it is as *strong* as new *and looks* like new.

When repairing rust-out, a body man must always determine what caused the rust-out to begin with. For example, if the rust-out was caused by uncontrolled *surface* rust, removing the surface rust and repairing the area will eliminate the cause. However, if the rust-out came through from *inside* the panel, the cause will be harder to eliminate.

Many times, clogged *drain holes* will cause rust-out. Drain holes are designed into auto bodies to let water and road dirt drain out, leaving the backside of the panel clean. If the holes become clogged, dirt, water, and chemicals can build up behind the panel, causing rust to start inside and work out. Clogged drain holes can be worked clear with a knife or other sharp pointed object.

Even when drain holes are kept open, mud and chemicals may still build up behind panels, such as in the lower parts of the trunk and many other cracks and "pockets." Whenever dirt and chemicals can become lodged, rust-out can begin on the backside of a panel and later break through underneath the paint. Usually, keeping a car clean underneath and at the bottom sides of the trunk will *help* prevent rust-out from beginning in these areas.

Beginning Rust-Out Repair

There are several basic methods by which rust-out may be repaired. Which method to use depends on the location of the damage, how much damage is present, how long the repair needs to last, and other factors. However, no matter which repair method is used, the *beginning steps* of rust-out repair are always the same. When beginning any rust-out repair, then, follow these steps in order:

1. Thoroughly look over the rust-out damage, as in Fig. 21-16. Notice the size and location of the holes or paint bubbles.

Fig. 21-16. Typical rust-out damage to be repaired.

2. Clean the paint and broken metal around the damage with solvent, as was shown in Fig. 21-6.
3. Grind the old paint and rust from around the rust-out area. See Fig. 21-17.

Fig. 21-17. Grinding the old paint and rust from around the rust-out area.

4. Examine the actual rust-out holes after grinding, as in Fig. 21-18.

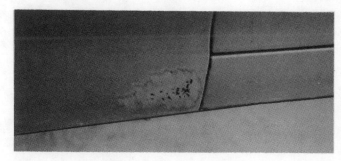

Fig. 21-18. When the paint around the rust-out area is ground away, the exact size and location of the rust holes can be seen.

5. Using tin snips, cut out any weak metal from *around* the edges of the rust-out holes. This metal is usually very weak due to rust and will cut easily.

6. Using a screwdriver or other tools, clean any dirt or other debris from *inside* the holes. Clean the area out well so that there will be nothing behind the repair to start the rust-out again after the repair has been made.

7. Treat the bare metal in and around the area with metal conditioner. *This is very important if any rust-out repair is to last more than a few months.*

8. Decide on the type of repair to be used and then make the repair.

Basic Types of Repair

There are three basic methods that may be used to repair rust-out damage. Which of these methods to use depends on how badly the affected area is rusted out.

1. Aluminum tape and plastic filler
2. Fiberglass mat and plastic filler
3. Metal patch and body filler (either plastic or lead)

If the metal is still intact and does not give in when pressed lightly, the damage is not serious. In this case, and if only *small* holes are present, the area may be filled with aluminum tape and plastic filler.

Often, a minor rust-out area will have larger holes after the old paint and metal have been ground away. In these cases, the rust-out damage must be repaired by patching with fiberglass and plastic filler. If the metal is weakened so much that the rust-out area is loose and gives in when pressed, the damage must be completely cut away before the fiberglass mat is applied.

If the rust-out area is extensive and has damaged a major area, the panel must be repaired with a metal patch and then levelled with body filler. To do this, the rust damage must first be cut back to solid metal, leaving a hole. Then, the edges of the hole are lowered with a hammer and chisel. A metal patch may then

be sized, cut, and placed over the area. Patches of this type are usually *brazed* or *riveted* in position. The patch and original metal may then be prepared, filled, and refinished.

Using Aluminum Tape—Making rust-out repairs with aluminum tape is an easy, fast method of repairing rust-out damage. The aluminum tape itself, of course, will not rust after it is applied. *If* it is used according to directions, it will last quite some time, although not as long as fiberglass or metal patch repairs. Fig. 21-19 shows aluminum tape being used. The product is bright on the top side and has a very sticky adhesive backing on the back side. The adhesive (glue) makes the tape stick tightly to *clean* metal.

Fig. 21-19. Aluminum body repair tape is sold in rolls and will firmly stick to properly cleaned metal surfaces.

One use of aluminum tape is on small rust-out holes such as those found under automobile rear windows. See Fig. 21-20. Most automobile rear windows (*backlights*) are accented with stainless steel *reveal moldings*. The moldings are held in place with spring steel molding clips

Fig. 21-20. Rust-out holes underneath a rear window. To make the repair, the molding clips along the bottom edge have already been removed.

all around the window opening. See Figs. 21-20 and 21. These clips hold the molding *against* the painted edge of the opening. The pressure of the clips *often causes the molding to chip the paint around the opening*.

Fig. 21-21. Molding clips are positioned all around the rear window opening. These clips hold the stainless steel molding in place around the rear window.

When the paint is chipped, of course, the bare metal under the paint begins to rust as the water trapped under the molding rests against the bare metal. After about a year, *holes* are rusted completely through the metal along the bottom edge of the glass. If the damage is not repaired quickly, holes may appear along the sides and top of the glass opening as well. These holes will allow water to leak into the car's interior and trunk.

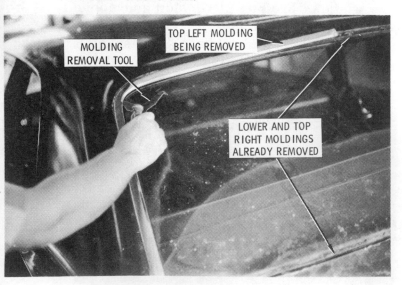

Fig. 21-22. *Step 1:* To properly repair rear window rust-out, first remove the rear window moldings. Use a molding removal tool to reach under the molding and pull the molding clips away from the molding one at a time.

Repairing rear window rust-out, then, is one of the more common rust-out repairs now done in most body shops. To thoroughly repair the damage, the rear window (backlight) should be removed. Figs. 21-20 through 21-29 show how aluminum tape may be used to repair rear window opening rust-out. Fiberglass or sheet metal patches could also be used.

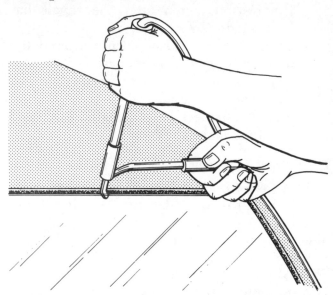

Fig. 21-23. *Step 2:* Use an electric hot knife to "cut" the adhesive sealer from the glass. This may also be done by cutting the sealer with a knife, although it is not as easy. Remove the rear window.

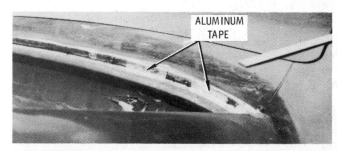

Fig 21-24. *Step 3:* Thoroughly clean the rear window channel. Remove any old sealers, paint, rust, and dirt. Grind off any old paint and surface rust in the repair area. *Step 4:* Treat the bare metal with metal conditioner. *Step 5:* Carefully apply small strips of aluminum tape over the rust-out holes. Proper fiberglass or metal patches could also be used.

Using Fiberglass Patches—Many times, the holes in a rusted-out area are too large for aluminum tape to support the repair area and make it as strong as needed. When this is true, or if a stronger *small* repair is needed, a fiberglass patch and plastic filler may be used to make the repair. Properly prepared and ap-

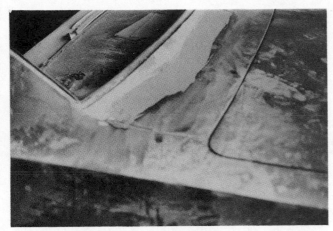

Fig. 21-25. *Step 6:* Apply plastic body filler to the repair area. Completely cover the tape with plastic filler. [If a metal patch was used, body solder ("lead") could be used for filler.]

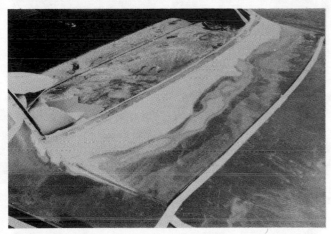

Fig. 21-26. *Step 7:* Featheredge and block-sand the plastic filler to restore the original contour of the back panel near the glass *and* the channel in which the glass sits. Finish the featheredging with #320 or finer paper.

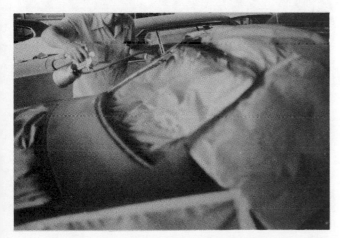

Fig. 21-27. *Step 8:* Mask off the entire area to be repainted. Apply primer-surfacer to the area. Allow the primer-surfacer to dry. At this time, replace or repair any molding clips that need attention.

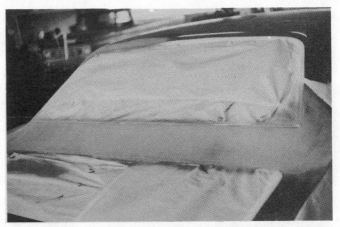

Fig. 21-28. *Step 9:* Wet-sand the primer-surfacer with #320 or #400 paper, preparing the area for the color topcoat. *Step 10:* Apply the color topcoat and allow it to dry.

Fig. 21-29. *Step 11:* Replace the backlight (rear window glass) as outlined in the Glass Unit. Replace the moldings around the rear window opening.

plied, fiberglass patch materials will do a good job of repairing rust-out damage. Most fiberglass repair kit manufacturers have complete directions included with their kits. These directions *must be followed carefully* if the product is to do a good job. Fig. 21-30 shows a typical, complete, fiberglass repair kit.

Fig. 21-31 shows typical rust-out damage on a lower body panel. After the metal has been cleaned, ground, and treated with metal conditioner, it can be seen where the panel has rusted through in several small areas. This rust-out damage is not major, but it does need more repair support than aluminum tape for a lasting repair. Figs. 21-32 through 21-39 explain how the fiberglass mat part of the repair should be done.

The fiberglass patch in Fig. 21-39 should then be allowed to *thoroughly cure* (harden)

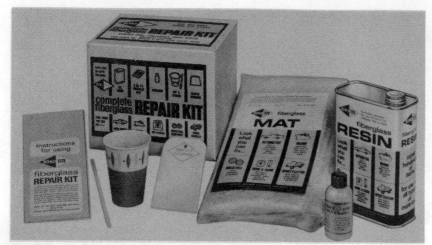

Fig. 21-30. A typical fiberglass repair kit that may be used to repair rusted-out sheet metal areas. (Courtesy of Oatey Co.)

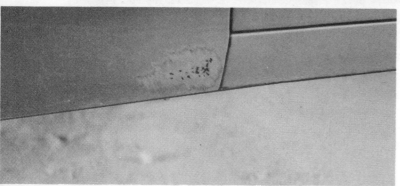

Fig. 21-31. A rusted-out area ready to be repaired with a fiberglass repair kit. The metal has been cleaned, ground, and treated with metal conditioner, the first steps for *any* rust repair.

Fig. 21-33. *Step 2:* Add several drops of hardener to the fiberglass resin *according to the manufacturer's directions.*

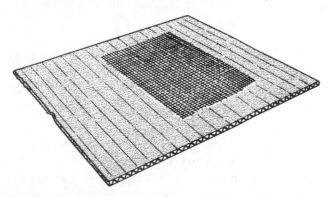

Fig. 21-32. *Step 1:* Cut a piece of fiberglass matting slightly larger than the hole(s) or area being repaired. For this repair, the mat should overlap the edges of the damaged area about 1" on each side.

according to the time recommended by the manufacturer. The hardened and trimmed repair may then be covered with plastic filler. Only *plastic* filler is recommended for use on fiberglass, and only a plastic filler sold for use *on* fiberglass should be used. The hardened

Fig. 21-34. *Step 3:* Thoroughly mix the resin and hardener with a wood mixture stick. After it is mixed, use the mixture quickly, as it will start to harden.

Fig. 21-35. *Step 4:* Pour and spread the resin and hardener mixture on the cut piece of fiberglass mat. Do this on wax-coated cardboard (or wax paper) so that the resin does not stick to the work surface.

Fig. 21-36. *Step 4,* continued: Thoroughly saturate the fiberglass mat with the resin and hardener mixture. Work the mixture well into *all* of the mat material.

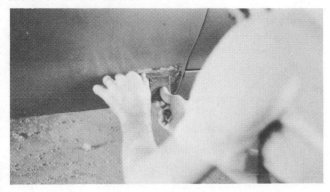

Fig. 21-37. *Step 5:* Carefully pick up the saturated, sticky fiberglass mat and apply it to the rust-out area being repaired.

Fig. 21-38. *Step 6:* Work *all* of the air bubbles on the repair area out of the fiberglass mat. Use a plastic spreader to do this. This also works the resin and matting down into the rust holes for a firm bond to the metal.

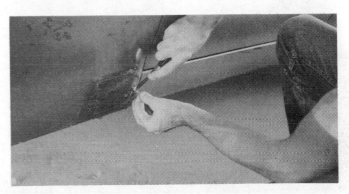

Fig. 21-39. *Step 7:* Trim the edges of the fiberglass mat so that the mat has no "strings" hanging out. This may be done with either a knife or a razor blade.

plastic filler may then be sanded smooth and prepared for refinishing.

Using Sheet Metal Patches—When a large *section* of a panel has been damaged or weakened by rust-out, a strong, permanent patch is necessary. A permanent patch must be a *metal* patch. This is necessary for strength and lasting contour. Metal patch repairs must be made differently than aluminum tape or fiberglass mat

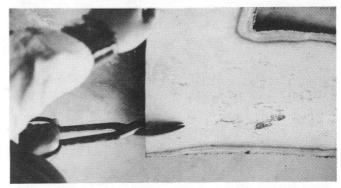

Fig. 21-40. Using metal snips to cut a sheet metal patch from a salvage panel. This is a good use for large, flat sheet metal panels that have been replaced during other repairs.

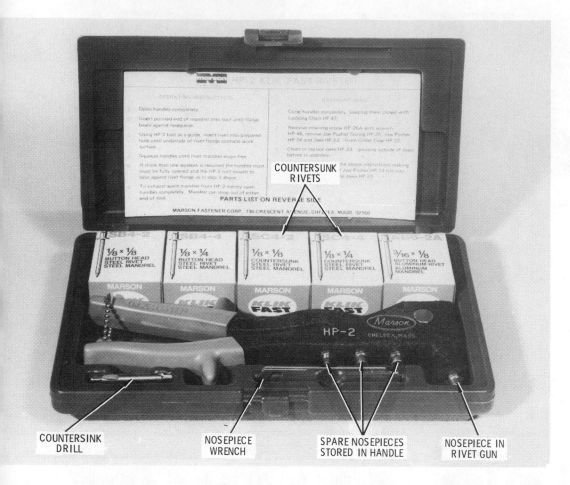

Fig. 21-41. A rivet gun kit. (Courtesy of Marson Corporation.)

Fig. 21-42. Rusted-out lower front fender. Because this damage is fairly large, a sheet metal patch will be used to repair the area.

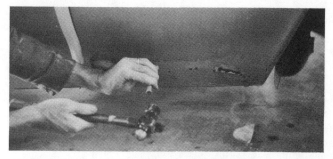

Fig. 21-43. *Step 1:* Use a *dull* punch and hammer to lower the rusted-out area. Keep in mind that the patch will make the area higher, so the area must be knocked down before the patch is installed. Otherwise, the repair will be higher than the metal was originally.

repairs because of the larger surface area being covered *and* because the repair is being made with metal.

Sheet metal patches are usually made from large, collision-damaged panels that may be cut to make small patches. For this reason, many body shops save damaged hoods, deck lids, and large fenders. These panels, even though bent, may be cut and used for smaller patches. Although a cutting torch may be used to cut

patches, they may be cut "cleaner" by using metal snips. See Fig. 21-40.

After a patch has been sized and cut, it may be attached to the damaged area by being either *brazed* or *riveted* in position. Fig. 21-41 shows a typical *rivet gun kit* that may be used to *rivet* patches in position. While riveting is

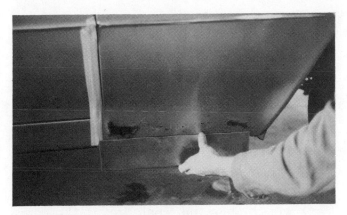

Fig. 21-44. *Step 2:* Prepare a metal patch to be placed over the rusted-out area. Trim the patch so that it fits the area *exactly;* the better the patch fits, the better the repair will look. If necessary, *bend* the patch so that it matches the contour of the area being repaired.

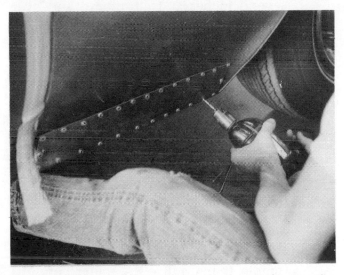

Fig. 21-45. *Step 3:* Fasten the patch to the area. In this example, *rivets* are being used. Holes must be drilled before the rivets are installed. A rivet gun, Fig. 21-41, will be used. *Brazing* could also be used but the old paint would have to be ground off first so that the brazing could adhere to bare metal.

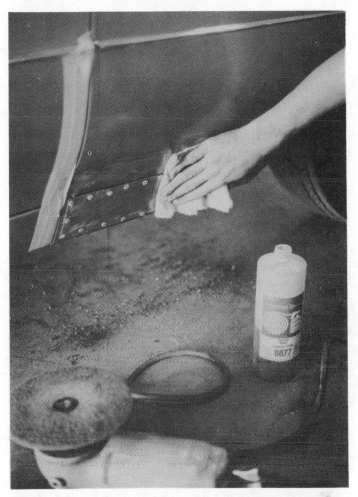

Fig. 21-46. *Step 4:* Prepare the repaired area for filling. Grind the area with a disk grinder and then treat the metal with metal conditioner. Be careful to *not* grind off the heads of the rivets. To avoid grinding the heads off, it is better to use *countersunk* rivets and the *countersink* drill shown in Fig. 21-41. These leave the rivet head flush (even) with the top of the patch.

usually easier and faster than brazing, brazing will produce the strongest rust-out repair if the brazing is done properly. When the patch is in position, either plastic or lead body filler may be used to complete the repair before refinishing.

Fig. 21-42 shows the lower part of a front fender that has rusted out from the inside. The rust-out was caused by moisture being trapped inside the panel. This damage is over a wide area; it needs the strength offered by a metal patch. Figs. 21-42 through 21-46 show how a sheet metal patch would be prepared and riveted in place to make this repair strong *before* filler is placed over the repaired area.

Permanent Rust-Out Repair

Rust-out is the result of a chemical reaction. Because of this, it is very difficult –if not impossible- to permanently stop this chemical reaction once it has started, especially on the backside of a panel. Even if the panel is treated with metal conditioner, the rust may continue "working" on the backside of the panel until the panel again rusts through. This usually happens around the *edges* of the first rust-out repair.

For the above reasons, no rust-out repair, *including* the procedure to be outlined here, can be thought of as absolutely permanent. Even the best repairs, after many years, may again rust out. By the time this happens, of course, the car may have been scrapped, wrecked, or purchased by someone who does not care that the rust-out has come back.

Every so often, however, a body man may have a customer who wants the very best type of rust-out repair *and is willing to pay the higher price required to have the job done very carefully.* For these customers, then, it is a good idea to know exactly what repair procedure will last the longest. It should be kept in mind that this is not the fastest, the easiest, nor the least expensive way to repair rust-out. For those customers who wish to keep their car quite some time –or to carefully restore an older car- the following procedure should be used:

1. If at all possible, *remove the rusted-out panel from the car.* This will allow you to work on the *back*side of the panel (where the rust began), as well as on the front side.
2. Remove *all* the dirt, old rust, undercoat, etc., from the backside of the panel. Carefully *clean* the metal *all around* the rust holes and note how far out from the holes the rust is actually continuing on the back of the panel.
3. Using metal snips *only,* carefully cut out *all* of the damaged metal. Remove all of the metal near the rust-out holes as well as the rust-out area itself. Cut back from the rust holes as much as needed until only *solid* metal remains around the edge of the large, cut-out hole.
4. From a good, sound piece of scrap metal, carefully cut a sheet metal patch to exactly fit the size and shape of the hole just cut in the panel. The patch should just fit inside the hole, *not* overlapping and *not* leaving any gaps between the patch and the panel. Take the time necessary to fit this patch correctly.
5. Carefully *braze* the patch in the opening from the *back*side of the panel, all the

way around. Tack-braze the patch in place *first.* Then, carefully braze all around the patch. Braze one area only a short time and then go across, to another edge of the patch. By changing braze positions, there is less chance of overheating and distorting the repair area. When finished, the braze should be *all around* the patch. By brazing the repair on the *backside* of the panel, the panel will be sealed so that no water or dirt can get through the repair area to the paint and filler on the front side.

6. Turn the panel over and begin working on the *front* side of the panel. Using a large disc grinder, grind an area back several inches and all around and over the patch repair, preparing the area for body filler.
7. Fill and level the area with *body solder,* not plastic filler. Keep in mind that this is a high-price, premium-quality, permanent rust-out repair. While good plastic fillers are excellent for virtually all filling jobs, they cannot be considered equal to body solder for the very best repairs.
8. Using body files and levelling tools, level the entire repair area. Finish the levelling by block-sanding the entire area with wet #320 or finer paper.
9. Wash the soldered area with lacquer thinner to neutralize the solder flux.
10. Treat the entire area with metal conditioner.
11. Wash the entire area with enamel reducer.
12. Prime the entire repair with *enamel* primer-surfacer. Allow it to dry thoroughly.
13. Turn the panel over and complete the following steps –14 through 18– on the *back* side. Protect the front side while doing this by putting old blankets or pads on the work surface under the front side.
14. Clean the back side of the *entire* repair area. Clean any *flux* off the brazing repair with a wire brush.
15. Treat the entire backside of the repair

area (patch, braze, and original metal) with metal conditioner. Do this only after the back side has been thoroughly cleaned.

16. Wash the back side with enamel reducer. Wipe off the reducer before it dries.

17. Brush or spray rust-proof red primer over the back side of the repair. Allow it to dry.

18. Brush or spray *undercoat* over the entire back side. Undercoat must not be applied too thick; a light-to-medium coat is heavy enough. Allow the undercoat to dry.

19. Turn the panel back over and finish preparing the enamel primer-surfacer for refinishing.

20. Apply paint putty to any small nicks or imperfections in the enamel primer-surfacer. Allow the putty to dry.

21. Block-sand the entire panel with #400 wet sandpaper.

22. Refinish the panel as outlined in the paint units.

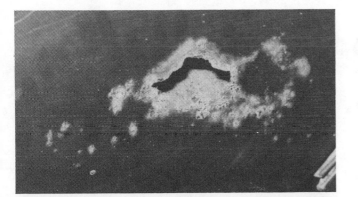

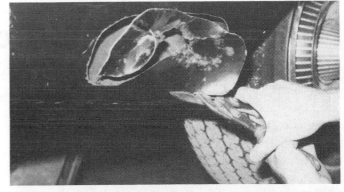

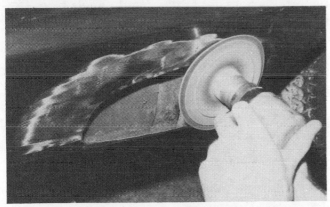

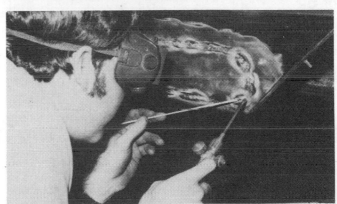

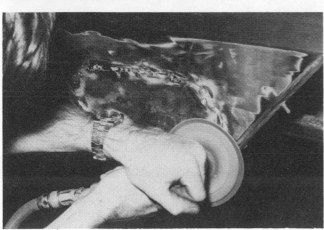

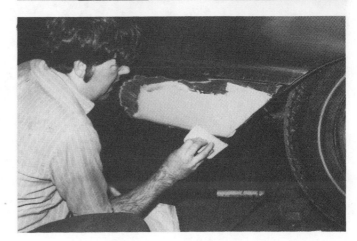

Unit 22

Auto Body Trim

Basically, any *trim* on a vehicle either beautifies the vehicle, adds additional strength to an area, and/or provides comfort. Many pieces of trim are bright moldings on either the outside or the inside of the car. Trim also includes dull ("flat", no gloss or shine) metal parts and many parts made of cloth, vinyl, rubber or plastic. These may be attached to either the exterior or the interior of an auto or truck body. See Figs. 22-1 and 22-2.

Repairing and replacing auto body trim is an important part of auto body work. During most auto body repairs, at least some exterior trim work will be necessary. Interior trim work may be necessary to get at damaged panels from the back side or for repairs to the trim itself. Because trim work largely affects the *appearance* of a repair, trim work must be done correctly for complete customer satisfaction on even the smallest repairs.

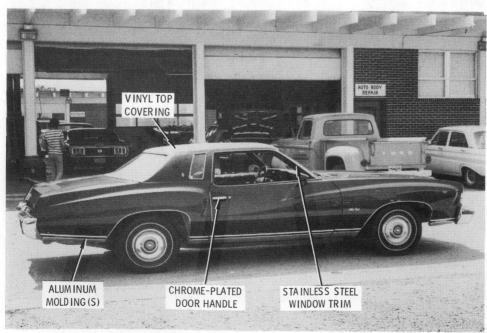

VINYL TOP COVERING

ALUMINUM MOLDING(S)

CHROME-PLATED DOOR HANDLE

STAINLESS STEEL WINDOW TRIM

Fig. 22-1. Many exterior parts of a vehicle are trim parts.

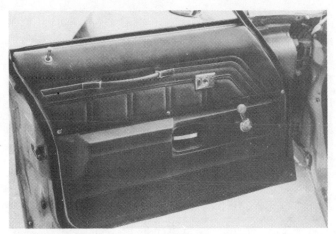

Fig. 22-2. Most of the interior parts of a vehicle are trim parts.

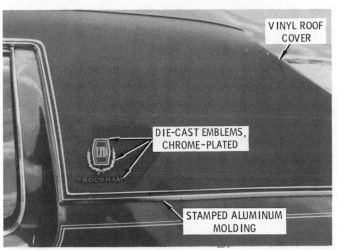

Fig. 22-4. Exterior trim includes vinyl roof covers and the moldings and emblems necessary for the vinyl cover's installation.

EXTERIOR TRIM

Most of the exterior trim moldings on an automobile are made of bright aluminum or stainless steel. These include side moldings, rocker panel moldings, grilles, and window trim pieces. Most of these parts are replaceable items because it is not practical to repair them; the cost of a new molding is less than the time it would take to repair the damaged molding.

Some exterior trim pieces are simply glued-on rubber or plastic parts. These may have an adhesive backing used to attach the piece to the vehicle. Fig. 22-3, for example, shows a strip of glue-backed plastic molding being pressed into place. Other pieces of plastic used for exterior trim include vinyl top materials. Vinyl top material, a type of plastic, is also cemented in place. See Fig. 22-4.

Types of Exterior Trim

Exterior trim moldings and pieces are made from many types of materials. Some of the more common molding and trim materials include:

1. Stamped Aluminum
2. Stamped Stainless Steel
3. Plastic
4. Die-Cast, Chrome-Plated Metal
5. Extruded Aluminum

Stamped Aluminum — Stamped aluminum parts are made from aluminum that has been *pressed* (stamped) into shape. The lettering in Fig. 22-5 is an example of *stamped aluminum trim.* Usually, stamped aluminum moldings and trim are polished to a bright finish. Sometimes, however, only a raised area, such as lettering, is

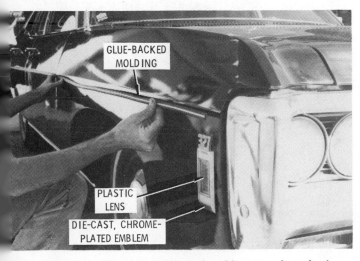

Fig. 22-3. Adding a glue-backed molding to a front fender.

Fig. 22-5. The letters on this fender are an example of *stamped aluminum trim.*

polished. Then, the lower part of the piece, at the base of the raised section, is left "flat" (unpolished) or is painted flat black. Stamped aluminum trim is rust-resistant, durable, attractive, and inexpensive. Many automobile manufacturers use stamped aluminum trim parts.

Stamped Stainless Steel—The most durable automotive trim is *stamped stainless steel*. This shiny trim may also be stamped into shape with contours to fit snugly against the vehicle's body. Stamped stainless steel moldings and parts are made bright by being polished to a high-gloss finish. Stainless steel moldings are used on many vehicles around the windshield and rear window (backlight). Here, they are known as *reveal moldings*. Many vehicle side moldings are also stamped stainless steel. Fig. 22-6 shows a stamped stainless steel drip rail molding. Often, aluminum moldings are used instead of stainless steel on newer cars due to the lower cost of aluminum.

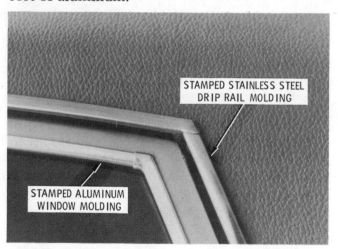

Fig. 22-6. Most drip rail moldings are *stamped stainless steel*.

Plastic—Plastic trim parts are formed in the desired shapes as they cool in the mold used to shape the hot plastic material. Different kinds of plastic parts are being used more and more on each model year of new cars and trucks. Plastic moldings, grilles, and many types of trim are made with either a *painted* color coat or a shiny "plating" made to look like chromium plating. Fig. 22-7 shows a plastic, "chrome" quarter glass molding.

Plastic moldings and trim parts may be either cemented to the vehicle's surface or held in

Fig. 22-7. A shiny *plastic trim molding* around a rear quarter glass.

place with screws or clips. Plastic trim may be formed to fit almost any contour. Repairing most types of collision damage will now include replacing one or more types of plastic parts.

Die-Cast, Chrome-Plated Metal—Die-cast metal parts are formed in factory shapes known as *dies*. As the molten metal injected into a die cools, the metal, under pressure, takes the shape of the die. Then, the new metal piece is plated with chromium. Die-cast trim pieces are hard and brittle. Door handles and some small trim are usually die-cast pieces. Sometimes, die-cast parts are known as "pot metal."

Aluminum die-cast trim is often used to make lettering strips. Fig. 22-8 shows an aluminum nameplate which has been die-cast to fit the vehicle's body contour. Aluminum die-cast moldings cannot usually be rechromed.

Extruded Aluminum—When a metal is forced through an opening so that it takes the shape of that opening, the shaped metal piece is known

Fig. 22-8. A *die-cast aluminum* nameplate.

as an *extrusion*. The process of shaping the pieces is known as *extruding*. When aluminum is shaped by this process, the parts become known as *extruded aluminum trim parts*. Common extruded aluminum parts include grilles and other pieces of trim.

Exterior Trim Fasteners

Exterior trim moldings, grilles, and many other pieces must be firmly attached to the body. Due to appearance and convenience, these pieces may be attached to the body by one or more of several different types of attachments. On any piece of trim, then, one or more of the following attachments may be used to hold the trim in place:

1. Glue Backing; shown earlier in Fig. 22-3.
2. Attaching Screws; Fig. 22-9.
3. Bolt and Clip assemblies; Fig. 22-10.
4. Molded Studs; Fig. 22-11.
5. Bathtub Clips; Fig. 22-12.
6. W-base Clips; Fig. 22-13.

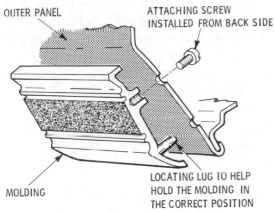

Fig. 22-9. A molding held in place with simple *attaching screws.*

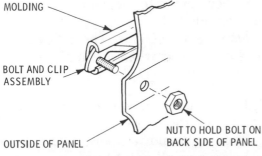

Fig. 22-10. A *bolt and clip assembly* used to hold a molding in place. To remove the molding, the nut holding the clip and molding in place must first be removed from the *back side* of the panel.

7. Welded Studs and Clips; Fig. 22-14.
8. Retainer Inserts; Fig. 22-15.
9. Self-Retaining Moldings; Fig. 22-16.

Wherever bolts, screws, or studs go *through* a panel, holes will be needed. To prevent water from leaking in the holes, the bolt, screw, stud, or hole must be surrounded with body sealer

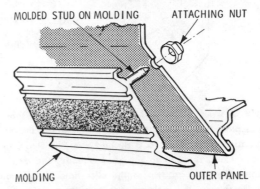

Fig. 22-11. A *nut* fastened to a *molded stud*. The stud is molded as part of the trim piece itself. To remove the molding, the nut must first be removed from behind the panel. When installing this type of molding, be careful *not* to overtighten the nut, because it is easy to break off the stud at the molding.

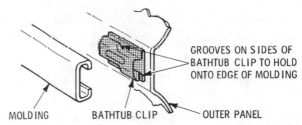

Fig. 22-12. A *bathtub clip*. Here, one part of the bathtub clip holds the clip to a hole in the panel. Then, the molding is snapped over the top of the bathtub clip and the clip holds the molding in place. To remove the molding, gently pry the molding off the bathtub clip with a putty knife.

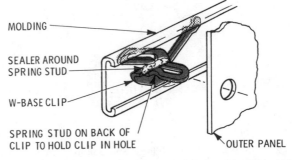

Fig. 22-13. A *W-base* clip. W-base clips snap inside the molding. A spring *wedge* on the back of the clip snaps into the hole on the panel, holding the clip and molding in place. To remove a molding held with W-base clips, use a putty knife to gently pry the molding and clip from the panel.

before the molding is installed. When exterior trim pieces are held in place with an attaching screw, Fig. 22-9, sealer should be placed on the screw *before* it is installed. This helps prevent water leaks around the hole in the panel.

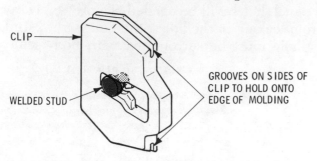

Fig. 22-14. A *welded stud and clip* fastener. Here, a short stud is welded in place along the side of the panel where the molding is to be installed. Then, the clip is pushed over the stud and moved sideways, locking the clip to the stud. Finally, the molding may be snapped over the grooves of the clip, holding the molding to the clip. To remove the molding, use a putty knife to gently pry the molding off the clip.

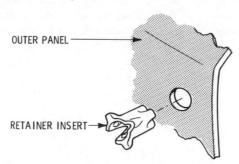

Fig. 22-15. A *retainer insert*. This fastener is often used for emblems and nameplates. Here, small metal or plastic pieces known as *retainer inserts* are *first* pushed into the holes in the panel. These inserts snap in place inside the holes. Then, an emblem or trim piece with molded studs may be pushed into the retainers. To remove emblems held with retainer inserts, use a putty knife to *gently* pry the emblem and its studs out of the retainer inserts.

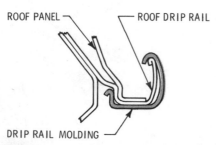

Fig. 22-16. Self-retaining moldings are usually stainless steel or aluminum, with tabs formed on the edges. These designs usually snap over the part they are to accent, such as the drip rail molding accent shown here. *Aluminum* moldings may have tabs on the edges; the tabs are bent around in back of the part being accented, holding the aluminum trim in place.

Most pieces of replacement trim (moldings, emblems, etc.) are sold in a wrapper that also contains the fasteners such as clips and screws that are necessary to install the molding. For this reason, be careful when unwrapping a new piece of trim so as to not lose any fasteners packaged with the trim.

Vinyl Top Coverings

Vinyl top material is made of a special cloth that has been coated with a plastic (vinyl) coating. Most vinyl top material is cemented directly to the steel roof panel itself. On some higher-priced vinyl top coverings, a *pad* is first cemented to the steel roof panel, using special vinyl roof cement. Then, the vinyl top covering may be cemented *over* the pad, but not to the pad itself. In this case, the vinyl is cemented and fastened along the *edge* of the steel roof panel.

In addition to being cemented in place, vinyl covering is often held in place by *molding strips* surrounding the top material. The edges of the vinyl are concealed beneath the molding strips. When the top covering and moldings are properly installed, the edges of the covering will not be visible.

Many times, work on vinyl top coverings must be done as part of auto body repair. When an automobile has gone through a fence, for example, the original top covering may have been torn and scratched and will need to be replaced. If collision damage has buckled a steel panel underneath the covering, but not the covering itself, the vinyl material must be pulled away from the buckled panel so that the panel may be repaired. Then, the vinyl covering must be recemented to the panel after the panel repair is completed.

Replacing a Vinyl Top—The following steps should be followed when a complete vinyl top covering needs to be replaced:

1. Place all the necessary tools and materials in the work area. These include molding removal tools, pliers, a putty knife, a small paint brush, and a pocket knife. Materials include the replacement top and vinyl top cement.

2. Remove the trim moldings around or on the vinyl top. These include the windshield and backlight moldings, drip rail moldings, upper quarter panel moldings, and any emblems or nameplates attached *through* the vinyl covering to the roof panel. The window moldings should be removed with a molding removal tool, as in Fig. 22-17. The other moldings and emblems can usually be carefully pried off with a putty knife.

Fig. 22-17. Using a molding removal tool to remove a windshield reveal molding.

3. Clean off any surface cement or caulking material from around the windshield and back glass openings.
4. Slowly pull the old vinyl material from the roof panel. Use the pliers or a putty knife to separate the top from the cement at the edges. Then, pull the material back from the edges.
5. Clean and smooth the entire roof area where the new vinyl top will be cemented. Use a good adhesive cleaner to remove any remaining old vinyl cement. The area *must* be smooth or high and low spots will appear under the installed top.
6. Lay out the replacement top material to make sure it is the correct replacement top for the automobile being repaired.
7. Mark both the roof panel and the underside of the vinyl cover to make sure of a proper fit. To do this, carefully draw and measure a chalk line down the center of both the roof *and* the underside of the vinyl material. *Be sure that the centers*

are measured correctly so that the top will fit properly. See Fig. 22-18.

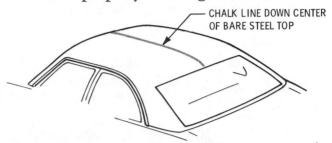

Fig. 22-18. To properly fit a replacement vinyl top, measure and draw a chalk line down the center of the roof panel to which the material will be attached. Do the same to the *underside* of the vinyl top material itself.

8. Lay the new vinyl cover material on the marked roof panel. Fold the vinyl cover material back over itself to the half-way mark (centerline) of the roof panel. See Fig. 22-19.

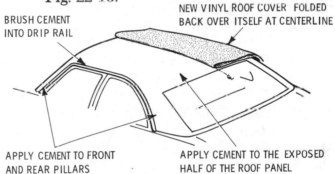

Fig. 22-19. Basically, a new vinyl top cover is cemented in place by working from the center line outward, one side at a time.

9. Apply rubber vinyl cement *to the half of the roof panel that is exposed.* Apply cement from the center line outward to the drip rail and the other edges. See Fig. 22-19.
10. Very carefully pull over and roll down the "folded over" half of the vinyl top covering. Quickly and carefully do this *while the cement on the roof is still wet.* As the cover is being rolled out onto the wet cement, thoroughly work the cover down to eliminate any wrinkles or air bubbles under the material.
11. Use a dull putty knife to work the material down into and around the edges of the window openings. Trim off any excess material with a sharp knife. Note if

any *drive nails* were used to hold the edges of the material in place. If so, install new drive nails at the edges of the material where the moldings will cover the nail heads.

12. When the one half of the material is thoroughly fitted and cemented in place, fold the "loose" side back over the newly cemented side.

13. Repeat the cement and application procedure on the opposite side of the roof panel.

14. Replace all the trim and moldings. Clean the vinyl top, windows and moldings as necessary.

Partial Vinyl Top Removal—Many times, a damaged panel is warped or buckled *under* the vinyl roof material. When this is true, a section of the vinyl material will have to be *carefully* pulled away so that the damaged area can be worked. Then, after the metal has been repaired, the vinyl material must be cemented back into place.

To temporarily remove part of a vinyl top, first remove any moldings and trim covering the edges of the vinyl section to be pulled up. After any trim has been removed, very carefully pull the vinyl material upward. See Fig. 22-20.

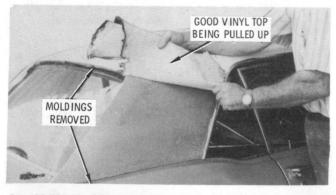

Fig. 22-20. Carefully pull back on vinyl top material to repair metal damage under the material.

When the metal repair has been completed, the vinyl top covering may be recemented to the roof. To do this, first brush new vinyl top cement on the roof area, as in Fig. 22-21. Then fold the vinyl material down over the new cement. Smooth the material down with the palm

of your hand, as in Fig. 22-22. Press any air bubbles out from under the vinyl material. Finally, replace the moldings and clean the repaired area. When the repair is complete, the top will appear as new; Fig. 22-23.

Fig. 22-21. Brush new top cement in place before refitting the top material.

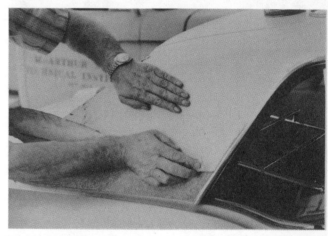

Fig. 22-22. Use both hands to stretch and smooth the top material as it is put back in position.

Fig. 22-23. The complete top repair. The vinyl top material has been recemented in place and the moldings reinstalled.

Heat Dam Asbestos Putty—To protect vinyl material, paint, trim, and glass from heat damage due to welding, putty-like asbestos material is available. This material, shown in Fig. 22-24, forms a "heat dam," absorbing heat so that it cannot damage trim pieces. This asbestos putty "heat dam" is used to protect vinyl, glass, and other trim whenever welding must be done in an area near the trim. Without the asbestos heat dam, the trim or glass would be damaged by heat.

To use this compound, pack it about ½-inch thick along and all around the area to be protected. The compound is designed to stick to any area and stay put while other work is being done. The asbestos in the compound will keep the heat from burning or discoloring the trim in the area, as in Fig. 22-24. This may be necessary, for example, if a new quarter panel is being welded near a vinyl roof covering. When the job is finished, the compound may be removed and placed back in the can. It may then be used again later.

INTERIOR TRIM

A complete automotive interior, Fig. 22-25, includes all the cloth, plastic, vinyl, carpet, and small rubber and metal parts used to make up the complete interior of the vehicle. Also included is the *headliner;* the plastic, vinyl, or cloth covering on the inside of the roof panel. Fig. 22-26, for example, shows a section of *cloth* headliner. The quarter and door *trim panels* are usually made of either fiberboard or plastic, and covered with vinyl, plastic, carpeting, or a combination of the three. Fig. 22-27 shows a typical door trim panel. Finally, a *moisture cover* underneath the trim panel protects the panel from any water that comes inside the door at the lower edge of the window.

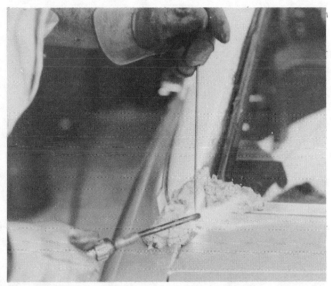

Fig. 22-24. Using heat dam asbestos putty. This material will protect glass and trim from heat damage if brazing or welding must be done in the area.

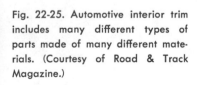

Fig. 22-25. Automotive interior trim includes many different types of parts made of many different materials. (Courtesy of Road & Track Magazine.)

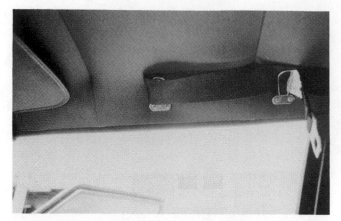

Fig. 22-26. Automotive *headliners* may be plastic, vinyl, or cloth.

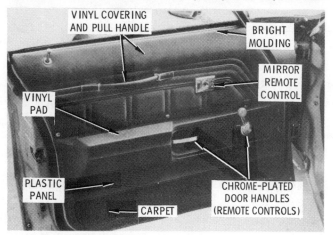

Fig. 22-27. A complete door *trim panel* may include many different parts and materials.

In Fig. 22-28 is the moisture cover behind the door panel shown in Fig. 22-27.

Floor coverings in an automotive interior may be either fabric, carpet (Fig. 22-29), or rubber mat (Fig. 22-30). These coverings, like headliners, are not normally replaced in an auto body shop. This type of work is usually done in an upholstery shop. However, the floor covering in an automobile may need to be completely removed, or at least moved back out of the way, for auto body repairs. This might be necessary, for example, to work on the metal floor inside a vehicle. Removing and cleaning floor coverings are simple jobs that are often done in a body shop.

Cleanliness and Detail—Successful auto body shops must pay close attention to the *interior*, as well as the exterior, of a car being repaired. A clean, neat interior leaves the customer with a good impression of the shop's work. Careful

attention to both the exterior *and* the interior shows that the shop does good work and is concerned about the entire automobile. Exterior repairs and sheet metal work will be more

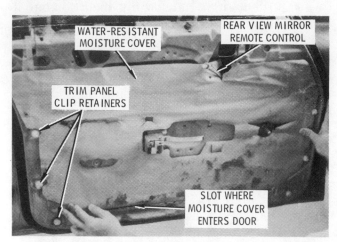

Fig. 22-28. Behind the trim panel, a moisture cover (sometimes known as a *water dam*) protects the inside of the trim panel from any water inside the door.

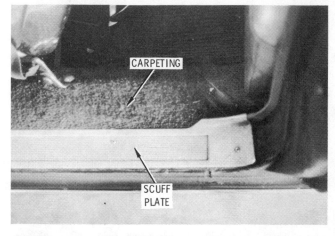

Fig. 22-29. Floor carpeting.

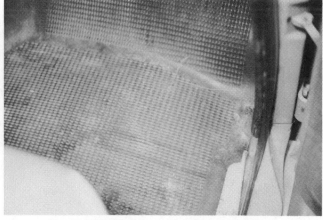

Fig. 22-30. Rubber or tough vinyl floor covering.

highly thought of if the interior is delivered neat and clean.

Trim Panels

The upholstered panels attached to the inside of the doors or quarter panels are known as *trim panels*. See Fig. 22-27. These are normally made of fiberboard and then covered with vinyl, plastic, or carpet. Sometimes, an interior trim panel may be damaged during a collision or may be accidentally cut. Also, if work is to be done inside the door or panel, the trim panel must be removed and replaced.

Removing and Replacing Trim Panels—Most interior trim panels are held in place in the same basic manner. For this reason, the general instructions below may be followed to remove and replace interior trim panels. (In some cases, special fastening methods or accessories

may exist on a given model. In these cases, a body shop manual may need to be used as a reference when removing and replacing these panels.)

1. Unscrew the *door lock knob*. Fig. 22-31 shows a trim panel from which the knob has already been removed.
2. Remove the door handles from the door lock and window regulator remote controls. These are held in place by screws or horse-shoe-shaped clips. Use a screwdriver or an allen wrench to remove the screws, depending on their head design. Use a *clip puller* to remove the clips from in back of the handles. See Figs. 22-32 and 22-33.
3. Remove any screws holding the trim panel in place. These may include arm rest retaining screws and any screws along the bottom of the trim panel.
4. Remove any accessories attached to the

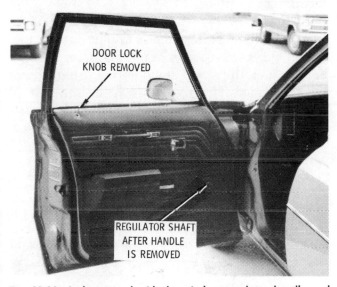

Fig. 22-31. A door panel with the window regulator handle and door lock knob removed.

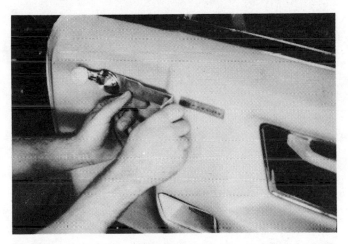

Fig. 22-32. Using a clip puller to remove a door handle.

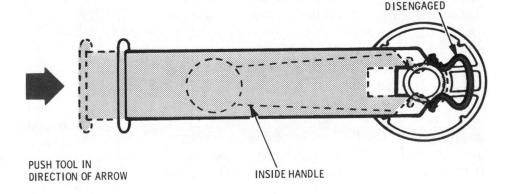

Fig. 22-33. How a clip puller works. The "teeth" of the clip puller push the ends of the clip out to one side. (Courtesy of Fisher Body Division.)

trim panel. A common example is an outside rear view mirror control, Fig. 22-27. Remove the screws holding the control in place and pull the control out slightly, allowing it to "hang" away from the trim panel.

5. Use an upholstery tool, Fig. 22-34, to pry the trim panel clips out of the inner door panel holes. These clips are located along the edges of the trim panel.

Fig. 22-34. A common upholstery tool. When removing door trim panels, this tool may be used to pry under the clips along the edges of the panel.

6. Remove the trim panel by pulling up and guiding the panel over the door lock shaft. Guide the rear view mirror control and any other accessories through their respective holes.

7. To install a new trim panel or reinstall the old one, reverse the procedure for removing the panel. Be sure that the trim panel clips are properly "started" in their holes before pushing the trim panel clips into the door panel.

Moisture Cover

A moisture cover, also known as a *water dam*, is used behind door trim panels. It is cemented in place on the metal inner door panel itself. This cover is important because whenever it rains or the car is washed, water passes *through* the inside of the door. Water enters the door at the door glass opening, runs *down* the inside of the door itself, and, finally, drains out the bottom of the door through the drain holes. If the moisture cover is not in place over the inner panel openings, water will stain and damage the door trim panel.

Fig. 22-28 shows a properly installed moisture cover. When replacing a moisture cover, be sure to put the bottom edge of the cover into the slot at the bottom of the inner door panel. If any water hits the moisture cover, the cover

guides the water down, through the slots. This forces the water to go down inside the door to drain out.

Headliner

The headliner in an automotive interior is the upholstery trim that covers the underside of the roof panel. Headliners may be made of cloth, vinyl-coated cloth, or, in some cases, plastic. Plastic or plastic foam headliners may be formed as "one piece" headliners. Headliners both beautify the car's interior *and* help insulate the interior from road noise.

Most conventional headliner material is held in position smoothly and tightly with listing wires, toothed holders, and cement. These are concealed between the headliner and the inner roof panel. Like other trim parts, there are many different types of fasteners used to hold headliners in place.

Listing Wires—Listing wires, Fig. 22-35, are used to hold most headliners in place at the top. These wires are about ¼-inch diameter and are held in a cloth pocket sewn across the inside of the headliner. The wires run from one side of the roof panel to the other. The *ends* of the listing wires are usually color-coded to fit color-

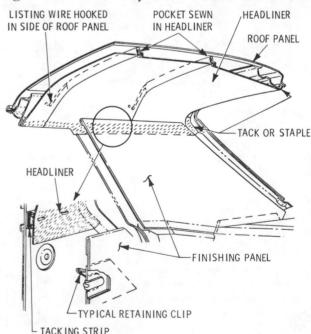

Fig. 22-35. Details of a typical headliner installation. Listing wires do most of the job of holding the headliner in place. (Courtesy of Fisher Body Division.)

coded holes along the side of the roof header plate.

Toothed Holders—The *outer* edges of headliner material are often held in place along the *sides* of the roof interior with toothed holders, sometimes known as *pronged retainers*. These are positioned between or around the listing wire holes. The holders are held in place on the roof header with sheet metal screws. See Fig. 22-36.

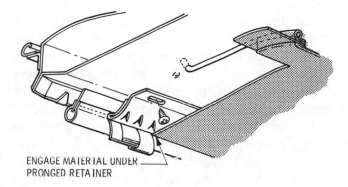

ENGAGE MATERIAL UNDER PRONGED RETAINER

Fig. 22-36. Toothed holders (also known as *pronged retainers*) hold the side edges of the headliner in place. (Courtesy of Fisher Body Division.)

Headliner Work—Usually, replacing a complete headliner is not done in a body shop. Instead, such work is normally done at an automotive trim shop specializing in upholstery work. However, if you need to only work on a small area *under* the headliner, it is not usually necessary to remove the entire headliner. In that case, only the headliner section covering the area to be repaired needs to be taken down. The following steps, then, may be followed to remove part of the headliner, as required.

1. Place a protective cover over the seat(s) in the area to be worked.
2. Remove the upper trim moldings and hardware surrounding the area to be removed.
3. Carefully remove any drive nails or staples holding the headliner to area being removed. See Fig. 22-35.
4. Pull carefully to remove the edge of the headliner from any cement along the area being removed. Avoid pulling too hard since too much sudden pressure might tear the material instead of pulling it away from the cement.
5. Use a wide-blade upholstery tool to pry up on the pronged retainers holding the headliner between the listing wires. This will release the material.
6. Work along the side(s) of the roof panel to disengage the listing wires from the roof header. To release the listing wires, simply pull the wires out of their holes. *Remove only as much of the headliner as is needed to make the repair.*
7. Make the needed sheet metal repair in the area. *Be careful about using any heat or flame* near the partially removed headliner.
8. Position the *sides* of the headliner on the roof panel. This is done by placing the listing wires back in the listing wire holes. Place each listing wire in the hole from which it was removed.
9. Secure the edges of the headliner under the pronged retainers. This can be done by pulling up on the retainers with a wide blade upholstery tool and then pushing the material into place. When the retainer is released, it will snap back and hold the headliner material in place.
10. Staple or tack the edges of the headliner if any staples or tacks were used along the edges of the original installation.
11. Use trim cement, as required, to secure the front and rear edges before, during, or after any tacking or stapling.
12. Install any trim moldings removed earlier.

Floor Covering

The *floors* of almost all vehicles are made of strong sheet steel and usually have some type of *covering*. The floor covering helps to insulate against road noise, seal out heat and cold, and beautify the vehicle's interior. There are two main types of floor covering: *rubber floor mats* and *carpeting*.

Often, there is an *insulation pad* installed between the floor and the floor covering. The pad material is a type of bulk fiber or foam. It is normally glued under the covering itself.

In body shop work, it may be necessary to remove all or part of the floor covering to repair floor damage in the metal *under* the covering. This is a simple task but should be done carefully to avoid damaging the floor covering. When *new* floor covering is needed, the job is usually done in an upholstery shop.

Removing Covering—Most floor coverings are held in place with glue, sheetmetal screws, and the door *scuff plates* shown earlier in Fig. 22-29. Sheetmetal screws hold the scuff plate and the floor covering in place. To remove a section of floor covering, first remove any screws in the covering itself and those in the scuff plate. Then, carefully pull the covering away from the area of the floor to be repaired.

Cleaning Interior Trim

Cleaning cloth and vinyl interior trim is an important part of auto body work. Most customers expect a thorough repair job and are impressed when a repaired vehicle is returned with "like new" interior trim. Therefore, removing any stains and dirt from upholstery will add to customer satisfaction.

Most stains are more easily removed while they are fresh, before they have dried and "set" into the fabric. Clay and mud, however, should be left to dry and may then be brushed off. Removing difficult stains is easier if the *type* of stain is known so that the correct cleaning agent may be used.

General Procedure—When cleaning any stain, use a clean cloth to absorb as much of the liquid as possible. Wipe very lightly with the cleaning agent being used, working from the outer edges of the stain to the center. Keep turning the cloth so that *clean* cloth is always being used. Depending on the type of stain, then, use one of the specific procedures outlined below.

Blood—Hot water or soap and water must *not* be used on blood stains. These will set the stain and make removing it all but impossible.

To remove a blood stain, then, rub the stain with a clean cloth saturated with *cold water* until no more of the stain will come out. Turn the cloth frequently so that only *clean* portions of the cloth are used to rub the stain. If this

treatment does not remove all of the stain, apply a small amount of household ammonia water to the stain with a cloth or brush. Wait about one minute. Then, continue to rub the stain with a clean cloth dipped in clear, cold water.

If the water and ammonia treatment does not remove the blood, a thick paste of corn starch and cold water may be used. Apply the paste and allow it to remain until it has dried and absorbed the stain. Then, pick off the dry starch. Brush the surface to remove any starch particles that remain. On very bad stains, several applications of the starch paste may be necessary.

Candy—Candy stains *not* containing chocolate can usually be removed by rubbing the stain with a cloth soaked in very hot water. If the stain is not completely removed after the area dries, rub the area lightly with a cloth wetted in cleaning fluid.

Candy stains due to cream or fruit-filled chocolates can be more easily removed by rubbing the stain with a cloth soaked in lukewarm soapsuds. Then, while the area is wet, scrape it with a dull knife. Follow this treatment by rinsing with a cloth dipped in cold water.

Chocolate stains can be removed by rubbing the stain with a cloth that has been dipped in lukewarm water. After the spot dries, rub it lightly with a cloth dipped in cleaning fluid. Use a clean white blotter to blot the area, removing excess cleaner and chocolate stain until stain is no longer transferred to the surface of the blotter.

Chewing Gum—To remove chewing gum, first use an ice cube to harden the gum. Then, scrape off the particles with a dull knife. If the gum cannot be completely removed by this method, moisten it with cleaning fluid and then work it out of the fabric with a dull knife while the gum is still moist.

Fruit and Liquor Stains—These stains can usually be removed by treating them with very hot water. Apply hot water to the spot with a clean cloth. Rub the spot vigorously with a cloth dampened in very hot water. Allow the fabric to dry.

If this does not remove the stain, first allow the fabric to dry thoroughly. Then, rub the stain *lightly* with a clean cloth dipped in cleaning fluid. This is the only further treatment recommended. Soap and water are *not* recommended because they may "set" the stain and cause a permanent discoloration. Using heat to dry the fabric is *also* not recommended.

Grease and Oil—If *grease* is on the material, scrape off as much as possible with a dull knife. Normally, then, the remaining grease or oil stain may be removed by rubbing it lightly with a clean cloth saturated in cleaning fluid. Be sure to rub toward the *center* of the stained area to avoid spreading the stain. Finally, use a clean white blotter to blot the area, removing excess cleaner and loosened grease or oil.

Ice Cream—Basically, the procedure recommended for removing ice cream stains is the same as that used to remove fruit stains. However, if the stain is stubborn, rub the spot with a cloth wetted in warm soapsuds *after* the treatment with hot water. Then, rinse the area by rubbing with a clean cloth wetted in cold water. After this dries, lightly rub the area with cleaning fluid on a clean cloth. This will clear up the last of the stain by removing any fatty or oily matter.

Vomit—To remove vomit, sponge the area with a clean cloth dipped in clear, cold water. After most of the stain has been removed, lightly wash the area with mild soap and lukewarm water. Use a clean cloth. If *odor* persists, treat the area with a water and baking soda solution of 1 teaspoon baking soda to 1 cup lukewarm water. Then, rub the area with another clean cloth dipped in cold water. If any

of the stain remains after this treatment, gently clean with a cloth moistened in cleaning fluid.

Shoe Polish and Dressing—To remove shoe dressings that contain starch, dextrine, or some water-soluble vehicle, first allow the polish to dry. Then, brush the spot vigorously with a stiff brush. This will probably be all the treatment that is necessary. If further treatment is required, moisten the spot with cold water and, after it has dried, repeat the brushing.

Paste or wax-type shoe polish stains may require using cleaning fluid. Rub the stain gently with a cloth wetted in cleaning fluid until the polish is removed. Use a clean part of the cloth for each rubbing. Rub the stained area from the outside toward the center. Blot the stained area to remove as much of the cleaner as possible.

Urine—To remove urine stain, first sponge the stain with a clean cloth saturated in lukewarm soapsuds. Then, rinse the area well by rubbing it with a clean cloth dipped in cold water. Saturate another clean cloth with a solution of 1 part household ammonia to 5 parts water. Apply this cloth to the stain and allow the solution to remain on the area for one minute. Then, rinse the area by rubbing it with a clean, wet cloth.

Lipstick—The composition (make-up) of different brands of lipsticks varies, making the stains very difficult to remove. For some brands, cleaning fluid may remove the stain. If some stain remains after repeated use of cleaning fluid, it is better to leave the stain than to try other measures.

Unit 23

Automotive Glass Work

Automotive glass and the hardware necessary to attach and move the glass are very important parts for safety and comfort. Because of this, the glass and its hardware in any vehicle must be in good condition. Replacing auto body glass is a common body shop job as part of collision repair. Sealing glass leaks and replacing and adjusting window regulators are also common body shop jobs.

The *glass itself* in an auto body may be either *fixed* (such as the windshield in Fig. 23-1) or *movable* (such as the large side glass in Fig. 23-2). Whether movable or fixed, damaged glass itself cannot be repaired. Instead, it must be replaced. The procedure is different for replacing fixed or movable glass pieces because they are fitted to the vehicle's body differently.

Glass *hardware* includes all the parts that are needed to hold or move the glass in the body. The largest pieces of glass hardware are the glass regulator assemblies. These units, the *regulators,* are the mechanisms that move the movable glass pieces up and down. The regulators are normally located between the outer door panel (the door *skin*) and the inner door, or in the quarter panels. Fig. 23-3 shows typical window regulator assembly and door lock parts.

FIXED GLASS

Fixed (stationary, nonmovable) glass is designed to stay in one place on the body. The most common piece of fixed glass is the *windshield*. Fixed glass parts may be held in position

Fig. 23-1. The largest piece of *fixed* glass on most automobiles is the *windshield.*

Fig. 23-2. Most of the glass in automobile doors is *movable* glass. Regulators in the door assemblies allow the glass to be moved.

378

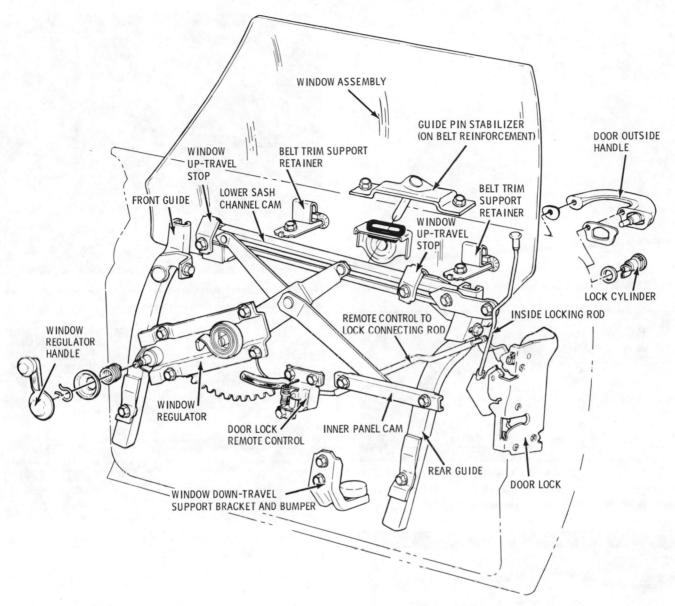

Fig. 23-3. A typical front door hardware assembly. The window regulator assembly forms most of the hardware in the door. (Courtesy of Fisher Body Division.)

on the body by one of two methods. These include *Butyl rubber sealer*, Fig. 23-4, or *rubber channels*, Fig. 23-5.

Butyl rubber sealer is used on both the windshield and backlight (rear window) of most late-model cars and some small trucks. This sealer is self-curing, *Butyl* rubber, adhesive material. It is fairly sticky, gummy, and usually comes in rolls about ten feet long. See Fig. 23-6. In Fig. 23-7, a roll of *Butyl* rubber sealer is being applied to the edge of a windshield. Some fixed side glass pieces are also held in place with *Butyl* rubber sealer.

On most older cars, a few newer cars, and many trucks, fixed glass pieces are held in place with a *rubber channel*. This channel is molded with *two* grooves, one on each side. The *inside* groove, Fig. 23-8, is the groove in which the glass fits. The *outside* groove, shown earlier in Fig.23-5, is the groove that fits around the glass opening in the metal body. Thus, the rubber seal has two grooves; one for the body and one for the glass.

When fixed glass pieces are damaged (or if a rubber channel is damaged), a body shop may have to make the repair or replacement as

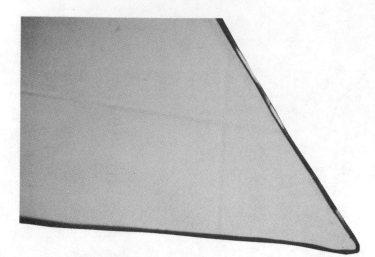

Fig. 23-4. *Butyl* rubber sealer around the edge of a window.

Fig. 23-5. The grooves inside a rubber channel. This groove holds the rubber channel in place in the window opening; the other groove holds the window in the rubber channel.

Fig. 23-6. A roll of *Butyl* rubber sealer.

part of normal body shop work. When replacing glass pieces or channel, they must be installed correctly. If they are not installed and sealed correctly, serious water and dust leaks may result.

Fig. 23-7. Applying *Butyl* rubber sealer to the edge of a new windshield before installing the windshield.

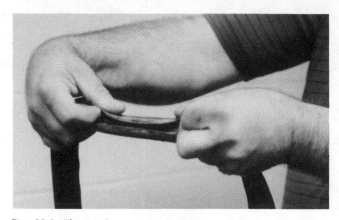

Fig. 23-8. The inside groove of a rubber channel weatherstrip. This groove holds the window in the weatherstrip.

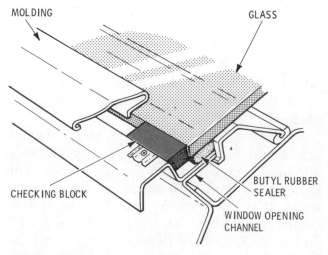

Fig. 23-9. Parts of a window installation using *Butyl* rubber sealer. *Checking blocks* are used to position the window squarely in the opening. (Courtesy of Ford Customer Service Division.)

Replacing Fixed Glass—
Butyl Rubber Seal

If either the glass or the *Butyl* rubber seal were damaged in a collision, the glass should be removed and replaced to repair the damage. During most body shop repairs of this type, one basic procedure may be used for all jobs. Although other procedures (methods) are available, learning just one procedure will be the easiest way to handle all the fixed glass/*Butyl*

rubber jobs that come into the shop. Figs. 23-9 through 23-25 outline the correct procedure and instructions for replacing a windshield held in place with a *Butyl* rubber seal. After the new windshield is in place and caulked, it should be tested for water leaks before the moldings are installed.

Fig. 23-12. *Step 2:* Use a molding removal tool to remove all the moldings around the windshield. Along the *bottom*, the moldings may be held in place by sheet metal screws. Remove any moldings around the windshield *inside* the car. If so equipped, disconnect the radio antenna from inside the windshield.

Fig. 23-10. A broken windshield to be replaced. A new windshield side molding will need to be installed after the windshield has been replaced.

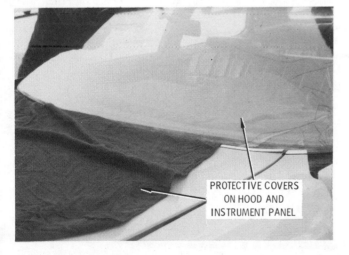

Fig. 23-11. *Step 1:* Place protective covers over the hood and instrument panel.

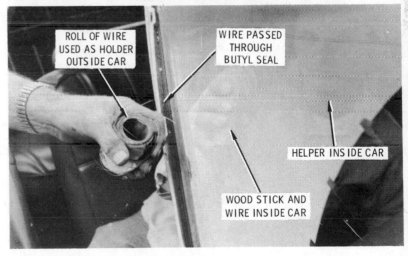

Fig. 23-13. *Step 3:* Cut the *Butyl* rubber seal from around the windshield. This may be done by one of three methods. Here, *Method A* is being used. In Method A, use needle-nose pliers to push a wire *through* the *Butyl* rubber seal somewhere around the windshield opening. Wrap each end of the wire around a firm wooden stick. With a helper *inside* the car holding onto one stick, *keep the wire tight and pull it all the way around the windshield*, cutting the *Butyl* rubber seal.

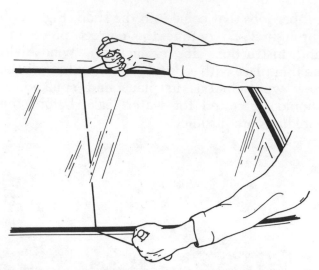

Fig. 23-14. *Step 3, Method B:* Cutting the *Butyl* rubber seal. By passing the wire through the seal *twice*, one person can pull on both wood sticks, cutting the seal with one pass.

Fig. 23-15. *Step 3, Method C:* Cutting the *Butyl* rubber seal. Here, a special knife is pulled around the windshield, cutting the seal.

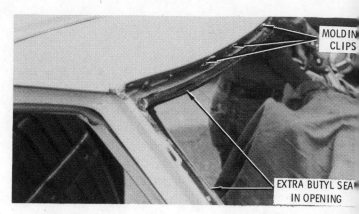

Fig. 23-17. *Step 5:* Inspect the molding clips around the edge of the window opening. Replace or reshape any clips that are bent away more than 1/16-inch. Make any needed repairs to the window opening.

Fig. 23-18. *Step 6: Temporarily* position the windshield in its opening. Shift the windshield as required until it fits the opening with a reasonably equal gap all the way around the opening. Shim or shave the checking blocks as required for a good fit. When the windshield fits properly, place several pieces of masking tape across the glass and body. Slit the masking tape along the side of the glass; these pieces of tape will serve as alignment marks when the windshield is permanently installed later. Remove the windshield from the opening and place the windshield upside down on a clean, soft surface.

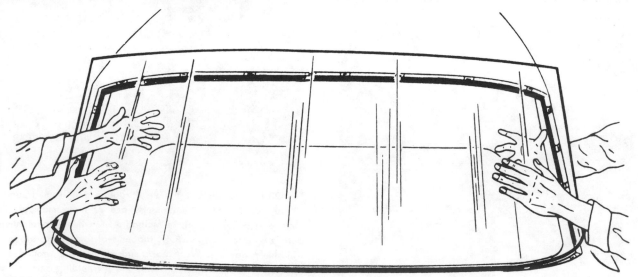

Fig. 23-16. *Step 4:* Remove the windshield. With a helper, support the windshield on both sides and remove it from the opening. If it is to be reused, place it on a soft surface. (Courtesy of Fisher Body Division.)

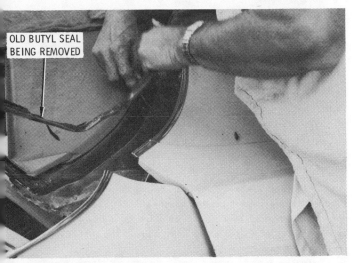

Fig. 23-19. *Step 7:* Thoroughly clean the windshield opening. Remove all the old *Butyl* rubber seal and any caulking sealer from the windshield opening. Thoroughly clean the opening with denatured alcohol.

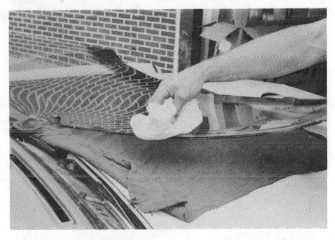

Fig. 23-20. *Step 8:* Thoroughly clean the windshield itself, whether it is the old windshield or a new one. Use a razor blade to remove any remaining *Butyl* material from around the edge of the windshield. Finally, clean the edges of the windshield with denatured alcohol on a clean rag.

Checking Blocks—Small hard rubber blocks known as *checking blocks* are used around the window opening on designs using *Butyl* rubber seals. Checking blocks help hold the glass in position inside the opening. In Fig. 23-9 was a checking block in position on a window held in place with *Butyl* rubber seals. When replacing a fixed glass held in place with *Butyl* rubber seals, *the checking blocks must always be in the correct position before the glass is permanently installed.*

Fig. 23-21. *Step 9:* Carefully position the new *Butyl* rubber seal on the edge of the windshield. Leave the wax paper covering on one side of the seal until the seal is completely installed around the edge of the windshield. Follow the specific directions outlined in the seal kit.

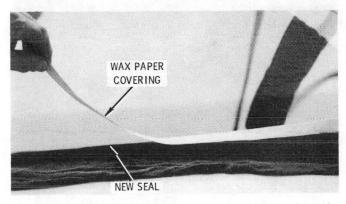

Fig. 23-22. *Step 10:* Remove the wax paper covering from the "body side" edge of the new seal.

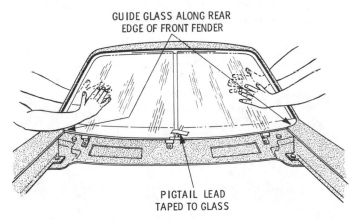

Fig. 23-23. *Step 11:* Lower the windshield into position. *Use a helper.* Be very careful to correctly align the windshield on the checking blocks; use the masking tape "alignment marks" made earlier to do this. Properly position the windshield *before* the *Butyl* contacts the windshield opening in the body. Once the *Butyl* has made contact, it is almost impossible to move the glass.

Fig. 23-24. *Step 12:* Carefully pound all the way around the windshield to push the glass firmly into position. This acts to "squeeze" the *Butyl* rubber, helping it adhere to the windshield and opening.

Fig. 23-25. *Step 13:* Apply caulking compound around the windshield. Here, compound is being applied before the windshield is installed. However, it is usually easier to apply the caulk *after* the windshield is in position.

Replacing Fixed Glass—
Rubber Channel Seal

If either the glass or the rubber channel seal were damaged in a collision, the glass must be

Fig. 23-26. *Step 1:* A broken rear window to be replaced. This is the rear window on a pickup truck, so there are no moldings to be removed. If there were, the first step would be to remove any moldings around the window after placing protective covers in the area.

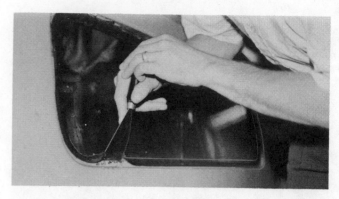

Fig. 23-27. *Step 2:* Use a putty knife to pry the outer edge of the rubber channel away from the pinchweld. (A heavy fiber stick would be preferred because it would be less likely to chip the paint.) Gradually pry the entire outer edge of the rubber channel away from the pinchweld.

Fig. 23-28. *Step 3:* Remove the rear window. This window can be pushed to the inside because it is flat. If the window was *curved*, such as a windshield, it would have to be pushed *out* from inside the car or truck.

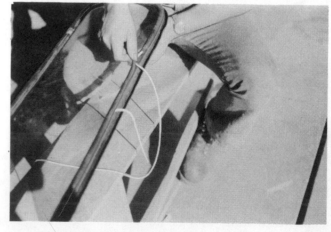

Fig. 23-29. *Step 4:* Prepare the new window for installation. Clean the edges of the glass and the window opening on the vehicle. Position the rubber channel around the outside of the new glass. Place a heavy cord in the pinchweld (body) groove of the rubber channel. Tuck the cord well inside the groove all the way around the channel. Leave both ends of the cord hanging free at about the same place. Many body men prefer to lubricate the cord and channel with ordinary soap or soapy water.

removed and replaced to repair the damage. During most body shop repairs, a common procedure using a putty knife and heavy cord is used to replace fixed glass held with a rubber channel. Figs. 23-26 through 23-31 outline the basic procedure and instructions for replacing a fixed glass with a rubber channel seal. After the new glass or channel is installed, the installation should be checked for leaks before the moldings are reinstalled.

MOVABLE GLASS

Movable glass pieces include those windows that can be raised or lowered, such as the rear quarter glass shown in Fig. 23-32. The rear glass in many station wagons is also movable. Most movable glass pieces can be moved up or down as desired, except *vent windows*. Vent windows, on cars so equipped, can normally be moved in or out to allow more or less air inside

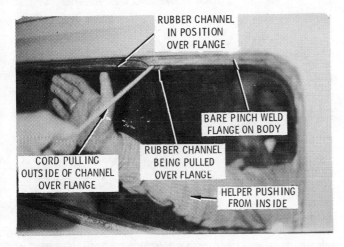

Fig. 23-30. *Step 5:* Install the rear window. Push the bottom of the rubber channel in position on the bottom of the body opening flange. Hang the cord ends out the backside of the window. Carefully pull the cord ends while a helper pushes the window in position. The cord will "pull" the outer edge of the rubber channel up and out, over the flange, as the cord is pulled out of the channel.

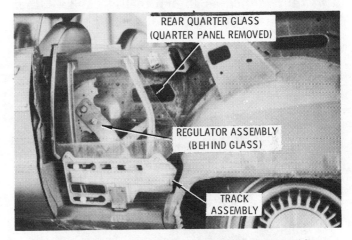

Fig. 23-32. Rear quarter glass and regulator assembly.

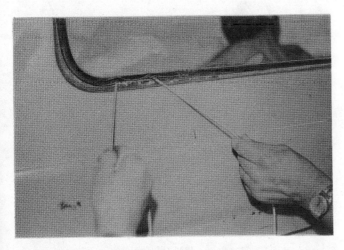

Fig. 23-31. *Step 5,* continued: When the window is almost completely in position, most of the cord will be completely out of the channel. Here, the last few inches of rubber channel are being lifted over the flange by the cord.

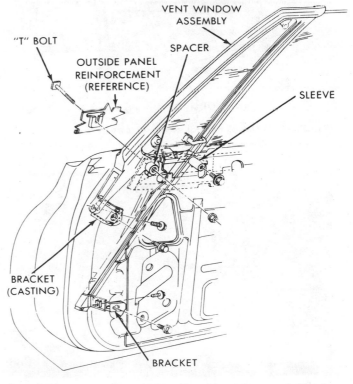

Fig. 23-33. A typical vent window assembly. (Courtesy of Chrysler Corporation.)

the vehicle. Fig. 23-33 shows a typical vent window assembly.

Movable glass pieces must have some type of *regulator* to move the glass (regulate it) up, down, in, or out. Regulators are either *manual* or *power*. These are discussed later in detail. Fig. 23-34 shows a typical *manual regulator*.

The glass itself in a movable window must be attached, usually at the bottom, to the regulator assembly. To do this, some designs use a *metal channel*, as shown in Fig. 23-35. Other designs have the glass itself *bolted* to the reg-

ulator by plastic-covered bolts and/or bushings to pass through the holes near the bottom of the glass itself. This design is shown in Fig. 23-36. These, too, are later discussed in detail.

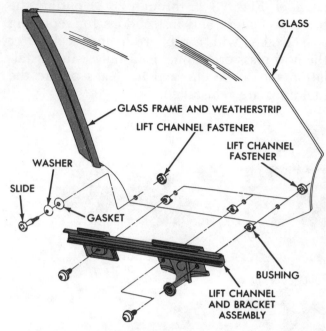

Fig. 23-36. A piece of glass held to the regulator track (lift channel) with bolts and bushings *through* the glass itself. (Courtesy of Chrysler Corporation.)

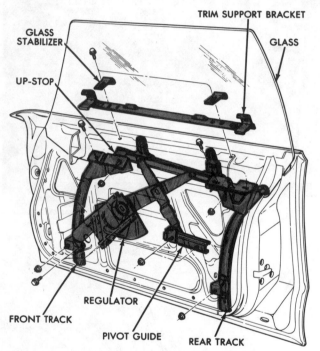

Fig. 23-34. A typical manual regulator assembly and installation. (Courtesy of Chrysler Corporation.)

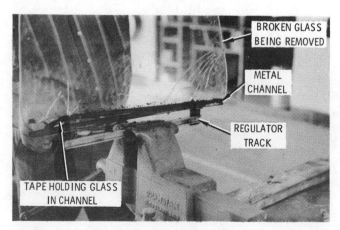

Fig. 23-35. A metal channel framework being used to hold a piece of movable glass.

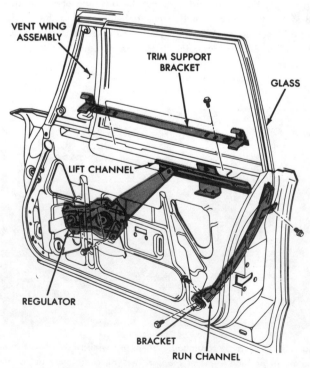

Fig. 23-37. Framed glass design with a manual regulator. (Courtesy of Chrysler Corporation.)

Protection—The opening all the way around the inside *and* the outside edges of a movable glass piece must be trimmed with some type of soft material. Normally, soft felt or rubber is used to form this "pad" around the window opening. This padding helps prevent the glass from breaking due to hitting the metal around the glass opening. The felt or rubber strips also help seal out water and wind, and help prevent rattles by holding the glass tight around the top and sides.

Types of Movable Glass

Any piece of movable glass on a car or truck may be one of two types. These include *framed glass* and *frameless glass*. Whether a glass is framed or frameless depends on how the glass is supported when it is rolled up. This can be easily seen by looking at the glass.

Framed Glass—Framed glass pieces are completely surrounded with the metal frame of the door or panel, or by chrome moldings around the edges of the glass piece itself. The "frame" helps protect the glass from chipping along the edge, or from hurting passengers when they have the door open. Most framed glass is lowered or raised by a *lift channel* attached to the regulator arm. The *run channel*, on the other hand, *guides* the glass while the lift channel is raising or lowering the glass. Fig. 23-37 shows a typical framed glass and regulator assembly.

Frameless Glass—Frameless glass pieces get their name from the fact that they are not surrounded by any type of frame. In most frameless glass designs, the glass itself is held on the regulator channel with the plastic-covered bolts and bushings discussed earlier. See Fig. 23-38. The plastic will help prevent the glass from breaking due to the pressure of the bolts and the regulator moving the glass up and down. When frameless door glass is raised and the door is open, of course, the edge(s) of the glass are exposed.

Regulators

All window regulators do basically the same job. They move the glass up, down, in, or out, *and* they hold the glass in position once it is moved. Different automobile manufacturers

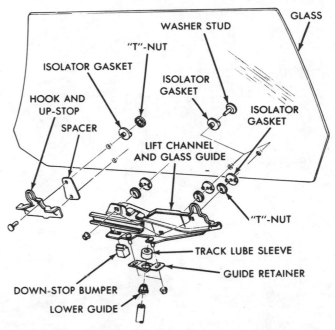

Fig. 23-38. Frameless door glass design. (Courtesy of Chrysler Corporation.)

have slightly different types of regulators, depending on the car and window glass design. Even so, important parts of any type of regulator design are the metal guides ("tracks") that hold the glass in alignment as it moves up and down.

Manual Door Regulators—Manual regulators are standard equipment on most cars. The mechanism if fairly simple, as in Fig. 23-37. Turning the crank (regulator) handle moves the regulator arm, causing it to push up or pull down on the front of the lift channel and glass. On some designs, a *second* arm holds the lift channel in alignment so that the window and glass do not "cock" in the door and become jammed.

Power Door Regulators—Power regulators work much like manual regulators and do the same basic job. The main difference is that power regulators have an electric motor to turn the regulator shaft. Fig. 23-39 shows a typical power regulator ("power window") installation.

Quarter Glass Regulators—Rear quarter window regulators are very similar to door glass regulators. However, *some* quarter window regulator designs have important differences from door regulator designs. This is because

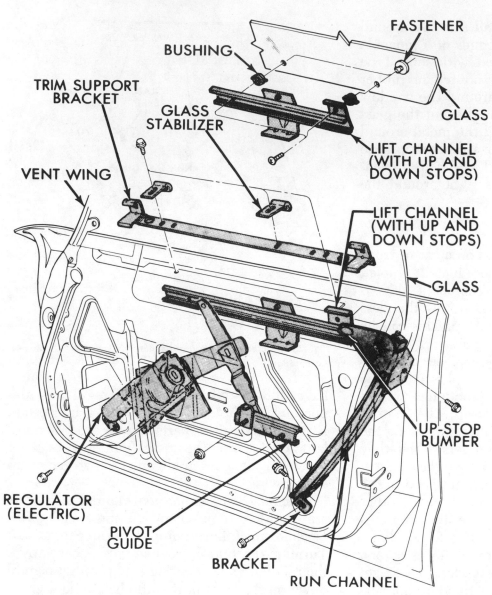

Fig. 23-39. A door assembly using a power (electric) window regulator assembly. (Courtesy of Chrysler Corporation.)

some quarter windows move up and down in a *curved* path rather than a *straight* up and down path. This difference is due to designing and placing the *guides* differently, depending on the car's design. For example, note that the quarter glass regulator in Fig. 23-40 has curved guides and that they are positioned at an angle. This is designed so that the glass will curve as it travels up and down, rather than travelling straight up and down.

Movable Glass Repairs

During ordinary collision work, or as a result of normal wear and tear, part of auto body repair will include making repairs to movable glass parts. The exact procedure for making these repairs will vary from one make or model to another, so it is almost impossible to outline all the details of each repair. However, the *general* procedure for each repair may be discussed. If a shop manual is not available for the specific make and model of car being worked on, then you must carefully reason out the exact procedure to use. Understanding the general procedure, however, will help you to better "think out" the details of each different job.

There are four general repairs that may be needed during automotive glass work on doors and movable glass parts. These repairs, listed below, will be outlined in the *general instructions* given later:

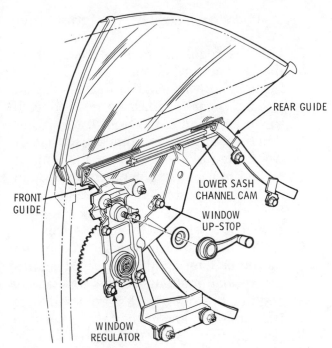

FRONT GUIDE

REAR GUIDE

LOWER SASH CHANNEL CAM

WINDOW UP-STOP

WINDOW REGULATOR

Fig. 23-40. A typical quarter window and regulator assembly. (Courtesy of Fisher Body Division.)

1. Replacing Regulators
2. Adjusting Regulators
3. Replacing Glass (Metal Channel Type)
4. Replacing Glass (Through-Bolt Type)

Replacing Regulators—When replacing regulators, it is helpful to remember that the lift channel (track) is *not* a permanent part of the regulator itself. Therefore, installing a new regulator does not necessarily mean that you must remove or replace the lift channel. As a general procedure, then, follow these steps to replace a regulator assembly:

1. Remove the door or quarter panel *trim pad*, as discussed in the Trim Work unit.
2. Carefully remove and set aside the *water dam* (moisture cover) behind the trim panel.
3. With the trim panel and water dam removed, *study* the door assembly *before* removing any screws. For example, notice the regulator attaching screws and parts in Figs. 23-34, 23-37, and 23-39. Determine which screws hold the regulator assembly itself and which screws hold the other parts of the door and window mechanism.

4. Raise the window to a point where the lift channel screws can be reached though a door panel *access hole*. On most door assemblies, this will be with the window about ¾ up.
5. Disconnect the glass and lift channel assembly from the regulator arm(s).
6. Grasp the glass on both sides and raise the glass up, out of the way. It may be necessary to remove the *up-stops* to do this.
7. Use a screwdriver or similar tool to *hold* the glass and lift channel up, out of the way. Usually, the screwdriver can be placed through a hole somewhere near the top of the inner door panel to hold the glass up.
8. Remove the regulator mounting screws themselves.
9. Move the regulator around as necessary to disengage the regulator arm rollers from their channels.
10. Remove the regulator through an access hole in the door.

To install the new regulator, reverse the basic procedure outlined above. Be sure to grease the regulator rollers and lift channels with a good amount of white grease before installing the new regulator. Unless the regulator itself is mounted in slotted holes —and many of them are not— no regulator adjustment should be necessary.

Adjusting Regulators—Before adjusting a regulator and the glass attached to it, the door itself *must be correctly fitted in its opening*. Also, the weatherstrip surrounding the door and glass must be properly installed. Therefore, regulator and window adjustment should not be done until the door and weatherstrip are installed correctly and are in good condition. When working on a car with no center post (a "hard-top"), the front glass should be adjusted *before* the rear glass is adjusted.

Correctly adjusting a regulator may include adjusting regulator *pivot guide tracks*, track *brackets*, *up-stops*, and, if so equipped, *stabilizer bars*. Again, these parts, their exact location, method of attachment, and method of adjustment will vary from one make and model to the next. For that reason, it would be almost impossible to outline the *exact* procedure for adjusting all the different regulator designs that have been used. However, if you understand the general procedure and the reason why certain adjustments are made, it will be easier to "figure out" and adjust any given regulator.

Before adjusting a regulator, *locate all the screws or bolts* (fasteners) *used to attach the above parts*. Place the tools needed to loosen the fasteners in the work area. However, do not completely loosen or remove the fasteners until necessary. With this preparation, then, the following steps outline how to adjust the typical regulator shown in Fig. 23-41. (Of course, the trim panel and water dam must be first removed before adjusting the regulator.)

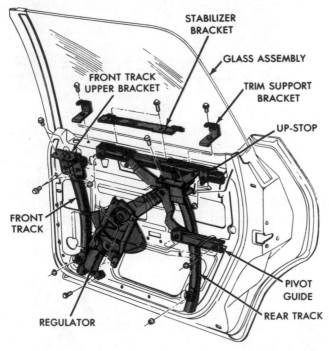

Fig. 23-41. A typical window regulator assembly as used with a piece of frameless window glass. (Courtesy of Chrysler Corporation.)

1. Raise the glass until it is ⅛-inch from the weatherstrip at the top of the window opening.
2. Loosen the nuts at the *pivot guide*. Adjust the pivot guide up or down until the top of the glass is *parallel to the top*

weatherstrip. Tighten the pivot guide nuts.
3. Use the regulator to raise the glass to the "full up" position.
4. Locate the *track* that is nearest the adjoining (nearby) glass or post edge. In this example, it is the front track. Adjust this track at its *upper* bracket so that the front edge of the glass (or molding attached to the glass) contacts the adjoining glass or post when the glass is in the *full up* position.
5. Lower the window to about ¼ up.
6. Adjust the stabilizer bracket to position the outer edge of the glass just against the rubber molding at the top outside edge of the door.
7. Raise the window to the *full up* position.
8. Loosen the upper and lower bracket screws on both tracks.
9. Position the *inside* edge at the *top* of the glass so that it firmly contacts the weather strip for a good seal.
10. Tighten all the track bracket screws.
11. With the window still up, adjust both *up-stops* down, against the top of the channel and bracket assembly at the bottom edge of the glass. Tighten the up-stop retaining nuts.
12. Operate the regulator through one cycle (glass full up to full down and back) to check the effort required and for interferences in the "scissors" action of the window regulator arms. Readjust if necessary.

Replacing Glass (Metal Channel Type)—When movable glass is damaged, it must be replaced. This is a common job in body shop collision work. If the glass is held in place by a *metal channel*, the glass and channel must together be removed from the inner door panel. Then, a new piece of glass may be installed in the channel. The channel and the new glass is then reinstalled in the door. Figs. 23-42 through 23-47 outline the procedure to use.

Replacing Glass (Through-Bolt Type)—When replacing a window glass held with *through bolts*, the procedure is easier than when

Fig. 23-42. *Step 1:* To replace a window held in a metal channel, first remove the inner trim panel. This will expose the regulator and lower edge of the window glass assembly.

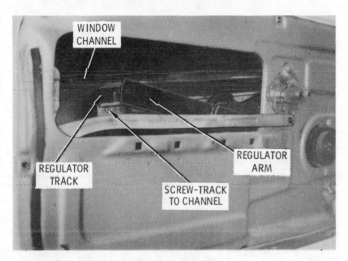

Fig. 23-43. *Step 2:* Remove the track-to-channel screws holding the regulator track to the window channel.

Fig. 23-44. *Step 3:* Remove the window and metal channel assembly from the door. To do this, it is often necessary to tilt the window as shown.

Fig. 23-45. *Step 4:* Remove the broken glass or glass pieces from the window channel. This may easily be done by first putting the window and channel in a vise. Then, soak the old window *tape* (the material between the glass and the channel) with lacquer thinner. This will soften the tape and make the glass easy to remove. When the lacquer thinner has softened the tape, pry the old glass out of the window channel with a screwdriver.

Fig. 23-46. *Step 5:* Prepare the metal channel and the new glass for installation. Clean the channel thoroughly to remove all traces of the old tape. Clean the bottom edge of the new glass and place a piece of window tape on the bottom edge of the glass. Fold the tape over the sides of the glass.

the window is held in a metal channel. Glass held with through-bolts, Figs. 23-36 and 23-38, must be carefully handled and installed, however. This is because almost all the sides of the glass are exposed. Since side glass is *tempered*, a slight chip on one exposed edge could shatter

Fig. 23-47. *Step 6:* Fit the channel onto the lower edge of the new glass. To do this, turn the new glass piece upside down on a piece of clean, soft wood. Then, use another wood block to carefully pound the channel onto the bottom edge of the new glass. Continue this until the new glass is firmly installed in the channel. Finally, put the channel and the new glass back into the door.

the entire glass. For this reason, the bushings and bolts must be carefully installed and tightened so as not to stress the glass.

The procedure to use is similar to that used to replace glass held with a metal channel. The trim panel is first removed and the regulator track is then separated from the regulator mechanism. Then, the window and track (also known as the *lift channel*) may together be removed from the door or quarter panel. Finally, the track is unbolted from the old glass and bolted to the new glass.

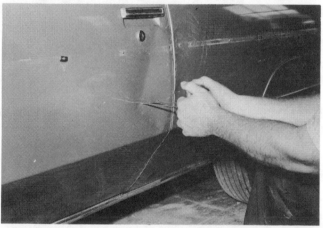

Automotive Painting

Unit 24

Automotive Painting and Equipment

An automobile would not be very attractive if it were not for the topcoat. It would be drab and would rust very shortly after leaving the factory. Therefore, an automobile's finish (topcoat) becomes a very important part of making the car attractive and protecting it from the rust and corrosion that would be caused by moisture and heat or salt and other chemicals. Because an automobile's topcoat is very important, then, automotive paint work is a very important part of auto body repair.

Job Opportunities

Anyone who chooses to make a specialty of automobile refinishing will find that the choice is a good one. Automobile refinishing and paint work has become one of the most important jobs in the auto body repair industry. Thousands of complete repaint jobs are done in body shops each year, such as the newly repainted automobile drying in the paint booth in Fig. 24-1. Equally important, and sometimes harder, is the job of painting only *part* of a car, as in Fig. 24-2. This may be more difficult because the painter is expected to *match* the new color to the older color already on the car.

BRIEF HISTORY OF FACTORY FINISHES

In a body repair shop, the types of paints used must be changed to keep up with changes

Fig. 24-1. A completely repainted automobile drying in a paint booth. (Courtesy of Binks Manufacturing Company.)

Fig. 24-2. Repainting only a part of one panel on a car. This job may be very difficult, since the color of the old and the new paint must match. (Courtesy of Binks Manufacturing Company.)

in the paints used at the *factory* by the automobile manufacturing industry. As manufacturer's paint ("factory paint") changes, older types of paint and material may not work well with the new factory material being used. For this reason, the auto body refinishing business, also known as the "aftermarket," must change with the automobile industry.

Early Factory Finishes

The very first automobiles, such as the restored antique car in Fig. 24-3, were painted with a *brush*. Lampblack color and varnish were used for the painting process. (*Color* is a pigment or substance which, when dissolved in a liquid, becomes an *ink*.) *Lampblack* is the very fine, black pigment of *carbon*. Originally, lampblack was collected as *soot* from the smoke of burning oil and other materials.

On these early factory jobs, each factory painter applied several coats of paint with a *brush*. Each coat was given plenty of flash-off time before the next coat was applied. Flash-off time is the amount of time needed for the thinner to quickly evaporate from the paint. However, the paint does not dry thoroughly in this period of time.

After each coat, the paint had to be sanded to a smooth finish with water and *pumice* (finely-ground volcanic rock used for polishing). This was repeated several times. After the last coat had thoroughly dried, *wax* was

Fig. 24-3. An antique car, a 1908 REO. At the factory, this car was originally painted with brushes.

rubbed over and into the finish. This complete method of painting usually took about 30 days. This process, of course, was not very adaptable to mass-production, since it was very time-consuming.

Later Factory Finishes

In the 1920's, the DuPont Company developed an entirely new type of finish. It was named *Duco*. Duco was the first type of modern *lacquer finish* and is technically known as *nitrocellulose lacquer*. Duco was applied with a spray gun instead of a brush, greatly speeding up automobile body manufacturing.

Later, in the 1930's, the first types of enamels were developed. These were known as *alkyd* enamels and were extremely tough, making them good for use on trucks as well as on cars. Alkyd enamel would dry with a high shine, so it did not require buffing to a high shine as did lacquer. Alkyd enamels and nitrocellulose lacquers, then, were used well into the 1950's. They are still available today, and alkyd enamels are still used as the factory finish on many imported cars and some trucks.

Current Factory Finishes

During the 1950's, the paint products used on most of *today's* new cars and trucks were developed. These include *acrylic* lacquers and *acrylic* enamels. The first of these to be developed was acrylic *lacquer*, and, in 1959, General Motors began painting all their new cars with acrylic lacquer, which they have continued to do through the 1970's.

Later, following developmental work in the 1950's, acrylic *enamels* were introduced in 1963. *Acrylic* enamel gradually replaced the older *alkyd* enamel that was used on production lines. Today, then, all new cars made in the United States are finished in either acrylic lacquer or acrylic enamel. Almost all the paint repair done in a body shop will be done with one of these two products. These paints, and their materials, are discussed in another unit.

PAINTING EQUIPMENT

No matter what type of paint is being applied, several basic pieces of *painting equip-*

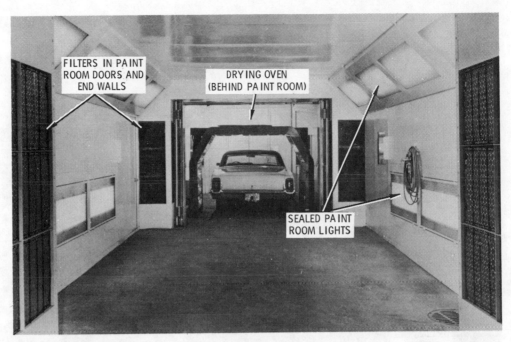

Fig. 24-4. A common paint booth and drying oven being used in a body shop. (Courtesy of Binks Manufacturing Company.)

ment are needed by any shop that does paint work. The size and amount of any shop's paint equipment depends largely on the shop's volume of business. A smaller shop, for example, may need only one *paint room*, Fig. 24-4.

To properly dry new paint, some shops have *heating ovens* to *heat* the surface, helping it dry. Behind the paint booth in Fig. 24-4, for example, is a large heating oven. Fig. 24-5 shows a smaller bank of "heaters" with infrared elements. These would be used for spot-drying both primer-surfacer and topcoat repairs.

Other equipment needed for auto body refinishing will be the *exhaust fans* discusssed

Fig. 24-5. A smaller bank of infrared heaters used to dry panel or spot repairs. (Courtesy of Refinish Division, Dupont Company.)

earlier. These will provide air circulation for good health and safety. Refinishing work will also require many pieces of tools and equipment, including, for example, the air compressors and separator-regulators discussed earlier. "Paint work only" tools include the paint spray gun itself and, in some shops, a paint thickness meter, used to measure the thickness of the paint on a vehicle.

Paint Booth

The size of a shop's paint *booth* (or booths) depends on the amount of refinishing business that the shop does. A large paint and body shop may have a large paint booth that can turn out more than one paint job per day. For example, notice the large paint booth in Fig. 24-4. This booth is designed for *spraying* the vehicle in one compartment (toward the front) and then *drying* the vehicle in another compartment (toward the rear). This allows two vehicles to be refinished at the same time.

The paint booth shown in Figs. 24-4 and 24-6 has all the features of a good, large, commercial paint booth. It provides a *totally enclosed* room in which to paint and dry an automobile or small truck. All the features of this booth make it ideal for fast, top-quality automotive refinishing. Many controls for the booth's dryers, ventilation, and other features are mounted

Fig. 24-6. The outside of the paint booth shown in Fig. 24-4. This booth provides a totally enclosed environment in which to do top-quality automotive refinishing. (Courtesy of Binks Manufacturing Company.)

outside the booth. Having the controls outside the booth allows the dryers and other features to be controlled without having to enter the booth itself.

Lighting—To be able to do good paint work, an automotive painter must have plenty of good *light*. This is necessary so that he can see exactly how the paint is going on, how the color is matching, etc. This is very important during good paint work. For these reasons, any paint booth must have many good, clean lights. Fig. 24-7 shows the fluorescent light fixtures on the side and top of the booth shown in Fig. 24-4 and 24-6.

In Fig. 24-7, note that the lights are mounted *outside* the booth so that they may shine *inside* the booth. This is done as a safety precaution. Paint fumes from automotive paint are very flammable and may explode if they are touched off with a spark or match. For this reason, the best paint booth designs have all the electric wiring and light fixtures *outside* the paint room itself. Then, the front sides of the lights themselves are sealed so that no paint fumes can enter the light fixture and, possibly, be ignited.

Ventilating and Filtering—While a car is being painted, there must be a constant flow of clean, fresh air in the paint room. This is neces-

Fig. 24-7. Sealed fluorescent lights, as seen from *outside* the paint booth. All the electrical wiring is outside the paint booth for safety. (Courtesy of Binks Manufacturing Company.)

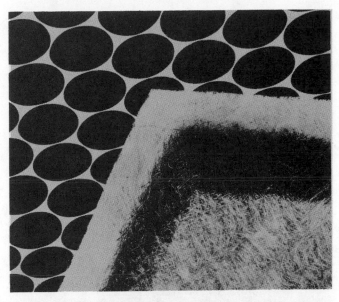

Fig. 24-8. The fine fiberglass filtering material used to make air filters for paint booths. (Courtesy of PPG Industries, Inc.)

Fig. 24-9. A typical exhaust fan as seen from outside a small body shop. For safety, a screen should be placed over the fan blades.

sary to remove paint particles and fumes from the air. If air was not "pulled through" as the painter sprayed the paint, the air would soon be so thick with paint particles that it would be difficult to see the car being painted.

Deluxe paint booths, Fig. 24-4, have filters built into the sides *and* doors of the booth itself. Many shops, though, have filters in only the *door of the paint room*. In either case, the filters themselves are usually a woven mat of hairlike fiberglass, as shown in Fig. 24-8. These filters are designed to be easily replaced. How often they are replaced depends on the amount of paint work done in a shop *and* on how dirty the shop's air is normally. However, they must always be replaced regularly.

To pull the air through the filters and paint room, some type of *exhaust fan* is needed. (In many areas, health and safety regulations require that a certain amount of air be circulated through paint booths.) A typical exhaust fan, Fig. 24-9, should be "standard equipment" in any body shop. No matter of what design, the fan should be large enough to quickly remove paint dust and fumes from the paint booth. Deluxe paint booths, Fig. 24-6, have built-in exhaust fans and air supply ducts.

A paint booth or room without an exhaust fan will cause trouble by allowing paint dust to settle onto the fresh paint and cause the

paint to *dull*. Without an exhaust fan, the shop may also have trouble with paint not drying (evaporating) correctly. Both lacquer and enamel paints need a good supply of fresh air to dry properly, even after the spraying has been done. If the paint room does not have the needed supply of fresh air, the paint may go flat, lack gloss, or be off-color.

Paint Measuring Meter

Many shops have a paint *measuring meter,* such as the one shown in Fig. 24-10. This instrument is used to determine the thickness of

Fig. 24-10. Paint thickness measuring meter. (Courtesy of PPG Industries, Inc.)

the paint on a vehicle. This meter works on electricity and a type of magnetic action. The meter measures the thickness of the paint and any body filler by "sensing" the magnetic pull of the metal *under* the paint and filler. If the paint and filler are *thick*, the magnetic pull will not be as great as if they are thin. The meter then changes this "pull" to read the approximate thickness of the filler or the paint.

The thickness of paint (or paint and filler) is measured in *mils*. A mil equals $1/1000$ of an inch. The paint thickness on most new cars is about three mils. This is the total thickness of the primer and the topcoats (color coats).

Usually, during auto refinish work, the total thickness should be no more than about *seven* mils after the new paint has been applied. Paint that is thicker than this may tend to crack.

Air Supply System

Important equipment for automotive refinishing is the shop's *air supply system.* The air supply system includes the air compressor, the air lines, the air separator-regulators, and the air hoses. These pieces of equipment are thoroughly described elsewhere in their own unit. Their job of supplying the shop with a good supply of clean, dry air is very important for quality auto body refinishing. For this reason, *a good auto body painter must know about and properly maintain the air supply system to the paint room.*

Paint Hoses—The air hose *from* the separator-regulator *to* the spray gun is an important part of the air supply system. *Regular shop air hose must not be used for this job.* Special *paint room* air hoses should be used for best results. The special hose is smoother inside and will not as easily lose pressure over the length of the hose as will regular shop air hose. Fig. 24-11 shows a group of paint room air hoses from one manufacturer.

Paint room hoses are available in *two* basic inside diameters: ¼-inch and 5/16-inch. For the best results, only 5/16-inch hose should be used. Regardless of the hose diameter, air pressure will be lost between the regulator and the spray gun. How *much* pressure is lost depends on three factors:

1. The *hose diameter.* A smaller hose loses more pressure than a larger hose.
2. The *age* of the hose. An older hose will lose more pressure than a new hose.

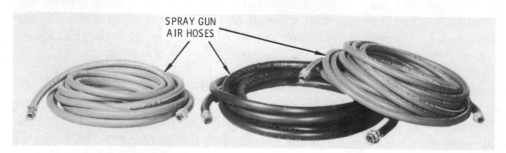

SPRAY GUN
AIR HOSES

Fig. 24-11. A group of paint room air hoses. (Courtesy of Binks Manufacturing Company.)

Fig. 24-12. Installing an air pressure gauge *at the paint gun* is the most accurate method to measure air pressure drop at the end of the hose. (Courtesy of PPG Industries, Inc.)

3. The *type* of hose connections used. Generally speaking, "quick-change" adapters will lose one pound of pressure when compared with threaded, screw-in hose connections.

There are two methods to determine the *actual* air pressure at the gun. The *best* way is to install an air pressure gauge *at the gun itself;* Fig. 24-12. Then, the air pressure at the gun may be compared with the air pressure at the regulator, as in Fig. 24-13. By using this method, the exact air pressure drop will be known.

The *second* method to determine the air pressure at the gun is to use Table 24-1. In this table, the approximate air pressure drop is listed for hoses of different diameters. These figures are for *new* hose and will not be exactly correct for older hose. Older hose will likely have several pounds more pressure drop than listed in the table. In any case, it is always

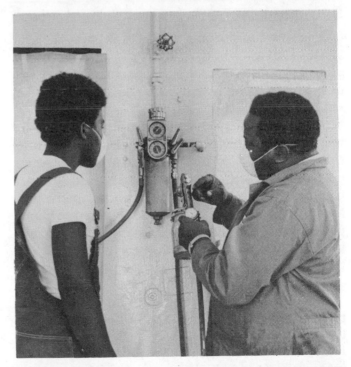

Fig. 24-13. Checking the air pressure drop at the end of a paint hose. Here, the regulator pressure is being compared to the actual air pressure at the gun.

Table 24-1. Approximate Air Pressures at the Gun
for Paint Room Hoses of Different Lengths

Hose Diameter	Regulator Pressure (lbs.)	Hose Length (ft.)					
		5	10	15	20	25	50
	30	26	24	23	22	21	9
	40	34	32	31	29	27	16
	50	43	40	38	36	34	22
1/4 inch	60	51	48	46	43	41	29
	70	59	56	53	51	48	36
	80	68	64	61	58	55	43
	90	76	71	68	65	61	51
	30	29	28	28	27	27	23
	40	38	37	37	37	36	32
	50	48	47	46	46	45	40
5/16 inch	60	57	56	55	55	54	49
	70	66	65	64	63	63	57
	80	75	74	73	72	71	66
	90	84	83	82	81	80	74

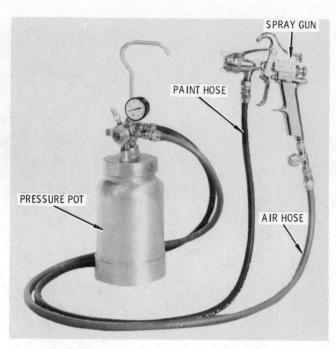

Fig. 24-14. A pressure pot spray gun. This type of gun is normally used in factory work for production spraying. (Courtesy of Binks Manufacturing Company.)

important for the painter to know the exact air pressure *at the gun* for the hose being used.

Spray Guns

The most important tool in the paint department of an auto body shop is the *spray gun*. All good automotive painters must master the skill of using a spray gun. This skill can only be learned by practice.

All spray guns are built to do one basic job: to break up the paint material (liquid) into tiny droplets ("atoms"). To do this, a spray gun needs clean, dry compressed air. It uses the compressed air to pull liquid paint up, through a tiny hole or holes. When the paint passes through the tiny holes, it is broken up into the small droplets. This process of breaking the liquid up into small droplets is known as *atomizing* the paint.

There are two basic types of spray guns that may be used in a paint shop. These are known as the *pressure pot* gun and the *siphon* gun. Either gun does the same job; it turns the liquid into a spray of droplets by using air pressure.

Pressure Pot Gun—A pressure pot spray gun, Fig. 24-14, works on compressed air and paint

supplied from a "pot". Air pressure forces the paint *from* the pot, out *through* a paint hose, and then *into* the spray gun head. After the paint is forced through the fluid hose, it is forced out the paint gun nozzle. When it leaves the nozzle, the liquid is mixed ("broken up") with air, *atomizing* the liquid and causing a fine spray.

Pressure pot spray guns are not widely used in the body shop trade because they weigh more than siphon guns and are harder to move around. Instead, they are more often used in industry.

Siphon Gun—A siphon gun, Fig. 24-15, works on a vacuum (suction) system. For this reason, siphon guns are also known as *suction* guns.

In a siphon gun, air rushes through the *air nozzles*, creating a suction in the *vacuum tube*, as shown in Fig. 24-15. This suction pulls the paint up, from the paint cup, into the paint gun. Here, the liquid paint is sucked out the tip by the compressed air leaving the tip. Finally the air "breaks up" the paint just outside the tip (head) of the gun, making the paint a spray of tiny liquid droplets.

Spray Gun Parts—Either type of spray gun (siphon or pressure pot) has many important

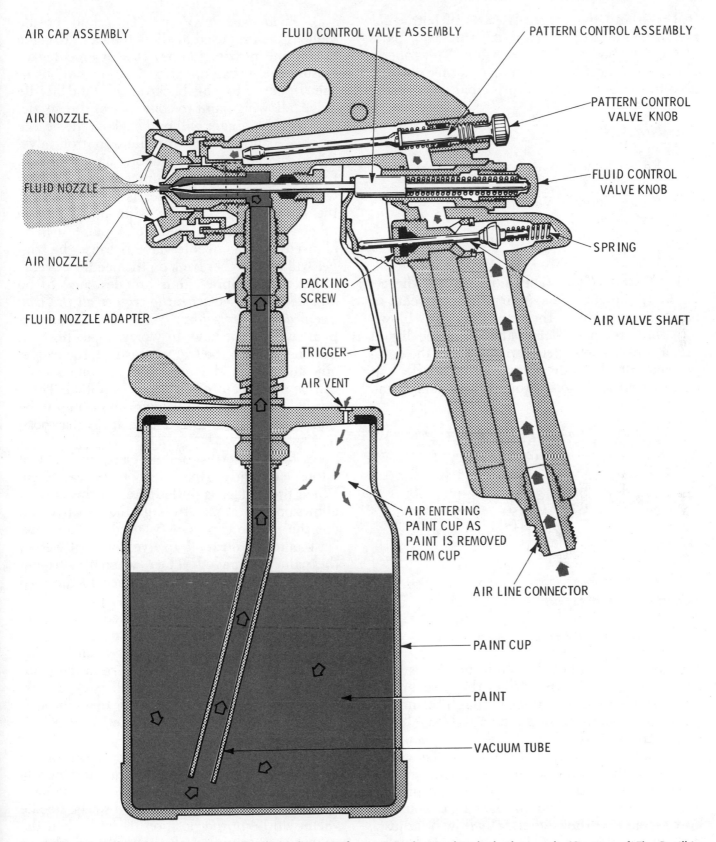

AIR CAP ASSEMBLY

FLUID CONTROL VALVE ASSEMBLY

PATTERN CONTROL ASSEMBLY

AIR NOZZLE

PATTERN CONTROL
VALVE KNOB

FLUID NOZZLE

FLUID CONTROL
VALVE KNOB

AIR NOZZLE

SPRING

FLUID NOZZLE ADAPTER

AIR VALVE SHAFT

PACKING
SCREW

TRIGGER

AIR VENT

AIR ENTERING
PAINT CUP AS
PAINT IS REMOVED
FROM CUP

AIR LINE CONNECTOR

PAINT CUP

PAINT

VACUUM TUBE

Fig. 24-15. A typical siphon (suction) spray gun. This is the type of gun most often used in body shop work. (Courtesy of The Devilbiss Company.)

features, and the principle parts of both guns are the same. Fig. 24-16 shows the major parts of an auto body paint spray gun. To properly clean and adjust a spray gun, a painter must be able to understand these principal parts of the gun.

1. Nozzle Cap
2. Fluid Nozzle
3. Fluid Needle Valve
4. Trigger
5. Fluid Control Valve
6. Air Valve Shaft
7. Pattern Control
8. Handle

1. *Nozzle Cap.* The nozzle cap directs (points) the compressed air into the stream of paint coming out of the gun. This air is blown into the stream of paint, atomizing the liquid into a spray. The nozzle cap may force the compressed air through holes in the nozzle cap horns *or* through holes around the center of the cap.

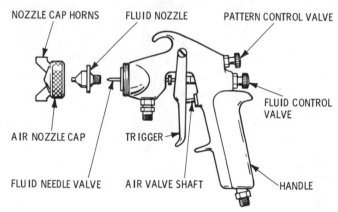

Fig. 24-16. The main parts of a spray gun.

2. *Fluid Nozzle.* The fluid nozzle is also known as the fluid *tip.* When the fluid nozzle is open, paint can be pulled through the nozzle by the air rushing through the nozzle cap holes. When the fluid nozzle is closed, no paint can come out of nozzle. The fluid needle valve, then, is in the center of the nozzle and controls whether the nozzle is open or closed. A painter can change how much the nozzle is open by how he handles the trigger *or* by how he adjusts the *fluid control valve.* The fluid control valve controls the *position* of the fluid *needle* valve.

3. *Fluid Needle Valve.* The fluid needle valve is the part used to allow the paint to come out of the nozzle. It does this by opening or closing the nozzle opening. One of the jobs of the *trigger* is to pull back on the fluid needle valve, allowing paint to come out of the nozzle.

When the trigger will pull back on the needle valve is controlled by the fluid control valve. When the fluid control valve is almost closed, for example, very little paint will come out of the nozzle when the trigger is pulled back. If the fluid control valve is wide open, on the other hand, a large amount of paint will be allowed past the needle valve because the trigger will pull farther back on the needle valve.

4. *Trigger.* Spray guns are designed to be adjusted and used *with the trigger all the way open during spraying.* With this feature, a painter does not have to worry about how far back he pulls on the trigger. Instead, the proper adjustments (fluid control and pattern control) can be made *before* the paint is applied. Then, during painting, the trigger may simply be pulled back all the way and held in that position.

As the trigger is pulled back, it has two "stops." The first "stop" is about ½ way open. When the trigger is pulled back to this stop, it allows only *air* to pass through the air valve and out the nozzle cap. This is used to blow any "last minute" dust off the vehicle just before the paint is sprayed. Then, when the trigger is pulled the rest of the way open to the final "stop", the fluid needle valve is pulled back, allowing paint to go past the needle valve and out the air nozzle cap.

5. *Air Valve.* The air valve, open in Fig. 24-15, is the main air control valve in the paint gun. When the trigger is pulled back, it first opens the air valve and allows air to go through the gun's air passages to operate the gun's air systems.

6. *Fluid Control Valve.* The fluid control valve controls the position of the fluid *needle* valve when the trigger is pulled all the way open. It *presets* the needle valve so the needle valve will be in the position desired when the trigger is later pulled all the way back during actual painting.

The fluid control valve is the *bottom* adjustment knob on the back of the spray gun. See Fig. 24-15. In Fig. 24-17, a painter is adjusting the fluid control valve. If the job to be done is a small spot repair, the fluid control valve would first be adjusted about ½ way open. When a large panel or a complete paint job is to be sprayed, however, the valve may be completely opened for a trial adjustment. In all cases, practice settings should be tested by being sprayed on scrap material before the actual paint work is done.

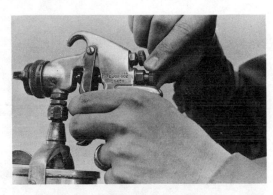

Fig. 24-17. Adjusting the fluid control valve. (Courtesy of Refinish Division, DuPont Company.)

Fig. 24-18. Adjusting the pattern control valve. (Courtesy of Refinish Division, DuPont Company.)

7. *Pattern Control Valve.* The pattern control valve sets the width of the spray pattern. Fig. 24-18 shows a pattern control valve, the *upper* knob, being adjusted. A small, round spray pattern is normally used for spot repairs. A large, oblong pattern is used for large panel repairs and for overall paint jobs.

When the pattern control valve is *closed,* the spray pattern is *round,* because the air is coming through the holes around the center of the nozzle cap. As the valve is opened, the spray pattern becomes more oblong (egg-shaped). This is because the air is also coming through the holes in the horns of the nozzle cap. This "blows" the paint up and down as it tries to come straight out. This produces a pattern that is not round.

Safety Equipment

Automotive paint, paint products, and the process of painting can all be very dangerous to good health if common "safety sense" is not used. Paint fumes, for example, can cause head and stomach aches if the fumes are breathed heavily. Paint *particles* (small droplets of paint in the air) can cause lung, chest, and breathing trouble because they will stick to the body's air passages and partially clog your breathing system.

Paints and paint products can also be damaging to your *eyes.* Several products may actually blind you if splashed into your eyes. All paint and paint products will cause at least *some* eye trouble if they are splashed into your eyes.

For these reasons, proper eye and lung (breathing) protection *must always be used when painting or working with paint and paint products.* Common shop painting safety equipment, then, will include three items:

1. Respirators
2. Face Masks
3. Safety Goggles

Respirators—A good *respirator,* with clean filters, is absolutely necessary for safe overall paint work or panel repairs. This tool, Fig. 24-19, thoroughly filters *all* the air breathed in from either the nose or mouth. The round filters on the side of the respirator may be easily replaced by unscrewing them and screwing new ones in their places. These filters take out *both* the paint particles *and most* of the paint fumes, so the filters must be replaced, not cleaned. For the safest breathing, the filters should be replaced after each overall paint job.

Face Masks—The simplest lung and breathing protection is given by wearing at least a *face mask.* Face masks, Fig. 24-20, *do not re-*

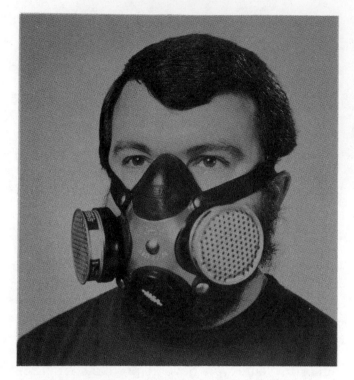

Fig. 24-19. A common respirator. This piece of safety equipment will correctly filter out most paint fumes *and* paint particles.

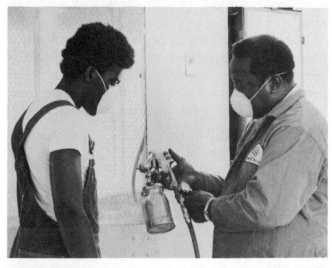

Fig. 24-20. Face masks being worn in the paint room. These masks provide good protection against paint overspray and shop dust.

sweeping down the shop. Since face masks are relatively inexpensive, it is a good idea to have a box of them on hand for use in the shop.

Safety Goggles—When working with paint or paint chemicals, *safety goggles* must be worn. In Fig. 24-21, for example, a painter is filling a spray gun cup with gun cleaning solvent. This product would cause severe eye damage if it was accidentally splashed in his eyes. For this reason, he is wearing safety goggles. Every shop, then, needs safety goggles in *both* the painting and grinding areas.

Fig. 24-21. Safety goggles being worn while working at the paint bench. These goggles provide good eye protection against the chemicals in paint and paint products that may cause eye damage.

Masking

Masking products and the masking process are used to protect the parts of a vehicle that are *not* to be painted. A good masking job will make the overall paint job easier by reducing the clean-up time needed after the paint has been applied. A good masking job also helps the overall paint job look better, too, since the paint will be exactly on the painted parts and not on other parts of the car, such as rubber weatherstripping, glass, and bright trim. Fig.

move paint fumes. Instead, they only remove paint particles; the small pieces of paint dust or overspray. For this reason, face masks should *not* be used during large panel repairs or overall paint jobs where a respirator should be used. However, face masks are useful for protection when painting spot repairs, applying primer, working down plastic filler, and even

24-22 shows a car that was properly masked for overall painting. The paper on the wind-shield was removed so that the car could be driven from the paint room.

Fig. 24-22. A car that was properly masked for repainting. The paper on the windshield was torn away so that the car could be driven from the paint room. (Courtesy of Binks Manufacturing Company.)

Masking Tape—The basic material for any masking job is *masking tape*. Most masking tape is ¾-inch wide and is sold in rolls, as shown in Fig. 24-23. Masking tape is also sold in very thin rolls of ¼-inch and ½-inch widths, and wider widths of one inch or more. Special masking tape is also available with *strips* that

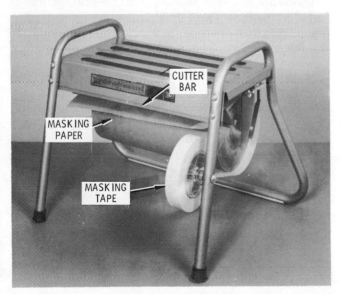

Fig. 24-23. A typical masking tape and masking paper dispenser. (Courtesy of 3M Company, Automotive Division.)

may be pulled out of the tape. This tape is used for making stripes. When this special tape is in position, one or more strips may be pulled out. Then, the stripes may be painted. See Fig. 24-24.

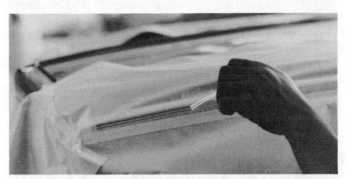

Fig. 24-24. Pre-cut masking tape has strips of tape that may be pulled out after the tape is in place. Then, the pulled-out areas may be painted to make stripes.

All masking tape should be stored in a cool, dry place, away from heaters or sunlight. This will help keep the tape sticky and flexible. Masking tape should be carefully removed *after* the paint work, when the paint on the tape is no longer *tacky*, but *before* the paint hardens. To see if the paint is tacky, touch the fresh paint that is *on the masking tape*. If your finger seems to stick to the paint when you pull it away, the paint is "tacky" and the tape may be removed. To do this, pull the tape straight up from the painted surface.

Masking Paper—To cover large areas not to be painted, masking *paper* should be used. See Fig. 24-23. Like masking tape, masking paper is available in different widths. The most common width is fifteen inches.

Masking paper is better to use than news-paper or other papers because masking paper is less likely to allow any paint to *bleed through*. When paint *bleeds* through paper, the paint soaks through the paper and reaches the glass or trim under the paper. Always using masking paper is the best way to help prevent paint bleed-through.

Cleanliness—Before applying masking tape to an area or a part, be certain that the area or part is *clean* and *dry*. If the car has just been washed, check to be sure that the areas around small parts have thoroughly dried. *Masking tape will not stick to even slightly damp surfaces.*

One sign of a good overall paint job is when the *rubber weatherstrip* around the doors and deck lid has been masked off. The paint job's quality looks much better when there is good, black rubber weatherstripping seen around the door jambs and deck lid opening. However, masking tape will not readily stick to rubber weatherstrip. To help the tape stick, then, apply *clear lacquer* to the weatherstrip with a rag, as in Fig. 24-25. Allow the lacquer to dry on the weatherstrip. Then, the tape will readily stick to the weatherstrip.

Basic Procedure—When masking tape and masking paper are applied, there are two basic "ground rules" to follow. The *first* of these, Fig. 24-26, is that masking tape should be applied

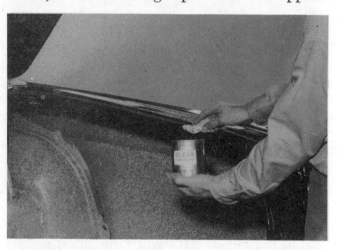

Fig. 24-25. To help masking tape stick to rubber weatherstrip, first apply clear lacquer to the weatherstrip and allow the lacquer to dry thoroughly. (Courtesy of 3M Company, Automotive Division.)

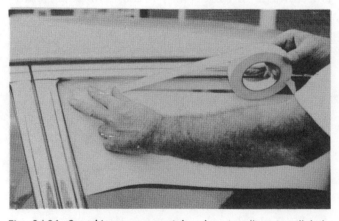

Fig. 24-26. Stretching tape out tight when installing it will help form a smooth, "clean" masking job.

firmly and stretched tightly as it is put in place. This is important if the paint is not to "creep" under the edges of the tape. Be certain that the tape goes *all the way* to the edge of the trim or piece it is protecting.

The *second* basic "ground rule" of masking is to *tear* the tape correctly when the tape needs to be torn off. Fig. 24-27 shows how this is done. Use your thumbnail to cut the tape while quickly pulling up on the roll. The key to properly cutting the tape is to cut or tear it *without* stretching or mangling the tape in the process. Correctly tearing the tape will help insure good, "clean" masking jobs.

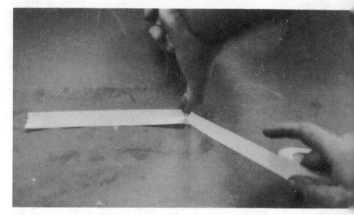

Fig. 24-27. To correctly cut masking tape, quickly tear it off by using the edge of your thumbnail as a cutter and quickly snapping up the roll of tape.

Masking Glass—Glass should be masked carefully to prevent any overspray from reaching the glass itself. Common 15-inch wide masking paper is wide enough and flexible enough to make masking glass an easy job. In Fig. 24-28, two widths of 15-inch masking paper have been overlapped to cover a windshield. Normally, two 15-inch widths are wide enough to protect even the largest windshields.

To install the paper, first use masking tape *alone* to tape along the very top and edges of the window moldings. The tape must be pressed down firmly along the outer edge of the molding. Then, use two pieces of masking paper to cover the upper and lower halves of the windshield. The tape on the *edge* of the paper should overlap the tape just placed on the molding. The top piece of masking paper should overlap the bottom piece of paper. This

Fig. 24-28. Correctly masked windows. Note that the top piece of masking paper on the windshield overlaps the bottom piece. (Courtesy of 3M Company, Automotive Division.)

helps to protect the glass from water and dust seepage. If need be, *fold and tape* any pleats in the paper so that sanding dust cannot collect in the pleats before painting.

Masking Antennas and Wiper Blades—To mask these small parts, first mask the very *base* of the part (where it meets the paint) with regular, ¾-inch masking tape. Then, wiper blades are usually removed before painting, since it is easier to remove the blades and arms from their shafts than it is to mask them. When the blades and arms have been removed, the small wiper shafts may then be taped with regular masking tape.

To mask antennas, an easy method is to place one ¾-inch width on one side of the antenna and another width on the other side, along the entire length of the antenna. Then, the two widths may be pinched together along the opposite sides of the antenna.

Masking Lights—Smaller widths of masking paper (3 to 6-inch widths, if available) generally work best around large lights such as headlights and taillights. Fig. 24-29 shows a typical masking job on a taillight assembly. Using smaller masking paper on these jobs makes the jobs easier because the papers are very flexible. They can be cut, folded, and worked around before being held down with ¾-inch masking tape.

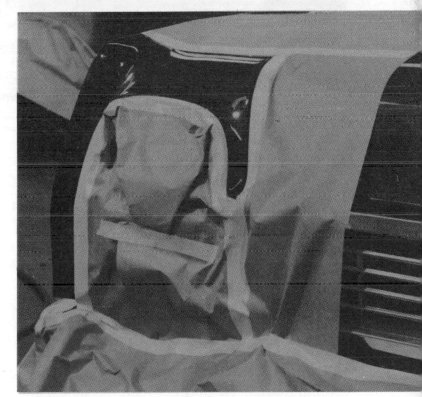

Fig. 24-29. Smaller widths of masking paper may be used to mask off light assemblies. (Courtesy of 3M Company, Automotive Division.)

Masking Door Jambs—Masking door jambs must be done carefully to avoid getting any paint on the car's interior. A 6-inch wide masking apron with ¾-inch masking tape is

Fig. 24-30. A door jamb partially masked for painting. Note that the striker bolt and door lock assembly have also been masked, a good sign of quality masking. (Courtesy of 3M Company, Automotive Division.)

Fig. 24-31. Very narrow masking tape is available to mask small trim and lettering. This job must be done very carefully, preferably by using a pocket knife to work the tape down into the small openings. If at all possible, it is better to remove very small trim and emblems than to take the time to mask them. (Courtesy of 3M Company, Automotive Division.)

usually wide enough to prevent overspray on the car's interior, when used as shown in Fig. 24-30. (Since the door jambs are sprayed at "close range," the entire interior does not need to be covered.) Before taping the rubber weatherstripping on the door, a thin coat of clear lacquer should be applied to the weatherstripping, as discussed earlier.

Masking Small Trim and Lettering—One sure sign of a first-class painter is the way that he tapes small trim and lettering on an automobile. Because these are difficult to mask, they are often *removed* during metal or paint preparation. However, if the job does not call for a good deal of metal work, it may be more economical to mask these small pieces. By masking these pieces, the possibility of *breaking* them when removing them is eliminated.

In Fig. 24-31, small lettering is being masked. This job, of course, can be more easily done

with narrow, ¼-inch wide masking tape. This tape is also very flexible and can be worked into small cracks. When applying this tape to small trim or lettering, care must be taken to press the tape down tightly on the edges of the trim. Often, painters use a pocket knife to work the sides of the tape in place on the edges of small trim.

Masking along Natural Breaks—Whenever only *part* of the car or *part* of one panel is to be refinished, the area to be painted should be masked along *natural breaks*. These breaks may be at the top of a fender at a sharp bend, at the edge of a door, or at the edges of moldings, for example. By masking along natural breaks, it is more difficult to tell that only part of the car or only part of a panel has been repainted.

In Fig. 24-32, note that the very top of the quarter panel (near the rear window) is *not* to be repainted. Instead, only the top of the quarter panel's *side* is to be repainted. Therefore, the area has been masked off along the sharp natural break at the top of the quarter panel. After the refinish work has been done, it will be difficult to see where the new paint stops because the line between the new paint and the old will be along the sharp natural break at the top of the quarter panel.

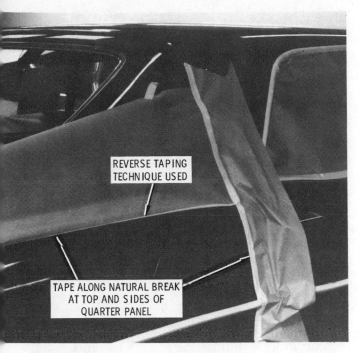

Fig. 24-32. Taping along the natural breaks of a quarter panel. In this example, the *reverse taping* procedure was used at the top crown (natural break) of the quarter panel. (Courtesy of 3M Company, Automotive Division.)

Reverse Taping—One method of reducing the definition line (the line between the old paint and the new paint) is by using the *reverse taping technique*. Reverse taping was used along the upper edge of the quarter panel (the natural break) in Fig. 24-32. Another advantage of reverse taping is that it reduces the chances of paint *bleed-through* along the edge of the masking job closest to the new paint. This is the area of the masking that gets saturated (soaked) with new paint when the paint is sprayed on the repair area.

To use the reverse taping technique, first apply the masking tape and paper *over the area to be painted.* See Fig. 24-33. Then, fold the paper (and the tape stuck to the paper) *back,*

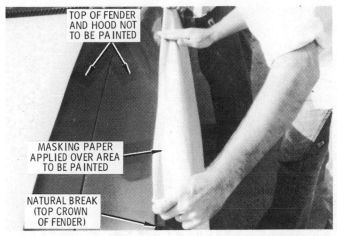

Fig. 24-33. *Step 1;* Reverse Taping. Place the masking paper over *the area to be painted* and tape the masking paper in place along the definition line.

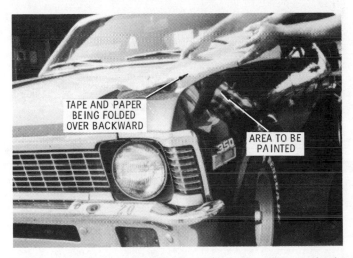

Fig. 24-34. *Step 2;* Reverse taping. Fold the paper and tape *back,* over the area to be protected. Make the fold neatly along the definition line. In this case, the definition line (the line between the old paint and the new) will be the natural break at the top of the front fender.

over the area to be protected. See Fig. 24-34. After the paper and tape is folded back, hold it back in the folded position with several small pieces of masking tape.

Unit 25

Automotive Paint and Paint Products

Fig. 25-1. A typical automotive paint; high-quality acrylic enamel. (Courtesy of Acme Quality Paints.)

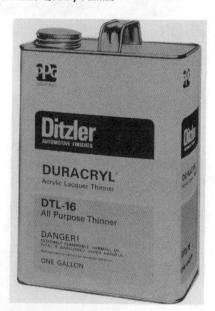

Fig. 25-2. A typical automotive paint product; lacquer thinner. (Courtesy of Ditzler Automotive Finishes Division.)

There are many different types and brands of automotive paints (Fig. 25-1) and paint products (Fig. 25-2). Several different product companies market good, complete lines of automobile paint materials. Usually, a body shop will use one company's line of products and get to know that company's local salesman. Then, he will be able to help the shop with any new paint products or problems that come up. Most paint company salesmen will also be able to provide the shop with specific literature and instructions on his company's line of products.

PAINT INGREDIENTS

Although automobile paints may seem very different, they all have basic ingredients. Actually, the word *paint* is a broad term. It is used to describe many different finishing materials with many different properties and uses. Such terms as lacquers, enamels, primers, sealers, putties, etc., all apply to some form of *paint*. Because they are all paints, *they all have several ingredients in common*.

In other words, no matter what the product is, *if it is a paint, it contains at least these three basic ingredients.* See Fig. 25-3.

1. Pigments
2. A Binder
3. A Vehicle

410

Fig. 25-3. All automotive paint contains three basic ingredients; *pigments* for color, a *binder* to hold the pigments together and to the car's surface, and a *vehicle* to make the pigment and binder mixture more liquid and easier to spray. (Courtesy of Refinish Division, Dupont Company.)

These ingredients (pigments, binders, vehicles) are found in all paints. Of course, there are different kinds of pigments, binders, and vehicles. Which *kind* of each ingredient and *how much* of each ingredient is used is what makes paints different.

Each of the ingredients has a different "job" to do for the final paint product. If the ingredient does not do its job properly, the paint may fail soon after it is sprayed, or it may cause trouble during spraying. It is a good idea, then, to understand what each ingredient is and what it does for the paint.

Pigments

Pigments are the paint ingredient that gives the paint its *color*. By themselves, pigments are dry and powdery; black pigments look like pure black coal dust, for example, whereas white pigments look like ordinary kitchen flour. Of course, there are many different colors of pigment, and the color of a paint depends on what color *pigment* is in the paint.

Some paints have very, very fine pieces of aluminum *metal* mixed up with the pigments. These small pieces of metal give the paint a "sugary" look, as if it was sprinkled with fine silver chips. These paints are called *metallic* paints and are discussed in detail later in the unit.

Binder

The second main ingredient of all paints is a binder. The binder is the paint ingredient that actually *sticks* the pigment to the car's surface. Without a binder, the pigments could be brushed off the car's surface like dust! Therefore, the binder is a very important part of the paint.

By itself, binder is clear or amber-colored, like very light syrup. Only when the pigment is added to the binder does the binder have any real color. The binder then, does not provide any color. Instead, it provides the "stick" to hold the color pigment to the surface.

There are thousands of different paint binders. At the present time, one of the more popular binders being used in paint is a type of plastic known as *acrylic*. From this binder, for example, comes the name acrylic enamel, such as the product shown in Fig. 25-1.

Vehicle

The third main ingredient in *wet* paint, ready to spray, is the *vehicle*. The vehicle's job is to allow the paint to be sprayed on the car's surface. Just as a vehicle (car, truck, etc.) moves people along a road, the *vehicle* in paint allows the paint to be moved from the spray gun to the car's surface. Without a vehicle, the combination of pigment and binder would be much too thick to spray; it would be like trying to spray thick syrup.

After the paint has been applied, however, the vehicle evaporates and leaves only the binder and pigment on the surface. This, then, is what happens as a paint job dries; the vehicle evaporates. If some vehicle is still present in fresh paint, we say that the paint is "wet" and it is sticky to the touch.

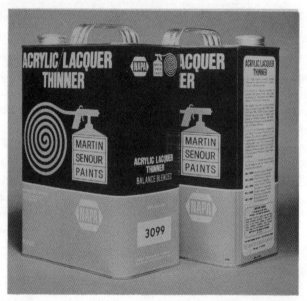

Fig. 25-4. A typical paint vehicle for *lacquer* paints; lacquer thinner. (Courtesy of The Martin Senour Company.)

Some vehicle is put into the paint when the paint is manufactured. However, *more* vehicle must be put into the paint before it is sprayed. This additional vehicle is known as either a *thinner* (for lacquer paints) or a *reducer* (for enamel paints). See Figs. 25-4 and 25-5. Both thinners and reducers are vehicles; they have different names because they are slightly different and the different names help keep them separate in the shop's paint department.

There are many different paint vehicles on the market. Each paint product company offers several different vehicles for both lacquer and enamel paints. Although all the vehicles on the market are different, there are only two *main* differences between any two vehicles:

1. How fast they *evaporate* (the *evaporation rate*).
2. How much they dissolve and thin the *binder* in the paint.

Because of these differences, it is very important that *only the vehicle recommended by the paint manufacturer be used for a given job.* Again, this is why many shops choose one paint manufacturer's products and then use those products with the help of that company's salesman. In any case, there are a few general rules about the different kinds of vehicles (thinners and reducers) that are available.

Fig. 25-5. A typical paint vehicle for *enamel* paints; enamel reducer. (Courtesy, Rinshed-Mason Products Division of Inmont Corporation.)

Thinners—Special paint vehicles known as *thinners* are to be used with lacquer paint. For this reason, these products are usually known as *lacquer thinners.*

Lacquer thinners from different manufacturers will have different numbers and different names, but they are all basically classified according to *how fast they evaporate.* Which thinner to use depends on the shop conditions where the painting will be done. Generally speaking, if the shop has a *higher* temperature, the evaporation rate of the thinner should be slower. Therefore, if the shop is fairly hot (over about 75°F), a *slow dry* thinner should be used. For average shop temperatures (about 68°-74°), a *medium dry* thinner should be used. Finally, if the shop is cold (67° or below), only a *fast dry* thinner should be used.

To properly mix lacquer and thinner for spraying, *first* read the manufacturer's directions for the products being used. See Fig. 25-6.

Fig. 25-6. Before using any paint or paint product, *read the manufacturer's directions on the product container.* (Courtesy, Rinshed-Mason Products Division of Inmont Corporation.)

Then, mix the lacquer and the *correct* thinner for the shop conditions. Usually, 1 part lacquer is mixed with about 1 to 1½ parts thinner. Any lacquer thinner should be thoroughly mixed in a container *outside* the paint gun cup before the mixture is filtered into the cup. See Fig. 25-7.

Reducers—Special paint vehicles known as *reducers* are to be used with *enamel* paint. For this reason, these products are often known as *enamel reducers.*

Like thinners, reducers from different paint companies will have different names and product numbers. Again, however, they are all basically classified according to how fast they evaporate; their *evaporation rate.* Slow-drying (slowly evaporating) reducers should be used when spraying enamel in a hot shop, whereas fast-dry reducers (those that evaporate quickly) should be used in a cold shop.

Enamel paints and reducers are mixed in very different proportions (amounts) than are lac-

Fig. 25-7. Straining (filtering) a mixture of lacquer and lacquer thinner into a paint gun cup. (Courtesy of Refinish Division, DuPont Company.)

quers and thinners. Where lacquer may be mixed at a ratio of 1 part lacquer to 1 or 1½ parts thinner, enamel is mixed at *2 to 4 parts* enamel to *1 part* reducer. Again, the exact amount varies according to the products used and the shop condition. It is *especially* true for enamels, then, that the manufacturer's recommendations be followed for the line of products being used.

TYPES OF PAINT

As discussed above under *Paint Vehicles,* there are two basic types of automobile paint: *lacquer* and *enamel. Any automobile paint is basically an enamel or a lacquer.* At times, other words such as nitrocellulose, acrylic, alkyd, polyurethane, etc., are used to describe automobile paints. However, these products are *still,* basically, lacquer or enamel paints. They have been made differently or with different additives or other properties so that they are slightly different. See Figs. 25-8 and 25-9.

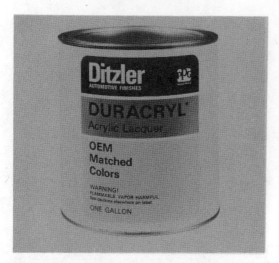

Fig. 25-8. Typical automotive lacquer. This product is acrylic lacquer. (Courtesy of Ditzler Automotive Finishes Division.)

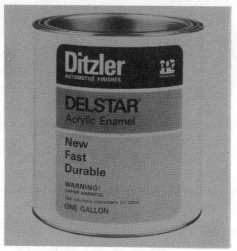

Fig. 25-9. Typical automotive enamel. This product is acrylic enamel. (Courtesy of Ditzler Automotive Finishes Division.)

The main difference between lacquers and enamels is how the paint film is formed *after* the paint has been sprayed. In other words, what happens to the wet paint; how it "dries" to form a smooth, hard film on the car's surface. The answer to this question is the difference between enamel and lacquer paints.

In *lacquer* paints, the film is formed *only* by the vehicle (the thinner) evaporating. Because only the vehicle (thinner) evaporates, the lacquer film and pigments left on the surface remain *soluble*. That is, if they are touched with thinner, they will again dissolve.

In *enamel* paints, however, not only does the vehicle (the reducer) evaporate, but the *binder*

gradually oxidizes as the paint dries. This means that part of the binder materials combine with the oxygen in the air, producing a hard, tough paint and film.

Because of their different properties, lacquer paints and lacquer products should not be mixed with enamel paints and enamel products. They would not mix or spray correctly, and would cause many paint problems. A good painter must understand the differences between lacquers and enamels *and* the differences between the different types of lacquers and enamels.

Lacquers

The first modern automotive paints to be used on new cars were *lacquers*. Since the earliest lacquers were developed in the 1920's, almost all new General Motors automobiles have been painted with lacquer at the factory. At the factory, the lacquer is usually baked at a *very* high temperature, sanded, and then baked again. The baking forces the lacquer to "flow out" and achieve full gloss.

To bake lacquer at a high enough temperature to make it flow out, a large amount of thinner and extreme heat are used in the factory process. The heat used at the factory is applied *before* the body's rubber, glass, and plastic parts are installed. In an auto body shop, it is not possible to bake lacquer at very high temperatures to make it flow out, because the car's glass, rubber, and plastic parts would be damaged.

In a body shop, then, lacquer paint must be compounded and polished to make it shine, because it dries without full gloss. This is known as "rubbing out" the lacquer. If lacquer paint is sprayed and then left on the car without "rubbing it out," the finish will look dull, as if the paint is bad.

The main *advantage* of lacquer paint in body shop use is the fact that it dries quickly. For this reason, lacquer paint is not as likely to dry with dirt or dust in it as is enamel. Lacquer, then, can be sprayed in conditions that are not as good as are required for enamel. Because lacquer dries quicker and does not require such clean working conditions, jobs finished with lacquer can be more quickly finished and moved out of the shop.

The main *disadvantage* of lacquer is that it must be compounded to full gloss after it has dried. This requires additional shop time and materials to complete each job, adding to the cost of making repairs with lacquer paint. Since enamel dries to a full gloss, no additional shop time or materials are needed to finish a job that has been painted with enamel.

Another disadvantage of lacquer is that it does not hide very small chips, nicks, and sand-scratches as well as does enamel. Enamels may "flow out" to partially cover such imperfections where lacquer on the same job would not. Finally, many painters feel that lacquer is not as "tough" as enamel, that lacquer is more likely to chip when hit by stones or gravel thrown up along the road. Newer lacquers, however, are "tougher" than older ones, so this tendency to chip has been reduced.

Types of Lacquer—There are two basic *types* of lacquer, depending on certain ingredients in the lacquer's *binder*. The two types of lacquer are *nitrocellulose* and *acrylic*. Because these lacquers have different qualities, it is important to know their differences and to *not* mix the two products.

Nitrocellulose lacquer was the first lacquer developed. It was used on most new General Motors cars from the 1920's until the late 1950's. Many painters refer to nitrocellulose lacquer as "old style" lacquer. One of the best-known nitrocellulose lacquers was *DuPont Duco* lacquer.

Only a few paint companies still manufacture nitrocellulose lacquer, and it is not very often used during body and paint repair today. For custom and restoration work on special cars, a few customers may prefer "old style" lacquer. In these cases, either the painter or the customer may need to search for some time to find a stock of nitrocellulose lacquer.

The newer, and most widely known and used, lacquer paints are *acrylic* lacquers. Acrylic lacquer was developed after WW II and, by 1959, all new General Motors cars were painted at the factory with acrylic lacquer. This product sprays on easily, dries fast, and blends

well with the original finish, even if the original finish was acrylic enamel. Properly cared for, acrylic lacquer will last for years without fading. Fig. 25-10 shows a typical can of acrylic lacquer.

Fig. 25-10. One manufacturer's acrylic lacquer paint. (Courtesy of The Martin-Senour Company.)

A common *advantage* of acrylic lacquer is that it can be bought locally in small quantities. This helps keep down the cost of repairs and reduces the paint stock needed by the shop. It is ideal for small touch-up jobs on either lacquer or *new car* enamel finishes. A very small brush may be used to touch up the small nicks or chips. Fig. 25-11 shows a touch-

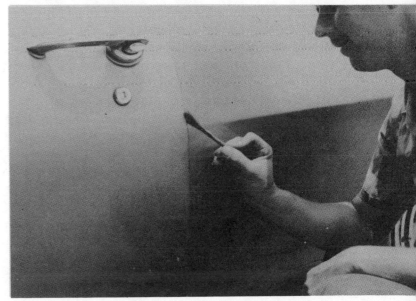

Fig. 25-11. Using a small touch-up brush to repair a door nick.

up job being done with acrylic lacquer. On factory-baked acrylic enamel paint, acrylic lacquer may be used for either spot repair (repainting a small area) or touch-up work.

The main *disadvantage* of acrylic lacquer is that it requires more coats than enamel to get the desired finish. This is because the finish must be compounded, and compounding removes some of the color (top) coat. To compound a complete car, for example, up to five hours is required *in addition to* the spraying time. This time must be added to the cost of the acrylic lacquer paint job, making the completed job more expensive.

Enamels

Enamel paints were developed during the 1930's. Since that time, most new cars and almost all new trucks have been painted at the factory with some type of enamel paint. This includes most foreign cars. Enamel paint is strong and durable. Properly applied, it will flow out to a high gloss and flow over very small imperfections that might otherwise show if the panel were painted with lacquer.

In automobile factories where enamel is used, the enamel is also baked on at a very high temperature, similar to lacquer. The temperature used to bake and flow out enamel, however, is not as great as the temperature used to bake and flow out lacquer. Even so, the factory bake-on temperature for enamel is too high to use in a body shop because it might damage glass, plastic, and rubber parts. As with lacquer, then, the enamel paints used in a body shop cannot be identical to the paints used in an automobile factory.

The main *advantage* of enamel paint is that it dries to a high gloss and does not need to be compounded. In fact, fresh enamel paint (less than 30 days old) must *not* be compounded or polished or the finish will be damaged. Other advantages of enamel include the fact that it covers small imperfections fairly well and the fact that good enamel paint is very durable and chip resistant.

For body shop work, the main *disadvantage* of enamel paints is that they are slow to dry when compared with lacquers. Because enamels are slow to dry, they are more likely to have dust or dirt settle in the wet paint while they are drying. This means that the shop and paint room conditions must be much cleaner when enamel paint is to be applied.

Because enamels must "flow out" and dry to a glossy finish, *how* the enamel is sprayed becomes very important. Generally speaking, more skill is needed to spray enamel than to spray lacquer. Even so, most enamel finishes have a slight amount of *orange peel* after they dry. This is a slight texture (appearance) like the surface of an orange. *Too much* orange peel in either lacquer *or* enamel is a paint defect. A *small amount* of orange peel is to be expected in all enamel finishes. For this reason, a good enamel finish may not be quite as slick and glossy as a carefully rubbed and polished lacquer finish.

Types of Enamel—There are *three basic types* of enamel paint in use today: alkyd, acrylic, and *polyurethane*. Each of them is used on some new cars and trucks throughout the world, depending on the manufacturer. Because of this, it is very important that a painter understand the different types of enamels, since all of them are in use today.

The first enamels, developed in the 1930's, were known as *alkyd* enamels. Alkyd enamels are still in use today. They are widely used in automotive refinishing work and are used on several new trucks, buses, and foreign cars. Because alkyd enamel was the original enamel, many painters refer to alkyd enamel as "old style" enamel. Fig. 25-12 shows one manufacturer's alkyd enamel product.

Fig. 25-12. One brand of alkyd enamel. (Courtesy of Acme Quality Paints.)

Alkyd enamels are widely used for overall refinishing repair work. Their *advantages* are speed of application, the ability to cover well, and the fact that they can be easily applied over other types of finishes. For example, preparing a surface for alkyd enamel may be done with sandpaper that is not as fine as for other types of paint; this makes the job faster. For this reason, alkyd enamel is often used to refinish used cars. The speed with which the job may be done and the fact that it does not need to be compounded make alkyd enamel refinishing popular for low-price work.

Very small scratches or chips are more easily covered with alkyd enamel paint than with either lacquer or acrylic enamel. If the paint on a vehicle is in fairly good condition, alkyd enamel may be used *after* the paint on the vehicle has been sanded with at least #240 wet sandpaper, preferably #320 wet. Then, the old paint would be sealed with enamel sealer before the alkyd enamel is applied.

The main *disadvantage* of alkyd enamel is its' slow drying time. This causes problems with dirt and dust getting into the paint before it is dry. If a defect (run, etc.) happens while spraying alkyd enamel, either the panel must be washed off and resprayed immediately or the painter must wait several hours for the paint to dry before correcting the problem. There is also a disadvantage if there is too much *orange peel* in the dried enamel. Finally, the slow drying time means that each paint job will require more time in the paint shop.

The most popular enamel in use today is *acrylic* enamel, Fig. 25-13. Almost all new trucks are finished in acrylic enamel. Many new foreign cars and the cars made by American Motors Corporation, Chrysler Corporation, and the Ford Motor Company are finished in acrylic enamel at the factory. Under factory conditions, of course, the acrylic enamel is baked on at very high temperatures so that it will flow out to a smooth, glossy finish.

The special ingredient in acrylic enamel paint is the transparent, thermoplastic resin known as *acrylic*. This acrylic is mixed into the *binder* part of the acrylic paint mixture. Because of this, there are special acrylic enamel

paint *products* (such as acrylic enamel reducers, Fig. 25-14), that are made to be used with acrylic enamel paints. For the best results with acrylic enamel paints, *as with any other paints,* only products recommended for use with the paint being used should be mixed with the paint.

The main *advantage* of acrylic enamels is that they are fast drying. Properly applied,

Fig. 25-13. One brand of acrylic enamel. (Courtesy of The Martin Senour Company.)

Fig. 25-14. Acrylic enamel reducer. This product should only be used with acrylic enamel. (Courtesy of The Martin Senour Company.)

they will dry to a beautiful, like-new look with almost no orange peel. Most acrylic enamels will dry fairly well in about 30 minutes. This helps eliminate long hours of drying time with the danger of dust and dirt settling on the wet paint. Because of this faster drying time, many more enamel paint jobs can go through a paint repair shop than if only alkyd enamel was used.

Acrylic enamel paint may be oven-dried in the shop. Or, it may be air-dried in an ordinary refinishing booth. Either way, properly-applied acrylic enamel will dry with a high, glossy shine.

Although acrylic enamel will normally dry with a high gloss, it *may* be compounded with rubbing compound to make it even smoother. This will also help eliminate the orange peel present in all enamel refinishing. Compounding can be a real advantage when correcting paint defects since it is much faster than sanding and repainting the defect. Under normal conditions, of course, compounding acrylic enamel is *not* necessary unless an even smoother finish is desired. For the best results, acrylic enamel should not be compounded until 30 days after it is applied.

Acrylic enamel blends well with original paint, especially original acrylic enamel. For this reason, acrylic enamel is the *best* enamel to use for making any spot repairs. This will usually allow a spot repair to be made on a panel without repainting the entire panel.

The main *disadvantage* of acrylic enamel is that it should *not* be recoated during the week after it was sprayed. After it has cured about six hours, there must be a waiting period of about one *week* before the vehicle can be recoated. If, for some reason, the job *must* be recoated during this week, *first* spray two coats of acrylic enamel recoat sealer on the job. Then, allow a one-hour drying time for the sealer *before* spraying the second acrylic color coat. Even so, this quick recoating method should be avoided whenever possible, since it may reduce the life of the paint job.

The third, and newest, type of enamel paint is known as *polyurethane* enamel paint. This type of enamel is a mixture of alkyd enamel and a clear epoxy activator. The basic color

portion (pigment) is the same as in the older alkyd enamel. The clear *epoxy* portion, however, contains additives to chemically activate the paint and cause the top film of the paint to become hard and durable. See Fig. 25-15.

Fig. 25-15. One manufacturer's brand of polyurethane enamel. (Courtesy of Refinish Division, DuPont Company.)

Polyurethane enamel has high gloss with good toughness and color retention. It also has the good chip resistance that is present in other enamel paints. Polyurethane enamel topcoats also have the so-called *wet look* of having been freshly painted for several months after they are applied.

A major *advantage* of polyurethane enamel over other enamels is its very short drying time. This means that the vehicle being painted can be delivered sooner than when working with other enamels. Some polyurethane enamels are designed to dry so quickly that they may be sprayed "on location" and will dry dust-free in minutes. This may be needed for off-road equipment such as construction trucks, bulldozers, etc. These can be painted with polyurethane enamel without having to be brought into a shop. Because of this, polyurethane enamel is popular for truck fleets, buses, construction equipment, aircraft, and boats.

A *disadvantage* of polyurethane enamel is that it is mixed differently than other enamels. Therefore, a painter must learn a new procedure to properly apply polyurethane enamel. When purchased, polyurethane enamel comes in two parts; alkyd enamel and the clear epoxy activator. The products must then be mixed by combining about 3 parts alkyd to 1 part epoxy, or according to the manufacturer's directions. As long as these products are properly mixed, polyurethane paint mixture may be sprayed full strength. No reducer is needed. However, *retarder* may be added to slow the polyurethane's drying time.

UNDERCOATS

The normal color paint (topcoat) seen on an automobile will not properly stick to bare metal. This is because properly-prepared bare metal is too smooth for the paint to grip the metal. If the metal was made rough enough so that the color could grip the metal, the finish would not be as slick and shiny as is desired.

For the color topcoat to be smooth and shiny *and* properly adhere (stick) to the material under the color, some type of *undercoat* must be used under the topcoat. Any undercoat, then, must do *two* jobs. It must firmly grip the surface on which it is applied (the *substrate*) *and* it must provide a good gripping surface for the topcoat. *Some* undercoats are also used to fill small imperfections, but not all undercoats do this.

Substrate—When an automobile body (or part of it) is painted, paint may need to be applied to many different types of surfaces. For example, part of a repaired surface may be bare metal while another part of the same surface would be plastic filler. Whatever the paint will be applied *to*, then, is known as the *substrate*. If the area is bare metal, then the substrate is bare metal. If the area is a combination of old paint, filler and bare metal, then we say that the substrate is a combination of old paint, filler, and bare metal.

When the body work has all been done, then, or when the old paint has been properly prepared, the smooth prepared area is known as the *substrate*. If the substrate is not properly prepared, there will likely be paint trouble during the paint work.

Some type of undercoat is nearly always applied to a substrate before the color coat (topcoat) is applied. One type of undercoat, *sealer,* is applied directly over the substrate *if the sub-strate is entirely old paint that is not cracked.* It is best to plan on using *some* type of undercoat under *all* topcoats, if this can be done without making the total paint film too thick.

There are four basic types of undercoats: primer, primer-surfacer, putty, and sealer. Although they are all undercoats, each is used for a different reason. *Primers* are used mainly to provide good adhesion for the topcoat, add to the topcoat's durability, and protect any bare metal from rust. *Primer-surfacers* do everything that primers do *and* fill small imperfections (such as sandscratches) in the substrate. *Putties* are used to fill any small nicks noticed in either primer or primer-surfacer. Finally, *sealers* are used to seal a substrate that may be a different type of paint than the topcoat to be applied.

Primer

Paint *primer* is normally used on all metals during new or replacement panel preparation. This includes galvanized metal, aluminum, and other alloy metals. Good production primers, properly applied on correctly prepared surfaces, do not normally require sanding. This is because primer is applied in thin coats and does not contain too many solids in the pigment. If any defects appear in the primer, however, they may be sanded with *fine* sandpaper.

Primers may be thought of as the filling in a sandwich, the part that holds the two pieces of bread together. See Fig. 25-16. One slice of bread is the substrate and the other slice of bread is the topcoat. Using a primer, especially on smooth, bare metal, will provide good topcoat adhesion.

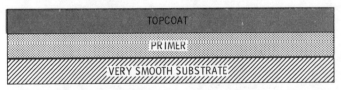

Fig. 25-16. Primer acts as the filling in the "sandwich" of a smooth substrate, primer, and topcoat.

Advantages—Good primers spread smoothly and adhere well to bare metal. Other properties of good primers are that they help prevent rust and help give the topcoat a full, rich, smooth appearance.

Disadvantages—Primers have several disadvantages. They are not good for use on rough surfaces because they have poor filling qualities.

For this reason, few shops use straight primers during repair work. Instead, primer-surfacers are more often used.

Types of Primers—Like other paints, different types of primers are available. The two common types of primers, enamel and lacquer, are those most often used in shops that use straight primers. While lacquer primer dries quicker, many painters feel that enamel primer is more durable. Either of these primers may need a light scuffing with #400 paper or steel wool to remove any *nibs* (small particles of dirt) on the primer before the topcoat is applied.

Special primers known as *zinc-chromate* and *vinyl wash* are also available. *Zinc-chromate* primer, for example, is used to protect steel and aluminum against heavy rusting and corrosion. It may also be used to prime aluminum truck bodies to insure good topcoat adhesion to the aluminum.

Vinyl wash primer, on the other hand, is used on either galvanized metal or aluminum alloy bodies to insure good topcoat adhesion. It is difficult to make topcoat colors stick to galvanized metal. For this reason, the proper use of a vinyl wash primer is very important when galvanized metal bodies are to be painted.

Primer-Surfacer

The most popular undercoat products used in body shops are *primer-surfacers*. These products are popular because they do both the job of a primer *and* they fill small imperfections and rough places in the prepared substrate. There are many different types, brands, and colors of primer-surfacers. Fig. 25-17 shows a primer-surfacer from one company, whereas Fig. 25-18 shows several primer-surfacers from different paint companies.

Fig. 25-18. Several primer-surfacer products.

Primer-surfacers may be used on bare steel, bare steel and filler, or old finishes; almost any type of clean, properly prepared substrate. In Fig. 25-19, for example, black lacquer primer-surfacer is being applied to a substrate of old paint, bare metal, and filler. This will help fill

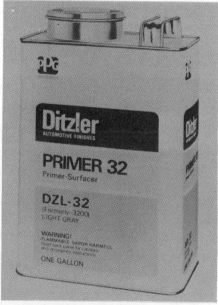

Fig. 25-17. One manufacturer's primer-surfacer. Primer-surfacers are available in either enamel or lacquer and in many different colors. (Courtesy of Ditzler Automotive Finishes Division.)

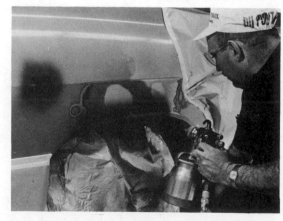

Fig. 25-19. Applying primer-surfacer to several different substrates. (Courtesy of Refinish Division, DuPont Company.)

and level the repair area, giving the topcoat a smooth, even undercoat on which to rest.

Advantages—There are many reasons why good primer-surfacers are popular body shop undercoats. They are good for use on slightly rough surfaces, since they will fill well and are easy to sand. The surfacer parts of primer-surfacers provide sanding ease because they do not dry gummy, as primers may do, and they have a high content of solids.

Both primers and primer-surfacers provide a good surface for topcoat adhesion, of course, but primer-surfacers fill better. They are able to fill small scratches, pinholes, nicks, etc. as in Fig. 25-20. However, primer-surfacers do not completely flow out over any nicks, etc.; primer surfacers *must be sanded* to provide the smoothest possible surface for quality topcoats.

Fig. 25-20. A primer-surfacer will fill small flaws such as nicks in the substrate. (Courtesy of Refinish Division, DuPont Company.)

Fig. 25-21 shows the qualities of a good primer-surfacer. It must resist settling into its separate parts, since this would cause it to not spread out uniformly. A good primer-surfacer must also have a good *sealing* quality. This gives the topcoat a full, rich appearance and

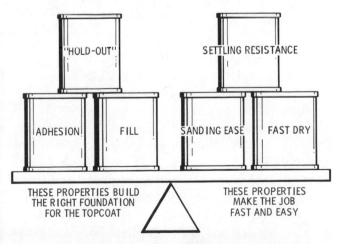

Fig. 25-21. A good primer-surfacer must have a balance of many properties since it does several different jobs. (Courtesy of Refinish Division, DuPont Company.)

helps prevent it from sinking into the primer-surfacer.

Even *alkyd enamel* primer-surfacers dry faster than do alkyd enamel topcoats, so all primer-surfacers speed up refinishing work. *Lacquer* primer-surfacers, of course, provide the fastest drying time and are the most popular of all primer-surfacers. However, enamel primer–surfacers should be used on large areas, when time permits, because enamel primer-surfacers generally have better flexibility and corrosion resistance than do lacquer primer-surfacers.

Disadvantages—One of the *disadvantages* of primer-surfacers is that they cannot adhere (stick) well to bare aluminum or galvanized metal. This is because of the chemicals in those metals. For this reason, it is best to use a vinyl wash primer, discussed earlier, on these types of metals.

The other main disadvantage of primer-surfacers is that they do not dry smooth. Instead, they dry to produce a thick, slightly rough film. For this reason, they *should* be sanded smooth before applying the topcoat. However, for commercial work (trucks, etc.) some enamel primer-surfacers are sold that dry smooth enough to not require sanding. Not sanding these primer-surfaces is only recommended for commercial work where speed and durability are more important than final gloss.

Types of Primer-Surfacers—There are two basic types of primer-surfacers: *lacquer* and *enamel*. Each type has its own advantages and disadvantages. For quality paint work, it is important that painters and body men know the differences between the two types, and when each type should be used. Generally speaking, lacquer primer-surfacers may be used over either type of old paint and *under* either type of topcoat. The same is true of enamel primer-surfacer *with one important exception:* enamel primer-surfacer must *not* be "sandwiched" between an old lacquer topcoat and a new lacquer topcoat. If this is done, the topcoat may lift after it has been applied.

Almost all spot repair work in body shops today is "primed" with *lacquer* primer-surfacer. It has many good qualities. The first of these is *speed*. Lacquer primer-surfacers are fast drying, making it easy to get repairs done fast. Properly applied, lacquer primer-surfacers are easy to sand. This makes the job of preparing the primer-surfacer much quicker and easier. A good lacquer primer-surfacer is probably one of the most frequently-used paint materials in body shops.

Enamel primer-surfacer, on the other hand, is recommended to "prime and surface" large bare metal areas, or for complete refinishing jobs where the old topcoat has been stripped off completely. Enamel primer-surfacer is generally more durable and flexible than is lacquer primer-surfacer, and offers better rust and corrosion resistance.

The big *disadvantage* of enamel primer-surfacer is that it is much slower drying than lacquer primer-surfacer. Since any primer-surfacer should be sanded to provide a smooth base for a good, glossy topcoat, there is a much longer waiting period before enamel primer-surfacer can be sanded and the job then completed. If *wet sanding* is to be done for the smoothest preparation, enamel primer-surfacer should first be allowed to dry *overnight*. If enamel primer-surfacer is wet-sanded before it is thoroughly dry, moisture may be trapped in the primer-surfacer. This could later cause bubbling or blistering in the color topcoat.

Putty

Putty is thick undercoat *filler*. Most of the time, it is used over primer-surfacers to fill deep imperfections that primer-surfacer cannot fill. See Fig. 25-22. In fact, putty is like very thick primer-surfacer, only in a tube or can. Because putty is very heavy, it cannot be sprayed. Instead, it must be applied with a rubber squeegee, as in Fig. 25-23.

Putty is sold under different names, such as the products shown in Figs. 25-23 and 25-24.

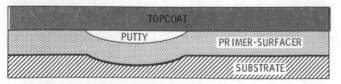

Fig. 25-22. A typical use of body or paint *putty*. (Courtesy of Refinish Division, DuPont Company.)

Fig. 25-23. Putty is applied with a *squeegee*. It cannot be sprayed because it is too thick. (Courtesy of 3M Company, Automotive Division.)

Fig. 25-24. A common tube of putty from one paint company. (Courtesy, Rinshed-Mason Products Division of Inmont Corporation.)

It may be known as spot putty, body putty, or, simply, *putty*. Some companies make one putty for use with lacquer paint and another for use with enamel paint. Good quality putties are fast drying, will sand smoothly, and have good adhesion and color holdout.

Using Putty—To use putty, apply the material with a squeegee over any spots or scratches. (Putty needs only to be applied where it is needed, not necessarily over the entire panel.) Then allow it to dry, one coat at a time. When one coat is dry, another coat can be applied if needed. Two thin coats of putty work better than one thick coat. If putty is spread too thick in one pass, the drying time is slow and the material may crack.

When putty has been applied and has thoroughly dried, it may be prepared for the topcoat in the same way as primer-surfacer. Putty may be wet or dry sanded as needed. Color (topcoat) or sealer (discussed next) may then be applied over any putty repairs.

Sealers

The last group of undercoat products are known as *sealers*. When sealers are used, *they are always used immediately under the topcoat.* They may be used under either lacquer or enamel topcoats. Although they may be used over primers and primer-surfacers, sealers are normally used over old finishes, as in Fig. 25-25.

The main reason for using a sealer is to improve adhesion between the old finish and the new finish. To insure good adhesion, a sealer should *always* be used over an old lacquer finish when the new finish is to be enamel. Under other conditions, a sealer may be desirable but is not absolutely necessary.

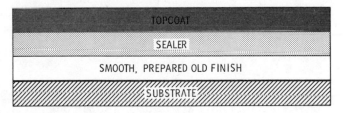

Fig. 25-25. Normally, a *sealer* is used to insure good adhesion between an old topcoat and a new topcoat.

There are three other times when a sealer may be used to "help" the topcoat:

1. To help a light color "hide" a dark color when the car will be repainted a different color or when the primer-surfacer is darker than the color will be.
2. To help reduce sandscratch swelling. See Fig. 25-26.
3. To provide uniform, even "holdout." This prevents the new topcoat from "sinking into" the substrate if the substrate is made up of different types of paint, such as primer-surfacer, old topcoat, etc.

Sealers are often misunderstood in the auto refinishing trade because they are thought of as "cure-alls" that will take care of any bad conditions on an old topcoat. Actually, this is not entirely true. For example, a sealer will *not* fill cracks or low places in an old topcoat and many sealers will not adhere well to bare metal.

Not all sealers will stop an old topcoat color from "bleeding" into a new topcoat color, such as when white is painted over red. Only a few sealers are marketed for this job.

Therefore, *like any other paint product,* sealers must only be used according to the manufacturer's directions and only on the job for which they are intended. Finally, one property of virtually all sealers is the fact that the sealer must not remain on the undercoat too long before the topcoat is applied. Usually, paint manufacturers recommend that the topcoat be applied *within one hour* after the sealer has been applied.

Like other paint products, there are two basic types of sealers: lacquer sealers and enamel sealers. Some sealers are known as *primer-sealers* and may be used over bare metal as both a primer and a sealer. Other sealers are known as *universal sealers* and may be used under any type of topcoat. Because sealer products vary widely from one paint manufacturer to the next, it is best to become familiar with the sealers offered by one manufacturer and then use them for all sealer jobs in the shop.

Using Lacquer Sealer—When a lacquer topcoat will be applied over an old enamel finish, a lacquer sealer *must* be used. If a sealer is not used over the old enamel paint, the new lacquer

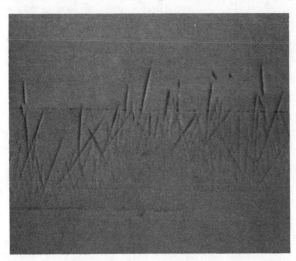

Fig. 25-26. Sandscratch swelling. This is a topcoat problem that may be controlled by using a sealer. Here, a sealer was not used. The solvent in the new topcoat paint softened the edges of these sandscratches in the undercoat. This caused the sandscratches to swell up, thereby producing a paint defect. (Courtesy of Refinish Division, DuPont Company.)

finish may crack or lift after it has been on the car for several months.

Lacquer sealer is not required for good adhesion when new acrylic lacquer is sprayed over old acrylic lacquer. However, using a lacquer sealer would help prevent sandscratch swelling on the areas when the old acrylic lacquer has been repaired. However, if the old lacquer finish is smooth and hard with no sign of cracks or sandscratches, it would usually *not* be necessary to seal the old finish.

Using Enamel Sealer—When enamel is sprayed over enamel, an *enamel sealer* should be used. The enamel sealer will do two jobs. First, it will help guarantee good adhesion between the two enamels.

Second, and most important, the enamel sealer will help seal and hold any dirt and dust *where it is*. This will help keep any small specks of dust in place, so they will not be blown out of cracks, for example, onto new paint. No matter how much an automobile is cleaned, there is always a chance that some dust may be present in joints or cracks in the body. A sealer will help prevent dirty paint by keeping the dust in place while the new paint is applied.

Enamel paint may be applied over a lacquer finish without using a sealer. However, using an enamel sealer *is* recommended when the enamel will be applied over a large area of lacquer paint, such as an overall repaint or a large panel repair.

Another advantage of enamel sealers (and primer-sealers) is that they may be lightly sanded. Therefore, after enamel sealer has been applied, it may be inspected to see if any dirt or nibs appeared on the sealer. If so, they may be lightly scuffed (removed) with #400 dry sandpaper.

TOPCOATS

Whether lacquer or enamel, a vehicle's *topcoat* is the actual paint that provides color and protection for the vehicle. For these reasons, of course, the topcoat is very important in auto body work. Customers usually judge the appearance of the topcoat as a reflection of the entire job, as in Fig. 25-27. Therefore, it is very

Fig. 25-27. Most auto body work is first judged by the appearance of the topcoat. (Courtesy of Refinish Division, DuPont Company.)

important that a painter know about the different types of topcoats and when each type might be used.

How Topcoats are Mixed

Since all topcoats are paints, all topcoat paint *mixes* are either lacquer or enamel. Topcoat *mixes* refer to how the paint is prepared (mixed) by the paint manufacturer or, as discussed later, by the paint dealer. Depending on how the paint will be used, it may be mixed slightly differently, as follows:

1. The number or color of *pigments* may be slightly changed.
2. The amount and type of *vehicle* may be slightly changed.
3. The amount and type of *binder* may be slightly changed.

There are three basic types of topcoats, only two of which are used during auto body repair. When a painter (or the shop) orders paint for a car, it is important that he know about the different types of mixes. Normally, the paint store will ask the painter or shop what type of mix is wanted.

New-Car Mix—The paint sprayed on a new car *at the factory* is known as *new-car mix*. Because new car paint is baked at very high temperatures, it is mixed differently than paint to be used in a body shop. New car mix is usually not available to body shops because even if the shop uses baking equipment, the conditions (spraying and baking) are still not the same as at the factory. For these reasons, painters do not need to know about new-car mix except to understand that it *is* different from the mixes available to a body shop, discussed next.

Factory-Packaged Mix—When a can of color (topcoat) is mixed *at the paint factory* and sold to the painter in a factory-sealed can, it is known as factory-packaged mix, or simply "factory package." When it is available, factory-packaged mix is the best mix to use, especially for spot repairs on late-model cars. Factory-packaged mix is designed to exactly match the color and gloss of baked-on new-car mix. To match the factory's new-car mix, *factory-packaged* mix is carefully designed to work well *under normal body shop conditions*.

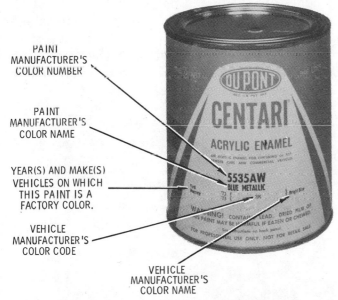

Fig. 25-28. Factory-packaged mix. This paint was mixed, packaged, and sealed at the paint factory.

Factory-packaged mix can always be easily identified because the label is clearly printed, *at the factory*, with the exact color and color number for that paint. See Fig. 25-28. This information usually includes the automobiles on which the color was used, the correct color code for those automobiles, and the paint manufacturer's product number.

Whenever possible, it is a good idea to use factory-packaged color mix. Factory-package color can be used for spot repairs, panel repairs, and overall refinishing. For the best spot repair color match on late-model cars, factory-packaged mix should always be used.

Custom Mix—Factory-packaged mix is not always available in all colors. After a certain numbers of years have passed, there is not enough demand for older factory-packaged colors, so they are "phased out."

When a color is not available in a factory-packaged mix, then, it is nearly always available in a *custom mix*. *Custom-mix colors are those colors that are mixed to order at the paint supply store.* A can of custom-mix color can always be identified easily because the contents of the can must be written on the label by the paint store that mixed the paint. See Fig. 25-29.

Fig. 25-29. Custom-mix color paint. This paint was mixed and packaged at a local paint dealer before being delivered to the body shop that ordered it.

To make custom-mix colors that match the original color, paint manufacturing companies must supply their paint stores with several basic items:

1. Paint Formulas
2. Paint Mixing Equipment
3. Custom-Mix Base Colors
4. Custom-Mix Special Ingredients
5. New Paint Cans
6. Paint Labels

With the above equipment, then, the paint store (or body shop) is prepared to accurately mix almost any color ever used on an automobile. (Many body shops prefer to have their own mixing equipment, since they can save time and money by mixing their own paints.) Each of these items is discussed below.

Paint Formulas are "recipes" that tell the paint mixer (person mixing the color) how much of each *base color* and *other ingredients* to mix together to produce the desired color. The base colors and ingredients are put into the mix by *weight*, not by volume.

Paint Mixing Equipment includes all the weighing, measuring, and mixing equipment needed to mix a can of color. Most of this equipment is shown below in Fig. 25-30.

Custom-Mix Base Colors are the basic colors (paints) used to prepare custom-mix colors. Base colors are not normally sold or used for refinishing all by themselves. Instead, they are first mixed with other base colors and ingredients to make the needed paint product. Fig. 25-31 shows an acrylic enamel base color from one paint company.

Custom-Mix Special Ingredients include products such as driers, binders, and aluminum

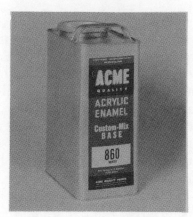

Fig. 25-31. A base color for custom-mix paints. This color will be mixed with other colors, as required, to make a given custom-mix color. (Courtesy of Acme Quality Paints.)

flakes that may need to be added to make up certain colors. There might be several special ingredients in certain colors, so a well-equipped paint store will need to have several special ingredients on hand to be able to mix any color required.

New Paint Cans and Labels will be necessary to package the mixed paint and send it out to a body shop for use and storage. Plain labels will identify what the paint product is (acrylic lacquer, for example) and allow the paint store to write on the label what color code and paint number is in the can. See Fig. 25-29.

Fig. 25-30. A typical paint mixing area. Many pieces of equipment are needed to accurately *weigh* and *mix* the ingredients in a can of custom-mix color. (Courtesy of Refinish Division, DuPont Company.)

There are two main reasons why custom-mix color would be used on a repair or refinish job instead of factory-packaged color:

1. Factory-packaged paint is not available in the color desired.
2. Custom-mix color is lower priced than factory-packaged color.

Properly mixed and applied custom-mix color will blend well with the original color, although possibly not as well as would factory-package color. For this reason, custom-mix color is more often used on overall refinishing than is factory-package. During overall refinishing, the very exact color match is not as important as when spot repairing and, since more paint is needed for an overall job, the cost of the paint becomes more important than when making spot repairs.

Both of the basic types of body shop mixes (factory-package and custom-mix) have the same appearance and actually appear to be the same product. This is not exactly correct, however, because the two paints were mixed in different places with different ingredients. Therefore, it is *not* a good idea to mix factory package paint with custom-mix, or vice-versa. If needed, however, one of them may be sprayed *over* the other if a flash-off time of 7-10 minutes is allowed for the thinner to evaporate (lacquer), or longer for reducer to flash-off (enamel).

Types of Topcoats

When the topcoat on an automobile or truck is clean and polished, it may reflect a bright, *solid* color, such as yellow, white, black, etc. Other topcoats may reflect a bright color *and* very small sparkles that look like "sugar" in the topcoat. How a topcoat reflects light and color, then, determines what type of topcoat it is. There are *two basic types of topcoats*, depending on how they reflect light. These are known as *solids* and *metallics*.

Solids—Many years ago, all cars were *solid* colors, such as maroon or black. Other solid colors include white, yellow, and some blues and greens. When polished up, these colors reflect light in only *one direction*, because the solids in the paint are all *pigments*, with no extra ingredients. Many cars today are still painted with solid colors. Solid colors pretty much look the same no matter from what angle you look at them.

Metallics—Many popular colors today have pigments *and* very small metal flakes mixed into the binder. When the paint is sprayed on a surface, the very small metal flakes are scattered in the binder along with the pigments. These flakes will then reflect light at different angles, especially when sunlight "hits" the paint. When the light is reflected at different angles, it makes the paint look "sugary" and glisten from different angles. These paints are known as *metallic* paints, or metallic topcoats. See Figs. 25-28 and 25-29.

Common metallic topcoats are silver and gold. Most green topcoats, many blues, and some reds are also metallics. When a metallic color is mixed, of course, a certain amount of the correct metal flakes (or "dust") must be added to the paint mixture. These flakes quickly settle to the bottom of the can of metallic paint, so *it is very important that metallic paints be stirred and mixed thoroughly before using.* If they are not, many metal flakes will stay at the bottom of the can and the paint will not match the same color on a car being repaired or refinished.

PAINT VEHICLES

Paint *vehicles*, of course, are one of the three basic ingredients in any paint. All paints are manufactured with *some* vehicle already in the paint when it comes out of the can. However, almost all paints must have *more* vehicle added to the paint before it may be sprayed. This is done for two reasons:

1. So that the painter can add the *correct* vehicle for the temperature and humidity shop conditions where the paint will be sprayed.
2. So that the paint will not have to be sold in such large quantities. If paint was sold with enough vehicle already in it, much larger cans of paint would be required.

The most *important* reason for adding vehicle at the shop just before spraying is so that the correct vehicle can be used for the existing shop conditions. The temperature and *humidity* (moisture in the shop's air) are very important when choosing a paint vehicle. Different paint vehicles are made and sold for different shop conditions. *Knowing about the different vehicles is very important for successful paint work under all shop conditions.*

What Paint Vehicles Do

The basic job of any paint vehicle is to thin the paint enough so that the mixture can be sprayed through a spray gun. The paint vehicle *dilutes* the paint (makes it thinner) so that the mixture can easily pass through the spray gun and be *atomized* as it leaves the gun and travels to the surface being sprayed. See Fig. 25-32.

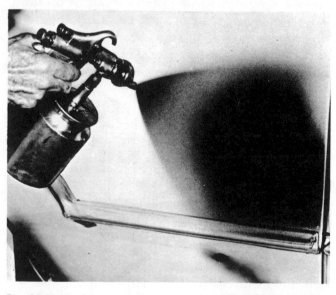

Fig. 25-32. As the mixture of paint and added vehicle leaves the gun, it is *atomized* (broken up into a fine, mist-like spray.) (Courtesy, Rinshed-Mason Products Division of Inmont Corporation.)

Then, when the mixture reaches the surface being sprayed, the vehicle must keep the pigments and binder in solution just long enough for the material to flow out and level to a smooth, even surface. On the other hand, it must *not* hold the paint in solution so long that the paint film can sag or run. Finally, the vehicle must evaporate completely over a period of time to leave a tough, smooth, durable film.

Selecting a Vehicle

As a general rule, the shop's *temperature* and the weather's *humidity* are the main factors to consider when choosing a paint vehicle. Hot, dry weather will require a vehicle that evaporates *slower* than when the weather is cooler and wet or humid. All paint manufacturers market several different vehicles for use with each of their topcoats. For the best possible results with any manufacturer's automobile paints, *use that same manufacturer's vehicle and use only the vehicle recommended by the manufacturer for the temperature and humidity conditions under which the paint and vehicle will be used.* No single item about choosing automobile paint products is more important for successful automobile painting.

Types of Vehicles

As discussed earlier, there are two basic types of paint vehicles: *thinners* for lacquer paints and *reducers* for enamel paints. Although they have similar jobs, they are given different names so that they will not be easily confused. If the two products are confused, the paint work will probably turn out poorly. For example, lacquer thinner *will* dilute enamel paint. However, it will *not* properly break up (dissolve) *all* the enamel paint pigments to hold them in the proper balance. On the other hand, if enamel reducer is used in lacquer paint, it will usually curdle the paint.

There is also a *third* type of vehicle on the market. In the trade, these are known as "universal" vehicles, or "universal thinners." These products are sold in bulk quantities and are designed to be able to do *both* vehicle jobs; *thin* lacquers and *reduce* enamels. Universal thinners are not normally used for high-quality paint work and are discussed more thoroughly later in the unit.

Thinners—Most lacquer thinners sold today are made for use with acrylic lacquer paints. See the thinners shown earlier in Figs. 25-2 and 25-4. If, for some reason, nitrocellulose lacquer is being used, be sure to use lacquer thinner that is also recommended for nitrocellulose lacquer paint.

Generally speaking, as the shop temperature goes up, a slower drying thinner should be used. It is a good idea to use as slow a drying thinner as the shop conditions will allow. This assures as smooth a finish as is possible, so that only a minimum amount of compounding will be needed.

Reducers—Many enamel reducers are sold that can be used in *both* alkyd and acrylic enamel. Even so, it is a good idea to check the paint manufacturer's literature to be certain that the correct reducer is being used. Most companies market several reducers for all types of enamel painting conditions. See Fig. 25-33.

As with lacquer thinners, slower-drying enamel reducers should be used as the shop temperature increases. These allow the enamel to flow out to the smoothest possible finish with a minimum amount of orange peel. For this reason, it is usually advisable to use the slowest-drying reducer that will work in the existing temperature and humidity of the shop.

Universal Vehicles—Some chemical companies market solvents known as universal *vehicles*, or, more likely, *universal solvents*. These products are made to be used as either thinners *or* reducers, in *both* lacquer *and* enamel paints. These universal solvents are usually high-quality products that will work with many types of paints. However, *they cannot be recommended for first-class automotive refinishing work*. This is because any automobile paint is designed to work *best* when it is mixed with a reducer or thinner made and recommended by the same company that made the paint itself. Those reducers or thinners will best dissolve the ingredients of that particular paint and will flow the paint out to its maximum smoothness.

There are some advantages for shops that use universal solvents to do all types of thinning and reducing. For example, universal solvent can be used for almost all paints or undercoats in the shop. This saves the trouble of having to stock all types of thinners and reducers. This reduces the storage space needed in the shop and the amount of money a shop has tied up in inventories (stock) of many different products.

The possible *disadvantage* of universal solvents is one of quality. While these solvents will normally work as advertised, the job may not be quite as good as if the paint company's *recommended* product is used. Universal solvent generally does not have all the high-quality material needed for the very best results in all types of paints under any different shop condition. To be sure of first-class paint work, then, it is always a good idea to use the thinners and reducers recommended by the manufacturer of the paint itself.

SOLVENTS

Before a damaged area is repaired and/or prepared for refinishing, the old paint should be cleaned with a precleaning *solvent*, Figs. 25-34 and 25-35. Each paint manufacturer usually has their own precleaning solvent product. Each of these products is basically the same and does the same job.

Fig. 25-33. One manufacturer's line of enamel reducers. (Courtesy, Rinshed-Mason Products Division of Inmont Corporation.)

Fig. 25-34. A typical gallon can of precleaning solvent. (Courtesy, Rinshed-Mason Products Division of Inmont Corporation.)

Fig. 25-35. Using precleaning solvent. Before an area is prepared for refinishing, it should first be cleaned with precleaning solvent. (Courtesy of Refinish Division, DuPont Company.)

The purpose of these solvents is to quickly remove road oil, tar, waxes, silicones, and old films from the existing paint surface. This is done so that grinding and sanding will not grind these chemicals into the bare metal. If these chemicals were ground into the bare metal, they would later cause paint troubles. The instructions for using these products are fairly similar. In general, they are "washed" on the surface with a rag and then wiped off, while wet, with a clean, dry rag.

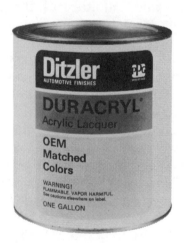

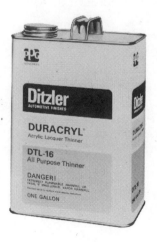

Preparing the Surface for Paint

To a very large extent, the success and appearance of a topcoat depends on how carefully the surface *under* the topcoat was prepared. The surface under the new paint work, of course, is referred to as the *substrate*, so the substrate must be in good condition if the new paint work is to be successful. Properly preparing the substrate, then, is known as *surface preparation.*

Surface preparation includes preparing *all* types of surfaces for new paint. These may include bare steel, aluminum, galvanized metal,

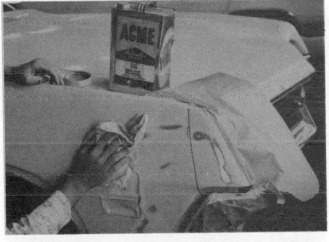
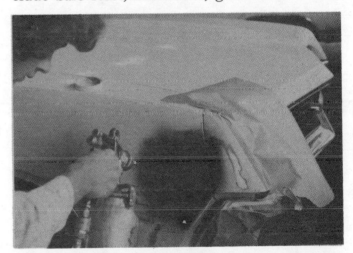

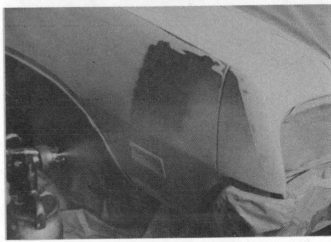

Fig. 26-1. Properly preparing the substrate is very important for successful automobile paint work.

and many types of old painted finishes. In any case, surface preparation is an important step. It can be compared to building the foundation of a house. A house is no better than its foundation; a paint job will be no better than the substrate. See Fig. 26-1.

PREPARING BASIC METAL SURFACES

Many times, it is necessary for a body shop to do paint work on one or more types of *basic metal surfaces*. These are surfaces that have *not* been repaired but *do* need to have paint work done to them. These include *replacement* panels, *aluminum* panels, and *galvanized metal* panels. Each of these panels is very different, and making paint correctly "stick" to each type of panel requires a *different* procedure, as follows.

Preparing Replacement Panels

The most commonly prepared basic metal panels are new *steel* replacement panels. This is because most car bodies (and the replacement panels made for them) are made of steel. Fig. 26-2, for example, shows a common steel replacement quarter panel.

Most steel replacement panels, such as the one shown in Fig. 26-2, are painted at the factory with a coat of primer, to help prevent rust on the panel before it is installed on a vehicle. Normally, this "factory primer" is not a very good basis for a smooth topcoat. This is because

Fig. 26-2. A replacement quarter panel. Preparing this panel for painting is the most basic replacement paint work in a shop.

it is usually applied unevenly and often has sags or runs in the corners or around holes and edges. For these reasons, replacement panels require normal preparation before they may be painted with a new color coat.

To prepare a replacement panel for painting, then, *first* figure out how the panel will be attached to the vehicle. If the panel is *bolted* to the vehicle, such as a complete door or front fender, then the panel is usually completely painted off the vehicle, before the panel is installed. On the other hand, if the panel must be *brazed* or *spot-welded* to the body (such as a quarter panel), the panel should first be attached to the vehicle and *then* painted.

A *second* item to consider before preparing a replacement panel for painting is whether all the trim attachment or other holes are already in the panel. If one panel is used for several models of a car or truck, not all the necessary trim holes for every model are drilled in the panel at the factory. For this reason, it is usually necessary for a body shop to drill holes in replacement panels for the specific trim on the car or truck being repaired. It is a good idea to drill these holes *before* the panel is painted, so that the holes will be painted along with the rest of the panel.

When a replacement panel has been installed (if necessary) and any trim holes have been drilled, the panel may then be prepared for final painting. To do this, proceed as follows:

1. Wash the entire panel with precleaning solvent. Wipe the solvent off with a clean rag *before* the solvent dries on the panel.
2. Block-sand the entire panel with wet #320 sandpaper. Pay special attention to any runs or sags in the factory primer.
3. The block sanding in Step #2 will usually leave a few bare metal places on the new panels where the sanding easily went through thin places on the factory primer. Treat these bare places with metal conditioner.
4. Note if there are any serious dents on the panel. If so, repair these with body filler.
5. Wash the entire panel, including any

body filler repairs, with enamel reducer. Be sure to wipe the reducer off the panel before it dries.

6. Apply primer-surfacer to any bare, thin, or repaired areas on the panel. Although *enamel* primer-surfacer would be preferred for this job, many shops use lacquer primer-surfacer successfully.

7. Allow the primer-surfacer to dry thoroughly.

8. Inspect the primer-surfacer for any nicks or small defects. If there are any, fill them with paint putty.

9. Carefully block-sand the entire panel, especially the new primer-surfacer areas, with wet #320 sandpaper. If an *enamel* topcoat will be applied, go to Step #11.

10. If a *lacquer* topcoat will be applied, block-sand the entire panel with wet #400 sandpaper.

11. Wash the entire panel with enamel reducer. Again, be sure to wipe the reducer off before it dries.

12. If enamel primer-surfacer was used and the topcoat will be *lacquer,* apply the correct *sealer* to the enamel primer-surfacer. When the sealer has dried, scuff off any nibs with dry #400 sandpaper.

13. Blow any dust or dirt out of the cracks around the panel if the panel has been installed on the car.

14. Tack wipe the panel with a tack rag. The panel is now properly prepared for the color coat.

Preparing Aluminum Panels

Fig. 26-3 shows a truck trailer with an *aluminum body.* Aluminum is more often used on truck trailers and van bodies than on automobile bodies. Even so, a body man may have to work on aluminum metal as part of auto body repair. Many times, owners of van and camper bodies may ask a shop to do repair or repaint work on bodies with aluminum panels. When this is necessary, a definite procedure *must* be followed if topcoats are to properly adhere (stick) to aluminum metal.

Aluminum and galvanized part manufacturers often spray their panels with an oily

Fig. 26-3. An aluminum trailer for a large truck. Many times, these trailers are not painted. However, if they are painted, a certain procedure must be followed for the topcoat to properly adhere to and protect the aluminum.

solution (or dip it in an oily solution) after the panel is manufactured. This is done before the metal is shipped from the plant to the assembly plant or to a body shop. Therefore, parts other than sheet metal usually have some type of oily coating applied to keep them from corroding.

To properly prepare *unpainted* aluminum panels for refinishing, then, any protective oily films or other material must be removed. This may be done as follows:

1. Wash the panel thoroughly with hot, soapy water. Rinse thoroughly and allow the panel to dry.

2. Remove any remaining oil or grease deposits with trisodium phosphate or steam cleaning.

3. Wash the panel with precleaning solvent. Wipe the solvent off the surface before it dries.

4. Treat any bare metal with a solution of metal conditioner. Wipe the metal conditioner off the panel before it dries.

5. Wash the panel with enamel reducer. Wipe the reducer off the panel before it dries. Tack wipe the panel.

6. Depending on how the panel will be used, complete *either* Step #6A or #6B, below. Then, proceed to Step #7.

6A. If the aluminum panel *will* come in contact with a panel of a different metal (for example, steel), apply *zinc chromate* primer to the bare aluminum. Allow it to dry 30 minutes before proceeding.

6B. If the aluminum panel will *not* be coming in contact with panels of a different metal, apply vinyl wash primer to the aluminum panel. Allow it to dry 30 minutes. Then, apply enamel primer-surfacer to the area. Allow the area to dry overnight.

7. Fill any remaining imperfections with paint putty. Allow the putty to dry.

8. Block-sand the zinc chromate primer or the primer-surfacer with wet #320 sandpaper.

9. Wash the surface with enamel reducer. Wipe off the enamel reducer before it dries on the surface.

10. Blow any dust out of the cracks near the panel if the panel is mounted on a body.

11. Tack wipe the prepared surface with a tack rag. The surface is now ready for an enamel topcoat.

Preparing Galvanized Metal Panels

Fig. 26-4 shows a school bus with a *galvanized metal* body. Galvanized metal is often used on lower automobile body panels and dif-

Fig. 26-4. A galvanized sheet metal body. Galvanized metal must be carefully prepared before it is painted or else the topcoat will have very poor adhesion.

ferent types of buses and commercial bodies. Most body men work less on galvanized metal than any other types of metal.

Often, truck and bus companies have their own body repair shops to repair damage to their vehicles. New body men must be employed by these shops as other men leave the shops to retire or work elsewhere. Also, more automobile manufacturers are using galvanized panels for rocker panels and other lower body pieces. For these reasons, then, body men must know how to work with galvanized metal and how to prepare it for painting.

How Galvanized Metal Is Made—Galvanized metal is actually normal sheet metal except that it has a very thin coating of *zinc* on it. When the sheet metal piece is coated with zinc, a thin layer of zinc is "floated" on the metal. This layer of zinc grips the metal and stays in place even when the metal is later bent into shape for a body part.

Procedure—Because of the zinc coating, galvanized metal is one of the most difficult metals on which to make paint "stick." For this reason, galvanized metal must be prepared exactly as outlined here if the topcoat is to properly stick to the substrate:

1. Wash the panel thoroughly with hot, soapy water. Rinse it completely and allow it to dry.

2. Thoroughly wash the panel with water and trisodium phosphate. Rinse it with clear water and allow it to dry.

3. Wash the panel with precleaning solvent. Wipe off the wet solvent before it dries on the panel.

4. Treat the bare galvanized metal with metal conditioner. Wipe off the metal conditioner before it dries on the panel.

5. Wash the panel with enamel reducer. Wipe it off the panel before it dries.

6. Blow out any cracks with a dust gun.

7. Tack wipe the panel.

8. Thoroughly *strain* and *mix* the correct amounts of vinyl wash primer and its activator. Follow the directions on the can carefully and do *not* substitute other products.

9. Spray a *thin* coat of vinyl wash primer on the clean galvanized metal.

10. Allow the vinyl wash primer to dry for 30 minutes.

11. Apply an *enamel* primer surfacer to the treated galvanized panel.

12. Allow the primer-surfacer to dry for 30 minutes.

13. Fill any imperfections in the primer-surfacer with paint putty.

14. Allow the putty and primer-surfacer to dry overnight.

15. Block-sand the putty and primer-surfacer with wet #320 sandpaper.

16. Wash the panel with enamel reducer. Wipe off the reducer before it dries.

17. Blow out any cracks around the panel with a dust gun.

18. Tack wipe the prepared surface with a tack rag. The panel is now ready for an enamel topcoat.

PREPARING PAINTED SURFACES

Most paint work done in a body shop is done on metal that already has *some* paint on it. This may be a panel that has been repaired or an old finish that will be covered when a new paint job (refinish) is applied to the entire car or panel. For these reasons, properly preparing (or, in some cases, *removing*) the old paint is very important for the life and durability of the new topcoat.

Choosing the Type of Repair

When a car is to be refinished after a collision repair, the painter and body man must decide how much of the car is to be repainted. This is determined by several factors, such as the type of metal repair that was done, the type and condition of the paint already on the car, and the cost of the total job. Once it is decided how much will be repainted, either *definition lines* or a *spot repair* must be decided upon.

Definition Lines—Whenever only *part* of a car is to be painted, the painter must decide exactly how much will be painted. That is, he must decide what area will have new paint and how big an area it will be. To do this, he must

decide what area to *mask off* so that it will not be painted. The *edges* of the area to be painted, then, are known as *definition lines*. Typical definition lines are the gaps between panels, at the edges where a panel is bent sharply for a contour, and along moldings. Fig. 26-5 shows several typical definition lines.

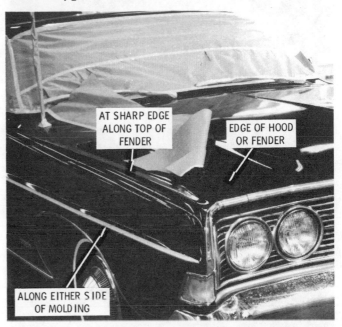

Fig. 26-5. Typical definition lines. When the new paint "stops" at a good definition line, it will be difficult to tell where the new paint begins and the old paint ends. (Courtesy of 3M Company, Automotive Division.)

Definition lines must be chosen carefully when only part of a vehicle is to be painted. If a length of masking tape and paper were put right down the center of a door, for example, there would be a definition line down the center of the door after the paint work had been done and the masking tape and paper removed. Because the definition line was in the center of the door, it would be easy to see the difference between the old and the new paint. Therefore, this would be a *poor* definition line. *Good* definition lines, on the other hand, make it very difficult to "find" the difference between the old and the new paints.

Spot Repairs—When an entire panel or an area is *not* painted but there *is* some new paint on the area, the new paint has been *spotted in*. This is known as a *spot repair*. Figs. 26-6 and 26-7 show a typical spot repair.

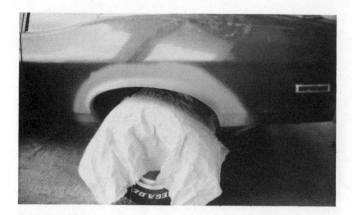

Fig. 26-6. A panel to be *spot repaired*. Here, a good painter will carefully "fade out" the new paint so that it blends in with the old paint on the same panel. Depending on the size of the "spot" to be blended in, masking may not be necessary when a lacquer spot repair is being made.

Fig. 26-7. A completed spot repair. The entire panel on this car (Fig. 26-6) was not painted. Instead, the new paint was carefully blended into the older paint around the spot.

When a spot repair is made, there are no definition lines. That is, there is no one line where the old paint ends and the new paint begins. Instead, the new paint gradually "blends" into the old paint around the spot. Making a good spot repair that blends well is a skill that can be "tricky," even for good painters.

Surface Preparation

As soon as you know exactly *what* area will be refinished, preparing the surface for the new paint may begin. Generally speaking, this procedure is the same for all types of repairs and painted surfaces. However, based on the *specific* job being done, certain procedures may need

to be done extra carefully, whereas others may not need to be done. For these reasons, the *general* procedure given here should be followed as closely as possible.

Wash the Car—This should always be the first step before *any* refinish work. Washing the *entire* car, Fig. 26-8, will help remove any dust or dirt that might otherwise be blown into the new paint, even if only part of the car is to be refinished. Washing the car also helps assure a good color match since the old color can be more accurately seen and matched. Finally, with no dirt and dust on the car, masking tape will more easily stick to the parts not to be painted.

Fig. 26-8. *Step* 1. Wash the car. This should be done *before* any other paint work preparation. (Courtesy of Refinish Division, DuPont Company.)

Clean the Area—After the entire car has been washed, work only on the area to be repaired. The first step is to clean the area with precleaning solvent. Wipe the solvent off the area *before* the solvent dries. See Fig. 26-9.

Fig. 26-9. *Step* 2. Clean the area to be repaired with precleaning solvent. (Courtesy of Refinish Division, DuPont Company.)

Making Metal Repairs—After the old surface has been cleaned with precleaning solvent, it may be ground off for repairs. If the old paint is ground off *before* it is cleaned, waxes and chemicals in the old paint might be ground into the bare metal. In the metal, the waxes or chemicals could later cause a serious paint problem known as *fish-eye*, discussed later.

Metal repairing will usually include grinding the old finish to remove it (Fig. 26-10) and filling the area with body filler (Fig. 26-11). Any different number of metal repair methods may be used to make the *substrate* as smooth and level as possible. These repair methods are discussed elsewhere in the book.

Fig. 26-10. *Step 3.* Make any needed metal repairs. Here, a grinder is being used to remove the old paint from a damaged panel. (Courtesy of Refinish Division, DuPont Company.)

*Featheredge Any Broken Paint—*Even if metal repairs were not made, most areas to be refinished will have small nicks and chips due to car doors hitting each other in parking lots or small stones being thrown up by the car's wheels and chipping the paint. In all these

Fig. 26-11. *Step 3,* continued. Any number of methods may be used to make the needed metal repairs. Here, plastic body filler is being used to finish levelling a damaged panel. (Courtesy of Refinish Division, DuPont Company.)

cases, the broken paint must be *featheredged* before primer-surfacer is applied to the bare metal left by the featheredging.

A *featheredge,* Fig. 26-12, is a tapered "feather" of the old paint that smooths down to the bare metal. This is done so that there is not a sharp edge around the paint break. A sharp edge would "show up" as a defect under the new paint and make the repair look poor. For this reason, featheredging broken paint is *very* important. *It must be done thoroughly and carefully all around the damaged area.*

Fig. 26-12. *Step 4.* Featheredge the broken paint. When a broken area is properly featheredged, there will not be a sharp line at the edge of the break in the paint.

There are two basic methods used to featheredge old paint: *mechanical* and *chemical.* Which method to use depends on personal preference. *Chemical* featheredging does require that the shop buy another solvent chemical, so many shops prefer to do mechanical featheredging.

During *mechanical* featheredging, *sandpapers* are used to knock down and taper the old paint. Mechanical featheredging, using sandpaper, *must be done with a sanding block.* If the featheredging is done without a sanding block (called "fingertip sanding"), the surface being sanded will not be cut evenly and the featheredge will not be as smoothly tapered as it should. See Fig. 26-13.

Sanding a featheredge may also be done with an orbital (power) sander. See Fig. 26-14. When this sander is used, #180 sandpaper should be used to *begin* the featheredge. If a sanding block is used, #220 paper would be used to *begin* the featheredge, as in Fig. 26-15.

To *finish* a featheredge, #360 or #400 *wet* sandpaper should be used. This paper should always be used *by hand, wet,* and *with a sanding block.*

To *chemically* featheredge broken paint, use a special solvent designed to dissolve the edges of broken paint. This special solvent is a prod-

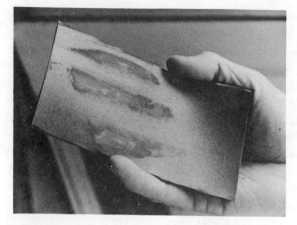

Fig. 26-13. *Step 4,* continued. As shown by this sanding dust, "fingertip" sanding does not cut a surface evenly. For this reason, a flat, smooth sanding block must *always* be used when featheredging. (Courtesy of Refinish Division, DuPont Company.)

Fig. 26-14. *Step 4. Mechanical Featheredging.* Using an orbital sander to featheredge broken paint. (Courtesy of Refinish Division, DuPont Company.)

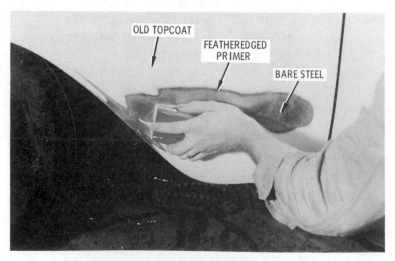

Fig. 26-15. *Step 4.* Mechanical featheredging, continued. Using a sanding block to featheredge broken paint.

uct marketed for just this purpose. See Fig. 26-16. Properly used, this product will *not* dissolve the car manufacturer's original undercoat primer. The instructions for using these products are usually printed on the can and should be followed carefully.

Fig. 26-16. *Step 4. Chemical Featheredging.* Special featheredging solvent is made to *partially* dissolve the paint on the car yet *not* disturb the factory primer underneath. (Courtesy of Refinish Division, DuPont Company.)

Prepare Any Remaining Areas—During a panel repair or an overall refinishing job, there are usually areas that do not need either metal repairs or featheredging. These are areas where the old paint has not been broken by chips or other damage. For these areas, it must be decided how the paint already on the area will be prepared.

There are *two* methods by which this old paint may be prepared; either *sanding* or *stripping.* If the old paint is in good condition, it may be block-sanded with *wet* sandpaper to prepare it for the new topcoat. If the new topcoat is to be *lacquer,* #400 sandpaper should be used. If the new topcoat will be enamel, #320 sandpaper may be used, although using #400 would produce a smoother topcoat.

The *second* method used to prepare an old finish for painting is to *strip* the finish. Stripping the finish means using heavy chemical *paint remover* to completely remove the old paint from the surface. If the old finish is badly weathered or scarred, it should be stripped. It would be a poor foundation for a lasting new topcoat. Paint remover should be used *accord-*

ing to the directions on the can and with good safety precautions. See Figs. 26-17 and 26-18. Stripping the finish will also soften and remove any plastic filler *under* the finish. Because of this, be prepared to replace any plastic filler in the area if paint remover is used to "strip off" the old paint.

Fig. 26-17. Stripping to prepare any remaining areas. If the old paint is in bad condition but does not need featheredging or metal work, it should be *removed*, down to the bare metal. This is done with *paint remover*. To use paint remover, it must be first brushed in place as shown here. (Courtesy of Refinish Division, DuPont Company.)

Fig. 26-18. *Step 5.* Stripping, if necessary, continued. After the paint remover has been on the paint for several minutes, the paint will wrinkle up and lift off the finish as shown above. Then, the old paint may be removed with a putty knife or water. (Courtesy of Refinish Division, DuPont Company.)

Treat Any Bare Metal—An important step to *lasting* paint work is to treat any bare metal with metal conditioner. This product will help to etch the metal for good paint adhesion *and* protect the metal from further rusting. Using this product is discussed elsewhere, but it must *always* be wiped off the bare metal before it dries. See Fig. 26-19.

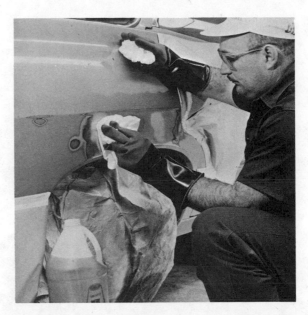

Fig. 26-19. *Step 6.* Treat any bare metal with metal conditioner. This will etch the surface for protection against rust and for good paint adhesion. (Courtesy of Refinish Division, DuPont Company.)

Wash the Area—After any metal repairs have been made, any featheredging completed, and any older paint prepared or stripped, the *entire area* to be refinished should be washed with enamel reducer. See Fig. 26-20. Washing the area with enamel reducer is a very important step. It will help to neutralize any chemicals and remove any sanding dust or other dirt on the surface.

Mask the Area—During almost all refinishing or repair work, there will be at least *some* bare metal that must be primed with primer-surfacer. Before this is done, it is a good idea to take the time to mask off all the trim and other areas that are not to be painted. This should be done carefully so that the same masking job may be left in place until *after* the new color topcoat is applied.

When masking the car, be certain to mask all around the area to be painted if the entire vehicle is not being repainted. See Fig. 26-21. Choose the *definition lines* carefully if a panel repair is being done, as in Fig. 26-22. Careful masking will help prevent excessive clean-up time and will do a good job of hiding definition lines.

Apply Primer-Surfacer—After the area has been masked and washed with enamel reducer,

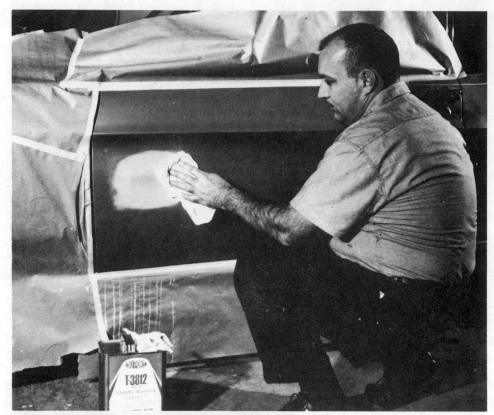

Fig. 26-20. *Step 7.* Wash the area. After any metal repairs and paint preparation are done, wash the area with enamel reducer. Be sure to wipe the reducer off *before* it dries on the finish. (Courtesy of Refinish Division, DuPont Company.)

Fig. 26-21. *Step 8.* Mask the area. Take the necessary time to carefully mask all the trim that is not to be painted. (Courtesy of Refinish Division, DuPont Company.)

primer-surfacer may then be applied. Whether lacquer or enamel primer-surfacer is used, it is important that the mixing and application instructions on the product's can be followed. The instructions will include *how much* thinner or reducer to use, *what type* of thinner or reducer to use depending on shop conditions, and the approximate *air pressure* to use at the gun.

Speaking in general, however, *lacquer* primer-surfacers are thinned with medium-dry ("mid-temp") thinners. About 1½-2 parts of thinner should be used with 1 part of lacquer primer-surfacer. See Fig. 26-23. When applying lacquer primer-surfacer to a *spot* repair, adjust the spray gun for a small pattern and use from 25-35 pounds of air pressure at the gun. See Fig. 26-24. For large repairs (panel or overall), 35-45 pounds of pressure may be used.

Again generally speaking, enamel primer-surfacers are reduced with either mid-temp or low-temp reducers, depending on the shop conditions. About 2 parts of enamel primer-surfacer should be mixed with 1 part of the correct enamel reducer for the best results. See Fig. 26-25.

If an *enamel* finish is being repaired, enamel primer-surfacer may be used to fill and prime any bare metal, featheredged areas on the surface. For these "spot-priming" jobs, about 35-40 pounds of air pressure at the gun should be used with a small spray pattern.

When spraying primer-surfacer, allow each coat to *flash off* (evaporate from wet glossy to a dull appearance) before applying the next coat. Do not build up too great a thickness of

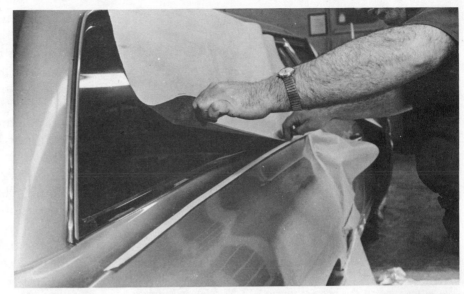

Fig. 26-22. *Step 8*, continued. When only a panel repair (or a spot repair) is to be done, mask off the surrounding areas that are not to be painted. Carefully choose the definition lines around a panel repair so that they will not be easily noticed. (Courtesy of Refinish Division, DuPont Company.)

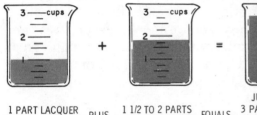

1 PART LACQUER PRIMER-SURFACER PLUS 1 1/2 TO 2 PARTS MID-TEMP THINNER EQUALS JUST UNDER 3 PARTS MIXED PRIMER-SURFACER READY TO SPRAY

Fig. 26-23. Mixing lacquer primer-surfacer.

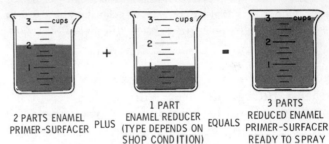

2 PARTS ENAMEL PRIMER-SURFACER PLUS 1 PART ENAMEL REDUCER (TYPE DEPENDS ON SHOP CONDITION) EQUALS 3 PARTS REDUCED ENAMEL PRIMER-SURFACER READY TO SPRAY

Fig. 26-25. Mixing enamel primer-surfacer.

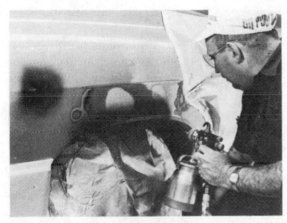

Fig. 26-24. *Step 9*. Applying primer-surfacer. Any bare metal in the repair area should be primed with primer-surfacer. Depending on the product being used and the area being covered, the air pressure and technique may need to be changed slightly. (Courtesy of Refinish Division, DuPont Company.)

primer-surfacer by using too many coats. Four to six coats of primer-surfacer are usually all that are required. Also, be careful to not make any one coat too heavy; a heavy coat of primer-surfacer will dry slowly and may crack.

Apply Paint Putty—If any large nicks or chips are noted in the surface of the primer-surfacer, paint *putty* may now be applied to fill them. See Fig. 26-26. Paint putty may be applied either before or after the primer-surfacer is block-sanded, which is discussed next. Applying the putty *before* the primer-surfacer is sanded has the advantage of only having to sand the area once. On the other hand, it is easier to see any small defects in the finish *after* the primer-surfacer is sanded, so that it may be desirable to apply the putty after sanding and then resand the area slightly to level the putty.

Block-Sand the Area—The area to actually receive the new paint must be block-sanded to prepare it for the final color coat. This is done to properly level the entire area and make it smooth enough for the new paint to flow out properly. If the block sanding is not done carefully, it will "show up" under the paint as uneven or rough areas and will make the topcoat look poor no matter how carefully the topcoat

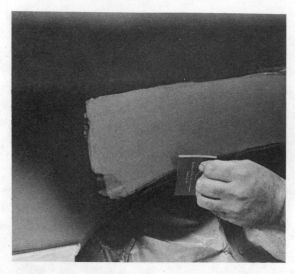

Fig. 26-26. *Step 10.* Applying paint putty. (This step may also be done after sanding the primer-surfacer.) To fill any minor defects in the surface or primer-surfacer, apply paint putty to the area and allow it to dry. (Courtesy of Refinish Division, DuPont Company.)

is applied. If any nicks or chips are noticed after block-sanding the area, fill the defects with paint putty and then resand the area where the putty was applied before going on to the next step.

Generally speaking, this is the final sanding preparation on an area to be refinished. This step is best done with wet sandpaper and must be done with a sanding block, as in Fig. 26-27. Which sandpaper to use depends on the type of

topcoat that will be applied. In all cases, #400 paper will produce the smoothest topcoat finish and is always required before a *lacquer* topcoat is applied. If an *enamel* topcoat will be applied, wet #320 paper may be used to speed up the job. However, the topcoat will not be as smooth as if #400 paper had been used.

It is important to *not* break through the old paint or new primer-surfacer during this final block sanding. If they are broken through to bare metal, the area will have to be spot primed and then resanded. Where hand sanding without a block must be done (such as around corners), be careful to *evenly* sand the area.

Finally, sand *only* the area that will actually be covered with new paint. For a *spot repair*, of course, there are no definitiion lines to determine where the new paint will stop. Therefore, wet-sand only the primer-surfacer area and about one inch around it for a spot repair. Then, as discussed next, rubbing compound will be used to prepare the *outer* area around the spot for the new paint.

Compound the Area—To prepare the good paint for "blending in" *around* a spot repair, the area must be compounded. To do this, either hand or "wheel" compounding may be done. See Fig. 26-28.

The good paint should be compounded about 10" around the repair to brighten up and thoroughly clean the paint. This allows the new

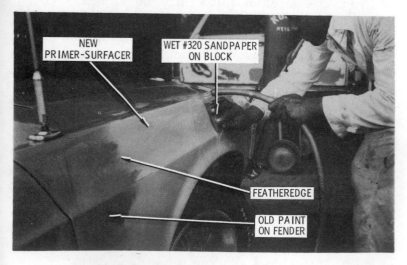

Fig. 26-27. *Step 11.* Block-sand the entire area to be refinished. Here, the front of the fender was repaired and the entire fender is being block-sanded to prepare the old finish and the new primer-surfacer for a new paint job on the entire fender.

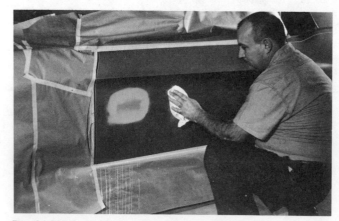

Fig. 26-28. *Step 12.* Compound the area around a spot repair. Use clean rags if the job is done by hand. A compounding "wheel" may also be used to compound a large area if the spot repair is fairly large. Note that compounding is done *only* around a spot repair. If a spot repair is not being made, this step should be skipped. (Courtesy of Refinish Division, DuPont Company.)

paint to more thoroughly blend into the old and allows it to more easily grip the old paint. For this reason, a good compounding *before* painting is necessary if a spot repair is to properly blend into the older paint on the same panel.

Wash the Area—The final cleaning for the area to be painted is to wash the entire area with enamel reducer. At this time, any area that was compounded should be carefully washed to remove any compounding sludge. In all cases, wash the entire area thoroughly and wipe the enamel reducer off the area *before it dries* on the area. See Fig. 26-29.

Fig. 26-30. *Step 14.* Dust and Tack. Blow out any cracks, around moldings, etc., to remove any dust or dirt "hiding" around the area to be painted. (Courtesy of Refinish Division, DuPont Company.)

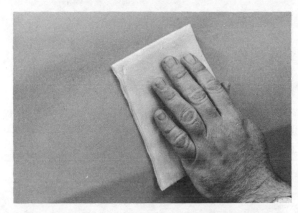

Fig. 26-31. *Step 14,* continued. After dusting, use a *tack rag* to remove any last specks of dust from the surface. (Courtesy of Refinish Division, DuPont Company.)

Sealing and Painting

After the surface to be repainted has been prepared and tack-wiped, it is then ready for repainting. At this point, the new topcoat color may be applied, as discussed in another unit. However, under some conditions, it may be necessary or desirable to apply *sealer* to the area before the topcoat is applied.

If sealer is to be applied, it should be applied just after the repair (or refinish) area has been tack-wiped. As usual, it is best to follow the directions listed on the can of the sealer. However, if these are not available, the following *general procedure* may be used.

1. Mix the sealer and the correct vehicle for the sealer according to the manufacturer's directions. Some sealers require no vehicle

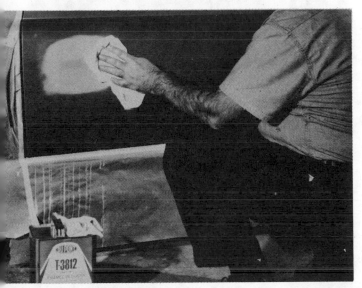

Fig. 26-29. *Step 13.* Wash the area. As a final cleaning for the repair area, again wash it with enamel reducer. Be certain to wash any areas that were compounded for a spot repair. In any case, wipe the wet reducer off the finish before it dries. (Courtesy of Refinish Division, DuPont Company.)

Dust and Tack—After the final wash, use a blow (dust) gun to blow any dust off the area. See Fig. 26-30. Also, use the gun to carefully blow any dust out from around cracks or moldings in the repair area. If dust remains in these areas, the air pressure of the paint spray gun may blow the dust out onto the wet paint.

Finally, tack wipe the entire area with a *tack rag*. A tack rag is a waxy, sticky cloth that will easily pick up any small specks of dust on the area to be painted. Tack rags are used *without* any kind of reducer or solvent. When a tack rag is dirty, it should be discarded. Tack rags cannot be cleaned and reused. See Fig. 26-31.

at all. In any case, *strain* the sealer or mixture as it is poured into the paint gun cup.

2. Set the air pressure from 35-45 pounds at the gun.

3. Apply an even, medium coat of sealer to the area. See Fig. 26-32.

Fig. 26-32. Applying sealer to the repair area. One even, medium-heavy coat should do the job. (Courtesy of Refinish Division, DuPont Company.)

4. Allow the sealer to dry for at least 15 minutes but less than one hour.

5. Very lightly scuff the area by hand with dry #400 paper to remove any nibs or overspray. Do *not* heavily sand the area; just a very light scuff is all that is required. See Fig. 26-33.

6. Tack-wipe the sealed area with a tack rag.

7. Apply the color topcoat.

Fig. 26-33. Using #400 sandpaper to *lightly* scuff the sealer to remove any small nibs or specks. (Courtesy of Refinish Division, DuPont Company.)

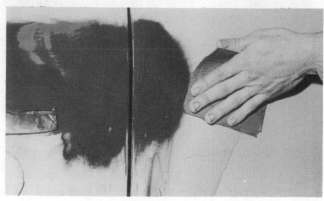

Unit 27

Applying Automotive Paint

The actual process of using a spray gun to apply paint is fairly simple. However, due to the many differences in paints, equipment, substrates, colors, etc., it requires a good deal of *practice* to properly apply automotive paint. A good automobile painter, then, must know a good deal about paint and painting equipment, *and* he must have a good deal of painting practice. See Fig. 27-1.

ORIGINAL PAINT TYPES

An auto body man must be able to identify the different types of paint that may be on an automobile. Almost all of today's *new* cars, of course, are painted with either acrylic lacquer or acrylic enamel paint. See Figs. 27-2 and 27-3. Most new trucks are painted with acrylic enamel, as are most foreign cars. A few foreign

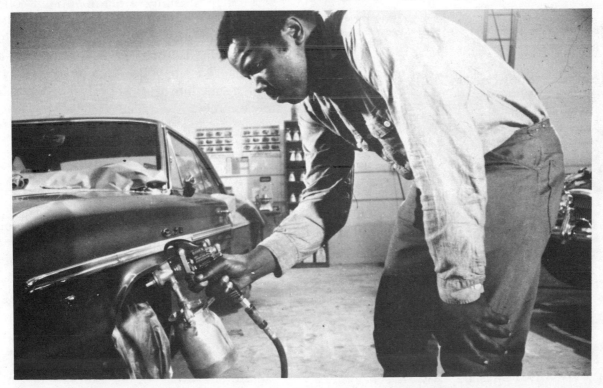

Fig. 27-1. A good painter must understand both paints *and* the painting process. (Courtesy of Refinish Division, DuPont Company.)

Fig. 27-2. An Oldsmobile Omega. This car, like other General Motors automobiles, is finished at the factory with acrylic lacquer. (Courtesy of Oldsmobile Division, General Motors Corporation.)

Fig. 27-3. An AMC Pacer. This car, like other automobiles from AMC, Chrysler Corporation, and the Ford Motor Company, is finished at the factory with acrylic enamel.

cars are factory-finished with alkyd enamel, as in Fig. 27-4.

Fig. 27-4. A Datsun 1200 Coupe. Like many foreign cars, this car was finished at the factory with alkyd enamel.

Lacquers

From a refinishing point of view, *lacquers* are more or less *soluble* (able to be dissolved) no matter how long they have been on the car. This means that the old lacquer finish will dissolve slightly when new lacquer is sprayed over it. This creates a good bond between the old lacquer and the new, and is known as *penetration*.

When refinishing a *lacquer* paint job, then, it is a good idea to use lacquer for the new paint. Often, however, a car that was originally finished in lacquer is refinished in acrylic enamel. This may be done successfully if the old lacquer finish is properly prepared for the new enamel.

Enamels

As enamels dry, they become *more* insoluble and "tougher" than lacquers. They are not easily softened by the reducer in new enamel paint when the new paint is sprayed on the surface. Old *enamel* finishes, therefore, must be carefully sanded before repainting so that they will have *pores* in which the new paint may grip.

Special Paints

Different areas of an automobile or truck may be painted with some type of special

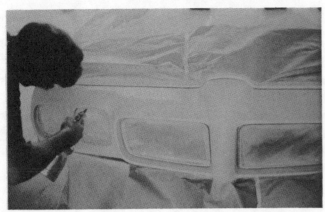

Fig. 27-5. Painting a flexible, urethane body part.

Fig. 27-6. Urethane additive; used to allow standard paints to be used when repairing urethane parts.

paint. A painter must be able to identify and apply these special paints when making routine body repairs on many newer vehicles. The most important of these, *urethane paints* or additives, are used on body parts made of urethane plastic. On the other hand, special *trunk paint* is available to refinish trunk interiors, whereas special *chassis paint* is packaged for use when painting chassis parts.

Urethane Paint—Many body panels are now being made with a special type of flexible, rubber-like plastic material known as *urethane*. Urethane parts are often used at the front and rear of some automobile designs, where they may partially take the place of a regular bumper. Fig. 27-5, for example, shows a painter refinishing a urethane front grille frame.

Special urethane *paint* is available and may be used on urethane body panels. On the other hand, special urethane *additives* are available, such as the product in Fig. 27-6. These products may be mixed with standard lacquers and enamels, *according to directions*, to allow "regular" paints to be used on urethane parts. If the additive is not used, regular enamel or lacquer may crack on the urethane's flexible surface.

Trunk Paint—Special paint for the inside of the luggage compartment (trunk) is known as

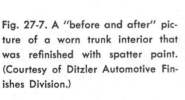

Fig. 27-7. A "before and after" picture of a worn trunk interior that was refinished with spatter paint. (Courtesy of Ditzler Automotive Finishes Division.)

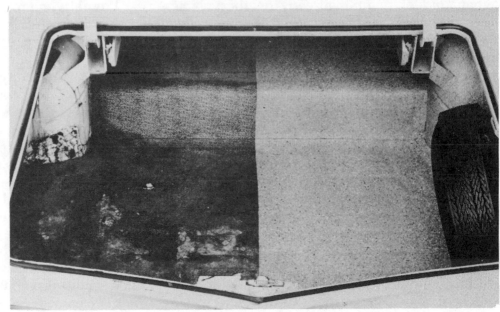

trunk paint. It is also known as *spatter paint*. In this product, small particles of a second paint color are suspended in the base color. These particles do not dissolve in the base paint because they are a different type of paint than is the base paint. When the paint is sprayed onto a surface, these particles hit the surface and spatter to make a speck of a second color in the base color. See Fig. 27-7.

Trunk paint can be bought in several basic colors to match the original color of the trunk interior. If necessary, the trunk may be spot repaired or completely refinished. All of the normal preparation steps should be followed, except that a paint undercoat does not need to be used unless there are rusted spots on the trunk floor.

Chassis Paint—Special tough, black enamel paints are made for chassis parts that need to be replaced or that have been repaired. Most chassis paints have an alkyd enamel base. They may be applied to new chassis parts before the parts are installed on the car. Chassis paint should also be used on areas underneath the car where heat, grinding, or hammering have broken the paint film.

MATCHING PAINT TYPES

When a vehicle (or part of it) is to be refinished, it is the painter's job to figure out what *kind* of paint is already on the vehicle. If the vehicle is fairly new and it is obvious that it has never been repainted, determining the paint *type* will be fairly easy. This is known as matching the original color. If the car has been repainted or spotted in, however, it will be more difficult to determine what type and color of paint is on the car.

Matching Undercoat Types

If it is necessary (or desirable) to match the manufacturer's original *undercoat,* it will be fairly easy. This is because all American manufacturers basically use the same materials and methods for the original *undercoating*: enamel primer or enamel primer-sealer. These are used because they have better adhesion, better color hold-out, and, when applied under factory con-

ditions, may not need as much sanding as would a lacquer primer. The original primer-sealer undercoat is a material that dries very hard. For this reason, it may be known as super-hard or *epoxyester* primer-sealer.

The original undercoat is applied on some makes by an *electrostatic* process. What this means is that the metal is given a *positive* electrical charge, and a big tank of undercoat is given a *negative* electrical charge. Then, when the positive-charge body and the negative-charge undercoat liquid come together, the electrical charge pulls the liquid onto the body, forming a tight bond. This process takes place when the body is completely dipped in the bath of undercoat. Fig. 27-8, for example, shows a new car body being dipped in an automatically-controlled bath of undercoat. After this dip, the undercoat is baked onto the body and dried in a high-temperature oven.

Matching Lacquer Types

General Motors Corporation is the only major American manufacturer that uses *lacquer* as the original topcoat on new automobiles. The lacquer General Motors uses on their cars (Chevrolet, Pontiac, Oldsmobile, Buick, Cadillac) is *acrylic* lacquer. For this reason, matching the original type of finish on General Motors cars should be done by using acrylic lacquer paint.

Presently, no major manufacturers are using *nitrocellulose* lacquer as their original lacquer finish. Therefore, it will not normally be necessary to match nitrocellulose lacquer on late-model cars. Today, nitrocellulose lacquer is more often used for restoration work on older cars, where desired.

Matching Enamel Types

Two types of enamel paints are being used today on new cars; acrylic enamel and alkyd enamel. Because of this, a painter must know which type of enamel is on a late-model car if paint work must be done on the car (or truck).

New cars made by AMC (American Motors Corporation), Chrysler Corporation, and the Ford Motor Company are factory-finished with *acrylic* enamel, generally beginning with the

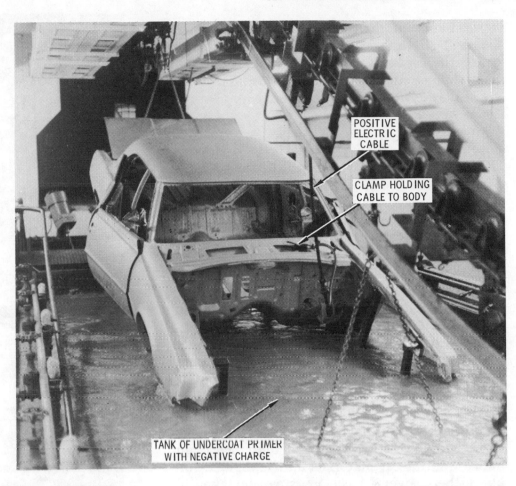

Fig. 27-8. A rustproofing primer bath. The positive electric cable charges the car body so that the negatively-charged primer will be drawn to the body. (Courtesy of Ford Customer Service Division.)

POSITIVE ELECTRIC CABLE

CLAMP HOLDING CABLE TO BODY

TANK OF UNDERCOAT PRIMER WITH NEGATIVE CHARGE

1965 models on up. Most small and medium-size American-made trucks are also finished in acrylic enamel, as are many foreign cars.

Some foreign cars are finished in *alkyd* enamel paint. When this is true, a sticker under the hood or on a door post may identify the paint as alkyd enamel. On the other hand, many large trucks and heavy, off-road equipment may be factory finished with *polyurethane* enamel.

Matching Repaint Types

If a car has been repainted, it may not have the original, factory-type paint on it. Because of this, a painter must be able to determine (figure out) what type of topcoat is now on the car. Most experienced painters are able to do this by simply *looking* at the topcoat very carefully.

For a new painter, however, or if there is a doubt about what type of paint is on the car, a simple test may be made to determine what

type of paint is on the car. To make this test, apply a small amount of lacquer thinner to a rag and rub the paint with the rag. This should be done under a fender lip or somewhere else near the bottom of the body where it will be out of sight. See Fig. 27-9.

ACRYLIC LACQUER THINNER

MARTIN SENOUR PAINTS

Fig. 27-9. Using lacquer thinner on a rag to test for the type of paint on the car.

After rubbing the paint with lacquer thinner, look at both the rag and the paint. If the paint colors the rag, the paint is lacquer. If the lacquer thinner curdles the paint, causing it to lift and bubble, the paint is enamel.

COLOR MATCHING

Matching the color of paint already on a car is one of the most difficult jobs in auto body repair. It is probably the most difficult part of automobile paint work. This is because there are so many factors that affect a color match. It is affected by paint booth lighting and ventilation, by how well the paint is mixed, by the quality of the materials and equipment used, and, especially, by the *techniques* (spraying methods) used to apply the color.

To properly match an automobile paint color, a painter must know a good deal about paint materials and how to use them *and* he must understand the equipment and tools used to apply the materials. For this reason, purchasing good-quality materials and equipment is one of the best investments that a body shop can make. With good materials and equipment on hand, then, several basic steps can be taken to help insure a good color match.

Matching the Original Factory Color

Generally speaking, it is easier to match a factory color than to match an unknown color on the car. As a first step to matching the original factory color, locate the body identification plate, as is being done in Fig. 27-10. The plate may be located on the cowl, on a door jamb, or elsewhere. Fig. 27-11 shows the identification plate with the paint (color) code circled. This color code can then be used to locate the correct color in a *color chip book*. The chip book will have a color chip of that code along with the code itself. *If the color chip for that code does not match the car's color, the car has been refinished in a color that was not the original color.*

Matching the Last Color Used

If a vehicle has been refinished, the color code of this color may not be known. In this

Fig. 27-10. Locating the body identification plate to find the vehicle's original color code. (Courtesy of Refinish Division, DuPont Company.)

Fig. 27-11. The manufacturer's original paint code is located somewhere on the body identification plate. (Courtesy of Refinish Division, DuPont Company.)

case, try to find a color chip sample of what looks to be the last color used on the vehicle. Place this chip over a clean, polished area on the present paint job. Wet both the chip and a spot on the paint, as in Fig. 27-12. Putting water on the old paint will give it a gloss so that it will have about the same lustre (shine) as the color chip.

While both the chip and the paint are wet, it is easy to determine whether or not the color chip is the same color as the color on the vehicle. If the colors look *at all* different, keep experimenting with different color chips until an exact match is found. When an *exact* match is found, the color code for that chip (printed

Fig. 27-12. To match the color on a vehicle when it is not the original color, *wet* the panel and a color chip to compare the two colors until an *exact* match is found.

in the chip book) may be used to order paint for the vehicle.

Sometimes, *no* color chips will appear close enough to the paint on the car. In this case, there may be a special color or a mixture of colors on the car. In these cases, paint will have to be custom-mixed to match the color actually on the car. To do this, remove a small part of the car that is painted with the special color. Then, *send this part to the paint store* and they will custom-mix an exact color to match the color on the part sent to them. Normally, custom mixes such as these *cannot* be returned to the paint store, so be certain that the customer has paid a deposit on the job to cover the shop's cost of this custom-mix paint.

Getting a Good Color Match

Having the correct color of paint in the can is only the *beginning* of a good color match. Even the correct color may not match perfectly the first time it is sprayed. This is because there are several *other* factors that definitely affect a good color match. Because of these factors, then, the following pointers should be kept in mind when trying to get the best possible color match.

Use Top-Quality Materials—When buying paint and paint *materials*, always deal with a product company and a store that *specialize* in automobile painting products. For the best results, do not buy from a store that sells the materials only as a sideline. Unknown paints and cheap reducers and thinners often do not

give as good resuts as do name-brand, quality products. Good paint materials, purchased from a reliable parts house or supplier, are good insurance for the best painting results.

Use Top-Quality Equipment—Buying paint *equipment* is like buying paint material. The best place to buy equipment is also from a supplier (store) whose main business is selling automobile paint equipment. They will be interested in selling only good equipment that will do a good job. The equipment they sell will have parts and service readily available if repairs are ever needed.

The spray gun itself is probably the most important piece of equipment, since it is used so often and must do so many jobs. For these reasons, many shops use *three* spray guns. See Fig. 27-13. One gun is used for lacquers, one for enamels, and one for the shop's undercoat, which is normally lacquer primer-surfacer. Of course, each spray gun must be thoroughly cleaned after each spraying job, but having three guns reduces the chances of getting different materials mixed up within the same gun.

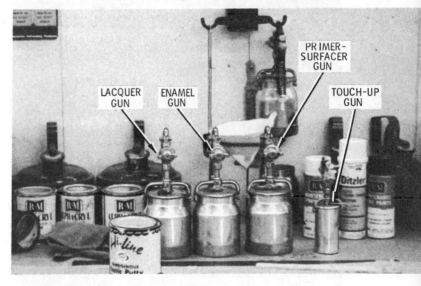

Fig. 27-13. Many shops use three spray guns plus a touch-up gun to keep the different types of paint materials separate.

Use Clean Air—Unbelievable as it may seem, *dirt* from compressed air lines often causes blemishes and trouble during paint work. For this reason, it is important that good separator-regulators be used to keep the air to the spray gun clean and dry. Equally important is keeping all the *air filters* in the compressed air system clean, and draining the separator regularly. See Fig. 27-14. The air compressor itself and any drops in the air system should also be drained regularly.

If dirt or moisture is suspected in the air lines during a paint job, turn off the exhaust fan and spray-paint a test panel in the paint room. Carefully look at the test panel for any dirt or moisture in the fresh paint. If there is any dirt or moisture in the fresh paint, stop painting until the problem is cleared up.

Fig. 27-15. Using a *handkerchief* test to reveal any dirt, water, or oil in the air lines.

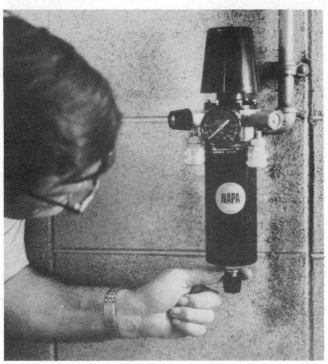

Fig. 27-14. Draining the separator-regulator.

Another method to check for dirt and moisture is to first remove the paint cup and air cap from the spray gun. Then, hold a clean white handkerchief over the gun nozzle and pull the trigger back *just far enough to release air,* not fluid. This way, any dirt, water or oil in the air lines will "show up" on the handkerchief. See Fig. 27-15.

Thoroughly Stir the Paint—Mixing the paint *in the can* is very necessary *before* adding any vehicle such as thinner or reducer. To properly stir and mix the material, use a paint paddle made of wood or metal, as in Fig. 27-16. The end of the paddle is sometimes tapered to a

Fig. 27-16. Paint must always be very thoroughly stirred *before* any thinner or reducer is added. (Courtesy of Refinish Division, DuPont Company).

sharp edge, like the edge of a chisel. This makes it easy to break up any material that has settled and stuck to the bottom of the can. Another method of thoroughly mixing the paint, of course, is to use a paint *shaker*, as in Fig. 27-17.

Paint must always be thoroughly stirred, especially after it has been in storage for a long time. While in storage, paint tends to settle

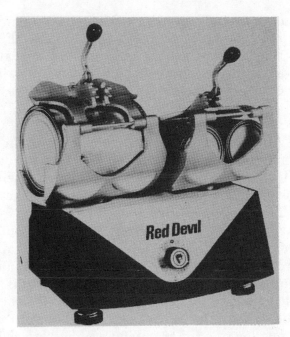

Fig. 27 17. A paint shaker. Many shops use a shaker to correctly mix paints before opening the can. (Courtesy of PPG Industries, Inc.)

into different parts, as in Fig. 27-18. If the paint is not stirred, all the parts of the paint will not be mixed thoroughly. This may cause it to not spray uniformly and will usually help cause a poor color match.

Then, after thinner or reducer has been added, the mixture must again be thoroughly stirred before being strained into the spray gun cup. One reason for this is that metallic flakes quickly settle to the bottom of the container

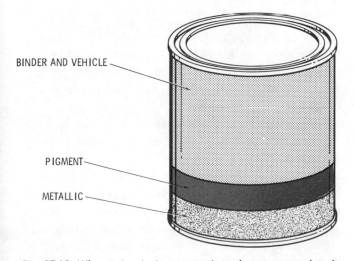

Fig. 27-18. When paint sits in storage, it tends to separate into its different parts.

after thinner or reducer has been added. This will nearly always change the topcoat color, causing a color mismatch on the finished job.

Judge the Color in the Correct Light—The *light* in a repair shop can be misleading. If the lights are regular *incandescent lamps* (ordinary light bulbs), the light will be slightly red when compared to daylight. Matching colors under this type of light is most difficult. See Fig. 27-19.

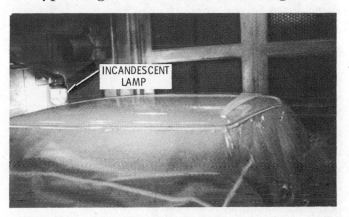

Fig. 27-19. A paint booth with artificial lighting from an incandescent bulb.

Fluorescent lights also give off a reddish color and it is also more difficult to match colors under this light than under natural light. However, flourescent lights are preferable to incandescent bulbs. Generally speaking, *all* artificial lighting makes it difficult to match paint colors.

The *best* light to use when matching paint is to paint in a room with *northern exposure* to as much *natural light* as possible. Natural light is the light of the sun; all other light is artificial light. Under natural light, color matching will be more easily done.

Judge the Color When It Is Dry—Generally speaking, new paint that is sprayed on a panel will darken slightly as it dries. Therefore, fresh, wet paint may be slightly lighter than the older, dry color. An experienced painter allows for this difference in color when judging a new color match.

MATCHING METALLIC PAINTS

One of the most skilled and difficult jobs that an automotive painter must be able to do is to match *metallic* paints. This is very important because paints with metallic *flakes* added to the pigment (metallic paint) are very popular original colors. Because the flakes reflect *light* while the pigments reflect *color*, how the flakes are arranged in the paint has a good deal to do with how well the new paint matches the old paint.

The metal *flakes* in metallic paint give the paint a sparkling, jewel-like appearance whenever light is reflected by the paint. Therefore, metallic paint is not only a color but also a color *effect*. Fig. 27-20 shows how the metallic flakes in the paint reflect light.

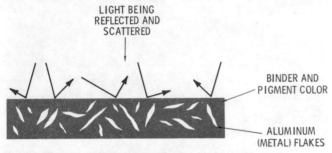

Fig. 27-20. In a *metallic* paint topcoat, small metal flakes (usually aluminum) are used to reflect light at different angles.

There are two main *variables* (items the painter can change) when applying metallic paints. A painter must know what can be changed and what the change will do to help a new metallic color match the color on the car. Generally speaking, these two items are the *spraying technique* and the *vehicle used*.

Test Card—To properly match a metallic color, it is best to "experiment" by painting

Fig. 27-21. Using a test card to practice the technique needed to match a given metallic color. (Courtesy of Refinish Division, DuPont Company.)

on a test card. Then, the card may be compared with the color on the car to be painted. See Fig. 27-21. Finally, when the test card and the car's color match, the same technique used to paint the card should be used to paint the car.

Spraying Technique

With exactly the same metallic paint in a spray gun, changing the *spraying technique* will change a metallic color to some extent. This is because metallic colors tend to change with the *wetness* (thickness) of the paint.

Wet Spray Techniques—If the spray gun is held close to the surface being sprayed and lower air pressure at the spray gun is used, more paint will be sprayed on the surface. This is called a *wet spray technique*. It causes the color to be *darker*. This is because the flakes are able to sink down in the wet paint and lay flat, as in Fig. 27-22. Because they lay flat and are deeper in the paint, they reflect less light. This makes the paint look darker.

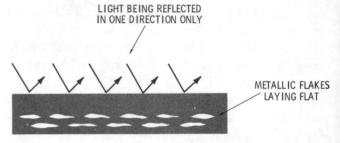

Fig. 27-22. When metallic paint is sprayed *wet*, the metallic flakes settle to the bottom of the paint. This makes the paint appear darker.

Other wet spray techniques include *opening* the spray gun's *fluid feed valve* more, *reducing* the size of the *spray pattern, slowing down* the *spraying stroke*, and allowing *less flash time* between coats. Any of these methods may be used alone or in combination, as necessary, to produce a *wetter* coat; making the metallic color appear *darker*.

Dry Spray Techniques—If the spray gun is held farther away from the panel, less paint will reach the surface. This is because a larger area is being sprayed than when the gun is held close, causing more paint to be lost in the air as *overspray*. This is known as a *dry spray technique*. It causes the color to be *lighter*. This is because metallic flakes stand up in the "drier" paint, rather than lay flat, as was shown earlier in Fig. 27-20. Because the flakes stand up closer to the surfacer of the paint, they reflect more light, and at different angles. This is because the paint is too "dry" for the flakes to have time to settle down to the bottom of the coat.

Other *dry spray techniques* include *closing* the *fluid valve* slightly, *increasing* the *spray pattern size*, increasing the *speed* of the *spraying stroke*, and *increasing* the *flash time* between coats. Any of these methods may be used alone or in combination, as necessary, to produce a drier coat and make the metallic finish appear lighter.

Vehicle Used

Many times, matching metallic colors is made more difficult by not using the correct thinner or reducer vehicle for shop conditions. Other times, problems can come up from using a cheap vehicle of poor quality. If cheap, poor quality vehicle is used, for example, the metallic flakes may not position themselves correctly in the wet paint. If this happens, some flakes will settle down and lay flat while others will stand up. This causes light and dark spots in the finish and is known as *mottling*.

Using Slow-Drying Vehicle—If metallic paint is applied with a slow-drying vehicle, the effect is the same as when spraying wet and close to the surface; the metallic flakes will settle closer to the bottom of the coat. They will also lay flat on top of each other, as shown in Fig. 27-22. This is because the flakes will have time to settle deeper in the finish by the time that the slow-drying vehicle "flashes off." This will produce a darker, stronger color.

Using Fast-Drying Vehicle—If metallic paint is applied with a faster-drying vehicle, the basic effect is the same as when spraying the topcoat dry and farther away from the surface. The metallic flakes will stand up and be "trapped" near the surface of the coat because the vehicle will allow the paint to "flash off" before the flakes have settled. This will produce a lighter, more metallic looking finish, as in Fig. 27-20.

PREVENTING DIRTY PAINT

One of the biggest headaches in the automobile refinishing business is the mysterious dust and dirt that seems to come from nowhere to mar freshly painted vehicles. Fortunately, this dirt can usually be prevented, but this takes extra time; some painters do not care enough about their work to take the extra time needed to help prevent dirty paint. For this reason, the dirt that spoils a nice, fresh paint job may come from the vehicle itself, the painter himself, the shop, or the paint materials. Discussed below, then, are the basic items to remember when trying to prevent dirty paint.

Clean the Car—Failure to remove dirt from the vehicle's cracks, underbody, and fenders is a main source of dirt. Dirt can fall or be blown off the vehicle and be carried into the fresh paint by the air currents (spraying and ventilating) in the booth while the spraying is being done. The slight additional time and cost to steam- or pressure-clean the underside of a vehicle is good insurance for clean, top-quality paint jobs.

Basic cleaning methods include washing the vehicle *thoroughly* with a water hose, as in Fig. 27-23. Then, a blow (dust) gun should be used with about 100 psi to blow any dirt and dust from body seams and under moldings. These cleaning jobs should be done before

Fig. 27-23. Washing the body underside with a water hose.

final preparation so that any dirt that is washed or blown out will not fall on clean, prepared surfaces.

Clean the Shop—Good "housekeeping" will help eliminate dust or dirt on the walls, floor, air hose, or spray gun that could find its way into wet paint. Clean the major shop areas before paint work is done by washing them down with a water hose or by dusting them with *clean* rags. To help keep any stray dust down on the floor, it is a good idea to always *wet down* the floor of the paint booth before spraying. See Fig. 27-24.

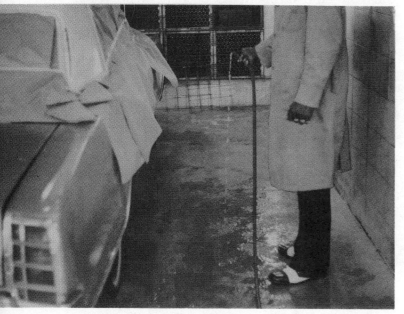

Fig. 27-24. To help keep any dust on the floor, wet down the paint room floor with a water hose.

Special oil-saturated sweeping compounds should be used to sweep in and around the paint booth. This will help collect floor dust or keep it settled. In the paint booth's *air exhaust system*, an automatic damper should be installed to prevent any air from blowing back into the paint booth and possibly carrying dirt back into the paint booth after the fan has been turned off. (The damper will also keep cold air out in the winter.) Finally, be sure that the paint booth is kept free of anything that might be called "junk," since these items will add to the dirt hazard in the booth.

Prepare the Car Outside the Paint Booth—Always complete all the body work and most of the paint preparation *outside* the paint booth. Check to be sure that no sanding or body work has been done in the paint booth. If this work *has* been done, the grinding grit and any sanding dust left by that work must be removed from the paint booth.

Prevent Drafts in the Paint Booth—Always keep the doors of the paint booth *closed* after the exhaust fan has been turned on. To do this, take enough paint, tools, and materials into the paint booth to complete the job *before* doing *any* actual painting. By doing this, you will be able to avoid opening any doors to go in and out for supplies while the new paint job is wet. To leave the booth after painting, use only the small door at the *fan* end of the paint booth. Leave the large door(s) to the paint room closed for about an hour after the job has been finished.

Use Clean Equipment—Be on the lookout for *dust* that may settle on the air transformer, the hoses, or any ledges in the booth. Clean these areas often. Any equipment that might be used during drying, such as travelling ovens or portable heat panels, should be dusted before using, kept covered, or stored in a separate compartment at one end of the booth.

Wear Clean Clothes—If street clothes or untreated coveralls are worn in the paint booth, a big chance is being taken on getting dust in the paint work. For this reason, it is a good idea to wear *starched coveralls* for painting, preferably *synthetic* (man-made) cloth with anti-static treatment. Gloves, if worn, should also be free of lint. If a customer wants to see his car being painted, it is better to buy a paint booth with windows in it than to let people inside the booth with their dusty clothes and shoes.

Prepare the Paint Properly—Be careful when choosing containers used to mix and prepare the paint being used. Mixing paint in old paint cans may cause the new paint to be contaminated by old paint skins, dried deposits, or dirt that may be in the can. These are sometimes fine enough to actually pass through the strainer and then show up on the painted car.

For best results, first mix the paint in its own container on a mixing machine. Then mix the paint and its vehicle in a separate, *clean* can. A large, clean coffee can is good for this job. Be sure to use the right vehicle for the job being done. (Using the wrong vehicle may cause rough paint conditions that look like dirty paint.)

After the paint and vehicle are mixed, the mixture should be *strained* to remove any fine dirt or paint scum. See Fig. 27-25. Regular paint strainers are either sold or given away by paint manufacturing companies and should be used to strain the mixture into the cup.

Fig. 27-26. Using a clean cloth to wipe build-up off the nozzle of the spray gun.

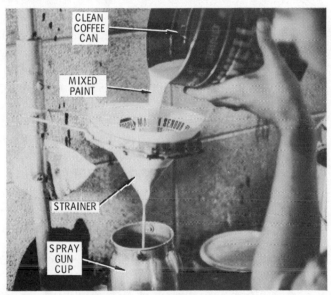

Fig. 27-25. Straining the mixed paint and vehicle into a spray gun cup.

Start Painting at Correct End of the Booth— When an overall paint job is being done, start painting at the end of the booth *opposite the end of the booth where the exhaust fan is located*. Then, move along the car *toward* the exhaust fan. By doing this, the spray mist is carried (pulled by the fan) over the panels that have *not* been painted, instead of over the finished work.

Keep the Gun's Nozzle Clean—During painting, paint particles will often build up on the spray gun's *nozzle*, forming a kind of fuzz. This build-up should be wiped off every so often with a *clean, lint-free* cloth. See Fig. 27-26. If it is not wiped off, it will continue to build up until parts of it blow off in globs, making a bad blemish on the wet paint surface.

Use Clean Masking Materials—It is best to use only good, clean masking materials. Name-brand masking paper will be fairly clean, as will good masking tape. Masking materials should be stored away from the dust and floor dirt of the shop. Before using any masking tape and paper, wipe off any shop dust that may be on the materials.

Use Clean Tack Rags—Have on hand a supply of clean, factory-varnished tack rags. When these are available, a painter will not have to use dirty tack rags. When the door jambs and trunk edges are sprayed, any dust blown out

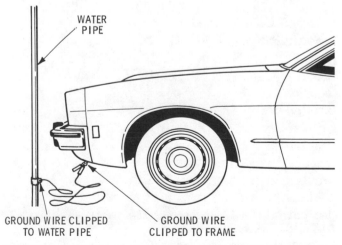

Fig. 27-27. Grounding the car helps prevent any dust from being pulled to the car by static electricity.

of these areas can be removed with a clean tack rag before painting the outside of the car.

Ground the Vehicle Electrically—During winter (or when humidity is very low), a vehicle will usually carry a small charge of *static electricity*. This electricity attracts dust like a magnet and makes removing the dust very difficult. To prevent this, run a ground wire from the car body (or frame) to a good ground such as a water pipe, but *not* to the booth itself. This should be done as soon as the car is in the paint booth, as in Fig. 27-27.

USING A SPRAY GUN

To be successful when using a spray gun, *two basic facts* must be kept in mind. *First,* the gun's paint and air controls must be *properly adjusted. Secondly,* the gun must then be *held and moved* correctly. When these basic facts are kept in mind, repeated practice will usually build up good painting results.

Adjusting the Air Pressure

Before adjusting the spray gun itself, adjust the air pressure at the regulator for the paint job to be done. Be certain to use a gauge *at the gun* to measure the *exact* air pressure *at the*

Fig. 27-28. Check the actual air pressure *at the gun* by installing a pressure gauge at the gun inlet.

gun. See Fig. 27-28. If no gauge is available at the gun, set the air pressure on the regulator gauge slightly higher than needed at the gun, to allow for a pressure drop in the hose. The approximate pressure drop may be figured by using the table given elsewhere in this section.

What Air Pressure to Use—Usually, the air pressure recommended for the paint being sprayed is listed on the paint can itself. In all cases, any recommendations *on the can* are the air pressures that should be used.

If no recommendations are given, the following *general recommendations* may be used. With *enamel* paints, for example, many painters are able to use lower pressures and move in closer to the work. By doing this, less dirt and dust is stirred up and less paint is lost as overspray. These recommendations, then, are only *general guidelines.* It is OK to use different pressures if better results are seen under given shop conditions. All pressure adjustments are made at the regulator with the spray gun trigger held all the way back and the gun empty.

Lacquers; spot repair: 30-35 psi.
Lacquers; overall refinishing: 40-45 psi.
Acrylic Enamels; spot repair: 45-65 psi.
Acrylic Enamels; overall refinishing: 50-70 psi.
Alkyd Enamels; panel or overall refinishing: 45-55 psi.

Adjusting the Spray Gun

Before a vehicle may actually be painted, the spray gun itself must be adjusted. There are two basic spray gun adjustments to make: the *fluid feed* and the *pattern control.* These must be adjusted *after* the paint is already in the gun and *after* the air pressure to the gun has been adjusted at the regulator.

Fluid Control—The *fluid control valve* adjusts the amount of *fluid* (paint) that is allowed to go through the nozzle. The valve must be adjusted differently for different types of jobs. Fig. 27-29 shows the fluid control valve being adjusted. For an approximate setting, first close the valve fully. Then, open it about halfway

Fig. 27-29. Adjusting the fluid control valve. (Courtesy of Refinish Division, DuPont Company.)

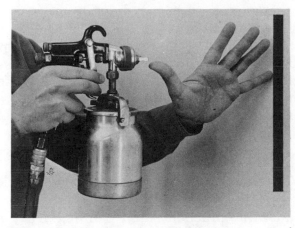

Fig. 27-31. To estimate the gun-to-work distance, open your hand and position the gun as shown. (Courtesy of Refinish Division, DuPont Company.)

for a small spot repair, or all the way for a panel or overall job.

Pattern Control—The *pattern control valve* adjusts the amount of air that is allowed to go out the air horn holes. This valve, like the fluid control valve, may need to be adjusted slightly for different painting conditions. However, generally speaking, it should first be adjusted like the fluid control valve; about halfway open for spot repairs and all the way open for panel or overall repairs. Fig. 27-30 shows the pattern control valve being adjusted.

Fig. 27-32. A normal test spray pattern. The pattern should be about 5" long for spot repair work or about 9" long for panel repair work and overall refinishing. (Courtesy of Refinish Division, DuPont Company.)

Fig. 27-30. Adjusting the pattern control valve. (Courtesy of Refinish Division, DuPont Company.)

Final Adjustments

Just before beginning a spray job, quickly "shoot" a test spot to check the gun and air pressure adjustments. This should be done on a card or piece of paper, *not* on the job to be painted. First, hold the gun about 6 to 8 inches from the surface used for testing. See Fig. 27-31. Then, quickly pull the trigger all the way back and release it immediately. This should leave a painted, oval pattern, as shown in Fig. 27-32.

After spraying the test pattern, look at it carefully. If it is too long or too short, adjust the pattern control valve slightly. If the pattern appears too coarse or too wet, Fig. 27-33,

Fig. 27-33. A test spray pattern that is too coarse and too wet. (Courtesy of Refinish Division, DuPont Company.)

close the fluid valve slightly or increase the air pressure slightly. On the other hand, if the pattern is too dry and powdery-looking, open the fluid valve and/or reduce the air pressure slightly. After making any adjustments, continue to "shoot" test patterns until the pattern is correct.

Operating the Gun

Generally speaking, the following "rules" for operating a spray gun should be kept in mind while practicing *and* painting. They are based on the recommendations of the Refinish Division of the DuPont Company and are listed here courtesy of the division.

1. Hold the spray gun at the proper distance for the material being sprayed: 6 to 8 inches for lacquers; 8 to 10 inches for enamels.
2. Hold the gun *level* so that it is at right angles to most of the car's surfaces, which are vertical. See Fig. 27-34. On *flat* surfaces (hoods, roofs) the gun should be pointed straight down, as in Fig. 27-35.

Fig. 27-35. When spraying a *flat* surface, hold the spray gun so that it points down. (Courtesy of 3M Company, Automotive Division.)

3. Move the gun *parallel* to the surface, as in Fig. 27-36. Generally speaking, do not *arc* the gun. However, when blending

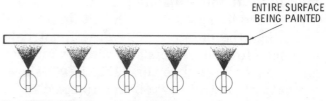

Fig. 27-36. Hold the gun *parallel* to the surface if the entire surface is being painted.

Fig. 27-34. When spraying a *vertical* surface, hold the spray gun level. (Courtesy, Rinshed-Mason Products Division of Inmont Corporation.)

in a spot repair, it *is* necessary to arc the gun. See Fig. 27-37.

4. Move the gun with a steady, deliberate pass, about one foot per second. Be careful to *not* stop in one place or the sprayed coat will drip and run.

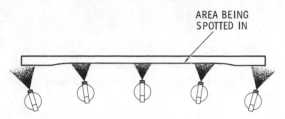

AREA BEING SPOTTED IN

Fig. 27-37. Arc the gun *only* during spot repairs, *never* during panel or overall refinishing.

5. Release the trigger at the end of each stroke or pass *when the spray is off the edge of the panel*. Then, pull back on the trigger as you begin the pass in the opposite direction. In other words, turn off the spray gun at the end of each sweep. This helps avoid runs, saves material, and helps reduce overspray.

6. If a panel is being painted off the car, *banding* may help produce a nicer job. Banding is a single coat applied with a small spray pattern to "frame-in" an area to be sprayed. It assures covering the edges of an area without having to spray a great deal beyond the spray area. See Fig. 27-38.

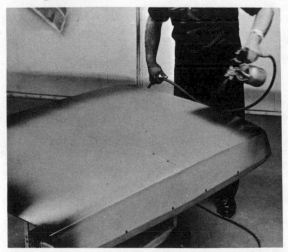

Fig. 27-38. The *banding* process; a first coat sprayed around the outer edge of a panel. (Courtesy of Refinish Division, DuPont Company.)

7. Generally speaking, start the *first* pass at the *top* of an upright surface. Here, the spray gun *nozzle* should be level with the *top* of the surface. This means that the upper half of the spray pattern will shoot off into space or will hit the masking around the area, which is OK.

8. Make the *second* pass in the opposite direction and *one-half* the width of the spray pattern. Hold the nozzle level with the lower edge of the first pass. Thus, one-half of the second pass overlaps the first pass and the other half is sprayed on the unpainted area, as in Fig. 27-39.

9. Continue back and forth passes, releasing the trigger at the end of each pass and lowering each pass one-half the width of the pattern.

10. Finally, make the last pass with the lower half of the spray being sprayed *below* the surface being painted.

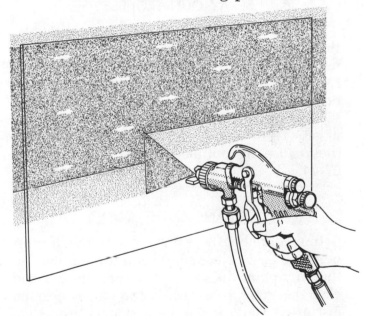

Fig. 27-39. The basic spraying procedure for a single coat. One-half of each pass should overlap the previous pass.

Types of Coats

The basic method of spraying, just described, is called a *single coat*. For a double coat, repeat the single coat procedure immediately. When spraying lacquer, double coats should always be used. Generally, two or more *double* coats are required to properly apply a lacquer topcoat, allowing a "flash-time" of several minutes between each double coat. At least two single coats are normally required to apply enamels. The first coat should be allowed to set up slightly (become tacky) before the second coat is applied.

Coat Thickness—There are three basic thicknesses of any sprayed coat: light, medium, and heavy. The easiest way to control the degree of thickness is the speed with which the gun is moved.

Besides the three basic coats just discussed, there are also coats known as *mist coats*. These are normally used as final coats over many types of color coats. Mist coats help to level the final coat and melt in any overspray. A mist coat is made by applying a rich, slow-drying vehicle with just a small amount of paint added for color.

SPRAY GUN TROUBLES

There are five major spray gun troubles that may happen while spray painting. These may be due to the gun being dirty or incorrectly adjusted, or they may be due to the gun not being handled correctly. Each problem will produce a certain type of defect in the finish. These major troubles and the defects they cause are outlined in Fig. 27-40 through 27-44.

CLEANING THE GUN

Immediately after using a spray gun, it must be *thoroughly* cleaned. This must be done so that any paint does not dry inside the gun and clog the gun's passages. If the gun is cleaned just after using, it will be easier to clean than if the paint dries in the passages and must be removed. Figs. 27-45 through 27-52 show how to clean a spray gun.

PAINT PROBLEMS

Although they have carefully prepared the surface, sometimes even the best painters have paint problems show up on a fresh paint job. These can be caused by any number of items

Fig. 27-40. DEFECT: *Faulty Spray Patterns.* CAUSE: Poor spray patterns from the gun are normally caused by clogged nozzle holes. Carefully cleaning the gun nozzle will normally solve the problem.

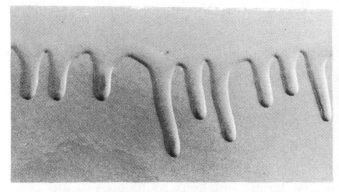

Fig. 27-41. DEFECT: *Runs and Sags.* CAUSES: Gun held too close or moved too slowly; fluid valve opened too far; too little air pressure. If runs and sags happen only in the center of the panel, it is probably caused by arcing the gun. (Courtesy of Refinish Division, DuPont Company.)

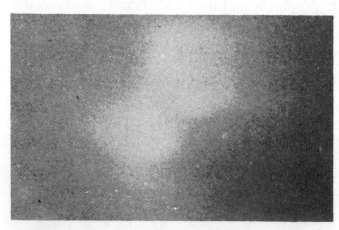

Fig. 27-42. DEFECT: *Thin Coverage.* CAUSES: Gun held too far away or moved too rapidly; fluid valve closed too far. (Courtesy of Refinish Division, DuPont Company.)

that may have been overlooked or simply not realized for the job being done. These problems and their probable causes are outlined in Figs. 27-53 through 27-67.

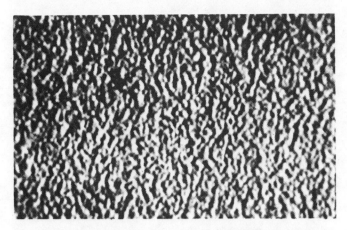

Fig. 27-43. DEFECT: *Excessive Orange Peel.* CAUSES: Some orange peel is normal in all finishes, including lacquers before they are compounded. Excessive orange peel may be caused by the gun being held too far away or excessive air pressure being used. (Courtesy of Refinish Division, DuPont Company.)

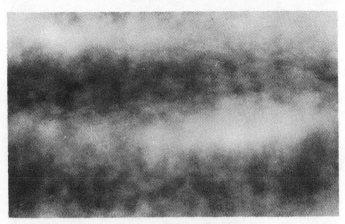

Fig. 27-44. DEFECT: *"Zebra Effect."* CAUSE: This condition is normally caused by tilting the gun so that one *part* of the spray pattern is reaching the surface first. (Courtesy of Refinish Division, DuPont Company.)

PROCEDURE: CLEANING A PAINT SPRAY GUN

Fig. 27-45. Cleaning a Spray Gun. *Step 1:* Unscrew the air nozzle cap about 3 turns. (Courtesy of Refinish Division, DuPont Company.)

Fig. 27-46. *Step 2:* Hold a cloth over the loosened air cap. Pull back on the trigger all the way. This will force most of the paint in the gun back into the paint cup.

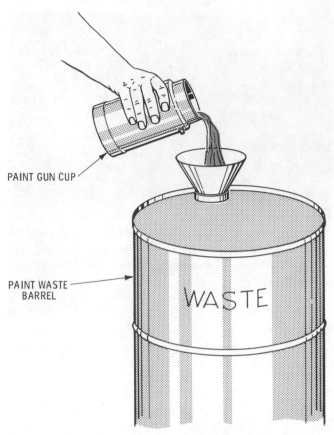

PAINT GUN CUP

PAINT WASTE
BARREL

WASTE

Fig. 27-47. *Step 3:* Pour all the paint mixture out of the paint cup.

GUN AND EQUIPMENT
CLEANER

Fig. 27-48. *Step 4:* Fill the paint cup about ⅓ full. Use lacquer thinner, cheap bulk thinner/reducer, or gun and equipment cleaner.

Fig. 27-49. *Step 5:* Position the gun back on top of the cup and tighten the air nozzle. Pull back on the trigger all the way. This will allow solvent to be drawn up through the gun and out the nozzle.

Fig. 27-50. *Step 6:* Remove the nozzle and clean all the gun parts in clean solvent. Thoroughly clean the paint cup.

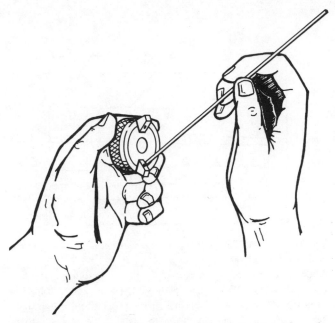

Fig. 27-51. *Step 7:* Use a broom straw or a toothpick to clean the nozzle holes in the nozzle cap. Do *not* use wire or nails to do this; they might damage the small holes.

Fig. 27-52. *Step 8:* Again, fill the cup about ⅓ full. Use more of the same solvent used in Step 4. Completely reassemble the gun. Wipe down the entire gun with a clean cloth.

COMMON PAINT PROBLEMS AND POSSIBLE REMEDIES

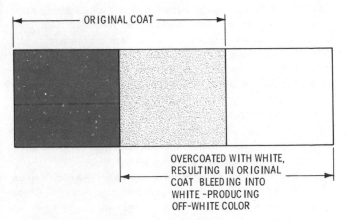

Fig. 27-53. DEFECT: *Bleeding*—a different color appearing within, and seeping through, a new topcoat.
CAUSE: Soluble dyes or pigments that were on the old surface before it was repainted. This is especially true with older *red* colors or dyes.
REMEDY: Seal the defective area with a bleeder sealer or primer-surfacer designed to help prevent bleeding. Avoid painting lighter colors over reds.

Fig. 27-54. DEFECT: *Blistering*—bubbles or pimples appearing in the paint film, sometimes months after the job was painted.
CAUSE: Moisture or air trapped under the paint film. Improper surface cleaning or preparation. Using the wrong (or cheap) vehicle. Excessive film thickness. Oil, water, or dirt in the compressed air that was used to apply the paint.
REMEDY: Sand or strip the finish to remove the blistered area and then repaint. (Courtesy of Refinish Division, DuPont Company.)

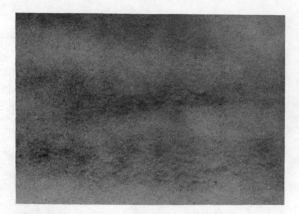

Fig. 27-55. DEFECT: *Blushing*—a milky-white haze or mist. Usually appears on lacquers only.
CAUSES: High shop humidity. Using cheap thinners.
REMEDY: Add a retarder to the last color coat or spray a medium-to-wet coat of retarder on the finish. (Courtesy of Refinish Division, DuPont Company.)

Fig. 27-57. DEFECT: *Crazing*—small cracks and fine splits all over the area. Also known as *cobwebs* or *crow's feet*.
CAUSES: Shop too cold. Original paint is under stress and breaks up due to the softening action of the solvents being applied.
REMEDY: Continue applying wet coats of color, using the wettest possible vehicle that shop conditions will allow. (Courtesy of Refinish Division, Dupont Company.)

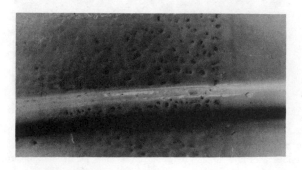

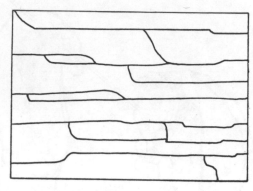

Fig. 27-56. DEFECTS: *Cracking* and *Line Checking*—actual cracks in the surface of the finish.
CAUSES: Excessive film thickness. Cracking: materials not mixed well; not enough flash time allowed between coats; using the wrong additives. Line Checking: Improper surface preparation.
REMEDY: Remove the color down to at least the primer and repaint. (Courtesy of Refinish Division, DuPont Company.)

Fig. 27-58. DEFECT: *Featheredge Cracking*—splitting to the substrate along the featheredge of a repair.
CAUSES: "Piling on" heavy, wet coats. Improperly thinning paint materials. Force-drying primer-surfacer by fanning it with compressed air from the primer gun. Poor surface preparation.
REMEDY: Remove the defective topcoat *and* primer-surfacer coat. Correctly prepare and repaint the area. (Courtesy of Refinish Division, DuPont Company.)

Fig. 27-59. DEFECT: *Fisheyes*—small, crater-like "holes" in a finish shortly after it has been applied.
CAUSES: Silicone particles and other dirt repelling the paint so that the paint cannot form a smooth film.
REMEDY: Remove the damaged new paint. Thoroughly clean the old finish or area *exactly according to directions*. Check for dirt or oil in shop rags, compressed air, tools, etc. In extreme cases, additives to help control fisheyes may be used in the topcoat mix. (Courtesy of Refinish Division, DuPont Company.)

Fig. 27-60. DEFECT: *Lifting*—distortion or shriveling of the topcoat as it is applied or as it dries.
CAUSES: Solvents in the new topcoat attacking the old topcoat. Improper flash or recoat time allowed between coats of alkyd enamel. Improper drying time. Can also be caused by applying topcoats over incompatible sealers or primers, by improper thinning or reducing, or by applying the topcoat over an improperly prepared surface.
REMEDY: Remove the damaged new paint and refinish the area. (Courtesy of Refinish Division, DuPont Company.)

Fig. 27-61. DEFECT: *Mottling*—metal flakes floating together in metallic colors to form a spotty appearance.
CAUSES: Using too much thinner or reducer. Not completely mixing the color and vehicle. Spraying too wet. Using too slow drying a vehicle in cold weather.
REMEDY: Allow the mottled color coat to set up. Then, apply a drier double coat or two single coats, depending on which topcoat is being applied. (Courtesy of Refinish Division, DuPont Company.)

Fig. 27-62. DEFECT: *Peeling, Poor Adhesion, Chipping.*
CAUSES: Poor bonding between the substrate and the topcoat due to not completely mixing the materials used. Poor surface preparation. Not using the proper sealer.
REMEDY: Remove the damaged area and a good deal of material *around* the area. Refinish. (Courtesy of Refinish Division, DuPont Company.)

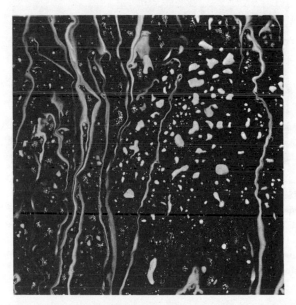

Fig. 27-63. DEFECT: *Precipitation*—paint curdles or breaks up.
CAUSES: Using the incorrect vehicle (thinner or reducer) or adding or mixing the vehicle incorrectly. Using old paint. Overheating the paint during spraying or storage.
REMEDY: Remove any paint that has been sprayed and refinish the area. Use the correct vehicle for shop conditions and mix the vehicle thoroughly with good, fresh color. (Courtesy, Rinshed-Mason Products Division of Inmont Corporation.)

Fig. 27-64. DEFECT: *Sandscratch Swelling*—sandscratches under the topcoat have been enlarged by being partially dissolved and swelled due to the solvents in the new topcoat.
CAUSES: Using too coarse a sandpaper to prepare the substrate. Using a slow-drying vehicle without having used a sealer.
REMEDY: Sand the surface down to a smooth finish and use a sealer before reapplying the topcoat. (Courtesy of Refinish Division, DuPont Company.)

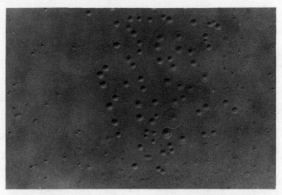

Fig. 27-65. DEFECT: *Solvent Popping*—blisters appear on the paint surface soon after refinishing.
CAUSES: Poor surface preparation. Using the wrong vehicle (thinner or reducer). Allowing too little drying time between coats; having "force-dried" the primer-surfacer.
REMEDY: If the blisters are not too severe, they may be sanded out and the area then refinished. If the damage is extensive, the area should be removed down to the bare metal and then refinished. (Courtesy of Refinish Division, DuPont Company.)

Fig. 27-66. DEFECT: *Water Spotting*—water stains on the finish.
CAUSES: Exposing a finish to water before it is completely dry; washing a car in bright sunlight.
REMEDY: Polish the area after the paint has cured for at least 30 days. Compound the area if polishing does not remove the stain. In severe cases, sand the area and refinish. (Courtesy of Refinish Division, DuPont Company.)

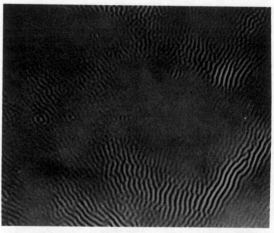

Fig. 27-67. DEFECT: *Wrinkling*—an enamel defect that appears while the enamel is being sprayed or while it is drying.
CAUSES: Baking or force-drying enamel too soon. "Piling on" thick, heavy coats. Warm air drafts in the shop; improper drying techniques.
REMEDY: Remove the wrinkled enamel and refinish. (Courtesy of Refinish Division, DuPont Company.)

Paint Rub-Out and Restoration

How *good* a vehicle's topcoat looks is very important for good customer satisfaction. Customers often judge the entire repair job on the appearance of the topcoat. "Spotted areas" that have been refinished and that blend in with the rest of the topcoat are very likely to impress customers with quality work. See Fig. 28-1.

Fig. 28-1. When a customer looks at a body repair, the first part of the repair that is noticed is usually the *topcoat*. (Courtesy of Refinish Division, DuPont Company.)

Wherever and whenever the topcoat is affected by a body man's work, it is an opportunity for him to build a good reputation. A vehicle's topcoat is usually the most impressive part of the vehicle since it is the part most often seen and noticed. Notice the body damage in

Fig. 28-2. In Fig. 28-3, the damage has been repaired. In the repair area, note that the refinished *topcoat* is the first part of the job that

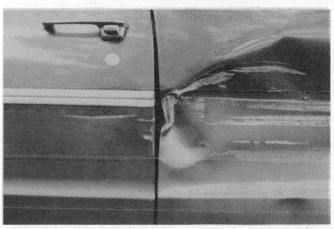

Fig. 28-2. Door and quarter panel damage. Because the damage to the *door* is slight, the door will be "spotted in."

Fig. 28-3. The completed repair of the damage in Fig. 28-2. The door was "spotted in" and the complete quarter panel was refinished. Since all the paint matches, the painter did a good job.

is seen. Even if the topcoat is *not* affected by the repair work being done, a good cleaning job on the topcoat will often impress the customer enough to bring him back for future repair work.

New Finishes

New automotive topcoats need almost no maintenance and upkeep right away. After new *lacquer* paint dries, however, even the best new lacquer paint job will need "rubbing out" with a product known as *rubbing compound*; Fig. 28-4. This is because lacquer finishes have an uneven, dull appearance until they are "compounded." Fig. 28-5 shows a magnified view of new lacquer paint before it is compounded.

Fig. 28-4. Rubbing compound. (Courtesy, Rinshed-Mason Products Division of Inmont Corporation.)

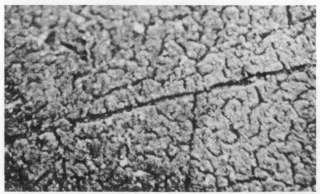

Fig. 28-5. A magnified lacquer surface before being compounded. (Courtesy of Ditzler Automotive Finishes Division.)

New *enamel* paint jobs, on the other hand, must *not* be compounded because of the way in which they dry. If paint defects "show up" in an enamel paint job and cause a dull finish,

enamel *may* be compounded after it has been on the vehicle for at least 30 days. This 30-day waiting period allows the enamel to "set up" hard enough so that it will not be damaged by *light* compounding.

Both enamel and lacquer paint jobs should be thoroughly washed with *mild* soap and water before being turned out of the shop. It is not necessary or desirable to further treat any new paint right away. *Polish* would not add to the shine at this time and it might damage enamel paint. *Wax* cannot be used until later on because the paint must be allowed to "age" about 90 days before it can be waxed.

Older Finishes

After a topcoat has been exposed to the elements (rain, sun, etc.) several weeks or more, it will begin to age and it will have picked up deposits of road grime. These deposits can be removed by cleaning the topcoat with a good grease and wax remover. This product should be used any time the topcoat needs to be cleaned of old wax, tar, stubborn stains, etc., and is the same product used before beginning any body repair on an area. In any case, precleaning solvent (grease and wax remover) must always be used *before* compounding an area, as in Fig. 28-6.

Fig. 28-6. Using precleaning solvent to remove road tar and old wax from a finish to be compounded.

After compounding (or polishing) an old finish, a good wax job makes a topcoat easier to keep clean because dirt will not readily adhere to a waxed surface. Because of this, wax is mainly used as a protective coating. Wax is especially useful on old, dull paint jobs *after* they have been compounded. For example, Fig. 28-7 shows an old paint job after being restored by compounding and waxing.

Fig. 28-8. Several different paint cleaning and protection products.

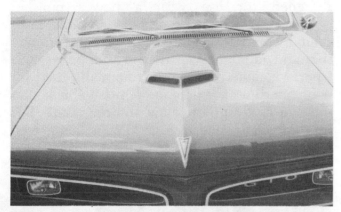
Fig. 28-7. An older paint job that was restored with rubbing compound and then waxed.

If an older paint job is only slightly dulled, the shine may be restored by waxing it with a "cleaner/wax" product. These products contain fine abrasive particles that lightly compound the paint to a smooth finish. Slightly dulled paint, then, can be restored by using these products instead of full hand or machine compounding. Of course, if an old finish is severely dulled, separate compounding and waxing are *both* needed.

Fig. 28-9. A common grease and wax remover product. (Courtesy, Rinshed-Mason Products Division of Inmont Corporation.)

PAINT REPAIR AND PROTECTION PRODUCTS

There are many different products made to clean and add a shine or gloss to a topcoat. These are known as *polishes* and *compounds*. Other products protect the topcoat from scratches and road grime, and make it easier to keep clean. These same products help *preserve* the topcoat so that it will not be broken down by the elements. These protection products include *waxes* and *cleaner/waxes*. Samples of all these products are shown in Fig. 28-8.

Grease and Wax Remover

Grease and wax removers, such as the product in Fig. 28-9, are also known as *precleaning solvents*. They are mild, solvent-type cleaners. They are designed to clean a surface by breaking up or dissolving any dirt, wax, or silicones

on the paint. Good precleaning products will remove wax, grease, oil, tar, silicone polish, road film, and other impurities. They are the same products that were used to clean an area before any paint or repair work was begun.

Rubbing Compound

Rubbing compounds, also known as *cutting* compounds, contain pumice particles. *Pumice* is very fine, ground volcanic rock. There are two basic types of rubbing compound: *hand* and *machine*. See Fig. 28-10.

All rubbing compounds actually remove part of the paint. As some of the old "dead" paint is removed, the surface becomes smoother and more even. As this happens, the pumice itself is broken up. Thus, it polishes the paint to a finer smoothness as it is broken up into smaller particles.

Rubbing compound is used to polish brand new *lacquer* finishes after they have cured at least four hours and, preferably, overnight.

Fig. 28-10. The two major types of rubbing compounds: *hand* compound and *machine* (wheel) compound. (Courtesy, Rinshed-Mason Products Division of Inmont Corporation.)

Compound may also be used to smooth defective *enamel* topcoats after they have cured. However, *acrylic* enamel does not cure until at least thirty *days* after it has been applied, and *alkyd* enamel is not cured until at least three or four *months* after it has been applied. Therefore, rubbing compounds must *not* be used on enamel paints unless they have been given time to completely cure.

Hand Compound—Hand compound contains fairly *coarse* pumice grit. This coarse grit does not require a lot of rubbing pressure to create friction and "cut" the paint. Hand compound is used mainly on small repair areas and may be applied with a rag or brush. Then, a clean

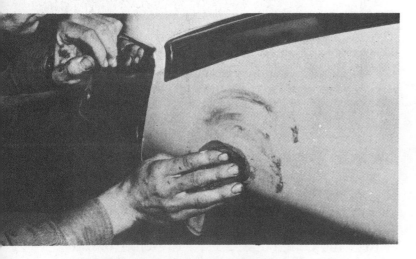

Fig. 28-11. Using hand compound. (Courtesy, Rinshed-Mason Products Division of Inmont Corporation.)

rag is used to work the compound until the finish is as smooth as desired. See Fig. 28-11.

Machine Compound—Machine rubbing compound contains *fine* particles of pumice and is designed for use with a power polisher ("wheel"). The coarse particles in *hand* compound would create too much heat and friction if hand compound was used with a power polisher. Machine compound is normally used for compounding jobs on an entire vehicle and may be used on both new and old paint. The machine compound in Fig. 28-12 is being used to rub out a new lacquer repair.

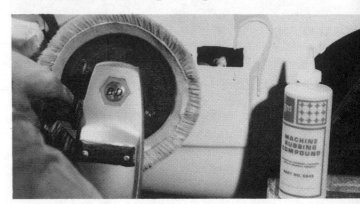

Fig. 28-12. Using machine rubbing compound. (Courtesy of 3M Company, Automotive Division.)

Polish

Most *polishes* contain both a cleaner and silicone material. The *cleaner* removes grime and stains from the topcoat and is actually like very fine rubbing compound. The silicone causes the surface to shine, improving the paint's gloss. A common polish product is shown in Fig. 28-13.

Fig. 28-13. An automotive polish product.

Polish is used to restore slightly dulled old paint jobs that are not in bad enough condition to need compounding. In all cases, the vehicle must first be washed with soap and water and grease and wax remover. Then, the polish may be applied by either hand or machine.

Wax

Most modern *wax* products contain *silicone* wax materials to help shine and protect the topcoat. They should be used *only* after grease and wax remover has been used to clean the vehicle and *only* after a new topcoat has cured for 90 days. Wax is especially useful for shining and protecting old paint that has already been restored by polishing or compounding. Fig. 28-8 shows a wax product among the other paint products.

Cleaner/Wax

Cleaner/wax products, basically, contain both polish *and* wax. Very small abrasive pumice particles and wax are combined in one product designed to smooth *and* wax the vehicle in one operation. These products are ideal for restoring slightly dull older paint jobs. Like other cleaners, the finish should be cleaned before using cleaner/wax. Applying cleaner/wax is similar to applying regular wax.

APPLYING COMPOUND

The process of applying rubbing compound, either by "wheel" or by hand, is known as *compounding*. Compounding may need to be done for either one of two reasons. The *first* reason, and the most common, is to compound the rough texture out of new lacquer topcoats. Even the best lacquer paints will leave *some* rough texture after they are sprayed, and this roughness must be removed to make the paint shiny and to bring up its full gloss. Compounding new lacquer paint is also known as "rubbing out."

The *second* reason for compounding is to brighten up (restore) an old finish. Compounding may be used in this way to restore an entire paint job, or to restore only one panel or a spot on the panel.

For best results, compounding should always be followed by waxing. However, on *new* paint jobs, it is a good idea to wait about 90 days before waxing the paint, even if the paint is lacquer. This is to allow the new paint to *cure* (dry) properly.

Hand Compounding

Hand compounding is normally used for only spot repair work. To hand compound an area, fold a damp, lint-free cloth into a ball. Then, put a small amount of compound on the bottom of the cloth, as in Fig. 28-14. Apply the compound to the area by rubbing back and forth on the area *in a straight-line motion*. Apply only enough pressure on the ball of the rag to actually make the "cut." When the surface has been smoothed enough, wipe off the compound residue with a clean rag.

This is the method used to prepare a panel for a spot repair by removing road grime and old film around the spot. This leaves the original color more visible, so that the new paint will match better and will be better able to grip the old finish.

Fig. 28-14. To hand compound an area, fold a lint-free cloth into a ball and put hand compound material on the bottom of the ball.

Machine Compounding

Most body shop compounding is done with a *power polisher*, also known as a "buffer" or a "wheel." These machines, Figs. 28-15 and 28-16, are normally used to quickly compound a large area. Of course, fine-grit *machine* rubbing compound should always be used when machine compounding. Fig. 28-17 shows a

Fig. 28-15. A power polisher with a short-hair *compounding* pad.

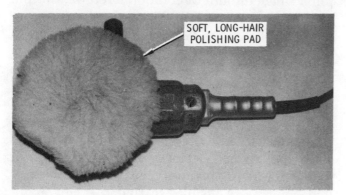

Fig. 28-16. A power polisher with a soft, long-hair *polishing* pad.

Fig. 28-17. Compounding a spot repair.

body man machine compounding a spot repair. This is also known as "wheeling off" the area.

Types of Pads—There are two different types of *pads* that may be used for compounding with a power polisher. These pads are known as *compounding* pads and *polishing* pads. Compounding pads are used to work down heavy roughness on new lacquer paints and for general machine compounding. Compounding pads have *short* lamb's wool, as shown on the pad in Fig. 28-15.

Polishing pads, on the other hand, have *long* lamb's wool, as shown on the pad in Fig. 28-16. Polishing pads do not cut as fast as do compounding pads, but they do produce a smoother finish. Polishing pads, therefore, are often used to "fine-polish" a new surface after compounding.

Compounding Heat—Both types of compounding pads create *heat* while they are being used, because they must rub the paint in order to work it down. For this reason, *always keep the machine moving whenever compounding or polishing.* All automotive paint will burn easily if the pad is held in one place while the machine is turning.

Typical Compounding Jobs

There are three basic compounding jobs that are done in auto body shop work. These include:

1. Compounding for a spot repair.
2. Compounding new paint.
3. Compounding older paint.

The first of these, compounding for a spot repair, is discussed earlier, in the unit *Preparing the Surface for Paint.* The other two basic compounding jobs are discussed here.

Compounding New Paint—After new lacquer paint has been sprayed and allowed to dry for at least four hours, it must be compounded to full luster. Large areas are difficult to compound all at once because it takes *time* to compound a large area. Some of the compound material may dry and harden on the finish, making it impossible to work. To avoid this problem, be sure to finish one small area at a time before moving on to the next section. The largest area compounded at one time should be no larger than about four square feet.

To compound a new *lacquer* paint job or spot repair, follow the directions outlined in Figs. 28-18 through 28-21. Before compounding new *acrylic enamel* paint, it is best to allow the paint to cure for at least 30 days. Then, do *not* wet-sand the paint before compounding. Also, it is a good idea to use *milder* compound on enamel paint than is used on lacquer paint.

Fig. 28-18. Compounding new lacquer paint on an automobile hood. *Step 1:* Wet-sand the new lacquer with wet #600 sandpaper. Be sure to use a rubber *sanding block* so that the finish is sanded evenly. Keep in mind that #600 paper is very, very fine; it will not harm the new paint if it is used correctly.

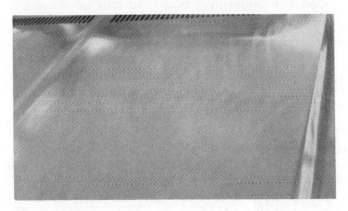

Fig. 28-19. *Step 2:* When the wet sanding is completed, *wash* the entire panel with clear water to remove any sanding residue. After the finish is washed, very small *sandscratches*, as shown, will be visible in the paint. Proper compounding will remove these scratches.

Fig. 28-20. *Step 3:* Compound the area with rubbing compound. Mix the compound until it is a watery paste. When using the "wheel," move it in an up-and-down or back-and-forth motion. Lift up slightly on the *side* handle for back-and-forth strokes. Lift up slightly on the *back* handle for up-and-down strokes. After compounding a small area, the compounding pad must be *cleaned* of built-up residue. *Have an experienced person show you how to do this.*

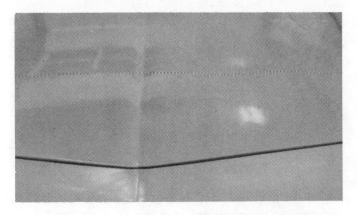

Fig. 28-21. *Step 4:* Polish the surface. On the left is the finish *after* compounding and polishing; on the right is the finish after compounding but *before* polishing.

Compounding Older Paint—It may be possible to compound any older finish, whether lacquer or enamel, back to "like-new" gloss when the finish becomes dull. Compounding will usually bring the luster back to an old finish. However, the old finish should also be waxed after compound has been used to restore the gloss.

The reason for waxing the restored finish is that the rubbing compound will remove any polish or wax on the surface. Then, the unprotected finish could be easily attacked by the weather and foreign elements such as bird droppings, bug juices, tree acids and sap, etc.

Restoring old paint by rubbing it out may be done in almost the same way as compounding new paint. To do this, follow the steps below:

1. Thoroughly wash the entire car with soap and water.
2. Clean the finish with wax and grease remover (precleaning solvent). Even after washing and cleaning, marks may remain on the paint, such as the damage on the fender in Fig. 28-22.
3. Apply a thin coat of fine, watery compound over a small area. See Fig. 28-23.
4. Compound the area with a *polishing* pad, unless the finish is in very poor condition. Hold the polishing machine slightly at an angle while moving the machine back and forth over the area. Allow about 3″ of the pad to touch the surface. See Fig. 28-24. Clean the pad as often as required.

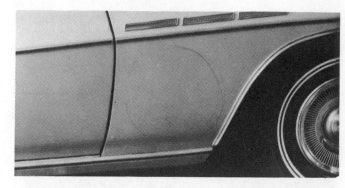

Fig. 28-22. A marred area on a fender. This mark will require compounding to be removed.

Fig. 28-23. Applying compound to the area needing repair.

Fig. 28-24. Compounding the area to remove the mark on the finish. Here, note that the *right* side of the wheel is being used. It is OK to use either the right side or the top side of the wheel.

5. Look at the paint to see if it has been restored to its natural color and gloss. If not, apply more compound immediately. *Be careful not to compound through the topcoat to the primer!*

6. Continue working around the vehicle from panel to panel until the entire top-coat has been restored.
7. Again wash the car with soap and water. Clean all the glass and chrome to remove the residue left by compounding.
8. Apply wax or a mild cleaner/wax to provide protection for the newly-restored topcoat.

POLISHING

Polish is used to restore slightly dulled paint, paint that is not badly enough weathered to need compounding. Polishing can be done by hand or by machine. In either case, *first* apply the polish to the vehicle by hand, as in Fig. 28-25. Always use a clean, slightly damp rag to apply polish. Depending on the temperature and humidity, the polish may be applied over the entire vehicle or over a small section. After the polish is applied, allow a few minutes for it to dry to a light-colored haze, as in Fig. 28-26.

If the vehicle is being polished by hand, wipe off the dried polish with a *clean* soft rag. *Turn* the rag often so that dried polish is not rubbing on the finish at the bottom of the rag. Use only a clean, dry, fluffy rag. Old towels, clean old diapers, and material known as *cheesecloth*, purchased new, are all good polishing rag materials.

Hand polishing may be difficult and time-consuming when an entire vehicle is being

Fig. 28-25. Applying polish. Always apply polish in a *circular* motion.

Fig. 28-26. After the polish has been applied, allow the polish to dry. If a vehicle is being polished on a hot, dry day, apply polish to only one panel at a time.

polished. In this case, or when a large-size area must be polished, *machine* polishing is much faster. To machine polish an area, use the "wheel" with a soft polishing pad to remove the dried polish. The polishing pad must be cleaned frequently, so, again, it is a good idea to have an experienced person show you how to clean the pad during the polishing procedure.

Polishing Heat—Polishing pads do not create as much heat as do compounding pads. For this reason, polishing pads are more often used for shining topcoats to a high gloss than are compounding pads. Since polishing pads do not create as much heat, there is less chance of burning the paint when using a polishing pad instead of a compounding pad. *Even so, the "wheel" must not be held in one position during polishing.*

APPLYING WAX AND CLEANER/WAX

After a new topcoat has cured 90 days (or after an old topcoat has been compounded), the finish should be *waxed*. Waxing alone is usually done to make it easier to keep the vehicle *clean* and to provide *protection* for the topcoat. Applying cleaner/wax is usually done to complete the restoration of an older paint job. Because cleaner/wax contains very mild abrasive particles, it may be used to restore slightly dulled old paint without having to compound the paint beforehand.

Applying Wax—Wax should be applied over a freshly compounded finish after it has been

washed with soap and water to remove the compound residue. Wax is usually sold in some type of *paste* form, although liquid types are available. Either type should be applied with a soft, slightly damp cloth.

Wax must only be applied to small areas at a time, no more than about two square feet. It is normally wiped off immediately, unless the manufacturer's instructions say otherwise. This process is then repeated over the entire vehicle. It is important that all excess wax be removed from the vehicle. If excess, dried wax is allowed to remain on the vehicle, it may dull the paint.

Applying Cleaner/Wax—To use cleaner/wax correctly, first wash the dulled finish with soap and water. Then, clean it with a precleaning solvent. This will leave the finish clean enough so that the mild cleaner in the cleaner/wax will only have to remove any "dead" paint.

Apply cleaner/wax with a soft, slightly damp cloth, over about two square feet at a time. After the product has dried, remove it with soft, *dry*, clean cloths. The entire procedure is similar to polishing, except that smaller areas should be done at one time.

ACCENT STRIPES

Most newer cars have one or more *accent stripes* on the car's finish. These stripes may be paint or tape and are a different color than is the regular topcoat. Accent stripes may be added to older vehicles to make them look more up-to-date. Accent stripes are also known as *pin stripes*.

By either name, stripes may be many different sizes. Some of them seem to be as narrow as a pin, which is why they are called *pin* stripes. Fig. 28-27 shows a pin stripe that has been added to a vehicle. Some stripes are fairly wide; others are made up of *groups* of stripes. Stripes that are not actually paint are made of *tape* with an adhesive backing. These stripes must be applied to *clean* paint or they will not be as durable as painted-on stripes.

Applying Stripes

Whenever body work is done on a late-model automobile, part of the paint work may include

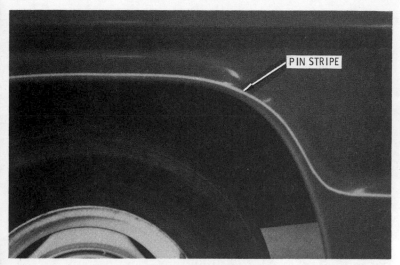

Fig. 28-27. An accent stripe (also known as a *pin stripe*) applied to a fender line on a small truck.

replacing stripes that were damaged or removed during the repair. For this reason, painters and touch-up men need to know how to add or replace accent stripes. Also, customers may want stripes added to a repainted car or to "dress up" an older car.

The easiest way to add or replace stripes is to use *striping tape*. Striping tape comes in many sizes and is available from various companies. See Fig. 28-28.

Fig. 28-28. Striping tape. This special masking tape has precut sections that may be pulled out to mask off an area where a stripe is to be painted. (Courtesy of 3M Company, Automotive Division.)

Striping tape is basically a special masking tape with a number of precut, pull-out sections. These sections may be pulled out as necessary

to mask off an area for stripes of different widths. Many different stripe combinations can be made by simply pulling out different sections of the tape. Figs. 28-29 through 28-39 show the procedure for using striping tape to add or replace stripes.

Fig. 28-29. Applying accent stripes. *Step 1:* Using enamel reducer, clean the area where the stripe is to be applied. If the finish is dull, lightly *compound* the area before washing with enamel reducer.

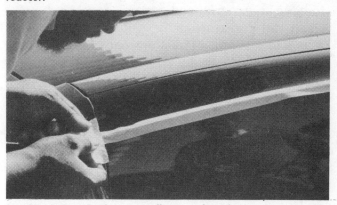

Fig. 28-30. *Step 2:* Place a small piece of masking tape across the end of the striping tape. This will keep the tape from spreading apart at the slits as the tape is applied along the vehicle.

Fig. 28-31. *Step 3:* Apply the tape along the vehicle where the stripe is to be made. Do this carefully so that the stripe will be *straight.*

Fig. 28-32. *Step 4:* Press the tape down firmly after it has been put in position along the car.

Fig. 28-33. *Step 5:* Mask off all *around* the strip of striping tape.

Fig. 28-34. *Step 5,* continued: The completely masked area. At this point, *all* the finish is covered with masking paper, masking tape, or striping tape.

Fig. 28-35. *Step 6:* Pull out the precut sections of the tape, as needed, to make the stripe(s) desired. Here, two strips are being pulled out. After the strip(s) have been pulled out, tack-wipe the area to be striped.

Fig. 28-36. *Step 7:* Apply *sealer* to the area being striped. Follow the directions for the sealer product being used.

Fig. 28-37. *Step 8, First Pass:* Apply a light mist coat of stripe color along the entire area. It is usually a good idea to use *enamel* paint at a slightly lower air pressure than if an entire panel was being refinished.

Fig. 28-38. *Step 8, Second Pass:* Apply a heavier mist coat on the second pass. *This is all that is necessary for complete coverage;* a common mistake is to spray too much paint on a striping job.

Fig. 28-39. *Step 9:* The finished job. Allow the enamel to dry before removing the masking materials. No further clean-up or compounding should be necessary.

Index